ALLEN WELLS AND GILBERT M. JOSEPH

# Summer of Discontent, Seasons of Upheaval

## ELITE POLITICS AND RURAL INSURGENCY IN YUCATAN, 1876-1915

STANFORD UNIVERSITY PRESS  STANF     CALIFORNIA  1996

Stanford University Press
Stanford, California
© 1996 by the Board of Trustees of the
Leland Stanford Junior University
Printed in the United States of America

CIP data are at the end of the book

Stanford University Press publications
are distributed exclusively by
Stanford University Press within
the United States, Canada, Mexico, and
Central America; they are distributed exclusively
by Cambridge University Press throughout
the rest of the world

*Photo sources*: Marie Robinson Wright, *Picturesque
Mexico* (Philadelphia: J. B. Lippincott, 1897); U. A.
Moriconi, *Album yucateco*, Latin American Library,
Tulane University; Archivo "Pedro A. Guerra,"
Facultad de Ciencias Antropológicas, Universidad
Autónoma de Yucatán

# Preface

This volume addresses a mutual interest that arose out of the work we did on our first books, *Yucatán's Gilded Age* and *Revolution from Without*. In these works, which overlapped thematically and chronologically, we documented a powerful plantocracy that kept the Mexican Revolution, which broke out nationally in 1910, at arm's length for almost five years, until a full-scale invasion by a conquering army from central Mexico preempted its power in March 1915. But while each of us had ideas about how Yucatán's henequen kings defused a series of violent challenges to their hegemony between 1910 and 1915, the conceptual frameworks and research bases of our first studies did not permit a systematic analysis of the politics and society of Yucatan's "extended Porfiriato."

We knew that such a study would have implications extending beyond the state's borders, for it would address a central problem largely ignored by students of modern Mexico: the breakdown of the traditional order during the first years of the revolutionary era. That process was more hotly contested and gradual in Yucatán than in any other Mexican region. Thus a close examination of it might also shed light on an issue of particular relevance to students of Central America (which structurally resembles Yucatán in many respects), South America's southern cone, and other postcolonial societies: namely, the capacity of local (or national) oligarchies (such as Yucatán's henequen planters or El Salvador's coffee barons) to "hang on," to resist seemingly inevitable structural change, even in the face of escalating social challenges, the outbreak of local rebellions, and ultimately the mobilization of multiclass coalitions. Indeed, it is striking that the Latin Americanist historiography has given so little attention to *integrating* the study of popular movements and rebellions with examinations of the efforts of elite establishments to prevent, depict, contain, crush, and ultimately, ideologically appropriate such rebellions. Most often, these problems are treated separately. The present volume seeks to redress this imbalance.

Although we have long since come to regard Yucatán affectionately as *nuestro terruño*—our (second) home—this study represents a significant redirection of our work there. Like many historians of our generation, we have shifted our focus from broader preoccupations with the political economy of development at a middle level of analysis to the complex, contested, and often maddeningly uncertain terrain of social history and political culture at the grassroots. Of course, the more intimate gaze reflected in this study was hard won, honed by more than twenty years of archival research, life experience, and intellectual exchange.

Happily, this exchange began with our immediate collaboration. Partnership is often more exciting in principle than in practice, and ours has had its share of trials and negotiations. Still, this volume offers testimony to the best that collaboration has to offer: respect for each other's strengths and openness to criticism. We conceived, researched, and wrote this book together. Wells initially drafted Chapters 2 through 6 and Joseph Chapters 1 and 7 through 10. Nevertheless, each put his stamp on the other's work; and our departure from alphabetical order in crediting authorship reflects nothing more than a desire to redress a longstanding "alphabetical inequity" built up through earlier writings published together.

We have also benefited from intellectual exchange with an array of friends and colleagues. The debts we have incurred along the way are far too numerous to hope to acknowledge here, but we will do our best.

It is widely remarked that Yucatecan historiography has been distinguished by a degree of international, interdisciplinary collaboration that is perhaps unique in Mexican or Latin American regional studies. Most of the arguments elaborated in the pages that follow have been substantially enriched by suggestions and more formal critiques provided by the following *yucatecólogos*: Hernán Menéndez, Othón Baños Ramírez, Alejandra García Quintanilla, Antonio Betancourt Pérez, Enrique Montalvo, José Luis Sierra, Francisco Paoli, Fidelio Quintal, Arturo Guémez, Susy Peniche, Teresa Ramayo, Iván Franco, Eric Villanueva, Blanca González, Carlos Bojórquez, Víctor Suárez Molina, Rodolfo Ruz Menéndez, Robert Patch, Herman Konrad, Sally Humphries, Kathleen Logan, Marie Lapointe, Lucy Defresne, Ben Fallaw, Christopher Gill, Jeffrey Brannon, Franco Savarino, and Paul Eiss. Many other Yucatecan colleagues, affiliated with the Centro Regional del Instituto Nacional de Antropología e Historia, the Centro de Investigaciones Regionales "Hideyo Noguchi," the Escuela de Ciencias Antropológicas (like "the Hideyo" an entity of the Universidad Autónoma de Yucatán), and the Academia Yucatanense de Ciencias y Artes, have generously engaged our work when we have periodically presented portions of it before their organizations.

We are also deeply indebted to the following individuals and institutions for their assistance in the investigative process: Beatriz Reyes, Juan Duch, and Piedad Peniche, the directors of the Archivo General del Estado during the course of our research; Juan Peón Ancona, director of the Biblioteca "Carlos R. Menéndez"; Roldán Peniche, director of the Hemeroteca "Pino Suárez"; Waldemaro Concha, curator of the Fototeca "Pedro Guerra" at the Escuela de Ciencias Antropológicas; and Maritza Arrigunaga, curator of Yucatecan manuscripts at the University of Texas-Arlington. We continue to reserve special feelings of gratitude and affection for Luis López Rivas (Archivo General del Estado), Alfredo Barrera Vásquez (Instituto Nacional de Antropología e Historia), and Clemente López Trujillo and Pedro Castro Aguilar (Hemeroteca "Pino Suárez"). All four of these modest, courteous men have now passed from the scene, but few did more to inspire and initiate neophytes to the study of the region's past.

We have also benefited from the generous and timely insights of a number of fellow Mexicanists and Latin Americanists, as well as those of several stimulating comparativists. Most notably (but more or less indiscriminately) these colleagues are Eric Van Young, Friedrich Katz, Alan Knight, Emília Viotti da Costa, Daniel Nugent, Florencia Mallon, Paul Vanderwood, Steve Topik, John Womack, Steve Stern, John Coatsworth, Bill Beezley, Romana Falcón, Jim Scott, Adolfo Gilly, Temma Kaplan, Cliff Welch, Francie Chassen, Jaime Rodríguez, Mark Wasserman, Tom Benjamin, John Hart, and Jeff Rubin. Bill Taylor and Linda Hall deserve special thanks for their thoughtful critiques of the entire manuscript. Our copy editor, Eleanor Lahn, deserves a special note of thanks.

We are also grateful for having had the opportunity to test early drafts of several of the chapters before particularly challenging audiences at the Center for U.S.-Mexican Studies, University of California, San Diego; the National Humanities Center; the Colloquium of the Mexico/Chicano Program, University of California, Irvine; the Alfredo Barrera Vásquez Institute for Yucatecan Studies, University of Alabama; the Conference of Mexican and U.S. Historians; the Latin American Labor History Conference; and the NEH/SSRC Research Conference on "Popular Culture, State Formation, and the Mexican Revolution."

Financial and institutional support has come from a variety of sources. We gratefully acknowledge seed grants from the National Endowment for the Humanities' Travel to Collections Fund, the American Philosophical Society, the Southern Regional Education Board, and the Faculty Research Councils of Appalachian State University, Bowdoin College, and the University of North Carolina at Chapel Hill and its Institute of Latin American Studies. From 1987 to 1990, the bulk of our research in Yucatán and Mexico City and much of the drafting of the manuscript was generously funded by an NEH Interpretive Research Grant (RO-21511) and an NEH Supplemental

Grant. The writing of the book was also facilitated by resident fellowships for Joseph at the Center for U.S.-Mexican Studies in 1988 and the National Humanities Center during 1992–93.

Given the collaborative nature of our work, most of our acknowledgments are mutual. There are, however, some very special people to whom we are individually indebted. Gil Joseph especially thanks his wife and best friend, Patricia Pessar, for her constant love and patience, and for improving everything she touches in his life, including what he writes. He dedicates this book to her. He also thanks their four-year-old son, Matthew, for making him a better historian by incessantly asking his daddy "why?" and not accepting half-baked answers. Allen Wells is indebted to Katherine, who has lived with this book from its inception in 1984. Her patience, understanding, and, most important, her perspective have made it possible to balance the often elusive priorities of family and work. To the extent that this project took away time to be spent with Anna, Emily, and David, finishing a manuscript like this causes one to reflect on the relative importance of scholarship in the larger scheme of things. He owes them a special thanks. Finally, Allen Wells dedicates this book to the late Robert Conant, who patiently followed this project from a distance, and who inspired our family by example. He is and will be sorely missed.

Today, as we bring this volume to a close, the "New World Order" busily entrenches itself on both sides of the Río Grande. The account that follows should leave little doubt, however, that the tune being played in Washington and Mexico City is one that was heard almost a century ago. And as intellectuals in the Distrito Federal and Mérida rewrite the schoolbooks in order to refurbish the liberal, modernizing discourses of yesteryear for the North American Free Trade Agreement of today, we can only speculate uneasily what the consequences of this new "summer of discontent" are likely to be. Will the campesinos of Yucatán and southern Mexico ultimately find more of a place in the "new North American economy" than they did in its previous incarnation? Or was the 1994 New Year's uprising in the highlands and jungles of Chiapas merely the first of many new seasons of upheaval, as those who are left behind desperately fight the future?

Gilbert M. Joseph                                            Allen Wells

# Contents

*Photographs follow page 92.*

# Tables, Figures, and Maps

The crisis consists precisely in the fact that the old is dying and the new cannot be born; in this interregnum a great variety of morbid symptoms appear.

—Antonio Gramsci, *Prison Notebooks*

## CHAPTER I

# Introduction

This is a book about unheralded people and events on Mexico's margins whose story has mainstream significance for the study of the nation's modern past. Focusing on the remote southeastern state of Yucatán, this volume most centrally examines the pivotal but still neglected period of transition joining the decline of the old regime of Porfirio Díaz and the emergence of the new revolutionary state. It is an enigmatic story, with twists and turns that run against the grain of most accounts of the Revolution of 1910—not least the Institutional Revolution's own Whiggish interpretation.

No telluric groundswell materialized around Francisco Madero's national liberal reform movement in Yucatán, the seat of Mexico's wealthiest planter class.[1] The seemingly "safe" mobilization of the countryside that was engineered against the regime by aggrieved planter factions under cover of Maderismo backfired, as local groups of beleaguered Maya peasants (campesinos) sought to redress their own grievances. By fits and starts throughout the Maderista period (1910–13), the countryside erupted into flames, forcing the plantocracy to paper over its differences and, ironically, reviving the political fortunes of an oligarchy that history seemed to have left behind. Whereas in much of the rest of Mexico, grassroots revolts in 1910 and 1911 led inexorably to civil war and the destruction of the oligarchical order, in Yucatán the development of a popular movement was severely stunted, and the old order survived until 1915.[2] Ultimately, the Mexican Revolution would have to fight its way into the peninsula with an army of seven thousand troops.[3]

This salient difference frames the central questions of this study of late Porfirian and early revolutionary politics and society. First, how did the old order manage, by mid-1913, to ride out the first challenges to its power, despite four years of frequent and widespread protest and revolt throughout the Yucatecan countryside? Second, what was the nature of this rural protest? What characteristic forms did resistance take among peasant villagers and hacienda peons? Equally important, how was such resistance woven into long-term patterns of adaptation? And finally, how was resistance repeatedly mobilized and then dissolved during the Maderista period, and what role did regional elites and the state play, both in fomenting and controlling this insurgency?

## Power, Resistance, and Hegemony

These questions suggest that we intend to do much more in this book than showcase the "exceptional" nature of Yucatán's early involvement (or lack of it) with the Mexican Revolution. At a deeper level, and for a longer haul (the late 1870s to 1915 and occasionally beyond), we will probe a set of linkages that is absolutely central to the study of Mexico's modern past: the complex, reciprocal relationship between modes of contestation and structures and discourses of power. In the pages that follow, we will trace the strategies—by turns coercive and more subtle—whereby factions of Yucatán's henequen plantocracy accrued power and wealth at the expense of the popular classes (and rival elites), then struggled to maintain their advantage. They were often aided in their efforts by international agents and events, by the national and local state, and occasionally by subaltern elements, who often had very different motives in mind. Such conditional alliances thereby formed part of an equally determined and varied (though far more checkered) effort on the part of the region's villagers, peons, and artisans to defend the remnants of their dignity and autonomy, and—in certain favorable conjunctures—to mount some telling offensives.

Students of Mexican and Latin American history will appreciate that this is hardly a new story; yet it is one that has rarely been told well. Long after the celebrated "turn" in social history and the human sciences toward a deconstructionist reading of historical texts and the study of political consciousness, and more than a decade after the first flowering of "resistance studies" and "subaltern studies" in other parts of the Third World, we still have few fine-grained accounts of how rule was accomplished, in political and cultural terms, in Mexico or Latin America across a medium or long duration. We have fewer still that meaningfully integrate analysis of the sinews and scripts of domination with the multiform "arts of resistance" that scholars like James Scott have celebrated with such gusto of late.[4] And perhaps the ultimate challenge—likely to be insurmountable, but one to which historians should at least aspire—is the daunting task of narrating such complex stories with clarity and verve while remaining sensitive to the multiple voices that inflect them. (This assumes, of course, that our sources admit these other voices, and that we have properly developed an ear for them.) Differences of class, ethnicity, and gender (among other factors) must inform any reconstruction of the past, and are themselves categories periodically constructed and reconstructed.

In clumsier hands, such narratives of resistance and accommodation can become reflexive, homogenizing accounts of thrust and parry.[5] Few would dispute that there has been of late a tendency to sentimentalize resistance, to lump all forms of contestation together as signs of the ineffectiveness of systems of domination and the indomitable creativity of the human spirit. Such telescoped readings, however, tend to neglect the multiple identities of resisters, to elide distinctions between forms of resistance, to shift attention away from conjunctures when historical actors move from one form to another, and to foreclose important questions about the deployment of power. Typically pressed into the service of some grander theory or ideological purpose, such essentialized treatments of domination and resistance have produced inadequate histories of both the subaltern and their rulers, and have shed little light on the workings of "hegemony."[6]

The issue of hegemony—which we do not burden with any *assumption* that "belief" or "consent" has been extracted from the ruled—is a particularly vexing one for Mexicanists.[7] More than a decade ago, Friedrich Katz engagingly set forth the terms of the puzzle surrounding hegemony, which social historians are only now beginning to address seriously. Mexico is the only country in the Americas where "every major social transformation has been inextricably linked to popular rural upheavals." Indeed, three times in a century—in 1810, in the 1850s and 1860s, and again in 1910—social and political movements emerged that destroyed the existing regime and most of the military establishment, then set up a new regime and army. Nevertheless, in every case, these popular movements ultimately wrought only rather modest changes in the countryside. Armies that began as campesino-based forces soon became the guarantors of an increasingly oppressive social order, which in time was itself challenged and toppled. Why have Mexico's embattled powerholders repeatedly called on campesinos, and why have campesinos so often followed? And perhaps more important, what were the terms of engagement, and how were they negotiated? These, Katz believes, remain the most tantalizing questions with which social historians of Mexico grapple.[8]

In effect, Katz has called on Mexicanists to historicize abstract, jargon-ridden notions of hegemony; to study it as a flesh-and-blood *process*, rather than posit (or reject) it, a priori, as an *outcome*.[9] In this book we take up that challenge, guided by a bit of wisdom dispensed in another context almost two centuries ago by Símon Bolívar: simply to "look from very close and analyze from afar."[10] Hence, this study provides a close examination of the state of play between Yucatán's dominant and popular political cultures. It was a dialectic of struggle that imbricated one with the other and invariably subjected elite and state projects of transformation and appropriation to some measure of negotiation from below.[11]

This is therefore a book that engages, unabashedly, in a fair amount of storytelling. It names names, insists on the specificity of particular times and places, and leaves a number of loose ends. After twenty years of listening to stories in the present and "taking" dusty testimonies from hundreds of informants from the past, it is the loose ends we find most interesting and revealing. They continually point up the complexity of the hegemonic process and compel us to think twice before imposing our own or others' analytical categories on them. If a critical reading of the "newer" social and cultural history has taught us anything, it is that the meanings of other people in other times are revealed *not* through the elaboration of models or statistical averages but through a careful consideration of particular sequences of action in particular social contexts.[12]

## Toward a New History

To conceptualize hegemony in a manner that examines the everyday and long-term articulations between dominant and subaltern cultures, between forms of the state and initiatives emanating from society's grassroots, is to attempt to reunite a history from above with a history from below. It is also to integrate social history with political history in a manner that transforms them both. In the process, new syntheses of research on both the Porfirian and revolutionary periods would appear to lie in the offing.

### THE PORFIRIATO

The past decade has witnessed a rich harvest of regional studies of the Porfiriato. In the recent literature, two currents predominate. One group of scholars has focused attention on the political sphere, examining the process whereby the Porfirian central state increased its power at the expense of the regional peripheries. Invariably, the federal cause was advanced by Don Porfirio's ability to bestow patronage and manipulate local factional struggles, playing off contending *parentescos*, or elite family networks.[13] This study will highlight the reciprocal dimension of the equation, demonstrating that the maneuverings among regional elite political factions, or *camarillas*, also had important consequences for the politics played out in Mexico City.

Another group of historians has explored the external context of the Porfirian regional economy, examining patterns of cooperation and conflict between local elites and foreign investors. The contradictory nature of such transnational alliances, and their social impact on lesser elites and the popular classes, have now been analyzed for several regions.[14] What has been called for but has yet really to emerge for Mexico (or for other Latin American nations), is a synthesis of these two literary currents—an enterprise that would constitute a "new political history" of the Porfiriato or other Latin American oligarchical formations.[15] This new political history (or politically informed social history) would transcend the traditional institutional narrative, examining the formation and struggles of notable family networks and their corresponding *camarillas* in a more ample, multilayered framework that would integrate locality, region, and nation into the larger process of world capitalist expansion.[16]

The first half of this volume seeks to provide just such an analysis. It shows that despite the fabulous wealth generated by Yucatán's late nineteenth-century henequen boom, the first decade of this century was a veritable "summer of discontent" for the vast majority of regional producers, merchants, urban workers, artisans, and campesinos. All found themselves increasingly subordinated in some way to the dominant oligarchical *camarilla* based on the *parentesco* of Olegario Molina and Avelino Montes. After 1902 this faction increased its clout considerably through an exclusive collaboration with the world's leading manufacturer of farm machinery and cordage products, the Chicago-based International Harvester Company. The mobilization of rival political groups, which began early in that decade and culminated in the years immediately following 1910, was a highly complex affair, one that grew out of deepening (and interrelated) political, economic, and social contradictions in the late Porfirian order. Thus far, the kind of *radiografía* of late Porfirian society that would reveal such dimensions of this summer of discontent has not been achieved for Yucatán or for any other Mexican region.

Although in reality these threads were tightly interwoven, for purposes of exposition our analysis will focus on each type of contradiction in turn. In Chapters 2 and 3, we trace the evolution of elite politics in Yucatán from the heyday of rivalry between narrowly based, personalistic factions, which engaged in stylized electoral performances for elite consumption around the turn of the century, to the rise of broader-based *camarillas*, which came to resemble rudimentary political parties on the eve of the Mexican Revolution. To our knowledge, this is the first study of the Porfiriato that integrates the dynamics of patronage politics at the national, state, *and grassroots* levels.[17] As such, it is also the first to examine the contested nature of Porfirian politics from the perspective of the popular classes—the artisans, workers, villagers, and peons whom Yucatán's elites were forced to recruit as political competition intensified and economic stakes soared at the height of the henequen boom. Of course, as factions led by the less wealthy and powerful of the planters used patronage to incorporate ever greater numbers of workers and campesinos into their incipient multiclass clienteles, these "parties" became more and more difficult to control. What began as an attempt by disgruntled elites to unseat an oligarchical *camarilla* soon evolved into an insurgency that called into question the very premise of elite rule.

How are we to understand the bitterness and envy that gnawed at Yucatán's "rank and file" planters and compelled them—against their better judgment—to engage in such risky political experiments in mass mobilization? Whereas previously the central government had, by and large, alternated rival elite *camarillas* in power, after 1902 Don Porfirio abetted the Molinista faction in its efforts to concentrate political power. In what rival elites regarded as a notorious Faustian bargain, Molina gave his blessing to Díaz's federal annexation of the territory of Quintana Roo in 1902 and its subsequent partition among foreign companies and a few cronies—Molina and Montes included. In one fell swoop, proud, chauvinistic Yucatán lost one-third of its territory, and rival elites were preempted from exploiting the rich tropical commodities they had always assumed would one day be theirs.

The "commodification" of the state's territory by executive fiat only underscored for Yucatán's *déclassé* elites the axiom that political patronage and wealth went hand in hand. Time and again during the Porfiriato, Yucatán's personalistic *camarillas* had, as incumbents, created economic empires within the boundaries of what were essentially their political fiefs. Now, however, the spoils that Molina and his *parentesco* were reaping were entirely unprecedented. This situation struck the other planters as obscene. Given the centrality of this political-economic nexus in monocrop societies, it is baffling how few detailed studies we have, either for modern Mexico or the rest of Latin America, that correlate the political and economic determinants of oligarchical power and document how each was deployed in the service of the other.[18]

Better documented are the often devastating economic and social *consequences* of oligarchy—which in Porfirian Yucatán were played out against the backdrop of the roller coaster rhythms of the henequen cycle. For example, during an extended economic crisis in the final years of the Porfiriato (1907–10), banks and businesses collapsed, estates sank into debt, landowners (*hacendados*) and campesinos alike lost their properties. As we will see in Chapter 4, Molina, Montes, and their associates invariably turned others' misery to their own profit. Buoyed by access to international capital, the Molinista *parentesco* acquired mortgages; purchased estates outright; and consolidated its hold on regional communications, infrastructure, and banking.

As if to add insult to injury, the Molinistas aggressively foisted their own version of developmentalism onto Yucatecan society during these unsettled times. Via infrastructural improvements and a blitz of moral injunctions against popular "vices"—all modeled on similar efforts introduced by their *científico* counterparts in the Federal District—the Molinistas sought to legislate not only the physical appearance of the urban landscape, but the sociological makeup of the citizen as well. As we will see in Chapter 5, their modernizing vision produced only checkered results while triggering a backlash of popular opinion that would feed into the Maderista seasons of upheaval a few years later.

The greatest burdens of Porfirian "modernity," however, were borne by the majority of the population, the Mayan campesinos whose labor fueled the region's monoculture. In boom times these Maya and smaller groups of imported workers were driven to step up production; when the market flagged, planters invariably passed the costs down to them, reducing wages and watering down customary paternalistic incentives. In Chapter 6, we provide a new conceptualization of monoculture's structure of domination and the forms by which campesinos accommodated and resisted it on hene-quen estates and in neighboring village communities. We argue that the Porfirian henequen estate was a transitional or hybrid institution. Its social regime combined both materialistic and personalistic idioms of power and deftly employed three complementary mechanisms of control: isolation, coercion, and security. In "normal" times, such a regime was particularly well insulated from both internal jacqueries and revolts mounted from neighboring villages; peons and villagers typically resorted to "everyday" forms of resistance and an "infrapolitics" of struggle. Yet as we will see in the second half of the book, in the political vacuum created when Díaz fell, Yucatán's monocultural regime would be hard pressed to enforce consis-tently any of the control mechanisms that had previously served it so well.

## THE MEXICAN REVOLUTION

The mobilization and demobilization of Yucatán's ensuing seasons of upheaval similarly speak to a variety of core issues now engaging students of the Mexican Revolution. Perhaps the central concern, around which con-flicting interpretations of the Mexican and other revolutions invariably order themselves, is the degree of continuity between revolutionary-era forms of authority and consciousness and those of the old order.

For example, who were the new men who led these Yucatecan revolts and filled the vacuum created by the weakening of the central state in 1910? How did they recruit and maintain their followers? To what extent did these local chiefs (contemporaries referred to them as *cabecillas* or *ca-ciques*) tap into local subcultures of resistance and represent truly "popu-lar," autonomous rebellions against the interests and values of the old re-gime? This is what Alan Knight, giving new voice to a venerable populist current of revolutionary interpretation, contends. Or were they more signif-icant in permitting new, upwardly mobile elements (with ties to existing elites) their first access to a clientele among the masses, upon whose backs they would one day consolidate a more efficient version of the old regime? This is what numerous self-proclaimed "revisionist" writers have argued.[19] No doubt, a compelling analysis of the historical role of these revolutionary "hingemen" would go a long way toward answering the salient questions by Katz posed at the outset.

Clearly, the revisionists have succeeded in situating the Mexican Revo-lution in relation to global forces of change and in focusing attention on important continuities between the Porfirian regime and the new revolutionary state. Yet along with Knight, we would contend that they often have reduced the revolution to "a series of chaotic, careerist episodes, in which popular forces were, at best, the instruments of manipulative *caciques*."[20] In the manner of Tocqueville's revision of the French Revolution, they posit the rise of a Machiavellian central state as the key element—some even argue the only important element—of the "epic revolution" (1910–17).[21] But such "statolatry," as Knight terms it, provides a false homogeneity to the complex history of the Mexican Revolution. Moreover, it ignores the pressures on the state from below; it mistakenly stresses the inertia of peasants and workers and the unbroken political hegemony of elites and middle strata.

Such a view is problematic for any decade after 1910 and particularly misguided for the period before 1920 and for the Cardenista administration (1934–40).[22] Finally, in spite of their reification of a "Leviathan state," revisionists have not been particularly clear, until now, about just what this state was or how "it" so successfully managed to swallow up Mexico's popular cultures like so many minnows. Indeed, the revolutionary state has remained something of a conceptual black box. Most often it has been cast as an ominous presence hovering above (but eerily removed from) the mundane workings of Mexican society.[23]

What is needed is a synthesis of populist and revisionist interpretations, one that integrates their contributions but in the process transcends them. This would entail, for starters, a more sophisticated reconstruction of peasant and worker mobilizations (and demobilizations) and a greater appreciation of the impact that these popular movements registered—locally, regionally, nationally, occasionally even internationally—on Porfirian and revolutionary state projects of social transformation. Here, analysis of revolutionary-era mobilizations must go beyond the kind of broad assertions of resistance and empowerment that populist scholars have provided in their national histories.[24] Instead, through close examination of popular political cultures, scholars must endeavor to deconstruct "the popular"; that is, to show how apparently "primordial" sociocultural forms—notions of community, the peasant economy, ethnic and gender identities—are actually historically constructed.[25]

In the process, such an approach would begin to generate empirical elaborations of both the character and the limitations of subaltern consciousness, situating the production of this consciousness in dynamic relation to ongoing—often quotidian—processes of domination and state formation. It would thereby avoid the excesses of much recent scholarship on resistance in Latin America and elsewhere that overemphasizes the "authenticity," the "irreducible integrity" of subaltern cultures and consequently ascribes an unwarranted autonomy to the politics and ideology of popular struggles.[26] Only then, with these conceptual elements in place, will we have any prospect of reconstructing more precisely how popular agency in the multiple arenas where state projects were promoted typically obliged powerholders to come to terms with those below them.[27]

## Recovering the Subaltern: Methodological Issues

In the second half of the book, "Seasons of Upheaval," we attempt to practice what we preach. In Chapters 7 and 8, we narratively reconstitute Yucatán's distinctive episodes of rural insurgency under Maderismo (1909–13). We then seek to plumb the meanings in them, particularly regarding the parameters of campesino consciousness. In Chapter 9 we probe the various strategies that ultimately enabled planters and the state to co-opt and contain campesino dissent, thereby keeping the Mexican Revolution at arm's length for two more years. Finally, in Chapter 10, after narrating how General Salvador Alvarado's Constitutionalist Revolutionary Army of the Southeast subdued the last stand of the oligarchs, we assess the legacies of Yucatán's seasons of upheaval for the region's subsequent revolutionary history and examine their implications for a broader reappraisal of Mexican revolutionary mobilization.

Our research is based in large part on an unusually rich set of personal testimonies from criminal court records in the Archivo General del Estado de Yucatán. These testimonies, along with oral histories; notarial archives; accounts in the partisan regional press; and government, church, and estate records, among other sources, enable us to focus on the villagers, peons, and artisans who participated in the revolts led by Yucatán's incipient revolutionary chiefs and statebuilders.

This is precisely what the "elite historiographies" of both the Left and the Right have failed to do. Most historians of Yucatán have passed over the Maderista period to focus on the more celebrated, radical regimes of Alvarado (1915–18) and Felipe Carrillo Puerto (1922–24), when Yucatán was hailed as the social laboratory of the Mexican Revolution.[28] When historians have addressed the Maderista seasons of upheaval, they have typically portrayed the violence in the manner of contemporary government officials: as the voiceless, brutish, and ultimately inconsequential outbursts of vengeful peons. Local writers of both conservative and Marxist stripe have "explained" the unleashing of these revolts as little more than the work of unscrupulous (choose: leftist or *hacendado*) "outside agitators" preying on the credulous minds of ignorant campesinos.[29]

Of course, this is not really surprising. Many modern scholars—too many of them, unfortunately, Latin Americanists—continue to deny peasants (and other subordinate peoples and groups) ideological attributes, as if they had no consciousness of their own, and hence no ability to make their own history.[30] While many scholars of the Mexican Revolution might not care to admit it, implicit in their work is some level of agreement with historian and literary scholar John Rutherford's contention that "like the pin-headed monsters of prehistory, the Mexican Revolution had inadequate mental control and direction to match the mighty physical forces at play in it."[31] Orthodox Marxist treatments of Mexico's twentieth-century revolution and other popular struggles are particularly vulnerable to this line of criticism, for they have served to empty subaltern movements of their specific types of consciousness and practice and to read in the past only the inexorable development of class consciousness.[32]

While social historians of the Latin American countryside are only just beginning seriously to ponder questions of political consciousness and the popular cultures in which such consciousness is embedded, the comparative literature on rural social action and mentality is richly innovative and provocative.[33] The grand studies of peasant insurgency and revolution of the 1960s and 1970s typically privileged elites, external agents, and the world-scale structural factors that conditioned agrarian society; but they frequently minimized the significance of peasant grievances and ideologies.[34] Now, by contrast, the nature of subaltern consciousness and agency is a blossoming concern. The process, as we have noted, has brought greater emphasis to "unlikely forms of resistance, subversions rather than large-scale collective insurrections, small or local resistances not tied to the overthrow of systems or even to ideologies of emancipation."[35]

Inspired by the axiom "the word is power," most of these recent contributions also share a critical intent to demystify and dismantle elite historiography in its several forms (colonialist, nationalist, Marxist, patriarchal, and so on). This new wave of resistance scholarship has engaged a diverse array of subordinate rural groups: indigenous New World peoples in the throes of conquest and colonization; plantation slaves and freedmen in the Caribbean, South America, and U.S. South; marginalized black peasant-workers in South Africa; and poor Indian and Southeast Asian village-based cultivators among them.[36] Such studies have argued, often with relentless power, that the time has long passed when peasantry could be equated with the "idiocy of rural life," or when it could be assumed that "the ideological content of peasant . . . consciousness must necessarily be imported from 'outside,' through the medium of urban contacts, the vanguard party or whatever external agency."[37] Of course, as the Mexican state's initial, re-flexive depiction of Chiapas's neo-Zapatista rebels in 1994 as poor rustics led astray by outside agitators attests, the conventional wisdom still possesses considerable power.[38]

Yet if such essentialist views do not easily wash for campesinos during the Mexican Revolution—or any other era—severe methodological problems stand in the way of a full-bodied alternative to elite historiography. Rural historian Eric Van Young recently observed that although the study of peasant politics has become something of a cottage industry, and although the will to probe the consciousness behind rural collective protest and violence is increasing, "there are almost insuperable obstacles in convincingly analyzing peasant political action at any time much before the middle of this century." Problems of conceptualization (and, more fundamentally, of epistemology) enter into the equation, to be sure; but ultimately the most intractable issue is one of sources: the scarcity and inherent limitations of the materials to make sense of the aspirations and moral criteria of "the inarticulate—or perhaps better said, of the illiterate, the preliterate, or the willfully non-inscribed."[39] Glossing some of the best writing on nineteenth- and twentieth-century Mexican peasant politics, Van Young is forced to conclude that while rural historians have taken pains to identify insurgents and their beliefs, most often they have tended to portray them as a "homologous magnitude"—Marx's proverbial sack of potatoes.[40]

A sample of these historians' own frequent disclaimers and admissions of frustration sheds light not only on the critical problem of sources but on the current state of Mexicanist scholarship on peasant consciousness. John Tutino laments the difficulty of directly "study[ing] the grievances that stimulate rural uprisings" and observes that the dearth of studies of village life impedes our ability to recover "the perceptions of the peasant majority."[41] Brian Hamnett points up "the difficulty of finding concrete evidence of individual or collective motivation for insurgent affiliation," which severely complicates fundamental determinations of cause and effect.[42] And Alan Knight, even as he powerfully demonstrates the peasantry's central involvement in the Mexican Revolution and persuasively argues that campesinos possessed distinctive forms of political consciousness, also bemoans historians' inability "to penetrate . . . the crucial but intangible [dimension of] . . . campesino mentality." Hence, he warns, "even qualified 'Mexicanists' run the old risk of listening to the articulate, literate voices of the past, while neglecting the inarticulate and rustic."[43]

Among such "qualified Mexicanists" must also be numbered the contributors to Friedrich Katz's rich collection *Riot, Rebellion, and Revolution: Rural Social Violence in Mexico.* In their case studies of rural insurgency, these authors, virtually without exception, masterfully account for causation by emphasizing long-term economic pressures in combination with short-term political crisis.[44] Nevertheless, also with few exceptions (most notably William Taylor's essay on late colonial banditry, which mines a particularly rich vein of criminal court testimonies), the authors are much less successful in linking their general causal explanations to flesh-and-blood rebels.[45] Basic questions go begging for answers: Who were the insurgents? What were their social origins and occupations? And what exactly did they want? William Meyers observes (regarding the social composition of the popular rebellion in the Comarca Lagunera during the first revolutionary decade), "the 'insurrectos' were generally described as a faceless mass, either hidden in the hills, terrorizing the countryside in small bands, or threatening the towns."[46] Unfortunately, hamstrung by official sources and elite historiography, Meyers, like most of the volume's contributors, is unable to sketch in his rebels' faces or flesh out their motivations with significantly greater clarity. All things considered, it is hard to argue with Van Young's summary judgment of Mexicanists' treatment of peasant consciousness: "When we generalize about political leaders, we tend to illustrate with biographical materials; when we generalize about peasants (with rare exceptions), we tend to illustrate with sociological generalizations."[47]

Yet, like Van Young, we would argue that, despite the attendant difficulties, there are indeed ways of getting at peasant consciousness. The first step, we believe, is to recognize both the possibilities and the pitfalls of elite-generated, often state-mediated sources.[48] By these we mean government reports and official correspondence, memoirs and eyewitness accounts of the *gente decente*, the partisan local and national press, and criminal court records, if one is lucky enough to have them.[49] This is, after all, the basic arsenal of sources that most Mexicanists have to work with in attempting an analysis of rural consciousness and popular culture. A favored few—ourselves included—have additionally gained access to so-called "popular" (or non-elite) sources: oral traditions and written folklore.

The value of elite sources as a staple of historical research is beyond dispute. They not only provide a corrective to the bias found in folklore; they overwhelm it in terms of sheer volume and accessibility. This is because the discourse on peasant insurgency is predominantly one of power, an outcome attributable to literacy levels as well as to the vested interests of the state and the dominant classes of society in monitoring gestures of defiance of authority.

By definition, then, elite-generated sources are fraught with their own biases and limitations. When used uncritically—as if the accounts they presented were transparent and authoritative—such sources inevitably distort or "socially foreshorten" peasants. They rarely focus on the social questions relating to the composition and motivation of campesino groups, which obliges the empathetic historian to engage in reasoned speculation. This gives rise, at best, to rather mechanistic treatments of causality, and at worst to some embarrassing, "tortured inferences."[50]

Without question, the richest elite-generated sources, in terms of the fine-grained personal detail they often contain, are criminal (that is, judicial and police) records. While such records have been a staple for some of the most innovative research in colonial social history, until now they have been largely neglected by Yucatecan specialists and have received relatively little attention from social historians of modern Mexico.[51] This is particularly unfortunate, because in addition to yielding biographical and autobiographical data, criminal records can often complement oral and written folklore by enhancing our knowledge of popular *attitudes* toward crime and resistance. Indeed, the "subaltern studies school" of South Asian historiography has demonstrated that a peasant discourse of insurgency often lies embedded in such official documents, and that historians can gain access to it in two ways.[52]

First, this political consciousness makes its presence felt "directly," either through insurgent messages and proclamations intercepted by state agents and included in court files, or through the personal testimonies of peasants under interrogation.[53] Of course, numerous difficulties attend the reading of these testimonies. Among the power-laden variables that frame such documents and inevitably shape their meaning are the ritualistic, confessional nature of trial procedure; the likelihood of coercive pretrial interrogation and the impact of fear on defendants' and witnesses' testimonies; linguistic and cultural barriers that skew communication with indigenous witnesses; and the calculated attempts by defendants to excuse themselves through recourse to familiar alibis, such as being under the spell of alcohol, being at the wrong place at the wrong time, political naiveté—all of which played on the dominant class's racial and paternalistic inclinations.[54] Nevertheless, because this kind of documentation was gathered to assist the state in controlling diverse forms of protest, its usefulness in that regard seems a measure of its authenticity as a window on peasant consciousness.

That consciousness, moreover, is at times validated more subtly by key indices in official discourse itself. Because all forms of political violence against the state were considered ipso facto to be criminal acts, police, judicial, and other classes of administrative documents often devote words, phrases, and occasionally even extended passages to condemnatory characterizations of the perpetrators as well as to denunciations of their deviance from the legal order. Read carefully, particularly against evidence from other sources (such as local press accounts, oral traditions), these "telltale signs" or "ideological birthmarks" can in certain cases mark the difference between two mutually contradictory norms or perceptions of society.[55]

Thus, by reversing the terms of official rationalizations, the reader often can detect the terms of an insurgent peasant discourse. For example, as we will see, references to a "district of bandits" might not describe a nest of thieves so much as a locality in which a sizable portion of the population was resisting the state's forces in some manner. The redundant invocation of the phrase *regional contagion* might reveal more about elite fears, and conjunctural solidarity and enthusiasm among groups of villagers and peons, than about the rapid spread of deviance. And habitual official references to "lawlessness" might tell more about collective defiance of what had come to be regarded as bad administrative practices than about rampant, wanton criminality. As Ranajit Guha, the principal theoretician of the "subaltern studies school," has trenchantly observed:

> The pressures exercised by insurgency on elite discourse force it to reduce the semantic range of many words and expressions, and assign to them specialized meanings in order to identify peasants as rebels and their attempt to turn the world upside down as crime. Thanks to such a process of narrowing down it is possible for the historian to use this impoverished and almost technical language as a clue to the antonymies which speak for a rival consciousness.[56]

Precisely because both peasant insurgency and certain kinds of rural crime have an "inversive function," Guha also argues that the "official mind of the state" has occasionally mistaken the former for the latter. Yet neither Guha nor we would suggest that the state consistently " 'misreads' the codes locked up in collective behavior." To do so, as Van Young correctly observes, would be to "paint 'the state' and its servants as slavering idiots, an assumption no more reasonable for this group than for peasants and other rural protesters." We would agree with Van Young that, more likely, a "realpolitik of reflexive regime self-defense" operated in rural Mexico; for in defining as crime what it knew to be protest, the state sought to strip the insurgents' actions of any claim to political legitimacy.[57] Indeed, elites may have perceived the use of "standard manipulationist vocabulary"—"dens of brigands," "disreputable elements," "regional contagion"—to criminalize popular protest as particularly necessary in the Mexican (or wider Latin American) context.[58] As Richard Morse and others have shown, doctrines supporting an inherent popular sovereignty dated from at least the sixteenth century and grew in tandem with a highly porous absolutist state.[59] Criminalization of popular protest and resistance was therefore essential to nullify protesters' claims to political legitimacy under the aegis of such doctrines.[60]

If in its healthy challenge of positivist or "realist" accounts of history the new linguistic turn in the human sciences has taught us anything, it is that "narration can only receive its meaning from the world which makes use of it."[61] Thus, we should not "mistake a 'meaning' (which is always constituted rather than found) for 'reality' (which is always found rather than constituted)."[62] Like Guha and many recent scholars of resistance, we would be careful to maintain a distinction between sociopolitical labels such as "bandit" and the events they signify. The actions of "bandits" may often be difficult to distinguish from those of other criminals and rural insurgents; nevertheless, as we will demonstrate in our treatment of Yucatán's seasons of upheaval, the label itself has often served, at strategic conjunctures, to crystallize images, recast allegiances, and mobilize public sentiment. In the hands of the state, the label has historically been employed to "normalize deviant behavior" (that is, to regulate defiant behavior). In the hands of insurgents, who have broken with the rules and interests served by such labeling and have set about inverting them, the label itself has often been refashioned into a badge of honor.[63]

## The Courtroom as Social Laboratory

The penal records found in the Ramo de Justicia of Yucatán's State Archive illuminate much more than the resistance that occurred during the Maderista seasons of upheaval. They constitute our principal resource for exploring the multifaceted relationships among state authorities, regional elites, hingemen, and the rural laboring classes throughout Yucatán's "extended Porfiriato." The judicial system of Porfirian Yucatán served several important functions. Perhaps most significant for this study, it was a forum where villagers, peons tied to estates by debt, landowners large and small, and all manner of merchants and itinerant traders voiced their grievances and petitioned for redress. When social relations turned excessively violent—and a low level of violence was endemic—or crimes were alleged, the court system moved swiftly to investigate. Hundreds of files consulted in the Ramo de Justicia, although uncatalogued and incomplete, provide a reasonably detailed picture of a legal order that offered the powerless as well as the powerful at least the opportunity to raise legitimate questions about their rights as Mexican citizens.[64]

The records of these criminal proceedings allow the social historian, amid a welter of testimony and cross-examination, to hear the voices of the dispossessed. Mostly through the accretion of mundane detail, but occasionally with distinct drama, court documents establish the connections between the Maya peasant and the larger world—a consciously "modernizing" society that typically advanced at the campesino's expense. Could the legal system of such a society work in the campesino's interest? And did the peasant's participation in it ultimately legitimate and reinforce larger mechanisms of social and ideological control by state authorities and powerful landlords? These are significant, complex questions that do not permit easy answers. As we will see, any strategy or mechanism of control, be it flogging by a *mayocol* (foreman) or *encargado* (overseer), the use of identification papers to inhibit worker mobility in the countryside, conscription into the despised national guard, or a byzantine criminal justice system, required a degree of flexibility to function with maximum efficiency. If the mechanism of control was too rigid or brutal, if it did not allow for exceptions, its utility was likely to diminish, because those for whom it was intended would increasingly balk at its implementation. Yucatán's plantocracy instinctively heeded Talleyrand's maxim: "You can do many things with bayonets, but you cannot sit on them" (that is, *rule* with them).

From late 1909 until the middle of 1913, Yucatecan authorities faced nothing less than the breakdown of law and order as numerous civil disturbances, particularly in rural areas, tore at the social fabric. Yet even in the veritable political vacuum created by the fall of Díaz in the summer of 1911 and later by the murder of Madero in the spring of 1913—both of which raised the specter of anarchy in the countryside—the laborious process of judicial review continued to operate in Yucatán. Indeed, we will see that it did more than operate; it continued to prove its mettle as a flexible instrument of social control. Unlike many other regions of revolutionary Mexico, where judges fled and courthouses were sacked, Yucatán's time of troubles appears to underscore Gramsci's observation that the judicial system is more than a mirror of class antagonisms; it reveals the dominant class's ability to contain conflict precisely when its legitimacy is most seriously questioned.[65]

Yucatán's courts were an important component in the old order's larger strategy to prevent a series of local brushfires from evolving into a peninsular conflagration, perhaps even a repeat of the apocalyptic nineteenth-century Caste War, the planter class's greatest fear.[66] Ironically, it was the success of the planters' strategy and the continuing operation of their judicial system through the Mexican Revolution's first, violent decade that provided us social historians with a body of documentation rich enough to enable us to sit in judgment of them.

Yet if the workings of the criminal justice system help to explain why revolutionary violence did not engulf Yucatán, they also reveal the bitter resentment that campesinos harbored toward planter hegemony. Through a myriad of cases indicting villagers and peons for everything from insulting, assaulting, or murdering a public official or estate employee to rebelling against the legal order, we come to appreciate the full range of direct campesino responses against Yucatán's monocultural regime. This same body of testimony, moreover, also documents behavior that lies in the much broader universe that James Scott calls "infrapolitics." Such "disguised, low-profile, undisclosed forms of resistance" ranged from everyday strategies of evasion and foot-dragging to more violent, clandestine activities such as arson and rustling.[67] The old order may have survived until 1915, but the campesinos challenged it on various fronts on a continuing basis. They also utilized the political instability of the post-Díaz years to secure some hard-fought concessions. In 1914, rural workers actually extracted from local authorities a decree abolishing debt peonage. Although it was never implemented and it represented an expedient means for the oligarchy to buy time, this reformist decree provided an important precedent for later revolutionary governments to build on.

Nevertheless, need it bear repeating, the records of judicial proceedings must be used with some care if they are to yield valuable insights. Despite the tremendous wealth of materials found in the Ramo de Justicia, it is impossible to gauge how complete the records are, or whether they typify criminal behavior and the workings of the judicial system across all of Yucatán's *partidos* (districts). The process is complicated, moreover, by the problems of determining motivation and bias. In his seminal study of rural crime and deviance in colonial Mexico, William Taylor observes that the personal statements taken at the beginning of each criminal investigation are frequently the most valuable component of the case record, because they are often spoken in the heat of the moment, sometimes only minutes or hours after an incident has taken place.[68]

We would certainly concur. In Yucatán's turn-of-the-century courts, however, these statements were typically entered into the record by a justice of the peace or some other court representative, occasionally written in the third person, and replete with interpolation. As the case unfolded over the succeeding weeks and months, additional witnesses were interviewed and supporting statements assembled. The resulting case record thus grew complex; the adversarial nature of the system constantly raised questions about the reliability of the testimony. More often than not, this leaves the historian with serious questions about circumstances, motives, and "the truth."

These doubts are further magnified by the ability of many poor rural offenders to "play the game." Clearly, the types of questions court interrogators asked often influenced or predisposed defendants' responses. For example, because premeditated crimes were known to be punished more severely, it was in a defendant's interest to argue that the offense was involuntary or unplanned. In a real sense, criminal proceedings were a learning experience for Yucatán's subaltern classes, one in which the dominant class taught the law as an institution of social control.[69] Knowing how well the peasantry mastered its lessons and used the legal system to its best advantage helps to explain how effectively this mechanism of control addressed rural unrest and defused a truly revolutionary challenge to the Porfirian dictatorship.

We have been able to overcome some of the methodological shortcomings of this rich documentary source by seeking corroboration in Yucatán's densely layered mainstream and ephemeral press, and whenever possible, in ethnographic accounts and oral histories. Ultimately, despite their limitations, criminal court records have been invaluable to this study in two crucial respects. On one level, they have helped us track the ebb and flow of individual and collective protest in the countryside, both everyday resistance and "seasonal" patterns of revolt.

On a deeper level, these trial records have revealed to us patterns of violent social acts against persons and property, which in turn have illuminated fundamental values and flash points in Yucatecan society.[70] Even when court testimonies are tendentious, polemical, or untrue, they hold great value. Indeed, the terms in which campesinos chose to represent their case to the authorities disclose some of the fault lines along which tensions in a village or hacienda community found their expression.[71] Here we would agree with Taylor that "it is primarily in the accumulation of individual coincidences that the delicate network of relationships and feelings can be made visible through written records by the social historian who has not directly experienced the time and place of the people he studies." Or, as E. P. Thompson put it bluntly, "History is made up of episodes, and if we cannot get inside them we cannot get inside history at all."[72]

# PART I

# Summer of Discontent: Oligarchy and Its Costs, 1876–1909

## CHAPTER 2

# Patrons and Clients

Personalistic political parties humiliate the individual and are the greatest insult to the people. . . . We would cease being democrats if we lent credence, even for one moment, to the theory of indispensable individuals.
—Ignacio Ramírez

I wish to know as soon as possible if the governorship of Yucatán would be convenient for you. . . . I expect that your definitive response will reflect the loyalty of a soldier and the sincerity of a friend.
—Porfirio Díaz to Francisco Cantón

Authoritarian rule at the regional and national level during the Porfiriato (1876–1911) was never absolute. Even after Porfirio Díaz reached the point of indefinite election in 1888, he still had to contend with power struggles in both the capital and the periphery. Díaz's consummate skill as a politician enabled him to set potential rivals against each other. Regional caudillos and powerful elite factions from Sonora to Yucatán were manipulated in a subtle game of Mexican realpolitik as Don Porfirio employed a classic strategy of divide and rule.[1]

Díaz's efforts at political centralization were aided by personalistic political parties, managed electoral campaigns, and limited criticism of state (but seldom national) politics in the local press. Limiting political participation became an effective tool of social control; the democratic facade that adorned Don Porfirio's dictatorial mansion served to mollify elite discontent in the provinces.[2]

## Defining the Rules of the Game, 1876–97

The dictator made a practice of personally selecting governors (*el destape*).[3] This proved an effective method of curbing—but not eliminating—the violence that had always accompanied local elections during the Restored Republic.[4] But embedded in this apparent strength of the Pax Porfiriana lay its most glaring weakness. Power-seeking *camarillas* incessantly sought to focus the dictator's attention on their particular needs. If an impatient opposition faction could demonstrate that the incumbent *camarilla* was unable to keep the peace, Díaz might be forced to intervene. On the other hand, incumbents were rarely content to bow out gracefully, because their factions stood to lose political influence and economic opportunities when they relinquished the statehouse. No one appreciated this more than the savvy Díaz: "the governors make up the core of our political system, and for that reason I wish to proceed in accord with them; but they do not go along easily for fear of losing their posts . . . nobody wants to bet on the cards he does not have."[5]

Because regional power could not change hands in the states without the consent of Mexico City, contending elites sometimes felt compelled to promote unrest if they wished to gain, regain, or retain power.[6] If Don Porfirio decided that a change was in order, he instructed the local federal garrison commander to seize temporarily, then redistribute, the gubernatorial reins of power. Invariably, the ousted incumbents would simply bide their time—sometimes not much time—and then renew their intrigues and plotting, ultimately precipitating the next round of national intervention. Chronic unrest at the local level was accordingly built into the Porfirian system.

The system entailed additional risks. Díaz had to keep the local *camarillas* beholden to him. As long as they accepted his rule without question, he would favor them with local power—in due time. What had to be prevented at all costs was the emergence of a truly independent party, one that might question the legitimacy of Porfirian rule. Díaz managed to forestall this threat in the Yucatán peninsula for 32 years. For their part, the regional *camarillas* had to take care not to let intra-elite power struggles mushroom into volatile conflicts that the popular classes of regional society could join. This was a particular concern in Yucatán, where bitter memories of the Caste War lingered.

Don Porfirio successfully alternated the *camarillas* in Yucatán, but such manipulation of the region's political carousel demanded his constant attention. In Yucatán, he did not so much twirl the merry-go-round as slow it down and regularize its pace. State politics had already achieved a well-deserved reputation for instability long before the Porfiriato. Or perhaps "instability" is too mild a description. Historian Serapio Baqueiro reminds us that during one 25-year period (1848–73), Yucatán had 26 governors.[7] In 1873 alone, the state may well have established a dubious record with 7 chief executives. A year later, perplexed Yucatecos witnessed the sorry spectacle of 3 competing legislatures, each designating its own governor.[8]

Yucatán's peripheral location, moreover, lent a measure of autonomy to its political affairs that accentuated elite divisiveness. Because no road or railway connected Mexico City and Mérida—only irregular steamship service between Veracruz and Progreso—federal authorities found it difficult to keep abreast of local affairs, and vice versa. Messages took weeks, and when

## TABLE 2.1
### Yucatán's Governors During the Porfiriato

| Governor | Term |
| --- | --- |
| General Protasio Guerra | 1877 |
| José María Iturralde | 1878 |
| Manuel Romero Ancona | 1878–1882 |
| General Octavio Rosado | 1882–1886 |
| General Guillermo Palomino | 1886–1889 |
| Juan Pío Manzano | 1889–1890 |
| Colonel Daniel Traconis | 1890–1894 |
| Carlos Peón Machado | 1894–1897 |
| José María Iturralde | 1897–1898 |
| General Francisco "Pancho" Cantón | 1898–1902 |
| Olegario Molina | 1902–1910 |
| Enrique Muñoz Arístegui (acting) | 1907–1911 |

they did arrive they were often rendered irrelevant by the rapidly changing circumstances. The bureaucratic maxim "obedezco pero no cumplo" (I obey but I do not comply), well known to colonial authorities, also was observed by Yucatecan governors. Not until the introduction of the telegraph (1870), the railroad (1881) and the telephone (1883) did the federal government exert greater influence on local politics.[9]

In an effort to mitigate elite factional bickering, between 1882 and 1894 Díaz and his "successor," Manuel González (1880–84), installed local military commanders—some of them non-Yucatecans—in the governor's palace.[10] Although these military governors did manage to curb overt violence and the worst excesses of factionalism, they themselves could not escape the entanglements of elite political rivalry.[11] Invariably, certain *camarillas* found some officers more acceptable than others.[12]

At times, Yucatecans even found federal commanders preferable to their own civilian nominees. The political infighting surrounding the 1886 gubernatorial campaign is illustrative. In 1885, partisans of former civilian governor Manuel Romero Ancona sent a delegation to Mexico City to lobby for their candidate. Romero Ancona's opponents warned Díaz that the delegation comprised little more than the former governor's personal emissaries. The visit, they contended, was "doubly deceitful": it sought to convince the president that the unpopular Romero Ancona enjoyed widespread local support, and it sent a false message to Yucatecos that the politician was Don Porfirio's choice.[13]

An influential group of Yucatecan expatriates living in the Federal District recommended a compromise candidate, General Guillermo Palomino of Veracruz, who had served as federal garrison commander in the peninsula and as Yucatán's congressman. Romero Ancona's shills responded that the general's candidacy was illegal under state law, because he was not a native and had not lived in the state for ten continuous years.[14] Mexico City newspapers chose sides and publicly debated the *destape*. After the sparring concluded, Díaz selected the Veracruzano general. Once "elected" governor in

1886, Palomino cultivated so much support that his partisans could collect thousands of signatures on petitions calling for a reform of the state constitution to permit his reelection in 1890. Díaz, moreover, appeared to be listening to his constituents, even while confirming his modus operandi in the provinces. By refusing to "elect" Romero Ancona to a new term, he emphasized the importance of rotating the regional *camarillas*.[15]

If gubernatorial nominees were unveiled in Mexico City and the results of each election were a foregone conclusion, why were elections always so bitterly contested? Why did regional *camarillas* go to such lengths to influence the *destape*? To understand political mobilization at the regional level—in "Los Porfiritos"—we first turn to patronage, the mortar and bricks that held together Díaz's mansion of power. Patrons and their clienteles exposed the contradictions inherent in a dictatorship uncomfortable with the formal democratic institutions—such as elections—that it appropriated to legitimate its rule.

## PORFIRIAN CLIENTELISM

To survive politically, to prosper economically, to advance socially, Mexicans of all classes found it imperative to join patron-client networks.[16] These were vertically linked to rival cliques, or *bloques del poder*, surrounding the president.[17] The nation's political culture was steeped in an "ideology of hierarchy," which Díaz exploited to strengthen the power of the central government.[18] Regional *camarillas* erected personalistic political machines that not only reached "up" to national cliques in the Distrito Federal, but also "down" through extended kinship networks and middlemen to villages, haciendas, and the barrios of the growing provincial cities. A *camarilla* that could not peddle influence up and down the political pyramid soon found itself bereft of power and economic advantage. Paternalism, so familiar to *hacendados* and their peons, also defined working relationships within the political arena.[19]

The strength of clientelism lay in its insistence on mutual obligations and its limited use of coercion.[20] The patron of the family-based faction offered positions, protection, and other inducements to his personal followers, who returned the favor by pledging loyalty and service when the politician demanded it. Reciprocity confirmed the existing social hierarchy: obedience and loyalty purchased favors, deference was expected, transgressions were not forgiven lightly.

This hierarchical pyramid was firmly rooted, especially at the regional and local levels, in the extended family. Melding ties of blood, marriage, and fictive kinship (*compadrazgo*), politicians relied on their relatives to create the nucleus of a devoted and dependable organization. With family and close friends placed in key leadership posts, politicians methodically broadened their appeal to embrace members of all social classes. Francisco Cantón's *camarilla*, for instance, had relatives and friends sprinkled throughout his Gran Club Liberal. His ties extended all the way to Díaz's cabinet, enhancing his political fortunes. His stepbrother, Joaquín Baranda, who served as minister of justice and public instruction for almost two decades, repeatedly lobbied on Don Pancho's behalf and was instrumental in persuading Díaz to "elect" Cantón governor in 1898.[21]

Because Pancho Cantón (1833–1917) cast such an imposing shadow over the entire period and because he, more than any other single politician, personified the pervasiveness of clientelistic politics in Yucatán, a brief sketch of his checkered career is in order.[22] A throwback to the chaotic age of *caudillismo,* Cantón was the epitome of the powerful regional chieftain. His victories and defeats in the Caste War and the War of the Reform had earned him a devoted following.[23]

Born and raised in Valladolid in eastern Yucatán, Cantón, like many in his political generation who had lost family and friends in the Caste War, became obsessed with the defeat of the "indios bárbaros" who refused to submit to white rule. In 1848, at the age of fourteen, he luckily had escaped with his family during the bloody Maya siege of Valladolid. When state authorities retook the city in December of that year, Cantón and his family returned, shocked at the devastation the *indios* had left. Young Cantón promptly joined the local militia to help protect Valladolid against further incursions. This was the beginning of a distinguished military career that featured numerous expeditions against the rebel Maya. Cantón would demonstrate similar resolve in defense of Maximilian's empire.[24]

Cantón's adversaries charged that he lacked formal military training, knew little about tactics and strategy, and evinced scant regard for discipline. Perceived by local politicians as a loose cannon, Cantón spent his entire political career leading "revolutions" against the Mérida establishment.[25] He instinctively grasped, however, that power and pride, not principles, were the essence of regional politics.

Pancho Cantón's reputation was validated in 1868, when, after an unsuccessful rebellion, the young *jefe* (chief) was forced into hiding in eastern Yucatán. With the help of friends and family, he evaded capture for fourteen months. When the federal army finally took the fugitive at Kantó, his hacienda outside Valladolid, on March 13, 1869, Cantón was summarily sentenced to be shot by a firing squad on the morning of the 17th in his native city. His friends worked tirelessly over the next few days to obtain a restraining order from the state appeals court in Mérida. On the morning of March 16, the presiding judge found in Colonel Cantón's favor. Two friends rode on horseback the 150 kilometers from Mérida to Valladolid, carrying the court documents granting a stay of execution. After riding all night, José Solís and Manuel Loría arrived moments before the scheduled 9 A.M. execution, just as the colonel—in formal military attire and smoking "an exquisite cigar"—embraced his friends who had come to say farewell to their patron, and made his way to the scaffold. Joaquín Baranda later embellished

Cantón's providential deliverance from the firing squad, delivering this melodramatic rendition of the colonel's difficult "last hours":

> The chapel, the last visits by his friends, the confessor, the final, tender farewell of his wife, the mournful tolling of the bells, the prolonged march to the scaffold. . . . Close to the scaffold, the stay of execution was received. Yet we can be sure that Cantón has already suffered the death penalty, because this sentence does not consist so much of the material act of dying, but that which precedes death itself; in the sight of the scaffold when one is still full of life. That is dying![26]

Thus reprieved, Cantón was eventually sent to San Juan de Ulúa military penitentiary in the port of Veracruz, where, in 1870, he and other recalcitrant imperialists were held until they could be court-martialed in Mexico City. Personal contacts again proved indispensable. Baranda's brother, Pedro, a colonel in the army, petitioned the minister of war to release Cantón from the fortress on his own recognizance. Then Joaquín, acting as Cantón's attorney, argued the case before the military tribunal and won his release. In his eloquent brief, Baranda not only earned Pancho Cantón the empathy of the judges but conveyed the impression that the colonel was a patriotic soldier grievously wronged by state authorities—an image that Cantón's political handlers would cultivate throughout his career.[27]

The rebellious caudillo wasted little time returning home to renew his ongoing feud with state authorities. He organized and led unsuccessful uprisings in 1872 and 1873; then in 1876 he belatedly answered Díaz's call to arms, trouncing the Lerdistas, Díaz's opponents, in the Tuxtepec rebellion's final battle in Mérida's Santa Ana Plaza. After countless political setbacks, Pancho Cantón finally was a winner. Díaz rewarded him with a promotion to the rank of general, a pardon for his imperialistic activities, and a post as subinspector of the military command in eastern Yucatán. In 1880 Díaz gave the caudillo one more lucrative plum: a railway concession from Mérida to his native Valladolid.[28]

Favors begat loyalty. As one fellow Tuxtepecista colonel who had fought alongside Cantón noted in a letter to the dictator:

> We are fighting and we will continue to fight with resolve, struggling against the intrigues and machinations of our enemies, because we have faith that our belief in you will not prove illusory. . . . We will always be your most constant and dedicated friends."[29]

Díaz's sponsorship, however, did not make the irascible caudillo any more acceptable to Yucatecan politicians. When Cantón's supporters tested the political waters in the 1878 and 1882 governor's races, Díaz and González wisely withdrew the former conservative (or *madruguete*, opportunist, as they were called in the peninsula) from consideration. Cantón's patrons in Mexico City did their best to keep the general away from political intrigues in Mérida, "electing" him a federal deputy from 1877 to 1885. In

an 1877 letter to the president, Cantón acknowledged that he was a liability
for the dictator in Yucatán: "I do not wish to create political problems there,
so I have decided to serve in the [federal] congress, unless you would prefer
some other thing."[30] Yet Cantón remained a formidable political force
throughout the Porfiriato precisely because his faction wedded his "outsider" persona to a statewide political machine that constantly competed
for power. No one understood the nature of patronage better than Pancho
Cantón. Even his critics grudgingly admired how he took care of his own.

> Accustomed to manage sufficient resources in order to live comfortably, he
> was more than willing to help those who requested it. He has been a tireless
> protector to his kin and has extended his assistance to other families and
> individuals, even to strangers.[31]

General Cantón's charismatic leadership aggravated liberal politicians,
who saw in his stormy past a painful reminder of Yucatán's notorious instability and in his former allegiance to the monarchy a proof that he was out of
step with Porfirio Díaz's modernizing vision. The general went to great
lengths to distance himself from his conservative past—indeed, his political
platform could have been written by his liberal opponents.[32] Even so, he
always maintained close ties to the military and church hierarchies, which
in turn actively supported his *camarilla*.[33] The Cantonistas' willingness to
cloak their reactionary past in liberal rhetoric raises significant questions
about the role that political principles played in that clientelistic regime.

## UNRAVELING THE IDEOLOGICAL THREAD

Did the Porfiriato mean "the end of ideology," as one scholar has recently maintained?[34] In Yucatán's case, the answer is equivocal. On the one
hand, the principles that local elites held dear never transcended their loyalty to Díaz's regime. They realized only too well that the Pax Porfiriana,
with its developmentalist impulse, suited their export interests to a T. But
the leaders of late nineteenth-century Yucatán, born in the chaotic 1830s
and 1840s, had cut their political teeth on the endless factional bickering
that culminated in the harrowing Caste War and the Reform.

The Caste War, especially the bloody first decade, from 1847 to 1857,
had a particularly profound impact on the historical memory of regional
politicians. Between one-third and one-half of Yucatán's six hundred thousand inhabitants died in the bloodbath; in some southeastern subregions,
the death toll reached an astonishing 75 percent. Nineteenth-century creole
historians—most of them politicians who had lived through the war themselves—later characterized the conflict as the result of the provincial elites'
cumulative failure to agree on a common vision of the future after independence. After 1840, chroniclers later lamented, partisan politics divided the
creoles as it armed the rebel Maya. By 1847 the distrust was so palpable that
conflict was inevitable.[35]

Luis González's *Pueblo en vilo*, an unconventional account of a small town in Michoacán, describes how historical moments can define an entire generation. But if San José de Gracia's generations were shaped by such natural or "supernatural" occurrences as snowstorms and comets, which were thought to presage the end of the world, Mérida's cohorts were nurtured by long-standing family feuds. Liberal-conservative sniping did not subside in the wake of Maximilian's defeat. In the provinces, grudges festered like sores; they were passed down from generation to generation.[36]

Even though ex-conservatives had to be more circumspect about verbalizing their sentiments during the Porfiriato, they were no less committed to preserving the institutions they revered, such as the church and the military. Through the beneficence of wealthy conservatives like the Casares, Ponce, and Cantón families, the church, in particular, made a dramatic recovery in Yucatán after Maximilian's defeat. Prestigious schools, such as the Colegio Católico de San Ildefonso and the Universidad Católica in Mérida, under the leadership of Bishop Crescencio Carrillo y Ancona and headmaster Norberto Domínguez Elizalde, opened their doors to a new generation of *gente decente*.[37] Indeed, an intriguing recent essay by Hernán Menéndez Rodríguez on the church's political and economic relationship with local factions argues that the diocese, while maintaining its long-standing ties to the Cantonistas, also sought to ingratiate itself with more pragmatic or opportunistic liberals like the Molina *camarilla*.[38]

In any case, the *madruguetes* took comfort in the realization that national elites were far less interested in wielding ideological axes than were local opponents. As the Porfirian state transformed liberalism into a unifying political myth, an uneasy ideological consensus emerged. Ironically, as former conservatives found shelter from the ideological storm, doctrinaire liberals, who believed the regime's adherence to scientific politics (or "liberal-conservatism") was a contemptuous perversion of Reform principles, were increasingly placed on the defensive.[39]

What complicates our understanding of Mexican liberalism is the realization that it meant different things to different socioeconomic groups and classes at different times. Some regional elites were most concerned with the federalist principles and political freedoms initially prescribed in the Constitution of 1824. Others were more committed to the institutional reforms embodied in the midcentury Reform Laws. Anticlericalism may have been an essential component of the liberal tradition for members of the urban middle class; it was anathema to most campesinos, who occasionally joined the fight against conservatives throughout the nineteenth century. Indeed, rural *caciques* and their clients viewed local autonomy and the protection of community rights as the most sacred tenets of the liberal creed. Regional elites, however, had a more pragmatic perspective on the relative importance of federalism and centralism.

Not surprisingly, those in power had a vested interest in maintaining the status quo, playing fast and loose with the separation of powers and individual freedoms. Conversely, those "on the outs" railed against the centralization of power. Moreover, an activist current articulated by lib-eral intellectuals like Ignacio Ramírez and Ponciano Arriaga, which de-manded a more egalitarian society, had little in common with the "liberal-conservatism" that became the mainstay of the Porfirian regime.[40]

In Yucatán, separatism, like liberalism, was a political football tossed around at opportune moments to rally *camarillas* during campaigns. Its slogans were a lament for losers; thwarted factions invariably railed against Mexico City's imposition of governors.[41] Yet there is little evidence that, with the exception of the sore losers and a few anachronistic zealots who reveled in past secessionist movements, regional autonomy was a burning issue among local politicians.[42] Regional elites did not repudiate their polit-ical patrimony; to deny those ideals would have been tantamount to admit-ting that the political battles fought since independence were irrelevant. But as the rules of the Porfirian *destape* became apparent, state politicians were forced to soft-pedal principles if they sought elected office. As yes-terday's conservatives, liberals, and separatists fought for political space, ideals were transformed into handy political slogans and used indiscrimi-nately to bash an opponent or justify an incumbent's policies. Personalistic politics and patronage made sure of that.[43]

Indeed, by the late Porfiriato, ideological differences were difficult to discern among rival factions. All actively supported Díaz's continuing re-election and paid lip service to liberal icons like Father Miguel Hidalgo, Benito Juárez, and the 1857 Constitution. Even Rafael de Zayas Enríquez, an enthusiastic supporter of the "liberal" Olegario Molina, admitted that the similarities between Cantón's and Molina's *camarillas* far outnum-bered their differences.

> I do not think that at present there are political parties in Yucatán, but instead two entirely personalistic groupings.... Both contain multimillion-aires, both enjoy a well-deserved prestige among all social classes and both entertain, as their strongest desire, the prosperity of the State. In both group-ings I can identify liberals, moderates, and remnants of the Conservative Party, all of which shows that political principles are not at issue in the peninsula but, instead, matters of order and public interest.[44]

Manuel Sierra Méndez, who kept the dictator abreast of local politics, echoed Zayas Enríquez's comments on the specter of personalistic politics, and was decidedly less sanguine about how meaningful political principles were to ambitious politicians: "the important thing is to achieve and wield power, without giving a thought to the well-being and the best interests of society."[45]

## PORFIRIAN CAMPAIGNS

However useful ideology or charismatic leadership might prove to re-gional *camarillas*, they were never a substitute for the organization of patron-client networks. Among the elite, recruitment was facilitated by a number of private clubs, literary societies, and Masonic lodges in Mérida and throughout the state. One group of intellectuals that played an active role in regional politics was led by Pancho Cantón's nephew, the poet Delio Moreno Cantón. This close circle of friends, many of whom had been class-mates at the Colegio Católico de San Ildefonso, met regularly at Waldemaro Ponce's downtown drugstore. The shop fronted the Gamboa Guzmán print-ing house, which published the group's literary magazine, *Pimienta y Mos-taza*. Moreno Cantón's literary society was largely responsible for churning out much of the political propaganda that blanketed the state during Pan-cho Cantón's successful run for the statehouse.[46]

To construct a multiclass coalition, however, politicians needed more than *hacendados*, merchants, and intellectuals; they required the assis-tance of middlemen or brokers—who, in Eric Wolf's words, stood "guard over the critical junctures and synapses of relationships which connect the local system to the larger whole."[47] These mediating agents, who moved easily between the city and the countryside, actively recruited followers for regional *camarillas*; and it was their consummate organizational abilities that would later fuel the first seasons of upheaval.

Electoral campaigns offered tangible proof of a *camarilla*'s ability to mobilize its partisans. Electoral triumph also validated the leadership abil-ities of the successful patron while simultaneously improving the bargain-ing position of clients because *camarillas* needed clients' votes and organi-zational muscle. Moreover, campaigns promoted the vertical integration of clientelistic politics from the smallest hamlet to the national arena, reen-forcing the prevailing hierarchy.[48] Electoral practices created a body of vot-ers for the personalistic political machines, even while replicating the in-equalities of society. Hilda Sabato has persuasively argued that throughout Latin America, the right to vote was granted as part of an elite project to impose the liberal model of an ideal citizen on the general population. Pol-iticians could also bestow legitimacy on their political institutions by creat-ing a malleable citizenry that willingly participated in the public sphere. But the politicians also had to be ever vigilant to maintain control over that potentially unruly multitude.[49]

Elite politicians were never interested in creating a community of equals. They did not conceive of voters as individual citizens in full com-mand of their political rights who periodically convened to cast their bal-lots peacefully. Instead, they saw voters as part of organized networks that served the politicians' interests. Newspapers and a variety of associations and organizations contributed to what Sabato has called "a culture of mobi-lization." Yet those who participated in the mobilizations often had their own agendas. Sometimes, members of associations marshalled to support a particular *camarilla* held meetings or outdoor public rallies to show au-thorities that their cause enjoyed popular support in its own right. And local authorities increasingly had to pay attention. As Fernando Escalante

Gonzalbo has shown in his study of nineteenth-century Mexican politics, "Undoubtedly, the 'pueblo' was an important actor in the political melodrama. . . . If the people were not the citizens fancied by the enlightened imagination of a political class, neither were they apathetic, or 'a flock of sheep.' "[50] After 1900 the electoral process was opened up, and constituents of different social classes were encouraged to participate. But this aperture only highlighted the growing contradiction between the republican rhetoric of citizenship and representation and the manipulative reality of machine politics.

*Camarillas* attracted partisans, moreover, because victorious political parties offered tangible rewards. Simply put, a victory at the polls generally meant an economic stake and/or post in the new administration. Machine politics meant access to lucrative government contracts, railway concessions, and land grants for those in power. *Empleomanía*, the Mexican spoils system that was firmly rooted in Yucatán throughout the nineteenth century, would reach epic proportions during the late Porfiriato, as each *camarilla* enriched itself while in power.[51]

The result was a civil service immobilized by inertia. Innovation and experimentation were frowned on; ingratiating oneself with powerful *hacendados* and merchants was expected; and since each new administration signaled a thorough housecleaning of the civil service, nearsighted policies and stopgap measures were the rule. Manuel Sierra Méndez decried the pernicious effects of clientelism.

> Unfortunately, a district prefect, a mayor, or any figure of authority is only interested in remaining in the position he occupies. His decisions, therefore, are generally not inspired by justice but by a desire to remain on good terms with the powerful individuals in each locality.[52]

*Científico* (technocrat) Francisco Bulnes, never one to mince words, fumed,

> the bureaucratic middle class . . . [has been] the real oppressor of the people, the octopus that has sucked the vital juice of all popular labor, of foreign and national capital, and of the patience of the victims who carried the weight of this race of vipers.[53]

Inertia gave way only at election time, as incumbent civil servants campaigned throughout the state, forming local clubs in every district seat (*cabecera*) and barrio, tacking up political broadsheets and posters, staging elaborate street demonstrations, and sending delegations to Mexico City to lobby Díaz and his lieutenants.[54]

Favorable publicity and the appearance of popular support had to be fabricated if they did not exist. Glossy pamphlets praising a candidate were distributed by organizers throughout the state and were sent to the halls of power in Mexico City. Each pamphlet, containing thousands of supporters' signatures, was specially designed to convince Díaz and his inner circle that a candidate enjoyed widespread popular support. Pamphlets became almost standardized. They expressed gratitude for Díaz's peaceful and "progressive" rule; they winked and nodded at liberal ideals; they praised their candidate's abilities; and they assailed the local opposition.[55]

Local and national newspapers were another tool employed by resourceful factions. Carlos Peón Machado's political handlers realized during the early 1890s that favorable press coverage in the national capital might enhance the prominent *hacendado*'s chances in the 1894 gubernatorial campaign. The ambitious Peón Machado, who was part-owner of a Mérida daily, *El Eco del Comercio*, commissioned his lieutenants to contact the Mexico City press, only to find that certain newspapers charged dearly for puff pieces. His assistants reported that Filomena Mata, editor of *El Diario del Hogar*, charged a hefty *embute* (in Yucatán, a bribe) for his services: "He asks for a substantial sum and told me that he has already named a person who will reach an agreement there with you."[56]

Ephemeral newspapers became grist for the patronage mill. The 1890 gubernatorial campaign, for instance, produced an avalanche of political propaganda. Twenty-eight periodicals throughout the state—fifteen in Mérida alone—postulated the candidacy of Colonel Daniel Traconis. With titles such as *La Sombra de Guttemberg* (Motul), *Del 90 al 94* (Ticul), *La Voz del Partido* (Hunucmá), *La Convención Radical Obrera* (Mérida), and *El Artesano* (Mérida), they obviously were aimed at Traconis adherents in all social classes. Traconis also enjoyed the backing of a bevy of newspapers in Mexico City. Two opposition *camarillas* played by the same rules, however, publishing nine newspapers statewide and enlisting endorsements from seven in the Federal District.[57]

The growing complexity and sophistication of gubernatorial campaigns intersected with two related trends: the growth of centralism and the national tendency, after 1882, to replace military governors with civilians.[58] In Yucatán, Colonel Traconis helped prompt the move away from military rule by his near-legendary incompetence. Before his term (1890–94) ended, Traconis—just to make ends meet—was compelled to borrow a total of fifty thousand pesos from the Banco Yucateco and the Banco Nacional, almost seven thousand from Mérida's municipal treasury, and twenty thousand from local merchants and *hacendados*. Finally, in a move that would earn him the lasting enmity of even his most ardent supporters, he impounded a portion of state employees' salaries.[59]

In 1894, after more than a decade of relatively peaceful military rule, local politicians demanded, and Don Porfirio permitted, the election of a civilian. They chose Carlos Peón Machado; and during his regime (1894–97), political activity increased in Mérida and various towns as members of the elite took advantage of the opening to organize for future campaigns.

By 1897, three rival *camarillas* were poised to enter the fall gubernatorial elections. After years of bitter disappointment, Pancho Cantón's faction had reason to believe that its persistence and loyalty would finally be rewarded. A new clique of moderate liberals led by Olegario Molina, a rising henequen merchant, began the arduous task of constructing a political machine. Although Molina realistically regarded himself as a longshot in 1898, it was clear that he had his eyes set firmly on a future gubernatorial bid. Finally, supporters of the incumbent Peón Machado stoked the fires of "continuismo."[60]

The trick for the *camarillas*, in keeping with the unwritten rules of the *destape*, was to delay public announcement of their nominee until it was certain that he enjoyed Don Porfirio's support. To commit prematurely might backfire; Díaz discouraged extended campaigns lest they ignite political passions. Delegations journeyed to Mexico City habitually in March and April before the November elections to approach Díaz on behalf of their candidates. Peón Machado, however, refused to follow the prearranged script, and dire consequences ensued. The bitterly contested election is fraught with significance for understanding the subsequent political unrest before and after the outbreak of the Mexican Revolution.

## ANATOMY OF A 'DESTAPE'

To begin with, Yucatán's 1898 gubernatorial campaign spotlights another set of actors in the Porfirian political process, the expatriate regional influence peddlers residing in the capital, and their relationship to the select circle of counselors to the dictator.[61] As illustrated in the case of Romero Ancona, a number of wealthy Yucatecos lived in Mexico City and used their clientelist connections with Díaz's lieutenants to lobby for favored regional candidates. Their opinions were seriously considered by the influential *bloques del poder* that surrounded Don Porfirio.[62] It was important for aspiring nominees to reside in the Distrito Federal for a period of time in order to "network," in today's parlance. Expatriates personally introduced their candidate to their *bloque* and, if possible, to Don Porfirio himself. Yucatán's last three Porfirian governors, Peón Machado, Cantón, and Molina, who administered the state from 1893 to 1910, all had extensive experience spinning webs of contacts in Mexico City.[63]

Because the final choice of governor was ultimately made by the dictator and not the governors of Yucatán, it might be argued that these informal lobbies, which had familial ties to powerful *parentescos* in the peninsula, were more important in determining the next governor of the state than the political preference of elites in Yucatán itself. Factions within the Yucatecan colony funneled their advice to Díaz's consultants on peninsular affairs, Manuel Sierra Méndez and Joaquín Baranda. These two aggressive power brokers represented rival national *camarillas*.[64]

One *bloque*—led first by Manuel Romero Rubio, minister of the interior, and after his death in 1895 by the minister of finance, José Yves Limantour—was the so-called *científicos*, comprising bankers, prominent landowners, government officials, and technocrats.[65] Its rival, composed of traditional regional strongmen, former military officers, doctrinaire liberals, and some bureaucrats, was sharply critical of the *científicos'* increasing power and influence.[66]

Given his military background and connections, Pancho Cantón was a natural choice for the latter clique, while Olegario Molina found favor with the former. Peón Machado's patron in Mexico City was Romero Rubio; their friendship dated back to the mid-1870s, when both served in Sebastián Lerdo de Tejada's administration. The interior minister's death late in 1895, however, left Peón Machado's *camarilla* without ties to either bloc and thus lacking clout in Díaz's inner circle, a weakness that would eventually prove politically fatal.

The campaign began in earnest on November 1, 1896, when the Cantonista newspaper, *La Revista de Mérida*, speculated that Joaquín Baranda would resign his cabinet post to become Yucatán's next governor.[67] When Baranda visited the state on January 28, 1897, he scotched rumors that he would leave the national political arena, but he met with prominent Meridanos and galvanized support for the Cantonista party, the Gran Club Liberal Porfirista Antirreeleccionista.[68] (The party's cumbersome name is itself instructive: the now "liberal" Cantonistas sought to shed their conservative baggage, to show their opposition to Peoncista "continuismo," and to confirm their allegiance to Porfirismo by invoking one of its most sacred, if not ironic, tenets: "no reelection." Yet Cantón's opponents never missed a chance to point out that the general's inner circle was filled with *madruguetes*.[69])

The Cantonista cause was enhanced by a precipitous decline in fiber prices that threw the regional economy into a tailspin. The recession, which coincided with the first three years of Peón Machado's administration, saddled the incumbent with some heavy political baggage.[70] Yet even though the Gran Club Liberal was poised to mobilize its partisans statewide, Pancho Cantón realized that the final decision rested with Don Porfirio. Soon after Baranda's return to the capital, Cantón received the news he had patiently awaited for three decades. On February 11, 1897, Díaz offered the caudillo the governorship, phrasing the proposition in the vernacular of patronage.

> I wish to know as soon possible if the governorship of Yucatán would be convenient for you. . . . I expect that your definitive response will reflect the loyalty of a soldier and the sincerity of a friend.[71]

Cantón responded in kind, thanking Díaz for his trust and his praiseworthy comments about Cantón's loyalty, and taking special pains to inform his patron that he would rely on his many "friends" rather than a political party. The last comment was meant to allay fears in Mexico City that the Yucatecan general was building a powerful personalistic organization. In reality, as Cantón was penning the words, the Gran Club Liberal was aggressively organizing electoral committees throughout the state.[72]

It is interesting that Carlos Peón Machado had written Díaz on February 6, urging the dictator to make his preference known.[73] Díaz's response, written on February 18, seven days after the decision had been made to name Cantón, was designed to keep the Peoncistas in the dark for as long as possible.

> For if, in fact, these things should not be left until the last moment, they should not be made known too many months in advance either, because this exposes the candidate to the different criteria found in public opinion that are not always healthy and prudent in their expressions.[74]

The decision to keep Peón Machado and his supporters guessing might appear to have been a serious lapse of judgment by the usually shrewd dictator, although ultimately it worked to his advantage. The longer the delay, the more the Peoncistas could hope to convince Díaz that the governor deserved reelection. Indeed, throughout the spring and summer of 1897, the governor's supporters, calling themselves the Convención Democrática Yucateca, systematically organized throughout the state, forming 112 electoral committees and collecting 35,781 signatures.[75]

Employing the tried-and-true measures of machine politics, the Peoncistas galvanized support, publicizing the campaign in their newspapers; staging demonstrations in Mérida, Progreso, and other *cabeceras* with peons and villagers brought in from the countryside; and showering Don Porfirio with letters and petitions in support of Peón Machado.[76] Incumbent campaigning was so fervent that the opposition press ripped Alvino Manzanilla, the abrasive *jefe* of the Convención Democrática, for hauling in "poor Indian laborers" to demonstrations in Mérida, plying them with alcohol, and then forcing them to listen to campaign rhetoric in a language they did not understand.[77]

This burst of electioneering, however, put the governor in a compromising position. He advised his followers to defend their liberal principles, but as a "loyal and unconditional friend of Porfirio Díaz" and a sitting governor, he had to remain above the fray and could not participate in the campaign.[78]

Because state law prohibited reelection, Peoncista deputies in the legislature proposed an amendment to the state constitution. Díaz moved quickly to nip this strategy in the bud. He wrote to State Deputy José Domínguez Peón that it would not be helpful to alter the constitution currently because such a blatantly political move would impair the perception of Peón Machado's impartiality. As a result of Díaz's lobbying, the state legislature let the matter drop.[79] The move alarmed the governor's supporters, who saw their candidate's chances slipping away.

Still unsure of Don Porfirio's intentions yet hopeful of swaying the *destape*, the Convención Democrática sent a delegation to Mexico City. The group, composed of prominent civil servants, had an audience with the dictator in late March.[80] Intent on delaying his decision, Don Porfirio refused to give the delegation a definitive answer. And a week later, he tersely wrote to Peón Machado that no more delegations should be sent until two to three months before the scheduled November elections.[81]

The Peoncistas now read the handwriting on the wall: the governor's reelection would not be permitted. Peón Machado was still confident, however, that his successor would be a bona fide liberal. Never before had Díaz permitted a *madruguete* to occupy the statehouse. On April 23, Peón Machado wrote to Díaz:

> With pleasure I will step down with the satisfaction of knowing that when I return peacefully to private life, the one who replaces me will be from the Liberal Party, which richly deserves to have your support, and not from the obstinate conservatives. Whoever replaces me will not be an enemy.[82]

When Olegario Molina saw which way the political winds were blowing in the capital, he threw his support to Pancho Cantón—despite their long history of political contretemps, dating back to the empire, when Molina fought alongside Peón Machado and the victorious liberals against Cantón and the imperialists. Now Molina used his political connections with the *científicos* to weaken the Peoncistas' bid.[83]

The ephemeral papers threw barbs at each other throughout the spring and summer. *La Opinión* zeroed in on the patronage issue, addressing the governor directly: "Sir, from the moment that a group of civil servants conceived of your reelection as state governor . . . the entire state began to vibrate as if shaken by a powerful electric current." The Peoncistas rejoined that the opposition press was composed either of former civil servants or those who "did not capture what they sought."[84]

By late spring, what Bulnes derisively called "bureaucratic cannibalism" was threatening to tear apart the body politic. A series of altercations in Mérida between incumbent bureaucrats and "oppositionists" heightened tensions. State authorities arrested a Cantonista for shouting "Death to Peón Machado!" at a Mérida rally in early May. In response to the arrest, Cantonistas allegedly set off a bomb next to the home of criminal judge Rogerio Aguilar. General Lorenzo García, the federal garrison commander and a close friend of Cantón, warned Díaz that state authorities were delivering arms and ammunition to Motul and Acanceh to bolster national guard detachments there, while Mérida militia battalions were conducting drills and occupying the heights of the city's taller buildings in preparation for expected violence.[85]

Even priests were caught up in the heated political campaign. A Tixkokob pastor, Manuel Ancona, went to the port of Progreso and championed the Cantonista cause at a Gran Club Liberal meeting. Peón Machado's campaign manager, Alvino Manzanilla, charged that prominent church officials had formed a Cantonista club surreptitiously. The hackneyed liberal-conservative debates over the church, publicly dormant for 30 years, now were revived by both sides.[86]

Díaz received a steady diet of detailed reports from both partisans and "impartial observers," all warning that the state was following the all-too-familiar path toward political violence. Serapio Baqueiro, who claimed to be nonaligned but openly criticized the incumbents, wrote to Díaz, "In Yucatán, Mr. President, political interests are disputed in a bloody way like no other state in the federation." Baqueiro suggested a compromise candidate, someone without ties to any political group. A Molina partisan, Agustín Vales Castillo, told Díaz that many of the signatures in the glossy pamphlets were those of hacienda peons. "By promising these peons something for signing, they [the incumbents] will no doubt disappoint them and create problems later." Vales Castillo reminded Díaz that the Caste War had come about because of promises made to Indians that were not kept. Prominent merchant Manuel Dondé Cámara added that he had heard reports that district prefects (*jefes políticos*) were rounding up opposition partisans, conscripting them in the national guard (*la leva*), and sending them to the frontier to defend against incursions from rebel Mayas—a charge commonly leveled at incumbents. He warned Díaz, "I know the Yucatecos well, and these measures will result in nothing but anger and hatred and will provoke disorder." Dondé Cámara closed his letter with an emotional appeal, pleading with Díaz to publicize his choice for governor. "All of this would disappear like smoke with just one word from you."[87]

Porfirio Díaz continued to play his hand close to the vest. As late as early June, he disingenuously wrote to Manzanilla that the will of the Yucatecan people would be respected in the November elections.[88] The Convención Democrática made one last attempt to influence the dictator: Manzanilla asked aging general Mariano Escobedo, a hero of the struggle against Maximilian, to appeal personally to Díaz's patriotism and ask that he "actively intervene and help to prevent the return of the representatives of the despised empire. Your decision is urgently required in these difficult moments." General Escobedo, a deputy in the federal congress, begged off, however, citing ill health and his imminent retirement. The Peoncistas, without a vehicle to influence the president, were left to stew over their own marginalization.[89]

In late July, the Gran Club Liberal sent its own delegation to the Distrito Federal. Led by Cantón's chief political aide, Alfonso Cámara y Cámara, the group met with Díaz on July 25 and learned that Cantón enjoyed Díaz's support. Díaz reportedly gave them a letter to deliver personally to Cantón, confirming *el destape*.[90] When the delegation returned to Progreso on August 7, Cantonistas came out on the docks to celebrate the good news. That night, the Gran Club Liberal turned a saint's day fiesta in the Mérida barrio of Santiago into a Cantonista rally, defying a ban against political demonstrations. From Santiago, partisans marched downtown to Cantón's home, where Cámara y Cámara presented Díaz's letter publicly to the general. Responding to the cheers of his supporters, Pancho Cantón accepted his party's nomination.[91]

As the news spread throughout the state, the Peoncistas, livid that Díaz had selected the caudillo they had spent their political lives battling, met and plotted strategy. Cámara y Cámara later claimed that former governor Manuel Cirerol, "due to his old vendetta with General Francisco Cantón," had offered the Peoncistas "his men, influence, and money" to fight the imposition.[92] From their actions over the next few days, it was apparent that the incumbents were unwilling to comply with Don Porfirio's wishes.[93]

## RIOT IN THE PLAZA

At first glance, the riot (tumulto) in Mérida's Plaza de las Armas on Wednesday night, August 11, 1897, appears to be an eminently forgettable episode. After all, political disturbances in "Los Porfiritos" were not unusual by any means. Up to the moment when violence erupted, political lieutenants for the rival camarillas had carefully orchestrated their partisans' actions. The showdown was the logical culmination of months of pent-up uncertainty, unleashed by two forces—one ready to celebrate after countless setbacks, the other to commiserate—both spoiling for a fight. And once this fit of violence had run its course, an eery silence fell over the remainder of the gubernatorial campaign. The central government's grip on Yucatán never was threatened, and at no time did the unrest arouse the political passions of the urban and rural working classes.

Yet the tumulto cannot be so readily dismissed. Yucatecan historians (as well as amateur chroniclers) have sensed its significance and recounted it in painstaking detail.[94] In retrospect, clearly few events in the recent past have engendered as much interest in Yucatán. Today, local intellectuals still debate, over cafecitos in their favorite restaurants, the finer points of what transpired that night. Everyone takes sides; some place the blame squarely on the incumbents, others castigate the Cantonistas, and most find the dictator culpable. One cannot help but come away from these passionate exchanges with the sense that in a provincial place like Mérida, the feuding of the past seeps unconsciously into the present. One thing is certain: Cantonista and Peoncista descendants care deeply about history's judgment.

With all the attention the narrative has received, why should we revisit the tumulto once more? First and foremost, it remains the most important political altercation of its kind in Porfirian Yucatán. It illustrates the risks that discontented patrons and their clienteles would and, more important, would not take. As such, August 11, 1897, stands as a perfect contrast to the rebellions that rocked the Yucatecan countryside during the violent phase of the Mexican Revolution—uprisings that were precipitated by similar elite factional infighting but that spun out of control and seriously threatened the oligarchical order. Furthermore, thanks to documentation uncovered in the Colección General Porfirio Díaz, we can present a more nuanced description of the tumulto than the extant primary and secondary accounts. Finally, for all the aforementioned attention, it is curious that so little effort has been devoted to interpreting the episode's implications.

Contemporaries, however, did not make the same mistake; they recognized the altered political landscape after that night. Elite-managed campaigns began to give way to a more sophisticated or "modern" brand of electioneering as constituents of all social classes became more comfortable with and more active in politics. As a result, staged unrest would now entail greater risks. *Camarillas* also stored away valuable lessons about the central government's response to the *tumulto*. During the 1906 and 1910 gubernatorial campaigns, incumbents and pretenders repeatedly invoked the disturbance either to justify their policies or to motivate their partisans.

It is somehow fitting that the *tumulto* should take place in the plaza.[95] Ever since the Spanish conquest, important matters had always been resolved somewhere near this fulcrum of power. The six-hundred-square-foot *zócalo* was the religious, economic, cultural, administrative, and military hub of the city and the state. The center of the square, bedecked with tufted laurel trees imported from Cuba by Governor Cirerol in 1870, was large enough to celebrate the numerous religious and political festivities regularly scheduled there. Streets intersecting the square were wide enough for marches, parades, and the growing number of trams and carriages that picked up and dropped off passengers each day.

Surrounding the square on its western, northern, and southern flanks were the principal centers of authority, the city hall, the recently completed governor's mansion, and the police station. A half-block away, behind the governor's palace on Calle 60, was the national guard headquarters. On the eastern side of the plaza stood the cathedral, the tallest building on the square, which served the state's three hundred thousand inhabitants. Although the market and the principal commercial houses were located a few blocks to the southeast, itinerant merchants and peddlers sold their wares along the bustling arcades and galleries adjoining the governor's palace.

On the morning of August 11, Convención Democrática partisans provoked an altercation with the Cantonistas. The governor's supporters spent the morning hours tacking over posters put up by their rivals along Calle 65 and Calle 59. When Cantonistas challenged them in the commercial district, a scuffle broke out, and the police moved in to restore order. Efforts to disperse the crowd met with resistance, however, when angry Cantonistas were joined by local merchants and workers unhappy with Peón Machado's tax reforms. The police fired shots in the air and then prudently retreated rather than use force.[96]

Bracing for the worst that night, however, authorities deployed a national guard detachment on the city hall balcony. It is curious that although political demonstrations had been banned, Mérida's *jefe político*, former governor Daniel Traconis, and his chief aide, Ceferino Montforte, did not postpone the regularly scheduled military band concert in the plaza.[97] It was therefore inevitable that large numbers of people would congregate in the zócalo.[98]

The governor's supporters met earlier in the evening at their campaign headquarters a few blocks off the plaza. An eyewitness, Felipe Pérez Alcalá, described their meeting as tempestuous and noted that following its conclusion at nine o'clock, Peoncistas joined the milling crowd of about three hundred Meridanos in the Plaza de las Armas.

Meanwhile, rumors had been racing through the city that federal commander Lorenzo García's troops were poised to seize control of the government. Pérez Alcalá judged the presence of federal troops in the plaza to be an ominous sign, because on a number of occasions in years past, zone commanders had meddled in local matters, and it was no secret that García's loyalties lay with General Cantón.[99]

Despite the ban on rallies, the Cantonistas came to the plaza that night determined to show support for their candidate. Why would the Gran Club Liberal court disaster by staging a demonstration when it had so little to gain from a violent encounter? The Cantonistas must have reasoned that Manzanilla and the Convención Democrática were intent on provoking a disturbance that would necessitate Don Porfirio's intervention. Then, who knew what might happen? Perhaps Díaz would present the reins of power to a compromise candidate, and Cantón's triumph would be snatched away by the same conniving Mérida political establishment that had blocked him so many times before. Perhaps by staging an impressive show of popular support for their nominee, the Cantonistas could convince the Peoncistas that further resistance was futile. Just in case the Convención Democrática did not get the message, however, the Cantonista partisans came to the plaza armed and ready to counter force with force.

At nine o'clock the crowd was treated to a unique demonstration of the impact of modern technology on a provincial political campaign. The Gran Club Liberal hired German photographers to project images of politicians on a makeshift screen hung from a rooftop adjoining the governor's palace. Cantonistas cheered wildly when the faces of Pancho Cantón, Porfirio Díaz, and *Jefe de la Zona* Lorenzo García appeared.[100]

The use of the "magic lantern" for fifteen minutes was apparently enough to incite the largely Cantonista crowd, which now turned its attention to the city hall. Egging on the crowd was Lieutenant Francisco Rivera Mutio, General García's aide. Cries of "Death to the governor!" and "Death to the *jefe político*!" were heard as demonstrators began pelting the municipal building with stones. Some of the rocks landed at the feet of Ceferino Montforte, the lone symbol of authority present, who was standing in front of the building.[101]

"Enough is enough!" Montforte admonished the crowd. Then he turned toward the police station and shouted, "Bring the police out!" With these words, 50 gendarmes filed out and placed themselves between the crowd and city hall. As if baiting the seething Cantonistas, Montforte added,

"*Muchachos*, what are you trying to do? Provoke a riot? Act in defiance of local authorities?" Montforte's outburst did little to calm the Cantonistas as the exchange of angry words continued in the plaza.

At that moment, Alfonso Cámara y Cámara and Delio Moreno Cantón, standing under the portals of the north side of the plaza, gained the crowd's attention. They persuaded their supporters to leave the plaza peacefully and walk to Pancho Cantón's home a block away on Calle 64. The candidate appeared on his balcony to greet the throng. He thanked them for their support, assured them that victory would be theirs, and asked them to retire peacefully.[102]

If the Cantonista faithful had followed the prearranged script, their political lieutenants, Cámara y Cámara and Moreno Cantón, would have judged the evening a complete success. The "magic lantern" had produced its desired effect, evoking an impassioned response from the partisans. And after the tense shouting match in the plaza, the leaders cleverly avoided a confrontation by shepherding their supporters to Cantón's residence. The general now was cast in the role of a dignified peacemaker, precisely the image his handlers had wanted to project. What better way to allay lingering fears among the *gente decente* that the old caudillo had not shed his rambunctious past. The evening's message was unmistakable: the 64-year-old Cantón was poised and ready to govern the state responsibly.

But only part of the crowd heeded the nominee's instructions. Those who lived in Santiago and San Sebastián to the west and south of the main plaza obeyed. Those who had to cross the plaza to find their way home to the northern and eastern barrios of Santa Ana, La Mejorada, and San Cristóbal soon became witting or unwitting participants in the night's bloody confrontation.

As the crowd passed through the *zócalo*, Cantonista Benito Teleo threatened the police, who promptly seized him and carried him off to jail. Large numbers of Cantonistas, some of them apparently armed, began congregating in front of the police station demanding Teleo's release. Suddenly, two or three bombs exploded.[103] Police Chief Francisco Irabién immediately ordered his men to fire into the air. In the confusion, some of the police fired at the crowd. As the shots rang out, the crowd, some of them innocent bystanders enjoying the evening's band concert, scattered in all directions. The national guard stationed on the city hall balcony, mistakenly thinking that the police station was under attack, also fired on the crowd. Militia reinforcements rushed into the plaza from their barracks and they, too, began peppering the crowd with gunfire.[104]

The *tumulto*'s price was high: nine dead and fifteen wounded. The dead included a printer, a medical student, a bricklayer, and a tram conductor.[105] National guard colonel Bibiano Traconis was gravely injured from three machete blows, lending credence to Peoncista claims that the Cantonistas were armed and prepared for violence that night.[106] Pérez Alcalá later wrote to Díaz castigating the Cantonistas for their disrespect for authority.[107] In reality, blame for the night's violence was ample enough to share. Government authorities permitted the concert and the "magic lantern" to take place and then baited the crowd, as if inviting a confrontation.

Two of the wounded were taken to General Cantón's residence, where they received medical treatment. General García deployed his troops and restored calm to the center of the city, while federal troops occupied the rooftops around the plaza for the next few days. Fearing more violence, Díaz ordered García to protect the armory and to station extra troops at Juárez Penitentiary, where the thirteen arrested for their part in the riot, including the Peoncista *jefe*, Manzanilla, were incarcerated after their arraignment.[108] But although isolated confrontations took place over the next few days, the episode did not precipitate widespread unrest.[109]

Parties on both sides of the conflict inundated Don Porfirio with "reliable" accounts. Federal troops had seized the telegraph offices, so Peoncista messages were intentionally delayed, while García's, Cantón's, and Cámara y Cámara's versions arrived promptly.[110] Díaz wired García to remove Peón Machado from the governor's palace and to keep the peace until the reins of power could be turned over to an interim governor, Cantonista sympathizer José María Iturralde. Díaz, however, did honor Peón Machado's request to come to Mexico City to tell his side of the story.[111]

The Cantonistas asked Díaz to take immediate action and make sweeping changes in state government. Cámara y Cámara reminded Díaz that it would be difficult to conduct a full investigation of the *tumulto* with incumbent judges on the bench. Meanwhile, the Peoncista-controlled legislature complained bitterly about the provocative actions of García's aide that precipitated the *tumulto* and the *jefe de la zona*'s blatant partiality throughout the entire campaign. The Peoncistas' heated reaction has to be one of the few public acts of defiance mounted by a state legislature during the Porfiriato.[112]

On August 22, Peón Machado arrived in the federal capital and requested an audience with Díaz.[113] Angered at the breakdown of law and order in Mérida, the dictator ordered Peón Machado to mail in his resignation and coldly postponed the meeting for a week. Díaz then sent instructions to acting governor Iturralde to replace Peoncista civil servants with loyal Cantonistas throughout the state. On August 31, a day after his resignation became official, Peón Machado finally had his interview with the president. Apparently, Díaz remained unmoved by the ex-governor's version of the *tumulto* and, in a humiliating note written immediately after their meeting, held Peón Machado personally responsible for the violence. Díaz went on to explain why he had ordered Iturralde to fire Peoncista civil servants.

> After the events of the 11th, I think it would be very difficult for the state if you continued as governor. You must accept all of the changes made by Iturralde. If you did replace Iturralde's choices with yours you'd have to put an armed guard around them to protect them, a force that would never be sufficient to expedite their ability to function in such a hostile environment.[114]

Although Díaz assured Peón Machado that García would no longer meddle in local politics, this was small consolation, since he ended his missive by admonishing Peón Machado to accept the consequences for the good of Yucatán.[115] The letter's forthright tone stands in sharp contrast to the president's ambiguous pronouncements throughout the *destape*. Peón Machado left Mexico City for New Orleans, where he stayed for a year before returning to Yucatán. He and his *camarilla* would never again be a factor in local politics.[116] Alvino Manzanilla and, to a lesser extent, Police Chief Irabién and his aides were also held accountable for the evening's hostilities, although all thirteen who were arrested, after spending several months in jail, were eventually acquitted. Manzanilla believed that he had been framed by the vindictive Cantonistas and appealed his case all the way to the Supreme Court. A few years later, a fascinating exchange of letters between Díaz and Manzanilla revealed that the president had personally intervened in Manzanilla's case.[117]

Iturralde completed Peón Machado's term. In stark contrast to the summer's violence, the November elections took place without incident. On February 1, 1898, Pancho Cantón was inaugurated as governor.

Why did Díaz delay the *destape* when he had ample evidence that the state was hurtling toward political violence? More significantly, why did he back a politician who was anathema to an influential segment of the Yucatecan elite? Knowing that his nominee was controversial, Díaz preferred to unveil his decision as close to the November elections as possible. Even though his "noisy silence" throughout the campaign heightened tensions, he must have reasoned that a premature announcement would give the Peoncistas time to organize their opposition to Cantón's appointment. Instead, he presented the Peoncista *camarilla* with a fait accompli late in the game and maintained the fiction that he was undecided for as long as possible.

But why select Cantón when another, less abrasive candidate from the Gran Club Liberal would have served the interests of alternation and patronage just as well? The answer to this enigma lies in the federal government's schemes for development in eastern Yucatán. This complex tale, which unfolded in the corridors of the National Palace, the Yucatecan forests, the British Foreign Office, international and national financial circles, and Yucatán's statehouse, deserves careful analysis; it has important ramifications for peninsular politics, and it helps to explain why Díaz was determined to run roughshod over local opposition and name Cantón chief executive in 1898. To unravel this story, we ask the reader to make a journey in space and time, one that goes well beyond the 1897 *tumulto* to the election of Cantón's successor, Olegario Molina, in 1902.

## The Political Costs of Development, ca. 1880–1902

Indeed, the *destapes* of Cantón and Molina ultimately had little to do with the standard practice of rotating the regional *camarillas*. They were really intended to further particular goals on the national government's development agenda. The costs of this federal-state collaboration were high; they included the creation of Quintana Roo, a federal territory carved out of the forest, which stripped from the state of Yucatán more than one-third of its territory. But in the final analysis, all the actors in this compelling drama were frustrated by the unforgiving tropical wilderness.

## PACIFICATION EFFORTS

Ever since the colonial period, British settlers in neighboring British Honduras (or Belize) had been a nuisance to peninsular authorities. They had engaged in contraband trade along Yucatán's Caribbean coast; and since the outbreak of the Caste War in 1847, British merchants had bartered with the rebel Maya (*cruzob*), whose stronghold, Chan Santa Cruz, lay deep in the eastern forest. The British traded arms for the mahogany, cedar, rubber, construction-grade lumber, and dyewoods found in abundance there. Although Mexican diplomats objected strenuously, the federal government (and its counterpart in Yucatán) could not muster a strong enough presence in the region to deter this illicit trade. Mexico, moreover, was concerned about Great Britain's intentions along the border, especially because the frontier was poorly defined and defended.

Díaz was unable to address these problems during his first term because Mexico's outstanding debts to British nationals delayed London's recognition of his government until 1884. An accord on the debt was not reached until two years later. Collectively, these factors provided some breathing space for the embattled *cruzob*, permitting them to forge an autonomous state during the latter half of the nineteenth century.[118]

The *cruzob* remained a thorn in the side of Yucatecan authorities, periodically attacking frontier settlements and then vanishing into the bush.[119] Time and again, state troops ventured into the interior only to be driven back by guerrilla attacks, as well as by disease and the hardships of transportation and communication. With each successive attack on a frontier settlement, emotions in Mérida approached fever pitch. Calls for military expeditions appeared in the press; patriotic societies were formed; men were dragooned into the national guard; and the state increased commercial taxes in an effort to raise revenue for the war effort. The prohibitive costs of the military campaigns and their meager results ultimately forced the state to reassess its policy, as government officials concentrated their efforts on protecting the frontier settlements of Tekax, Peto, and Valladolid.[120]

The state invested as heavily as its finances would permit in the effort to sustain these outposts. On February 6, 1886, however, the state's perimeter defenses were easily pierced when *cacique* Aniceto Dzul and four hundred *cruzob* daringly assaulted, sacked, and burned Tixhualahtún, leveled Tekom, and advanced as far north as Dzonotchel in Peto *partido*. Néstor Rubio Alpuche, vice president of the Sociedad Patriótica Yucateca, implored the state legislature to send two thousand to three thousand troops to retake the port of Bacalar near the Belize border and defeat the "barbarous Maya race" once and for all.[121] The proposal fell on deaf ears. Patriotism was one thing, but few state officials wanted to pay the expedition's costs. Henequen *hacendados* worried that a call-up would deplete their already scarce labor force, and the state's working classes bitterly opposed the *leva*.

By 1890, however, all but the most chauvinistic Yucatecos had realized that federal assistance was necessary to end the Caste War, and they welcomed the national government's cooperation.[122] Years later, Porfirio Díaz stated what had become patently obvious: "I am convinced that Yucatán cannot by itself, as it has not been able to do for more than half a century, recover, pacify, and maintain the southeastern region, much less colonize and develop it. . . . I believe firmly that only the Nation has the means to achieve such goals."[123] Governor Daniel Traconis, a Caste War hero, especially welcomed the opportunity to work with federal authorities.[124] On July 30, 1891, for instance, at a public ceremony commemorating both the death of Father Hidalgo and the Tepich uprising that ignited the Caste War, the state government presented Porfirio Díaz with a letter written by veterans soliciting federal assistance.[125]

Even though Díaz was concerned about the *cruzob* (he received a steady stream of reports on their military capabilities), his government dragged its feet. Not until foreign and national forest-extraction companies, previously based in Veracruz and Tabasco and driven by the chewing gum craze in the United States, expressed an interest in exploiting the rich stands of chicozapote (chicle), cedar, and mahogany in the forest did the federal government take steps to deal with the rebel Maya.[126] If foreign and national entrepreneurs exploited this region with the appropriate concessions from the federal government, Díaz and his technocrats reasoned, they simultaneously would colonize the forest and create a buffer against worrisome British expansion.[127] In addition, Díaz adviser Manuel Sierra Méndez contended that the exploitation of the forest would alleviate some of the federal government's costs in the upcoming military campaign.[128]

Of course, the war against the autonomous Maya was part of Díaz's project to pacify and then economically develop Mexico's frontiers. The Apaches, Yaquis, and Mayos of the northern frontier suffered the same fate as the *cruzob*: over the course of the Porfiriato, federal armies drove these "indios bárbaros" from their homelands; built roads, railways, and communication lines; and parceled out lucrative concessions and enormous federal land grants to foreign and national investors.[129]

Díaz and his officers harbored few illusions about the nation's ability to "civilize" Mexico's rebellious Indians. The term *pacification* became a euphemism for genocide. General Ignacio Bravo, chosen for his track record against the Yaqui of the northwest, directed the successful federal military campaign in the forest and later was named military governor of the new territory. Bravo and Díaz shared similar perceptions of the rebellious Maya. As Bravo wrote to Díaz from Chan Santa Cruz,

Your description of them [the *cruzob*] could not be more perfect. They are a race that for humanity's sake must be extinguished, because they will never amount to anything good. . . . I am convinced that the only way to guarantee the interests of the zone in general is to finish off the race, if that would be possible.[130]

To "extinguish" the *cruzob* and make the forest safe for investment, however, the national government first had to negotiate a treaty with Great Britain regarding Yucatán's disputed southeastern border. In 1887 the *cruzob* had attracted Díaz's attention when rebel *caciques* petitioned British authorities to annex their state. Still, the proposed boundaries turned over a sizable chunk of Yucatán's borderland to British Honduras; this angered outspoken Yucatecan politicians, who delayed treaty deliberations.[131] The Mariscal–St. John boundary treaty was finally signed on July 8, 1893.[132] Although it avoided the question of Mexican recognition of British sovereignty over Belize, the British left the bargaining table with implicit recognition, as well as generous borders. In return, Article 2 insisted on Great Britain's cooperation in curbing arms supplies from Belizean merchants to the *cruzob*. The Foreign Office also agreed to provide Mexico with intelligence, logistical support, and an increased naval presence off the coast during the upcoming pacification campaign. Documents recently discovered at the Colonial Record Office indicate that the British actively participated in the planning and direction of the campaign and made sure that the *cruzob* could not easily flee to safety in Belize.[133]

Although some Yucatecos remained unhappy with the boundary treaty, the state legislature voted its approval on January 25, 1894. The legislature's resolution demonstrates that local authorities concurred with the federal government and viewed Mariscal–St. John as an essential prelude to the pacification campaign. The Peón Machado administration was ready and willing to participate in the war effort.[134]

## AMBITIONS OF A PATRON

The entire development scheme was spearheaded by the *científico* Sierra Méndez, who traveled extensively between Mexico City, Belize, Mérida, and eastern Yucatán, where his family had significant landholdings.[135] Free with his advice, military and otherwise, Sierra Méndez sent lengthy memoranda to Díaz on the *cruzob*, on the Icaiché and Xkanhá Indians (or *pacíficos*) in Campeche who had assisted the rebels in the past, on British smugglers, and on Yucatecan politicians.[136]

Throughout the 1890s, Sierra Méndez urged Díaz to create a federal territory, although he insisted that this move should be temporary and that the lands should revert back to Yucatán after the *cruzob* were defeated.[137] The federal government, he added, "must also assume command of military operations, because it is doubtful that Yucatec Maya conscripts would obey their *dzul* [white] officers." More idealistic than Generals Díaz and Bravo, he recommended that the federal government make available vacant public lands in the forest to coax the Indians to submit to federal rule. Finally, he urged the national government to pressure Yucatán's and Campeche's leaders to initiate legislation, forming special battalions and raising funds for the war effort.[138]

The peninsula was certain to greet this agenda with mixed emotions. When rumors surfaced in 1896 that the federal government had plans to partition the state and make the forest a federal territory, Yucateco separatists raised their fading banner and demonstrated in Mérida.[139] Whether the rumor was a trial balloon floated by Díaz or a political bombshell unintentionally leaked from the National Palace remains a mystery, but after Yucatecans publicly voiced their displeasure, the partition plan was kept under wraps for five years, until federal troops had accomplished their objective and driven the *cruzob* out of Chan Santa Cruz.

Sierra Méndez had nothing but contempt for the "reactionaries" who opposed the new territory. Although the dissenters now called themselves liberals, in his eyes they had been and always would be recalcitrant obstructionists, intent on reviving the secessionist illusion of 1843. They had opposed the treaty with Britain and now were determined to disrupt development in the peninsula. In a detailed memo written in June 1897, Sierra Méndez made it abundantly clear that the Peoncista *camarilla* was the chief obstacle blocking the federal government's path through the forest.[140] Although he did not mention names, it was also clear that Peón Machado's trusted political lieutenant, Yanuario Manzanilla, was the ringleader.

Sierra Méndez's political salvo against the incumbents raises intriguing questions about Governor Peón Machado's position on the impending partition. Because he never publicly voiced his feelings on the subject, historians have speculated that personal considerations may have diminished his political will to confront Don Porfirio. For instance, Marie Lapointe notes that in 1897 the governor's wealthy in-laws, the Escalantes, had just purchased a sizable interest in Compañía Agrícola de El Cuyo y Anexas, or "El Cuyo," a two-hundred-thousand-hectare tract of adjacent properties along the northeast coast devoted to the exploitation of sugarcane, rubber, chicle, and logwood for the production of railroad ties, construction lumber, and cabinet woods.[141]

The *cruzob*'s defeat would have been advantageous for the Escalantes' investment, but whether this influenced Peón Machado's position on Quintana Roo is conjecture. Peón Machado's biographer, Menéndez Rodríguez, with access to the governor's personal correspondence, contends that he vehemently opposed the new territory; and in large measure, his *camarilla*'s opposition to the partition sealed its fate during the 1897 gubernatorial campaign. Yet documentation found in the Díaz archives does not sustain this view. Apparently, Díaz authorized Joaquín Baranda to inform the governor about the new territory as early as the spring of 1895. Following Díaz's instructions, Peón Machado kept the matter quiet because "it was

such a touchy subject." In a May 1, 1897, letter, the governor, perhaps sensing the inevitable and recognizing that his *camarilla* was under the gun,
told Díaz that he supported the partition.[142]

With the federal government poised to initiate military operations, Sierra Méndez not only sought to undermine the incumbents' credibility but
insisted that Pancho Cantón was not the right choice either, at this critical juncture. The initiative had to be presented delicately to the proud Yucatecos.

> At the moment when a portion of Yucatán's territory has been separated
> temporarily by virtue of a decree turning it into a *federal territory* [emphasis
> in original]; at the moment when a border treaty, such as that with Belize,
> has been concluded and which, without good reason, has made some Yuca-
> tecos unhappy, it would be inconvenient for the State to have a soldier as
> governor, because a long time must pass before Yucatecos will give up the
> notion that the Center tends to weaken Yucatán and seeks to turn it into a
> simple puppet of the national government's will. And as it is generally
> believed that the military, due to its condition, obeys the Supreme Chief of
> the Nation without question, if the future governor of Yucatán were a sol-
> dier, he could not count on the support of Yucatecos in the campaign, and
> they would not participate in it or they would do so under pressure. On the
> other hand, if the governor were a civilian, more civilians would respond
> and volunteer and provide resources for the pacification campaign, and it
> would be more successful.[143]

It would be better to proceed as he suggested, Sierra Méndez added,
because "the two elements would then be in better harmony—the civilian
in the government and the soldier on the front—rather than a military man
in both posts." He went on to identify a third faction, a moderate liberal
cohort that had abstained from politics during the "disastrous" Peón Machado administration and that now wholeheartedly supported the Caste
War intervention. This progressive group—"the soundest group in Yucatán"—was the aspiring Molinista *camarilla*.[144]

Thus, Sierra Méndez's critique was not motivated by patriotism alone.
Furthermore, he had proprietary reasons for masterminding the pacification campaign and advocating Olegario Molina for governor. First and foremost, he wanted to exploit his family's extensive holdings in the forest. In
January 1896, he secured a concession from Díaz and the Ministry of Development for the Belizean logging agent J. E. Plummer to exploit his family's properties near Bacalar Lake and the Río Hondo. Two months later, his
client, Molina, also sank capital into the forest, purchasing shares in the
Compañía Colonizadora de la Costa de Yucatán—a mirror image of the
aforementioned El Cuyo operation—which hugged the Caribbean coast of
the peninsula from Cabo Catoche to Puerto Morelos.[145]

In addition to developing properties in the forest, the patron and his
client became partners in perhaps the most ambitious undertaking yet conceived in Yucatán: the building of a railway through the forest to connect

Peto and Valladolid, the southern and eastern outposts of *civilización*, with the Belize border. Three lines, totaling 450 kilometers through the heart of the forest, would facilitate the deployment of troops and chase the Indians from their secure position.

The Compañía de los Ferrocarriles Sud-Orientales (FCSO) was awarded a concession by the Secretaría de Comunicaciones y Obras Públicas on March 19, 1897, just as the federal government prepared to move against the *cruzob*. Also on board as partners, besides Sierra Méndez and Molina, were Rosendo Pineda and Joaquín D. Casasús, two powerful *científicos*. A year later, Pineda and Casasús won an additional concession to survey and exploit all public lands along the route. The promoters contracted with Porfirio Díaz y Compañía, an engineering concern established by the president's son, Porfirio Díaz, Jr., for the surveying. If all 450 kilometers of track were completed, more than 1.8 million hectares might be redeemed in federal subsidies. At $2 per hectare—the prevailing price of vacant lands at the turn of the century—the total projected value of lands surveyed amounted to more than $3.5 million. Key members of Molina's *camarilla* invested in the fledgling company and served on its first board of directors. No wonder the Molinistas welcomed the partition.[146]

Although he recognized the *científicos'* ambitious plans for developing the new territory, Díaz rejected Sierra Méndez's advice and once again placed a soldier in Yucatán's statehouse in 1898. He needed a governor who would commit the necessary resources—troops, materiel, and funds—to assist the federal government. No one was better qualified to promote the war effort than Pancho Cantón, who to many Yucatecos embodied the epic struggle between "civilization and barbarism." Fifty years after the razing of Valladolid, Cantón had lost little of his determination to defeat the hated *cruzob*.

## AMBITIONS OF A SOLDIER

Anticipating the impending federal-state pacification campaign, soon after learning that he was Díaz's choice for governor, the 64-year-old general was as eager as a new recruit before his first battle. On April 28, 1897, he congratulated Díaz on the Senate's recent ratification of the Mariscal–St. John treaty and, unaware of Mexico City's plans for the eastern forest, waxed enthusiastic about the prospects for the state's economic revitalization after the inevitable triumph.[147] In accepting the nomination of the Gran Club Liberal in August, only days before the *tumulto*, he told his supporters what his administration's principal objectives would be.

> To all the motives mentioned that have led me to sacrifice the repose of private life and enter the commotion of public life, I must add the desire to cooperate with all my energies with the noble propositions of the President of the Republic to end once and for all the dreadful Caste War that for 50 years now has constrained the prosperity of the state in the rich southern

and eastern zones. This is the greatest glory to which I could aspire, my lifelong goal, and the objective to which I devoted the best days of my youth.[148]

Díaz heeded Sierra Méndez's recommendation that the war effort be placed under the direction of the secretary of war, but rejected his counsel on military strategy. The principal military offensive was aimed not at Bacalar and the Bahía de Ascensión, near the Belize border, as Sierra Méndez had urged (and where he owned property), but at Chan Santa Cruz.[149] Federal troops and Yucatán's national guard, with the assistance of impressed campesinos, would depart from Peto and hack their way through the forest to the Maya bastion. Military encampments would be constructed along the road to protect the rear guard and provision the soldiers. The federal army's principal task during this early phase was to protect the Yucatecan work gangs clearing the roads and building the encampments.[150] As this military plan illustrates, the secretary of war required state authorities to play a vital role in the pacification campaign.

Porfirio Díaz's faith in Pancho Cantón's sense of duty was richly rewarded. The state poured money into roads, telegraph and telephone lines, and armaments. Under Cantón's stewardship, the state spent $849,354.19, more than 25 percent of each year's budget.[151] By 1901 the state was sending four hundred men a month to the forest. Of Cantón's commitment to the cause, Baranda later wrote,

> General Francisco Cantón, who just after childhood was torn from his home to fight against the rebellious Indians and who stood out in various encounters because of his unquestioned bravery and daring, made the greatest efforts to include in the federal forces state militia troops, who had considerable experience in the type of campaign being undertaken.[152]

Cantón was promoted to brigadier general on October 19, 1900, for his indispensable role in the Quintana Roo campaign.[153]

More than two thousand Yucatecan soldiers perished during the expedition, mostly from disease and privation. *Hacendados* soon lost their taste for the war and openly criticized Cantón for dragging able-bodied workers off to the forest. Cantón and Molina later pleaded repeatedly with Díaz to reduce the state's share of soldiers. After several years of slogging through the forest, the numerically superior federal forces finally routed the "indios bárbaros" in a number of small skirmishes.[154] In 1901 the federal troops occupied Chan Santa Cruz, and Yucatán greeted the news enthusiastically.

But the euphoria proved short-lived: Cantón was notified that fall of the federal government's plans for territorial partition. The incredulous governor wrote Díaz a series of letters, ardently pleading that the creation of Quintana Roo endangered the economic security of the peninsula. By stripping the state of such fertile properties, he argued, the federal government was actually condemning Yucatán to continue its precarious monocrop existence based on henequen.[155]

Cantón's outspoken reaction to the new territory appears out of character. Nowhere else in his correspondence with the president does he exhibit such boldness. Why would the usually deferential client, who valued duty and loyalty so greatly, object so strenuously to his patron?

The Quintana Roo surprise must have been especially painful for Cantón. So many Yucatecans had died in the half-century struggle and now, just at the moment when the state could profitably develop the interior, the forest was to be turned into a federal preserve. Just as significant, the general had spent almost two decades building a railway from Mérida to Valladolid in the hope of bringing about the revitalization of his home region. The financial success of his railroad—managed and run by his family, of course—was predicated largely on the development of the forest. Now, as construction on the Mérida–Valladolid advanced slowly toward completion, the general had to reassess his railway's future. He had incurred a $1.5-million debt from this enterprise, and now its prospects for success were clouded. Thus, while he made his anguished objections to the Quintana Roo initiative, Cantón also took action: within a year, he sold off his railway to a group of Mérida investors.[156]

Cantón tried to persuade Don Porfirio to redraw the partition lines so that Yucatán would not lose so much territory, but the federal government stood firm. Mérida was politically powerless to do more than meekly object. In February 1902, the federal congress passed legislation creating the new territory. The president's legislative liaison, responsible for guiding the bill through, was the ubiquitous Sierra Méndez.[157]

For Díaz, Cantón had served his political purpose well. Now, with only mopping-up operations left, a soldier was no longer needed to rally Yucatecans to fight the good fight against barbarism. It was time for a civilian politician to soften the blow of partition. In December 1901, during his run for the statehouse, Olegario Molina promised Díaz that his newspapers would convince Yucatecos that the federal initiative was in their best interests. Articles followed in *El Eco del Comercio*, a Mérida daily, and in the Molinistas' ephemeral press proclaiming "the advantages" of development for Yucatecan entrepreneurs.[158] The chief justification for partition centered on the high cost of developing the forest and the state's inability to fund such initiatives.[159]

Naturally, Molina's political loyalty was rewarded. Indeed, a number of key supporters of partition were repaid handsomely between 1902 and 1905 with huge federal concessions in the new territory. Molina was recompensed for his "damage control" with 328,000 hectares surrounding the Bay of Chetumal. J. E. Plummer, who was an agent for C. C. Mangel and Brothers, came away with an additional 165,000 hectares near the Río Hondo. FCSO director Rafael Peón Losa received 279,680 hectares.[160]

The president, just to show that he was not playing favorites, spread his largesse around generously, and *científicos* were not the only ones to benefit. Rodolfo Reyes, son of Secretary of War Bernardo Reyes, received 270,000

hectares near Lake Nohbuc. General Ignacio Bravo secured a small, 6,000-
hectare parcel. Bravo, moreover, remained military governor of Quintana
Roo until 1912, a position that offered ample opportunity to reap favors
from grateful developers in return for protection. In all, nearly 3.5 million
hectares of land were doled out to Mexican, Belizean, and Yucatecan concessionaires, most fronting for North American and British companies.
Mexico City attorneys closely connected to the *bloques del poder* pro-
cessed the contracts.[161]

After the concessions were granted, the difficult task of developing the
interior remained. Commercial activities increasingly came under foreign
control, and the foreign companies relied on imported seasonal labor to
export chicle and hardwoods. Of the original contracts, however, six failed
outright; and of the five survivors, only three original concessionaires completed their initial contracts. In most cases, the concessions failed to secure
the attention and capital required to succeed. The *cruzob*, now on the run,
nevertheless continued to prey on forest settlements. The presence of federal troops was required to ward off recurring ambushes. The national blueprint's twin objectives—development and pacification—were never realized. As historian Herman Konrad concludes, "Contrary to official claims,
the interior of the territory was neither peaceful nor safe for capitalist
development."[162]

## The Political Landscape Redrawn

Yucatán's late Porfirian governors became witting (Olegario Molina) and
unwitting (Pancho Cantón) pawns in the central government's plans. As a
result, the rules of the political game changed in some respects after 1897.
Although Díaz continued to impose his will through the *destape*, he did so
now to satisfy his own agenda, not to reconcile competing elite factions. The
Porfirian political carousel that had accommodated rival *camarillas* and
had given each its brief moment to rule also changed. Unlike the *destapes*
of 1878, 1882, and 1886, in which Díaz (and Manuel González) skillfully
averted the accession of unpopular politicians, appointments were now
made almost contemptuously, with little regard for local sensitivities.

The partition, moreover, made clear to state politicians that Yucatán
was not an equal partner with Mexico City in the national march toward
modernization. Its territory was viewed as a commodity, something national politicians, foreign entrepreneurs, and a select few local compradors
could milk for their material benefit. As one Maderista critic would later
lament, "Mexico during the last ten years of the Porfirian government had
been transformed into an enormous market to which people of all nation-
alities flocked to make their fortunes, until it became a land of adventurers,
without country, religion, or family, whose god was gold and who, like the
gypsies, pitched their tents on the spot that Mercury designated as propitious."[163] In true mercantilistic fashion, Yucatán and the rest of "Los Porfiritos" existed for the benefit of the Distrito Federal.

The lesson was not lost on local politicians. In the same manner that federal authorities plundered the tropical forest, the Cantonista and Molinista administrations set out to fleece the regional economy. As we will see, new "standards" of corruption and influence peddling would be set during the last decade of the Porfiriato, precipitating a crescendo of political unrest among Yucatecans of all social classes.

The *tumulto* in the central plaza also revealed the dictatorship's new clothes. Díaz's willingness to risk political violence to nominate Pancho Cantón exposed the charade of "democratic elections" for what it was. An authoritarian regime intent on costuming itself in formal democratic institutions could expect its citizens to suspend their disbelief only as long as the dictatorship paid lip service to those institutions. As Alan Knight has aptly put it, "Eventually, as Díaz found, the constitutional chickens come home to roost."[164] Much political capital—and, indeed, legitimacy—was carelessly spilled along with the blood in the Plaza de las Armas.

Yet although the *tumulto* had momentarily ended the Pax Porfiriana in Yucatán, Díaz did act swiftly and decisively to stop the spread of further unrest. To be sure, the Cantón–Peón Machado campaign evoked bitter memories that many thought had been put to rest after 1867. Nevertheless, in retrospect, August 11, 1897, never amounted to more than a nasty spat between personalistic elite *camarillas*. The tense electoral season never unleashed the popular classes. The fears voiced by Serapio Baqueiro, Agustín Vales Castillo, Manuel Dondé Cámara, and Manuel Sierra Méndez proved groundless. The Peoncistas never had any intention of contesting the Porfirian regime. Their local organizing, which formally extended throughout the interior of the state, never penetrated to society's roots, and with good reason: it was designed merely to "demonstrate" to the president their nominee's popularity and to protect their jobs, not to contest state power.

Thus, when Peón Machado became the president's scapegoat, his *camarilla* disappeared from the political landscape. Its sudden demise underscores the limitations of personalistic politics during the Porfiriato. With their leader in exile and the *madruguetes* in power, the Peoncistas had little hope of—or even much interest in—reviving the "liberal" cause. Smarting from their fall from grace, opportunistic Peoncista bureaucrats shifted their allegiance: most gravitated toward the state's new breed of *científicos*, the Molinistas.

Although Cantón's *destape* noticeably shook the political establishment, regional politics remained unchanged in three fundamental respects. First, with only two *camarillas* left after 1897, it would now be easier than ever to present state politics as simply an epic confrontation between "continuismo" and "antirreeleccionismo." During the 1902, 1906, and 1910 electoral campaigns, the "outs" and the "ins" would repeatedly trot out the same worn political slogans and clichés that *camarillas* had employed so persistently throughout the spring and summer of 1897.

Second, the essence of Porfirian authoritarianism, patronage politics, had been preserved. As the Cantonistas and Molinistas battled for the state-house, they continued to rely on their clientelistic networks in Mexico City and throughout the state to make their case. However, as the monocrop economy entered a boom of unprecedented proportions after 1898, the political stakes rose significantly. Patronage came to mean much more than a post in the bureaucracy; with national politicians leading by example, political power and personal enrichment became synonymous in Yucatán. Never had the advantages of clientelism been so apparent.

Finally, as might be expected, political infighting between rival blocs in Mexico City would continue to dictate the terms of the debate in Mérida. As the *científicos* increasingly took the measure of their opponents after 1900, it became painfully clear to the Cantonistas that it would be difficult to dislodge Molina from power. Because the Porfirian state would not permit a truly independent party, the Cantonistas' only recourse would be to take their case directly to Don Porfirio, as well as to redouble their efforts to build their political base throughout the state. In the following years, the more the Cantonistas organized the urban working classes, villagers, and indebted peons, the more the Molinistas worried. Perhaps the most strategic lesson Olegario Molina and his political aides learned from the 1897 *tumulto* was that popular mobilization, initiated by elites in the city and the countryside, was a volatile, potentially dangerous enterprise and had to be stopped in its tracks at all costs.

For their part, the Cantonistas would make sure that their partisans never forgot it was their blood that had been shed in the plaza that August night. Twelve years later, on the eve of another gubernatorial election, they reminded their supporters of the massacre.

> This history is sad but necessary: sad because the memory of our brothers' blood spilled needlessly will bring back the blackness of that sinister night to the minds of the survivors of the victims and of those responsible for so much destruction. It is necessary, because the memory of the mistakes and the impropriety of yesterday's politics encapsulate for the politics of today a great lesson—namely, that the abuse of power does not always lead to victory; and the rights of the people, even those who are unarmed, will always be victorious, even in the face of tyranny.[165]

## CHAPTER 3

# Oligarchs and Pretenders

If a man is not a republican at twenty, it is because he has no heart, and if he is one at forty, it is because he has no brains.
—Victor Hugo

If we don't do anything and continue to accept the tyranny, what will become of the people?
—Manuel Damosein, bootblack

By the mid-1890s, Porfirio Díaz's hold on Mexico was secure.[1] No longer tested by political adversaries or regional strongmen, the dictator now turned his attention to fashioning a compliant bureaucratic state. As he gained experience and confidence, Don Porfirio displayed a more assertive role in managing affairs of state, delegating less and less authority to his ministers. The more engrossed in administrative detail the president became, however, the less give-and-take took place at the highest levels, and the more shrouded in secrecy his actions became. Although Don Porfirio continued to consult his most intimate advisers, this newfound self-reliance meant that he was less responsive to public opinion than he had been during his first terms in office.[2]

Díaz responded to constituents' requests only when he absolutely had to, usually scribbling barely legible, cryptic rejoinders. And this meant that his correspondents (and historians who have immersed themselves since in the Colección General Porfirio Díaz) had to read between the lines to discern his motives. Not surprisingly, contemporaries and historians alike have disagreed on Don Porfirio's persona. Some have viewed him as a cunning, sinister despot who manipulated his rivals to remain in power. Others have contended that he was an indecisive ruler whose mixed signals betrayed a fickle personality that confounded supporters and opponents alike. Certainly the Peoncistas would vouch for this second interpretation.[3] Científico Justo Sierra offered his own explanation for the apparent incongruity.

Many who have tried to analyze the psyche of President Díaz . . . find in his mental processes a noticeable inversion of logic: his decisions are quick, and deliberation follows the act of will, deliberation that is slow and laborious and modifies or even nullifies the original decision. This mental pattern . . . has given rise to imputations of political perfidy (deceiving in order to persuade, dividing in order to rule).[4]

Although his motives were sometimes enigmatic, historians sifting through the ambiguous evidence cannot help but come away with a grudging admiration for Díaz's uncanny instincts and his ability to survive in a hostile environment. Whether he was the prescient puppeteer who toyed with his ministerial marionettes or the canny prestidigitator who simply knew how to react instinctively to the changing political atmosphere, his rule was never seriously in question until 1910.

## National Rivalries, 1890–1904

With the president firmly ensconced in the National Palace, journalistic repartee was relegated to speculation about the frequent changes in his cabinet. The members of Díaz's brain trust must have sensed that they were all interchangeable cogs in a well-oiled machine. The notable exceptions were the president's father-in-law, Interior Minister Manuel Romero Rubio, who shrewdly managed the bickering regional *camarillas* until his death in 1895; Treasury Minister José Yves Limantour, whose able stewardship of Mexico's finances made him indispensable to the success of the Porfirian development model after 1893; and Joaquín Baranda and Ignacio Mariscal, fixtures for two decades at the Justice and Foreign Relations ministries, respectively. The remaining cabinet ministers and the scores of deputies, senators, judges, and military officers counseling the general were not permitted to rest secure in their posts for too long. Until his last two terms in office, Díaz rotated and recycled his most reliable clients within the upper echelons of the national bureaucracy.

Don Porfirio's preference was for aging warhorses who understood the value of loyalty and deference. "The Senate was an asylum for gouty decrepits," the caustic Francisco Bulnes later recalled, while government offices were "a home for the aged, with a standing account at the druggist's."[5] By 1910 the gray eminences in the cabinet bore an average age of 67. New—albeit seldom young—blood occasionally made its way up the clientelistic arteries from the provinces to the national capital, and in two cases obtained prominent cabinet portfolios.[6] Nevertheless, the corridors of power became increasingly sclerotic during the Porfiriato's last decade. Bulnes's comments are revealing.

Without renewal there is decay, and decay leads to the grave. General Díaz's ideal was the petrification of the State. He had permitted himself to be led into the irreparable error of fearing any change in the personnel of his immediate political entourage, and in that of the civil branches as well.[7]

Don Porfirio's sycophantic councilors not only served as willing instruments of his repressive regime, but insulated the dictator from an increasingly restive public. Porfirian deputy Ricardo García Granados, who in the 1920s wrote what is arguably the best political history of the dictatorship, deplored the absence of integrity in Díaz's cabinet.

> Those who advised him to suppress liberty, persecute the press, and annul the Congress; those who, in the name of science, justified systematic fraud and the violation of the most solemn promises; who taught the dictator to scorn public opinion; who made him believe in his immense intellectual superiority in the face of the "ignorant masses," the rabble who had to be handled with the utmost sternness; who heralded as expressions of incredible talent whatever banal ideas emerged from his lips—all of those individuals renounced their dignity to become instruments of despotism.[8]

Although these feckless "instruments of despotism" went about enforcing what Justo Sierra euphemistically termed "the political religion of peace," they were certainly no models of decorum around the National Palace. The dictatorship's credo, *poca política y mucha administración*, may have made good copy for government propagandists, but in truth the regime was beset by chronic political infighting. Moreover, the struggle between the national power blocs had great significance for regional elites. Local politicians read the comings and goings of ministers like so many tea leaves; their political future depended in large part on their contacts in the cabinet.

Eventually, familiarity bred contempt, as Díaz's ciphers turned against each other and marshaled their forces for the moment when the president would die or step down. Nevertheless, the prospect of dueling power blocs had certain inherent advantages for the dictator. Come election time, the president invariably pitted the national cliques against each other until each cohort reached the same conclusion: it was better to keep the seemingly ageless dictator in the National Palace than to contend with one of their adversaries as chief executive.[9]

Determined to outlast the pretenders to his throne, Díaz wrote a similar script with the same cast of characters in 1896, 1900, and 1904 to ensure his reelection. He staged and directed a three-part political drama (García Granados aptly called it "the electoral comedy"), which on the surface sought to reconcile the feuding factions. In the first act, Díaz would profess a desire to step down and would instruct his aides to develop a strategy to ensure an orderly transfer of power.[10] Act 2 thus opened with Mexico City abuzz with rumors as the intrigues (and character assassinations) began. Both camps would besiege Don Porfirio with nominations. Cast always in the role of peacemaker, the president would then step in to broker a settlement between the rival factions. During the 1900 campaign, Díaz went so far as to propose a compromise: Limantour as president and General Bernardo Reyes as secretary of war.

In the tense third act, the sniping *camarillas*, abetted by venomous smear tactics from their subsidized newspapers and pamphlets, would refuse to set aside their differences and agree on a successor.[11] Instead, each clique met privately with the president and melodramatically implored him to serve another term for the good of the nation. In 1904 the third act had two intriguing twists that provided Don Porfirio with additional breathing space: the office of vice president was created, and the presidential term was extended from four to six years. Although these changes delayed the next round of plotting and scheming until 1910, they did little to placate the disgruntled power blocs.

State governors tethered to the national *camarillas* (or *facciones, bandos*, or *banderías*, as the Mexico City press referred to them) had proprietary reasons for seconding the calls for Díaz's reelection. Enjoying the fruits of their own *destapes*, they obsequiously petitioned the president to stay in office lest the nation return to the chaos and instability that had plagued it since independence.[12] The moral of the drama was not lost on the actors or the public: Mexico was not yet ready for democracy; Don Porfirio, ever the reluctant public servant, would stay the course until the nation came of age.

Yet few observers were fooled by the smoke and mirrors. Although less cynical than Bulnes, García Granados recognized the despot's Machiavellian tactics.

> In fact, everyone knew that the reelection of Don Porfirio would not be the work of his friends or followers but the result of his own designs, and not so much because of his accomplishments in the mind of public opinion but because he simply was not willing to leave office voluntarily.[13]

This high-stakes political theater was not without its rough rehearsals. At times Díaz had to grant concessions to the *camarillas* in return for their willingness to follow the script. The balancing act grew more difficult in the late 1890s as Don Porfirio became more dependent on the financial expertise of technocrats like Limantour and Joaquín D. Casasús, who coped with sensitive economic issues, such as the abolition of the regional sales taxes, banking and monetary reform, refinancing the foreign debt, and a rising tide of international capital that was threatening to swamp the nation. As the aristocratic *científicos* exerted more control over the nation's financial portfolio, the president was forced to counter their growing power, wealth, and influence by strengthening their rivals' political position.[14]

## '¿POCA POLÍTICA?'

The dictator's not-so-subtle maneuvers to bolster the visibility and credibility of General Bernardo Reyes must be seen in this light. The pomp and circumstance associated with Díaz's eight-day visit to Governor Reyes's Nuevo León in December 1898 is a perfect illustration of Porfirian realpolitik. The normally taciturn dictator, who seldom voiced his opinions publicly, turned positively effusive on the final day of his visit to Monterrey, extolling the governor's abilities as an administrator: "General Reyes, this is the way to govern; this is how one reciprocates the trust that the people have placed in you."[15] His bold move less than two years later in appointing the popular, 50-year-old general—a veritable youngster in Porfirian terms—to the cabinet as secretary of war offered further proof of Díaz's desire to prop up the Reyista clique.[16]

*Científicos* like Bulnes were well aware of the president's tactics, and recognized that such a risky action was destined to backfire.

> [General Díaz] authorized, even incited, his friends, preferably the most discriminating, to pick flaws in his work, to point out the failures, lapses, even infamies that stood out like putrefying ulcers, so long as they were laid at the door of the *científicos*, who were his subordinates, and for whose actions he was responsible. . . . General Díaz's supreme delight . . . was to hear the *científicos* calumniated, and to realize that, as public opinion gradually accepted the dictum of his friends, which transformed Señor Limantour and his colleagues into monsters, it thundered back replies charged with hate that shook the nerves of even the most complacent.[17]

Because Limantour was the likely heir apparent, Díaz made every effort to impede his treasury minister's chances of securing the presidency. In early 1898, right on cue, Don Porfirio informed both Limantour and Reyes that he would not stand for reelection in 1900. He wished the treasury minister to succeed him and Reyes to work closely with the new president as secretary of war. Apparently Limantour and Reyes agreed to the plan, and the president's visit to Nuevo León in December 1898 offered seemingly incontrovertible proof of his desire to pass the torch. On the face of it, the compromise seemed like a stroke of genius: it would bring the competing factions together while reenforcing Don Porfirio's image as a patriot who placed the welfare of the nation above petty politics.

No sooner had the stage been set, however, than the plan fell apart. During the winter of 1899, while the treasury minister was abroad renegotiating Mexico's foreign debt and bolstering his fragile health, a cause célèbre developed over the question of Limantour's nationality. Limantour was born in Mexico, but his parents were of French descent and never became naturalized citizens. Although he obtained his Mexican citizenship when he turned 21, the 1857 Constitution stated that only "Mexicans by birth" could serve as president (or as cabinet ministers, for that matter). When Díaz had run into similar constitutional obstacles in the past, he had simply rushed legislation through to circumvent the problem. In this case, however, Díaz took the dubious step of turning the matter over to Secretary of Justice Joaquín Baranda—hardly a neutral party. True to form, Baranda's legal brief concluded that the treasury minister could not become president. Limantour was finished as a pretender to the throne.[18]

Díaz also undermined *científico* influence in "Los Porfiritos." After the death of Romero Rubio, the clique's *compadre*, the president named as interior minister a nonentity, Manuel González Cosío, passing over ambitious politicians like Romero Rubio's private secretary, Rosendo Pineda. *Gobernación* was a key ministry. In addition to monitoring the governors, it had dominion over provincial elections, the rural police, *jefes políticos*, customs officials, and the governance of the federal territories, including the Federal District. Díaz's father-in-law had deftly employed the carrot and the stick for more than a decade, sometimes gently persuading regime opponents that it was in their enlightened self-interest to cooperate, sometimes brutally stifling press freedoms and crushing student dissent in the national capital.[19] Don Porfirio's selection of a colorless, pliable successor went along with his new, interventionist approach. He easily manipulated González Cosío and took a more active role in the *destapes*.[20] His conspicuous actions in the selection of Pancho Cantón in 1897 are but one example of this meddling. With the *científico* Romero Rubio no longer involved, it was not surprising that by the turn of the century the "anticientíficos" enjoyed the backing of more of the nation's governors than did their opponents.[21]

### 'LOS ANTICIENTÍFICOS'

Díaz's attempts to weaken the *científicos* brought together some strange bedfellows. Some historians have characterized the *anticientíficos* as "traditional"—a nostalgic collection of veteran officers, backward-looking landowners, former monarchists, and shopworn regional caudillos like General Cantón, who had come to terms with Porfirian patronage.[22] In truth, this label misses the mark; this bloc included an eclectic mixture of conspirators in both the capital and the provinces who either resented the *científicos'* ascendancy or opposed their developmentalist project. Technocrat Ramón Prida recalled that they all shared a common hatred for the *científicos*.

> For the liberals, the *científicos* represented reaction; for the Catholics . . . [they] represented atheism; for the friends of General Díaz, the *científicos* were the disguised enemies of the government; for the public at large, they were the favorites of the administration. For the military, the *científicos* embodied antimilitarism and were strongly opposed by General Reyes and Brigadier Félix Díaz; and for the people they were the pillars of the dictatorship.[23]

One important constituency disturbed by the *científicos'* infatuation with "scientific politics" (a pastiche of positivism, Social Darwinism, and liberalism) was the *puros*. These doctrinaire liberals viewed the Constitution of 1857 as a sacred text and Díaz's dictatorship, prosperous though it might be, as an interminable detour on the road to republican democracy.

The *puros* were outraged by Díaz's systematic abuse of constitutional guarantees, and they beat a steady drum of protest in the press. The *científicos*, for their part, viewed the *puros* as hopelessly misguided Jacobins who misunderstood the fundamental nature of Mexican society and wanted to wed the nation to a constitutional artifact that was entirely inappropriate for Mexican political culture.[24]

By the mid-1890s, with the dictatorship in full flower, the "Jacobins'" message was increasingly marginalized. Their cause took a severe blow in late 1896, when two key liberal newspapers, *El Monitor Republicano* and *El Tiempo*, shut down their presses. The *puros*, who had inherited their ideological mantle from Benito Juárez and Miguel Lerdo de Tejada, were left without a public voice. Their only options were to attack Porfirismo more openly, running the risk of certain reprisal, or to work within the regime, casting their lot with other *anticientíficos*.

Those Jacobins who chose to work from within joined Joaquín Baranda's bloc. A stalwart liberal whose family had fought the good fight against the conservatives in Campeche and Yucatán throughout the nineteenth century, the justice minister had first served as governor of Campeche under Lerdo. President Manuel González brought him to national prominence, appointing him secretary of justice and public instruction in 1881. Díaz inherited the eloquent Baranda from González in 1884, and Baranda became a fixture in the general's cabinet, his opposition to the Tuxtepec rebellion and his Gonzalista baggage notwithstanding. Prida believed that Díaz elevated Baranda in his inner circle to counter the growing influence of Romero Rubio, a likely successor at the time. Dogmatic *científicos*, such as Bulnes and Antonio Manero, may have exaggerated when they tagged Baranda a Jacobin, but they had every reason to fear his considerable influence with Don Porfirio.[25]

How *puro* was Baranda? To survive in an atmosphere that openly discouraged advocacy of political principles must have demanded circumspection. Although one historian has characterized him as impetuous, Baranda was really a wily political operator; his longevity was a testament to his pragmatism. Moreover, it was widely rumored that Baranda had presidential aspirations of his own. The minister's working relationship with *puros*, conservatives such as Pancho Cantón, old-guard Tuxtepecistas like longtime Veracruz governor Teodoro Dehesa, and discontented journalists and students is best understood as a marriage of convenience. By 1900, Barandista clients were placed in statehouses throughout southeastern Mexico.[26]

In his own way, Baranda was just as indispensable to Don Porfirio as Limantour or Romero Rubio. One of the linchpins of Díaz's personalistic regime was a submissive judiciary that outwardly appeared independent but in reality was kept on a short leash. Baranda staffed his ministry with political hacks who understood the rules—punish dissent and restrict freedom of the press.[27] García Granados, who had been a target of judicial authorities, was especially critical of the shortcomings of Barandista justice.

> Licenciado Joaquín Baranda was a fairly erudite and intelligent man, but more given to political intrigues than to the study of truly worthwhile causes. Thus, the most enduring legacy of his many years as Secretary of Justice and Public Education was his total corruption of the administration of justice and the complete destruction of the independence of the judicial branch of government.[28]

Even the Supreme Court became a malleable tool of the dictatorship as distinguished jurists were replaced by nondescript, albeit loyal, Barandistas. In 1891, for example, Baranda appointed former Yucatecan governor Eligio Ancona to the high court, where the old Lerdista remained until his death in 1893. An insider later remarked: "The authority and the prestige of the Court proceeded in inverse terms to the authority and the prestige of the dictatorship, until it became, in underhanded fashion, a dependency of the Ministry of Justice."[29] It is significant that when the *científicos'* National Liberal Union convention met in 1893, one of the central planks of its political platform was a clarion call for the immovability of judges.[30]

In the long run, the *anticientíficos* achieved only limited success. Both Baranda and Reyes became casualties in the factional power struggle. When Díaz was reelected in 1900, the *científicos*, led by Rosendo Pineda and Federal District governor Ramón Corral, waged a ruthless campaign to sabotage their two most prominent opponents. On April 12, 1901, without warning or explanation, Baranda "resigned" as secretary of justice and was replaced by *científico* Justino Fernández. After an extended vacation in the United States, Baranda returned with a sinecure from Díaz as comptroller of the Banco Nacional and a largely ceremonial post as senator from the Federal District.[31]

Then, in 1902, in a dramatic showdown, the usually quiescent Limantour, whose presidential aspirations had been stymied by the bellicose Reyista leadership, turned the tables on his opponents and demanded a vote of confidence from Don Porfirio.[32] Apparently, this vote meant more than just a rhetorical pat on the back. Díaz was given an ultimatum: either the popular Reyes must step down or Limantour would resign. On December 22, 1902, just two years after General Reyes had been brought from the provinces to the cabinet with much fanfare, he tendered his resignation as secretary of war and returned to govern Nuevo León.[33]

Although Baranda and the Reyistas had denied Limantour the presidency, the costs to their own blocs were considerable. Díaz tried to cushion the shock to the *científicos'* opponents by taking the extraordinary step of personally writing the Reyista governors and the federal garrison commanders to explain that their leader had not lost the president's confidence.[34] The letter put the best face on a difficult situation. In reality, after 1902, *científicos* dominated the cabinet; and although they remained unpopular in the provinces, their control of the political and economic levers of power in the capital upset the careful balance that Díaz had labored to maintain. Insult compounded injury in 1904 when Corral, Limantour's close friend and the man the Reyista leadership held responsible for thwarting their general's ambitions, was "elected" vice president.[35]

## REGIONAL REPERCUSSIONS

The jockeying for power in Mexico City continued to cause ripples at the nation's periphery. Baranda had been instrumental in swaying the dictator's choice in Yucatán's 1898 *destape;* and the intimate working relationship between Manuel Sierra Méndez and Olegario Molina on the Quintana Roo misadventure had influenced Díaz's selection of the henequen merchant as governor in 1902. But Baranda's and Reyes's precipitous fall from grace signaled a new *científico* hegemony.[36]

Of course, Molina's *camarilla* was elated by the sudden turn of events in the Federal District. Their patron's election in 1902 coincided with the *científicos'* successful offensive against their adversaries in the cabinet. Predictably, Molina cleaned house, sweeping the Cantonistas from the state bureaucracy and replacing them with his clients. But the new governor's agenda went far beyond the conventional spoils system of his predecessors. Don Olegario, who shared a similar modernizing vision with his technocratic counterparts in the capital, moved expeditiously to revitalize Mérida and its environs. Aided by a fortuitous rise in the price of fiber, Molina taxed henequen production and used the funds to address a multitude of urban ills, undertaking public works improvements with reckless abandon. This assault at first baffled his political opponents, who watched sullenly, while the Molinista press trumpeted the governor's projects.

In contrast, Joaquín Baranda's ouster dealt an especially telling blow to Francisco Cantón's *camarilla*, which now saw its chances of regaining the statehouse in 1906 fade away. Like the Peoncistas before them, the Cantonistas would henceforth have to do battle without a helping hand from the National Palace. Their only recourse was to organize more systematically statewide and resort to the tried-and-true tactics employed by factions that had been on the outs before them.

The most viable option left to the Cantonistas was to force Don Porfirio to intervene in Molina's administration by demonstrating that Molina could not keep the peace. To that end, between 1902 and 1906 the oppositionists would aggressively mobilize the new urban working classes in Mérida and Progreso. And Molina and his lieutenants, aware that this opportunistic political marriage between the elites and the lower classes might sow the seeds of another *tumulto*, would respond to the Cantonista grassroots mobilization with what local critics aptly called *la mano dura*, the heavy hand. Before that confrontation took place, however, Yucatecans had to experience the political consequences of Molina's modernizing project.

## Breaking the Rules, 1902–9

To a far greater extent than his more traditional predecessor, Pancho Cantón, Olegario Molina was driven by the desire to make Yucatán a dynamic contributor to the modernization of Mexican society. Yucatecans remember him best as "El Constructor," the builder. The embodiment of nineteenth-century Mexican positivism, the state's own *científico*, Don Olegario reasoned that to the extent that he and his class prospered, so would Yucatán. For Molina, who had earned degrees in topographical engineering and law, Yucatán's future lay with its educated creole elite, not with the mass of illiterate Maya Indians who toiled on the henequen estates.

Governor Molina's regard for Yucatán's working classes might best be described as paternalistic. Although he is still lionized in the region for the number of schools he built (most of which were constructed by his firm, Olegario Molina y Compañía), although he raised teachers' salaries and pensions and had the state overhaul Mérida's floundering public school system, the governor did little to introduce education to the tens of thousands of peons who lived on haciendas in the henequen zone. Like other *científicos*, Don Olegario believed that, at least in the short run, the modernization of Yucatán and Mexico depended on the appropriation of foreign ideas, capital, and technology by an enterprising and educated native elite.[37]

Molina coaxed wealthy henequen producers to supplement state funds by underwriting a spate of capital improvement projects in Mérida, including the paving and draining of the downtown and the construction of O'Horan Hospital, Juárez Penitentiary, Ayala Asylum, and Mérida's grand boulevard, the Paseo de Montejo. In addition, he reorganized the state's property registry to make tax collection more efficient. During his tenure, state revenues almost doubled, and a surge in henequen prices enabled the state treasury to balance its books—a stunning accomplishment considering the sizable debt Molina inherited from the Cantón administration. Molina also found time to rewrite the state constitution, reform the penal and civil codes, and reorganize both the state national guard and the Mérida police.[38]

While only a few bitter opponents dared to speak out against Molina's dazzling public works projects and reforms, critics lambasted the governor on a variety of other issues: his purported role in the loss of Quintana Roo to the federal government; his numerous tax levies; his insatiable political ambitions (specifically his alleged yearning for the vice presidency of the republic); the state's bureaucratic intrusion into the private lives and pastimes of ordinary citizens; his reorganization of the national guard and the nefarious *leva*; his frequent leaves of absence for health and business reasons (locals joked about an *interinato*); and perhaps most galling, his questionable practice of handing out government positions, lucrative concessions, and contracts (such as the street paving) to business associates and

TABLE 3.1
*Nepotism During the Olegariato*

| Relative of Olegario Molina | Relationship to Molina | Position |
| --- | --- | --- |
| José Trinidad Molina Solís | Brother | President of Board, United Railways of Yucatán |
| Juan Francisco Molina Solís | Brother | Attorney for Olegario Molina y Cía |
| Augusto Molina Solís | Brother | Director, School of Medicine; Deputy, State Congress |
| Manuel Molina Solís | Brother | Interim Governor |
| Rogelio Suárez[a] | Son-in-law | Director, Banco Yucateco; Manager, government dynamite concession |
| Avelino Montes | Son-in-law | Agent, International Harvester; City Council; board member, local banks, railways; director, binder twine factory |
| Carlos Casasús | Brother-in-law | Deputy, State and Federal Congress |
| Luis Demetrio Molina Cirerol | Nephew | *Jefe político*, Mérida; Deputy, State Congress |
| Ignacio Molina Castilla | Nephew | Director of services, Hospital O'Horan |
| Vicente Molina Castilla | Nephew | Chief engineer, United Railways of Yucatán |
| Manuel Molina Castilla | Nephew | *Juez de paz*, Mérida |

SOURCE: *Yucatán Nuevo* (Mérida), Nov. 6, 1908, no. 8.
NOTE: This brief list covers only the most obvious political linkages as reported by this ephemeral Cantonista newspaper. The paper was published in neighboring Campeche because of the Molina regime's harassment of the press in Yucatán.
[a]Rogelio Suárez apparently was the most independent of the Molina relatives, as attested by his bankruptcy during the 1907–8 panic. To our knowledge he is the only Molina relation who succumbed to the hard times of the last years of the Porfiriato.

family members.[39] Those who attacked Molina on the nepotism issue took great pains to print long lists of Molina relatives who had profited politically and economically from their association with the governor. Table 3.1 illustrates the validity of those charges.[40]

What worried elite factional opponents most was Don Olegario's consuming ambition. Unlike Cantón, Molina had little intention of stepping down at the end of his first term. It was one thing to engage in patronage for his family and cronies; it was quite another to create a dynasty of privilege and wealth. How Molina dealt with his opponents to ensure "continuismo" is a textbook case of late Porfirian regional power politics.

STIFLING DISSENT

First, the governor inhibited the political activities of rivals by harassing the Mérida-based opposition press. Just as the pretense of open elections was maintained in Yucatán, so was the sham of a free press. Reporters who raised substantive complaints about Don Olegario's rule found themselves languishing in Juárez Penitentiary; nettlesome editors had their newspapers shut down. Journalists were taken "out of circulation" for months, even years at a time. Several came to know intimately the not-so-friendly confines of the state prison, nicknamed the Hotel Bolados after the despised warden, Leonardo Bolados Garza.[41]

The most blatant example of press harassment was Don Olegario's handling of the satirical liberal weekly, *El Padre Clarencio*. Indeed, Carlos Escoffié, the newspaper's 26-year-old editor, wrote many of his columns while serving time in the Hotel Bolados.[42] Molina also "persuaded" local printers not to work with Escoffié; for several issues *El Padre Clarencio* was scrawled longhand. On still other occasions, local authorities closed down the paper's operations and confiscated entire issues. Finally, Escoffié was driven from the state. He went to neighboring Campeche, where he resumed publishing. Unfortunately, Campeche was not far enough away; Yucatecan authorities had him arrested on libel charges, bringing him back to his second home in the penitentiary in December 1909.[43]

Don Olegario's heavy-handed tactics resembled those of the federal government.[44] In 1901, for instance, federal authorities arrested the brothers Ricardo and Enrique Flores Magón, editors of the liberal newspaper *Regeneración*, and sent them to Belém prison for their vituperative exposé of a corrupt and brutal Oaxacan district prefect. After their release, the harassment continued, until the Flores Magón brothers fled to the United States, in January 1904. There they continued to publish *Regeneración* and to smuggle thousands of copies across the border.

The parallels between Yucatán's *El Padre Clarencio* and the nationally circulated *Regeneración* are striking. Both papers started out as essentially anticlerical tracts that found a small readership among urban intellectuals and professionals; but soon, social questions came to dominate their agendas, as the editors focused on the grievances of the urban and rural working classes. As the newspapers continually tested the limits of press freedom, authorities labeled Escoffié and the Flores Magóns as dangerous subversives and singled them out for special persecution. The months and years in jail and on the run served only to sharpen their pens, however, as they became increasingly critical of authoritarian rule at the state and national levels.[45]

The two newspapers joined forces in January 1905 when *Regeneración*, from San Antonio, Texas, published the sensational allegation that slavery was being practiced in the Yucatecan countryside. "The Social Question in Yucatán—Does Slavery Exist in the Peninsula?" was written in the form of an open letter by a henequen worker, Antonio Canché. The peon's testimonial documented his mistreatment by the overseer of Hacienda Xcumpich and by the *hacendado*, Audomaro Molina—a brother of Don Olegario. Brutally flogged, Canché had escaped from Xcumpich and found shelter in the state capital in the home of 40-year-old Tomás Pérez Ponce, a lawyer, journalist, and indefatigable advocate for Yucatán's working classes.

For more than a decade, Pérez Ponce, like Escoffié, had been a thorn in the side of local officials. His ardent defense of campesinos throughout the Yucatecan countryside had earned him the enmity of the *henequeneros*. An unrepentant Jacobin, Pérez Ponce once boasted, "I was educated in the schools of pure, radical, and reformist liberalism." He dedicated his life to defending the rights of peons and workers and to defeating "all tyrants, all dictatorships, all human injustices in their four fundamental forms: clerical, economic, political, and military." During the mid-1890s, judicial authorities periodically shut down his newspaper, *El Libre Examen*; confiscated his printing press on at least three occasions; and repeatedly jailed him and his brothers, Tirso and Teodoro. It was no coincidence that the Pérez Ponce brothers were in the thick of the *tumulto* of August 11, 1897, mobilizing urban and rural workers against the incumbent Peón Machado administration. Teodoro paid for his commitment with his life when he was slain in the plaza that night. But if anything, his death only reenforced his brothers' resolve as they threw themselves into organizing the first labor unions in Mérida and Progreso.[46]

It is therefore understandable that Canché sought out these organizers when he fled Xcumpich in late 1904. Tomás Pérez Ponce harbored the fugitive peon, transcribed his story for publication, conspired with the gadfly Escoffié to smuggle the story out of the peninsula and find a national forum in *Regeneración*, and then gave José Vadillo, the editor of another working-class newspaper, *Verdad y Justicia*, the "open letter" to publish locally. For his part, Escoffié added the descriptor "antislavery" to the masthead of *El Padre Clarencio* to accompany "liberal" and "independent," to make clear where his sympathies lay. Predictably, Pérez Ponce, Escoffié, and Vadillo soon found lodging in the Hotel Bolados.[47]

Naturally, the Xcumpich affair proved especially embarrassing to Don Olegario, as a number of Mexico City dailies picked up the story. With the 1906 gubernatorial campaign under way, state authorities decided to shelve the trial until well after the election. The much-delayed proceedings proved frustrating for the defendants, who had intended to use the trial to prove Canché's charges and indict the plantocracy. The state circuit court ruled narrowly, however, that the contents of the "open letter" were irrelevant to the case.[48] The defendants also received harsh treatment: all were convicted and sent to Juárez. Pérez Ponce alone was sentenced to three years and ten months; Escoffié received "only" one year, seven months, and nine days and a fine of $486. Escoffié refused to pay the fine on principle, so seven more months of jail time were tacked on.[49] One of Pérez Ponce's attorneys, Urbano Espinosa, was held in contempt of court for this outburst after the sentencing:

> Tomás Pérez Ponce has been tried already and probably sentenced and condemned by a small group of select individuals who dominate through their power, their money, and their influence.[50]

The Xcumpich affair was so politically explosive its aftershocks were felt in the Federal District. Attorneys for Pérez Ponce and Escoffié appealed all the way to the Mexican Supreme Court, arguing that the Penitenciaría Juárez used an unconstitutional ordinance that denied the defendants an opportunity to receive legal counsel while incarcerated.[51]

While Escoffié languished in prison, his staff published a few more issues of *El Padre Clarencio*; but the newspaper's tone was subdued, perhaps out of fear of further reprisals against its embattled editor. In the spring of 1906, *El Padre* suspended publication and did not reappear until Escoffié was released from prison in 1908.

In 1907 the Molinistas silenced another social commentary newspaper, *La Humanidad*, which scandalized the *gente decente* with such strident articles as "The Only Way of Transforming Society Is Through Social Revolution." The editor, Agustín Pardo, a native of Puebla, and his chief reporter, José Dolores Sobrino Trejo, a twenty-year-old student from the eastern Yucatecan pueblo of Dzitás, sought to raise working-class consciousness. The issue of September 1, 1907, certainly raised state officials' ire. It appealed to both urban and rural laborers with statements such as the following:

> The slave, the serf, the subject, or the proletarian who tries to achieve his emancipation, is a dead person who rises up from the ashes to conquer life. . . . Yet the emancipation referred to here is a sad commentary, the result of social despair, of the differences between the rich man who has laid his hands on everything that serves to enhance life, and the unfortunate, the worker, the proletarian whose life is reduced to nothing more than work, indigence, and misery.[52]

What especially worried local authorities were *La Humanidad*'s blatant attacks on the plantocracy.

> The potentate could not accept that his goods and riches, of which he has an ample supply, might be distributed more fairly in fraternity, equity, and harmony . . . or that these victims [the workers] might sit by his side and all differences be eradicated so that all are equal: neither oppressors nor oppressed.[53]

For such class-based invective, Sobrino Trejo and Pardo were convicted on the overblown charge of "thwarted rebellion." Each received a sentence of two years, three months, and sixteen days.[54] Meanwhile, the police destroyed *La Humanidad*'s tables and desks, and all furniture belonging to Pardo.[55]

Although Sobrino Trejo and Pardo were freed after serving a year, the Molinista strategy was obvious: take opponents out of the public eye. Dissidents had to wait months for their cases to come to trial. Pérez Ponce spent a year and five months beyond his sentence in Juárez, clearly a Molinista ploy to prevent him from organizing workers in Mérida and the port of Progreso or publishing *Verdad y Justicia*. Even though Molinista judges

doled out some relatively light sentences, and legally the time spent awaiting trial was considered time served, some dissenters spent twice as long in
jail awaiting trial as the actual sentence handed down by the judge. Here
again, the similarities between provincial Mexico and the federal government were striking.[56]

Mérida's two mainstream newspapers read the handwriting on the wall
and practiced self-censorship, seldom criticizing the governor during his
first term. Indeed, following Don Olegario's election, *El Eco del Comercio*
functioned as a government mouthpiece, and it was ultimately bought by
Molinista interests in 1904. The Cantonista paper, *La Revista de Mérida*,
initially ripped Governor Molina over his handling of the Quintana Roo partition but subsequently reined itself in. More than anything, *La Revista*'s
meek stance illustrates Molina's tightfisted control of the press. The paper
had not felt similarly constrained during Peón Machado's administration.[57]

Nowhere was self-censorship more evident than in *La Revista*'s reluctance to exploit the Xcumpich controversy. The story broke nationwide
during the first half of 1905, just as local attention was focusing on the
upcoming gubernatorial campaign. By all rights, the story and its timing
were tailor-made for the Cantonistas, who needed to mount a concerted
attack on the formidable Molinista *camarilla* if they entertained any hopes
of recapturing the statehouse. Yet *La Revista*'s owner, Delio Moreno Cantón, the nephew of Pancho Cantón, refused to seize the opportunity. The
paper's unwillingness to debate freely the "open letter" suggests that the
jailing of Pérez Ponce, Escoffié, and Vadillo intimidated the Mérida press.
But this is not the only explanation for the silence. Yucatecan *henequeneros*, highly defensive about the charge that they were slaveholders, perceived any attack on Audomaro Molina—particularly one emanating from
Mexico City—as an attack on all property holders. Moreno Cantón and his
editor, Carlos R. Menéndez, most likely felt it best just to let the matter
die.[58]

Press censorship was only one of the Molina administration's strongarm
tactics. The governor rewrote the state constitution to give his administration greater latitude over the judicial and executive branches. Article 59, for
example, gave the state executive the right to name judges of the first instance, while justices of the peace were approved from a slate submitted by
the state appeals court.[59] Article 58 gave the governor sweeping powers to
name, without the consent of the state legislature, his lieutenant governor
and treasurer, along with any other civil servant not already appointed by
someone else.[60] Finally, Article 42 provided the governor with the power to
remove all judges without the consent of the legislature. This last change
did provoke a vigorous protest from 52 lawyers, many of them prominent
Cantonistas, who understood only too well the implications of such a
move.[61]

During his first term, Molina also reorganized the local constabulary
and brought in Spaniards and Cubans to direct a new bureau of investigation

with the forbidding name of secret police. The new agency was charged with ensuring the Molinistas' primacy in local politics.[62] Tomás Pérez Ponce, who was targeted for surveillance, wrote in *Verdad y Justicia,*

> It is reported that for some time back there has been a slow rise in the number of agents from the Secret Police who shadow those considered suspicious (in other words, those who are against the government and do not want reelection). These police outnumber the regular police, something which is totally new in this city, and which proves that they fear those who are dissatisfied and are trying to instill fear in those who are against the government.[63]

The secret police worked in tandem with the *jefe político* of Mérida.[64] The recent literature has made much of the prefect's status as an outsider, a functionary selected by and answerable to federal officials and therefore perceived as a threat by state authorities.[65] In Yucatán this was clearly not the case. There the *jefe* was part and parcel of the lucrative state system of patronage; each gubernatorial administration was empowered to clean house and appoint new prefects.[66]

## AWAKENING OF THE URBAN LABOR MOVEMENT

The changing nature of the urban labor movement was one potential threat to this intensification of state authority. A turn-of-the-century boom in fiber prices had triggered a prodigious spending spree by *henequeneros* and officials in the state capital, Mérida, and the principal port, Progreso. Employment opportunities encouraged workers to leave rural areas and attracted immigrants from outside the state, many of them Mexican nationals, Cubans, and Spaniards. Dockworkers, stevedores, carriage drivers, pushcart operators, printers, barbers, railway employees, binder-twine workers, carpenters, machinists, and even secondary school teachers responded to the influx by organizing in the two cities during the late Porfiriato, and with good reason. Management-labor relations in Yucatecan commerce and industry up to that time resembled those of the paternalistic world of the henequen hacienda.[67] In lieu of a legitimate union that could resolutely protect their interests, urban workers typically fashioned a relationship with management that provided them with some measure of protection and security. In return, individuals and small groups were compelled to petition on an ad hoc basis to present their grievances against management's often arbitrary measures.[68]

Not until the late Porfiriato did this patriarchal order begin to break down. Then, as businesses were progressively transformed from family ownership to joint-stock management and, in some instances, concentrated into regional oligopolies, clientelism gave way to partial proletarianization, a decline in real wages, and the formation of an urban trade union movement.[69] While the growth of the regional economy did not end paternalistic practices in the urban workplace, it did "distort them, emphasizing their coercive or oppressive aspects, while stripping away what reciprocity formerly existed."[70]

Moreover, unlike Mexico City and elsewhere in central Mexico (Orizaba and Puebla, for example), Mérida did not develop a sturdy "proletarian" class in the modern sense of the word. Monoculture's appeal and the peninsula's dearth of natural resources persuaded *henequeneros* to invest their venture capital in light industry and infrastructure that complemented the export economy, rather than take a chance on new manufactures. A few admirable experiments in industrial capitalism were initiated, most notably La Industrial, a modern binder twine factory just north of Mérida, which for twelve years competed unsuccessfully with North American cordage manufacturers. Ultimately, it proved too expensive to import machinery, equipment, and expertise from the United States and to train an unskilled or semiskilled work force.[71]

Trade unions, such as the Sociedad de Trabajadores Marítimos and the Alianza Mutualista de la Compañía de Trabajadores Ferrocarrileros, were therefore the exception in Yucatán. The union leaders, like their counterparts throughout Mexico, faced the daunting task of organizing the rank and file, raising workers' consciousness through the publication of working-class newspapers and pamphlets, sponsoring cultural evenings and discussion groups, and searching for nonconfrontational ways to petition management to improve their membership's standard of living.[72]

It should be emphasized that Yucatán's first hesitant steps toward worker solidarity pale beside the more militant union mobilization in other parts of Mexico during this era. The peninsula's isolation impeded the incorporation of Mérida's workers into national and international trade unions. Yucatecans and Mexican nationals, furthermore, filled most of the worker and management positions in Mérida. Whereas the visible presence of foreign workers sparked the growth of nationalistic unions elsewhere in Mexico, their relative absence in Yucatán inhibited the formation of a strong urban proletariat.[73]

If Yucatecan monoculture precluded the possibility of a characteristically "modern" industrial regime, it did not inhibit the growth of a strong urban artisanate. Maya villagers, mestizos, and immigrants all found gainful employment in the numerous public works projects, and the ubiquitous service sector. For example, jobs in the state's construction industry doubled during the last ten years of the Porfiriato alone. Skilled and semiskilled laborers found employment in the burgeoning public utilities, in printshops and foundries, and in trades such as carpentry, plumbing, and bricklaying.

Mutual aid associations appeared in working-class barrios such as Santiago, San Sebastián, and San Cristóbal. These incipient workers' groups sought to educate their membership and set up a rudimentary social net for their families, earmarking funds for workers' disabilities, retirements, and layoffs.[74] Night classes were held and libraries opened. Local intellectuals occasionally came to lecture, give literary readings, or discuss issues of the day. Former artisan leader Ceferino Gamboa recalled a stimulating evening held by the Unión Obrero on September 17, 1907, in which a number of local journalists, including José María Pino Suárez and Ricardo Mimenza Castillo of *El Peninsular*, Pardo and Sobrino Trejo from *La Humanidad*, and Julio Río, publisher of *La Campana*, delivered speeches.[75]

The power of the patron-client networks made it inevitable that incumbent and opposition *camarillas* would woo, and in some cases win over, these fledgling associations. Although documentation on the relationship is limited, we can speculate, from what we know about how the Porfirian regime operated nationally and the strategies the Molinistas employed locally, that state authorities would have been particularly aggressive in befriending and co-opting workers' associations.[76]

Whatever their working relationship with rival *camarillas* may have been, the artisanate's literati recognized all too well that workers' interests and needs differed from those of their patrons. *Artesanos cultos* soaked up ideas like sponges and then educated their membership through their cultural events and newspapers. Socialism, anarchism, and Catholic social action all came to Yucatán via foreign and domestic travelers. Literate artisans appropriated these ideologies, mixing and matching them syncretically with old-fashioned liberalism.[77]

It is understandable that these aspiring artisans had more in common (and were more comfortable interacting) with the city's petty bourgeoisie and professionals than with the peasants and peons in the countryside. But some elements of the artisanate's leadership, most notably the Pérez Ponce brothers and Gervasio Fuentes, sought to close the gap between the urban and rural working classes. As investigators have shown for other regions of Mexico, worker-peasant alliances were initiated in Yucatán during the late Porfiriato.[78] Campesinos who migrated to provincial capitals in search of jobs made contact with mutualist societies and trade unions. Although the evidence is fragmentary for Yucatán, we know that the Pérez Ponces and other "agitators" not only organized recent migrants in Mérida's and Progreso's working-class barrios but also went to the countryside to "educate" peons and villagers about their rights. These mediators, who empathized with the exploitation of the working classes but were not workers themselves, took a keen interest in the heated political environment and were actively recruited by regional *camarillas* during the 1906 and 1910 gubernatorial campaigns.

State authorities, for their part, blamed such "agitators"—especially outsiders and foreigners—for exacerbating the tensions between management and labor. This was not surprising; for years, public officials and *henequeneros* had insisted that relations between capital and labor were harmonious, and it was essential for the plantocracy to maintain that paternalistic fiction.[79]

As a result, Governor Molina and his successor, Enrique Muñoz Arístegui, kept President Díaz fully informed of the comings and goings of suspicious agitators from abroad or elsewhere in the republic who might "infect" Mérida's and Progreso's workers. Words like *anarchist* and *socialist* appear so often in their correspondence that it is occasionally difficult to discern whether these were merely convenient labels or accurate descriptions of the Spaniards, Cubans, and Italians to whom they were applied. Certainly the visit of the prominent anarchist Giuseppe Garibaldi in 1905 startled local authorities, especially when he met publicly with Yucatecan labor organizers, such as the Duch brothers, Valeriano Martínez, José Catalá, Emilio Sadó, and Emilio Rodríguez.[80] That same year, Molina wrote to Díaz that he had ordered the secret police "to watch with the usual discretion" the arrival from Havana of "a Jew whose name is not known and an Italian, Stutezzo Filippo, both of bad backgrounds," adding,

> There are four or five Catalans recognized as anarchists in Mérida who maintain contact with their coreligionists in Cuba. They get anarchist papers and newspapers. We are watching them. Also there are others coming from Cuba who are probably fleeing authorities there. They are a bad influence here.[81]

The harassment of working-class organizers continued undiminished throughout the last years of the Porfiriato. Gamboa recalled that after the Unión Obrera held a series of meetings at its Mérida headquarters between September 27 and October 14, 1908, *jefe político* Agustín Vales Castillo ordered the union leaders arrested, once again labeling them anarchists. Gamboa himself escaped arrest by fleeing to neighboring Campeche. Tomás Pérez Ponce's Círculo Libertario met similar treatment.[82]

The 1906 gubernatorial campaign pitted the Molinista *mano dura* against this growing urban artisanate, its politically engaged leadership, and Cantonista politicians desperate to prevent Don Olegario's reelection. This constellation of forces would open up the elite electoral game and expose how tenuous the Pax Porfiriana really was.

## Political Baptism, 1905

Making the most of the considerable advantages of incumbency, the Molinistas spared no expense in mobilizing their supporters for the 1906 gubernatorial election. By early April 1905, their newspaper, *La Democracia*, was churning out propaganda, electoral committees were constituted in every *cabecera*, and peons and villagers were hauled in from the countryside by rail, tram, and cart to attend elaborately staged rallies in the state capital. The government press published fragments of correspondence between Molina and Díaz giving the appearance that the dictator endorsed Molina's reelection. Molinistas also made use of their allies in Mexico City, who lavished praise on the governor's modernization campaign in the *científico* daily, *El Imparcial*.[83]

More important—and much to the chagrin of the Cantonista opposition—the Molina administration rushed a bill through the legislature amending the state constitution to permit the governor's reelection.[84] This was no small matter. Since independence, Yucatán's political carousel had never permitted a governor to serve two consecutive terms. Moreover, just eight years earlier the Peoncistas had tried the same maneuver, only to see Díaz quash the initiative before it could be debated in the state congress. The ease with which the Molinistas steered this measure so expeditiously through the legislature was yet another sign that Don Porfirio approved of Don Olegario's reelection.

On the night of August 10, 1905, Molina accepted the nomination of his party, the Unión Democrática, before eight thousand supporters in front of Mérida's Circo-Teatro.[85] From start to finish, the theatrics were indeed impressive; they deserve description, because this kind of stylized campaigning stood in stark contrast to the Cantonistas' grassroots organizing. The Mexico City newspaper *El País* filed this report:

> Never before had Yucatecans witnessed such a political demonstration. . . . The Circo-Teatro, profusely illuminated all the way to the top with tricolored lights, was an impressive sight. . . . In the center of the stage, decorated like a real living room, hung a beautiful portrait of our illustrious president, General Díaz, as if he were presiding over the event.[86]

The nominating committee members spoke in turn. After cataloguing the governor's considerable accomplishments, each implored Don Olegario, who sat in the seat of honor, to accept the party's nomination. Dr. José Patrón Correa, vice president of the Unión Democrática nominating committee, pleaded,

> And now answer. Say the one word that we all wish to hear; the only one that will produce the applause of this multitude imbued with a sacred love for the Motherland; the only one worthy of the sublimity of your civility, of the sublimity of your heart, of the sublimity of your conscience. . . . Speak, Señor Molina. The people anxiously await your answer. History is listening to you. Speak![87]

After Patrón Correa's oratorical flourish, Don Olegario graciously accepted the nomination, and the Yucatecan hymn was solemnly played. A triumphal recessional followed as the candidate and the nominating committee led a parade to his home on Calle 57. The governor then greeted the crowd from his balcony, watching as his supporters filed past carrying lanterns and placards. A number of musical bands from different parts of the state marched and played, while a fireworks display in front of Don Olegario's mansion added to the festivities.

A strong believer in temperance, Molina made sure alcohol was not available for consumption. Police on foot and horseback were prominently placed along the route to ensure responsible behavior. After wellwishers sauntered past Molina's home they found themselves in the Plaza de la

Mejorada. The demonstration continued in orderly fashion as Unión Democrática supporters walked over to the *zócalo* (about ten blocks) and then trekked back again to the Ferrocarriles Unidos train station just off the Mejorada. Here the directors of the various reelection clubs organized their workers and peasants for the ride home later that evening aboard specially commandeered trains paid for by the party.[88]

That August evening the governor's clientele, who had traveled to Mérida from all over the state, received a civics lesson in how a respectable gubernatorial candidate should be presented to his constituents. It followed the script to a T. No outbursts of any kind were noted.[89]

After his nomination, Don Olegario took a leave of absence, ostensibly for health reasons, and traveled to Havana, Puebla, and Mexico City, naming Izamal's district prefect, Braulio Méndez, to govern in his place. Although he returned to Mérida in October, Molina did not assume his gubernatorial duties until after the November elections. It might appear odd that a candidate for reelection would leave the state precisely when the campaign was heating up; but given the nature of the *destape* during the Porfiriato, it made good sense. The candidate preferred to remove himself from the campaign because he wished to appear above tawdry "politics," leaving the day-to-day organizing to his lieutenants. Just as important, with the governor out of the state for much of the campaign, the repression visited on his political opponents would be carried out by two relative unknowns, Méndez and Mérida's district prefect, Enrique Muñoz Arístegui. The timing of the personal leave therefore could not have been accidental.[90]

## REORGANIZED OPPOSITION

In response to Molinista electioneering, the Cantonistas formed the Convención Liberal Antirreeleccionista. Its leadership was intent on persuading the redoubtable Cantón to run again. But the 72-year-old patriarch was ailing; he had suffered a stroke just six months after he became governor that had "completely debilitated him." Still, in that age of personalistic politics, *camarillas* were so closely identified with their *jefes* that it was politically risky to sever Cantón from the clientele he had assembled over the preceding four decades. In this respect, the Cantonistas must have learned an important lesson from Peón Machado's ouster and subsequent exile in 1897, when the Peoncista party machine had disbanded overnight. Aged and infirm as he was, General Cantón's name still carried resonance throughout the state.[91]

In July, however, the Convención Liberal Antirreeleccionista suffered a serious setback: Molina sent word that the dictator did not want Cantón to run for governor. Wary of openly confronting Díaz, the Cantonista leadership publicly announced the dissolution of the Convención Liberal.[92] Almost overnight, however, a new party, the Unión Popular Antirreeleccionista, was cobbled together with a fresh slate of officers. Manuel Meneses, a little-known Mérida attorney, served as president, while Alfonso Cámara y Cámara and other Cantonista politicians quietly worked behind the scenes to gather firm support.

Aware that the new party could no longer be openly associated with Pancho Cantón, Meneses took special pains to inform General Díaz that the Unión Popular should not be confused with the Cantonistas. The modifier *popular* was chosen deliberately. Discontent percolated throughout the state, cutting more deeply than conventional elite rivalries; Meneses and his political patrons sensed that the working classes were ready to make their presence felt in the electoral arena.

True to form, the Unión Popular sent the president pages of petitions and propagandized in ephemeral newspapers.[93] It also went a step further, providing Díaz with a detailed account of the abuses committed by authorities statewide. Under normal circumstances, prudent historians would dismiss (or at the very least, treat with a healthy dose of skepticism) complaints from a disfavored *camarilla*; after all, the unending tale of woe was meant to persuade Don Porfirio to change his mind. But in this case, we have already witnessed how Molinista officials hounded labor organizers and journalists before the gubernatorial campaign. Both the Unión Popular's leadership and its rank and file had faced the identical pattern of around-the-clock surveillance, falsified arrests, and lengthy jail detainment to which union leaders and newspaper editors had been subjected during Don Olegario's first term.[94]

Even more significant, the repressive measures are corroborated by an extraordinary 28-page, typewritten report compiled by the Molinista secret police, a copy of which was sent to the dictator by Don Olegario's patron in the national capital, Manuel Sierra Méndez. The state bureau of investigation scrutinized every move the opposition made over a two month period, lending credence to Unión Popular claims that the incumbents had used any means at their disposal to ensure their triumph. The secret police infiltrated antireelectionist rallies, documenting their time, location, and site; recording names; estimating crowd size; and paraphrasing or quoting verbatim from speeches delivered by organizers and followers. Moreover, authorities planted agents as Unión Popular coreligionists, who even ascended the rostrum at rallies and delivered impassioned speeches criticizing local officials.[95]

The report also illustrates how the Unión Popular leadership made use of local power brokers, specifically union activists and *artesanos cultos*, who aggressively took the campaign to every barrio and working-class suburb in Mérida and Progreso. It also teases out how Mexican workers responded to those pleas and became engaged by the political process. The secret police's meticulous surveillance provides a window on the political baptism of Yucatán's working class, as traditional politicians sought to broaden their base and to empower and politically energize the grassroots.

Finally, the report confirms that throughout the summer and fall of 1905, the Cantonista leadership was conspicuously absent from these meetings and rallies, publicly distancing itself from the fledgling Unión Popular. Playing by the rules of the Porfirian *destape*, Cámara y Cámara and Delio Moreno Cantón could not openly commit their *camarilla* to a candidate without the dictator's consent. Instead, Cámara y Cámara wrote to Don Porfirio like an informed bystander, criticizing the incumbents and reminding the president that the Molinistas did not enjoy the people's support.[96]

## "ALL OF US FREE, HONEST WORKERS"

Three aggressive labor activists, Tirso Pérez Ponce, Gervasio Fuentes, and Urbano Espinosa, joined *jefe* Manuel Meneses to spearhead the Unión Popular's campaign. Pérez Ponce, who had lost one brother in the *tumulto* while another languished in jail awaiting trial for his role in the Xcumpich controversy, was a key figure throughout the summer and fall of 1905, speaking at virtually every meeting and demonstration.

Given the Pérez Ponces' numerous run-ins with the law, it is clear why Tirso was so committed to the task of organizing Yucatán's working classes. But why these activists would do the Cantonista leadership's bidding deserves some discussion. Yucatán's labor organizers realized that the nascent working class could not oppose the Molinista regime alone. Only by working with traditional politicians could labor leaders buy enough time to educate and mobilize workers. The Cantonistas not only gave these activists a certain degree of legitimacy; they would soon provide the perfect vehicle to raise workers' consciousness.

Spirited meetings were held in Progreso; the Mérida barrios of Santa Ana, Santiago, San Sebastián, and San Cristóbal; and Mérida's growing working-class suburbs, Kanasín and Chuburná. Typically, the Unión Popular scheduled evening meetings in private homes in a different barrio or town every few days. But often the crowds attending the meetings—the secret police estimates ranged from 50 to 200—were so large and boisterous they spilled into the streets, occasionally precipitating confrontations with the local police. An August 19 rally in Kanasín, for instance, held at 5:30 P.M. in Pedro Pablo Herrera's home, was attended by 50 to 60 local community residents and another 100 from Mérida. At the conclusion of the rally, a local band played, *aguardiente* (the sugarcane alcoholic beverage of the working classes) was passed around, and a raucous celebration began. The secret police reported that oppositionists yelled *mueras* against Olegario Molina and *vivas* for Pancho Cantón. Mérida's mounted police detachment was dispatched to quiet things down, but it was met by rock-throwing partisans. The police responded with arrests.

A core group of speakers addressed the membership at each rally, but they were invariably joined by barrio residents who chimed in with their particular concerns and grievances. Artisans, labor organizers, and even parish priests took to the podium and spoke to their families, friends, and neighbors. At the meetings, which usually lasted an hour and a half, party officials made sure to mention their organizing efforts, the necessity of raising funds to support the families of jailed party members, the dates and locations of future rallies, the difficulty of securing permits for demonstrations from local authorities, and their desire to send a delegation to Mexico City to speak with the president. Organizers were proud that their rallies, although relatively small and spontaneous in comparison to the Molinistas' elaborately scripted demonstrations, were entirely voluntary, and that peons and campesinos were not forcibly brought in from the countryside. José G. Corrales told a Progreso meeting,

> As you have all seen, the demonstration that took place today (in Mérida) with great enthusiasm and pomp, was very well attended by thousands of free and honorable people who paid their own way; none wore a suit, nor were they transported like pigs in a cart to the Circo-Teatro, but they went freely and spontaneously. That miserable reporter from *El Imparcial* must surely be convinced by now that we are not fourteen nor twenty, but many thousands, all of us free, honest workers.[97]

Corrales's stinging criticism of *El Imparcial* acknowledges that the antireelectionists—their working-class appeal notwithstanding—understood the necessity of taking their message to the national capital. The Unión Popular's "manifesto," published in Filomena Mata's *Diario del Hogar*, another Mexico City newspaper, excoriated state officials for

> the painful prostitution of justice, the abandonment of individual rights, the flourishing of ruinous monopolies, the unchecked speculation, the abhorrent favoritism, the systematic cruelty, the continuous arbitrariness and other evils, which have caused a profound discontent among the Yucatecan people.[98]

The publication of such a statement, furthermore, leaves little doubt that the antireelectionists' political spadework in the Federal District could only have been accomplished by seasoned Cantonista politicians taking advantage of their contacts.

"Down with reelection" was the Unión Popular's battle cry. The complaints were fleshed out at the rallies, as speakers cited countless examples of how *la mano dura* had made life miserable for the party. Not only was it difficult to get permits for rallies, José Espinosa alerted his audience, but authorities had pressured the railway companies to deny the party access to special cars to carry the faithful from Progreso and the countryside to Mérida demonstrations. Partisans instead had to come by "coach, car, on horseback, and mostly on foot." *La Revista de Mérida* corroborated Espinosa's charges later when it obtained and printed a copy of the letter *jefe político* Muñoz Arístegui had dispatched to the Mérida–Peto railway company prohibiting the management from providing trains for the August 19 Kanasín rally. The newspaper publicly ripped authorities for their high-handed tactics: "it now seems that Mérida's *jefe político* . . . can officially engage in the persecution of all those who do not side with the government."[99]

Speakers further alleged that party leaders were jailed for no good reason, that judicial authorities arbitrarily suspended due process, and that the ephemeral press was harassed. Tirso Pérez Ponce told one rally, "Day by day, señores, the injustice increases, the abuses, the arbitrary imprisonment against the antireelectionists. They throw our brother into prison, the brave octogenarian Don Bernabé Moreno, for the grave offense of stating that Yucatecans are a noble people." The Molinistas contended that Moreno had been arrested because he threatened the governor's life. Pérez Ponce retorted that the only ones who had heard Moreno threaten the governor were the secret police.[100]

State authorities retaliated by going for the jugular. Meneses was arrested and taken to Juárez Penitentiary only hours after the massive Unión Popular rally in Mérida on September 3, and kept out of commission until well after the November elections. The timing outraged antireelectionists, who informed Díaz that the arrest, whether deliberate or not, "would provoke a riot." Meneses was arraigned on civil charges stemming from his wife's disputed estate. He wrote to Díaz from prison that the authorities were beating a dead horse; his relatives had dropped this suit six years earlier. "My only crime," he added, "is to be president of the opposition." Meneses closed his letter by informing Díaz that two of the three judges reviewing the case for the state court of appeals were "blind instruments" of the regime. Díaz's terse response—he could not interfere in judicial matters—proved that he did not object to the Molinista *mano dura*. If that were not enough, Meneses, who was later moved to the Hospital O'Horan because of his failing health, wrote to Díaz that authorities had seized his home and sold it at auction for considerably less than it was worth.[101]

Meneses, however, was fortunate. Another antireelectionist, journalist Abelardo Ancona, left Juárez Penitentiary that fall in a casket, the victim of a grisly stabbing.[102] State officials were so wary of criticism of any kind that they closed down José María Pino Suárez's newspaper, *El Peninsular*, in October for having the temerity to argue that Molina did not deserve a second term. Pino Suárez was not a Cantonista and had no association with the Unión Popular.[103]

The leaders were not the only ones to suffer. Some oppositionists were hauled off to serve in the *leva*; the most unfortunate were taken to the frontier to protect outlying settlements from the *indios bárbaros*. Nicomedes Acosta (alias "La Rosca") reminded a Santa Ana rally in late August, "More than a year ago a worker named Antonio Madero was sent to the disease-ridden Bahía de Ascensión [in Quintana Roo near the Belize border], better known as the slaughterhouse, and we still don't know what has become of him. His family has sent letters that have not been answered." Moreover, antireelectionists who had paid the two-peso monthly fee exempting them from militia service were made Molinista block captains by the district prefect and were forced to attend the governor's demonstrations.

The party leadership also told Díaz of cases in which members were forced to serve in the auxiliary police force or do *corvée* (or *fagina*, as it was locally known) in their communities (cleaning streets, road construction, and so on) without remuneration. In Kanasín, oppositionists who refused to perform *corvée* were taken to jail. Residents who did not attend Molina's nomination at the Circo-Teatro either had to deliver three *cargas* of *sahcab* (quantities of quarried calcium carbonate) or pay its equivalent in cash to their block captains.[104]

Similar abuses were documented throughout the state, many in Sotuta, a southeastern *cabecera* on the fringes of the henequen zone and a purported hotbed of antireelectionist activities. The Unión Popular complained to Díaz that overzealous state authorities forcibly took campesino partisans by train to Mérida and ordered them to sweep the streets, in the middle of the spring planting season. The only oppositionists spared national guard service were those exempted by Sotuta's *jefe político*, "who makes them work on various estates administered by Olegario Molina's relatives."

The litany continued in other *partidos*: "Señor Molina and his relatives" who had recently purchased numerous sugar mills in Espita district "forced villagers to build roads near their fincas."[105] Francisco Gamboa Contreras, a mestizo typesetter who, notably, worked for the government newspaper, *El Diario Oficial*, went to the heart of the matter before the Kanasín faithful: "This is the first time I have had the pleasure of speaking, and I do it because every day I am more convinced of the abuses and capriciousness of those in power." *El Diario del Hogar* echoed Gamboa's complaints: "It is difficult to imagine how arbitrary the government's repression of public opinion has become, yet the facts speak for themselves."[106]

The Unión Popular also decried the pernicious effects of "continuismo" in Yucatán. La Rosca alerted a crowd in Santiago: "Don't worry about the spies or informants among us; they covet a position in the secret police or the national guard or another job that means nothing more than a measly salary." Felipe Paredes, who identified himself as a poor artisan, added bluntly: "[the civil servants] are vampires and parvenus who are afraid their party will lose and that they too will fall from grace." Paredes understood all too well the benefits of incumbency. He drew an effective contrast between the hard-working urban poor and government bureaucrats who lived off the dole and took advantage of workers by speculating in corn, beans, and other staples.

> The working people, who are at this moment united in struggle against the reelection of this despot and tyrant, are a people who earn their livelihood from the sweat of their work; they are not a handful of civil servants who live off of the taxpayer, nor do they hoard the basic commodities which the people need.[107]

Other speakers complained bitterly about the new taxes Molina had imposed to fund the seemingly endless array of construction projects. Here, activist José D. Espinosa drew explicit comparisons between Molina's and Pancho Cantón's handling of fiscal matters.

> Cantón made improvements during his administration without fanfare and without taxing the people. If it is true, in fact, that he negotiated a loan with the banks near the end of the [Quintana Roo] campaign, it was repaid within two months . . . while the improvements undertaken by Molina . . . have taxed the pockets of many.[108]

Tirso Pérez Ponce went to great lengths to belittle Molina's modernizing project. At a Kanasín rally, he derided Don Olegario's well-publicized role as topographical engineer and superintendent of the region's first railway, built in the late 1870s. "What has this engineer ever done to demonstrate his intelligence? Nothing! Well, the design and construction of the Mérida–Progreso railway that everyone called a mule cart at the time, that was no technological feat!" He ended his speech by blasting the incumbents for raising the art of corruption to a science: "And what has he accomplished as governor?" The crowd roared back in unison, "Enriched himself!"[109]

Gervasio Fuentes, president of the Unión Obrera, decried the costly paving of Mérida's downtown, informing those in attendance that Molina's decision to award the contract to a Philadelphia company was an egregious error. The company had a disastrous record, proving itself negligent in paving the streets of its own hometown.

> [It] will have the same effect it had in Philadelphia, namely that after ten years the governor there had to order the construction of cisterns to provide water to the town because people were dying of typhus as a consequence of the poisonous water they drank.[110]

Pérez Ponce refused to credit the governor for the myriad changes in Mérida's physical appearance but instead praised the urban construction gangs that had performed the paving and drainage of the city center, as well as the rural peons who toiled on the henequen haciendas.

> And they mention the paving of the streets as something that Molina should take credit for. We all know that task was not due to Molina nor to the group of landowners, or better put, slaveholders, that surround him. It is our brothers, the poor Indians of the haciendas. It is the sweat of these unfortunate souls who work in the henequen fields to enrich their executioners.[111]

*Hacendados* would have bristled at Pérez Ponce's use of the term *slaveholder*; the class character of the appeal could not have been more unmistakable. Aware that a wide gulf existed between the countryside and the city, Pérez Ponce sought to narrow that chasm and accentuate common ground between the urban and rural working classes. If his description of

hacienda peons was typically patronizing, his linkage of the wealth generated by monoculture to the developmentalist impulse that had transformed
the state capital was compelling. Nowhere was this more evident than in
his blistering attack on the governor's renovation of the Hospital O'Horan.

> The hospital—that overgrown shed covered with zinc—that's good for noth-
> ing. Well, the humble people would rather die in their miserable ham-
> mocks, with their family by their side looking after them, than in that
> degrading mansion that was made through the sweat and floggings of the
> people.[112]

The labor organizer reminded his followers why his brother Tomás was
rotting in Juárez Penitentiary. Hacienda Xcumpich was a perfect symbol of
the regime's repression of the urban and rural poor and their leadership. It
spoke volumes about the mistreatment of the peons, the persecution of
urban working-class organizers, and press censorship. After all, Pérez Ponce
reminded his listeners, vocal opposition to Molina's reelection had begun as
a response to the persecution of Pérez Ponce, Escoffié, and Vadillo.

> During the first months of this year, Tomás Pérez Ponce published some
> broadsheets denouncing crimes committed at Don Audomaro Molina's Ha-
> cienda Xcumpich, and instead of opening an investigation to determine
> what was happening, they sent the accuser to prison. At that moment no
> one had thought of opposing Señor Molina's reelection. Afterward, there
> were new attacks against journalists like José Vadillo and Carlos Escoffié,
> and it was then that the people began to become aware, and fixed their
> attention on the antireelectionist party.[113]

Finally, Tirso Pérez Ponce explicitly raised the specter of armed struggle
with authorities. He often closed his speeches by categorically stating that
the Unión Popular would oppose Molina's imposition "whatever it takes."
Once he concluded by throwing down the gauntlet: "If anyone dies in this
struggle, it will be the government's fault."

The urgency of the Unión Popular's oratory is also displayed in the
speakers' persistent call for a return to constitutional democracy. Just as the
1857 Constitution was a crucial symbol for Mexico City's "Jacobin" intellectuals, it was also a formidable part of the ideological repertoire of these
activists and *artesanos cultos*. Sometimes they invoked specific articles;
one artisan who felt betrayed by the regime's constant infringement on the
working classes' rights read particular clauses verbatim.[114]

At other times, speakers were more playful. Rosalío Dávila remarked,
"Oh, Indian of Guelatao [Benito Juárez]! What do you make of our problem?
If you would rise up from the grave and see how the Constitution of 1857 is
being trampled, you would drop dead again."[115] Here Dávila exploited a
powerful rhetorical device, invoking the liberal patriot to remind workers
that the Porfirian state was systematically violating their fundamental
rights as Mexican citizens.

Appropriating the 1857 Constitution as a symbol was especially effective, considering that this very same symbol had been jettisoned—or better put, mocked—by the Porfirian regime. Historian James Epstein has found that early nineteenth-century English artisans were similarly preoccupied with appropriating historical symbols for their own purposes. His conclusions help make sense of why the leadership of Yucatán's urban working classes was so devoted to a political icon that might have meant little to the rank and file.

> The obsessional concern with such symbolism was linked to questions of power: the power to move within public space, the power to speak, and the power to give definition to words, visual symbols and actions. Ultimately what was at issue was the power to provide an interpretation of Britain's past, and, therefore, to give direction to the nation's political and social future.[116]

At stake was how power at all levels of society was to be defined and exercised. From the artisans' perspective, it meant articulating an alternative vision, one that constantly constructed and reconstructed itself in opposition to the hegemonic interpretation preferred by national and local elites.

That is why the symbols always served to place the heroic past in stark contrast to the corrupt present. Sometimes the names of prominent Yucatecan liberals, such as Lorenzo de Zavala, Juan Miguel de Castro, or Father Vicente Velázquez, replaced the national icons, Juárez and Hidalgo. At a Progreso rally, Pedro P. Avila praised Castro, the recently deceased founder of the port, calling him a patriot of the same caliber as George Washington. The *empresario*, Avila declared, would have been horrified at the despicable actions of this repressive regime.

> People of Progreso, you, whose honest brows are kissed by the waves of the sea, should proudly support the good intentions of the founder of this port: with good reason he gave it the name of Progreso, because he surely believed that its sons would keep its name in dignity and would move it ahead and not backward. You must know that before the tyrant there was a Castro, an honest and progressive man, of good and noble feelings, who was the founder of our beloved town. Honor his memory and never take a step backward, always forward; do not fear tyranny and government repression, which mean nothing. We are not living in the times of Napoleon III, we live in the century of lights and we should admire Washington, Hidalgo, and others; furthermore, we must assure respect for the Constitution of 1857 that was bequeathed to us by the venerable Juárez. The people are governed by the people and that must be respected.[117]

These *artesanos cultos* had to walk a fine line. Even though they never criticized Díaz personally, they explicitly attacked his regime's contempt for workers' constitutional right to free expression and organization and its exaction of onerous contributions without consent. Free elections, representative democracy, an independent judiciary, and municipal autonomy were part and parcel of their rhetoric.[118]

The artisans shared the same principled moral outrage—what Barrington Moore has termed "justice untarnished by compromise"—that historians generally associate with peasant leaders deprived of their ancestral lands. Justice meant more than mere adherence to the law; it was infused with moral content. A young bootblack, Manuel Damosein, who plied his trade in front of the Hotel Llano in Mérida, must have touched a responsive chord in his fellow workers when he addressed a Progreso rally as follows:

> If we don't do anything and continue to accept the tyranny, what would become of the people? What would we have said if Hidalgo had asked us, "Where is the liberty that I spilled my blood for?" What would we say if Juárez had asked us, "What has become of my constitutional laws that I bequeathed you at great sacrifice and suffering?" What shall we tell our sons if we continue to accept the repression and tyranny? Nothing, citizens. We must respect ourselves and respect our laws. If you are worthy and brave, you should not permit our flag's colors to be trampled by any tyrant—unless you are cowards and desire the lasting shame of our sons![119]

Damosein's folk liberal rhetoric—and the feisty way he delivered it—must have appealed to workers who yearned for dignity and respect. His provocative mixture of past liberal heroes, the present call to action, and the future "curse" for their children (if the workers failed to redress the dictatorship's wrongs) was simultaneously nostalgic and confrontational. No wonder the secret police tried to drive Damosein away from his regular spot in front of the Hotel Llano.

Alan Knight notes that "organic intellectuals" like this shoeshine boy "did not have to 'go to the people,' they were already there. They enjoyed, furthermore, a measure of popular trust and sympathy; they had no mountain of prejudice to traverse; and by their very presence they could act as a screen against intellectual co-option and control from outside."[120] Damosein and others, whether they emerged from the working class or the middle class, were part of a protean force, consciously reproducing or conveying ideas to their adherents and exerting influence far beyond their numbers. Their primary task was to persuade the rank and file that they shared a common vision for the future and a yearning for self-improvement. To be truly effective, these "organic intellectuals" had to feel the same passions as the workers, making use of a distinctive language of culture to express, with conviction and eloquence, the experiences and feelings the masses themselves could not so readily verbalize.[121]

Yet oratory, as powerful a tool as it was, was not enough; nor was social class background. Antonio Gramsci maintains that "organic" intellectuals have to integrate themselves into the organization or culture of the movement to be truly effective. It was less important for these leaders to have the same occupation as their adherents than to play a functional role "in direct-

ing the ideas and aspirations of the class to which they organically be-
long."[122] This perhaps explains why the leadership of Mérida and Progreso's
artisans was peppered with lawyers, journalists, and other professionals,
like the Pérez Ponces, Escoffié, and Fuentes. Imbued with a zeal for individual independence and an utter contempt for authority, these leaders had
their feet firmly planted in both worlds, and fed off their own marginalization from a dominant culture that increasingly viewed them with fear and
suspicion.

Epstein argues that "the rhetoric of radical persuasion must be expansive, touching deep emotional chords if intellectuals are successfully to
challenge ingrained structures of understanding."[123] These Yucatecan per-
suaders had to paint a verbal canvas that spoke to a larger national culture.
It is not surprising, therefore, that another common refrain among these
speakers was the glorification of past struggles against the Spanish, French,
and North Americans, painting these foreign enemies with a very broad
brush. Tirso Pérez Ponce again: "The Spanish race from the beginning was
bad, because it must be said, it drank the blood of the Inquisition. Because of
this, they shot the venerable Hidalgo in the back."[124] This nationalistic
rhetoric took some resonance from the actual presence of recent Spanish
immigrants in Yucatán, as in other parts of Mexico, often hired by creole
landowners and industrialists as overseers, managers, and foremen. Workers perceived this new generation of *gachupines* as just as cruel and exploitative as the conquistadors.[125]

The *artesanos cultos'* ideological construction of a heroic liberalism
must be understood, moreover, as a conscious effort to instill in workers a
sense of *mexicanidad*. Benito Juárez's victory against Maximilian and the
French, in particular, had indelibly entwined liberalism with patriotism in
the minds of many Mexican workers. Here we would concur with Rodney
Anderson: "Their nationalism did not dilute their demands for social justice; it stimulated them, giving them form and strength. In effect it legitimized the workers' demands in their own eyes, casting their movement as
patriotic, not revolutionary, and placing their cause squarely in the mainstream of Mexico's historical development."[126]

RALLY IN MÉRIDA

The Unión Popular's barrio-hopping antireelection campaign culminated on September 3, 1905, with a three-and-a-half-hour demonstration in
Mérida. Supporters were brought to the capital from as far away as Valladolid to the east, Peto to the southeast, and Chocholá to the southwest.
A machete-swinging scuffle took place in Progreso when the notoriously
heavy-handed *jefe político*, Primitivo Díaz, blocked Unión Popular supporters from boarding a train to the state capital. Although the party had paid
four hundred pesos to the Ferrocarriles Unidos de Yucatán for extra railway
cars, only 120 supporters were able to board.

The secret police, whose informants provided headcounts at railway stations throughout the state, estimated that the party brought 470 partisans to Mérida by train. Authorities estimated that an additional eight hundred to nine hundred Meridanos participated in the September 3 demonstration, although Unión Popular leaders later boasted that "thousands" were present.

Rather than hold one large rally in a central spot with dozens of speakers, the Unión Popular opted for a novel strategy, turning the gathering into a parade. It began in San Cristóbal at 8:30 in the morning and then moved to different barrios or parks throughout the city, stopping at predetermined sites along the route where one or two short speeches were delivered, usually from the back of a small cart. Authorities commented that the rally grew larger as it progressed. Finally the floating rally wended its way back to where it had begun in San Cristóbal. In that working-class barrio, five Unión Popular leaders delivered impassioned speeches.

As the rally moved from barrio to barrio, it was led through the streets by twelve men on horseback; a band of musicians; 25 partisans carrying flags, banners, and posters; another musical group from Kanasín; and carriages transporting the Unión Popular leadership. The banners and posters reiterated the campaign's themes: *vivas* to Cantón, Meneses, and Díaz; "Down with reelection"; "Victims of reelection—Pérez Ponce, Escoffié, Vadillo, Peñalvert, Cámara, Zavala, and the Erosas"; "Monopoly, insults, compulsion, abuse, arbitrariness."

Authorities prepared for the worst, marshalling police, state militia troops and plainclothes agents. National guard troops brought in from Tixkokob were kept at a police station in Hidalgo Park, while other contingents from Hunucmá and Sotuta kept an eye on the suburbs. Still others were stationed in the barrio of San Sebastián. The police surveyed not only those attending the rally but those who stayed away. The upper classes, for instance, were conspicuously absent: "There was no one present of any social standing." Pancho Cantón's whereabouts were a special concern: informants reported that he took the 5:30 A.M. Mérida–Valladolid train that morning, bound for Motul.[127]

The absence of such luminaries as Cantón and Cámara y Cámara from even this culminating demonstration reflected the *camarilla*'s unease about the Unión Popular's chances in the November elections. Deprived of influence in Mexico City and convinced that Don Porfirio had already made up his mind, the Cantonistas continued publicly to distance themselves from the campaign, even though authorities alleged that Cámara y Cámara and his aides were still working behind the scenes.[128] The government newspaper, El Eco del Comercio, tried its best to link the Unión Popular to the former governor after the Mérida rally, declaring that "the demonstration had a markedly 'Cantonista' color to it" when the parade surged past General Cantón's downtown home.[129]

Despite the encouraging Mérida rally, Unión Popular hopes were dashed by a September 8 telegram to the leadership from Díaz, innocuously proclaiming, "elections are a fundamental right of the Yucatecan people." The antireelectionists tried to put the best spin on the cable, reading it aloud at their rallies and asserting, "these words guarantee the failure of Señor Olegario Molina's plans." But Cámara y Cámara, who had witnessed this type of Porfirian posturing from the opposite side of the fence in 1897, understood what the telegram meant: Molina's reelection was a foregone conclusion. Manuel Sierra Méndez, who was in Mérida during the summer and fall and who peppered Díaz with reports about the campaign, opined that Cámara y Cámara was disgusted because Díaz publicly had led his *camarilla* on while secretly working to ensure Molina's victory.[130]

The final twist of the political knife came in mid-September, when General Cantón learned indirectly that Díaz was planning a trip to Yucatán to help inaugurate Molina's public works projects. Cantón wrote Don Porfirio that he would be honored if the president would stay at his home, but Díaz tersely replied that he was coming to Yucatán as Governor Molina's guest. Local arrangements for the presidential visit—the first time a Mexican president had deigned to visit the state—would be handled by Sierra Méndez and a local organizing committee of prominent Molinistas. We can only surmise how devastating the events of that autumn must have been to the loyal Cantón. Not only would he and his party be denied the statehouse, but he would be pushed ignominiously into the background while his rival garnered the accolades during the president's historic trip.[131]

With Meneses in jail, Martín Romero Ancona assumed the presidency of the Unión Popular, while Pérez Ponce was promoted to party secretary. On September 19 the new leadership tried to force the issue, announcing their intention to send a delegation to the National Palace. They cabled the president a list of five possible candidates, including former governors Cantón and Daniel Traconis and respected judge José Encarnación Castillo. Díaz's reply nine days later was as ambiguous as his earlier telegram: "The electoral matter is to be decided by the people of Yucatán, and I cannot and must not tell you anything else."[132]

The Unión Popular still refused to accept the inevitable. The party informed Judge Castillo of its willingness to nominate him for governor at its upcoming October 22 demonstration. The judge immediately wrote to Díaz that he wanted nothing to do with the nomination, protesting that the antireelectionists were using his name without his permission. The leaders went ahead anyway, publicly announcing their support for the reluctant candidate before six hundred supporters in Mérida. The day after that rally, Castillo took the extraordinary step of placing an advertisement in *La Revista de Mérida* disavowing his candidacy. Intent on keeping a low profile, Castillo refused to come to Mérida for the rest of the fall, tending to his hacienda in Maxcanú district.[133]

Faced with the embarrassment of nominating a candidate who wanted nothing to do with their party, Romero Ancona and Tirso Pérez Ponce had little choice but to make the best of their defeat on their own terms. They published a broadside urging their supporters to abstain from voting on November 5. Disillusioned by the political process, partisans vented their frustrations. In Kanasín, violence erupted and, in a skirmish with authorities, two antireelectionists were killed and five more were arrested.[134]

## VIOLENCE ON THE OUTSKIRTS

The unrest in Kanasín is a fitting episode with which to conclude this examination of the 1905 campaign. It sets in sharp relief what transpired when the traditional brand of patronage politicking came together with the Cantonistas' expanded organizing efforts. Throughout the campaign, the suburb of Kanasín had been a tinderbox of political tensions awaiting a spark. After the Unión Popular's August 19 rally culminated in a skirmish between state authorities and the opposition, prefect Muñoz Arístegui stepped up surveillance and refused to permit concerts or dances in Kanasín. On September 20, *La Revista de Mérida* foreshadowed the coming violence when it reported that there was "bad blood" and that "for political reasons, the residents of this pueblo are badly divided."[135]

Pedro Pablo Herrera, host of the boisterous August 19 rally, was a prominent Unión Popular organizer and a Kanasín native with the familial connections to build a strong base of support for the party in his village. Herrera publicly lambasted the incumbents throughout the campaign. As the campaign season drew to a close and government officials moved to preempt disturbances by arresting a number of key antireelectionists, Herrera, fearing the worst, went into hiding and stayed out of sight until well after the elections.

Three weeks after Molina's victory at the polls, violence erupted. On November 28, an ambush designed to capture Herrera backfired when national guard commander Porfirio Solís, who had set the trap, was shot and killed under shadowy circumstances. Herrera's son Magdaleno was also shot and injured in the fracas. The next day, police lieutenant Leopoldo Buendía led a manhunt to find Solís's assailants and was himself injured in a shootout that claimed the lives of two Indians working on their *milpa* on nearby Hacienda Santa Rita. Adding to the confusion surrounding these two days of violence was that one of the victims, Teófilo Baas, had recently deserted from the national guard. *La Revista de Mérida* speculated that it might have been Baas who had killed national guard commander Solís.

Although it is impossible to discern exactly what transpired in Kanasín on November 28 and 29, subsequent newspaper reports make it abundantly clear that the Herrera and Solís families had been feuding for decades. During the 1878 gubernatorial campaign, Solís's father, an overseer of a hacienda owned by then gubernatorial candidate Miguel Castellanos Sánchez, purportedly had brandished a machete in front of national guard headquarters in Kanasín and demanded that one of Castellanos Sánchez's peons be let out of prison. Herrera's father, the commander of the Kanasín national guard and a strong supporter of Governor Manuel Romero Ancona, shot and killed Solís's father in the incident and was later found innocent of any wrongdoing. More than 25 years later, the tables had eerily turned: Porfirio Solís was now national guard commander and a fervent Molinista, while Herrera was a member of the political party on the outs. *La Revista de Mérida*, all too willing to paint a nefarious portrait of the incumbents, reported that throughout the electoral campaign Solís had "persecuted the antire-electionists . . . which at the same time satisfied his desire for vengeance."

Leaving aside the political opportunism of the Cantonista press, it is clear that the mayhem in Kanasín was the result of a blend of "old" and "new" politics. The Unión Popular's grassroots organizing, the Molinistas' *mano dura*, clientelistic politics at the local level, and a blood feud pure and simple; all combined to lead the younger Solís and Herrera to reenact their troubled past. *La Revista de Mérida* put it bluntly: "There was no government there, only friends and bitter enemies."[136]

Kanasín's behavior, moreover, was not anomalous, according to the newspaper: "Some parts of the state have found themselves in a very sad situation, similar to that of Kanasín, where the residents emigrate to other towns or flee to the countryside; where they live isolated from the civilized world, or they remain in their homes; where they either experience the government's heavy hand or wait for a spark to suddenly catch."[137] The newspaper's admonition proved prophetic: state authorities would not be able to manage the "sparks" so effectively during the 1909 gubernatorial campaign.

## An Uneasy Peace, 1905–9

On November 5, 1905, Olegario Molina was reelected—the state's first governor since independence to succeed himself. His victory was soon overshadowed, however, by the excitement surrounding Don Porfirio's impending trip to the peninsula. The meticulously organized presidential visits to the provinces accomplished several important objectives. First and foremost, they provided an opportunity to confirm the dictator's popular appeal. The gala affairs, which generally lasted less than a week, comprised a long succession of parades, banquets, concerts, and speeches, carefully scripted to emphasize the president's virtues. The pretext for one of these infrequent excursions to the *patrias chicas* might be the inauguration of a new public works project or the unveiling of a statue to a national or regional hero. By his attendance, the president reminded his constituents that he, like the hero so honored, was a patriot who deserved their gratitude, not only for his ardent defense of the motherland against foreign intervention but, just as important, for his laudable efforts to transform Mexico into a modern nation.

In Yucatán's case, Manuel Sierra Méndez and his local arrangements committee chose to emphasize Molina's modernization campaign. Don Porfirio would personally inaugurate the Hospital O'Horan, the new mental asylum, and the expanded penitentiary. Patriotism would be given its due a few weeks before the presidential trip, when Justo Sierra Méndez, Manuel's brother and the recently appointed secretary of public instruction, would pay homage to their father, Justo Sierra O'Reilly, by unveiling a statue of the prominent liberal intellectual on the Paseo de Montejo.[138]

More pragmatically, the visits were an important political plum for Don Porfirio's most trusted clients in the provinces. The dictator came always as a "personal" guest of the sitting governor. The entourage's magisterial luster invariably rubbed off on provincial oligarchs. In Molina's case, the visit was especially propitious, coming just weeks after he was sworn in for a second term. Friends and foes alike could reach only one conclusion: the president had journeyed to Yucatán personally to bestow his political blessing on the governor. For the local press, the only remaining question was, would Don Olegario complete his second term, or would he be swept away to the Distrito Federal and rewarded with a position in Don Porfirio's cabinet? Such a move had a precedent, the elevation of Governor Bernardo Reyes to secretary of war soon after Díaz's triumphal visit to Monterrey in 1898. And the rumors proved true within the year, when Molina was appointed secretary of development (fomento).

Molina baffled many Meridanos, however, by naming Enrique Muñoz Arístegui to complete his second term. Although Muñoz Arístegui, a shoe merchant, had a modicum of political experience, having served on the city council during the first half of the 1890s and as Mérida's district prefect for part of Molina's first term, most of the plantocracy regarded him as little more than a cipher, and an officious one at that. As jefe político, he had gained notoriety by rounding up antireelectionists and journalists during the 1905 campaign.[139]

The decision to hand over the statehouse to a colorless, albeit loyal, hatchet man with little education and no kinship ties to prominent Meridano families must have shocked the gente decente. "El Zapatero," as he was derisively called, was widely viewed as Don Olegario's puppet, someone who could be easily shoved aside when the governor returned to the peninsula. In retrospect it is easy to see that Molina made a serious error in judgment. Moreover, as the economy unraveled and political tensions heightened during the last years of the Porfiriato, Muñoz Arístegui, who never outgrew the "interim" tag even though he served almost a full term, increasingly had to resort to repression to keep the peace.

Meanwhile, the Cantonistas regrouped for the next elections. Now that the dictator had broken the rules of alternation, the Cantonistas needed to rebuild their political bridges nationally and extend their clientelistic networks statewide. Even more essential was to choose a new candidate to replace the ailing Pancho Cantón. The most likely heir apparent was the general's nephew, the poet and newspaper publisher Delio Moreno Cantón.

The disparity between the party's past and its future could not have been more obvious. Pancho Cantón was a man of action, a soldier, a leader who hailed from the countryside. Although regarded as an outsider by Mérida politicians, the general enjoyed widespread popularity in southeastern Yucatán. Moreno Cantón, who, like his uncle, hailed from Valladolid, grew up (and was educated) in Mérida. He was an intellectual with virtually no political experience, and although his romantic, stylized poetry was highly regarded by the local literati, he had inherited little of the general's charisma.

Moreover, not all Cantonistas agreed that Moreno Cantón was a suitable replacement. Alfonso Cámara y Cámara in particular had doubts about Delio's leadership abilities. He preferred General Luis C. Curiel, who had served as federal garrison commander in the peninsula during the early 1890s. Even though Curiel was not a Yucatecan, Cámara y Cámara reasoned, he was precisely the kind of candidate that Don Porfirio favored. The aging military officer had ample political experience, serving as governor of the Distrito Federal and his native Jalisco and as a member of the national congress. He was highly regarded locally.[140]

As the Cantonistas pondered a replacement for Don Pancho, the state's volatile export economy further complicated matters. Both Cantóns became unfortunate casualties of the 1907 panic. Moreno Cantón had to declare bankruptcy and sell his interest in *La Revista de Mérida* to his uncle. He would ultimately "survive" to claim the caudillo's political mantle, but his position would always be a precarious one.[141]

Nationally, the last years of the Porfiriato were uncertain ones for the Cantonistas. Their patron, Joaquín Baranda, died in 1909. Although Baranda had lost much of his power after his 1901 ouster from the cabinet, he had continued working to undermine *científico* influence. Baranda's longtime ally, Governor Teodoro Dehesa of Veracruz, was regarded as vice presidential timber for the 1910 elections. And because Dehesa and Pancho Cantón were old friends who had fought for Díaz in the Tuxtepec rebellion, it was understandable that after Baranda's death, the Cantonistas gravitated to Dehesa's camp.

Even though the 1905 campaign had proven unsuccessful, the Cantonistas had used it to solidify their *camarilla*'s clientele. Even in defeat, the Unión Popular had served a useful purpose, energizing Mérida's and Progreso's working classes and introducing them to Porfirian electoral politics. A few individuals would participate in the political conspiracies against the Molinista regime in 1909, but for the present, the urban working classes were unable to capitalize on their political organization; state repression made sure of that.

If the political baptism of Yucatán's urban working class proved frustrating for the Pérez Ponces, Escoffié, and Fuentes, it also made clear to these labor activists and to the Cantonista leadership that recruitment was sorely needed in the countryside. That is why, soon after his release from Juárez Penitentiary in 1908, Tomás Pérez Ponce traveled throughout the henequen zone, mobilizing villagers and hacienda peons. By 1910 most observers agreed that despite the advantages of incumbency enjoyed by the Molinistas, the Cantonistas were the strongest political *camarilla* in rural Yucatán.

Worsening economic conditions abetted the Cantonistas' organizing. The 1907 panic devastated the regional economy and affected all social classes. The price of henequen plummeted, haciendas went onto the auction block, credit evaporated, and wages were slashed across the board. The construction boom quickly became a memory, leaving many artisans out of work. The unpopular Muñoz Arístegui became a handy target for disgruntled *hacendados*, small businessmen, professionals, and the working classes.

The Cantonistas did not hold a corner on disaffection, however. Some members of the local intelligentsia searched for a different option, one that could promise more meaningful reform. Such an option coalesced in artistic societies, such as "La Arcadia," "La Bohemia," "Lord Byron," and "Eligio Ancona." These circles served as forums where political, economic, and social issues were aired. Respected intellectuals like Moreno Cantón and playwright and journalist Manuel Sales Cepeda assembled teams of idealistic writers, doctors, engineers, and lawyers, while Rodolfo Menéndez de la Peña, José Montes de Oca, and Juan López Peniche, faculty members at the Escuela Normal de Profesores, lectured their students on the importance of public education. It should be stressed that these groups were not purely "middle class." Some members were sons of the plutocracy whose own livelihood depended on their parents' and relatives' economic interests. Furthermore, given the suffocating political climate, many of these academic and literary societies were understandably reluctant to voice their concerns publicly. Some groups shied away from provoking a confrontation by concentrating entirely on apolitical issues. For instance, the Liga de Acción Social, founded in 1909, was a small group of "progressive" *hacendados* committed to improving conditions on haciendas and opening rural schools. Taken together, however, these diverse groups of *hacendados*, lawyers, educators, civil servants, journalists, and white-collar employees generally believed that some type of change was necessary.

For many of these educated professionals, the Cantonistas were nothing more than loyal Porfiristas, committed to perpetuating the status quo. In 1909, some of these intellectuals joined journalist José María Pino Suárez to find common cause with the national reform movement of Francisco Madero. Under Pino's banner they began the arduous task of creating the infrastructure for a competitive political party for the next gubernatorial campaign.[142]

Porfirio Diaz (*Picturesque Mexico*)

Governor Carlos
Peón Machado
(*Picturesque Mexico*)

General Francisco
Cantón, caudillo,
governor, and railroad
entrepreneur (Latin
American Library, Tulane
University)

Minister of Justice and
Education Joaquín
Baranda, anti-*científico*
and stepbrother of Pancho
Cantón (*Picturesque
Mexico*)

Governor Olegario
Molina, prominent
landowner and henequen
merchant (Latin
American Library,
Tulane University)

Enrique Muñoz Arístegui, district prefect of Mérida (1905) and interim governor (1907–11) (Latin American Library, Tulane University)

From left to right, José María Pino Suárez, Francisco Madero, and Serapio Rendón, ca. 1911 (Archivo "Pedro A. Guerra")

Calle 59, downtown Mérida, ca. 1900 (Archivo "Pedro A. Guerra")

On August 11, 1897, political violence rocked Mérida's main plaza; soldiers fired from the balcony of the city council building, pictured here (Archivo "Pedro A. Guerra")

Military band similar to the one that played *serenatas* in Mérida's Plaza de las Armas on the night of the *tumulto* (Archivo "Pedro A. Guerra")

Scene along the arcade in the central plaza of Mérida (Archivo "Pedro A. Guerra")

Juárez Penitentiary, aka "Hotel Bolados"
(Latin American Library, Tulane University)

Tirso Pérez Ponce referred to Mérida's
Hospital O'Horan, pictured here, as "an
overgrown shed with a zinc roof" (Latin
American Library, Tulane University)

Portrait of an oligarchical family at the height of Yucatán's henequen boom (Archivo "Pedro A. Guerra")

Palacio Cantón, the ornate mansion of General Cantón, on the Paseo Montejo in Mérida (Latin American Library, Tulane University)

*Jornaleros de campo*
(henequen field
workers) (Archivo
"Pedro A. Guerra")

Peons and armed overseers haul henequen leaves on a mule-drawn tram (Archivo "Pedro A. Guerra")

Torres de Regil (Towers of Regil), a palatial residence on a henequen hacienda (Latin American Library, Tulane University)

*Labor omnia vincit*, "work conquers all": a hacienda community assembles for a religious procession (Archivo "Pedro A. Guerra")

Maya wedding portrait, ca. 1900 (Archivo "Pedro A. Guerra")

Yucatecan state militia troops on the southeastern frontier during the final campaign of the Caste War, ca. 1900 (Archivo "Pedro A. Guerra")

Yaqui Indians deported from the northwestern state of Sonora to work on the henequen plantations during the late Porfiriato (Archivo "Pedro A. Guerra")

## CHAPTER 4

# Economic Contradictions

We see Montes, the hero of Yucatán, going out among the planters and say-
ing that the Great White Father in Chicago will pay them a half a cent per
pound more for their fibre. [I]f we were an American farmer we would not
have a bale of sisal . . . put onto our binder next harvest.
    —Cordage company pamphlet, 1910

The turbulent 1905 gubernatorial campaign revealed to both
oligarchs and pretenders how the political landscape was
dramatically changing during the late Porfiriato. Despite
the heavy hand state authorities applied to stifle dissent, Mérida and Progreso's disgruntled urban classes and their elite sponsors were more determined than ever to oust the incumbents in the next round of gubernatorial
elections, in the fall of 1909. If the Cantonistas were concerned about the
Faustian bargain they had struck with this feisty group of artisans, they
failed to show it. If anything, the Cantonistas escalated their efforts to
broaden their political base by appealing to disgruntled Yucatecos of all
social classes. One of the most promising groups they targeted was the
growing number of disaffected *henequeneros* who, despite rising world demand for hard fiber, had ample reason to feel insecure about henequen
monoculture's (and their own) uncertain future.

To untangle further the twisted skein of Yucatán's summer of discontent, we now turn our attention to the economic origins of elite factional
strife during the late Porfiriato. What follows is an analysis of four pivotal
episodes during and after the 1907–8 financial panic, episodes that crystallize the severe economic contradictions embedded in the prerevolutionary
order. The first of these was a futile attempt by *henequeneros* to organize a
producers' association. The second was the turn-of-the-century merger of
four family-owned railway companies into one powerful trust, and its accompanying problems and pitfalls. Third was the failure of a powerful henequen exporting house (*casa exportadora*); and fourth, the celebrated at-

tempt in 1909 by Avelino Montes S. en C. and the International Harvester Company (IHC) to corner the local fiber market.

Collectively, these cases demonstrate the planters' failure to contest the economic control of Molina-Montes and International Harvester in Yucatán. In each instance, the weakness and divisiveness of competing elite factions nullified the factions' efforts to assert some measure of independence. Finally, in all four cases, Molina, Montes, and Harvester became convenient scapegoats for planter misfortune, although apparently they justly deserved much of the criticism. It is our thesis that the frustration the *henequeneros* experienced as a result of these confrontations would be expiated in a torrent of political activity during the last years of the Porfiriato and the first years of the Mexican Revolution. Before analyzing these four episodes, however, let us briefly sketch the contours of Yucatán's political economy during the late Porfiriato and the economic contradictions that led to a pitched battle among competing elite *parentescos* for control over the spoils of monoculture.

## Heyday of the Oligarchical Order, ca. 1902–9

Mexico in 1910 had one of the highest proportions of foreign investment in Latin America.[1] Close to two billion dollars, roughly 70 percent of the total capital invested in the country, permeated railroads, mines, commerce, land, and industry. Certain export commodities required heavy capital investment—well beyond the means of national entrepreneurs—to import new technologies and improve infrastructure and marketing. Foreign capitalists often established economic enclaves in mining and commercial agriculture, which entailed the construction of "company towns," as well as an extensive network of associated companies in other sectors—in other words, horizontal and vertical "linkages"—in the foreign country. This foreign-dominated export model carried heavy costs: it exposed the domestic economy to violent shocks brought on by changes in external demand; it exacerbated inequality while ignoring social reform; and, most important for the Yucatecan case, it favored the political dominance of landowner-exporters, who played an increasingly oligopolistic role in regional economies.[2]

By 1910, Mexican exports, although certainly diverse, were dependent on the North American market. Indeed, three-quarters of the nation's exports found their way north. Despite efforts by the Porfirian state to diversify its dependence by entering into trade treaties with a number of countries, only Cuba—by then a virtual colony of the United States—exhibited a greater reliance on the U.S. market. Infrastructural improvements, North American investments in Mexico, and the Europeans' turn toward their colonies all contributed to this phenomenon. Unfortunately for the Mexican economy, the United States produced many of these same commodities in larger quantities (silver, gold, copper, petroleum, cotton), or sometimes shut them out by prohibitive tariffs (wool, cattle, lead), or allowed them in only as long as they did not challenge U.S. producers. Tropical commodities not produced in the United States also ran into problems: the merger movement in the United States since the 1880s had created oligopolistic buyers that enjoyed tremendous political clout, such as the U.S. Rubber Company; Crossman Brothers; Arbuckle Brothers (coffee); the American Sugar Refining Company; and the American Chicle Company (chewing gum).[3]

The *científicos* encouraged the importation of foreign theories, capital, and technologies. Positivism, Spencerian Social Darwinism, and liberalism were appropriated and adapted to Mexican realities. To persuade foreigners that Mexico was an appealing site for investment, Porfirio Díaz bolstered the army and rural guard to make the countryside safe, made regular payments on the nation's debt, balanced the budget for the first time in its history, and eventually moved the nation to the gold standard. A North American writing in *Harper's Magazine* in 1897 wryly remarked that Díaz's administration may not have been republican, but it certainly was "business."[4]

In sharp contrast to past administrations, which had discouraged entrepreneurial activity, Díaz and his brain trust gave foreign and national elites "an economic hunting license with a perpetual open season."[5] While urban or rural enterprises historically had used kinship ties and political muscle to overcome a capricious economic environment, now, for the first time, companies could utilize these very same strategies under the watchful eye of an accommodating state. Employing the tenets of economic liberalism loosely, the Porfirian government intervened repeatedly to encourage investment, providing subsidies, tax breaks, and tariff protection. Through legislation and persuasion, moreover, the state invited mergers and other anticompetitive strategies, contending that these tactics were needed to overcome the obstacles that plagued nascent industrialization. In this manner, the Porfirian state of mind justified the privilege of the rich while it rationalized the creation of an authoritarian regime determined to unify its stubborn *patrias chicas*.

Yucatán was thoroughly transformed by the requirements of North American industrial capitalism and governed by its fluctuating rhythms during the last quarter of the nineteenth century. Henequen production increased furiously as annual exports rose from 40,000 bales of raw fiber to more than 600,000 bales. By the turn of the century, the peninsula's colonial-style haciendas had been transformed into modern henequen plantations. Contemporaries chronicled how the green cornfields and idly grazing cows of the northwestern part of the state were replaced by rectilinear rows of bluish-gray spines. The final destination of this raw fiber was the cordage factories of the United States, where manufacturers converted it into binder twine for the grain farmers of North America.[6]

The henequen estate differed from the classical pattern of late nineteenth-century plantation agriculture in several important respects.

Land tenure and ownership of the means of production were almost exclusively in Yucatecan hands. There was no major influx of technology from abroad; indeed, Europeans and North Americans had miserably failed to invent the machinery required to make henequen processing economical on a commercial scale. Nor was management brought in from the outside; it, too, was completely Yucatecan. Finally, while capital was ultimately imported from the United States, it was made available and distributed, as far as the producers were concerned, on a local basis.

When fiber prices were high, *henequeneros* secured bountiful profits. But local *hacendados* needed sizable amounts of capital to purchase machinery for processing the fiber, as well as to build tramways, clear and cultivate the land, and then wait seven years for their fiber plants to mature. For this they had to borrow money in advance from *casas exportadoras*. The *casas*, in turn, borrowed capital from banks and buyers in the United States. A small *hacendado* class, numbering between three hundred and four hundred, promised its fiber to the *casas* in exchange for cash advances.

From the 1870s on, local business leaders served as fiber-purchasing agents and financial intermediaries for foreign loan capital. Thus North American brokers and manufacturers operating during the first decades of the boom, such as the Thebaud Brothers and the National Cordage Company, enlisted the services of the large Yucatecan export houses of Eusebio Escalante and Manuel Dondé, among others, in their bids to corner the local market. For their own part, these "collaborators" realized sizable profits, usually in the form of commissions and kickbacks but also through the usurious lending practices that access to foreign capital allowed. Ideally, just as the foreign investor sought to carve out a durable monopoly or "corner" on the trade, so the collaborator wished to enjoy the benefits of an exclusive relationship with the controlling foreign interests.

These limitations made it difficult for *henequeneros* to adjust productivity or predict prices. As a result, local landholders were particularly vulnerable to the repeated boom-and-bust cycles that afflicted the hard-fiber market. Although henequen provided 85 percent of the fiber for the profitable binder twine industry by the turn of the century, it had enough competition from manila and other hard fibers, as well as occasional attempts by North American buyers to corner the market, to create alternating shortages and gluts. This chronic price instability, coupled with the producers' inability to diversify, meant that Yucatán's regional economy as a whole, and the henequen sector in particular, experienced severe dislocations in the midst of sustained growth.

Despite these continuing fluctuations, henequen represented a bonanza for those elites savvy enough to understand how political influence and economic leverage might complement each other. The capacity of merchant and planter families to adapt to changes in the political arena amid the boom-and-bust shocks of the regional economy produced a tangled web of power relationships in the peninsula throughout the fiber boom.

TABLE 4.1

*Political Factions and Their* Casas
*Exportadoras, 1890—1910*

| Faction | *Casas exportadores* |
|---------|----------------------|
| Peoncistas | E. Escalante e Hijo |
| | Manuel Dondé y Cía. |
| Cantonistas | Urcelay y Cía. |
| | Ponce y Cía. |
| Molinistas | Molina y Cía. |

TABLE 4.2

*Two* Casas' *Shares of Henequen Exports to
the United States, 1897–1905*

| Year | Urcelay y Cía. | Urcelay and Ponce |
|------|----------------|-------------------|
| 1897 | 0.0 | 7.0 |
| 1898 | 12.0 | 28.0 |
| 1899 | 15.2 | 21.1 |
| 1900 | 6.7 | 11.0 |
| 1901 | 14.8 | 15.3 |
| 1902 | 17.3 | 17.3[a] |
| 1903 | 9.5 | 9.5[a] |
| 1904 | 1.8 | 1.8[a] |
| 1905 | 1.7 | 1.7[a] |

SOURCE: Peabody Records, HL-1, 254–74; U.S. Senate, *Importation of Sisal*, 2: 963; *Boletín de Estadística*, July 15, 1905, no. 14, May 21, 1906, no. 15.

[a]After 1902, José María Ponce y Cía. exported so few bales of henequen that the name is not specifically listed with the leading exporters but lumped together with other sundry merchants. All the "other" producers combined accounted for a negligible percentage of exports, especially after 1903, when the Molina *casa* increasingly monopolized the henequen trade.

Stepping back from the political and economic fluctuations of the period, we can construct a basic typology that links the henequen *casas exportadoras* to the personalistic political *camarillas* of the 1890s and early 1900s (see Table 4.1). Each of the three political factions in late Porfirian Yucatán had the backing of at least one powerful export house.[7]

Escalante, Dondé, Ponce, Urcelay, and Molina were all active family enterprises in the local agrocommercial bourgeoisie. While the henequen economy was the motor that drove their regional economic empires, these commercial houses also benefited at key junctures from their political connections. A clear illustration comes from the Cantón administration (1897–1901), when the general's political rise catapulted to new heights the fortunes of those loyal merchants who had supported him. As Table 4.2 demonstrates, Carlos Urcelay y Compañía saw its share of the fiber market soar during the Cantón years, from almost nothing in 1897 to a high of 17.3 percent in 1902.

Combining the export shares of Urcelay and Ponce reveals that in 1898 and 1899 (the first two years of Cantón's term), the two *casas* had a greater share of the market than the perennially powerful Escalantes, who saw their own share dip to 17.4 percent in 1898 and 16.7 percent in 1899—their lowest totals ever. Not coincidentally, the Escalantes' link to the state-house was severed with the unceremonious dumping of Carlos Peón Machado in 1897. Conversely, the Urcelay and Ponce market share of 28 percent in 1898, the first year of the Cantón era, represented a whopping 21 percent increase over the year before Cantón assumed his duties. A year later, Cantón's business associates (taken together) were the second-largest exporters in the state.[8]

While these statistics must be used with care because "nonpolitical" factors certainly influenced the fiber trade during these years, the meteoric rise of the Cantón-allied houses and their subsequent precipitous collapse after the general's four-year term lead to the conclusion that political power and economic success went hand in hand in Porfirian Yucatán.

If the Cantonistas understood how patronage and profit complemented one another, the Molinistas would easily surpass them in siphoning off the growing wealth of the henequen boom. Although a prosperous merchant before 1902, Olegario Molina, like Pancho Cantón, saw his economic fortunes rise dramatically on becoming governor. After taking office, Molina became the most powerful economic force in the region. Unquestionably, he was aided by his business relationship with the International Harvester Company; but this collaboration, which was cemented during the first years of the century, cannot be explained or evaluated without reference to Don Olegario's political power. By the end of the Porfiriato, Molina had become the largest single landowner in the state and was cultivating more henequen on his haciendas than any other planter. As Chapter 3 noted, numerous family members and business associates profited politically from his influence and stature. In short order (aided by bright and able lieutenants like his son-in-law, Avelino Montes), Olegario Molina created an economic empire within the boundaries of what was essentially his *camarilla*'s political fief.

Before 1902, a truly exclusive and powerful collaborator mechanism had never characterized the Yucatecan henequen industry. A secret contract consummated between IHC and Molina y Cía. in October 1902 dramatically transformed the political economy of Yucatán by weeding out competitors and forcing down the price of fiber. With increasing frequency throughout the period from 1902 to 1915, members of the planter-merchant bourgeoisie became indebted to Molina and Montes and were forced to advance their future product at slightly less than the current market price to cover present obligations. Moreover, the access to foreign capital, and International Harvester's capacity to funnel large amounts of it at critical junctures, enabled Molina and his faction to acquire mortgages, purchase credits outright, and consolidate their hold on regional communications, infrastructure, and banking—all of which guaranteed control of local fiber production and generally worked to depress the price.

Backed by a continuous supply of foreign capital, Molina and Montes were able to invest even when the economy was depressed and prices were low, precisely when most planters and merchants faced capital shortages. This strategic position enabled them to buy when most investors were compelled to sell out their interests at rock-bottom prices merely to escape financial ruin. Then, when fiber prices rose, along with local property values, the Molinas had the option of selling their newly acquired assets for a tremendous profit or adding them to their expanding empire.

The ascendancy of the Molina *parentesco* coincided with International Harvester's takeover of the farm implement and binder twine industries in the United States. The very establishment of the new "International," a combination of five of the largest U.S. harvesting machine companies (McCormick; Deering; Plano; Wardner, Bushnell, and Glessner; and Milwaukee Harvester) with an initial capitalization of U.S. $120 million, eliminated the bulk of existing competition in the two industries and placed at the manufacturer's disposal organizational and financial resources that had never existed before.[9]

The groundwork for Harvester's rapid rise to prominence in the binder twine industry was laid during the 1890s, when the two largest harvesting machine companies, McCormick and Deering, became increasingly dissatisfied with the practices of cordage companies and fiber buyers. Twine was an important secondary line for farm implement manufacturers. North American farmers needed a regular supply of twine to operate their binders (mechanical attachments to reapers that bound the cut bales). If McCormick or Deering could not supply it, sales of their farm machinery would suffer.

Deering was the first harvesting machine company to build its own twine mill. To ensure that farmers would use its line of twine, Deering refused to guarantee its binders if farmers used other twine. For its part, McCormick bought out a number of cordage mills and fronted U.S. $75,000 to one of the largest fiber buyers in Yucatán, Henry W. Peabody and Company. Moreover, it decided to act as a silent partner for La Industrial, the intriguing experiment to manufacture binder twine in Yucatán. Olegario Molina and several other Yucatecan *henequeneros* recruited local capital and solicited a loan from McCormick plus the most up-to-date North American machinery. Molina reasoned that La Industrial, if successful, would enable Yucatán to reap the value traditionally added by North American cordage manufacturers. McCormick provided technological supervision and influenced the plant's day-to-day operations by dictating production, shipment schedules, and quality standards. The Chicago-based company also became La Industrial's largest customer.

With the outbreak of the Spanish-American War in 1898 and the suspension of shipments from henequen's chief competition, manila fiber from the Philippines, henequen prices soared. Interest in La Industrial's twine production waned in Yucatán, and efficiency in the plant deteriorated. McCormick executives concluded that La Industrial would not become the company's principal source of binder twine. By 1899, McCormick was already constructing its own stateside twine mill, which opened in Chicago in 1900. By the time International Harvester was created in 1902, the conglomerate was committed to providing for most of its own twine needs. Harvester went to great lengths to diminish its dependence on henequen and manila. It purchased fiber plantations in Baja California, Mexico, Ecuador, and Cuba and experimented unsuccessfully with flax twine as a homegrown alternative to the two tropical fibers. Despite these efforts, binder twine continued to be manufactured with Yucatecan henequen and Philippine manila until after World War I.

Challenges to the Molina-Harvester partnership and the *casa exportadora*'s control of the regional economy took different forms; all had important ramifications for the state political arena.

## Challenging Molinista Hegemony, 1906–8

Like modern scholars, the planters, merchants, politicians, and journalists of the time openly discussed the impact of International Harvester's collaboration with the Molina-Montes *parentesco* on both the regional economy and their own investments. In the local press and at the seemingly endless round of parties in the elite's posh villas along the Paseo de Montejo or the resplendent homes on the haciendas, the perception was widely shared that the machinations of "the trust"—as the Molina-IHC partnership was called—were bringing financial ruin to all but a select few. Harvester became a target in the regional press, especially after 1905, when the Díaz government began to take a decidedly more nationalistic posture toward foreign investments.[10] Indeed, the perception of guilt seemed proof enough for many intellectuals and planters, who were disposed to saddle the collaborators with more blame than they probably deserved for the ills of an inherently unstable economy.

The price of henequen plummeted from an artificial high of almost ten cents a pound in 1902 (inflated by the Spanish-American War) to just under four cents a pound in 1911. As it dropped, criticism of "the trust" became increasingly strident. Words were replaced with action in 1906–7, when disgruntled landowners and merchants formed the Cámara Agrícola to fight the power of the *casas exportadoras*. This Chamber of Agriculture was the most sophisticated planters' association yet created in Yucatán. A list of its committees suggests its ambitious scope: Agriculture, Statistics, Economy, Propaganda and Immigration, Agricultural Machinery, and General Matters.[11] Perhaps most important, the chamber spawned an activist group of *hacendados* determined to forge a more competitive balance in the henequen trade. They formed the Compañía Cooperativa de Hacendados Henequeneros and, late in 1907, secured a loan from the Banco Nacional's Mérida branch office to enable producers to hold 16 percent of their fiber off the market and force the price to rise.[12]

## WITHHOLDING PRODUCTION

The compañía's plan called for growers to deliver fiber to the compañía at central points—but not in Progreso—and to receive advances in cash equal to two-thirds of the value of their production, based on the market price on the day of delivery. The decision to keep the henequen away from the principal port of commerce was deemed essential by some planters and speculators, because North American buyers always underscored the number of bales stored in Progreso in determining their pricing policy.[13] The compañía also agreed to charge interest at a fair rate (compared to local usurers) for the advances, while planters pledged not to withdraw from the scheme for one year. Finally, heavy penalties would be assessed to planters who violated the agreement.[14]

Earlier attempts (in 1876, 1887, 1890, 1894–95, 1902, and 1904) to withhold production and create a shortage of fiber on the market had failed miserably. Invariably, agricultural societies like the compañía had lacked the capital to compete with powerful *casas* that had foreign backing, such as Molina y Cía. or Peabody and Company. While many *henequeneros* may have wished to improve their ability to influence the price of henequen, they could not participate in these cooperatives because their product was already fully or partially promised to Molina or Peabody for advances tendered in years past. *Casas exportadoras* extended short-term contracts of three, six, or twelve months, as well as agreements that lasted up to seven years. Whether the contract was for a brief period or the long term, the agreements always covered a planter's entire delivery at a fixed price. Peabody and Company records demonstrate that advances were a fact of life in the fiber business, even when the price of henequen was high (see Table 4.3).[15] Growers who had their henequen under contract to one of the *casas exportadoras* might agree in principle with the cooperative societies, but they lacked the independence to join in such valorization schemes.

Capital-starved planters also had themselves to blame for the failures of these associations. A contentious lot even under favorable market conditions, the planters were hampered from the start by a lack of solidarity. An undercurrent of distrust, which set family-based elites at odds throughout the Gilded Age, worked to inhibit these cooperatives. *Henequeneros* prided themselves on their individualism, and when they needed assistance to weather the bust cycles, they preferred to rely on extensive kinship networks rather than to unite to do battle against the powerful *casas exportadoras*.[16] Generally speaking, planter cooperative societies coalesced only when the price of henequen dropped so low that it cut into the planters'

TABLE 4.3
*Peabody and Co.'s Average Monthly
Advances, 1892–1904*

| Year | Average advances (in pesos)[a] | Fiber prices (pesos per pound) |
|------|------|------|
| 1892[b] | $97,333 | $.033 |
| 1893[b] | 132,000 | .033 |
| 1894 | 126,417 | .025 |
| 1895 | 96,250 | .023 |
| 1896 | 109,667 | .025 |
| 1897 | 109,083 | .026 |
| 1898 | 96,083 | .062 |
| 1899 | 44,083 | .062 |
| 1900 | 40,167 | .063 |
| 1901 | 77,917 | .062 |
| 1902 | 177,167 | .098 |
| 1903 | 380,833 | .082 |
| 1904[b] | 391,333 | .075 |

SOURCE: Peabody Records, HL-1, "Mérida Advances."
Price data from Gonzalo Cámara Zavala, "La industria henequenera desde 1919 hasta nuestros días," in C. Trujillo, *Enciclopedia yucatanese*, 3: 779. All averages computed by the
authors.

[a]Before 1905, one U.S. dollar equaled one Mexican peso.
After 1905 two pesos equaled one dollar.

[b]Data available for only three months in each of these
years.

considerable profits. This was precisely the worst time for such a maneuver
to succeed, because money was stretched thin. In short, these *compañías*,
*sindicatos*, or *sociedades* had functioned as short-lived, complaining con-
fraternities, usually folding only months after their formation.

The *casas exportadoras*, however, did not take lightly any demonstrations of incipient planter solidarity. Montes was particularly concerned
about the formation of the Cámara Agrícola. In a series of telegrams, he
warned Harvester that a powerful syndicate of planters and henequen speculators had been formed with capital of six million dollars, "the object of
which is to advance the price of sisal [that is, henequen] and to maintain the
high price for this commodity during this year."[17] Horace L. Daniels, the
head of International Harvester's fiber division and Montes's chief contact
in Chicago, passed on Montes's concerns to Harvester corporate executives,
such as James Deering, a member of the Executive Committee. Montes
urged Daniels to persuade his superiors to lend Montes's firm ample capital
"to make advances for deposits of sisal which could be shipped to us [Har-
vester] for our immediate use, but price of which could be fixed, at any time
during the next four months by planters who have made the deposit [of
fiber]."[18]

Such a proposal was certain to appeal to local producers, who would
have some flexibility in determining when their fiber might fetch the highest price. In addition, this proposed corner on the market by Montes would

have destroyed the nascent planter association. After carefully considering Montes's scheme, however, Harvester decided not to lend the capital, at least for the time being. But an important seed had been planted in the minds of Harvester's Executive Committee members; and in 1909, after three full years of depressed henequen prices and tight money, Montes and Harvester would attempt a similar corner in an effort to ensure their continued domination of the henequen trade.

According to many accounts, Montes found other means to shatter the planters' cooperative.[19] In 1908 the Banco Nacional's branch in Mérida, which held the stockpiled henequen as collateral on the loan, shocked the planters by selling off the fiber at a low price.[20] Critics of the Molina-Montes economic empire have pointed out that one of the principal board directors of the bank was Olegario Molina.[21] Faustino Escalante, in testimony before a U.S. Senate subcommittee investigating the fiber trade in 1916, claimed that Molina, then Díaz's secretary of *fomento* in Mexico City, used his considerable influence with fellow *científico* and secretary of *hacienda* José Limantour, "who compelled the bank to sell said bales . . . to Montes."[22]

Whether such contemporary allegations of complicity in the bank's sell-off were true will probably never be known.[23] It is likely, however, that the Compañía Cooperativa's plan to withhold production would have failed on its own. The association could not have picked a worse time to get its cooperative venture off the ground. The 1907 panic started in the financial markets of the United States and set off a chain reaction that extended throughout Mexico. Two of the oldest and most respected names in the financing and marketing of henequen, New York–based Thebaud Brothers and Yucatán's Eusebio Escalante e Hijo, were casualties. With money in short supply and apprehension growing daily, fiber prices began to tumble. Even the nominally supportive *Revista de Mérida* termed the Banco Nacional's loan to the planters an "illusion."[24] With many *hacendados* heavily in debt to the *casas*, the newspaper warned, the amount of henequen the compañía might control would prove to be insignificant. From New York, *Cordage Trade Journal*, the trade publication of the binder twine industry and never an advocate of planter unity, offered its "condolences" to the growers.

> If such a project has really been started on the foregoing lines, those who are in it should receive, in advance, sympathy, for there has never been a worse time to launch such a scheme as just now; with money conditions all over the world what they are, and the Winter grain crop planted here [in the United States] probably less than the short acreage a year ago . . . the prospects are that the project will mean loss for all concerned.[25]

Such prophetic words in the press may well have contributed to the crisis of confidence that spread among the planters themselves. Once again, their lack of solidarity proved a liability. Speculators, playing on the *henequeneros'* fears and anxieties, manipulated stocks of henequen and circulated wild rumors of the fiber market's imminent demise. As the news spread throughout Mérida, growers, fearing a further price drop, sold their fiber to the speculators, who turned a tidy profit.[26] The local press reported that Manuel Zapata Martínez and many other prominent *hacendados* who initially had supported the Compañía Cooperativa's efforts broke faith with the combination and began dumping fiber on the market in the spring of 1908.[27] The association's officers, facing the prospect of rapidly tumbling prices brought on by the introduction of these stocks, quickly sold off twenty thousand bales (each bale equaled 350 pounds) to Avelino Montes S. en C. Although the compañía failed to end Harvester-Molinista control of the market, at least one outspoken critic of the Molinista *camarilla* later admitted that the collapse of the valorization scheme was instrumental in reawakening the political consciousness of disgruntled *hacendados* who, whether rightly or wrongly, blamed Molina and Montes for the economic crisis now gripping the peninsula.[28]

### "EL TRUST" AND RAILROAD POLITICS

The lack of cooperation Yucatecan *henequeneros* displayed during the 1907–8 crisis was compounded by loose credit practices and the planters' own unfortunate speculations in the regional economy. Bonanza fiber prices from 1898 to 1904 had pushed property values up, giving producers a false sense of security. Many borrowed heavily during the boom, securing additional mortgages on their properties. As Table 4.3 demonstrates, Peabody and Company advanced planters substantially more money during the 1902–4 period than in the previous decade. In addition, peninsular banks, such as the Banco Yucateco and the Banco Mercantil de Yucatán, extended credit to growers in ways that give the term *creative financing* a new meaning.

> One of the ways that credit was most abused, the most troublesome and perilous . . . was in the fabrication . . . of falsified letters of credit. We are referring to the promissory notes that are extended to secure money from a bank or an individual or to guarantee payment of an existing obligation. These promissory notes are extended to a party on behalf of another for the express purpose of signing an endorsement on behalf of a third party or a bank or in order to obtain the signature of the aforementioned as endorser on other letters of credit of equal value and type.[29]

These growing credit abuses were detailed in both the local and the Mexico City press, but not before many *henequeneros* found themselves teetering on the brink of financial ruin.

The easy money made available by banks was linked both to local *casas exportadoras* and to foreign lenders. The Banco Yucateco, for instance, was firmly under the control of the Molina house, while the Banco Mercantil was tied to Eusebio Escalante e Hijo. These links were crucial, because a weakness in a major *casa's* economic armor could undermine the fiscal well-being of the regional banking industry. Foreign lending institutions like Crédit Lyonnais were also vulnerable because of their indulgent investments in peninsular banks. As late as May 1906, French banks lent three million pesos to the Banco Yucateco, an unwitting show of confidence in a monocultural economy that was about to come apart at the seams.[30]

*Henequeneros'* frequent speculations in peninsular joint stock companies further destabilized the regional economy. Again the boom compounded problems, as many members of the agrocommercial elite took advantage of easy money to invest in local industry and infrastructure.

The balance of power among regional *camarillas* was first threatened in 1899, when a new joint stock company dominated by Molinista shareholders, the Compañía del Ferrocarril, Muelle y Almacenes del Comercio, was formed. The board of directors announced its intention to build a third railway line between Progreso and Mérida and to acquire docks and warehouses in the port and the capital. Perceiving a threat of potentially ruinous competition, rival *camarillas* initiated serious discussions proposing to derail the new competitor by merging all the railway companies in Yucatán.[31]

The groundwork for the merger began during the late 1890s when the wealthy Peón y Peón family acquired stock in both the Campeche and Progreso e Izamal lines. Two brothers, Augusto and Joaquín Peón y Peón, became directors and board presidents of the respective railways. By 1900 the Mérida–Progreso railway held 447 shares of the Campeche line, and a number of Peón relations controlled a substantial portion of the Campeche's remaining shares. In addition to his management role, Augusto, one of the largest *henequeneros* in Yucatán, lent the Campeche line a two-hundred-thousand-peso mortgage.[32]

With these two lines under the Peóns' control, and with the Molinistas threatening to build a third line in Progreso, the Escalantes began to take a serious interest in acquiring railway properties. Eusebio Escalante e Hijo, one of the pillars of the fiber trade since the mid-1870s, had watched its share of the market steadily decline throughout the 1890s. The Escalante *camarilla* decided to put much of its considerable financial muscle into the regional transportation sector. The Escalantes and their extended relations, including former governor Carlos Peón Machado and wealthy merchant Pedro Peón Contreras, systematically began to accumulate shares of railway stock. By 1902 they had acquired a majority interest in the Mérida–Progreso, the Mérida–Campeche, and the Compañía Constructora del Muelle Fiscal de Progreso, and were in a position to become the chief architects of a merger. They achieved their goal that fall by purchasing the Mérida–Valladolid line from Pancho Cantón for a record five million pesos. Cantón unloaded his railway not only because of the inflated price paid by the Escalantes, but because his debt had risen to one-and-a-half million pesos.[33]

Within weeks of the sale announcement, the Ferrocarriles Unidos de Yucatán was born. All the peninsular railway companies except Rodulfo G. Cantón's Mérida–Peto had been acquired, and the new company, under the direction of Nicolás Escalante Peón—manager of and son (*hijo*) in Eusebio Escalante e Hijo—was capitalized at a highly inflated $23 million. Escalante Peón received the unheard of salary of $24,000 a year, four times that of other regional railway directors.[34]

The merger of the peninsula's three principal railway companies into the Ferrocarriles Unidos de Yucatán (FCUY) in 1902 touched off "a wild speculation in the shares of the railway company . . . two banks, and also in the buying and selling of plantations."[35] Rumors that International Harvester was going to buy the new company only fueled the activity, as railroad shares originally offered at one thousand pesos now went as high as two thousand.[36] Tomás Castellanos Acevedo, a prominent planter, would later lament that the wave of "speculation fever" accompanying the railroad merger had contributed to the first bankruptcies of the 1907 panic.[37] While the Escalantes appeared to reward themselves by overvaluing their own lines, they actually put themselves in an untenable situation. William James, a North American import-export agent then living in Yucatán, would later comment,

> The original owners of the railroads, taking advantage of the situation, increased the real costs of the line. The new company made an additional increase in the valuation when they organized, and then the general public speculated on a structure that wasn't firm to begin with.[38]

Organizational problems plagued the merger from the outset. Escalante Peón estimated that more than $2 million was needed to modernize and integrate the lines. But even though the Escalantes controlled more than $14.7 million in FCUY shares—in comparison to the $8.3 million worth of stock the Molinistas retained in their company—Escalante Peón could not persuade the shareholders, many of whom had purchased stock at very high prices, to divert their dividends toward improvements. Escalante Peón argued that if a portion of the dividends were used as collateral, the company could secure low-interest mortgage bonds from abroad. When the shareholders refused, management was forced to seek a less advantageous loan from North American bankers. On August 21, 1906, the FCUY borrowed one million dollars from Ladenburg, Thalmann and Company of New York.[39]

The FCUY was hindered by sagging passenger and cargo revenues, which peaked in 1903 and declined thereafter.[40] To add to its difficulties, Escalante Peón had the railroad trust purchase two properties, one the shareholders knew about and another that was kept secret. In 1904 the FCUY added the Escalantes' own urban tram company to its holdings for a hefty price.[41] Two years later, just as the consolidation loan was being negotiated with the New York bank, the railroad trust, unbeknownst to its stockholders, bought Escalante's Agencia Comercial for just under two million pesos, more than double its real value. The Escalante faction took both these actions to raise cash to repay a debt of more than one million dollars that the Escalante *casa exportadora* owed Thebaud Brothers, its New York fiber buyer.[42] By early 1907, the FCUY's debt service had reached $5,106,427.63.[43]

Another factor that hurt the entire regional economy and especially the *casas exportadoras* was the Mexican government's decision in 1905 to adopt the gold standard and peg the value of the standard silver peso at U.S. 50¢.[44] Henequen interests for years had bitterly resisted the switch to gold, because they had benefited by paying most of their expenses domestically in silver while selling their fiber abroad in gold (in dollars or pounds sterling). The reform outraged local *casas*; prices of foreign imports increased almost overnight by 10 to 25 percent. Because Mexico, and especially Yucatán, conducted most of its foreign trade with the United States, the silver peso's lower value also exacerbated inflationary pressure in the peninsula.[45]

From 1904 to 1907, with inflation rising and the price of henequen sagging, the artificially high peninsular stock prices could not be maintained. When the bubble burst in 1907, the first local casualty was the Escalante house. As a result of its failure, on September 1, 1907, the Molinistas took control of the FCUY. José Trinidad Molina, Olegario's brother, became the new president of the railroad trust's board of directors. The first report issued by the new management team was, needless to say, highly critical of the Escalante regime.[46]

Assailing the secret purchase of the Agencia Comercial, the Molinistas asserted that the FCUY had lost more than $1.2 million on the sale. Austerity measures were implemented, including the wholesale sacking of 254 employees, and wages were cut across the board. Salaries were reduced by $24,000 a month, and another $20,000 was saved monthly by cutting costs.[47] The lesson drawn by railway workers, watching helplessly as "el trust" scaled their wages back to pre-1898 levels in the teeth of the recession, was that the monopolization of the railway industry had left more Yucatecos vulnerable to monoculture's bumpy ride.

Even after the Molinista takeover, the railway trust was far from healthy.[48] In the depths of the crisis, the value of railway shares had plummeted from $1,000 to $250.[49] The FCUY was forced to take out a $4 million loan from the Banco Nacional and an £800,000 loan from English financiers over the next couple of years to shore up the company's shaky finances.[50]

At first glance, it may be difficult to understand why the railways engendered such fierce competition among regional elites. Many investors went bankrupt during the financial panic, and the dividends realized from the railway trust never met shareholder expectations. But the competing *camarillas* also realized significant benefits from their control of the railways. Years later, testimony before a U.S. congressional subcommittee would go a long way toward explaining why the Escalantes and Molinas vied for control of the FCUY. Dr. Víctor Rendón, manager of the Comisión Reguladora del Mercado del Henequén, recalled,

In Yucatán it was a thing of common knowledge that Mr. Montes paid some money to railroad officials, from the superintendent to the general manager to the brakemen, to have all the cars they needed and to withdraw cars from their competitors. It was common knowledge that in the days of General Díaz, that he [Montes] had bribed the operatives and the telegraphers in such a way that he knew every telegram that was passed by his competitors.[51]

Leo Browne, FCUY assistant general manager, added,

I found that Mr. Blake would daily get a memorandum from Mr. Montes of purchases of sisal that he had made; that is, a memorandum of the bills of lading covering his purchases. . . . In the distribution of cars, Mr. Blake would first take care of Mr. Montes and Montes's requests for cars.[52]

These two quotations attest that even if the railway trust itself did not prove profitable, Avelino Montes's control of it helped ensure bountiful profits for his multiple investments in the regional economy. Control of the railway was indispensable to the Molinista empire, which had the political connections to complement its formidable business holdings. In contrast, the Escalantes, who lacked political clout at a crucial moment, watched their fortunes tumble.

## HOUSE OF CARDS: THE ESCALANTE FAILURE, 1907–10

Rumors of the collapse of Eusebio Escalante e Hijo circulated in Mérida throughout the first months of 1907. The Escalante house was the oldest *casa exportadora* in Yucatán, and although it could no longer lay claim to dominance in henequen sales, it still held considerable investments in the Yucatecan economy. Besides the commercial house in Mérida, the firm owned the Agencia Comercial, whose warehouses, docks, lighters, and other means of transport enabled the Escalantes to move fiber from hacienda to steamship. The agencia, created in the late 1880s in a partnership with another prominent *casa*, Manuel Dondé y Cía. (which succumbed to bankruptcy in an earlier bust cycle, in 1895), owned much real estate in the port of Progreso.[53] In addition, Escalante e Hijo had invested heavily in the FCUY, tramway companies, banks, urban properties and haciendas, a variety of attendant service industries, and some chancy agricultural companies in the eastern portion of the peninsula.[54]

Like all the *casas*, Escalante e Hijo served as creditor to a great number of *hacendados*. In some cases, it made cash advances; in others, it provided mortgages to planters. Finally, many wealthy businessmen and individuals in Mérida and elsewhere had invested in the Escalante *casa*, including such notables as former governor Carlos Peón Machado and the wealthy merchant Pedro Peón Contreras. Thebaud Brothers, which had first financed the Escalantes in the 1850s and in large measure had helped create the henequen industry in Yucatán, had running accounts with the *casa* that exceeded one million dollars.[55] Clearly, many people and enterprises stood to lose through association with this collapsing economic powerhouse.

In a desperate but futile effort to avoid bankruptcy, Nicolás Escalante Peón went to Mexico City in May and June of 1907 to speak with Ministers Molina and Limantour. More was at stake than just the failure of one of the peninsula's largest henequen firms. Yucatecan banks, especially the Banco Mercantil (the Escalante bank) were also in imminent danger of default. Treasury Secretary Limantour agreed to bail out the Yucatecan banks by authorizing the Banco Nacional de México to loan ten million pesos to the Banco Yucateco and the Banco Mercantil under certain unspecified conditions. Later, in 1908, Limantour would agree to the fusion of the two weakened banks into one stronger institution, the Banco Peninsular Mexicano.[56]

Although the federal government intervened to prop up the peninsular banking industry during this financial crisis, it did not rescue the Escalante *casa*. Nicolás Escalante Peón and some of his creditors would later suggest that Molina had intentionally worked to subvert any type of financial settlement that would save the Escalante house.[57] Although we will probably never know if this is true, the Molinista faction certainly had little interest in propping up Escalante. As a direct result of the Escalante failure in July 1907, Avelino Montes S. en C. would scuttle one of its principal rivals in the henequen trade, obtain control of the Ferrocarriles Unidos de Yucatán and the peninsular banks, and then use its new clout to purchase a steamship line in 1908. Rarely has one business profited so well from another's misfortune. Escalante's demise ensured Molinista dominance over the key facets of the regional economy.

When news of the Escalante failure was made public, financial circles in Mérida, Mexico City, Paris, and New York were shaken. There is ample evidence to suggest that the Escalante bankruptcy induced a similar failure for Thebaud Brothers.[58] Crédit Lyonnais, the French bank that had invested large sums in peninsular banks, closed its doors in September 1907.[59] Indeed, this whole episode demonstrates the little-studied impact that peripheral areas can have on the world financial system during such perilous times.[60]

Locally, the failure precipitated the bankruptcies of several allied joint stock companies and prominent members of Mérida's elite, among them Peón Machado and Peón Contreras. Loan capital became even scarcer as banks provided funds only to their most preferred customers. Private moneylenders offered capital at 2 to 3 percent interest a month to the most desperate *henequeneros*.[61]

Each Meridano involved seemed to have different ideas about how best to minimize losses. In an effort to avoid an endless, expensive round of lawsuits and to mollify nervous creditors, a *comisión liquidora* was formed on August 22, 1907, to dispose of the Escalante *casa*'s property and holdings. The *comisión* was headed by the acting state governor, Enrique Muñoz

Arístegui, Olegario Molina's hand-picked replacement when the latter became minister of *fomento* in 1907.[62] The decision to place the governor in the middle of this financial disaster demonstrates the gravity of the matter for the Mérida elite. Only someone at the highest level of the state would be in a position to ensure credibility. On the other hand, Muñoz Arístegui was perceived first and foremost as a Molinista, and his injection into the midst of a sensitive financial matter only served to exacerbate factional tensions among the *henequeneros*.[63]

The *comisión's* task was to sift through the morass of charges and countercharges made by creditors and debtors. As the *casa's* books were studied, numerous irregularities appeared. Escalante e Hijo had been broke almost a year before the bankruptcy was announced, and all its holdings and properties had been systematically overvalued to prop up the ailing firm. In addition, the *casa* evidently had continued to pay off selected creditors with its assets even after the business was dissolved. Questions were also raised about the propriety of some last-minute mortgages that the Banco Yucateco and the Banco Mercantil had granted on the Escalantes' valuable henequen haciendas.[64] No doubt many *henequeneros* would have agreed with Peabody and Company vice president Edward B. Bayley, who observed, "when houses fail in Yucatán, the procedure is quite different from what it is in this country [the United States]. They seem to go on until they evaporate."[65]

Charges of fraud heightened tensions at the *comisión's* open meetings as creditors harangued each other about the best course to follow. Many creditors themselves desperately needed capital to pay off their own debts. Yet they also realized that if the properties were auctioned off during this downswing in the regional economy, the holdings would fetch only a fraction of their worth. Naturally, those wealthy creditors who could afford to wait counseled patience, while more desperate merchants and planters demanded their money immediately.[66]

What made the process drag on interminably (until 1910) was the *comisión's* inability to prevent the largest creditor, the receivers of the now-defunct Thebaud Brothers, from litigating its claims. The Escalante bankruptcy languished in the courts of Mérida, Mexico City, and New York for four years. The biggest losers were not the Escalantes, who, in the manner of many familial elites, somehow rose from the ashes of this financial disaster and recouped some of their losses.[67] Although local judges issued a formal arrest order for both Eusebio Escalante Bates and Nicolás Escalante Peón in 1909, the two were warned by a highly placed "government functionary" of their impending arrest a full two months before the order was issued. This advance notice gave them enough time to flee to New York.[68] The lawyers for the receivers tracked them down in the suburb of New Rochelle and, through an international legal instrument called letters rogatory, made them take the stand in New York.[69]

The Escalantes personally appealed to General Díaz for relief from prosecution. And despite the numerous legal and ethical questions raised during the trial, the Escalantes received a *juicio de amparo*, or protection, from the Mexican courts and were ultimately exonerated from any criminal wrongdoing.[70] Although their name was dragged through the mire, they escaped relatively unscathed, much to the consternation of the Thebaud receivers. Indeed, the biggest losers were the creditors themselves, who, after years of waiting, only received eight cents back on every dollar the Escalantes owed them.[71]

Governor Muñoz Arístegui finally extricated himself from the *comisión liquidora* in the fall of 1909, and the Banco Peninsular took over the task of dealing with the embittered creditors. The bank and private investors formed a Compañía Comercial de Fincas Rústicas y Urbanas, with a working capital of three million pesos, to auction off the Escalantes' properties. In the depressed economy, many valuable estates were sold for a song.[72]

The Escalante collapse graphically demonstrated to many *hacendados* just how little control they had over their own destinies and how unforgiving the monocrop economy could be. But in truth, the *henequeneros* were their own worst enemies. Lessons begged to be learned about the dangers of loose credit practices and speculation. And as we have seen, many planters' lack of solidarity and resolve in the face of powerful vested interests only contributed to the dire consequences of the financial crisis.

Still, it was always easier to blame someone else, and the Molina *parentesco* and International Harvester, the North American "trust," were inviting targets. As many planters fell by the economic wayside, the Molinistas' economic and political fortunes continued to rise. A trail of circumstantial evidence tying Molina, Montes, and Harvester conspiratorially to the fall of the Escalantes' house of cards only provided more ammunition for the political opponents of the dominant oligarchical faction. The *henequeneros'* worst fears seemed to be confirmed when Montes and Harvester compounded the growers' problems by attempting to corner the henequen trade.

## Tightening the Noose: Montes's Corner, 1909–10

The attempt to seize control of the fiber market in the spring and summer of 1909 is one of the more tantalizing topics in modern Yucatecan economic historiography. The principals have alternately been hailed as saviors of an ailing regional economy and excoriated for their sinister manipulations of the market on both sides of the Gulf of Mexico. While inflammatory rhetoric has further muddied this complicated affair, the short- and long-term consequences of the corner for politicians, planters, and merchants can now reasonably be explained.

Montes's motives seem clear enough. After three years of depressed fiber prices, planters were being foreclosed in alarming numbers. Hundreds of mortgage judgments fill the Archivo Notarial and the Ramo de Justicia of the Archivo General del Estado. These materials document not only the problems of beleaguered planters in meeting their financial obligations but the role that speculators played in an economy in flux. Treating haciendas as little more than liquid assets, speculators bought and sold mortgage credits during this downturn, creating a highly unstable real estate market. And if low henequen prices and frequent foreclosures were not enough to worry the *casas exportadoras*, a drought worked to diminish the harvest for the dependent growers in 1909.[73]

Against this backdrop, Montes stood to lose considerably if his firm could not meet advances, credit lines, and mortgage payments. Fiber division chief Horace L. Daniels, in his testimony before the U.S. District Court of Minnesota in the Harvester antitrust trial years later, summarized Montes's precarious position.

> Mr. Montes was writing us continuously that something had to be done to advance the price of sisal or the country would be ruined. He and his family and his associates were among the largest planters in Yucatán as well as merchants in sisal. And not only the interests and those of his family and associates were in peril; there was more or less insurrection and revolution, incipient in form, taking place. Some plantations had been burned by the workers who were dissatisfied because they did not get more pay or did not get their pay.[74]

While the last statement may be somewhat exaggerated, the rest of Daniels's testimony is an essentially accurate assessment of the henequen economy in the spring of 1909.[75] M. J. Smith, who was Montes's agent in New York during the corner, would later echo Daniels's sentiments, testifying before a U.S. Senate subcommittee in 1916 that Montes had "many high-interest loans and he was afraid he might lose them."[76]

Given Montes's extensive investments in the regional economy, moreover, his fiber loans were not the only ones that might suffer. Carlos Escoffié, a harsh critic of the Molinista faction, satirized Montes's enormous hold on the *hacendados* and implicitly recognized the high stakes Montes was playing for.

> Oh, poor Yucatán! For almost eight years you have been selling your henequen at a price that suits Don Avelino Montes; you have been eating beef at the price set by Don Avelino; you have been buying corn at a price set by Don Avelino; you have been paying railway passages at a price that Don Avelino thinks best; you have been paying interest on your loans at the bank at the rate stipulated by Don Avelino; and you have watched your newspapers and magazines disappear because of Don Avelino.[77]

With henequen market conditions at rock bottom, Daniels and Montes met in Havana in April 1909. (They agreed to meet in Cuba because a yellow fever epidemic had broken out in Mérida.) Both expressed their concerns about the difficulties in the peninsula. Daniels, moreover, emphasized his own problems in the stateside binder twine industry, what with rival cordage companies and prison twine factories now challenging Harvester's leadership. Although twine profits were always small in comparison to receipts from Harvester's major lines of harvesting machines (binders, mowers, and others), twine nevertheless constituted an important secondary line; and as competition began to intensify in the harvesting machine field, the company paid increasing attention to its fiber and twine production.

The key to Harvester's dominance of the fiber trade was not profit but control of production and supply. The availability of fiber was much more significant in both the short and the long run than the return per unit of twine. North American farmers needed a regular supply of twine to operate their binders; if Harvester could not supply twine, its sales of farm machinery would suffer. The actual profit that Harvester and other manufacturers made on twine fluctuated from year to year with the price of the raw material and the level of competition.[78]

If a Montes corner on the market, funded by Harvester, succeeded, it would not only assure Montes a favorable market in Yucatán but would also assure Harvester a supply and simultaneously deprive stateside competitors of raw material. According to the terms of the contract that Montes and Daniels worked out (and Daniels later spelled out in a detailed letter to Harvester executive Alexander Legge), beginning on May 20, 1909, Montes would fill contracts with local planters for 220,000 bales, almost one-third of Yucatán's annual production. The contract was to be guaranteed over the next twelve months at 5 1/8¢ a pound, substantially above the current market quotation.[79] (Later the number of bales contracted would be increased to 400,000.[80])

For its part, Harvester agreed to front six hundred thousand dollars as working capital. Why did Montes need such a large amount of money? If the corner was to succeed, Daniels explained to Legge, Montes was "compelled to advance between four hundred thousand and five hundred thousand pesos in gold to planters who previously had advances from H. W. Peabody and Company. Montes was enabled to secure the contracts from these people for furnishing them the money to pay their indebtedness to Peabody."[81] Despite Daniels's claims, however, it seems unlikely that this money would go solely to Peabody's debtors. Given Montes's own precarious position, much of it would have to be utilized to support loyal planters who had borrowed heavily from his own *casa*.

The contract was greeted favorably by merchants and planters in Mérida when it was announced in late spring. Indeed, it was the first good news many entrepreneurs had received in a long time. Joaquín L. Peón, a powerful *henequenero* and erstwhile Molinista, remarked that the contract was a godsend and that the high price of the planters' contracts would not have been realized without Harvester's support. In a candid interview in the *Diario Yucateco*, Peón admitted, "It is obvious that the American henequen market is completely dominated by 'the International' and for some years this company has imposed these prices and buys the major portion of the production here at a price it establishes through its principal agent."[82]

Peón added that although Harvester and Montes would undoubtedly make higher profits from this corner, money was not the most important reason for the combination. Demonstrating his keen awareness of the binder twine industry in the United States, Peón correctly surmised that what Harvester really wanted was to buy out half the stocks of fiber, force fiber prices upward, and make its chief competitors in the binder twine industry—numerous midwestern prisons and the Plymouth Cordage Company—buy the rest of the stocks at even higher prices.[83] If Harvester could control the supply of fiber, prices would eventually take care of themselves.

While Joaquín Peón may have downplayed the potential profits for Montes and Harvester, M. J. Smith, who was intimately involved, later admitted that Montes's commissions from this venture alone exceeded U.S. $103,000.[84] Because the collaboration also protected Montes's outstanding credits and weakened his competition in the local market, Montes's gains were substantial.

Planters were "encouraged" to act patriotically and support the local economy by signing up with Montes S. en C. Alexander Legge would later relate his impressions of Mérida's reaction to the individual contracts.

> And in order to put the thing through there was a meeting in the chamber of commerce [Cámara Agrícola] and all farmers were advised to sign this paper. Then various committees were sent to the towns. . . . Why, I think they were inspired by Montes, but I think they were nominally from the chamber of commerce, and these committees held public demonstrations in the town [Mérida] calling on the farmers as a patriotic duty to sign these contracts, so that these higher prices of sisal could be realized.[85]

Ironically enough, a year earlier Montes had been perceived as the arch-enemy of the *henequeneros*. But now, at least for the short term, he was viewed as a hero who offered a way out of the financial crisis. Daniels was optimistic about the success of the venture. In a letter dated June 30, he chortled, "We feel more confident of the final and perfect success than we have felt at any time since this campaign began."[86] A week later, Daniels wrote to Montes, instructing him to keep the market up by warehousing some 75,000 to 100,000 bales of fiber in Progreso. If more space were needed, he added, Harvester could hold 30,000 to 40,000 bales in Chicago, "in addition to our daily requirements at the mills."[87] By purchasing and warehousing all available fiber, the collaborators realized their plan to force higher prices. Competitors had to pay as much as 6½¢ per pound to secure any henequen. A pitched battle ensued as the Plymouth Cordage Company and other buyers tried to advance the market to prevent planters from fulfilling the contracts they had made with Montes at 5⅛¢ a pound.[88]

It looked on the surface like a successful corner. Harvester purchased 454,786 bales from Montes in 1909, almost 200,000 more bales than it had bought the previous year.[89] But the arrangement began to unravel as the competition, principally Plymouth, decided to fight the combination. This

Massachusetts-based company, one of the founders of the binder twine industry, had successfully opposed an earlier corner by the National Cordage Company in the 1890s.[90] This time, Plymouth's cause was favored by a rare occurrence in the twine trade: the inflated price of henequen was now pegged higher than its chief competitor, manila or *abacá* fiber from the Philippines. Manila had higher tensile strength than henequen but cost more to produce, so it was often blended with henequen to make a stronger twine. In a fascinating letter to his agent in Mérida, Peabody vice president Bayley describes Plymouth's maneuvers to fight the Harvester corner.

> I have got this week some inside information on Plymouth's policy which bears very strongly on this question. They had been experimenting for some time with manila fibre in short-length twines, when Montes started his corner, which caused them to redouble their efforts. In June, they made several hundred tons of a 500 ft. twine without using a pound of sisal, and which they found they could sell at about a half cent below the price of similar sisal twine. This they put out in the English market at a low price to make sure of its selling, some of which we placed through our London house. It met with instant popularity . . . they state very frankly that it is very much superior to Plymouth's sisal twine.[91]

Bayley was particularly concerned about Plymouth's decision to switch to manila because his company had sold the cordage company 150,000 bales of henequen in 1908. As a result of Plymouth's decision to "make the full assortment of twines in the various lengths of 500, 550, 600, and 650 ft. without using a pound of sisal, if necessary," Peabody stood to lose considerable business.[92] And as it turned out, Peabody's sales to Plymouth in 1909 amounted to only 50,000 bales of henequen.[93]

Plymouth also fought the Harvester corner with an extensive propaganda campaign geared to persuade North American farmers to buy manila. In a hard-hitting pamphlet titled *What Every Good Farmer Should Know About Binder Twine*, which was widely distributed in 1910, Plymouth railed against the monopolistic practices of the Chicago-based corporation in tirades such as the epigraph at the beginning of this chapter.[94]

The campaign to thwart the IHC-Montes combination succeeded largely because the contracts that were filled with Yucatecan producers in 1909 quickly acted as a dead weight on the market. By 1910 the price of henequen had reverted to pre-corner levels. Bayley had predicted as much in September 1909.

> The I. H. Co. are very powerful and the collapse to the sisal corner may not come until next summer, but come it must. Then we are going to be in for a bad time and will just have to wait until sisal settles to a point that will allow it to be bought in competition with manila. The only thing for us to do is to get everything as snug as possible at the Yucatán end and shorten sail until after the crash. . . . We are not in the least discouraged in regard to the business in the long run, but do feel very bitter over this disaster to Yucatán

and check to our business that will be brought about by Montes's pig-headed attempt to make water run up a hill.[95]

Bayley's prognostication of a collapse in the local fiber market proved correct. Although henequen would recapture its market share of the binder twine trade and manila once again would be relegated to its role as a secondary fiber, the failed corner left its mark on the henequen industry and the planters of Yucatán.[96]

The planters' initial euphoria over Montes's contracts soon melted into the bitter realization that the success of the 1909 season would be paid for with low fiber prices for the next several years. Montes S. en C. had used the 1909 corner to rescue its own investments in the regional economy, and it would continue to reign over the fiber trade until General Salvador Alvarado's arrival as revolutionary governor in 1915. Harvester's massive loan had enabled Montes to save the planters (and himself) by paying higher prices. But in the bargain, IHC had also enabled the Molinista oligarchical faction to acquire additional mortgages and haciendas, thereby gaining control of an even greater percentage of current and future fiber production. Thus, Harvester's temporary largesse permitted its local collaborator to exercise an even greater sway over the market, forcing the price upward in the short term but guaranteeing Harvester a continuing, dependable supply of fiber—always its principal object. The 1909–10 episode only shows the great lengths to which Harvester would go to preserve the collaborator mechanism; in this case, even at the risk of greatly diminished short-term profits.

## Oligarchical Control in Broader Perspective

What the foregoing four episodes make clear is that Yucatecan entrepreneurs were very much at home in the tumult of Porfirian high finance. Steven Haber, in his impressive study of the Mexican manufacturing industry, has also documented a cohesive, indigenous oligopoly that "knew how to structure the market in order to avoid competition and had the economic and political clout to do so." Social, family, and political connections were utilized to build economic empires and to restrict entry to the market and the control of capital.[97] In the late Porfirian corporate environment, survival of the fittest meant the concentration of wealth in fewer and fewer hands. Not surprisingly, the New York Times reported in December 1902 that "nearly all the principal branches of industry" in Mexico were controlled by trusts and combines.[98]

Such powerful economic combinations were not always lucrative for the capitalists involved.[99] Nevertheless, investments by these diversified oligopolies were part of a larger strategy of profitability; losses in some areas would be compensated by high profits in others. This allowed entrepreneurs to control both new, promising areas of activity, such as railroads and manufacturing, and the older, more established options of land and commerce. And this is precisely why many Yucatecan *henequeneros* kept such diffuse investment portfolios. Haber's insights on the bonds between entrepreneurs in Mexican industry apply as well to Yucatán's factionalized agrocommercial economy: "Because no individual would risk his entire fortune on any one enterprise, this tightly knit group combined again and again to finance a variety of undertakings."[100] The dearth of profits never discouraged Yucatecan elites from waging an intense battle over the spoils of henequen monoculture.

Spirited competition was not confined to the peninsula. Indeed, Harvester's actions in Yucatán throughout the summer of discontent are more comprehensible considering the significant changes the North American private sector underwent at the turn of the century. Harvester's 1902 consolidation was part of the wave of mergers that swept U.S. industry between 1895 and 1905, when more than 1,800 firms were reorganized into "horizontal combinations."[101] One-third of these consolidations commanded more than 70 percent of their markets; Harvester's share of the North American harvester and reaper market approached 85 percent immediately after its merger. Although economic historians disagree on why these combinations occurred and what their relative impact was at home and abroad, they generally concur that this process of horizontal consolidation set the stage for the "managerial revolution" that followed—a revolution that effectively altered the way business was conducted throughout the world.[102]

Whether these combinations coalesced to escape ruinous competition, to coordinate better the flow of production, to respond to federal antitrust legislation, or to take advantage of bountiful capital markets, modern, multi-unit enterprises like Harvester had powerful advantages over their smaller rivals. According to Alfred Chandler, these oligopolistic "first movers" invested in plants large enough to capture economies of scale and scope, and embraced new technologies to increase throughput. They were, moreover,

> well down the learning curve in each of the industry's functional activities before challengers went into full operations. Such advantages made it easy for first movers to nip challengers in the bud, to stop their growth before they acquired the facilities and developed the skills needed to become strong competitors. And such advantages could be and often were used ruthlessly.[103]

Nevertheless, these turn-of-the-century conglomerates were never assured of survival, let alone success. Harvester, for instance, earned less than 1 percent of its net assets during the first fifteen months after the merger. Not until 1906 did the company take advantage of its "first mover" strengths by consolidating the other companies into the core organization of the old McCormick Harvesting Machine Company.[104] Horizontal combinations of capital-intensive industries proved effective only if they fashioned an efficient managerial hierarchy that coordinated purchasing, pricing, production, and marketing. Salaried managers developed long-term and short-term strategies to integrate their horizontal enterprise vertically. Integrating "backward," they secured access to raw materials; linking "forward," they created a modern, responsive sales organization to market their goods and services efficiently.

Where raw material supplies were limited or were controlled with relative ease by a small number of firms, as in the Yucatecan case, first movers aggressively sought to assure a steady supply for their factories. The Harvester-Molina working arrangement provided the manufacturer with a measure of relief against erratic pricing and fluctuating production levels. Moreover, as shown by the *henequeneros'* futile attempts to withhold production in 1907 and 1908, it diminished the likelihood that producers' associations like the Compañía Cooperativa de Hacendados Henequeneros could successfully elevate the price of their commodity.

Backward integration in the twine industry also meant the creation of purchasing departments to replace the costly middlemen, such as Thebaud Brothers and Peabody and Company. The establishment of Harvester's Fiber and Twine Division, ably stewarded by H. L. Daniels in Chicago, provided the company with skilled buyers who understood the vagaries of the hard-fiber market, actively sought new supply sources, and contracted with their suppliers on pricing, specifications, and delivery dates. In addition, the Fiber and Twine Division worked hand in hand with the twine mills to schedule the arrival of raw material; and with the traffic department, which was responsible for the shipment of fiber to the mills. Career professionals like Daniels preferred "policies that favored the long-term stability and growth of their enterprises to those that maximized current profits."[105] Division heads and upper-level managers were ultimately more willing than shareholders to reduce short-term dividends in favor of long-term staying power.

The strategy of backward integration led the trust to build its own twine mills, which led to the need to acquire a dependable source of supply. We would argue that this change prompted Harvester to sign the "notorious" contract with Governor Molina's *casa exportadora* in 1902.

The Harvester consolidation clearly altered the character of the binder twine and farm implement industries. In the 1890s, McCormick and Deering had competed equally in the harvesting machine market; fierce competition also had characterized the cordage industry. The merger dramatically changed the distribution of the two sectors into one giant, multiplant firm and a number of smaller independents.

In the 1890s, moreover, tight competition gave cordage companies an incentive to cut prices and increase market share at competitors' expense. After 1902, Harvester adopted what economic historians have subsequently defined as a "dominant-firm" strategy. To secure supply and deter price cutting, Harvester permitted independent cordage factories, such as the Plymouth and several small, midwestern prison twine mills, to sell as much output as they wished, so long as their competitors acceded to the seasonal prices set by Harvester's Fiber and Twine Division. A dominant firm held the prospect of price warfare over the collective heads of its smaller rivals, enabling it to enforce cartel-like behavior. If the competitors played along, Harvester did not have to maintain prices, especially during downturns like the 1907 panic. Dominant-firm strategy not only inhibited price cutting but also gave Harvester the opportunity to teach recalcitrant rivals a lesson by switching price competition on and off.[106]

Harvester's decision in 1909 to float Montes six hundred thousand dollars and to elevate fiber prices not only bailed its Yucatecan agent out of a tough predicament; it also served as a perfect example of that lesson. If Harvester could have kept the market up, it would have put its rivals' backs to the wall. Even though Plymouth successfully fought the corner by swamping the market with manila twine, Harvester managed to weather the storm, running its mills with a steady supply of henequen fiber and disciplining its rivals by keeping fiber prices down until the start of World War I. Not until Alvarado's revolutionary government committed state resources to a valorization scheme in 1915 did planter solidarity effectively confront the fiber buyers.

Depressed fiber prices did serve to heighten existing tensions within the regional elite during the last few years of Porfirio Díaz's dictatorship. The attempted corner, the Escalante failure, the fight for control of the railway trust, and the collapse of the producers' cooperative crystallized the belief among most planters that the Molinista *camarilla* and its patrons in Chicago were unwilling to countenance any loss of economic control in the peninsula. Accommodation no longer seemed possible. Political activity and, if necessary, violent rebellion increasingly were perceived as the only means to restore a more equitable reapportionment of the spoils of the henequen economy. Nowhere were these contradictions more painfully evident than in the rapidly expanding provincial capital, Mérida.

## CHAPTER 5

# Growing Pains in the White City

Mérida is probably the cleanest and most beautiful little city in all of Mexico. It might even challenge comparison in its white prettiness with any other in the world. The municipality has expended vast sums on paving, on parks, and on public buildings, and over and above this the henequen kings not long since made up a rich purse for improvements extraordinary.
—John Kenneth Turner, 1910

Nowhere in the world, probably, is money so absolutely God as here.
—Arnold and Frost, 1910

I f the Porfirian export model favored the political dominance of landowner-exporters throughout Mexico's regions, it also promoted the assimilation of new modes of thought about people's ability to harness the environment. Not only did local elites pour their profits into the advancement of their primary commodity and the infrastructure to market it; they also sought to perfect the world in which they lived, to recast their provincial communities as modern societies.

Change began at home; and for Yucatecan *henequeneros*, home was the state capital, where they actually resided, not the haciendas they inspected from time to time. By any measure, Mérida underwent a glistening facelift during the late Porfiriato; yet this metamorphosis came at some cost. The growth of the state capital meant much more than expensive macadam, streetlights, sewer lines, and the construction of opulent suburbs; these, after all, could be defrayed by windfall fiber revenues. Urban renewal entailed another set of consequences, some unforeseen, that disrupted the social fabric of city life. Ultimately, Mérida's extraordinary growth during the fiber boom contributed significantly to the climate of unrest that gripped Yucatán during the final years of the Porfiriato.

A discussion of Mérida's growth during Yucatán's Gilded Age will also shed light on what has been a rather neglected chapter in the historiography of Porfirian Mexico: the impressive development of the nation's provincial capitals. Inexplicably, Mexicanists have yet to examine the extent to which

Mérida or other state capitals replicated in miniature the institutional and ideological blueprint for modernization that Porfirio Díaz's advisers had designed with the national metropolis in mind. At the same time, this chapter will emphasize the pitfalls local *científicos* encountered in their efforts to tailor that urban model to the very different set of geographical and social specifications in peripheral centers like Mérida.

Before we can document Mérida's transformation and its concomitant growing pains, however, we must turn our attention to the Porfirian urban policies that ushered in those changes, as well as the broader rationale that inspired them.

## *Modernizing Visions and 'Chilango' Blueprints*

National and regional leaders during the Porfiriato shared an unshakable belief in the universal benefits of modernity. Although the elites often were educated abroad and were enamored of foreign ideas and innovation, it would surely be an exaggeration to maintain (in overwrought *dependentista* fashion) that the Porfirian blueprint for progress represented simply the appropriation of Western European and North American models. Like their counterparts elsewhere in Latin America, Mexican elites in both the capital and the provinces perceived themselves as more than mere imitators of and collaborators with foreign interests. They staked their own claims to modernity and a shared Western tradition. They had well-defined ideas about what progress meant and what a prosperous and civilized Mexican nation would look like in the not-too-distant future. (Indeed, in their own developmentalist scenarios, foreign investment and technology played a pivotal yet diminishing role. Late Porfirian economic policies, which attempted to restrict North American control, bear this out.)

President Díaz and his optimistic technocratic ministers sought to harness an increasingly muscular central state to the task of creating this thoroughly modern Mexico. Bold plans were drafted, new laws passed, and old codes rewritten by federal bureaucrats and, in turn, by like-minded state officials. Their project would begin in the nation's urban centers and would address not only the physical appearance of the city (and countryside) but also the sociological makeup of the Mexican citizen.

In essence, Porfirian developmentalist "ideology" sought to guide the invisible hand of the liberal state so that it might implant both the institutions and the "morality" of modern capitalism. Modernity meant more than introducing new methods, machines, and the wage; it implied the assimilation of a new ethic based on "time and work-discipline."[1] And because Porfirian reformers subscribed to racial and biological explanations of historical development, this project took on a special urgency.

Immorality posed great threats to Mexican society. Uncontrolled alcoholism, prostitution, gambling, and vagrancy promised physical degeneracy and debilitation of the Mexican race—a crisis not only in personal terms but to future political liberties. Alcoholism and venereal disease represented the greatest evils, but degeneracy could be moral as well as physical. Unregulated vice destroyed virtue, provided poor moral examples for the youth, . . . created men useless to society. The struggle to impose morality thus transcended politics and the workplace and became a patriotic duty—at stake was the future of the country and the people.[2]

Faced with such a daunting responsibility, only the inculcation of a "burning morality" (in the words of one prominent Chihuahuan reformer) would suffice. During the last decade of the Porfiriato, police surveillance and coercion became the most immediate means of enforcing this zealous new morality among a "disorderly" populace.[3] Conjuring up an "urban geography of vice" in the manner of their European contemporaries, national and provincial elites sought to expunge popular vices from city centers by regulating cantinas and brothels and limiting amusements in general. By controlling the popular classes for their own good—"immobilizing them," as it were, "in time and space"—the *gente decente* could reserve important public space for themselves.[4] But such campaigns to legislate urban morality (and more generally to implant a "dominant ideology") never met with notable success.[5]

While regional elites may have shared the national rulers' vision, decades of bitter feuding had left them suspicious of a central government that repeatedly had sought to limit their autonomy and siphon off their wealth.[6] Ultimately, it was the demonstrated power of the Porfirian export model that won them over. Provincial power holders recognized the substantial benefits that could accrue from a closer alignment to a federal government that now enthusiastically supported (and partially subsidized) their economic interests. By the late Porfiriato, local elites and officials had become true believers, championing the "progressive" ideas radiating from the national metropolis.

Yucatán's henequen boom was one of the shining successes of the Porfirian economic miracle, and the newfound wealth generated by the worldwide demand for the green agave assuaged any lingering doubts among chauvinistic Yucatecos about collaborating with the central government. As other regional elites accepted the ineluctable federal hegemony and hitched their fortunes to its economic star, Díaz's ministers began to implement their modernizing project, revitalizing the nation's urban centers, which they envisioned as the beachheads of progress.[7] Mexico City in particular became both a showcase and a social laboratory, where experiments were performed to promote the transformation of every aspect of daily life.

## THE FEDERAL DISTRICT

The late nineteenth-century export boom enabled federal authorities to finance ambitious public works projects that would have been unthinkable

during the Restored Republic of Juárez and Lerdo. And while federal subsidies were distributed for the construction of railways, ports, and dams in
the provinces, the capital (not surprisingly, given the Porfirian regime's
increasingly centralized power structure) received the lion's share, a staggering 80 percent.[8] Thus, although Mexico City had always dominated the
country's political and economic life, during the Porfiriato the capital's primacy was further enhanced.[9]

What makes the Distrito Federal's performance especially impressive is
that it did not directly benefit from the contemporaneous booms in mining
and agricultural exports. Products were shipped directly out of the country,
not funneled through the metropolis.[10] Even though Mexico City was the
hub of the national railway grid, the iron horse brought more economic
advantages to regions directly tied to that export trade than to the capital.[11]

In the Federal District itself, Díaz's advisers arrogantly believed that urban revitalization demanded federal oversight.[12] Through a series of shrewd
political maneuvers, the executive branch wrested control of public works
projects from the Mexico City Council; and on March 26, 1903, the National Congress passed a bill that placed the Federal District under the
political and administrative control of the executive branch. The bill created three new bureaucratic posts: district governor, general director of public works, and president of the Board of Health, all of which served at the
pleasure of the Ministry of *Gobernación*. Engineer Alberto Pani would later
argue that this decree was one of the most harmful legacies of the Porfirian
era, because its impact extended far beyond the Distrito Federal. "It is also
known that in all the other Federal States the municipal institution has
been likewise emasculated, making it utterly subservient to the Executive,
through the oppressive action of the *jefe político*."[13]

Armed with expanded powers, the architects of Díaz's plan set out to
recast the Federal District into a New World Paris or London. Travelers'
accounts and contemporary diplomatic reports attest to striking changes
not just in the physical ambience, but in virtually every aspect of residents'
lives.[14] It would be incorrect, however, to speak of an orderly master plan
mandated from above by prescient *científicos*. In reality, urban transformation often occurred in fits and starts, suggesting that planners frequently
reacted to changes already under way.

A case in point was the long-overdue drainage and sewer project, which
cost sixteen million pesos and preoccupied officials from 1886 to 1900.[15]
Heralded by Porfirian publicists as one of the wonders of the modern world,
the system included a 30-mile canal and a 6-mile tunnel. It was designed to
end the harmful effects of constant flooding during the rainy season.[16] The
herculean construction task was entrusted to S. Pearson and Son, Ltd., the
British engineering firm that had dredged the East River Tunnel in New
York and the Blackwell Tunnel under the Thames in London. The drainage
project generated a host of ancillary activities to introduce municipal services to the rapidly mushrooming suburbs that the new sewer system would

reach.[17] Trams, trolleys, electric and gas streetlights, running water, refuse pickup, professional police and firefighters, and a host of other services had to be coordinated for a population and a city that were steadily expanding.[18]

As might be expected, the public works binge benefited some classes of Federal District society much more than others. As the plutocracy moved out of the increasingly congested downtown, developers created new neighborhoods, such as Roma, Cuauhtémoc, and Juárez, which extended westward along the Paseo de la Reforma.[19] It was in this new zone that most of the aesthetic changes were introduced during the Gilded Age. The Paseo de la Reforma and other avenues were spruced up and widened; streets were paved (and repaved); and theaters, opera houses, and statues were rapidly constructed. All of this caught the eye of diplomats, entrepreneurs, and other visitors, who lavished praise on the dictator for the handsome improvements.[20]

Yet the trappings of modernity in this section stood in stark contrast to the overwhelming poverty, filth, and disease endemic in many working-class barrios and hastily constructed suburbs.[21] And Díaz's advisers placed the blame for social ills—alcoholism, vagrancy, gambling, homosexuality, pornography, illiteracy, abandoned children, overcrowded prisons, begging, indolence, and a deplorably high murder rate—squarely on the shoulders of the "vice-ridden" urban working classes.[22] The *científicos* were also ambivalent about the growing middle class, many members of which worked as civil servants. Even Justo Sierra, perhaps the most progressive of Díaz's advisers, believed that while this largely mestizo class had potential,

> there is a constant infiltration between the social classes, an osmosis. . . . Thus, the middle class has never been cured of either alcohol or superstition. Those are sociopathogenic microbes that pullulate in colonies where the culture is propitious to them.[23]

Although Sierra and penal authority Julio Guerrero believed that these social ills had no quick solution, they were optimistic that, with continued economic development as well as political stability, the middle and lower classes would eventually be "civilized."[24]

The linchpin of this grand urban design, then, was the maintenance of social control. This required a more activist state that knew how strategically to combine bread (*pan*) and the stick (*palo*). Mexico City became the national proving ground for moderate social reform (*pan*), as the *científicos* waged battles against society's social ills armed with mortar and bricks. Wherever visitors went in the Federal District, they commented on the highly publicized new structures—hospitals, mental asylums, health clinics, sanitary facilities, public schools, the ultramodern Lecumbérri Penitentiary, markets, slaughterhouses, and cemeteries.[25]

Physical improvements were matched by a comprehensive schedule of legal and moral reforms, as codes were rewritten to reflect modern Western advances in criminology, medicine, health, and other fields. Yet although Porfirian publicists showcased the inauguration of each new modern advance and decree, their reformist campaign fell far short of success. In 1911 Mexico City was saddled with the dubious distinction of being "the most unhealthful city in the whole world."[26] According to Alberto Pani, in virtually every category, from morbidity to infant mortality, the Mexican capital's statistics had no rival in Africa, Asia, the Americas, or Europe. Pani's exposé, *Hygiene in Mexico*, lambasted the Porfirians for what in reality had been only a halfhearted attempt to improve health and sanitation for the masses, an effort that only confirmed "the sin of inefficiency that stains the administration of our sanitary authorities."[27]

When positive remedies proved inadequate to maintain social control, coercion (*palo*) provided the ready answer. The death penalty was instituted for certain crimes, forced labor for others, and prohibitions were enacted against a variety of lower-class "vices." Yet even though *científico* reformers sought to legislate mores and alter the character of the lower classes by curtailing drinking hours at cantinas and *pulquerías*, penalizing the sale of erotica in bookstores, prohibiting illicit gambling, and rounding up vagrants in business districts near the downtown, these tougher laws were largely observed in the breach and only sporadically enforced.[28]

While the government certainly felt compelled to keep the peace, law and order in a violent place like turn-of-the-century Mexico City was a relative concept. The police force was generally instructed to protect private property (and persons) by keeping the "rabble" out of the city's more affluent neighborhoods. Likewise, popular celebrations and festivities were forced out of the *zócalo* and into the new working-class barrios. Meanwhile, the newly professionalized police saturated wealthier neighborhoods—suggesting a formidable presence to foreign visitors—but largely left the poor to their own devices.[29]

Of course, politically motivated opposition to the dictatorship was another matter and was dealt with severely. The secret police, based in the capital, rooted out dissidents, especially anarchist union organizers and outspoken journalists, and left them to languish in prison.[30] *Científico* planners thus set definite limits on moderate co-optative strategies for maintaining social control.

In sum, Mexico City's political power and economic dominance enabled public officials to embark on an ambitious public works program, which transformed the physical appearance of the Federal District yet did little to arrest the serious everyday problems that plagued many of its middle- and working-class residents. In comparison, to what extent did Porfirian urban policies make their presence felt in the provinces? And how successful were regional elites in addressing the problems caused by the growth of their state capitals? An analysis of Mérida at the turn of the century will elicit some answers.

## MÉRIDA'S PRIMACY

Because they have generally ascribed the Porfirian economic miracle to mineral and agricultural exports, historians have often overlooked the secondary cities (usually, but not always, state capitals), whose growth that export wealth made possible. During the 35-year dictatorship, the nation's population rose by a respectable 61 percent, but that of the state capitals increased by 88 percent. Moreover, Mexico's fastest-growing cities—Chihuahua City, Veracruz, Monterrey, and Mérida—expanded by more than 4 percent a year, outpacing 2.5 percent for the Federal District and 1.2 percent nationwide.[31] Not surprisingly, all the secondary cities that experienced demographic growth were tied by rail or sea to the burgeoning export trade.[32]

Unlike many provincial capitals that stagnated through much of the nineteenth century, Mérida expanded steadily after independence. A sleepy little city of ten thousand in 1803, the former colonial capital grew appreciably during the first 25 years of nationhood as the entire regional economy prospered.[33] Local entrepreneurs, whose agricultural and commercial holdings were spared the destruction that central Mexico experienced during the independence wars, took full advantage of the lifting of colonial mercantile restrictions as interstate and intrastate trade blossomed. Sugar, cotton, dyewoods, and a bustling trade in grains fueled the development of the southeastern zones of the peninsula.

Mérida shared the fruits of that agrarian boom with Valladolid and Campeche. Indeed, even though it often exercised its political clout at the expense of its chief urban rivals, it was not the dominant city in the peninsula at midcentury. An 1846 government report indicates that the state capital *partido* was only the third-largest in the state.[34]

A tragic byproduct of development, however, was the escalation of tension between Maya villagers and opportunistic sugar planters on the state's southeastern frontier. The disastrous Caste War that erupted at midcentury decimated Yucatán's population by more than one-third. Ironically, Mérida (and the entire northwestern quadrant of the peninsula) benefited demographically from the hostilities as Valladolid, Peto, and Tekax, its principal urban rivals to the south and east, suffered the worst ravages of the war. Residents of these cities and hinterlands fled from the attacks of the rebellious Chan Santa Cruz Maya, and Mérida's population swelled.[35]

Political squabbling among elites in Mérida and neighboring Campeche during the first half-century after independence also contributed indirectly to the state capital's growth. When the Campechanos finally seceded from Yucatán in 1862, Mérida remained the only viable commercial center in the state. By 1877 the city's population had grown to roughly 30,000, the only state capital to register a sizable increase during that turbulent period (see Table 5.1).[36]

By the onset of the Porfiriato, then, Mérida was in a good position to assume a commanding role in the rapidly expanding fiber trade. The sur-

TABLE 5.1
*Mérida's Growth*

| Year | Population | National rank |
|------|-----------|---------------|
| 1803 | 10,000[a] | 12 |
| 1877 | 30,000[a] | 5 |
| 1895 | 36,935 | 9 |
| 1900 | 43,630 | 5 |
| 1910 | 62,447 | 5 |

SOURCE: For 1803, Boyer; for 1877, 1895, 1900, and 1910, *Estadísticas sociales*, 9.
NOTE: Figures are for the city of Mérida, not Mérida *partido*.
[a]Estimates.

rounding agricultural zone was converted into vast henequen estates; *henequeneros* lived in the capital and managed their haciendas through administrators.[37] During the henequen boom, a peninsular railway network, built, financed, and managed by native entrepreneurs, was routed through Mérida to transport the monocrop. Much of the raw fiber (pressed into 350-pound bales) was kept in city warehouses until it could be transported by rail to the port of Progreso, 35 kilometers north, on the first leg of its journey to North American and European cordage and binder twine factories. The *casas exportadoras*, also headquartered in Mérida, facilitated the movement of more than six hundred thousand bales of fiber in peak years. Perhaps historian Serapio Baqueiro did not exaggerate when, in 1881, he expressed the prevailing perception in Mérida that "all the State is for henequen, and outside of [henequen] is nothing."[38]

The city's growth spilled over into its suburbs and neighboring pueblos. Whereas just before the Caste War broke out, Mérida *partido* had held less than 15 percent of the state's population, by 1883, with the fiber industry flourishing throughout the northwestern henequen zone, the city and its environs had mushroomed to almost 35 percent of the state total. (That year, no other urban center in the state had more than 6,000 inhabitants.[39]) As the pace of monoculture intensified, Mérida's preeminence remained unchallenged. By 1910 the capital's population had grown to more than 60,000, while Valladolid, the state's second city, had fewer than 12,000 residents.[40] As one student of Yucatán's economic history has surmised, "In a sense, the whole of Yucatán became the hinterland of the capital."[41]

Mérida's growth was impressive even by Porfirian standards. During the dictatorship, Mérida leapfrogged over such provincial capitals as Guanajuato, Durango, Chihuahua, Morelia, Oaxaca, Veracruz, and Zacatecas. By 1910 it trailed only Guadalajara, Monterrey, San Luis Potosí, and Puebla. And during that last decade of the Porfiriato, it experienced the third-highest growth rate of any city in Mexico.[42]

Two infrastructural improvements, the railroad and the steamship, played key roles in reenforcing Mérida's primacy.[43] Like the spokes of a

TABLE 5.2

*Passenger Travel to and from Mérida, 1910*

| Route[a] | Total tickets sold[b] | Percentage of travel |
|---|---|---|
| Mérida–Progreso e Izamal | 234,945 | 80.4 |
| Mérida–Peto | 321,751 | 64.8 |
| Mérida–Valladolid | 261,635 | 67.5 |
| Mérida–Campeche | 285,309 | 53.4 |

SOURCE: AGN, SCOP, 23/460-1, *Informes del Consejo de Administración del FCUY de 1910* (Mérida: Imprenta de la Escuela Correccional de Artes y Oficios, 1911).
NOTE: Comparative 1908 and 1909 passenger traffic falls within percentage points of the 1910 data, suggesting that the figures cited are not anomalous.
[a]After the FCUY merger in 1902, the four lines were renamed the Divisiónes Norte, Sur, Oriente, and Oeste. For clarity, this table uses the original names.
[b]Includes first-, second-, and third-class tickets.

wheel, the four major railway lines locked outlying villages and haciendas into a tight orbit around their Mérida hub (see Table 5.2). The affordable railroad contributed significantly to the vitality of the capital, placing travel in reach of the peninsula's working classes. A third-class fare on the Mérida–Peto railway in 1901 was calculated at 2 centavos per kilometer. This meant that a roundtrip fare from Acanceh, a *partido* seat about 25 kilometers from Mérida, cost 1 peso.[44] Rural workers' wages ranged from 75 centavos to 1 peso a day in 1900, so railway fares were not too expensive for most rural inhabitants. Figure 5.1 breaks down the tickets sold between 1881 and 1913 into the three customary fare classes to demonstrate that the working class provided by far the highest percentage of riders on the Mérida–Peto line during the Porfiriato. (Furthermore, the commute from Acanceh, Tixkokob, or Hunucmá, important *partido* seats in the henequen zone, took less than an hour.)

As Table 5.2 clearly illustrates, travel to and from Mérida dwarfed passenger traffic in the rest of the state. Even setting aside the high percentage of Mérida traffic on the Progreso e Izamal line due to the disproportionate travel between the state's capital and port, the percentages for the Mérida–Peto and Mérida–Valladolid lines show that the railroad stimulated the capital's growth. Only the Mérida–Campeche portion, at 53.4 percent, is relatively low, and this figure is explained by Campeche's position as a second, smaller hub on this railway.

Data on volume of cargo corroborate Mérida's economic importance as a hub. In 1896, a staggering 90 percent of the cargo carried by the Mérida–Peto line went to or from the capital.[45] In 1900 and 1901, the figures for Mérida "dipped" to 69.5 percent and 72.3 percent of all cargo handled by the railway.[46]

The steamship, which doubled cargo capacity and halved sailing time, strengthened Mérida's already formidable commercial sector. Tariffs on inbound steamship freights were drastically reduced to allow shippers to fill their vessels on the return trip. Because Mérida's *casas exportadoras* contracted with foreign shippers, such as Ward and Company, to move their fiber, it made good business sense to take advantage of reduced shipping rates and flood the greater Mérida market with foreign grain, foodstuffs, manufactured goods, construction materials, and luxury items. With additional refinements, such as refrigeration and improved handling, during the last decades of the nineteenth century, even perishable products found their way to inland capitals.[47] *Henequeneros* purchased corn, beans, sugar, and other basic commodities for their hacienda stores from foreign suppliers through the *casas exportadoras*, thereby undercutting southeastern grain producers.[48]

Cargo was funneled through the new port of Progreso, which had been built with a combination of government subsidies and private initiative. Inaugurated in 1870, Progreso served as a feeder for Mérida, a second commercial hub with the carrying capacity needed to handle efficiently the ever-increasing volume of goods entering and leaving the state.[49]

Not surprisingly, Mérida was the only banking center in Yucatán. Besides cash advances doled out to *henequeneros* by local *casas exportadoras* in return for fiber, Yucatecan *hacendados* and merchants had the option of opening running accounts with three banks: a branch of the Banco Nacional (opened in 1883), the Banco Mercantil de Yucatán (1889), and the Banco Yucateco (1890). More than a few proprietors opened accounts with all three banks simultaneously, overextending themselves in the process.[50]

The henequen boom, however, meant much more for the state capital than commercial, financial, and infrastructural changes. Greater employment opportunities encouraged migrants to leave rural areas and attracted immigrants from abroad. The newcomers included Maya campesinos, Spaniards, Cubans, and *turcos*.[51] Asians—usually Chinese and Koreans—were

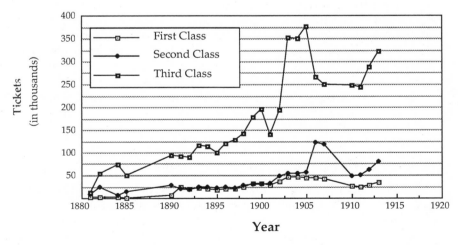

*Fig. 5.1.* Mérida–Peto passenger ticket sales by class, 1881–1913. AGN, SCOP: 23, *passim*. Data unavailable for 1883, 1886–89, 1908, and 1909.

contracted to work on the henequen haciendas. After they fulfilled their contracts, many moved to Mérida and found work in small commercial establishments. Mexican nationals came in increasing numbers.[52] They found gainful employment in the numerous public works projects, the professions, artisanal trades, factories, and the ubiquitous service sector.[53] For example, the numbers of construction and professional jobs both doubled during the last ten years of the Porfiriato alone.[54] Urban directories published during the last two decades of the Porfiriato attest to a dramatic increase in virtually every occupational category.[55]

As the boom progressed, the now overburdened state capital began to lose much of its colonial charm. Like many early Spanish American cities, Mérida had been laid out by its founding fathers in the classic style of the Spanish Renaissance. Royal authorities had insisted on the traditional grid of broad, straight streets intersecting at right angles to form rectangular blocks and open squares.[56] But now the neat and orderly grid pattern belied the same deadly problems that residents of Mexico City regularly confronted. "Her streets were saharas of ill-smelling dust . . . in the dry season, and sloughs of despond in the wet," noted two travelers.[57]

Matías Romero, an adviser to Porfirio Díaz, wrote in 1883 that Mérida's working-class housing was worse than the Maya's humble huts in the countryside, its streets were filthy, and its milk and food supply adulterated. Families kept animals in the home, drinking water was scarce, and taking a bath was next to impossible, except for a few privileged people. Yellow fever and malaria epidemics recurred with frightening consistency in Mérida and smaller urban centers throughout the state. "If we continue like this," Romero concluded, "we should put a funeral home on every corner."[58]

Little changed until state authorities generated enough revenue to share the costs of modernization with the private sector. Knowing the monocrop's periodic boom-and-bust cycles, local *henequeneros* and merchants were understandably reluctant to invest in costly urban improvements in such a volatile economy. Little help was forthcoming from the federal government. Not until the Spanish-American War sent fiber prices rocketing to a record ten cents a pound did state government officials and the private sector decide to invest in the sorely needed, urban public works projects. It was during Olegario Molina's tenure as governor that the oligarchical state presided over a full-scale effort to remake Mérida into a Porfirian showcase.

## Urban Renewal Under Mérida's Own 'Científico'

The Molinistas embraced the *científico* program in full, although previous governors had made individual moves in this direction.[59] Urban tramways had been built, public lighting and telephones installed, rubbish collection introduced, government offices in the Plaza de las Armas refurbished, new plants and tufted laurel trees imported from Cuba to spruce up the *zócalo*, and a new, more sanitary public market constructed several blocks away from the city center.[60] But none of Governor Molina's predecessors had enjoyed the fortuitous combination of plentiful local resources and federal inspiration and encouragement that Molina now boasted. The changes affected most areas of urban life, as the Molinista regime and the private sector (sometimes with the assistance of foreign companies) joined together to transform housing, transportation, communications, public health, sanitation, education, the arts, the business community, and the urban landscape itself.

In each of these areas, Mérida traveled in lockstep with the Federal District, a more modest provincial echo of the national capital's style and substance. The quaint town of 1840 picturesquely described by John Lloyd Stephens bore little resemblance to the bustling Porfirian city portrayed by John Kenneth Turner in 1910.[61]

Perhaps Molina's greatest accomplishment as a modernizer, the paving and draining of Mérida's streets, became the showpiece of his administration. Imitating the national leaders and their extensive pavement and drainage project in Mexico City, the governor levied a special tax (on henequen) to help defray the cost of public works. He then commissioned O. Molina y Compañía, in collaboration with the Mérida Water Company (based in Philadelphia, despite its name), to undertake the enormous task of constructing sewers, building sidewalks, and laying more than 350,000 square meters of asphalt, concrete, and brick in the downtown area. Ignoring cries of conflict of interest from his political enemies, Don Olegario spent more than five million pesos on paving and drainage, transforming Mérida into Mexico's most modern provincial capital.

Molina prevailed on a number of prominent *hacendados* to supplement state funds to finance a number of key capital improvement projects in Mérida, including O'Horan Hospital, Juárez Penitentiary, and Ayala Asylum. A showplace for the arts, the new Peón Contreras Theater, was built near the plaza, with an imposing foyer, marble balconies, velvet upholstery, and the latest lighting and stage equipment.[62] To encourage financial contributions and demonstrate civic spirit, Don Olegario himself gave fifty thousand pesos to these projects (out of more than a million pesos raised from the community) and returned one year's pay from his governor's salary to the state treasury.

Again guided by Federal District precedent, Governor Molina moved to expand the physical boundaries of the state capital, pushing outward toward the periphery. As the downtown became increasingly more congested, upper-, middle-, and lower-class neighborhoods were built on the city's perimeter—always under the state authorities' watchful direction and regulation. While expenditures were greater in the more fashionable neighborhoods, each barrio had its own miniplaza, church, police station, public market, and professional offices and stores that catered to its residents. Within a radius of roughly twelve blocks, local residents of Santiago (west of the downtown plaza), San Sebastián (southwest), San Cristóbal (southeast), La

Mejorada (northeast), or the more fashionable haunts of Santa Ana to the north could find just about any occupation or skill they required, including doctors, dentists, tailors, shoemakers, chemists, barbers, blacksmiths, and milkmen. Many of the more humble barrios, despite their poverty, developed a measure of cohesion and solidarity as recent arrivals from the countryside tried to recreate elements of the social environment they had just left behind.[63]

Meanwhile, Governor Molina and Mérida's *gente decente* sought to duplicate Mexico City's Paseo de la Reforma—which itself emulated Paris's Champs Élysées. They designed Mérida's stunning Paseo Montejo north of Santa Ana on the route to Progreso. After several false starts, construction of the tree-lined boulevard began in 1904. By 1910, elegant, horse-drawn carriages (and automobiles) were parading down the avenue in the evening, as *nouveaux riches* and old money alike vied to express who they were and whom they aspired to be.

Olegario Molina's achievements did not go unnoticed in the Federal District. Local public works projects were lauded in the Mexico City press; *El Imparcial* regularly carried stories of Mérida's dazzling transformation.[64] These journalistic puff pieces, plus the goodwill and influence of the *científico* bloc in the capital, persuaded President Díaz that it now made good sense to override an established Porfirian rule and permit Yucatán's dynamic and loyal governor to run for a second term. In the fall of 1905, with the state constitution amended by the Molinista legislature, Don Olegario's candidacy was declared. More important, as we have seen, it was also announced that the president of Mexico would come to Yucatán in early 1906 to inaugurate a variety of public works projects in Mérida.

In addition to legitimizing Molinista hegemony, in a symbolic sense Díaz's journey signaled the Mérida elite's coming of age, as well as its reconciliation with the national regime's modernizing project. Local *henequeneros* threw themselves into preparations for the presidential visit, determined to impress on Don Porfirio that they were in the vanguard of Mexican progress.[65] Native son Justo Sierra, returning as part of the presidential entourage, observed with great satisfaction, "Yucatán's reconquest by the *patria grande* is now sealed. . . . No longer do the peninsula's forests echo with separatist shouts or the bloodcurdling screams of Maya rebels, but with the whistle of the locomotive." And "the new force for progress, which had transformed the region like a magic wand, was an erect spine of henequen."[66]

Don Porfirio enthusiastically concurred that the region was no longer a refractory provincial backwater but an integral part of the rapidly modernizing Mexican nation. If the local elite had become a regional bulwark of his national development strategy, it was also clear that Olegario Molina and his *camarilla* were among that strategy's chief architects. It was hardly surprising, therefore, that only months after his triumphant visit to the peninsula, Díaz named Molina secretary of *fomento* (development). Don

Olegario represented the best that the provinces had to offer, and his incorporation into the national superstructure illustrated the co-optative nature of Porfirian politics.

## LIFESTYLES OF THE RICH

Wealthy *henequeneros* purchased properties along the Paseo Montejo and built palaces designed by architects from Paris and Brussels. Opulent mansions like the Cantón and Cámara homes, with their imposing entrances and elongated balustrades, demonstrated that the enclosed patio architecture of colonial-period houses was now out of vogue. The home was no longer a familial sanctuary from the outside world; it was an expression—or better put, an advertisement—of the power, wealth, and status of Mérida's plutocracy.[67]

Even though the *gente decente* moved out to the suburbs in increasing numbers, they did not abandon the downtown. Many retained their hermetic homes in the center of the city even as they built new, more fashionable residences along the Paseo or in Santa Ana. The central Plaza de las Armas (also called the Plaza de la Independencia since 1821) was still the commercial and bureaucratic locus of power for both the city and the state. Local elites understood the advantages in maintaining a residence in or near the *zócalo*. Moreover, the preponderant share of urban renewal and modern amenities had already been added precisely in the central zone.

Because members of Yucatán's most powerful families regularly cooperated in building economic empires, pooling risk capital, and forming joint stock companies, it is not surprising that they lived in close proximity. Indeed, the combined effect of this residence pattern was to create veritable familial power domains in the downtown area. For instance, the Casares family all lived within a block of each other. Eulalio lived on Calle 61, no. 511 with sister Raquel, while another sister, Prudencia, lived across the street at no. 516, and brothers David and Arturo lived nearby at Calle 63, no. 475. The Molinas followed the same pattern: Olegario lived on Calle 57, no. 459; brother Ricardo lived three houses away at no. 465; another brother, José Trinidad, two houses in the other direction at no. 455; son-in-law Avelino Montes across the street at no. 470; and son Augusto Molina Fajardo down the block at no. 457. The Peón y Peóns, the Cantóns, and the Escalantes orchestrated their family geographies in a similar manner. Mérida's most valuable urban properties were thus acquired by *henequenero* families intent on maximizing and diversifying their investment portfolios. In the process, local elites fueled a speculative urban real estate market that drove housing prices ever higher during the henequen boom.[68]

Economic power also permitted *henequeneros* to partake of unbridled conspicuous consumption, and like their peers in Mexico City, they imported many of the trappings—from fine Spanish and French wines to commode fixtures—from Western Europe and the United States. The Yucatecan plutocracy basked in the glow of Mérida's reputation as the Paris of Mexico; as in the Federal District, *francomanía* was rampant. Advertisements regularly ran in *La Revista de Mérida* for a men's clothier, Au Petit Paris, while a pair of women's clothing stores, Au Paris Charmant and La Ciudad de Londrés, sold muslin from India and Persia as well as English and French cashmere.[69] French restaurants, clubs, and theaters began to appear in the downtown and the more fashionable suburbs.

Mérida's *carnaval*, which rivaled the pre-Lenten celebrations in Venice and New Orleans, was another opportunity for the *gente decente* to show off their Parisian finery and validate their status. The wives of wealthy *henequeneros* sponsored allegorical-theme floats and paraded in their carriages and cars through the downtown. Masquerade balls were held at two private clubs, La Unión and El Liceo; more than five hundred couples typically attended. Sunday of *carnaval* week witnessed a battle of flowers and confetti at La Unión and a midnight dance at El Liceo featuring *calaveras* (skeletons) and other allegories of death.[70] Such ostentation prompted the British travelers Arnold and Frost to comment sarcastically in 1910, "Nowhere in the world, probably, is money so absolutely God as here."[71]

## THE SQUEEZE ON WATER AND HOUSING

By any yardstick, Mérida's downtown underwent a radical facelift. No longer the dingy, overgrown town of 1850 with horses meandering down muddy streets, by 1904 it was the republic's "white city": clean, well lit, increasingly motorized, and paved with glistening asphalt. Nevertheless, every aspect of this transformation came with costs and new obstacles, as imported ideas and technologies had to be adapted to local conditions. Mérida's *científicos* might look to federal urban planners for guidance, but tropical Yucatán was a far cry from the central valley surrounding the Federal District.

The roller-coaster cycles of the regional henequen economy made access to urban services highly problematical, creating dilemmas for state bureaucrats, private firms, and residents alike. As urban problems lingered and deepened, moreover, they nurtured resentment toward officious Molinista bureaucrats. At first, the complaints were muted; few city residents chose to voice their opposition to the regime's ambitious agenda of physical improvements. But as the Porfiriato drew to a close and Yucatán's boomtime economy fell victim to a worldwide financial panic, strong public resentment of Molina's long-running oligarchical regime began to surface as well. Two pivotal issues, water and housing, will illustrate how changes projected in one area often had unfortunate and unintended consequences in another.

Scarce water resources had always limited the quality of life in this arid northwestern quadrant of the peninsula. Under the traditional arrangements of water supply, torrential seasonal rains filtered through the surface layer of the ground and, by the time they reached a depth of 30 feet (that is, sea level), lost most of their contamination. At that depth, shallow wells collected the water. Wind power raised it from the wells into iron storage tanks; some 3,500 windmills blanketed Mérida during the Porfiriato, earning the "White City" the additional sobriquet "City of Windmills." People who could not afford artificial wells simply collected water, especially during the rainy season, on the roofs of their houses and stored it in tanks. So many unprotected reservoirs and private storage tanks, however, proved ideal breeding grounds for mosquitoes. As a result, Mérida gained notoriety for yellow fever and malaria epidemics throughout the nineteenth century.[72]

The difficult access to water rendered fire-fighting capabilities inadequate. Blazes would rage out of control until they subsided. Fiber warehouses were particularly vulnerable, especially during the last month of the dry season, when intense heat and scant water produced potentially disastrous conditions. Not surprisingly, insurance companies either wrote policies reluctantly or raised premiums precipitously, so that many city businesses opted to go uninsured and risk the consequences.[73]

While all Meridanos agreed that this state of affairs was unacceptable, the municipality and the state lacked the financial resources to address the problem seriously until the late Porfiriato. When funds materialized during Molina's administration, civil servants pushed ahead with plans to construct a new waterworks similar to the system just completed in Mexico City. They reasoned that the water problem could not be cured by itself but had to fit into an overall strategy for the renovation of the downtown. First, the streets had to be paved, sewers dug, and water lines built (with funds realized from the special henequen tax). By 1904 this stage was complete. But in the process, Mérida's antiquated water retrieval system turned positively venomous. Surface water, instead of filtering gradually, as it had under the old natural system, was now channeled directly through the new drains and sewers into the old water supply. As William James, manager of the Mérida Water Company, later noted, "This let the water down without any straining process. . . . Unfiltered water from the asphalt streets found its way through these many wells lying about, rendering them deadly."[74]

This turn of events prompted Governor Molina to solicit bids from foreign companies to repair the sewer and water system. The Mérida Water Company won the concession in 1904, and over the next three years it installed an expensive water plant. Wells had to be drilled to a depth of more than one hundred feet below a bed of nearly impervious clay that protected the water from contamination. Hydrants were built, and the company agreed to keep them in working order and to furnish water to the city at no charge when fires broke out. The system was finally completed in 1907. Preliminary testing, however, revealed that the city's water was still impure. James insisted on making new tests, but public officials unexpectedly balked. Not until 1909, after two years of further wrangling between the company and the state, was the way cleared to retest the water. This time, after a successful battery of tests, Mérida's snakebitten waterworks were officially inaugurated.[75]

The government's timing suggests motives for its reluctance to open the new water plant. When the contract was drawn up in 1904, the henequen economy was barreling along at full speed, driven by high prices on the world market. By 1907, however, the bottom had dropped out of the market and the entire regional economy was in the throes of a terrible slump. The tax revenues generated from the sale of henequen also declined during the financial panic. No longer could state officials tap the private sector, which was equally strapped by the precipitous fall in the price of fiber. As we have seen, a tight credit squeeze drove the powerful *casa exportadora* Eusebio Escalante e Hijo into bankruptcy, dragging down a number of *henequeneros* along with it. Moreover, all state funds had been used to pay for the costly street paving and other urban improvements. Not until 1909 could the state pay the Mérida Water Company for services rendered.

The water company was not the only aggrieved party. Even as downtown residents (including the elite) were asked to do without city water, lucrative concessions and contracts—most notably, the downtown paving—were doled out to Molina y Compañía and other business associates and family members. To be sure, influence peddling and patronage were nothing new in Yucatecan political life. But the spoils of henequen monoculture that the Molinistas had inherited during the boom from 1898 to 1904 now made political power that much more rewarding for them, and the inconveniences attending modernization that much more galling for Molina's political opponents and the public at large.[76]

The unstable regional economy also had an unsettling effect on the urban real estate market. The construction industry boomed in turn-of-the-century Mérida as housing for all classes, business establishments, and the formidable public works sector grew by leaps and bounds. In 1895, 131 houses were under construction in Mérida; by 1900 the number had grown to 489; and by 1910 it had reached 693.[77] The Compañía de Tranvías opened up new suburbs like Itzimná and Chuminopolis, while working-class barrios like Santiago added twenty new blocks in a matter of years, and observers commented on the addition of second floors on top of existing structures. Indeed, during the early years of the boom, housing could not keep up with the steady influx of migrants from rural areas and outside the region.[78]

The demand for housing, a fiber market that increased the local money supply, and the rising value of both rural and urban real estate all contributed to an across-the-board rise in the capital's housing prices. Then, in an effort to generate additional revenues to underwrite his urban renovations, Governor Molina reorganized the Registry of Property and ordered it to reassess the value of all urban real estate. A retrospective newspaper article persuasively argued that the new catastral assessment led to a rapid turnover in the housing market, giving rise to a speculative frenzy among Mérida's developers.[79] The combination of an overheated economy, housing shortages, and speculation led *El Eco del Comercio* to lament in 1903 that urban properties were scarce and rents dear.[80] *El Peninsular* noted three years later that housing was just about out of reach for the middle class; many public employees, petty merchants, and artisans had to pay more than half of their salary in rent.[81]

When the bubble burst and the price of fiber collapsed in 1907, housing values plummeted, and many speculators were caught in the downturn. *La Revista de Mérida* remarked a year later that any proprietor would be more than happy to sell his city properties for the 1903 assessment.[82] As the construction industry cooled during the panic, a crescendo of complaints arose about Molinista patronage practices. In 1909, Arsenio Rodríguez Caballero, whose company imported building materials for windmills in Mérida, wrote to President Díaz that he was unable to obtain essential materials from Monterrey and San Luis Potosí because Adriano Erosa enjoyed a government monopoly on their sale throughout the state. When Rodríguez Caballero defied the state monopoly, imported the parts, and sold them for half price, Erosa sued and, not unexpectedly, won a judgment in the Molinista-controlled courts. State monopolies on imports were just another irritating example of Molinista privilege. In addition to building materials, exclusive import licenses for gunpowder and livestock were handed out to trusted Molina clients.[83]

Mérida's growing pains went beyond physical discomforts and a nagging irritation with bureaucratic arrogance and corruption. The city's physical transformation both altered and reflected the way urban groups and classes perceived themselves and each other, escalating tensions among them. The concentration in one primate city of regional population, infrastructure, and wealth, and the increasing monopoly on political power and privilege by one elite faction, contributed significantly to the unsettled political climate that marked the final years of the Porfiriato in Yucatán.

## Curbing Social Ills

Another significant and more sinister factor was the Molinista effort to enforce social control. No sooner was he inaugurated in 1902 than Don Olegario, emulating his counterparts in Mexico City, began a concerted effort to inject the pristine morality of the modern state into the workaday lives of Mérida's urban poor. In an attempt to curb lower-class "vices," which, Yucatán's *científicos* believed, abetted criminal violence while undercutting labor productivity and efficiency, Governor Molina pushed ahead with a battery of reforms aimed at regulating the very leisure pursuits that had previously given the popular classes some measure of independence and satisfaction.[84]

Critics like Carlos Escoffié Zetina, editor of *El Padre Clarencio* and a frequent victim of Molinista harassment, had a field day mocking the

Olegariato's futile attempts to legislate popular morality in the early 1900s. Always walking the dangerously thin line between political satire and libel, Escoffié embellished his bitter broadsides with humorous, hand-drawn caricatures that critiqued the state's intrusion into the private lives of ordinary citizens. On one front cover, for instance, Molina was sketched in the guise of the pope, broadly inveighing against drinking, gambling, vagrancy, prostitution, pornography, and homosexuality.[85]

Escoffié, moreover, took great pains to illustrate some of the new morality's unintended consequences. For example, Molina's stiff temperance measures were "clandestinely circumvented," as social drinking was driven out of the dank, unpleasant confines of Mérida's cantinas (sans tables, chairs, or windows) and relocated to working-class homes where additional family members, especially women, joined in the "diversion." Now that public drinking establishments were closed on Sundays, Escoffié added, "San Lunes" was living up to its name as the preferred day of drunkenness and disorder.[86] No doubt Escoffié and other opposition satirists struck a common chord with the public when they mocked the self-righteous morality of Yucatán's rulers.

Don Olegario's peremptory reforms met with little success. Penal statistics published in the *Diario Oficial* chart an increase in urban and political crimes during the late Porfiriato.[87] As we have seen, state authorities responded by upgrading the city's police force, instituting a state bureau of investigation—with the same foreboding name as its Federal District counterpart, the secret police—and spending massive sums on a renovation and expansion of the state penitentiary (see Table 5.3).

Opened in 1895 during Carlos Peón Machado's administration, Juárez Penitentiary became Mérida's Lecumbérri, a state-of-the-art facility that, in theory, offered inmates an opportunity to repay their debt to society through rehabilitation. Molina's renovations enlarged the facility to 182 cells (including isolation cells) and provided schools, workshops, lecture halls, libraries, recreation areas, and gardens for the prisoners. Many prisoners wove hammocks and did woodwork, and their handiwork was sold at a prison store.[88]

Yet no matter what spin Molina's publicists (and later his apologists) put on his renovations, disturbing reports on actual conditions inside the penitentiary directly refuted the progressive image. Escoffié, who spent more than two years there and was arrested 51 times for his repeated political attacks on the regime, wrote that rehabilitation was a joke; that the prison served as a glorified holding tank to keep so-called "dangerous elements"—alarmingly on the rise—off the streets until their trials. He added that because state officials were in no hurry to prosecute, prisoners sometimes stayed longer in jail awaiting trial than they would spend for the crime itself.[89]

Serapio Rendón, a prominent Mérida lawyer and public defender who ran afoul of Molinista interim governor Enrique Muñoz Arístegui, came

TABLE 5.3

*State Expenditures for Juárez Penitentiary*

| Governor | Term | Amount (in pesos) |
|---|---|---|
| General Guillermo Palomino | 1886–1890 | $47,214.95 |
| Colonel Daniel Traconis | 1890–1894 | 29,364.37 |
| Carlos Peón Machado | 1894–1897 | 109,034.59 |
| General Francisco Cantón | 1898–1902 | 1,798.18 |
| Olegario Molina | 1902–1909 | 359,771.82 |

SOURCE: Casasús, 75–77.

to know intimately the confines of the Hotel Bolados. He served three months in 1909 for allegedly obstructing justice. Rendón wrote a blistering memorandum to Porfirio Díaz about his incarceration, titled "How Life Is in Juárez Penitentiary, Mérida, Yucatán."[90] The most vexing problem, he noted, was the noxious combination of insufficient ventilation and Mérida's "suffocating climate." Sleeping was a painful experience. Prisoners were permitted to bring their own thin sleeping pads, which may have sufficed on their hammocks at home but were next to useless on the meterwide wooden platforms that served as beds. Ampler mattresses that might alleviate the pain were not permitted. Rendón added that more comfortable (six-meter-square) rooms, available to those inmates who could afford to pay two pesos a day, were for unknown reasons unavailable during his incarceration. Cells in corridor 5—death row since Molina's new decree instituting the death penalty—were so overcrowded that two inmates slept on the floor and one on the wooden platform. And those who needed to be disciplined received a steady regimen of solitary confinement.[91]

Personal hygiene was impossible in the Hotel Bolados. Prisoners were allowed to shave only twice a month; personal effects like shaving cream, scissors, or a mirror were forbidden; and the prison barber, himself an inmate, used the same razor on every prisoner. Bathrooms were unventilated, and the odor was sickening. A detailed, day-by-day menu documented a poor, repetitive diet. What little meat was provided following the weekend's bullfight was supposed to be mixed with a gruel made of beans, chickpeas, or lentils, but jailers often pilfered the beef. Family and friends could bring food to supplement the diet, but only twice a month. The results of this prison regimen were predictable: rampant tuberculosis, scurvy, conjunctivitis, rheumatism, and intestinal diseases.[92]

Invasion of privacy was the rule at Juárez Penitentiary. Warden Leonardo Bolados Garza opened and read all mail. Prisoners were not permitted to receive newspapers, and the library opened by Governor Peón Machado in the mid-1890s was now off-limits to inmates. The work therapy heralded by prison authorities amounted to little more than slave labor. While workers did receive 40 centavos for each hammock they made, they had to pay for the thread, which was so sensitive to the extreme indoor humidity that it regularly broke on the looms. By the time a hammock was finished,

Rendón reported, it had cost prisoners more than the pittance they earned. Finally, prisoners had only limited access to their lawyers. During his three-month nightmare, Rendón never even saw the prison oversight board that was supposed to compile prisoners' complaints.[93]

Clearly, despite Juárez Penitentiary's thoroughly modern veneer and reformist agenda, its treatment of prisoners was entirely consistent with the disciplinary strategies that the state employed to limit dissent. In a Foucaultian sense, then, Juárez, like Lecumbérri and its contemporary European counterparts, represented merely one of several social institutions in which diverse "disciplinary techniques" were deployed to regulate or "normalize" behavior and preserve the existing social order.[94]

## The Porfiriato's Achilles Heel

Thus did the political-economic model elaborated in Mexico City and implemented by Yucatán's own *científico* clique ultimately prove as destabilizing in the peninsula as everywhere else in Mexico. With no political freedom and no real share in Porfirian growth, the majority of Yucatecos in Mérida and the countryside, like Mexicans elsewhere, found the Porfirian formula of Order and Progress too costly to follow. As we will see, the Molinista *camarilla* managed to ride out the seasons of upheaval that threatened the oligarchical order between 1909 and 1913, but the economic and political promise of the Pax Olegariana was shattered long before the Molinistas were defeated by Alvarado's Constitutionalist revolutionary army in 1915.

We would therefore contend that Porfirian Yucatán and its capital city experienced a late-century transformation that was quintessentially modern in terms of its origins, ideology, and consequences. The urban histories of most of Mexico's other provincial capitals still remain to be reconstructed. We would expect that their elites, like those of Mérida, undertook urban renewals inspired by, and often strikingly congruent with, the blueprint of the national metropolis. In the process, these provincial oligarchs no doubt encountered many of the same problems that Yucatán's plutocracy experienced as it sought to tailor Mexico City's pattern to the rigors of the regional environment. And it is quite likely that these provincial elites elicited the same backlash and provoked much of the same popular discontent as their Yucateco counterparts.

The prevailing current in Mexican revolutionary historiography emphasizes popular agrarian insurgency as the key to understanding the essential character or "logic" of the revolution. Nevertheless, as Alan Knight, the doyen of the new populist interpretation, and other writers have documented, the greater rural upheaval that was unleashed in 1910 was often triggered by an earlier round of plotting and Maderista political activity in the republic's urban areas.[95] This being the case, it is high time we knew more about the late Porfirian city and its deepening political, economic, social, and ecological contradictions. The Porfirians hailed the nation's cities as both the engines and the showcases of their modernizing regime. Ironically, by 1909, given the problematic nature of their transformations, Mexico's provincial capitals had themselves become one of the *lados flacos* of the old order.

Of course, unrest was hardly confined to the state capital and its port. In the next chapter we turn our attention to the Yucatecan countryside, to examine the consequences that export monoculture had for estate workers and independent villagers alike.

## CHAPTER 6

# The Gathering Storm in the Countryside

Yes, they are aware! . . . Deep within them the indebted peons feel hatred and a desire for revenge against their masters and the authorities who helped their masters to enslave them!
—Tomás Pérez Ponce

A sensational interview in 1911 with that public defender and labor organizer extraordinare, Tomás Pérez Ponce, must have profoundly unsettled Yucatán's *henequeneros*, accustomed as they were to dictating the terms of debate both in the local press and on the estates.[1] Belittlingly dubbed "the peons' leader" in the planter press, Pérez Ponce now had the temerity to demand an end to debt peonage, freedom of movement for all agricultural laborers (*jornaleros de campo*), and wage increases for henequen workers.[2]

The upstart attorney observed in the interview—aptly titled "The Grave and Pressing Rural Question"—that the real evil driving this heinous labor regime was henequen monoculture. Arguing for diversification, he warned planters that unless the relentless pressure of monocrop production was tempered with the cultivation of corn and beans and perhaps even the return of cattle raising in the henequen zone, peons resident on the henequen estates (*peones acasillados*), tired of being tricked and exploited by landowners and politicians, were likely to resort to violence against their masters or else to flee the estates for nearby villages, *cabeceras*, or the state's urban centers.[3] Indeed, Pérez Ponce urged *jornaleros* to do just that—to forget about their "illegal" debts and abandon the haciendas. He even counseled that if district prefects should arrest and return peons to the estates, their relatives should contact him, and he would make sure that "the authorities upheld the laws."

Such blatant rabble-rousing would have been unthinkable a decade earlier. The publication of the interview in *El Ciudadano*, the organ of one of the planter factions opposing Molinista rule, signaled an elite recognition that the rural "labor problem" was something that needed to be addressed—at least rhetorically—if planters hoped to gain the support of influential political brokers and agitators such as Pérez Ponce. Of course, the labor mobility that Pérez Ponce advocated would have threatened the traditional tenor of Yucatecan monoculture, undermining the social relations of production in the henequen zone. If *jornaleros* left their estates for nearby villages and towns and became, in the regional vernacular of the day, *hombres libres* (free men), the world the *henequeneros* knew would turn upside down.

Pérez Ponce's diatribe attests to the cleavages that existed in late Porfirian Yucatán. Widespread rural discontent from 1907 on enabled disgruntled elites struggling for political control of the state to enlist hacienda peons and marginalized villagers, both in the henequen zone and on its periphery, to participate in a mosaic of jacqueries, riots, and rebellions that rocked the peninsula during the first years of the Mexican Revolution.

It is interesting that, perhaps because of comparisons with other Mexican regions that experienced more violent revolutionary histories, modern historians have consistently underestimated the resistance of Yucatán's peasantry before the overthrow of oligarchical rule by General Salvador Alvarado's Constitutionalist Army of the Southeast in March 1915. Particularly misunderstood is the social behavior and political consciousness of the *peones acasillados*. Unlike the Porfirian *hacendados* and their nemesis, Tomás Pérez Ponce, modern writers have dismissed the peons' capacity to oppose or protest the demands of their masters. To be sure, *henequeneros* effectively utilized both the carrot and the stick, blending paternalist incentives and a measure of security with restrictive mechanisms of coercion and isolation. It is hardly surprising, therefore, that their servants lacked the revolutionary potential—or, as Eric Wolf has put it, the "tactical mobility"[4]—manifested by the villagers, cowboys, miners, and *serrano* peasants who made up the revolutionary armies of central and northern Mexico.

By the same token, however, the *peones acasillados* who toiled on Yucatán's henequen estates were not inherently passive. Their characterization in the historical literature as a lumpen mass of docile retainers is a profound exaggeration. Ironically, such a portrayal harks back to the contemporary stereotypes put forward (for very different reasons) by foreign muckrakers and *henequenero* apologists alike.[5]

Our own research in the Ramo de Justicia of the Archivo General del Estado de Yucatán prompts a very different characterization of the late Porfirian peasantry. It recasts prevailing notions about resident peons' inability to resist their masters. If henequen monoculture's characteristic structure of domination restricted the potential for self-generated insurrection on the estates, it still could not prevent *acasillados* from joining the revolts that originated on the periphery of the henequen zone during the early years of the revolutionary era. Moreover, although Yucatecan peons were not as overtly rebellious as villagers outside the henequen zone, this does not mean that they did not resist the monocultural regime. On the contrary, their personal testimonies, as well as other local documentation, suggest that they partook of quieter, "everyday forms of resistance" that were, in the long run, safer and more successful for contesting materially and symbolically the exploitative aspects of henequen monoculture.

The goals of this chapter are threefold: first, to make explicit the structure of domination of planter and state that hampered the prospects for mobilization in the henequen zone during the fiber boom; second, to examine the range of "routine" or "everyday" responses that peons made to monoculture's escalating demands; and third, to paint, with broad strokes, the social contradictions that fueled repeated cycles of unrest throughout the Yucatecan countryside during the final years of the Porfiriato. First, however, let us briefly characterize the henequen estate, focusing on the special problem that monoculture presented for labor relations.

## A Hybrid Institution

The largely self-contained world that Yucatecan *hacendados* and peons fashioned on henequen estates during the late nineteenth-century boom was rife with inconsistencies. The boom came so suddenly that the henequen estates could not erase vestiges of their predecessors, the cattle-and-maize haciendas that had dominated the northwestern region from 1750 to 1850. Moreover, unlike their more progressive Caribbean counterparts, the sugar plantations, henequen estates never evolved into modern commercial plantations during the boom.

Whereas the Caribbean sugar industry during this same period utilized new techniques to separate the agricultural and industrial sectors and thereby increased productivity and efficiency, Yucatecan *henequeneros* never substantially altered their means and factors of production. The agro-industrial sugar complex was characterized by corporate ownership, ample capitalization, profit maximization, and a variegated yet dependent labor force organized to supply a distant yet substantial market—all characteristics of the prototypical plantation. By contrast, Yucatán's syncretic henequen estate fell under the rubric of family ownership. It featured an entrepreneurial class that desired to follow in the footsteps of its forebears, entertaining lavish status aspirations that inhibited the reinvestment of profits. It faced chronic capital shortfalls brought on by volatile fluctuations in the world market price of fiber. The result was an estate geared to modern commercial operations but lacking a farsighted, sophisticated ownership and management class that could complete the transformation.[6]

While the henequen estate may have physically resembled a modern commercial plantation—with modern machinery, narrow-gauge tramways, and land-intensive cultivation of the staple crop—its family ownership, management, and mentality perpetuated the pre-henequen hacienda. Emblematic of a rural society in the midst of a complex transition, the henequen estate is best viewed as a hybrid. Moreover, the emergence of a full-fledged plantation society apparently was also inhibited by lingering vestiges of the earlier institution, particularly the way *hacendados* confronted their labor problems.

In the classic plantation model, corporate managers take advantage of a free (or relatively free) labor market and pay cash wages.[7] Unlike the hacienda, the modern plantation does not have to rely on debt or cultivate a paternalistic relationship. But the henequen estate, like the poorly capitalized corn-and-cattle hacienda, bound "labor by means other than money wages."[8] Landowners continued to rely on traditional labor practices, such as debt peonage and the hacienda store, to inhibit mobility and ensure a dependent labor regime. Coercive techniques such as naked force and the manipulation of debt were coupled with more subtle, indirect methods, such as the parceling out of subsistence plots and the "institutionalization of personal relationships between employer and employee."[9]

Given this preference for dependent labor, as well as the henequen boom's rapid takeoff, Yucatecan *henequeneros* faced the unenviable task of converting the traditional labor relations of the hacienda to the ironclad discipline required for henequen production. As the demands of international capitalism increasingly engaged and ultimately subordinated the henequen economy, labor conditions inevitably grew more rigorous. Overseers (*encargados*) and their Maya foremen drove work gangs of peons who cleared, planted, weeded, and harvested fiber year-round. The *desfibradora*, the henequen estate's industrial equivalent of the sugar mill, required disciplined teams of workers to decorticate and press thousands of henequen leaves a day.

What is interesting, however, is that the idiosyncratic nature of henequen production did not necessitate a battery of trained specialists to take care of specific agricultural and industrial tasks. Although technological advances would increase production capabilities, the henequen industry never demanded a skilled work force. Instead, it needed a large and flexible group of laborers to work in all phases of production as circumstances warranted. Because the fibrous agave was harvested throughout the year, unlike sugar, it required a permanent labor supply and ruled out—from management's point of view—more cost-efficient seasonal employment schemes.

In essence, henequen monoculture produced labor relations that in some ways resembled those of a rural proletariat (routinized work gangs, piecework, daily wages, and a quasi-cash economy) but in other ways continued to embody the earlier paternalism. Although working conditions on the henequen estate were certainly more onerous than those of its labor-extensive predecessor, the new hybrid continued to offer *peones acasillados* an essential measure of security, at least until the final years of the Porfiriato. The new land and labor arrangements meant that the Yucatecan Maya on the estate were now totally dependent on the master and his *en-*

*cargado* for food, firewood, water, famine relief, justice, protection, medical care, and other services. For these peons, life on the henequen estate represented a compromise of sorts: minimal security, but at the cost of their autonomy.

Yet if stability and security most concerned resident peons, *henequeneros* pursued a very different agenda, one that diminished their direct contact with their workers. Unlike their parents and grandparents, this generation of landowners saw their estates as business investments first and patrimonies second. Speculation in rural real estate—particularly during bust cycles in the regional economy—forced entrepreneurs to consider henequen haciendas as liquid assets. In this freewheeling investment climate, peons had difficulty maintaining a close relationship with their masters. While patron-client relationships did exist in the henequen zone, they never approached the level of sophistication that prevailed in the antebellum U.S. South, simply because most henequen producers never invested the time and effort required to nurture them. As the boom wore on, business investments multiplied, and mortgage credits were swapped at a dizzying pace, clientelistic bonds on the estate inevitably suffered.

The flagging paternalistic ethos and the incomplete transformation of the northwestern haciendas caused social tensions to run high among state authorities, *hacendados*, *encargados*, and peons. Although the mechanisms of social control utilized by estate managers and local authorities throughout the Porfiriato kept a lid on collective action, they did not prevent *peones acasillados* from demonstrating their unhappiness with the changing order.

## The "Idiom of Power"

Why did henequen workers obey their masters even to the degree they did during the Porfiriato? Force (or the threat of force) alone would not have kept the peons subservient.[10] Furthermore, armed repression cannot be applied everywhere at all times. While the fear of retribution is an essential ingredient of all coerced labor systems, force must be combined with an underlying obedience to authority to ensure compliance. The ultimate success of such asymmetrical systems has historically depended on the ability of elites to convince their workers that such an existence was, on balance, in their best interests. Even the most heinous forms of servitude have had elements that at least paid lip service to dependent workers' "rights" and needs.[11]

The subordinate classes must somehow be led to believe that such a repressive system is part of the logical, immutable order of things, and that collective action therefore is not a viable option. Moreover, as long as the subordinate classes do not compare their own lot with that of their masters (implicitly accepting their own inferiority), the prospects for rebellion are greatly diminished.[12]

To appreciate how obedience to authority was conveyed to *peones aca-sillados* by *henequeneros* during the Porfiriato, let us briefly focus on "idioms of power"; that is, on the various ways the coercive aspect of domination has been represented to subordinate classes throughout history.[13] In many premodern, traditional societies, force was presented directly, in face-to-face relations, most often transparently. Although this personalistic idiom of power was at times camouflaged by such strategies as *compadrazgo* (fictive kinship), paternalism, and asymmetrical gift exchanges, the superordinate and subordinate elements had little doubt that domination was the essence of the relationship.

More recently, a second, materialistic idiom of power emerged, in which the unequal relationship was represented as power over commodities rather than people. As modern capitalism evolved, labor-management relations became increasingly depersonalized, as both parties grew more detached from the commodities they produced. Dependency was "disguised under the shape of social relations between the products of labor."[14]

The social relations of henequen monoculture represent something of a halfway point along the continuum joining the personalistic and materialistic idioms of power. Just as the syncretic henequen estate combined characteristics of both the traditional hacienda and the commercial plantation, its labor relations represented an amalgam of the two modes of coercion. Indeed, many of the elements that constituted the personalistic idiom found in traditional societies—paternalism, *compadrazgo*, the ever-present agency of human force exemplified in floggings meted out by overseers—carried over to the new plantation society.

To illustrate more fully how henequen monoculture's idiom of power adapted some of the characteristics of traditional labor relations to the requirements of a more "proletarianized" regime, it is helpful to conceive of three complementary mechanisms of social control: isolation, coercion, and security. Underwritten by the state political apparatus, these mechanisms allowed *henequeneros* to maintain the disciplined work rhythms of monocrop production. Isolation, coercion, and security worked together to cement a structural relationship that suited not only the production requirements of management but also the subsistence needs of workers, at least until the eve of the Mexican Revolution.[15]

## ISOLATION

*Henequeneros* inculcated obedience to authority through their deft management of physical and social space. Utilizing four reenforcing spheres of isolation—we have conceptualized them as concentric circles in Figure 6.1—Yucatecan landholding elites and their ally, the state, effectively channeled and tied *jornaleros* to the haciendas while closing off other options and avenues of escape.

At the core of the isolation mechanism was the henequen hacienda

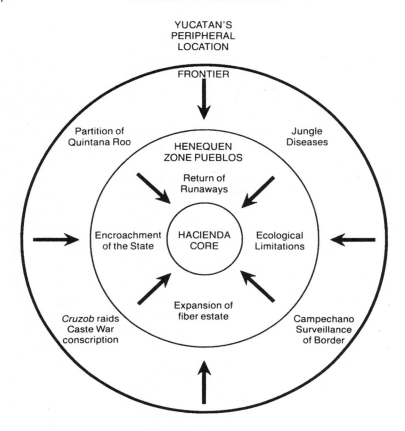

*Fig. 6.1.*   The isolation mechanism.

itself. *Peones acasillados* could leave the estate only with their *hacendado*'s or overseer's express written consent. A series of positive and negative inducements ensured that peons remained trapped on the estate. Workers were constrained by debt, the hacienda store, corporal punishment, arranged marriages, and identification papers; at the same time, their lot was made more tolerable by piecework wages, medical care, and funds advanced for weddings, funerals, and baptisms.

*Henequeneros* attempted to regulate workers' communication with the outside world. Although individual villagers were periodically granted access to the estate as part-time workers and, less frequently, as petty traders, landowners discouraged fraternization or intermarriage between their peons and residents of other estates and villages. Sometimes *hacendados* arranged marriages for their peons, not only to produce future laborers but to give workers a compelling reason to stay put. Recent studies of matrimonial records for a parish in the henequen zone between 1860 and 1900 revealed that the number of exogenous marriages between Maya of different villages and haciendas accounted for less than 15 percent of the total.[16]

*Hacendados* also altered housing patterns during the boom to maintain a dependent labor force. A recent study of three haciendas on the henequen zone's southwestern periphery, Tankuché, Uxmal, and San Simón, found that patrons purposefully resettled their peons closer to the center of the hacienda. Whereas workers' huts had previously been scattered throughout these estates, as the boom lengthened, planters consolidated these dwellings according to a grid pattern extending outward from the hacienda core.[17]

As a general rule, *hacendados* limited the access of city visitors and peddlers to their estates while keeping peons within their borders. Of course, Yucatán's primitive internal road system impeded such relationships and exchanges anyway. Finally, the heterogeneous composition of the work force augmented the prevailing climate of isolation. To meet escalating fiber demand after 1880, *henequeneros* diluted the majority of indebted Maya peons and village part-timers with admixtures of Yaqui deportees, indentured Asian immigrants, and contract workers and prisoners of war from central Mexico. The strategy of "importing" ethnic and linguistic strangers, whom the *henequeneros* euphemistically called "foreign colonists," addressed an endemic labor shortage, but also dampened possibilities for the creation of viable workers' communities.

Of course, *henequenero* power and influence transcended the physical boundaries of the estate. Proprietors regularly engaged bounty hunters and *jefes políticos*—the latter typically members of their extended families and clienteles—to return peons who escaped to urban areas or, more likely, to villages or neighboring estates. During the early years of the fiber boom, *henequeneros* advertised in Mérida's newspapers offering rewards for the return of escaped servants. Only when Mexico City journalists cited the advertisements as clear proof of the existence of slavery in the peninsula did these notices disappear.[18] The introduction of tram lines and telephone service on many estates after 1890 improved communication between *encargados* and district prefects and made it easier to apprehend runaway peons.[19]

So precarious was life in the zone's pueblos that they themselves collectively constituted a second, complementary sphere in the landowners' mechanism of isolation. That *henequeneros* could exercise their power so freely and that runaways had such bleak prospects for refuge suggests something of the villages' miserable existence during the late Porfiriato. As economic options narrowed and the social fabric of village life in the zone frayed, ever greater numbers of campesinos were channeled to the great fiber estates.

Quite simply, the logic of monoculture's expansion consigned traditional peasant life in the zone to oblivion. As the boom intensified, henequen cultivation required ever greater amounts of labor and land. Planters

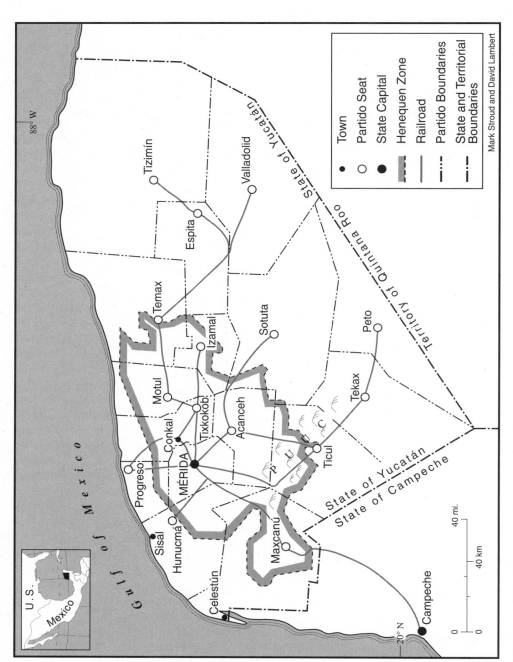

*Map 6.1.* Yucatán, ca. 1910.

bought out neighboring smallholders as much to acquire their labor as to expand production on their fields.[20]

*Henequeneros* were aided in absorbing these smallholdings by the agrarian policy of the oligarchical state. Under the provisions of the 1856 reform laws, all corporate forms of land ownership had been abolished, and village (*ejido*) lands were to be divided among heads of families, each receiving a small parcel. With the fiber boom under way, *hacendados* wasted no time in buying up *ejido* lands from individual heads of families throughout the zone. Sixty-six *ejidos*, totaling 134,000 hectares, were purchased by encroaching estates and given over to henequen cultivation between 1878 and 1912.[21] Sometimes disputes and violence accompanied the surveying and parceling of *ejidos*, particularly on the less controllable fringes of the henequen zone. Ultimately, however, villagers and smallholders were powerless to stop the expansion of the large estates.

Sooner or later, most of the villagers based in the zone went to work on the henequen estates as tenants, part-time workers, or, most commonly, *peones acasillados*. Late nineteenth-century censuses reveal that the number of peons rose from 20,767 in 1880 to 80,216 in 1900, an increase of 386 percent in two decades.[22]

As the estates waxed, the henequen zone's Maya pueblos waned. The boom transformed not only the social relations of production on the henequen estate but also the cultural character and demographic composition of villages and *cabeceras*. Spanish authorities had stripped these pueblos of the wealth of their religious brotherhoods (*cofradías*) at the end of the colonial period. Now, the legislated erosion of village lands rendered obsolete the extended patrilineal kin networks that had sustained reciprocal labor exchanges and had underwritten a hereditary political-religious elite. By presiding over the yearly round of fiestas central to the community's religious experience, this Maya elite had orchestrated a syncretic Catholicism that culturally resisted white domination—promoting what Nancy Farriss has termed a "collective enterprise of survival."[23] But by the end of the Porfiriato, many villages, lacking the collective human infrastructure that the traditional *ejidos* had provided, could not sustain that community or that resistance.

The hacienda's assault on the village's land, labor, and cultural resources was intensified by the state's increasing involvement in rural life, beginning in the last half of the nineteenth century. Increased taxes, frequent military levies, and arbitrary *corvée* labor obligations further undermined corporate village bonds and weakened whatever symbiotic relationship had previously existed between the villages and the great estates. With some notable exceptions—such as Hunucmá, a *cabecera* 25 kilometers from Mérida that consistently and often violently opposed both hacienda encroachment and state exactions—peasant villages in the henequen zone were reduced to a shadow of their former, semiautonomous selves by the end of the Porfiriato.

Those campesinos who opted to stay in pueblos, now bereft of land and with only the most fragile sense of community, found it increasingly difficult to sustain themselves. Most were forced to accept irregular work on the neighboring henequen estates, where they were paid the piece rate for cutting henequen leaves or clearing new fields. A lucky few found work at the railway station loading bales of henequen fiber onto the rolling stock. Others took jobs in the state militia (national guard) returning runaway peons to neighboring haciendas or enforced tax collection and road *corvée* for the *jefe político*. Still others worked in local mercantile establishments or wove henequen hammocks and bags to be sold in Mérida. Sometimes villagers had to combine several of these tasks as they struggled to maintain a marginal existence as "free men."

The region's ecological limitations further exacerbated conditions for villagers.[24] The northwest's foundation of porous limestone rock made water an even more precious commodity than land. With no rivers and only a few scattered sinkholes to draw from, Yucatecos tapped water from deep underground canals with the assistance of costly pumps and windmills. The growth of large landholdings during the boom concentrated scarce water resources in the hands of aggrandizing *henequeneros*, giving them one more tool to recruit villagers for their work force.

Even where water was not a problem, the dearth of topsoil often was. Low corn yields were a persistent problem for Maya campesinos.[25] The intense demand for firewood by the steam-driven decorticating machines, as well as the railroad locomotives, led to the deforestation of the henequen zone, diminishing much-needed shade for corn and beans.[26] Yet another scourge were the recurring locust plagues.

Faced with meager employment opportunities and an inhospitable social and physical environment in the surrounding pueblos, most campesinos made an economically rational decision in opting to reside on the haciendas. Not only did the estate provide work and life's basic necessities (corn, water, and firewood), it also offered legal exemptions from military levies and road work.

And in reality, the henequen zone presented few viable alternatives. Even flight to Mérida or Progreso, the principal urban centers, offered runaway peons or beleaguered villagers little advantage. A Maya campesino might find temporary refuge in the rapidly growing slums. But with little knowledge of Spanish or of the city, no job, and the all-too-visible gnarled hands of a leaf cutter, the *jornalero* would ultimately prove an easy target for the authorities to discover.[27] If he were lucky, he might be returned to his estate to be whipped or jailed; otherwise, he might find himself dragooned into the state militia by a district prefect in search of able bodies to fill his quota (*la leva*).

A third reenforcing sphere of isolation further reduced the possibility of escape from henequen cultivation. No longer could these Maya campesinos find refuge in the open southeastern forest.[28] The brutal midcentury Caste

War had effectively precluded that possibility by dividing the peninsula into two distinct zones: the northwestern zone of commercial agriculture, dominated by white Yucatecan elites, and the dense forest of the southeast, the last refuge of the rebel Maya. Even at the turn of the century, much of the southeast was still held by the implacable, marauding *cruzob* and the somewhat more tractable, semiautonomous *pacíficos*. And even if the acculturated northwestern Maya could somehow make their way to the forest, past all the obstacles imposed by state authorities, they would find little in common with their now culturally distinct brethren. It is not surprising, then, that despite vast extensions of cheap, fertile land, the southeast remained undeveloped, a virtual no-man's-land during the second half of the nineteenth century.

One of the peninsular authorities' major preoccupations during the boom was to keep the northwestern henequen zone safe from *cruzob* incursions. From a Maya villager or peon's perspective, however, *mala suerte* meant being taken to the frontier to serve on the state militia's first line of defense against the *cruzob* in remote hamlets like Xoccén or Chemax. As we have seen, when President Díaz sent a federal army to root out the *cruzob* once and for all, in 1901, he insisted that Yucatecan troops participate in the "pacification" campaign. More than two thousand Yucatecans perished in the military expedition, the majority of them Maya villagers from the henequen zone.[29]

To motivate those Maya to serve in the extended campaign against the *cruzob*, as well as to further their unquestioning acceptance of white rule in the northwest, the *henequenero* elite effectively reinvented the prevailing terms of regional ethnicity. For decades they worked assiduously to accentuate in their discourse the differences between the northwestern Maya and their estranged *cruzob* brethren; simultaneously they attempted to bridge the cultural chasm that separated them from their Maya subordinates. For example, during the darkest days of the Caste War, when Maya rebels besieged the whites in Mérida, those peons and villagers who fought with the whites or performed essential tasks for their troops were accorded the title *hidalgo* for their efforts.[30] Then, once the whites had gained the upper hand and the so-called *indios bravos* had retreated into the bush across the Quintana Roo and Campeche frontiers, the Maya who remained in the northwestern hacienda zone came to be known euphemistically as mestizos. Thus, at least in the realm of official discourse, the classification of Indian ceased to exist in Yucatán.[31]

Although northwestern villagers and peons would come to refer to themselves before the turn of the century as mestizos or *macehuales* or campesinos, or simply as *pobres*, and rarely as *indios* or Maya, they held few illusions that the *dzules*—the *señores*, their white masters—regarded them as anything other than *indios ignorantes y borrachos* (stupid, drunken Indians).[32] These were certainly the terms planters often used in their "offstage" descriptions of their workers; the same terms repeatedly found their way into contemporary criminal court records.[33] The classic and revealing planter aphorism regarding the Maya work force was *El indio no oye sino por las nalgas*, a sardonic justification of the lash best translated in polite company as "The Indian only hears with his backside."[34]

Yet if the northwestern Maya would not be hoodwinked into answering the state's patriotic appeals to fight the *cruzob*, even the fabled ferocity of the *indios bravos*, so indelibly etched in the regional consciousness of all classes, worked to reduce campesino options and channel workers into monoculture. Males between the ages of 15 and 60 were required to serve in the militia each year. Exemptions from the dreaded *leva* could be secured in only three ways: paying a set fee or finding a replacement to serve; having a debilitating illness (a doctor's affidavit was required as proof); or being classified as a permanent laborer attached (read: indebted) to a hacienda.[35] Because the first option was typically out of reach for many campesinos and securing a medical certificate also cost dearly, villagers who wished to avoid military service on the frontier or in the state militia often found refuge (in debt) on the hacienda.

Thus the encroaching state and the local interests it often served created a mechanism that aided the federal government in its campaign to eliminate the *cruzob*, even as it ensured *henequeneros* a permanent labor force. Significantly, the conscription statutes gave villagers the illusion of a choice by making it appear that they themselves chose servitude on the estate over "freedom" in the pueblos.

Villagers' "choices" were further circumscribed in 1902 when the national government officially partitioned the peninsula, creating the federal territory of Quintana Roo. The pacified interior was now transformed into a vast federal prison for Mexican criminals, recalcitrant deserters, and Yaqui prisoners of war. Opponents of the Díaz regime served their sentences in malarial labor camps patrolled by the federal army, cutting mahogany and cedar trees or working on government-sponsored chicle concessions. Yucatán's southern neighbor, Campeche, provided no better prospects. Campeche was essentially a scaled-down version of Yucatán during the Porfiriato, complete with henequen haciendas, its own *leva*, a similarly hostile frontier, and a state militia patrolling the border with a keen eye out for wayward *jornaleros*. In short, the peninsula's outer rim hemmed in villagers like a vise, making them aware that their best option was steady work on henequen haciendas.

Finally, Yucatán's remoteness from the rest of Mexico constituted a fourth circle of isolation that buttressed the idioms of power conveyed by *henequeneros* and state authorities. As far as localistic Maya campesinos were concerned, Yucatán was an island unto itself. Even if campesinos had wanted to leave their homes and their *patrias chicas* entirely (and they did not, for any number of culturally sound reasons), they would have found it very difficult. Railway or road connections with the rest of the nation would not be realized until well after World War II. At the turn of the century, the only way to reach the Mexican mainland was an irregular steamship service with the port of Veracruz. Geography reenforced the overarching control mechanism by constricting freedom of movement for Yucatán's laboring classes.

If that lack of mobility tied the Yucatec Maya to the henequen zone, Yucatán's distance from the capital diminished the campesinos' prospects for social justice. Existing documentation suggests that the federal government turned a deaf ear to campesino complaints during the Porfiriato. Until his celebrated visit to the peninsula in 1906, Díaz remained very much an abstraction to most Yucatecan country people. Among the tens of thousands of letters written to the president during his long tenure, only a handful came from Yucatecan villagers (and fewer still from *peones acasillados*).[36] Although the Porfirian polity was hierarchical and based on patronage, it seems clear that the Maya felt excluded from that hierarchy. They seldom took the opportunity to appeal directly to the *Gran Patrón* in Mexico City, although, no doubt, many peons would have felt too constrained even to think about doing so.

On the occasions when campesinos did find a sympathetic lawyer to set down their grievances in a letter, their chances of receiving a meaningful response from the dictator were slim. Díaz generally answered all mail in a perfunctory and cryptic manner; many letters apparently elicited no response at all.[37] The dictator's evident disdain for purely local matters seems to have been matched only by his constituents' unwillingness to petition their grievances to a higher authority. Yucatecan campesinos during the Porfiriato did not exhibit the same feeling their ancestors did for their colonial sovereign, the king of Spain. Reverence for the presidential office was conspicuous by its absence. Particularly after 1910, the Maya looked to local institutions, such as the judicial system, to seek redress for unjust treatment.

In sum, four concentric circles of isolation acted like magnetic poles, creating a force field that propelled campesinos (and wayward peons) away from the pueblos, Mérida, and the southeastern interior and toward the fiber estates. This was accomplished most often by diminishing the attractiveness and feasibility of other choices. The mechanism of isolation not only predisposed *jornaleros* to obey hacienda authority and facilitated the coercive aspect of power relations; it also gave villagers a distorted view of the henequen estate, making it appear more secure than their own emiserated pueblos.

It is important to keep in mind that the mechanism of isolation did not completely take away independent villagers' ability to make decisions about their own (and their families') future. Such circumscribed choices— whether to accept resident status, hire out as a part-time worker, or stay put in the declining villages of the henequen zone—gave Maya campesinos the sense that they were independent actors involved in a decision-making process, even if the options framed by the landholding elite and the state amounted to little more than a choice of the lesser of evils. Those who did opt for permanent resident status on the henequen estate came up against the mechanism of coercion, which exploited their labor through an effective combination of the personalistic and materialistic idioms of power.

## COERCION

If the isolation mechanism gave the northwestern Yucatec Maya a somewhat illusory set of choices, the messy business of coercion reminded resident peons on the estates that naked force could and would be used against them if disciplined work rhythms were not maintained. But even coercion was a variegated mechanism, imparted sometimes with cathartic fury and other times more subtly to intimidate or "make an example." It was this ambiguous quality that conveyed diffused images of power to *jornaleros*.

Like the sugar plantations of the Caribbean, the henequen estate was a world unto itself. With the state's blessing, *hacendados* fashioned a powerful extralegal system of justice to reenforce the estate's relative isolation. Overseers—referred to variously as *encargados*, *mayordomos*, or *personeros* in the haciendas' account books—answered only to their employers, who on average visited their properties one weekend a month.[38] As a result, until the national Madero rebellion opened up greater political space, peons rarely registered complaints of *encargado* brutality or other abuses to unsympathetic state authorities on the outside.

The personalistic idiom of power was most transparently represented by corporal punishment. Whipping was believed to be an overseer's most effective tool in controlling his laborers. The most graphic representation of this venerable practice is found in a photograph that appeared in Henry Baerlein's muckraking account, *Mexico: Land of Unrest* (1914). The photograph displays the scarred back of a Maya servant on the hacienda of Don Rogelio Suárez, Olegario Molina's son-in-law.

*Encargados* inflicted the lash for a variety of reasons: insubordination, shirking, dissimulation, flight, and as the standard antidote against the generalized violence that was so much of a part of the daily routine on henequen haciendas. Whipping, after all, did not cost the *hacendado* his *jornaleros'* daily labor; placing them in the hacienda jail for any length of time did.[39] Thus the aphorism "The Indian hears only with his backside" was more than just black humor; it reflected a widespread belief among the dominant class that discipline needed to be reenforced by stern example. Governor Santiago Méndez reaffirmed this arrogant sentiment.

> As a rule the Yucatecan Indians are regarded as being meek, humble, and not easily stirred to ire and cruelty; . . . the most customary punishment among them was a whipping applied with moderation. This kind of punishment did not offend them, if they were informed of the reason why it was meted out to them, nor did they consider it degrading.[40]

Although we now recoil at the idea, the notion that flogging "in moderation" reenforced discipline at the workplace and served as an effective tool of social control was shared by many *encargados*.[41] Maya *jornaleros*, another observer commented, were "docile, obedient, and compliant with their master's orders, the application of a few strokes being, in the last resort, invariably effective."[42] The *henequeneros'* rationalization implied an unmistakable message to the laboring classes: *jornaleros* were subordinates who required, indeed expected the lash, just as children expect to be disciplined by their parents. In Yucatán, this explicit dehumanization took on a racist character because *mayordomos* and other managers invariably had Spanish surnames, while henequen workers were mostly Yucatec Maya.

Resident peons contested whippings in only a small number of cases. The record of one of them demonstrates why such episodes were rarely brought before the state judiciary. In 1912 the stepparents of a sixteen-year-old servant who was whipped for insubordination took the *mayordomo* of a small hacienda in Sotuta district to court. As the case unfolded, however, the plaintiffs retracted their original story and said that the *mayordomo* was only disciplining their unruly stepson, who sorely needed it. The stepmother actually contradicted her own earlier testimony, denying that the boy had been whipped, despite a medical affidavit filed by the plaintiffs corroborating the corporal punishment. Needless to say, the charges were dropped. While we may never know exactly what happened, the implications are clear: the *hacendado* (in this case, Hernando Ancona Pérez) had so many ways to "convince" his servants of the importance of settling their affairs outside the courts that few *acasillados* sought to press their rights as Mexican citizens.[43] This minimal recourse to legal redress by resident peons stands in sharp contrast to the practice of free villagers on the fringes of monoculture, who regularly petitioned judicial authorities with their grievances.

Hacienda "justice," or coercion, was further dispensed through hacienda jails, which were designed to lock up peons temporarily for infractions. Alcoholism was a pervasive problem; many peons who created disturbances while intoxicated found themselves sleeping off their binges in the jail. On Hacienda Tamanché, along the road from Mérida to Progreso, the jail attached to the hacienda store was not much larger than a cell for solitary confinement. With low ceilings and only two small windows to counteract the stifling tropical heat, it must have made even a short stay a hellish experience.[44]

Two indispensable components of the *henequeneros'* personalistic idiom of power that were adapted from the traditional cattle-and-corn hacienda were the debt mechanism and its complement, the hacienda store. Together, these institutions reenforced henequen workers' immobility. An 1882 state law, the *Ley agrícola industrial del estado de Yucatán*, reiterated earlier peonage laws, stipulating that the peon who left work without paying the sums he owed might be legally prosecuted. In addition, if an indebted servant escaped and took refuge on another estate, the landowner who hid the servant could be arrested.[45] By contrast, Article 5 of the 1857 Constitution stated, "no one shall be obliged to render personal service without proper compensation and full consent," a clause that should have rendered debt servitude illegal. It was ignored by elites, who breached the spirit of the federal law by euphemistically justifying debt peonage as a "simple contract convenient to both parties."[46]

Debt was, after all, an established labor practice dating back to colonial rule that historically had permeated social relations throughout the peninsula. The peon had two running debts: *chichán cuenta* and *no hoch cuenta*. The former was a small debt for daily purchases and weekly wages; the latter was a large account used for important rites of passage, such as marriages, baptisms, or establishing a household, from which a servant rarely extricated himself. Indeed, debt peonage was so ingrained in local labor practices that Yucatecan railway entrepreneurs utilized the institution to limit the mobility of their own scarce labor force. Local legal statutes, moreover, accepted the valuation of workers' debts as a legitimate expense, thereby granting the practice further legitimacy, not to mention a financial advantage. Specifically, Article 2030 of the state civil code stipulated that peons' debts should be included in a property's inventory. Néstor Rubio Alpuche, a prominent local lawyer, put it bluntly in an 1895 legal brief: "In Yucatán, loose teams of peons do not exist. . . . A hacienda that does not have persons obligated by personal contract . . . is not worth anything."[47]

If debt labor was an established practice, what intensified during the boom was *henequeneros'* compelling need to make sure that their *jornaleros'* debts were never paid off.[48] As a result, the relatively mild relations that had characterized the pre-henequen labor regime hardened. *Henequeneros* now enlisted the aid of the burgeoning state bureaucracy. Local justices of the peace and district-level *jefes políticos* cooperated to make it difficult for debtors to find relief in the court system. In many cases, collaboration was cemented by kinship ties between *hacendados* and state officials.

The case of Juan Bautista Chan provides a useful illustration of such collaboration among elites. By 1912, Chan, a *peón acasillado* on Hacienda San José in Hoctún municipality, had run up a debt of about four hundred pesos. He fled San José (for unspecified reasons) and took up residence in a distant pueblo, Tahmek. According to him, he tried to pay off his debt by giving the sum to Tahmek's justice of the peace, Segundo Sergio Echeverría.[49] The judge refused to accept the payment because the matter was out of his jurisdiction, and advised the peon to go back to Hoctún and pay the debt at the business office of his own *hacendado*, the politically powerful Aurelio Gamboa. Chan's lawyer pointed out that his client had a legal right to repay the debt at the venue of his choice, and petitioned the state court of appeals to order the judge to accept the payment. For his part, Justice Eche-verría denied that he had ever seen Chan and paraded witnesses before the court who supported his contention. Not surprisingly, the higher court found for the judge. The case implicitly illustrates the collegial relationship between *henequeneros* and the court system and indicates how difficult it was for *acasillados* to repay their debts, even in those rare instances when they could. It also suggests that Chan was unwilling to return to Hoctún because he might be snared by local authorities in cahoots with Gamboa and remanded to Hacienda San José.

If authorities worked hand in glove with *henequeneros* to preclude re-payment of debts, the hacienda store *(tienda de raya)* offered an excellent opportunity to increase those debts. Peons' wages were paid in scrip re-deemable at the hacienda store.[50] Workers had little access to "real" money; the wages they earned were deducted from a running account that was rarely repaid.[51]

Conceivably, the peon never had to leave the sanctuary of the hacienda. In terms of convenience, the store offered a wide variety of goods, including food, unfinished cloth, and household items; shotguns and gunpowder for hunting; and last but by no means least popular, liquor. Account books from the Compañía Agrícola del Cuyo y Anexas, S.A., a multifaceted enterprise in the eastern hinterlands, testify to the considerable income that a cantina attached to the *tienda de raya* generated for its owners.[52]

While some estates had no such facilities on the premises, most ha-ciendas sold cane liquor *(aguardiente)* to their workers. Social critics, fond of needling Governor Molina for his blue-nosed temperance exhortations to Yucatán's laboring classes, gleefully pointed out this apparent hypocrisy. *Hacendado* Manuel Arrigunaga y Gutiérrez de Estrada was firmly con-vinced that alcoholism on henequen estates was rising during the fiber boom. (Even a cursory reading of the era's criminal records bears him out.) In a report presented to the Cámara Agrícola in 1908, Arrigunaga exhibited the characteristically patronizing rhetoric shared by many of his colleagues: "Money in Indian hands come Sunday, with *aguardiente* available, can only mean a day of excess followed by an evening of want. . . . The head of the household, his wife and children soon find themselves at week's end living on loans and handouts."[53]

A flexible mechanism of coercion that combined elements of corporal punishment, a proprietary, extralegal system of justice, debt peonage, and the hacienda store was thus a powerful weapon in the *henequenero*'s arse-nal of social control. And the juxtaposition of such personalistic institu-tions, singularly and in combination, with the materialistic mode of pro-duction enforced on the estates fostered henequen monoculture's greatest social contradictions. Because the ultimate goal remained the maximi-zation of fiber production, however, *hacendados* understood that heavy-handedness could be overdone, and that force was often most effectively applied "in moderation." That is why coercive institutions such as debt and the *tienda de raya* were closely linked to another more amenable mechanism, security.

SECURITY

Resident peons had to be induced to think that the estate's social relations, as exploitative as they were, offered them something more than an occasional whipping and a lifelong debt. The co-optative security mechanism was the "flip side" of isolation and coercion: it provided something tangible—a fundamental security of subsistence[54]—in return for the peons' labor. As one student of peonage explains: "peons stayed on the plantations (maltreatment notwithstanding) because it was a rational as well as a customary thing to do."[55]

By providing a continuous supply of imported corn, beans, and meat at the store and by diminishing the *acasillados'* ability to provide for their families, *hacendados* ensured that they alone controlled the means of subsistence in the henequen zone. After 1880, with monoculture's bounteous profits plainly in view, many *henequeneros* eschewed self-sufficiency and rapidly converted their estates' corn plots to henequen.[56] The higher prices of imported Mexican and foreign corn notwithstanding, it made good business sense to purchase the basic foodstuffs to feed *peones acasillados* from grain merchants in Mérida. With imported corn now available at the hacienda store, *henequeneros* no longer needed to provide corn plots (*milpa*), which, in addition to removing land from henequen cultivation, cost them labor time as well.

The loss of *milpa* had far-reaching social implications for both *acasillados* and villagers in the henequen zone. Corn cultivation had been central to Maya cultural identity for millennia. The gradual loss of their *milpa*, like the loss of the *ejidos*, not only deprived campesinos of the sense of community they enjoyed in planting and harvesting their fields; it also created serious nutritional problems for their families. Arrigunaga noted that imported grain was just too expensive to use as feed for the pigs and fowl that many campesinos kept to supplement their diet. The problem of protein deficiency was further exacerbated in 1884, when state authorities prohibited small groups of campesinos from hunting. The law was enacted to keep shotguns out of Maya hands and to diminish the prospect of rebellion—another communal activity that had been practiced throughout the peninsula since the colonial era. The 1884 edict required peons to obtain written consent from *hacendados* or *mayordomos* to hunt on their lands.[57]

Henequen workers complained bitterly about the poor quality of imported corn. Some called it rancid and mistakenly believed that it encouraged outbreaks of pellagra, a nervous disorder caused by a vitamin B deficiency. Nevertheless, by 1910 imported maize had supplanted homegrown as the staple of the Yucatecan campesino's diet.[58]

TABLE 6.1
*Corn Cultivation in the Henequen Zone,*
*1896–1912*

| Partido | Average hectares cultivated |
|---|---|
| Acanceh | 2,332 |
| Hunucmá | 4,515 |
| Izamal | 4,225 |
| Maxcanú | 3,461 |
| Mérida | 579 |
| Motul | 1,800 |
| Progreso | 313 |
| Temax | 2,792 |
| Tixkokob | 1,073 |
| Henequen zone overall | 2,343 |
| Outside henequen zone | 5,683 |
| Yucatán | 3,805 |

SOURCE: For 1896–1901, *BE*; for 1907–12, *DY*, Feb. 22, 1910; *EA*, 1907–8; *BE*, 1908–10.

NOTE: Reliable data exist for individual *partidos* for 1897–1901, 1908–10, and 1912. Data on Yucatán's average cultivation include these years plus 1896 and 1907. Las Islas *partido*, part of Yucatán before the 1902 partition, was factored out for 1896–1901. *Partido* averages computed and rounded off by the authors. Caution: these figures represent *milpa* planted on haciendas and in villages, not final production figures. Unfortunately, data on statewide corn production were too erratic to prove statistically useful.

Significantly, the entrepreneurial brokers of this profitable trade in foreign corn were the very same *casas exportadoras* that bought the *henequeneros'* fiber. The losers, again, were the villagers of the henequen zone, who for more than a century had enjoyed an appreciable market, selling the surplus maize and beans from their *milpas* to the nearby haciendas. Monoculture's infrastructure—the four railway lines that articulated agricultural zones with Mérida and the port of Progreso—abetted the economic decline of the zone's pueblos, transporting imported corn, beans, and beef from the port throughout the peninsula. According to the *Boletín de Estadística*, from 1894 to 1914, Yucatán imported 493,279,979 tons of corn.[59]

By about 1910, corn cultivation in the zone was in an irreversible decline. Production levels for zone *partidos*, such as Maxcanú, Mérida, Motul, and Tixkokob, demonstrate the extent to which the tentacles of monoculture had choked *milpa* lands in the northwest (see Table 6.1). The zone's cultivation figures pale in comparison with those of the "fringe" *partidos*. Indeed, in districts where henequen did not overrun the countryside and where peasant communities remained relatively intact (*partidos* such as Tekax, Valladolid, Ticul, Espita, Tizimín, and Sotuta), the average cultivation of maize more than doubled that of the henequen zone. Whereas a half-century earlier the northwestern *partidos* had supplied the product of primary necessity to peripheral districts, now they imported it. Thus the parasitic henequen economy not only siphoned labor and land from henequen-zone villages but also denied those communities a meaningful role in the wider regional economy, effectively condemning them to a slow and painful economic death during the Porfiriato. And obviously, with corn no longer plentiful in village communities, the hacienda store's abundant reserves took on greater importance as a tactic in the *hacendado*'s overall strategy to lure and tie workers to the estate.

The shift away from the *milpa* also must have undermined the division of labor among campesino families. As long as the *hacendado* permitted the peons access to their cornfields and extended the privileges of hunting and purchasing alcohol for leisure consumption, the male peon could provide for his family and enjoy a small measure of autonomy. By the close of this period, however, the ability to provide primary necessities for the nuclear family, tenuous in the best of times, was out of the indebted peon's hands.[60]

Also figuring in the mechanism of security was the tepid brand of paternalism practiced on henequen estates. As we have seen, Yucatecan *hacendados* were, for the most part, absentee landlords who left the daily operation of their haciendas to their overseers. The *jornalero* typically directed his problems, complaints, and requests to a hired employee. Conscientious planters occasionally visited their estates on weekends, preferring to spend the rest of their time in Mérida, where they could monitor their myriad investments and enjoy the cultural amenities of urban life. This is not to say that certain Yucatecan *hacendados* did not take a special interest in their peons, or that paternalistic relationships based on mutual obligations and responsibilities did not exist in Porfirian Yucatán. The institution of *compadrazgo*, or fictive kinship, for example, tied the peon somewhat loosely to his master.[61]

Perhaps masters and servants did find common ground in their perceptions of the role Maya women should play on the estates.[62] First and foremost, they agreed on the necessity of a rigid division of labor. *Acasillados* toiled in the fields, performing all the tasks related to planting, harvesting, and processing fiber on the estates. If daughters or wives occasionally worked in the fields to remove the spines from the henequen leaves after cutting (just as they had helped in the past with harvesting the *milpa*), they were accompanied by their fathers or husbands and were never paid in scrip for their labors. Those males who continued to have access to *milpa* not only tended their plots but also conducted the sacred Maya religious ceremonies associated with cultivating the grain. Men, moreover, hunted to supplement the family diet, although, as we have seen, the state sought to curtail that activity as the boom progressed.

Not surprisingly, women on henequen estates were relegated to the domestic sphere. Their tasks centered on raising the family, cooking, cleaning, retrieving water from the well and firewood from the forest, bringing lunch to their husbands in the fields, and tending the fruits and vegetables in the family garden. Ledger books occasionally listed women as domestics who worked in the landlord's "big house" or as hammock and sack makers and corn grinders; but they were not identified as henequen workers. Indeed, it appears that the fiber boom brought little change to the campesinas' regimen, for this strictly observed division of labor on the estates was consistent with pre-boom patterns. Even at the boom's height, when planters were desperate for workers, Maya women apparently were not used in the fields.

Why was this the case? Planters regularly complained about the scarcity of labor in the henequen zone and, as we have seen, did not shrink from employing coercive strategies when it suited their purposes. Christopher Gill and Piedad Peniche Rivero, who have begun the task of investigating gender relations in the henequen zone during the boom, both emphasize that masters and peons alike sought to maintain the patriarchal order. By permitting the peon to earn "wages," to provide for his family through access to *milpa* and hunting (during the early stages of the boom), and to exercise "de jure and de facto power over women in his household," the *hacendado*, according to Gill, was securing the loyalty—and limiting the mobility—of his worker.[63] As a consequence, families were rarely separated in the henequen zone; nor, apparently, did *hacendados* use the threat of separation to ensure loyalty—even if children were sometimes taken to planters' homes in Mérida to work as domestics.

*Henequeneros* applied a thin veneer of reciprocity, which formalized gender relations on the estates. When they arranged weddings for their peons, they provided grooms with a loan—their first debt—to pay for the religious and civil ceremonies and a fiesta. Victoria Catzín, a resident of Hacienda Santa María Campos, remembered, "On the hacienda, there was no such thing as [marrying for] love. The patron came and said to you, 'That man is going to be your husband.' And then he [the *señor*] would give you what you needed to work."[64] Neighboring villages occasionally provided prospective brides, but most marriage partners came from the same or nearby haciendas. A recent study of Umán parish records from 1860 to 1900 found that more than 70 percent of the marriages recorded were made within the hacienda system, and that most commonly it was the woman who moved to join her new husband.[65]

The result was a complicitous arrangement among males on the estate in which the master permitted the peon to preside over his own household as a subordinate patriarch. If this led to cases of domestic violence, they were most often handled circumspectly on the estate. Rarely did grievances find their way into the local courtroom. Typically, *hacendados* and overseers put gross offenders in the hacienda jail.

Such campesino patriarchy, however, had limits. Often the *henequenero* or his overseer invaded the peon's hut and violated his spouse or daughter, exercising the humiliating "right of first night." While such an affront undermined the reciprocal nature of the shared sense of patriarchy, it did provide the peon with one more object lesson in where power ultimately resided on the estate. The servant would seldom take revenge on his boss;

more often, we learn of unfortunate cases of misdirected rage, as *acasillados* abused their wives to reassert their dominion in the home.

Peniche Rivero argues that planters were reluctant to tamper with the peons' patriarchal control of their families because, in the long run, it suited their economic interests. As far as the *hacendado* was concerned, the principal task of Maya women was to procreate and raise the next generation of henequen workers. To permit women to work in the fields would undermine that role and upset social relations on the estate. At the same time, however, *hacendados* had little compunction about utilizing imported female contract laborers in the fields. Some planters boasted that Yaqui widows performed twice as much weeding as their Maya *acasillados*. Perhaps because female contract laborers worked for a fixed period of time and were not perceived to be an integral part of the hacienda community, planters were more willing to break with tradition and maximize their investment.[66]

At any rate, it would be a mistake to assume that either paternalism or a shared ethos of patriarchy ever fostered strong bonds of attachment, let alone cultural understanding, between the acculturated Maya and their masters.[67] The Maya servant and the *dzul* were separated by a cultural polarity that undermined trust.

A clear example of how that cultural divide weakened paternalism is reflected in the different perceptions of medical treatment between the *dzules* and the Maya during the Porfiriato. *Hacendados* provided a modicum of health care on the hacienda. Because doctors were not permanent fixtures on any save the largest estates, most servants when seriously ill were transported by train to their master's villa in Mérida, where the family doctor treated them until they recovered. If *acasillados* required admission to Mérida's O'Horan Hospital, the only legitimate medical facility in the state, they needed to be accompanied by their master or to have the written permission of hacienda authorities.[68] The rural Maya, however, were reluctant to entrust themselves to their master's personal doctor, let alone to a hospital, given what they regarded as culturally bewildering, even frightening, practices on the part of city doctors.

A case in point is the unfortunate story of Eleuteria Ek, a young girl growing up on Hacienda Santa Bárbara near Cansahcab in Temax *partido*. On October 8, 1907, Ciriaco Santos, the *mayordomo* of Santa Bárbara, demanded that the parents of the ailing twelve-year-old deliver her to the main house. Eleuteria was stricken with influenza, Santos later testified, and it was hacienda policy to isolate such contagions. Initially, Eleuteria's parents, Crisanto Ek and Micaela López (who was from nearby Cansahcab but now lived on the hacienda) refused to hand over their daughter, claiming that she was needed to help with household chores. According to their testimony, the *mayordomo*'s men then physically hauled Eleuteria off to the main house, warning the parents that they would be beaten if they continued to object. The next day, Eleuteria was taken by train to Mérida to receive medical treatment and to convalesce in the home of the *hacendado*, Pedro Luján.[69]

The scene—emotionally described in the parents' court testimony—of a child wailing hysterically as her mother and father watched helplessly at the train station in Cansahcab points up the different worlds of the rural Maya and their paternalistic masters. Although, as a rule, families were not broken up during the boom, Maya campesinos had legitimate reason to fear that once their children were taken to the master's residence in the capital, they might stay on there as domestic servants. Perhaps because she was a villager who had married and moved onto the hacienda, Micaela assertively filed the grievance with Cansahcab's justice of the peace. The judge granted the mother permission to go to Mérida to pick up her daughter and return her to the estate. The case record closes with an interesting affidavit from Micaela attesting that Eleuteria was well treated in Mérida—a reassuring judicial epitaph for an unsettling incident. Clearly, the court wanted it known that while the parents were permitted to bring their child home, the *hacendado*'s reputation also required that he be absolved from any suggestion of mistreatment.

Eleuteria's story graphically illustrates the lack of trust between Maya and *dzul*. Something as seemingly innocuous as medical treatment is inflected with cultural tensions that weaken rather than strengthen clientelistic bonding. Perhaps Nancy Farriss's observation on the colonial Yucatec Maya is apt for their more acculturated descendants of the late nineteenth and early twentieth centuries: "The Maya had no hospitals nor any desire for them, having come to the not wholly unfounded conclusion from their observations that these European institutions were for dying."[70]

It is ironic that Maya families harbored such suspicions precisely when the master's intentions were so overtly altruistic, however paternal. Apologists have taken great pains to laud benevolent *hacendados* who took care of ailing servants, either transporting them to their homes in Mérida or taking them personally to Hospital O'Horan.[71] Eleuteria's case and others like it call for a reexamination of paternalism on henequen estates; altruism may well be in the eyes of the beholder.

While the cultural dissonance between master and servant tempered patron-client relations, henequen monoculture's fundamental security of subsistence throughout most of the Porfiriato, coupled with the economic demise of nearby village communities, enlisted workers for and harnessed them to the disciplined work rhythms of fiber production. *Henequeneros'* skillful management of the three complementary mechanisms of social control—isolation, coercion, and security—kept *jornaleros* tied to the estates. Yet although *jornaleros* found themselves very much on the defensive during the boom, they often responded to the structure of domination in a number of creative ways.

## Forms of Resistance in the Henequen Zone

Formidable as it was, henequen monoculture's structure of domination did not—indeed, could not—completely deprive *peones acasillados* of the means to protest and express their humanity. Even the most coercive labor systems must have a certain amount of "play." The implementation of any means of social control, be it flogging, the use of identification papers, manipulation of the *leva*, or the operation of the court system, requires a measure of flexibility to achieve its ends. If the system of control is too rigid, its value is sure to diminish, because those for whom it is intended will increasingly contest its strictures. Not surprisingly, we have found that despite its coercive aspects, henequen monoculture's characteristic idiom of power still afforded resident peons a certain latitude to adapt to changing circumstances, tapping the cultural resources at their command. In the process, they became active agents in shaping the terms of their own oppression.

Here, our argument buttresses recent findings for the roughly contemporary slave regime that drove Cuba's sugar monoculture. Despite profound differences on other matters, both Manuel Moreno Fraginals and Rebecca Scott agree that Cuban slaves successfully forged a countervailing culture.[72] Even under the brutal working conditions found on sugar estates—where slaves would labor up to twenty hours a day during the harvest, literally sleepwalking among scalding boilers and dangerous machinery that cost limbs and lives—deracinated slaves did not acquiesce to, or allow themselves to be broken by, the treatment their masters meted out. Scott concludes, "Slaves could be cheated, yet participate in a money economy. They could be ill housed, yet struggle to maintain families. They could be treated worse than beasts, yet not become like beasts."[73]

Compared to the African-born and creole slaves who toiled on Cuban sugar plantations, Yucatán's resident Maya peons—who always made up the vast majority of the fiber estate's labor force—enjoyed distinct advantages that enhanced their capacity to resist. As we have seen, despite their isolation and subordination by the *dzules*, the northwestern Maya still possessed a distinct culture, based on nuclear and extended family units that were seldom broken up, and reenforced by syncretic religious beliefs and practices. Even the chronic labor scarcity that characterized the boom limited workers' movement among the estates. *Acasillado* family units lived in wattle-and-daub huts, not the gender-segregated, impersonal barracoons that held as many as two hundred slaves on large Cuban sugar plantations.

The Maya's cultural heritage was further reenforced by their language, which, throughout the Porfiriato, remained the lingua franca of the henequen zone. Yucatán outranked the rest of Mexico in its percentage of native speakers. While the national portion of Spanish-speaking inhabitants in 1895 was 83 percent, in Yucatán seven out of ten citizens spoke Maya.[74] At the very least, then, family cohesiveness and the persistence of language and cultural traditions offered the Maya a degree of solace and refuge against the ravages of an exploitative system.[75]

No doubt, the intensification of the labor regime during the boom impeded peons' ability to fashion a countervailing culture. Nevertheless, *henequeneros* continued to view potential Maya solidarity with some alarm and, as we have seen, they consciously diluted communities of Maya *acasillados* with groups of ethnic and linguistic strangers. Cuban sugar planters adopted a similar strategy, employing Chinese contract workers and even, during the Caste War, imported *cruzob* prisoners. Ultimately, however, neither master class succeeded in eliminating the cultural space that legitimized challenges to its hegemony. Yet it seems clear that Yucatán's indigenous Maya had a greater capacity for resistance than Cuba's slaves, many of whom were themselves "outsiders," uprooted and transplanted from abroad.[76]

Of course, the *forms* of resistance that Yucatán's peons were able to mount against monoculture were shaped by the relations of domination at particular historical junctures. Until the final years of the Porfiriato, Maya peons in the henequen zone, like their counterparts in more formal slave societies, rarely took the risks that attended violent collective action against the plantocracy. Given the multitiered repressive mechanism that the *henequeneros* fashioned in collaboration with the state, such jacqueries, insurgencies, or even just organized bandit operations were doomed to eventual defeat, if not violent suppression. To be sure, sporadic flare-ups did occur, signaling desperate local responses to particularly egregious abuses and typically provoking excessive retaliation. Yet by and large, Maya peons, like slaves in the U.S. South and the Caribbean, were not suicidal; they, too, appreciated that while "a man may perish by the sword . . . no man draws the sword to perish, but to live by it."[77] Moreover, other alternatives were open; more modest strategies by which *peones acasillados* could deal a blow, materially and symbolically, against the exactions and domination of their masters.

Such quieter or "everyday forms of resistance," as James C. Scott terms them, might include small, self-serving acts of noncompliance, footdragging, shirking, and flight; or more aggressive, clandestine acts of theft, arson, and sabotage. While social scientists have given it short shrift, this "small-arms fire of the class war," these "weapons of the weak" that act outside the bounds of organized movements, have always constituted the greatest part of peasant (and working-class) politics.[78] And as Scott persuasively argues, they have probably accomplished what futile armed resistance could not. They "confer immediate and concrete material advantages while at the same time denying resources to the appropriating classes."[79]

In the henequen zone, such "routine" resistance or "infrapolitics" was eminently suited to the highly controlled, socially heterogeneous plantation milieu. It required little planning and only a modicum of room to maneuver, and it could be carried out secretly by *jornaleros* acting alone or in the smallest, most informal of groups. Moreover, it avoided any direct (and inevitably costly) confrontation with the master or his overseers. The thrust of such resistance was not the impossible goal of overthrowing monoculture's system of domination, but of surviving—today, this week, this season—within it. For, as Eric Hobsbawm conceives it more generally, the campesinos' fundamental aim has always been to work "the system to their minimum disadvantage."[80]

Such day-to-day resistance poses a challenging methodological problem for the social historian. It is little noticed in the official records of the state because it does not generate the programmatic statements, violent encounters, and public demonstrations that tend to rivet the state's attention. Indeed, the perpetrators' goal is precisely not to draw attention to themselves. Moreover, state bureaucrats and local landowning elites have little interest in publicizing the incidence of campesino insubordination, for to do so would be to acknowledge unpopular policies and hegemonic limits in the countryside. Thus, with good reason, Scott argues that the historiography of class struggle has been "statolatrous." Minor, doomed revolts that have left an impressive paper trail continue to preoccupy scholars out of all proportion to their impact on class relations, while "unheralded acts of flight, sabotage, and theft that may be of greater long-run significance are rarely noticed."[81]

While social scientists like Scott engage in participant observation to understand such nonconfrontational strategies firsthand, historians are left with an incomplete written record that systematically understates everyday forms of resistance. For example, all but a few instances of shirking, dissimulation, and insubordination—the principal forms of protest by peons on the henequen estates—have fallen through the cracks. Agents of the state found such behavior too insignificant to document—except in rare, vexed bureaucratic asides—while *henequeneros* chose not to belabor the underside of plantation life in the lofty memoirs they commended to posterity.[82] Unfortunately, regarding the peons themselves, few then old enough to remember have been interviewed, and few old-timers now remain to give testimony. Moreover, the several incomplete oral histories that have been taken treat the past in nebulous terms that do not permit a thorough understanding of everyday forms of resistance.[83]

This methodological dilemma goes a long way toward explaining the rather monochromatic, static portrait of Porfirian life in the henequen zone that emerges in the historical literature. As we have noted, the peons are characterized as cowed and docile retainers, the planters and their agents as omnipotent and omnipresent masters who refused to countenance the slightest rebuke to their authority, let alone a consistent challenge to the boom's regimented rhythms of production. Of course, such a portrait omits not only routine forms of resistance but also the more violent and coordinated acts of protest that peons initiated or joined during the final years of the old order.

Although they are incomplete, disorganized, and rife with official bias, Yucatán's criminal records nevertheless help to redress the methodological and interpretive shortcomings of the historical literature. Court testimonies document instances of even the most routine forms of protest on Porfirian estates (shirking, footdragging, and insubordination).[84] They also capture more aggressive forms of resistance (rustling and theft, arson and sabotage).[85] Ultimately, they provide a window onto the riots, jacqueries, and revolts that erupted during the Madero era. Beyond that, such personal court testimonies graphically—often poignantly—reveal larger snatches of working-class life during the henequen boom, documenting a rigorous quotidian struggle to cope and survive. While we cannot reconstruct the texture and nuance of the larger process here, we can illustrate the broad range of resistance that culminated in waves of insurgency during the first years of the Mexican Revolution.

## THE POLITICS OF DAILY LIFE

Despite the various forms of coercion that were brought to bear, shirking and absenteeism remained a problem throughout the boom, especially for the overseers, who were entrusted with maintaining production levels on the estates. *Hacendados* and their personnel continually groused about the lazy, shiftless Maya. The hacienda account books regularly list peons who, for one medical reason or another, did not work on a given day. How much of this illness was feigned it is impossible to say.[86]

Clearly, *henequeneros* failed to inculcate a "proletarian" attitude in their *acasillados* during the boom. Then again, their hybrid labor regime was not suited to produce such a transformation in mentality. Peons physically coerced to cut fifteen hundred to two thousand spiny leaves a day under the relentless tropical sun, who existed in a perpetual state of indebtedness, whose mobility was severely constrained, still found ways to avoid work. Piece wages may have been paid, but debts grew so large at the end of the Porfiriato that few peons saw any real prospect of liquidating their accounts. Indeed, what incentive did peons have to complete their assigned tasks (let alone develop a work ethic) when all that their toil yielded was an inconsequentially smaller debt?

It was more likely that the *jornalero* found escape in alcohol, with intoxication exacerbating the problem of absenteeism. Even systematic whippings failed to prevent the popular custom of extending weekends to include "San Lunes." Alcohol was, of course, the principal release for resident peons; its ready availability in the hacienda stores indicates that, on another level, *henequeneros* appreciated its value as a mechanism of social control. Alcohol abuse was therefore a complex matter in social terms; alcohol probably both augmented and diminished resistance on the henequen estates.

Intoxication appears to have figured heavily in much of the crime and low-level violence that were endemic in rural Yucatán during the Porfiriato. In 1906 and 1907, for example, arrests for drunken disorderliness accounted for 55 to 70 percent of all arrests by state authorities.[87] Although such government statistics are notoriously unreliable and reflect urban as well as rural patterns, they point up the staggering incidence of alcohol abuse. Moreover, government figures do not include those incidents handled more quietly, outside the state judicial system, by *hacendados* and overseers on the estates themselves.

The criminal records abound with deaths and crimes that the courts found were either induced or mitigated by alcohol.[88] The crimes run the gamut, from simple theft and cattle rustling to arson, from domestic quarrels and assault and battery to murder. In a great many (and likely most) instances, peons victimized other peons, the obverse of Scott's notion of "routine" resistance.[89] Scott argues plausibly that to the extent that campesinos are reduced to lashing out at or preying on their peers, appropriation by the dominant classes is aided, not resisted.[90]

Recent research has made clear that adult Maya males often masked their feelings and denied the daily humiliations they suffered at the hands of their masters, while displacing their rage onto family members, usually their wives. In one revealing episode, a campesino who had meekly watched Hacienda San Simón's *encargado* force his wife to spend the night with him later vented his rage by beating his spouse and shaving her head.[91]

Nevertheless, the criminal records also contain a variety of cases in which peons robbed, rustled from, even assaulted and killed overseers and *hacendados*. Invariably, defendants and witnesses invoked excessive drinking as either an explanation or a mitigating factor. It appears that the types of questions prosecutors posed influenced or predisposed defendants' responses, suggesting that poor rural offenders could "play the game." Because they knew that premeditated crimes were punished more severely, it was in the defendants' interest to assert that their offenses were induced by an alcoholic stupor or merely unplanned.[92]

It is quite likely, then, that the criminal records overrepresent unpremeditated acts. Authorities understood the significance of alcohol as a release for the peasantry, and judges appear to have indulged their stereotype of "the ignorant and drunken Indian."[93] Yet these same judges—usually planters or their clients—also appreciated the notion that if every infractor, drunk or sober, received a "just" sentence, the jails would overflow, and few laborers would be left to work in the henequen fields.[94]

In rare instances, prima facie cases of resistance—episodes of rustling, theft, and sabotage—portray peons caught in the act. Arson, for example, became a formidable mode of resistance in the henequen zone, looming as a constant threat to production during the Porfiriato. In 1908, Santiago May, a Maya *jornalero*, was caught, matches in hand, torching 120 *mecates* of henequen (valued at three thousand pesos) on his hacienda, San Pedro, in

Izamal *partido*.[95] Although the peon claimed he had been drinking *aguardiente*, the judge, relying on the testimony of numerous eyewitnesses, concluded that May had acted with premeditation and had never lost control of his faculties. May was convicted and sentenced to six years in prison, an extraordinarily harsh sentence, more severe than what murderers often received during that epoch.

The harshness of this and other sentences related to the destruction of hacienda assets can only be interpreted as the oligarchical state's clear signal to peons that crimes against property constituted the gravest of offenses and would not be tolerated.[96] Arson, moreover, represented one of the few instances in which state authorities, reflecting the interests of the large landowners, felt compelled to meddle in the hacienda's internal affairs. A fire in a henequen field could wipe out a *henequenero*'s life savings in a matter of hours.

The clear-cut verdict in the May case notwithstanding, rulings in arson cases were often complicated by considerations involving the region's tropical climate. Accidental fires were common in the henequen zone during the long dry season from October to April, and particularly during the last two parched months, March and April. It was during these months that campesinos in nearby villages, employing swidden techniques, set their *milpa* ablaze to clear land for the next planting season. Occasionally, a change in wind direction would blow sparks into neighboring henequen fields.

Once a fire ignited, *encargados* could do little to stop it; the region's scarce water supply hampered firefighting capabilities. One of the largest fires of the late Porfiriato took place on Hacienda Temozón, about 40 kilometers from Mérida, during the hottest part of the dry season, late April 1908. Up in smoke went 31,700 *mecates* of prime henequen, valued at more than four hundred thousand pesos.[97] Although Porfirian judges regularly ordered investigations following the destruction of henequen fields, given the nature of the ecology, they were hard pressed to find culprits, let alone assess guilt.[98]

Clearly, considerations such as the peon's mental state and the region's ecology, as well as the representativeness and bias of the official documents themselves, render problematic any conclusions regarding the incidence of "conscious resistance." James C. Scott argues that the social historian is unlikely to understand completely a campesino's motivation. Everyday resistance depends for its effectiveness and safety on secrecy and the appearance of conformity; moreover, intentions may be so embedded in the rural subculture and the day-to-day struggle for security of subsistence as to remain "inarticulate." Ultimately, lacking definitive evidence, the historian must assess the local setting and infer intention or motivation from the acts themselves. Where the material interests of the dominant classes directly conflict with those of peasants or peons (over such issues as access to land, wages, or work conditions), Scott suggests that acts of rustling, theft, and sabotage may often be presumed to be resistance.[99] Scott would be likely to view the courtroom defenses that Yucatecan peons advanced—impaired mental state, accidents of the environment—as convenient alibis that masked clandestine acts of class struggle.

Scott may well overstate the case for a consistent strategy of everyday resistance, particularly where arson is concerned. If resistance is to be inferred from the social context, the historian should be prepared to make a compelling, if not gilt-edged case.[100] In any event, our data for Yucatecan henequen estates are sufficient to conclude that *peones acasillados* challenged the monocultural regime through a variety of forms, which escalated in terms of the damage they inflicted and the risk they entailed.

No doubt the most poignant, negative, and "total" response to exploitation was suicide. The judicial records document a frightening number of self-inflicted deaths, many induced by pellagra, which in its advanced stages produces mental disorders. A 1910 article in the *American Medical Journal* estimated that in 1907 a staggering 15 percent of the population in Yucatán had that disease.[101] When coupled with endemic alcoholism, pellagra often had tragic consequences. That so many peons hung themselves from trees or house beams or threw themselves into wells testifies to their poor diet, inadequate medical care, and feelings of desperation—conditions that became increasingly acute during the final years of the Porfiriato.[102]

The judicial investigation of José María Eb's death provides a grisly case in point, and also illustrates the deterioration of paternalism and security on late Porfirian estates. Eb was a 70-year-old Maya peon on Hacienda San José, midway between Cacalchén and Motul. His fellow workers Isidro May and Toribio Escobarrubias discovered him in a field, completely buried under henequen leaves. A concentration of buzzards hovering overhead led them to his body. They found that the buzzards had eaten the body almost beyond recognition; identification was possible only from Eb's characteristic clothing and sack. The medical examiner found the corpse covered with the telltale lesions of an advanced case of pellagra. May and Escobarrubias testified that because of the disease and heavy bouts of drinking, Eb had periodically fallen down and passed out during the previous few weeks. Occasionally he had even forgotten where he was and had to be led to his work in the fields.[103] His case was not ruled a suicide but instead ascribed to acute alcoholic congestion.

Significantly, the many Maya peons who did commit suicide often adhered to traditional ritual and custom, hanging themselves from trees or house beams.[104] Pre-Columbian Maya religious beliefs held that suicide victims, unlike most of the dead who faced an arduous journey to the underworld, were rewarded with a direct trip to paradise. In effect, they would be assigned to a special heaven, where they, along with other unfortunates, such as unweaned children, would rest forever from labor and enjoy "a life of happy leisure with all imaginable delights beneath the shade of a giant ceiba tree (the sacred *yaxché*)."[105] Indeed, suicides were taken to this heaven by the Maya goddess Ix Tab (translated alternately as She of the Cord and Goddess of the Hanged), who is depicted in the Dresden Codex hanging from the sky by a rope looped around her neck. "Her eyes are closed in death, and a black circle, representing decomposition, appears on her cheek."[106] In his *Relación de las cosas de Yucatán*, Bishop Diego de Landa speculated on the motives behind such ultimate acts.

> They also said and held it as absolutely certain that those who hanged themselves went to this heaven of theirs; and thus there were many who on slight occasions of sorrows, troubles, or sicknesses hanged themselves in order to escape these things and to go to rest in their heaven, where they said that the Goddess of the Gallows, whom they call Ixtab, came to fetch them.[107]

Archaeologists have not clearly determined why the northwestern Maya accorded such special distinction to suicide victims. Yet the persistence of this cultural belief, possibly into the twentieth century, confirms our argument that the plantocracy and the church never fully succeeded in ideologically recasting these acculturated Maya in their image. The Maya's particular treatment of suicide suggests that other indigenous traditions and beliefs may have underwritten daily acts of resistance, and that the Maya may have reshaped other cultural forms of the dominant society and invested them with a different, empowering significance.[108]

The sustenance of indigenous traditions and beliefs was facilitated in large measure by the Catholic church's meager presence in the Yucatecan countryside. A recent examination of the church's role in Yucatán during the Porfiriato concludes that in quantitative and qualitative terms, its influence on the Maya was very limited.[109] Financially weakened by the mid-century Reform Laws and by the Caste War, which forced the religious to flee to the security of the state capital, the church never regained sufficient strength in rural areas seriously to contest indigenous religious practices. At the turn of the century, Yucatán's entire diocese was staffed by only 76 priests—half of them foreigners—catering to the spiritual needs of more than three hundred thousand inhabitants. A disproportionate number of the priests still served Mérida's barrios and rarely ventured out to the rural parishes. As late as March 1909, Archbishop Martín Tritschler y Córdoba lamented,

> the great majority of the rural parishioners do not live in the *cabeceras*, but in pueblos and haciendas and they rarely (and then hurriedly) come to the parish. . . . And because they lack any semblance of religious instruction, they exist in a state of profound ignorance and have abandoned [Catholic] religious practices. Their spiritual needs are dire.[110]

Some landowners even obstructed priests' visits to their estates, which suggests how far *hacendados* would go to enforce their peons' isolation.[111] And when priests did travel to outlying haciendas to perform mass and administer the sacraments, their fleeting presence did little to counteract indigenous folk practices. Patronal fiestas sponsored by religious brother-hoods dotted the calendar throughout the state, but these popular folk cel-ebrations reflected the Maya's ability to refashion Catholic holy days to suit their own spiritual needs. Although further work remains to be done on the church's role in the Yucatecan countryside, it is apparent that the Yucatec Maya managed to preserve some measure of spiritual and cultural autonomy.

## 'ACASILLADO' PROTEST

If the "quieter" forms of resistance utilized by *acasillados* in many re-spects resembled those employed by slaves throughout the Americas, the cultural resources the Maya had at their disposal made those strategies more effective. With the notable exception of suicide (which had its own cultural rationale), such forms reveal a tenacious will to persevere and, when opportunities presented themselves, to contest *henequeneros'* de-mands without risking open (and unequal) confrontation.

After 1907, however, new historical conjunctures facilitated more dy-namic patterns of *acasillado* resistance. The consequences for Mexico of the worldwide financial crisis of 1907–8, particularly its role in eroding the Porfirian regime, have been the subject of recent debate.[112] There can be little question, though, that the international panic had a profound impact at all levels of Yucatán's dependent monocrop society. With fiber quotations plummeting in 1908 (and generally declining thereafter until 1912) and with credit in short supply, a chain reaction of commercial failures and bankruptcies swept the peninsula, claiming many small and medium-sized *henequeneros*.

The straitened planters, their backs to the wall, passed the burden downward, reducing wages, restricting initial advances to peons while con-tinuing credit at the hacienda store and slashing traditional paternalistic benefits and incentives. At the same time, *henequeneros* stepped up the pace of production. Heightened labor demands left peons little time or en-ergy to tend small, traditional *milpa* plots—in those increasingly rare in-stances where estates had not already converted them to monoculture. In addition to the extra labor they extracted from the *jornaleros* themselves, according to recent research, planters may have begun to appropriate the labor of servants' family members. Peons had long augmented their house-hold income through the extra wages of adolescent sons and the domestic labor provided by wives and daughters. Now the *henequeneros* tapped that labor directly, particularly the unpaid labor of the women, and to that ex-tent deprived the *acasillados* of a strategic resource in their continuing struggle to maintain a security of subsistence.[113]

In this new environment, resident peons could only reflect that their calculated exchange of autonomy for security was no longer working. Peri-odic droughts and almost annual locust plagues between 1907 and 1911 further eroded peons' expectations. It is hardly surprising, therefore, that violent confrontation, previously the last and most dangerous resort, became a more frequent response after 1907.

One need not espouse a simplistic "volcanic" theory of collective violence to account for the local riots and jacqueries that occurred in the henequen zone between 1907 and 1911 or the broader waves of rural revolt that swept the state in 1911 and 1912, enlisting substantial *acasillado* support. Such "volcanic" or J-curve models suggest that worsening economic conditions generate relative deprivation and discontent, which eventually trigger mass rage and collective action.[114] To be sure, where the peons were concerned, deteriorating, increasingly "involuted" conditions of labor and economic well-being lowered the threshold of the peon's tolerance toward his oppression and likely generated multiple local—albeit isolated—encounters after 1907. But, as we will see, worsening economic conditions never triggered a more generalized tide of protest and violence in the state, let alone an incipient mass movement that would topple the oligarchical order.

The regional press reported a variety of violent disputes over wage cuts, deteriorating labor conditions, and physical abuse in the face of declining fiber prices during the 1907–11 period. For example, in 1909, an *encargado* cut the wages of four platform drivers who refused to work Sundays at Hacienda Eknakán. When violence erupted, the national guard was sent in to restore order. The captain of the guard unit was wounded and forced to withdraw; reenforcements from Mérida had to be rushed in to quell the disturbance. One peon was killed and eight others injured.[115]

In other reported episodes, *jornaleros* protested abusive treatment and punishment on the estates. Late in 1907, 110 peons marched from Hacienda Oxcúm, owned by Don Olegario's son-in-law, Avelino Montes, to the municipal hall of nearby Umán to protest the imprisonment of three co-workers. National guard troops were dispatched from Mérida, six kilometers away. Undaunted by the show of force, six Oxcúm peons later assaulted the estate's hated overseer. The national guard was called in again, this time to arrest the six offenders.[116] In March 1911, a notoriously brutal labor regime on the Hacienda Catmís, a more isolated southern estate near Peto, provided the spark for perhaps the most violent episode of *acasillado* protest during the Porfiriato. Exploding in cathartic rage, peons destroyed machinery and carved up the *hacendado* and members of his family and staff.[117]

Almost always, violence came in response to specific local causes, and was isolated and quickly repressed by state authorities. As we have noted, such riots and jacqueries occurred from time to time throughout the Porfirian fiber boom. Although they caused some immediate concern, they presented no real threat to the modernizing plantocracy. Indeed, after 1890, these violent episodes in the henequen zone served to showcase the regime's technological superiority, providing the occasion for veritable "rituals of order and progress."

The detailed . . . step-by-step coverage of [such outbreaks] indicates the elite in Mérida relished the experiences of the 1890s. The . . . elite felt a sense of well-being and empowerment through the use of telegraphs, telephones, railroads, and armed troops to quash minor revolts.[118]

Between 1907 and 1911, however, the incidence of violent protest appears to have steadily increased. By 1911, both in the henequen zone and on its suddenly less-controllable fringes, such uprisings (*motines*) and *tumultos* had become principal forms of resistance among the Maya peasantry, while (often related) acts of rustling and theft had reached epidemic proportions.[119]

## Agrarian Conflict on the Henequen Periphery

Ultimately, it was the villages and hamlets on the fringes of monoculture that most preoccupied the plantocracy in the first chaotic years of the revolutionary era. Grievances had simmered for decades along the southern range of stunted hills known as the Puuc near the Campeche border, and in the area south and east of the prime henequen haciendas of Izamal and Temax districts. Independent smallholders tenaciously guarded their lands against the incursions of local *hacendados* and the *jefes políticos* who were their partners, clients, and, not infrequently, relatives.

From about 1870 through the 1890s, as henequen cultivation pushed outward from its northwestern base, planters worked assiduously to appropriate the land and labor of those transitional Maya pueblos that lay in their path. By the turn of the century, the frontiers of henequen expansion extended in a broad arc that swung from the western municipalities of Hunucmá and Maxcanú through northern Ticul and northeastern Sotuta, and ultimately bisected the district of Temax (see Map 6.1).

While the precise phasing and outcome varied with the locality, everywhere the scenario was roughly the same. Maya villages on the periphery were penetrated by white proprietors and labor contractors, who came to exercise patronage and control over significant numbers of the *comuneros*. In the process, existing divisions within pueblos were exacerbated. Not surprisingly, in such "open," factionalized peasant communities, the distribution of the *ejidos* in fee simple to household heads became a complex, hotly contested matter.[120] Some *comuneros* favored the distribution of lots and complained that the process moved too slowly; others favored the survey of *ejidos* but not their distribution; still others favored distribution, but only with the assurance that procedures would be honestly administered, survey fees affordable, and planters prohibited from buying *ejido* parcels.[121] Of course, *henequeneros* and their agents routinely exploited such contentiousness to purchase, confiscate, or otherwise acquire bundles of individual lots when village *ejidos* were parceled.[122]

On the near eastern periphery, in Izamal and the western half of Temax district, powerful planters like the Manzanillas, Regils, Cámaras, Méndezes, Castellanos, and Torreses rapidly transformed newly purchased ejidal lots into productive henequen fields. Kantunil pueblo's *ejido* was partitioned in 1884 (by entrepreneurial engineer Olegario Molina) into 192 lots, only 15 of which were subsequently retained by *comuneros*. In 1906, the *ejido* of Sudsal was divided among 70 villagers; 61 immediately sold their parcels to neighboring estates. Similar outcomes could be recounted for Hoctun, Tepekan, and Tekantó in Izamal, or for Dzilam González and Hoydzonot in Temax.[123]

Nevertheless, when a pueblo's traditional lands hung in the balance, *comuneros'* normally attenuated bonds of solidarity could gain strength. This was often the case in the eastern half of Temax, in the Puuc (particularly the less accessible areas of Ticul and Maxcanú districts), and in smallholding pockets of Maxcanú's northern neighbor, Hunucmá *partido*. In these locales, most villagers opted collectively to protest the parceling of their *ejidos* or, if division did occur, to resist the planters' pressure on their parcels and implicitly on their labor. Resistance assumed a variety of adaptive forms throughout the 1880s, 1890s, and 1900s, beginning with petitions and litigation but invariably escalating to hit-and-run acts of sabotage, land invasions, and violent encounters with surveyors, bureaucrats, *jefes políticos*, *hacendados*, and their personnel.

The unremitting struggle was occasionally crowned with success. Puuc villages and *cabeceras* like Muna, Santa Elena, and Peto managed to avoid ejidal survey throughout the Porfiriato. No doubt, the sierra's deeper soils (henequen thrived best in the rocky northwest) and remote locations made them a bit less desirable for henequen cultivation. Santa Elena, for example, a pueblo of about one thousand campesinos, was situated almost 70 kilometers from Mérida; separated by rugged foothills from the nearest railhead in Ticul, the district seat; and, except for a few small settlements, was the only real pueblo in the southern Puuc between Ticul and Bolenchenticul, Campeche.

All these southern pueblos, moreover, lay in reasonable proximity to the frontier of *pacífico* settlement in the Chenes region of neighboring Campeche. The Yucatecan state had accorded the *pacífico* peasantry semiautonomous status in 1853 in return for their agreement to lay down their arms in the Caste War. Now, decades later, regional elites were loath to engage in any aggressive acts that might trigger new hostilities in the south—particularly before the more ferocious *cruzob* were subdued in the east. Thus, by blunting agricultural expansion and restricting the application of military force in the southern Puuc, geopolitics gave the *comuneros* of villages like Santa Elena greater tactical mobility and worked to nourish strong local traditions of protest.[124]

Known as Nohcacab before the Caste War, Santa Elena stood in sharp contrast to Ticul, its white-dominated *cabecera*.[125] Although some whites had always resided in the pueblo, John Stephens reported in the late 1840s

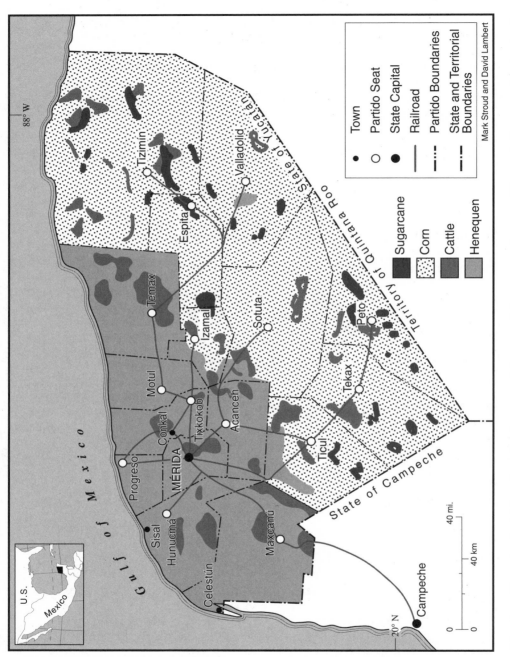

*Map 6.2.* Yucatán: Agricultural production around the turn of the century. Sources: "Censo de fincas rurales de 1890"; *La razón del pueblo*; adapted from Villanueva Mukul, "La formación del las regiones de Yucatán," 171.

Mark Stroud and David Lambert

**Legend:**
- Town ●
- Partido Seat ○
- State Capital ●
- Railroad
- Partido Boundaries
- State and Territorial Boundaries

- Sugarcane
- Corn
- Cattle
- Henequen

that Maya villagers participated in an Indian government that decided *milpa* allocations. Even before 1847, the villagers clashed with one of the state's most powerful *hacendados*, Simón Peón, over the extension of the village's *ejido*. Deserted during the Caste War (we have no record of which side the villagers supported), the town was renamed Santa Elena in 1848; but a proper Spanish name did nothing to blunt the ferocity with which its Maya villagers defended their lands in succeeding decades.

On several occasions in the 1880s, armed villagers invaded the fields of Miguel Peón, which they claimed as their own. When Agustín Cuevas, a white politician imposed on the village as municipal president in 1885, began to work with the *jefe político* of Ticul to repel one such invasion and punish the leaders, his body soon turned up outside the pueblo. In the late 1890s and early 1900s, the villagers obstructed surveyors and knocked down markers when the Southeastern Railway Company attempted to alienate their *ejido*. In 1900, one of the railroad's surveyors disappeared without a trace.[126]

Villagers on the far more accessible western and eastern peripheries, in the districts of Maxcanú, Hunucmá, and Temax, had a much tougher time of it. In western Maxcanú and Hunucmá, henequen fields had pushed their way almost to the Gulf of Mexico by the late 1880s (see Map 6.2). Although pueblos were typically forced to parcel their *ejidos*, large numbers of villagers in Cepeda, Halachó, and Opichén in Maxcanú *partido* and Tetiz, Kinchil, and Ucú in Hunucmá *partido* struggled to hold on to their individual plots in the face of substantial pressure from planters such as Arcadio Escobedo, Eusebio Escalante, Augusto L. Peón, Diego María Solís, and Gonzalo Maldonado Solís.[127]

A celebrated incident in 1908 outside the pueblo of Cepeda richly illustrates the nuances of the adversarial relationship between expansionist *hacendados* and a determined, though by no means monolithic, peasantry.[128] An aged smallholder, Feliciano Chi, was brutally murdered while tending his *milpa* on his parcel, San Francisco. Chi had been a spokesman for the nearby town of Halachó in its dispute over ejidal lands with the powerful *hacendado* Arcadio Escobedo. The landowner (who would later become governor during the regime of Victoriano Huerta) was in the midst of a fourteen-year battle over land with both Halachó and Cepeda. Escobedo hired one of the best trial lawyers in Mérida, Serapio Rendón, to defend his overseer, who was implicated in Chi's murder.[129] Later Escobedo published a pamphlet, *En defensa de Faustino Méndez (el crimen de Cepeda)*, to clear his own name.

During the trial—which Mérida's elite followed closely—the prosecution alleged that Escobedo's *encargado*, Méndez, had paid several servants from his estate, Dzidzibachí, the sum of $80 to murder Chi. The prosecutor felt that the overseer was the chief architect of the crime, and in his brief he commented at some length on the intimidation that patrons and their personnel exercised over their peons.

Cepeda was a new town, founded in 1876—named after the Liberal hero of Yucatán who had defeated the imperialists in 1867. Created after the Reform Laws were introduced, Cepeda was not formally entitled to ejidal lands; it had to apply to the federal government for them. The courts reached a compromise in 1894, declaring that Cepeda's villagers were entitled to lands, but that these should come partly from Escobedo's holdings and partly from the *ejido* of Halachó.

The ruling pleased no one. Escobedo was so upset he went back to court to regain his lost lands, and simultaneously pressured for the parceling of Cepeda's fledgling *ejido*. The villagers of Halachó complained about the land they had been forced to relinquish; their counterparts in Cepeda groused bitterly about the piddling amount they had received (no more than eight hectares per household head). Indeed, Escobedo's attorney, Rendón, asserted during the trial that some of Cepeda's residents, who participated in the homicide, had been upset with Feliciano Chi for the settlement he had helped to work out. The prosecutor countered that Escobedo was enraged with the residents of Halachó for his ongoing difficulties; just months earlier, he had lost another round in the seemingly endless judicial proceedings. It was that aggravation, the prosecutor contended, that eventually boiled over and led to the "Crime of Cepeda."

In reality, in Maxcanú and Hunucmá *partidos*, long litigations ending favorably for *comuneros* were less common than violent denouements perpetrated by impatient *henequenero* entrepreneurs. When petitions and lawsuits to prevent hacienda usurpations availed little, and land invasions and riots in the district seats were quashed by the national guard, disgruntled *comuneros* in these *partidos* often shifted their strategy to banditry in the late 1880s and 1890s. Time and again, the elite press reported that small groups of "known bandits" burned dyewood stands and henequen fields. On one occasion in July 1895, such brigands sneaked onto the estate of the *jefe político* of Hunucmá and murdered him in his hammock.[130]

In more remote eastern Temax, the struggle for land was particularly acute by the first decade of the twentieth century. Although it was 80 kilometers distant from Mérida, the area was reasonably accessible via the Mérida–Valladolid railroad (with a station in Temax, the district seat), and it harbored prime terrain for fiber cultivation. The lots that had once formed the *ejido* of Dzilám González, located at dead center of the *partido*, had been sold under duress to the large planter Atilano Torres. Still, a few *comuneros*, led by Juan Campos, a petty merchant and smallholder, stubbornly clung to their parcels and, it was rumored, engaged periodically in banditry against the neighboring estates.[131]

As one moved farther east in the district, the number of viable smallholders steadily increased. In Buctzotz municipality and that of the *cabecera*, for example, large planters, such as the Cámaras, Méndezes, Castellanos, Manzanillas, and Olegario Molina himself, had been able to buy up only a small fraction of plots from the former *ejidos*. Further henequen expansion would not be easy; it would have to come at the expense of *comuneros* like Pedro Crespo, a middle peasant and small merchant in Temax who himself had bought up an extra parcel or two and desperately feared losing his autonomy to an expanding monoculture.[132]

It is hardly surprising, then, that these transitional zones proved to be fertile recruiting grounds for both the *cabecillas* and the clienteles of the first rebellions of the revolutionary era. It was not just that almost all the villages on the periphery of monoculture were in the midst of protracted agrarian struggles with *henequeneros*. They also nursed resentment on a broad range of issues that had come to be regarded as common denominators of Molinista administrative abuse: political imposition, nepotism, and "continuismo"; personal enrichment, including the arbitrary use of unpaid labor (*fagina*); increased taxation; and last but not least, implementation of the hated *leva*. As we shall see in the chapters that follow, time and again the rural chiefs of Yucatán's contending factions were the economically threatened smallholders of these villages (many of whom were also petty traders or artisans), who had been humiliated by corrupt, arrogant, often brutal Molinista *jefes políticos* or their subordinates.

Thus, Pedro Crespo, along with Manuel Fausto Robles (Temax), José Loreto Baak (Santa Elena), and Juan Leal (Espita), had been arbitrarily imprisoned by district prefects. While Crespo was in the local jail, his father was shot in cold blood for refusing to perform illegal *corvée* labor. Baak and Leal were repeatedly harassed by Molinista thugs for backing opposition candidates in their pueblos; Robles received a particularly excessive sentence for a routine fracas with a petty civil servant.[133] Yet, judging from their testimonies and those of their lieutenants, relatives, and followers, these local leaders rarely drew a distinction between "political" and "economic" (or "cultural") grievances. Instead, they spoke more generally of "tyranny" and the loss of freedom and dignity. They identified local authorities as cronies of the *dzules*, whose henequen fields would advance to the extent that the *señores* could erase their status as *hombres libres* and reduce them to servants.[134]

Militia officers (Crespo was one), traders in provisions (Campos), town-based artisans (Santa Elena's Baak, Peto's Elías Rivero, Temax's Robles), reasonably prosperous smallholders (Leal, Campos, and Crespo)—each of these incipient *cabecillas* had one foot in the world of the *comunero*, the other in that of the *dzul*. In most cases, they were "mestizos de buen hablar," Maya campesinos who spoke Spanish well enough and could handle themselves in town.[135] In short, they were ideally suited to broker the politics and translate the ideologies and programs of the new era that was about to dawn in the peninsula in 1909.[136]

# Seasons of Upheaval: Oligarchy in Crisis, 1909–15

How did Yucatán's bickering summer of discontent fester into several violent seasons of upheaval that shook the oligarchical order? And once such insurgency had been unleashed in 1910–11, how did the old order successfully forestall a general conflagration until the Mexican Revolution was imported from outside the state in 1915? In the second part of this book we focus on the mechanisms and consequences of both the mobilizations and demobilizations that were carried out in Yucatán between 1909 and 1915. In the process, we attempt to mark out the agendas and political consciousness that elites and campesinos brought to the insurgencies of the period.

However outraged they may be, campesinos generally wait for evidence that powerholders are weak or divided before they take the risks attending insurrection. We will see that in Yucatán, news of such opportunities for revolt was brought to campesinos by dissident elites—in some cases their own patrons—or by strategically placed individuals, whom we would call "hingemen."[1] These were typically the local *cabecillas*, whose origins we have already examined; actors who had some experience in the dominant society that complemented, indeed often enhanced, their standing in the subordinate rural society. Although such brokers did not cause Yucatán's rural revolts, as we will see, they often precipitated them, played a role in organizing rural insurgents, and helped establish their links with other groups. Thus, to paraphrase one recent commentator, John Tutino, from the perspective of poor campesinos, rural rebellions result from "critical meetings of grievances and opportunities."[2]

From late 1909 through the middle of 1913, tightening economic prospects plus widening political space in Yucatán would give some country people with room to maneuver both the incentive and the opportunity to join new planter-financed coalitions, and even to lead local revolts. And that same combination of circumstances would put others, particularly peons on rural estates, in a position to be mobilized and armed by these contending elite factions.

Throughout 1910 and early 1911, this tenuous alliance between dissident elites in the cities and influential rural brokers in the interior would continue to develop as the elites secured arms and cash and the new local *cabecillas* recruited in their pueblos and, increasingly, on neighboring estates. Yet regional elites would soon come to reconsider the wisdom of their mobilization of villagers and peons. By the spring of 1911, the latest round of local riots and revolts was beginning to spin out of control.

Surprisingly—particularly given the searing memories that lingered from the apocalyptic Caste War a half-century earlier—the Yucatecan elites never really considered that their erstwhile clients and proxies might have different stakes and strategies. To their horror, and rather quickly, campesino mobilization began to develop a logic and an organization of its own. Try as they might, Yucatán's bickering elites would be unable to contain the rage unleashed on the periphery of the henequen zone. Even more frightening was that at various junctures between 1911 and 1913, such popular insurgency would threaten to ignite the henequen zone itself.

In Chapters 7 and 8, we reconstruct a narrative of these complex revolts; at the conclusion of the latter chapter, we scrape away the political veneer of events to plumb some of their deeper meanings. Apart from assessing the nature and historical impact of these insurgencies, our aim is to glimpse in them—if only through a glass darkly, given the limitations of largely "official" sources—the political consciousness of everyday Yucatecans. Finally, in Chapters 9 and 10, we probe a variety of strategies on the part of both *henequeneros* and the state. These, in combination with important structural and attitudinal factors, explain why, in Yucatán, political conflict and popular insurgency stopped short of the generalized rebellion that occurred in many other parts of Mexico.

## CHAPTER 7

# 'Primeras Chispas' (First Sparks), Fall 1909–Spring 1911

I have more faith in the people of the pueblos than in those of Mérida.
—Alfonso Cámara y Cámara

Our goal is to overthrow the authorities and then see what happens.
—Pedro Crespo

Francisco Madero's national political campaign against the Díaz regime emboldened two disgruntled *camarillas* of the planter class and their middle-sector allies to organize parties for the purpose of challenging Molinista rule in the November 1909 elections.[1] Officially formed midway through 1909 (though they had really begun to operate several months earlier), the Centro Electoral Independiente (CEI) and the Partido Antirreeleccionista (PA), were known popularly as the Morenistas and the Pinistas, after their respective standardbearers, journalists Delio Moreno Cantón and José María Pino Suárez.[2] In truth, they resembled loose political coalitions more than proper parties. The CEI was the latest incarnation of what had originally been Don Pancho Cantón's Gran Club Liberal of 1897 and the short-lived Unión Antirreeleccionista of 1905. Both of the latest "parties" were financed by their planter supporters, and each hastily attempted to construct alliances reaching into the intelligentsia, the small urban working and artisan class, and—perhaps most important but least examined—into the large and potentially explosive Maya peasantry.

Although Molinista domination of late Porfirian Yucatán was qualitatively different than past rule by competing *camarillas*, rival elites still believed that the tactics that had worked well in the past deserved to be tried again. For example, in the first part of 1909, the Morenistas began to employ the same strategy that they had used so effectively as Cantonistas in 1897. They plotted and intrigued, seeking to draw national attention to themselves and the region so as to embarrass the local authorities and, ultimately, to force the federal government to intervene in local politics. The ploy had worked well enough twelve years before, when Díaz had sided with the Cantonistas and toppled the incumbent Peoncista faction.

The Morenistas reasoned that Don Porfirio would, as usual, play one faction against the other, and that they would eventually emerge holding the reins of power. What they did not see at first was that the flexible system of power sharing that had served Don Porfirio so well for three decades had calcified by 1909. Too much lucrative speculation was now riding on the maintenance of the status quo. As one historian has affirmed more generally for late Porfirian Mexico, "politics meant business. In maze upon maze of graft and collusion between politicians and businessmen . . . [change] meant renegotiation of a myriad of shady deals."[3]

The writing was on the wall; the Morenistas chose not to read it. Including Don Olegario on his team as secretary of *fomento* in 1906 signaled the aging dictator's decision to stay with the Molinista incumbents during the last years of his rule. Yet it would be a costly mistake, one that soon revealed how badly the *científico* clique in Mexico City and Mérida underestimated the determination and resilience of competing Yucatecan *camarillas*. When, late in 1909, in the wake of unceasing government harassment, the Morenistas came to realize that the old rules no longer applied and that power would have to be taken forcibly, they broadened their political organization and intensified their recruitment of campesinos in the outlying rural areas. Then they planned a wave of armed attacks on state authorities. Let us tease out the chronology of events that led inevitably to insurgency so that we can better examine the responses of both the elite factions and the popular classes.

## Campaigns and Conspiracies: "La Candelaria," Fall 1909

Francisco Madero's weeklong visit to Yucatán in late June 1909 had encouraged elite opponents of the regime to believe that change might still come by traditional political means. While in Mérida, Madero had urged the leaders of both parties, Pino Suárez and Moreno Cantón, to patch up their differences and present a unified front against the Molinista incumbent, Enrique Muñoz Arístegui.[4]

In class terms, there was little to distinguish between the rival elitist parties with respect to either political platform or constituency. A Molinista political commentator wryly observed that some elites consistently hedged their bets regarding affiliation.

> *Hacendado* Don Fulano gave one [opposition] club ten pesos, the other five pesos, all the while subscribing to the governing party's publications. Merchant Mengano sides with the Molinistas, his younger brother with the CEI,

and his older brother is a Pinista; that way the family is secure and might even extract a position in the next administration.[5]

Beyond the doses of anti-Molinista propaganda that saturated their broadsheets, both parties were moderate, indeed ambiguous, in their political pronouncements. The Pinistas were a bit more specific with regard to "the social question," but neither group called for significant changes in the structure of regional monoculture.[6]

Perhaps the chief difference between the two *camarillas* was rooted in their respective stances toward Díaz's national leadership. Always the opportunists, the Morenistas sought to work within the Porfirian system, at least until the system turned overtly against them. By far the more visible of the two movements, they had the benefit of more than a decade of political organizing to draw on as they went about the task of forming political clubs in rural communities and enlisting the participation of middle- and upper-class women in the capital and the port.[7] By contrast, the Pinistas were a component of Madero's new national movement, had only a small organizational base in Yucatán, and were determined (at least in principle) to peacefully oust the national dictatorship.[8]

The Morenistas showed their true Porfirian colors in September 1909 when they sent a delegation to Mexico City—just as they had done in 1897—to seek Díaz's blessing in the upcoming elections. The delegation carried three names as possible CEI candidates: Delio Moreno Cantón (who had been the party's clear choice at its recent convention), José E. Castillo, and General Luis Curiel.[9] Don Porfirio muttered that the military man, who had served in Yucatán during the 1890s, would make a fine candidate; Curiel, however, refused the party's nomination. The CEI subsequently held a second convention and nominated Pancho Cantón's nephew for the governorship.[10]

What little trust had existed between the two rival opposition parties began to dissipate as a result of the Morenista expedition to Mexico City. Madero, unhappy that the Morenistas had tried to accommodate themselves with the president, still realized that his organization in the state left much to be desired. Accordingly, he suggested that his followers take the tactical step of supporting Moreno Cantón for the governorship in return for a CEI promise to support Madero in the forthcoming presidential elections.[11] Thus, even though Pino Suárez agreed not to run for governor, the coalition was never more than a marriage of convenience, and a brief one at that. Both parties mobilized followings in the cities and the countryside during the summer and early fall of 1909, and often stepped on each other's toes.

This friction is clearly demonstrated in a letter Pino Suárez wrote in September 1909 to Rigoberto Xiu, a twenty-year-old campesino and political organizer from Muna, a town on the fringes of the henequen zone about 50 kilometers south of Mérida. Xiu had a running feud with the Molinista president of the local municipal council, who made a practice of forcing campesinos to provide him with free labor. Xiu spoke out against such treatment and began to organize Muna's populace during the summer of 1909. Although he had initially pledged his support to Pino's Antireelectionist cause, by September Xiu had shifted his allegiance to the more popular Morenistas. Pino's letter to Xiu implores the *cabecilla* to abandon the CEI. Ironically, Pino, himself a Tabascan, accuses the Morenistas of trying to bring in an outsider for governor, General Curiel from Jalisco. He also attacks the CEI's Porfirian orientation: "these Morenistas say they have the support of the President, but so do the supporters of the administration [Molinistas], which just goes to show that they are both deceivers, since the President cannot support both of them."[12]

While both parties worked at cross-purposes, state authorities knuckled down on CEI electioneering. Early in August, Muñoz Arístegui had confided to Don Porfirio, "I will work to ensure that their group loses ground and fails to root itself in local society."[13] Díaz apparently was pleased; he himself had just ordered the federal zone commander to "use force against opposition groups when necessary."[14] On September 11, the national guard and the state police wielded billy clubs against Morenista demonstrators in Mérida's central plaza. Thirty prominent CEI members were arrested and kept in jail for a month, deprived of the opportunity to post bail, pay a fine, and get back to the campaign. Morenistas immediately invoked memories of the bloody *tumulto* in the *zócalo* twelve years before.[15]

Strong-arm tactics were brought to bear in the countryside as well. In the pueblo of Chemax, just kilometers away from the Morenista stronghold of Valladolid, several members were arrested trying to organize a political club. The *jefe político* jailed the Morenistas, claiming he had it on good authority that they were "about to create a disturbance."[16] A spate of similar crackdowns in other pueblos and *cabeceras* throughout September, followed by a state ban on all political demonstrations, street processions, and even musical concerts (again, shades of 1897) amply convinced the CEI president, Alfonso Cámara y Cámara, that traditional Porfirian political options had been exhausted.[17] Meanwhile, Muñoz Arístegui bragged to Díaz (very prematurely), "these [opposition] clubs appear totally disbanded," and promised to "keep all leading Cantonistas under strict surveillance."[18]

Cámara y Cámara, scion of a wealthy planter family, well remembered the events of 1897. That year, he had served as president of Pancho Cantón's Gran Club Liberal and had been a highly visible participant in the violent events of August 11. Now, he began to prepare his forces statewide to overthrow the Molinista government.[19] The CEI had been thrown back on its heels by government repression; while the party exhorted supporters to mobilize, its broadsides candidly observed that "the people of Yucatán are not yet ready for a revolution, much as they deserve one."[20] The resulting October conspiracy, which came to be called "La Candelaria," was therefore rather premature.[21] It included plans to capture the armories in Mérida; take control of the electric plant; cut telegraph and telephone lines; apprehend the governor, the city council president, and various deputies; and then storm the house of Avelino Montes for money to pay the expenses of the rebellion—a tall order indeed.

The leadership anticipated that the conspiracy in Mérida, set for October 14 to coincide with Díaz's meeting with U.S. President William Howard Taft at the border, would be joined by similar uprisings throughout the state, particularly in the Mérida suburb of Kanasín and in Cuzamá, Muna, Peto, Tizimín, and Valladolid. The Morenistas had key people in each of these places, all of whom had been laying in caches of machetes and some small arms. Despite the uneasy pact between the two opposition parties, Pinista clubs in the interior had agreed to participate in the revolt. Cámara y Cámara was reported to have said at one meeting: "I have more faith in the people of the pueblos than in those of Mérida."[22]

Cámara y Cámara's faith in the countryside's support was not misplaced. Despite government harassment and Muñoz Arístegui's boasts, the ranks of both opposition parties continued to expand in the interior. Maya villagers, after all, had even more reasons than disgruntled *hacendados* had to despise Molinista rule. The mix of grievances and claims varied with the history of the locality. As we saw in the last chapter, many communities on the fringes of the henequen zone remained embroiled in struggles over what remained of their ejidal patrimonies; most others within the henequen zone had lost their lands long before. Yet virtually everywhere, pueblos nurtured the bitterness that had accumulated with years of Molinista political abuse, and they were now emboldened to do something about it. Extensive CEI files, seized by the secret police in Mérida and several key pueblos in the aftermath of the failed conspiracy, reveal the scrawled signatures and marks of literally hundreds of campesinos, artisans, petty merchants, and young people, each of whom paid party dues of 12, 25, or 50 centavos in the fall of 1909. This represented a good day's pay for many *jornaleros* at a time when the agricultural economy was heading into a tailspin. The captured files also document that hundreds of people turned out for Morenista rallies in small communities like Santa Elena and Muna, as well as in larger centers like Valladolid and Peto.[23]

Moreover, communication between these new clubs and their party headquarters in Mérida, achieved through a network of couriers, agents, and spies (known colorfully as *orejas* and *madrinas*; literally, ears and godmothers), was already surprisingly extensive.[24] In Muna in September, Rigoberto Xiu bluntly requested from the CEI sufficient machetes, guns, and money "to meet the needs of our 150 exploited compañeros." Arms had apparently arrived by early October, when tensions rose to a fever pitch. Only days before the projected October 14 uprising, Xiu and his brother Claudio taunted their nemesis, the town's Molinista mayor and *cacique*, Serapio Cabrera, then beat him soundly with a length of metal pipe. In Cuzamá, in the very heart of the henequen zone, CEI organizer Moisés

Montero, a 43-year-old carpenter, told a courier from Mérida that local Mo-renistas had one hundred homemade bombs and enough machetes "to bring down the bosses." One of Montero's fellow conspirators, Pablo Cámara, a campesino in his early fifties, rehearsed a litany of grievances against "the son-of-a-bitch authorities," then swore to the party agent that a reckoning was imminent: "Very soon we'll put an end to the way they screw us . . . very soon we'll burn their asses good [quemar el culo]."[25]

In Peto, the plot was hatched by a local committee that included several campesinos, artisans, and a hacienda foreman. The foreman assured CEI headquarters, "you can count on me and maybe five hundred others. . . . provided there will be arms." After reporting on their agreed plans to take the local militia barracks, these dissident Petuleños made sure Mérida knew that they also intended to kill Casimiro Montalvo Solís, the despised prefect who had been the district's cacique for nearly fifteen years, and his chief ally, "the notorious slaveowner of Catmís, Arturo Cirerol."[26]

All these preparations were for naught, however, because state authorities got wind of the conspiracy.[27] Secret police agents had managed to infiltrate a number of CEI clubs.[28] On October 9, arrest warrants for Moreno Cantón and Pino Suárez were issued and the two parties' Mérida offices were searched. Although both opposition leaders went underground, a host of their partisans, including Cámara y Cámara, Xiu, Moisés Montero, Pablo Cámara, Loreto Baak, and about 30 other cabecillas—mostly Morenistas— were immediately rounded up and thrown into Juárez Penitentiary.[29] The opposition press, which had been quick to lampoon the regime for its acute case of "morenophobia," was closed down, and arrest warrants were issued for the editors.[30] As the witch-hunt expanded over the next few days, Muñoz Arístegui called in Luis D. Molina, Olegario's nephew and Mérida's new prefect, to supervise the repression. With the jails overflowing, Muñoz Arístegui and Díaz made sure that the compliant state and federal judiciary denied all prisoners' requests for amparo (appeal).[31]

Francisco Madero had suspected that dislodging the Molinista oligarchy would prove exceedingly difficult. As the number of political prisoners mounted into the hundreds, he wrote to Pino Suárez, "You always knew how obstinate Don Olegario Molina was. Now you can be sure that his grip will not loosen easily." Madero shrewdly advised Pino to sit tight, bide his time, and then pick up the pieces after the more visible Morenistas had borne the brunt of the regime's displeasure.[32]

In the short term, the repression of "La Candelaria" gave the Molinistas some breathing space; but the conspiracy's greater importance lay in the contacts the Morenistas, and to a lesser extent the Pinistas, made in the countryside. The incipient partnership between planter factions in the cities and individual smallholders, artisans, and small traders in several interior villages would consolidate in the months and years ahead. The elites provided a measure of cash and weapons, and these local chiefs recruited in their villages and, increasingly, on nearby haciendas.

## "La Primera Chispa de la Revolución Mexicana"? Valladolid, Spring 1910

It is interesting that until recently, much of the literature on the Mexican Revolution in Yucatán before General Alvarado's arrival focused on the failed rebellion in Valladolid in early June 1910. Indeed, many Yucatecan writers, most notably Carlos R. Menéndez, the longtime editor of *La Revista de Mérida* and an ardent Morenista, proudly boasted that the Valladolid revolt constituted *la primera chispa* (the first spark) of the Revolution of 1910. As such, Menéndez argued, it preceded the national upheaval's traditionally accepted November commencement date by almost six months.[33]

We would contend that, far from being epochal or "revolutionary," the uprising in the eastern part of the state should be regarded more as an example of the kind of conspiracies and violent outbreaks that surfaced periodically during Yucatán's "extended Porfiriato" (1910–15). Because "La Candelaria" provided the organizational impetus that facilitated subsequent revolts in 1910 and early 1911, we have chosen to emphasize its precursor role here. It is significant that the Molinista regime, just like its opponents, portrayed the Valladolid episode as something of a delayed reaction to the government's suffocation of the Candelaria eight months earlier.[34] Despite the Valladolid rebellion's dramatically larger size, its circumscribed locale, and the violent manner in which the regime suppressed it—all of which set it apart from the uprisings that preceded and followed it—a strong argument can be made for including it in the period's characteristic seasons of upheaval.[35]

Little changed between October 1909, when the Candelaria was thwarted, and June 1910. Meridano officials of the CEI and the PA and local *cabecillas* had been obliged to cool off during short stays in the Hotel Bolados. Once the electoral farce had been played out (Muñoz Arístegui was announced to have officially defeated his "closest challenger," Moreno Cantón, by 76,791 votes to 5!), the Molinista governor had been imposed for a full term in February 1910.[36] It is hardly surprising, therefore, that the Morenistas would attempt violently to contest power again, this time concentrating their efforts in an area where they were traditionally strong, Valladolid *partido*.

They had grounds for optimism. Valladolid (160 kilometers southeast of Mérida) and its hinterland were the Cantonistas' home territory. Hacienda Kantó, the greatest estate in the *partido*, belonged to Don Pancho; his *camarilla* owned a variety of other haciendas capable of rallying hundreds of peons. Moreover, support, if not wholehearted enthusiasm, had been pledged by certain prominent local Pinistas, such as Crescencio Jiménez Borreguí.[37] Indeed, Morenistas could count on the sympathies of most of the district's residents, who had been alienated by the excesses of Luis Felipe de Regil, the high-handed Porfirian military officer who was Valladolid's prefect. Appointed in the wake of the Candelaria, the dandified, austere Regil had immediately boasted to Vallisoletanos that he would put an end to dissent in the district and "maintain the most absolute calm."[38]

The rebellion was plotted throughout the spring and drawn up in the Plan de Dzelkoop on May 10, 1910. Dzelkoop was the small estate of Morenista *cabecilla* Maximiliano Ramírez Bonilla, a 45-year-old merchant, who had languished for periods in Juárez Penitentiary for his coordination of the Candelaria in Valladolid and other activities. Also leading the revolt was Claudio Alcocer, the overseer of Hacienda Kantó. Apart from his personal ties to the Cantón family, Alcocer had a grudge to settle with Regil. The *jefe político* had recently banished him from the city as his mother lay dying there. The third leader of the revolt was Alcocer's *compadre*, Miguel Ruz Ponce. A former schoolteacher and now an accountant in the commercial house of Marcial Vidal (the director of the local CEI), Ruz Ponce, like Ramírez Bonilla, was a Candelaria veteran who had served jail time. He quickly assumed leadership of the tactical aspects of the rebellion and came to be acknowledged as the movement's chief by both its adherents and the regime.[39]

Like the conspiracies that characterized the Candelaria, the Valladolid rebellion had a distinctly local flavor. The Plan de Dzelkoop was thick with liberal platitudes and general statements of discontent (in the manner of most Maderista pronouncements), but it made no mention of Porfirio Díaz. This omission fit with Morenismo's ambivalence about perpetuating the national regime and the reign of its living icon. Instead, the plan excoriated Muñoz Arístegui and his local agents, those who maintained "an order run by one large family of slaveowners whose only ambition is to monopolize all the wealth in the land and reduce the suffering population to the status of laborers on its highly profitable estates."[40]

Practically speaking, the revolt's mobilization hinged on local discontents and social networks. To be sure, Ramírez Bonilla, a close political associate of Alfonso Cámara y Cámara, made several brief trips to Mérida to secure CEI support in the west of the state. Nevertheless, far greater effort was made to cultivate venerable patron-client networks to drum up a local military force. Several prominent Morenista *hacendados* enlisted their peons on the eve of the uprising. At Hacienda Kantó, *mayordomo* Alcocer left nothing to chance, telling Don Pancho's 35 peons that their master was being held prisoner in the Valladolid jail and was counting on them to free him.[41] En route to the plaza, when some expressed second thoughts, Alcocer fortified their resolve with a few rounds of *aguardiente*.

The Molinistas would later paint the rebellion as a great deceit perpetrated on Maya campesinos by their Morenista patrons, and some local historians (armed with very different ideological agendas) have concurred.[42] Such a bluntly conspiratorial view does not square with either the bulk of the evidence or the ethnohistory of the district. To be sure, the Kantó peons were manipulated, although we should not discount the pull of paternalism on Kantó and other estates in the district. Valladolid was far away from the impersonal, factorylike rhythms of the henequen zone, and cultural dependency still remained a vital force in rural social relations.[43] It also appears that Ruz Ponce deceived the leaders of several of the surrounding Maya pueblos, obliging them to support the uprising by counterfeiting orders that appeared to come from *jefe político* Regil. Nevertheless, many of the villagers, who made up the majority of the rebel fighting force, likely joined the revolt for good reasons of their own.

Local Maya campesinos had struggled to protect their economic and cultural autonomy from the encroachment of the *dzules* for generations even before the Caste War. Aided by their remote geographical location and proximity to both *cruzob* and *pacífico* settlements, the local Maya possessed substantial tactical mobility. Villagers routinely circumvented elite exactions and authority (for example, the *leva*) through flight or permanent migration into the *pacífico* zone. They were much more successful at maintaining control over local government (and even the police) than their counterparts on the western or eastern fringes of monoculture. The history of the district as one of the bloodiest theaters of the Caste War only exacerbated the locals' reputation among the *dzules* as truculent Indians.

Regil's exactions and abuses (*corvée* labor, forced conscription, increased taxes), coming on top of generations of moral claims and ethnic conflict, therefore, provided the neighboring Maya with more than enough motivation to join the revolt.[44] (Indeed, most of the revolt's second-line leadership, whose names appear on the Plan de Dzelkoop, were Maya *comuneros*.[45]) By the time the revolt broke out, on June 4, 1910, Ruz Ponce had a force of fifteen hundred under his command.[46]

Lacking effective leadership, sufficient firepower, and any support in the western part of the state, the Valladolid rebellion played itself out tragically. Armed mostly with machetes and old hunting pieces, the rebels overwhelmed the city's small garrison, killing Regil and several others in the assault. Claudio Alcocer, aided by the peons of Kantó, settled his score with the *jefe político* in particularly brutal fashion: he stopped Regil in his tracks with a shotgun blast, then finished off the mortally wounded man with a flurry of machete blows.[47]

After Ruz Ponce read the Plan de Dzelkoop aloud in the town square, the rebels emptied the municipal treasury and demanded provisions and "contributions" from Molinista commercial and landed interests at gunpoint. Each day, for example, several steers were brought in from the countryside and slaughtered to feed the rebel band. But although Ramírez Bonilla led his men in looting and roughing up members of the elite, no massacre or general sack of the city like the 1847 Caste War episode occurred. The six-day occupation of Valladolid provoked minor disturbances in the countryside and peon desertions from Molinista *fincas* (as well as some unanticipated desertions from Morenista estates.)

While the campesino insurgents celebrated in the district seat, the regime orchestrated its counterattack. Muñoz Arístegui wired President Díaz complete details following the rebels' seizure of Valladolid, and in hours received a commitment of federal forces. On June 8, six hundred fresh, well-armed troops from the Tenth Federal Battalion and four hundred state militia (mostly conscripts) fell on the city. After two days of stiff combat, the rebels surrendered.[48] Justice was served in draconian fashion: although Ruz Ponce and Alcocer managed a daring escape, the state punished hundreds of the insurgents.[49] Several of the leaders, including Ramírez Bonilla, were publicly executed; others received long jail sentences to be served in Mérida. Most of the lesser lights were sent out of the state to penal servitude in the jungles of Quintana Roo or the federal army in Veracruz. A subsequent public outcry for amnesty, spearheaded in Mérida by several of Yucatán's most prominent opposition planters and timed to coincide with the one hundredth anniversary of Mexican independence in September 1910, was rejected outright by Muñoz Arístegui.

The dramatic failure of the Valladolid revolt casts into bold relief some of the weaknesses and limitations of the elite-led mobilizations that characterized Yucatán's seasons of upheaval. The revolt was logistically isolated, poorly organized, and inadequately armed, largely because competing Morenista and Pinista elites could not set aside their differences and intelligently coordinate their statewide efforts. Despite Ramírez Bonilla's frequent visits to Mérida and the optimism they generated, when push came to shove neither the CEI nor the PA was willing to commit sufficient materiel, let alone broad-based support, in the western part of the state. Nor did Ruz Ponce think to leave Valladolid in search of broader support when he had the chance to do so, just before the regime's counterattack. Given the level of popular opposition to Molinista rule throughout the state and the large size of the rebel force, some contemporaries believed that had the Valladolid insurgents marched on Mérida immediately, before federal reinforcements arrived, the state might have fallen into their hands.[50] Such indecision and elite factionalism gave Molinista authorities the respite they needed to regroup, seal off the troublesome area, and prevent the rebellion from spreading, particularly to the strategic henequen zone.

Of course, we must also ponder whether the specter of another Caste War gave CEI and PA elites second thoughts about undertaking a full-scale mobilization and military campaign. Before the revolt, for example, Ramírez Bonilla and Ruz Ponce had had extensive discussions as to which Indians were "peaceful" enough to control.[51] Yucatecan *hacendados* had grown up with their families' bitter memories of how similar internecine political disputes during the 1840s had led to the arming of Maya campesinos and their emergence as an independent, hostile force. Few could forget—least of all in Valladolid, where depredations on white elites were perhaps greatest— a war that had reduced the peninsula's population by up to one-half and razed the profitable sugar industry on the southeastern frontier. Thus, although many elites virtually itched to defeat Molina's *camarilla* in 1910, the majority feared that fully unleashing the rural masses would destabilize the elaborate mechanisms of social control that were fashioned in the wake of the Caste War and had so successfully underwritten the henequen boom.

As we have seen, this finely tuned system of coercion and co-optation, managed by both private landowners and the state, balanced a brutal agricultural regime with sophisticated use of the judiciary to redress the worst excesses. In 1910, if *hacendado*-supported revolts were to blossom into social revolution, Yucatán's contending elites might lose everything once again. That dissident elites, such as Valladolid's Morenistas, would even risk going down that road by mobilizing campesinos in their locality underscores not only the deepening contradictions within the late Porfirian elite but also the Morenistas' rising level of desperation.

Ultimately, therefore, the Valladolid rebellion was undercut by powerful tensions within the elite parties that sponsored it and within the revolt itself. Even as Delio Moreno Cantón publicly called for the overthrow of the Molinista order in 1909–10, the CEI chief was privately impressing on his lieutenants the importance of counseling their followers "to maintain order."[52] Even as villagers and peons were recruited by elite *camarillas* and prepared to unseat "the son-of-a-bitch authorities," they were deprived of the firepower they needed to succeed. More often than not, at Valladolid and in the insurgencies that followed, they carried their own machetes.[53]

The circumstances surrounding the execution of *hacendado* Ramírez Bonilla themselves contain an irony that highlights the rebellion's essential paradox. Only hours before he faced the firing squad, the Morenista spoke with a small group of fellow prisoners. He had become a colonel in "this revolution," he told them, because "our land has degenerated into a slave plantation." Not long afterward, Ramírez Bonilla drew up his last will and testament, in which he settled a five-hundred-peso debt by leaving his creditor one of his own debt peons.[54]

## A Spark Poorly Snuffed Out: Rebellions on the Fringes of Monoculture, Spring 1911

To no one's surprise, Porfirio Díaz was overwhelmingly "reelected" for another term in late June 1910. Yet while the Maderista movement built tremendous momentum throughout the republic the following fall, things became rather quiet in Yucatán. No doubt the Molinistas' harsh response to Valladolid played a role in temporarily muting political activity by the opposition parties. Short-term economic conditions also registered an impact. At least partly as a result of the manipulations of the price of fiber by the International Harvester Company and the Molina-Montes *parentesco*, the henequen market hit bottom in the year 1910–11. Commercial bankruptcies and foreclosures rocked the peninsula, caused partly by the steep drop in fiber prices, partly by the lingering effects of the panic of 1907–8. Once again the oligarchy, with its access to capital, took advantage of the situation, while lesser elites were caught in the credit squeeze.

Meanwhile, in the countryside, as if things were not bad enough, a severe locust plague in 1910 ravaged the campesinos' cornfields. Locusts are a formidable foe. Creatures of the wind, they fly by day; at night they eat anything that grows, consuming their weight in vegetation and leaving the land barren behind them. A 40-square-mile swarm of these migratory grasshoppers is not uncommon; some Yucatecan old-timers recall several immense swarms in their lifetime. A sun-blackening swarm of that size weighs up to ten thousand tons, a biological mass equivalent to the weight of a good-sized ocean freighter.[55]

In 1910, with their food supply destroyed, many Maya villagers were no longer able to resist falling into debt servitude on the plantations. But moving onto the estates was now an even less attractive option, for planters in financial straits passed their burdens downward, further emiserating their peons. Wages for weeding, for example, plunged four centavos in 1911.[56] Moreover, the locust plague worsened the *acasillados'* diet and increased the incidence of pellagra to near-epidemic proportions. All the while, the state kept the popular classes busy, implementing a public labor levy that compelled campesinos and workers to combat the locusts when and where it dictated. For many hungry and weary campesinos, this proved to be a hellish assignment. For example, residents of Espita returned from a national guard stint fighting the rebels in Valladolid to find their cornfields devoured and their presence immediately requested for locust service many kilometers away.[57]

Although worsening economic conditions must certainly figure in any explanation of Yucatán's volatile political climate during the period 1910–15, it is hazardous to attribute reflexively either rural insurgency or quiescence to fluctuations in the economy. In contrast to once-fashionable "volcanic" theories of collective violence, we now appreciate that hunger and misery likely impede political mobilization more often than they abet it.[58] During the seasons of upheaval that gripped Yucatán intermittently between 1910 and 1913, it was the combination of tightening economic prospects *and* widening political space that facilitated rural mobilization, providing both the incentive and the opportunity to rebel. As Díaz's national regime began to crumble in the face of Maderismo's armed challenge throughout the spring of 1911, political space began to widen, even in remote, oligarchical Yucatán. The peninsular version of this Maderista opening witnessed a revitalization of Morenista and Pinista elite political activity and a reactivation of their networks in the countryside. That spring, Yucatán saw a chain reaction of rural revolts and local riots that paralyzed the Molinista government and soon began to pose a threat to elite rule itself.

What dissident elite *camarillas* had originally envisioned as a *controlled* mobilization, à la the Candelaria and Valladolid, for the purpose of wresting the spoils of monoculture from an overweening oligarchy now began to veer out of control. Valladolid may not have been the "first spark" of a revolution, but elites understood that it had been a potentially dangerous spark nevertheless. No doubt even many Morenista planters in the northwest rested more easily when that single, isolated spark had been vanquished. Now, however, the sparks were multiplying, the tinder seemed inexhaustible, and elites were growing increasingly uncertain of their ability to forestall a conflagration.

While we will argue that the participants did not intend these episodes of local rural insurgency to be "revolutionary," they did have objectives and consequences that would pose serious problems for the hegemony of Yucatecan monoculture. Given the opportunity, as they were in the spring of 1911 (and would be throughout much of 1912 and early 1913), Yucatán's subaltern groups—free campesinos and groupings of hacienda peons—would turn elite feuds to their own advantage, lashing out at hated targets, settling old scores, exercising new-found mobility, pressing traditional claims and resisting new demands by the state and elites, and, in certain individual cases, carving out new bases of political power. The kaleidoscope of local revolts and riots that convulsed the countryside that spring season provides all the clues we need to appreciate the disjuncture between popular and elite politics (see Map. 7.1). We begin by reconstructing the revolt that most preoccupied the Molinista regime, led by Pedro Crespo in the strategically located north-central district of Temax.

## PORTRAIT OF A 'CABECILLA' AND A REVOLT

In 1911, as it still is today, the *cabecera* of Temax was at the end of the road. A few blocks north of its weatherbeaten plaza, the serviceable road from Izamal ran out. Farther on, *camino blanco* (dirt tracks) wound for about fifteen kilometers through scrub, then mangrove swamp to the Gulf of Mexico. Eighty kilometers west of the town was Mérida; en route, one journeyed through the very heart of the henequen zone. Henequen fields lined both sides of the highway, crisscrossed here and there by the narrow-gauge rails of imported Decauville tram tracks. Tall chimneys and elegant dwellings in the background bore witness to the flush times of monoculture. To the east of Temax, henequen's bluish gray spines almost immediately gave way to denser scrub and clearings of grazing cattle; beyond the neighboring village of Buctzotz there was virtually nothing for another seventy kilometers, until the town of Tizimín.

Temax district had figured significantly in regional affairs since the Caste War. Poised as it was between the henequen zone and the sparsely populated hinterland, between the settled, dominant plantation society and the frontier zone of refuge for the rebellious Maya campesinos who had resisted encroachment on their traditional way of life, Temax constituted a strategic periphery. Moreover, the Mérida–Valladolid railway ran through

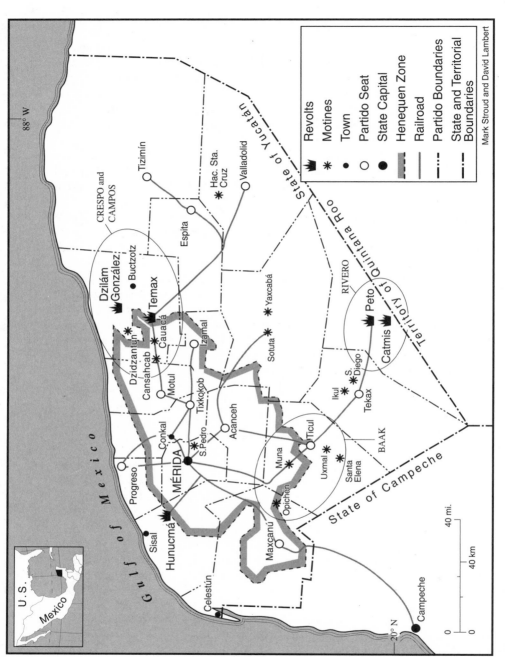

*Map 7.1.* Yucatán: Spring 1911.

Mark Stroud and David Lambert

the *partido* and its district seat. If rebels held Temax, Valladolid and points southeast could effectively be cut off from contact with the state capital. Control of Temax was therefore of great concern to the Molinista regime. And beginning in March 1911, the Molinistas would come to appreciate that Temax's political disposition was closely linked to the fortunes of an extraordinarily shrewd rural *cabecilla*, Pedro Crespo.[59]

Born in Temax about 1870, Crespo, like many campesinos on the fringes of the expanding henequen zone, grew up determined to preserve his family's status as small but free cultivators. It is quite likely that he chose to enlist in the state national guard to avoid the mechanism of debt that tied an ever-increasing number of villagers as peons to the large and powerful henequen estates.

In short order, Crespo demonstrated his prowess as a soldier and was made an officer in the local guard. How Crespo regarded his duties—which included hunting down and returning runaway peons to their masters; quelling worker protests against brutal, slavelike conditions; and implementing the hated *leva*—we will never know. Ironically, it seems likely that Crespo even was one of the leaders of Temax's contingent of conscripts that helped subdue the Valladolid rebellion in June 1910.

Crespo came to know the social world of north-central Yucatán more intimately than the average country dweller. Temaxeños remember him as a clever politician, a "mestizo de buen hablar"—a Maya campesino who spoke Spanish well and could operate in *dzul* society.[60] Through his work, young Crespo was introduced to the milieu of urban politics, to the ever-shifting, multilayered networks of patronage and clientele that tied the powerful local planters to even more powerful patrons in the state capital.

As a rising officer in the guard, Crespo was compelled to play the exacting, dangerous game of late Porfirian politics. His ability to bridge the cultural distance between *dzules* and campesinos made him a valuable asset, and he was wooed by incumbent and dissident *camarillas* alike. Although he initially flirted with the intrigues of Morenista elites in 1909, by the eve of the gubernatorial elections that year, Crespo had allied himself with the Molinistas. Along with Temax's other prominent functionaries, Colonel Antonio Herrera, the *jefe político*, and Nazario Aguilar Brito, the municipal tax collector, Crespo joined the local chapter of the Unión Democrática, Muñoz Arístegui's campaign organization. When the oligarchical regime stood firm in its repression of the Candelaria and Valladolid conspiracies, Pedro Crespo stood with it.[61]

What, then, turned this cautious policeman into an insurgent? Quite likely he was unable to ignore ties of blood and a claim of vengeance. Like Pancho Villa (whose sister was raped) and countless others who rebelled in Yucatán and throughout the republic in 1910–11, a sense of deep personal outrage set Crespo at odds with the Porfirian authorities. Although details are sketchy, press accounts and judicial proceedings, corroborated here and there by local tradition, indicate that Temax's corrupt prefect, Colonel Herrera, who was also Crespo's superior officer in the local guard detachment, left Crespo to languish for 30 days in the unfriendly confines of Juárez Penitentiary. Crespo would later speak vaguely of "differences he had had with the Temax authorities," and his lieutenants would cite "tyrannical abuses" by Herrera's local rule.[62] Some old-timers recall that Crespo was openly critical of the *jefe político*'s high-handed tactics in meetings with Temaxeño campesinos.[63] For Crespo, however, a much more compelling reason fueled his anger: while he was in jail, Herrera killed his father, Don Cosme Damián Crespo, under shadowy circumstances. Apparently Don Cosme balked at Herrera's arbitrary order to do road labor, whereupon the prefect ordered his thugs to gun down the old man in broad daylight.[64]

Soon after his release from prison, Pedro Crespo sought revenge. He mustered a small band of kin and clients—most of them Temaxeño villagers—and exploded into revolt. Operating in the chaotic political climate that was Maderismo in Yucatán, Crespo elected to burn his bridges behind him, joining his local vendetta to the evolving regional movement against the Molinistas and, by implication, the national Díaz regime. On March 4, 1911, he led his column in a lightning predawn raid on the district seat.

The rebels easily overwhelmed the nine-man guard detachment just off Temax's central plaza. (Later, the town police commander would charge that the sentries had been sleeping on the job.) Crespo immediately rousted Colonel Herrera and the treasury agent, Aguilar Brito, from their beds and hauled them, clad only in their skivvies, to the plaza. All the while, as members of his band shouted "Down with bad government!" and "Viva Madero!" Crespo vented his rage (in Spanish) on the stunned Herrera: "You bastard, you killed my father! For nine years you were on top and screwed me and the pueblo, but now it's my turn!"[65]

The tables indeed had been turned. Hand-picked as district prefect about 1900 by Temax's great Molinista planters, the Manzanillas, Peóns, Regils, Méndezes, and Cámaras, Herrera was the dominant figure in the *partido*'s political life. His physical presence made him even more menacing to local campesinos. Hulking in stature, with his shaved head and long gray beard, Herrera often took on the dimensions of a mad monk or an avenging prophet. Only days before, during the carnival revels of Shrove Tuesday, although too cowed to make a statement about the *jefe político*, Temaxeños had mocked his subordinate, Aguilar Brito, as "Juan Carnaval," shooting an effigy of the tax collector in front of the municipal palace. Now, in the same central plaza in the wee hours of the morning, Pedro Crespo was cutting the despised prefect down to size. In a final act of humiliation, Crespo strapped Herrera and Aguilar to chairs and riddled them with bullets in the same spot where Aguilar had been "executed" during Carnival. Their bodies were piled into a meat wagon and dumped at the gates of the town cemetery. (In a ghastly ironic twist, the treasury agent later was interred in the same coffin that "Juan Carnaval" had occupied on Shrove Tuesday.[66])

Before he left town later that morning, Crespo emptied the municipal jail, freeing some campesinos who had been imprisoned by Herrera for refusing to do *fagina*. Crespo armed his new recruits with guns and ammunition seized from the guard barracks—slim pickings, on the whole—and then, in the manner of the Valladolid rebels, demanded food and "contributions" from local merchants and took the three hundred pesos in the municipal treasury.[67] Yet Crespo had learned some valuable lessons from the Valladolid debacle. He made sure that Temax's prominent families were not physically harmed, and he strictly limited his men's intake of *aguardiente*. (Indeed, Crespo instructed the town's merchants not to make liquor available to them.) There would be no premature celebrations in Temax. Crespo saddled up his force—now swollen to about 80—and divided it into two bands, one to head west toward Cansahcab, the other east, under his direction, towards Buctzotz. All wore on their hats the characteristic red ribbon of Morenismo.

In the weeks and months that followed, Pedro Crespo became Yucatán's most successful insurgent. His hit-and-run tactics, based on an intimate knowledge of the local terrain, were celebrated in the pueblos and hacienda communities of north-central Yucatán, and his ranks continued to multiply. One week after his raid on Temax, his troops had mushroomed to two hundred; by mid-April some estimates placed his strength at four hundred, and in May, close to one thousand. Many free villagers and some hacienda peons joined his campaign willingly, eager to strike a blow against the *dzules*, particularly the district prefects, municipal presidents, and hacienda overseers who symbolized the encroachments and abuses of the oligarchy. Other campesinos provided his forces with intelligence in the form of a far-flung network of *madrinas*, who reported on strategic political developments and government troop movements.

In Buctzotz, on Crespo's arrival, a group of villagers rose up, took the national guard barracks, and cut out the tongue of the municipal president before executing him. In Dzilám González, villagers freely offered Crespistas liquor and cigarettes. Then dozens of campesinos, including the town band, defected en masse to the rebellion. The musicians brought their instruments and enlivened the guerrilla campaign in the following weeks with a series of impromptu Saturday night *jaranas* (popular dances) in remote backcountry hamlets. In Tixbaka, a tiny settlement in the neighboring district of Espita, for example, Crespo and his men danced the night away with the settlement's several-score inhabitants, then slept off the painful effects of their revels most of Sunday. On finally arising, the Crespistas received a delegation of Morenista organizers from Motul, Maxcanú, and Valladolid, with whom they conferred for several hours. This piece of evidence suggests that despite its grassroots origins, in the spring of 1911 the revolt may already have been feeding into a more coordinated Morenista effort than is immediately apparent.[68]

Although the rebels recruited many hacienda peons at gunpoint, Crespo also sought to erode planter paternalism and social control with clientelist measures of his own. At Cauacá, Chacmay, and San Francisco Manzanilla—the haciendas of the largest *henequeneros*—he declared "liberation," canceling all the *acasillados'* debts. Crespo provided amply for his recruits, moreover, raiding police stations and guard barracks for munitions, and levying forced loans on local planters and merchants. At Cauacá, 150 peons joined him, and suddenly Maya surnames greatly outnumbered Spanish ones in his ranks. Crespo also managed to enlist the support of several overseers and foremen—one of whom, Carmen Castillo, became a trusted lieutenant—as well as a local priest.[69] Many planters, hoping to avoid the total loss of their work force, immediately ordered the temporary evacuation of their peons to nearby *cabeceras*, where they would wait out the rebellion. "The district of Temax is becoming depopulated," the regional press reported, "even though the district seat has been well fortified. Nights in this town have a funeral air about them."[70]

Crespo's guerrilla campaign forced the Molinista regime to expend great amounts of time, money, and manpower in a futile effort to pin down the rebels. As the spring of 1911 wore on and other local revolts sprang up, the Mérida government found itself unable to do more than hold the district seats, leaving the hinterland to the insurgents. Crespo moved freely throughout Temax *partido*, and penetrated neighboring Izamal to the south and Espita and Tizimín to the east.

Early on, Crespo reached an understanding with Juan Campos, another Morenista *cabecilla* who had also risen against local abuses and then conveniently labeled himself a Maderista. Campos, as we will see in the next chapter, was already carving out a power base (*cacicazgo*) north of the town of Temax, in the area around Dzidzantún and Dzilám González. Beginning with a number of joint operations in the spring of 1911, Crespo and Campos together came to control all of north-central Yucatán throughout the 1910s and 1920s. Old-timers still recall the two chiefs as local instruments through which the Mexican Revolution put an end to "the age of slavery." Campos is said to have been even more audacious and vengeful than Crespo in his dealings with the local planter elite. Lore has it that he would arrive at an estate, hear the peons' grievances, and then mete out the appropriate number of lashes to the *hacendado* (which is likely apocryphal) or his overseers (more plausible) before distributing merchandise from the estate store.[71]

In late May 1911, after both Díaz and the Molinistas had fallen, Pedro Crespo and Juan Campos disbanded their forces. All along, Crespo had said that his aim was simply "to overthrow the authorities and then see what happens."[72] For his part, Campos had rebelled "to fight tyranny and remain a free man."[73] Far from being finished, however, their careers and *cacicazgos* were only beginning. Crespo's ability to survive, come what may, is unique in the local history of twentieth-century Yucatán. For the next 30 years, Crespo would arbitrate the political affairs of Temax, brokering power among elites, villagers, and peons during the most volatile juncture of the revolutionary period.[74]

## STRUGGLES FOR LAND AND AUTONOMY IN AND AROUND THE PUUC

As Crespo was launching his popular revolt on the eastern periphery of the henequen zone, insurgency had already broken out on the zone's volatile southern fringe, along the range of foothills known as the Puuc (see Map 7.1). Here, as we have seen, at various junctures between 1880 and 1910, Maya villages had repeatedly contested state authorities' attempts to limit, seize, survey, and parcel out their traditional *ejidos* in the interests of capitalist proprietors, real estate speculators, or railway companies. Pueblos in the sierra had suffered setbacks, to be sure, but on the whole they had fended off the proprietors and investors who coveted their land and labor more successfully than had the *comuneros* of Temax *partido*. For example, whereas the communal lands of Temax and Dzilám González (the pueblos of Crespo and Campos, respectively) had been surveyed, parceled, and virtually devoured years earlier by the district's prime henequen haciendas, southern villages such as Muna, Santa Elena, and Peto continued fiercely to resist ejidal survey in 1911. Other pueblos, such as Halachó, Maxcanú, and Opichén, gamely struggled against further agrarian encroachment. As impoverished and marginal as life was on the fringes of monoculture, it was here, along the arc of pueblos that swung from Maxcanú and Halachó on the northern border of Campeche through Opichén, Muna, and Santa Elena to Peto, that the notion of *el hombre libre*—a free and independent man—remained most vital.[75]

All along the Puuc corridor, the perpetually simmering agrarian question was perceived as inseparable from the issue of Molinista administrative abuse. Put simply, what remained of an independent peasantry felt increasingly hemmed in by aggressive haciendas and a regime that catered to their needs. Molinista *caciques*, typically prefects and municipal presidents who often doubled as *hacendados* or gouging merchants, frequently greased the machinery of the surveying process or influenced the courts to redefine *ejidos* as vacant public lands. Of course, as we have seen, the pueblos' loathing of these officials did not stop here. The morally felt grievances and personal vendettas that had underwritten the Candelaria in villages such as Peto, Muna, and Santa Elena in October 1909 had only festered in the intervening year and a half. Now, in 1911, with the national and local regimes' power and legitimacy in precipitous decline, these outlying communities were in a position to take action.

Before dawn on March 3, 1911, an armed group of about two dozen of Peto's Morenistas—campesinos and artisans led by Elías Rivero, a silversmith, and Antonio Reyes, a laborer from Veracruz—attempted to do what they had been preempted from doing in 1909: take the local guard post and "bring that bastard, Casimiro Montalvo Solís, to justice."[76] Shouting "Viva Madero!" the rebels assaulted the guard barracks. The post, manned largely by inexperienced conscripts who were both outnumbered and taken by surprise, offered little resistance, yet just enough to allow the hated prefect to make good his escape a block and a half away.[77] By the time the town hall doors had been battered in with machetes, Don Casimiro, still agile enough at 70, had slipped into the bush and headed for Tzucacab. The rebels had to content themselves with the capture of his clerk, Fernando Sosa. Pulled from his hammock, Sosa was led, tied elbow to elbow and clad only in his underwear, to a clearing outside town. Angry at being deprived of Montalvo Solís, the Morenistas showed no pity, taunting Sosa that his comfort was over: "those were other days; now we command." The unfortunate scribe protested that he was not well and needed to return home to take his pills. Elías Rivero responded, "Don't worry, we'll give you your medicine. In fact, why don't I just complete your cure right now." Drawing a revolver, the *cabecilla* shot Sosa point-blank while his men fell on the victim with their knives.[78]

The Morenista insurgents returned to town to fortify themselves with supplies from the barracks. They made off with an artillery piece, 32 Remington rifles with numerous rounds of ammunition, and half a case of dynamite. They were then able to set their sights on their second principal target, the district's largest hacienda, Catmís, located in the neighboring *municipio* of Tzucacab. Labor conditions on this profitable sugar estate—where a number of the Petuleños' friends and relatives had become tied by debt—were notorious, reflecting the worst aspects of the contract labor system, including the exploitation of Yaqui deportees. According to old-timers in the district, workers were forced to cut and grind cane a minimum of eighteen hours a day.[79] Peons' houses resembled slave barracks, "human beehives inhabited by 30 to 50 people, including many families."[80] Roofs were inadequate, water scarce, medical attention and schools nonexistent. At Catmís, the infamous designation "age of slavery" really lived up to its billing.[81]

The Cirerol family had run the plantation for twenty years and had benefited immeasurably from its alliance with the district's prefecture.[82] For the past decade, the eldest brother, Arturo, had developed a tight partnership with Colonel Casimiro Montalvo Solís. Petuleños portrayed the hated prefect as utterly Cirerol's creature: Montalvo Solís had supported the wretched conditions on the sugar estate by hunting down runaways. He had used his influence to abet the Cirerols' acquisition of small parcels of land around Tzucacab, "threatening the [campesino] owners to sell at laughable prices set by the buyer."[83] Thus far, however, it seems that neither Montalvo Solís nor the Cirerols had been as successful in breaking up the Peto *ejido* as they had been in Tzucacab, although rumors of an imminent renewed effort hung over the pueblo in 1911 and certainly must be numbered among the social determinants of the March revolt.[84]

Finally, and perhaps most profoundly offensive, the prefect had turned a blind eye to (and occasionally actively abetted) Arturo Cirerol's long-running habit of claiming the "right of first night," not only with brides-to-be on his estate but often in the district at large. According to several of the rebels, some grooms actually attempted to flee the area with their brides, only to be apprehended and jailed by Don Casimiro, thereby giving "this Don Juan . . . the critical access he required to fulfill his ends." "These are *the facts,*" insurgent Máximo Sabido angrily observed, "and they will be remembered two generations from now."[85] Indeed they are. Old-timer Marcos Ku Peraza recalled in an interview, "Back then, they didn't charge you anything to get married. But first the *señor* took your woman, first *he* had her and *then* you got married."[86]

It was this corrupt partnership between the Molinista *cacique* and the *patrón* that the villagers correctly identified as the source of their oppression. "Arturo Cirerol set himself up as the master of lives and haciendas, and Casimiro Montalvo let him do it with absolute impunity."[87] Unless one appreciates this partnership and the Petuleños' graphic perception of its consequences, it is difficult to make sense of the brutal events that unfolded when the rebels arrived at Catmís.

Following their uprising in Peto, the insurgents visited several outlying hamlets and recruited additional campesinos. Far from being contested, their arrival on March 6 at the sugar plantation was cause for celebration among the peons. After about two hundred workers, including the Yaquis, had pledged Rivero and Reyes their support, the rebels purposefully set about destroying the planters' machinery and cane. (Damages would later be estimated at a whopping half-million pesos.[88])

At about this time the Cirerol brothers arrived, at the head of a national guard column of about 150, determined to recapture the estate. (Colonel Montalvo Solís, who had earlier returned to Peto with the reinforcements, stayed behind to defend the *cabecera.*) The Cirerols, however, overestimated the morale of the government forces, who were conscripts dragooned mostly from other villages in the state. They also underestimated the fury of the Petuleños and their own peons. Part of the guard company immediately sided with the insurgents, and the remainder were routed. As one participant recalled the pivotal moment of the encounter,

> The shootout was intense, ugly. . . . The battle lines were drawn amid the cane. . . . Cane all around. . . . Our leader [Reyes] gave the order to set the cane around the national guard ablaze, and we ran like the devil. No more than 60 of them left that canefield alive.[89]

The surviving guard fled, along with Arturo Cirerol, leaving his two younger brothers, Enrique and Antonio, to their fate. The two Cirerols attempted to evade the rebels, hiding in the hut of peon José Salazar, who was Don Enrique's *compadre.* But in this instance, the bonds of *compadrazgo* had eroded beyond repair: Salazar himself informed Rivero and Reyes of the *patrones'* whereabouts.[90] After brutally carving them up with machetes, the insurgents shot the brothers. The Morenistas fled immediately into the bush and remained at large for a month and a half, until an amnesty was decreed following the fall of Muñoz Arístegui.[91]

Like Crespo and Campos, Elías Rivero, the village jeweler who formerly had tended the municipal clock for Don Casimiro, would soon become a political force in his district and ultimately a bona fide revolutionary *cacique* who endured in the Puuc until the 1940s.[92] Yet throughout March and the first half of April 1911, he and his movement remained virtually anonymous, a bad dream that obsessed Yucatán's elites. For days after the grisly events in Peto, the *gente decente* in the Puuc's neighboring *cabeceras* and Mérida harbored strong fears that another "race war" was brewing. Rumors were rampant. On March 4 the morning edition of the Molinista paper announced that "reputable sources" in the Puuc had spotted five hundred "Indians" outside of Oxkutzcab. Could it be, the paper wondered, that the southern *pacíficos* were no longer pacified, and indeed were ready to consummate an alliance with the hostile *cruzob*? Were the events of the past two days merely the first hostilities of a new Caste War? Hours later, the newspaper reported in its afternoon edition that the "revelations" in the morning paper had been premature. No formidable Indian alliance appeared to be in the offing; the rebels were fewer in number and indigenous to the Puuc. Most reassuring to Yucatán's *catrines* (white city folk) was the story's final sentence: "Many of the assailants spoke Spanish and wore trousers."[93]

Still, as we will see, the same racial fears would be rekindled every time a revolt broke out in the Puuc or on the fringes of the eastern forest between 1911 and 1913.[94] Until Yucatecan elites could ascertain that indeed the rebels wore pants, no one in polite society in the northwest or the larger interior towns breathed easily.

For the plantocracy, being able to label the rebels mere "bandits" and "assailants" rather than *indios bravos*, while consoling, did not solve the larger problem of subduing these "criminals." Yucatán's villagers increasingly resisted the government's attempts to recruit them to fight against the rebels, or mutinied and deserted following recruitment.[95] Some local historians have read class solidarity into this behavior, arguing that "now campesinos were no longer willing to attack their class brethren."[96] Such emphasis on a developed class consciousness seems unwarranted for these episodes of draft resistance and desertion (or for the seasons of upheaval as a whole), for a variety of reasons that will be discussed later. But certainly these "routine" forms of resistance shed light on the larger struggle of Yucatecan rural communities and campesino groups for greater autonomy and dignity at a juncture when they had more "tactical power" to make themselves heard.[97]

Let us consider the collective act of civil disobedience that precipitated revolt in Yaxcabá, in the district of Sotuta on the day following the Peto uprising.[98] Sotuta was one of Yucatán's poorest *partidos*, perpetually at the bottom of the Porfirian statistical rankings in terms of both agricultural production and consumption. Lying roughly midway between Temax and Peto at the geographical center of the state, Sotuta was devastated in the Caste War, and it never really recovered. As northwestern monoculture waxed and southeastern commercial grain production waned after the war, Sotuta probably fared worse than any other district in this marginal zone. On the plus side, however, its Maya campesinos preserved their traditional *ejidos*. Despite the virulent *caciquismo* of a series of abusive Porfirian prefects and municipal officials—Spanish-speaking *catrines* who lorded it over the Maya majority—the latter managed to eke out a living from their traditional plots. But as henequen production continued to expand in the 1880s and 1890s, Sotuta became a transitional zone for the cultivation of fiber, and pressure on the communal lands increased. Although henequen itself never deeply penetrated Sotuta *partido*, commercial interests came to covet Yaxcabá's *ejidos* for maize production to supply the henequen sector (see Map 6.2). Moreover, as we have seen, such a strategy would also yield badly needed workers for those enterprises by depriving villagers of their land base.

In Yaxcabá, as in the Puuc, Molinista officials worked hand-in-glove with *hacendados* to indebt campesinos and undermine their hold on the land. Juan Evangelista Díaz, Yaxcabá's municipal president and self-styled *tatich* (a Maya term meaning *cacique*) in the years before 1910, was himself a large landowner, as was the district's *jefe político*, Pedro Pablo Ruz. Much later, septuagenarian campesino Clotilde Cob recalled that Díaz and Ruz jointly ran profitable commercial maize estates by hooking children into debt relationships. "They gave the kids *aguardiente* when they were very young; then, when they reached their tenth birthday, they wanted to drink but didn't have the money. The *tatich* was there to lend it, and that's how they came by many of their servants."[99]

Abuse of *fagina* also enriched these public officials-turned-entrepreneurs. Another old-timer recollected, "Ruz . . . was famous for his ability to screw folks. He had people at his beck and call. . . . His corn operation . . . was run by personal guards. He must have planted more than a hundred mecates of oranges . . . without paying a centavo."[100] And woe to the *faginero* who failed to show the proper respect to either the municipal president or the prefect: "If someone passed in front of [one of them] without removing his hat, he would be cited and hauled off to Sotuta for punishment."[101]

In the spring of 1911, pressure continued to build to divide Yaxcabá's *ejidos*. Rumors predicted the imminent arrival of armed teams of surveyors from the Puuc. Clotilde Cob later recalled that everyone remained alert for such an intrusion. In the evening, sentries were posted at the westernmost point of town on the Sotuta road, the route by which outsiders would arrive. "When there was a full moon, we didn't sleep in our hammocks but on the ground, to be closer to sounds in the night."[102]

As it turned out, the military recruiters arrived before the surveyors. On

March 4, the district prefect instructed the new municipal president, Clau- dio Padilla (picked for the job "because he knew how to command") to assemble for the draft all but 22 of the men then present in the pueblo.[103] (Many villagers were a good distance out in the countryside clearing their fields, and thus were ineligible to answer the call.) Troops were needed immediately to form a guard unit to subdue Peto's Morenista insurgents, and Yaxcabá's draftees were to leave for Sotuta that very afternoon.

The men, although disgruntled, began to prepare for the journey, until Yaxcabá's women intervened. First they confronted the municipal pres- ident and gave him a piece of their mind, ultimately obliging him to call the prefect to rescind his order. Before the prefect they argued that the pueblo was working under a tight deadline to finish preparing its cornfields, and that the men's absence would jeopardize the town's livelihood (tra- ditionally, only men made *milpa*). Furthermore, they pointed out that in these times of violence, the men were their only protection. East of Yaxcabá no settlements stood between them and the *indios bravos;* southwest of the town the rebellion was gathering. When the *jefe político* refused to rescind his order, the women, led by Asunción Carrillo, exhorted their men to resist the call-up.

Ultimately, rather than marching to Sotuta, the conscripts marched into Miguel Carrillo's cantina late that morning. One of them remarked years later, "In those days, Miguel carried some fine *aguardiente* from Cam- peche. We drank it by the gourdful until we had our fill. Then we paid the justice of the peace a visit."[104] The justice of the peace was none other than Juan Evangelista Díaz, the former municipal president and still very much the town's *cacique*. Suddenly, weeks and months of worry about the pueb- lo's lands and years of exploitation by the *tatich* and the other *dzules* were building toward an unanticipated catharsis.

The justice, however, was not at home, and his absence saved his life. The campesinos sacked his house and moved on to the office of municipal president Claudio Padilla. Padilla's son counseled a quick exit, but the fa- ther, who had been a Porfirian official for decades, demurred. He knew "his Indians" after all these years, and "these stupid Indians I have well un- der control."[105] The ensuing siege of the municipal hall ended tragically for Padilla. The official was shot badly, then passed around by the campe- sinos to be finished off with their machetes "that justice might properly be served."[106] Packing up the arms and ammunition that were stockpiled in the municipal hall, the rebels fled into the bush, shouting "Viva Madero!" Although the *tatich* organized a column to pursue them, apart from one Claudio Cuxim, who was still drinking at Carrillo's cantina, none were apprehended. All were given amnesty when the Molinistas fell a week later.

## DON PORFIRIO IMPOSES A MEDIATOR

Peto, Yaxcabá, Temax . . . the revolts followed one another in staccato fashion, depriving the regime of the possibility of isolating each episode as it had done at Valladolid. Moreover, in the days that followed, Catmís-style jacqueries erupted in a new area: the *partido* of Tekax, just west of Peto in the Puuc. Insurgent peons killed the administrator of Hacienda San Diego and badly beat up his counterpart at the neighboring sugar mill, Ikul. Violence also erupted at several sites on the Campechano side of the sierra; ejidal unrest was alleged to have sparked these *tumultos*.[107]

Even with recourse to conscripts, state troops were now stretched too thin to put out all these fires. As the Yaxcabá episode illustrates, moreover, campesinos wanted no part of the draft and were prepared—women and men alike—to stand up to recruiters. The government failed utterly in its attempts to muster troops against the Crespo rebellion in the pueblos of Muxupip, Calotmul, Baca, Mocochá, Dzidzantún, and Buctzotz. Almost a year earlier, the regime had drawn on these pueblos in the districts of Motul, Izamal, and Temax to defeat the Valladolid rebels. Now it was Crespo, and not the Molinistas, who was successfully recruiting in north-central Yucatán.[108] Governor Muñoz Arístegui despaired, "When called to serve . . . [villagers] flee, hide, afraid they'll be designated to fight for the federal army. . . . Others rebel in towns and won't fight for the [state's] national guard. Troops are in short supply and needed throughout the state."[109]

Increasingly, the regime was forced to rely on conscripts from Mérida, even as fears mounted that the state capital might itself become vulnerable to attack by the Crespo band. Nor was reinforcement by additional federal troops likely; the Third Military Zone, which included Yucatán, had its headquarters in Santa Cruz de Bravo, Quintana Roo, where (even after 1901) it remained preoccupied with containing raids by *indios bravos*. And federal troops could not be spared from central Mexico, where the Madero rebellion continued to gain ground.[110]

With the Molinistas' dilemma increasing daily, and with no prospects of militarily defeating the insurgents or even intimidating them, President Díaz opted to use the carrot rather than the stick. On March 11, 1911, he replaced Governor Muñoz Arístegui with General Luis del Carmen Curiel, a shrewd but tactful military politician, who had served as governor of Jalisco and also, briefly but effectively, as the federal military zone commander for Yucatán and Campeche. For Díaz, this was essentially an old ploy; he had often turned to outside military men to put down insurrections or settle disputes that bickering regional elites were incapable of resolving. As we have seen, he had used this tactic to good effect before in Yucatán.[111]

General Curiel already had the critical support of the Morenistas, who had a hand, it seemed, in several of the spring revolts. Even before his arrival, the CEI was hailing him as the "Savior of Yucatán."[112] Curiel had been a serious contender for the party's gubernatorial candidacy in 1909, and the Morenistas now believed that he might help them achieve their principal aim: to end Molinista control of politics and regional monoculture. While the Pinistas had understandable reservations about Curiel's impartiality, they, too, hoped that he would undermine oligarchical hegemony and, more immediately, restore social control in the countryside. For their part, the Molinistas bided their time. Later they would insist on the inviolability of existing economic arrangements and would attempt to turn the new political conjuncture to their advantage. Like their elite counterparts in the other *camarillas*, they knew that a change in government was inevitable and that social control was now first priority. After all, Muñoz Arístegui had been no Olegario Molina; perhaps Don Porfirio had sent them someone who could halt the rampage in the countryside that victimized them most of all.[113]

Nevertheless, the general's task was daunting. He had to navigate the intrigues of three rival elite factions (all of which knew that his boss, Mexico's octogenarian dictator, would soon fall from power) while placating an angry peasantry. Curiel did not sugarcoat the situation for Díaz.

> There is disorder almost every day in the pueblos and on the haciendas, and there would be in the *cabeceras* as well if I did not station my best soldiers there. But now I lack sufficient forces to control the insubordination that is multiplying so rapidly. In the pueblos there are uprisings against the municipal presidents, as well as against the tax collectors—none of these exercises authority. On the haciendas the owners, administrators, and foremen are continually in danger of attack. Bands of 30 to 40 carry out hit-and-run operations, then hide out in the bush or head for the unpopulated coast. They simply disperse when we go after them. Those from the haciendas are frequently apprehended in a state of drunkenness. We wait for them to sober up, then return them to the estates. If we were to arrest them, their labor on the estates would be missed.[114]

Under these near-impossible circumstances, Curiel succeeded admirably. First he abolished the nefarious draft, replacing it with a voluntary, paid battalion. The state legislature quickly approved a special fund of two hundred thousand pesos for the contingent, which was named the Cuerpo Activo de Seguridad Pública "Cepeda Peraza," after the beloved liberal native son who had defeated the imperialist forces in 1867. The Cepeda Peraza battalion scrounged for recruits in the months that followed. Repeatedly, the government was forced to reduce the minimum service requirement while increasing the monetary enlistment bonus. Nevertheless, Curiel's cancellation of the *leva* was an extremely popular measure in the interior villages and towns.[115]

Curiel also paid attention to other rural concerns. For the first time, significant numbers of peons from henequen estates began to petition the government regarding *fagina*, wages, and working conditions. The political opening actually emboldened several to leave their estates, make their way to Mérida, and present their complaints in person. During his brief tenure, the general listened sympathetically, then worked with a committee of progressive planters from the Cámara Agrícola to explore ways to improve conditions on the estates and thereby defuse increasing peon militancy.[116]

As we have seen, another flashpoint of grievance in the countryside was *caciquismo*. Apart from the rebellions examined in this chapter, a plethora of small village riots, bombings, and assaults took place. The great majority were directed at unpopular bosses imposed from above. Responding to these violent local "referendums" and to a host of petitions, Curiel made a number of adjustments, some of them particularly timely. In Peto, for example, he replaced prefect Casimiro Montalvo Solís with Máximo Sabido, one of the March insurgents. (Unfortunately, he then inflicted Don Casimiro on the *partido* of Acanceh, in the more tractable henequen zone.) Another Petuleño rebel, a relative of Sabido, became the *cabecera*'s justice of the peace. In perhaps his boldest move, General Curiel named Morenista leader Alfonso Cámara y Cámara, the chief strategist of the 1909 Candelaria (and, significantly, his *compadre*), the new *jefe político* of Mérida *partido*.[117]

In short order, the general also sent secret envoys into the countryside to negotiate with the insurgents of Temax, Peto, and Yaxcabá. The result of these parleys was a blanket amnesty, dated April 19, 1911, with highly generous terms. All those who had committed political crimes ("rebellion, sedition, uprisings, and riots") could present themselves to the *jefe político* of their *partido* within one month and thereby avoid prosecution. The decree was retroactive to July 1, 1909; thus all political prisoners in Juárez Penitentiary, including the Valladolid rebels and several prominent intellectuals, *hacendados*, and merchants imprisoned by the Molinistas, were immediately set free.[118] The Morenistas and Pinistas in Mérida, who had sent so many "guests" to the Hotel Bolados, were ecstatic, and most rural *cabecillas* seized the opportunity to end their revolts.[119]

Pedro Crespo and Juan Campos, however, refused to lay down their arms until the Díaz regime itself fell. Moreover, Curiel also had to deal with two new village-based revolts in Hunucmá district and the municipality of Muna. Both had a familiar ring: after years of poor but uninterrupted peasant existence, commercial agriculture and the Porfirian state were wreaking havoc with village life.

Hunucmá, bordering the Gulf of Mexico, and neighboring Maxcanú were the westernmost districts of henequen penetration (see Map 6.2). Several pueblos in the center of Hunucmá District—Tetiz, Kinchil, Ucú, and the *cabecera* itself—clung as best they could to their traditional agriculture in 1911. *Ejidos* had been surveyed in virtually all the villages, and distribution of the lots was well advanced in some of them. In the district seat, villagers protested distribution irregularities that had enabled some of the state's largest planters (including Augusto L. Peón and Gonzalo Maldonado Solís) to enlarge estates that already pressed up against the village itself. Receiving no satisfaction from the Molinista authorities, a sizable portion of the community—branded "agitators" and "bandits" by the big planters—took matters into its own hands.[120] General Curiel found himself facing an outbreak of rustling, arson, robberies, hit-and-run attacks on henequen estates, and bombings of the municipal and prefectural offices.[121] The Hunucmá insurgents wanted social redress, not amnesty, and they continued their guerrilla campaigns throughout Curiel's short administration. In the months and years ahead, similar episodes of social banditry would spread to neighboring Kinchil, Tetiz, and Ucú, and into Maxcanú as well.

The general had more luck in Muna, in the Puuc. There the rebellion broke out on May 23, just as Díaz and Madero, meeting at Ciudad Juárez in Chihuahua, were reaching an agreement on the transfer of power.[122] The origins of this revolt dated back at least a decade, to Santa Elena, a few kilometers south of Muna. As we have seen, in 1900 and 1901, villagers had harried surveyors and toppled markers when the Southeastern Railway Company attempted to grab their communal lands.[123] The land issue, accompanied, as usual, by official arrogance and abuse, had sparked Santa Elena's involvement in the Candelaria in 1909. That failed conspiracy also marked the emergence of José Loreto Baak as a *cabecilla* to be reckoned with in the Puuc. A carpenter and smallholder then in his late twenties, Baak recruited hundreds of campesinos into the CEI before being harassed and jailed for 30 days that October by the Molinistas.

Subsequently he became the Morenistas' principal chief in the western Puuc, conferring frequently in Mérida with both Delio Moreno Cantón and Alfonso Cámara y Cámara. Indeed, while it is difficult to assess how much communication transpired between CEI headquarters and the revolts led by Crespo, Campos, Rivero, and other popular *cabecillas* in the spring of 1911, it is certain that in the case of Baak's uprising, such communication was extensive. In late 1910 and February 1911, Santa Elena's and Muna's *ejidos* were again threatened; once more, markers were knocked over, surveyors put to flight, and their maps destroyed. In May, Baak and Manuel Mendoza Rosado, a white Morenista politician originally from Campeche, galvanized about seven hundred campesinos throughout the district of Ticul—almost five hundred from Santa Elena and Muna alone—around the issues of vulnerable *ejidos*, rising taxes, and bad government, and stormed the Muna barracks. After seizing Muna's small supply of arms and exhausting the town's possible sources of forced loans, the rebels used Muna as their base while they roamed the countryside demanding provisions and money from Molinista and Pinista haciendas.[124]

Manuel Arrigunaga observed that the *revoltosos* had hit the estates of Molinista Augusto L. Peón particularly hard. "They were in Uxmal dining at Uncle Augusto's table. How is it that they did not touch the *fincas* of Don Olegario? His turn and Don Trinidad's [Molina] will come."[125]

On May 25 President Díaz resigned. True to their word, Crespo and Campos laid down their arms in Temax. Curiel's final accomplishment was to reach an accommodation with Baak and Mendoza Rosado and bring peace to the Puuc. He succeeded by sending Alfonso Cámara y Cámara, Baak's principal Morenista contact in Mérida, 52 kilometers south to Uxmal to negotiate on his behalf. When Baak realized that both Cámara y Cámara and Moreno Cantón were behind Curiel's offer of amnesty, he and

Mendoza Rosado surrendered their 671 troops, on May 27. Cámara y Cámara personally made sure that "the servants were returned to their respective *fincas*."[126] Like Pedro Crespo, Juan Campos, and Elías Rivero, José Loreto Baak's career as an insurgent and local boss was only just beginning. But now, at least for the moment (and with the unsettling exception of Hunucmá), the countryside was relatively peaceful.

## CHAPTER 8

# Another Caste War?
# Spring 1911–Spring 1913

¿Eran de pantalón? (Did [the rebels] wear trousers?)
   —*Dzul* preoccupation, 1911–13

I've got Pino and Madero here with me. What do you want me to do
with them?
   —José Loreto Baak to Morenista party headquarters, 1911

O f the three contending elite factions, the Pinistas seemed
the least capable of ruling Yucatán following Díaz's ouster.
Perceived as outsiders, they did not have a strong political
base of support in the state to begin with—in contrast, say, to the Morenistas. Economically, their clout was also limited. The Molinistas, despite
their political defeat, still maintained a stranglehold on the region's monocrop. Nevertheless, the Pinistas did enjoy the imprimatur of Francisco Madero himself, and even in these chaotic times, backing from Mexico City
was an enormous asset. While Madero at first appeared an unlikely caudillo,
both in physical demeanor and in political rhetoric, he was quickly obliged
to learn the part—at least where the timely application of patronage and
force was concerned. As the local beneficiaries of central power, the Pinistas
never endeared themselves to Yucatecan society; yet, like Madero, they
managed to cling precariously to power for almost two years.

At least in the beginning, early June 1911, Pinismo's elite rivals were
prepared, for tactical reasons, to acquiesce to Madero's designation of José
María Pino Suárez as provisional governor. Madero had promised to guarantee democratic electoral competition, and certainly the Morenistas (if
not the politically tainted Molinistas) intended to contest state power in
elections already scheduled for September. Yet even more immediate for
all three factions was the task of ensuring the continuation of elite rule
itself.

## Pinismo in Power

The "social question" (as elites often referred to it in a kind of euphemistic shorthand) loomed ominously on the horizon. For the rural insurgents in the western *partido* of Hunucmá, it made little difference which *dzules* ruled in Mérida; "banditry" and more clandestine, informal acts of rural violence continued daily. Elsewhere in the state as well, acts of peon defiance were occurring with greater frequency, even in the heart of the henequen zone.

For example, on June 29, less than a month after Pino Suárez took office, *jornaleros* rioted en masse at Hacienda San Pedro Chimay on the outskirts of the state capital.[1] Significantly, the *motín* erupted not long after 27 of the estate's resident peons had returned from Mérida, where they had protested to the new governor that their wages were excessively low. When Pino delayed acting on their petition, the peons began to drag their feet in the henequen fields and to grumble bitterly to their *encargado*, Carlos Sánchez. Finally, unleashed by *aguardiente* during the festival of their patron saint, their anger overflowed. As Sánchez distributed rations of meat to the peons at the fiesta, they began to excoriate and threaten him in Maya.

> We're going to cut you up into little pieces like this meat you parcel out in such a miserly way to us. Then we'll carry you home in our pockets and dice you up like *salpicón*.[2]

The peons never made good on their threat, but before the national guard arrived and rounded up six alleged ringleaders, they did sack the hacienda store and attack the landowner's big house. At the subsequent trial, although the Maya workers alleged that the overseer had stolen food and wages from them regularly, the defense attorney petitioned the court for leniency on other grounds.

> The Indian servants work in the fields like beasts of burden . . . ignorant that they have any rights . . . virtually indifferent to right and wrong itself.[3]

Whether the court was swayed by this rather crude, racially tinged appeal to paternalism, or merely acted leniently to defuse further unrest, the defendants were detained for several months before the charges were dropped.[4]

When, two weeks after the incident at San Pedro, an almost identical jacquerie ignited workers at the Hacienda Santa Cruz in eastern Espita District, planters and politicians began to speak of a growing "contagion" that had to be treated immediately before it "infected" the entire state.[5] Hardliners argued that the state had to suppress these pockets of disorder to prevent them from gathering into a regional insurrection. By contrast, their more progressive counterparts in the Cámara Agrícola and the Liga de Acción Social maintained that only substantive changes—particularly improved working conditions and educational opportunities—had any prospect of defusing dissent among *jornaleros,* let alone transforming them into more efficient and disciplined workers.[6]

Governor Pino Suárez was disposed to follow the second course of action, but not before strengthening the state's military capacity to confront a rural rebellion. In the wake of a visit to Mexico City by a delegation of frightened planters pleading for greater protection against "a repeat of the unforgettably tragic events of 1847," when "civilization was at the point of disappearing," Pino requested at least one more federal battalion and a large shipment of machine guns from President Madero.[7] He pointed out "the seriousness of the threat to society" that "destructive criminal acts" and "bloody rampages by *jornaleros*" continued to pose.[8] But when the troops and materiel arrived in August, the governor emphasized his intention to use them as a last resort, in the event that a stepped-up program of private and state reforms failed to curb rural violence.[9]

Taking its cue from Pino Suárez, the Liga de Acción Social devoted the summer of 1911 to hammering out a planter consensus regarding the substance and implementation of labor and educational reforms. The Liga's initiative built on discussions that had taken place several months earlier between then-governor Luis Curiel and progressive planters in the Cámara Agrícola about how to ameliorate working conditions for peons. Those talks had produced recommendations to prohibit *fagina,* establish a standard minimum wage, regulate the abuses of monopoly and gouging perpetrated by hacienda stores, combat alcoholism among peons, and promote mandatory primary education at newly created rural schools. Of course, the recommendations had also made very clear statements about the inviolability of property rights and had stressed the importance of enforcing existing legislation regarding idleness ("vagabondage") and debt. Equally significant, they had made no mention of how to implement such guidelines on estates. Planters were merely exhorted to adopt them voluntarily "to advance the well-being of our agriculture."[10]

The Liga de Acción Social, which, like the Cámara Agrícola, included progressive planters from all three elite factions, debated the issue of peonage (or, as many of its members called it with greater candor, "the Indian problem") for a full month. Yet ultimately it produced no more concrete proposals than did the Cámara Agrícola. Pino Suárez participated fully in the deliberations, advising prudence throughout. Indeed, rather early in the process, he reassured local society that until things changed—which would be gradual—workers would "remain in their present enslaved state to prevent brusque transitions that might injure their well-being."[11]

Pino's emphasis on evolutionary change in the "glorious work of regenerating the Indian race" was captured in the Liga's rather vague, largely procedural recommendations on peonage issued in late July. First, planters should "confer" with representatives of their workers to "define the issues" most in conflict. Second, the governor should "name a commission" to hear discontented workers when problems arose on estates. Third, the state should "create an agency" to regulate planter-*jornalero* relations. Last, the government should "continue to study" the problem of debt peonage with a view to "finding a solution that is not only just and legal but will not hinder the state's economic progress."[12]

In its report, the Liga also reemphasized the need to establish rural schools on the estates, and this recommendation became the focal point of its work in the months ahead. It is here, in the planters' deliberations over education, that we gain further insight into their "modernizing" vision, and particularly the contradictions and limitations that such a vision held for their workers. The Liga had been founded in January 1909 in an effort to apply such liberal tenets as self-help and private initiative to the ills of a society held back by corporate groups and privileges. Liga spokesmen never tired of pointing out that these values could be said to have triumphed only if they truly engaged "the most elemental part of Yucatecan society": the Maya *jornalero*. The worker's socioeconomic and spiritual liberation was essential if the region was to continue to advance.[13] Yet ironically, when it came time to formulate a concrete plan for the education of their work force, the planters could reach agreement only on an arrangement that kept the *jornalero* immobilized as a dependent peon, so as to guarantee the short-term interests of the plantocracy.

The Liga's socially minded president, Gonzalo Cámara Zavala, had organized twelve conferences throughout 1910 and early 1911 to galvanize support for a rural education plan among his fellow *hacendados*, the majority of whom remained opposed to any education of peons. The conferences gave Yucatecan planters of diverse ideological persuasions an opportunity to vent their hopes and fears about the Maya's potential for advancement and rebellion, and ultimately to fashion a policy for rural schools that reflected a basic consensus. The curriculum of the new rural school would be designed to produce "a salubrious effect." This meant that religious education would be mandatory, as a safeguard against the "contaminating socialist ideas" being propagated by "dangerous agitators" like Tomás Pérez Ponce and Felipe Carrillo Puerto.[14]

In reality, the debates at these education conferences suggest that the more reactionary planters frankly opposed the idea of "outsiders" coming onto their estates to teach anything—even constitutional principles that spelled out the fundamental rights of Mexican citizens. Moreover, planters across the ideological spectrum feared the power of "radical socialism" to corrupt the Maya. For, as the moderate Cámara Zavala warned,

> We should not forget that socialism is traditional with this race. The ancient Maya were essentially communists. The Indian still has not forgotten old grudges . . . he obeys whoever commands him, and under these conditions it is not difficult for socialism to spread.[15]

Conservative planters like Leopoldo Cantón Frexas not only accepted Cámara Zavala's anachronistic depiction of pre-Columbian communism;

they freely admitted that contemporary Maya *jornaleros* had every reason
to nurture class grievances.

> How can [the *jornalero*] not compare his miserable existence, the difficulty
> of his labor, and the scanty wage he earns with the little work his master
> does and the great wealth and luxury he reaps? The Indian will find Marx's
> views acceptable and useful; revenge will cry out in his heart and he will
> decide to take from his master that which he feels belongs to him.[16]

According to Cantón Frexas, only Christian instruction had any prospect of
instilling in the exploited peon a respect for nonviolence, as well as preserving the notions that work was sacred and social inequality was part of the
natural order of things. Thus, certain conservatives argued, if it remained on
a "moral plane," rural education made good political and economic sense.[17]

Progressive planters like Cámara Zavala, Alonso Patrón Espadas, José
Patrón Correa, and Víctor Rendón adduced other arguments. While they
tended to emphasize the moral (and patriotic) duty involved in "regenerating an impoverished, ignorant, and decadent people," they linked the Maya
*jornalero*'s moral salvation to his transformation into an efficient worker.
In the words of Patrón Correa, "We want to convert our workers from the
simple animate machines that they are, into conscious beings . . . able
to apply reason to the tasks that they are assigned."[18] Rendón pointed out
that a thinking worker was a profitable one, less likely to be driven to the
"fatal vices and diseases" that traditionally impaired and decimated Indians. Sooner or later, moreover, the peon would seek out education if it
were not brought to him.

> Not one cunning trick . . . can prevent [it]. If the planters make no attempt
> to educate the Indians at their homes, they will eventually leave . . . the
> estates.[19]

Yet despite such pragmatic appeals to political economy as well as to
morality, most planters remained unconvinced that literate workers would
be easy to supervise, let alone control as cheaply as before. As the debate neared its conclusion, it was Ricardo Molina Hübbe, Don Olegario's
nephew, who summarized the position of the Liga's pragmatic moderates.

> Rural schools will not awaken ambitions in the Indian contrary to tradi-
> tional rural life, nor will he become so studious that he will acquire extra-
> ordinary knowledge. . . . Sooner or later, whether it be through peaceful
> means . . . or through bloody convulsions . . . the education of the Indians
> will be accomplished . . . with or without us. We can choose.[20]

In late July 1911, the Liga forwarded to Governor Pino Suárez a recommendation for the establishment of rural schools. On August 25, the state
legislature passed the governor's bill to that effect.[21] Once again, however,
the new measure lacked teeth. Sensing opposition among the planter rank-
and-file and hamstrung by low fiber prices, Pino committed no appreciable

public monies to rural education. Proprietors were merely encouraged to organize schools on their estates and offered certain tax incentives to construct appropriate facilities. And whereas the new law stipulated the educational responsibilities of students, teachers, parents, and even overseers, the planters' obligations were not specified. Sadly, over the course of Pinista rule, only three proprietors—Alonso Patrón Espadas (Sacapuc), Alvino Manzanilla (San Francisco), and Manuel Rodríguez Acosta (San Diego)—took the initiative to establish schools on their estates.[22] It is therefore difficult to argue with the assessment of one historian, who contends that most planters (and Pino himself) were merely willing to *entertain* the concept of rural education as "a political gesture during a period when certain issues *had* to be addressed, if not necessarily adopted."[23]

If Pino's approach to labor and educational reform was cautious, it is not surprising that his policy was even more conservative on the complicated, highly charged issue of ejidal distribution. As we have seen, there were compelling reasons for the state to revise its ejidal policy. Most obvious was the simmering discontent of pueblos in Hunucmá, the Puuc, and other transitional zones, where villagers struggled to preserve their shrinking agrarian patrimony from acquisition, legal or otherwise, by commercial estates. But even in those cases where, for a variety of reasons, campesinos participated willingly in the survey and sale of their plots, a plethora of abuses had occurred. Most common was the exaction of exorbitant fees by shady engineers who sought to acquire estates for themselves or worked in league with neighboring planters. Characteristically, on August 9, the governor created a Commission of Engineers to investigate such abuses and eventually to correct irregularities.

Unfortunately, Pino's cautious agrarian policy managed to alienate most campesinos while pleasing no one. Not only did the governor defer the return of ejidal lands that *hacendados* had expropriated during the Porfiriato; he also indicated his intention to continue the survey and distribution of *ejidos* in those areas previously unaffected, "with the aim of . . . promoting their allocation to small agriculturalists."[24] Such a policy, of course, was anathema in Sotuta and remote areas of the Puuc, where *comuneros* knew firsthand the full implications of liberalism's project to implant "small agriculture." At the same time, Pino's agrarian program moved too slowly for those who did favor parceling. Deprived of adequate funding, the Commission of Engineers never published its report on agrarian conditions—which was to be a prelude to further parcelization.[25]

Under the circumstances, Pino's halting, contradictory social initiatives won the regime few adherents in the countryside. Even had the rhetoric of Pinismo been sincere, social reform could not have come overnight; and while the fall of the dictatorship raised expectations, the patience of most countrypeople had already worn thin. Patience and trust were compromised by the legacy of a cynical political process that had always promoted the enrichment of a few at the expense of the majority. As the 1911

TABLE 8.1

*Henequen Exports, 1911*

| Exporter | Bales | Percentage of total |
|---|---|---|
| Avelino Montes | 431,917 | 63.40 |
| Arturo Pierce | 150,077 | 22.30 |
| Compañía de Hacendados Henequeneros de Yucatán | 91,799 | 13.50 |
| Alonso Escalante y Cía | 4,630 | 0.54 |
| Escalante y Cía | 2,283 | 0.26 |
| Antonio Cirerol | 177 | — |
| José Vela | 100 | — |
| Banco Peninsular Mexicano | 3 | — |
| Cámara Agrícola de Yucatán | 2 | — |
| Miguel G. Gutiérrez | 1 | — |
| Julio Blanco | 1 | — |
| Total | 680,990 | 100.00 |

SOURCE: *EA*, Jan. 1912, p. 417.

"summer of reform" ran its course, peons and villagers were under few illusions. Large estates continued to expand at the expense of Maya villages. Planters and officials abused their authority with virtual impunity; flogging and *fagina* remained hallmarks of the rural labor regime.[26] Debts mounted on the plantations.[27] Bounty hunters continued to track down runaway servants.[28] Government commissions might come and go, but the plantocracy's underlying strategies of social control remained rather transparent to the region's campesinos. As grievances in the Yucatecan countryside continued to peak, violence simmered. But the social cauldron threatened to blow sky-high, given the right political opportunity.

That political conjuncture would be provided by the upcoming fall elections. At best, elite unity was but a brittle facade late in 1911, and that facade would be shattered by the forces and passions unleashed in the turbulent gubernatorial campaign.

Since the nineteenth century, the governorship had afforded the winning *camarilla* greater access to patronage and wealth at both the national apex and the regional base of the Mexican pyramid of power. Indeed, as we saw in Part I of this book, if the statehouse were not won, the difficulties of consolidating and then maintaining patron-client networks at the federal and local levels were almost insurmountable. For the Pinistas, an electoral triumph that would institutionalize their tenuous hold on the governorship was essential if they were to build a real political network in the state, overcome their perception as a "*camarilla* of outsiders,"[29] and gain a more equitable share of the spoils of monoculture, which the Molinistas still dominated.

For the Morenistas, of course, the governorship continued to represent something of an irredentist obsession, a return to the dominance and wealth they had enjoyed under Don Pancho Cantón but had been fraudu-

TABLE 8.2

*Henequen Exports, 1912*

| Exporter | Bales | Percentage of total |
|---|---|---|
| Avelino Montes | 506,659 | 62.27 |
| Arturo Pierce | 183,155 | 22.81 |
| Compañía de Hacendados Henequeneros de Yucatán | 68,480 | 8.42 |
| Comisión Reguladora del Mercado del Henequén | 42,273 | 5.20 |
| Negociación Exportadora del Henequén | 11,068 | 1.36 |
| Escalante y Cía | 1,873 | 0.23 |
| Agencia Comercial de Ferrocarriles de Yucatán | 100 | 0.01 |
| José Juanes G. Gutiérrez | 2 | — |
| Total | 813,610 | 100.00 |

SOURCE: *EA*, Jan. 1913, p. 631.

lently deprived of ever since. Unlike the Pinistas, they enjoyed a far-flung, multilayered network of patronage throughout the state. They would now seek to persuade President Madero that it was in Mexico City's interest to accept their return to the statehouse. Last were the Molinistas, forced to accept that their *camarilla* was, at least temporarily, politically discredited by the overthrow of Díaz. It behooved them to keep a low profile during the election campaign, then to try to exercise as much power as they could over the new administration through their control of the regional monocrop (see Tables 8.1 and 8.2).

The political economy of henequen, and particularly the fluctuations in the fiber market, had always kept *camarillas* permeable and pragmatic. According to a regional aphorism, "To play politics in Yucatán is to be open to the possibility of an *acomodamiento de desleales"*—an alliance with one's rivals.[30] As we have seen, on several occasions before 1910, dissident planters in the Cantonista and Peoncista *camarillas*, working through the Cámara Agrícola and other more ephemeral cooperative associations, had attempted unsuccessfully to combat the monopsony that the Molina-Montes *camarilla* and the International Harvester Company had established shortly after the turn of the century. Both before and after the 1911 elections, the Pinistas and Morenistas joined forces in latter-day valorization schemes aimed at breaking the Molinistas' grip on the local fiber industry.

The most celebrated attempt before Salvador Alvarado's revolutionary administration was the Comisión Reguladora del Mercado del Henequén, founded in 1912. Unlike its predecessors, which were limited cooperatives voluntarily organized and financed by minority groups of *henequeneros*, the Comisión Reguladora was a government agency, supported by the overwhelming majority of Yucatán's producers and financed by a state law sanctioning an extra impost on production. By the end of 1912, the commission's membership included all but the largest Molinista planters and those very small producers who found themselves trapped in the web of debts and mortgages spun by Montes and his associates.

Like its predecessors, however, the Comisión Reguladora operated in an open market, which was still controlled by the Molina-Montes faction. It therefore had little hope of achieving even its modest goal of maintaining a reasonable and remunerative price. More often than not, when it eventually sold the fiber it had, with some difficulty, held off the market, the sale was to Montes himself. Such valorization schemes thus typically broke up with the erstwhile Morenista and Pinista allies pitted against each other, amid bitter accusations that one side or the other had sold out to Montes. Invariably, the only clear winners were the Molinistas.[31]

## Porfiriato Redux?

This legacy of frustration on the economic front only raised the stakes for the Morenistas and Pinistas in the political arena. In preparation for the 1911 election campaign, both *camarillas* scurried to deepen their existing networks of patronage in the countryside. The Morenistas enjoyed a tremendous advantage here: as we have seen, some of their local political clienteles had been recruited before the turn of the century. In other instances, however, the rival elite factions made appeals to village communities and (through intermediaries) to settlements of peons that had yet to be enlisted in partisan politics. As elites attempted to choose up sides, they invariably injected themselves into local factional rivalries and vendettas that had their own complex histories. In the weeks and months ahead, regional politics would more often than not serve as a pretext, an overlay for deepseated local conflicts over land, cattle, labor relations, and commercial rights. As rival elites distributed money, arms, and promises to prospective clients, they typically polarized politics and exacerbated patterns of factionalized violence in villages and haciendas, between neighboring villages, or between villages and adjacent estates—of which more presently.[32] The consequences of this strategy would soon come back to haunt Yucatán's elites.

The 1911 campaign operated on two levels. In their high-profile urban campaigns and in the regional and national press, gubernatorial candidates Pino Suárez and Delio Moreno Cantón both professed the highest ideals, pledging to uphold platforms that stressed gradual reform and social peace. At the same time, each candidate excoriated the other for unscrupulous demagoguery and political agitation that could only rend the region's fragile social fabric. Moreno Cantón, for example, repeatedly emphasized his party's commitment "to redeem and rehabilitate the Indian in a responsible, evolutionary manner . . . one that would not strip the gears of [Yucatán's] dynamic social mechanism."[33] All the while, however, Morenista lieutenants and sympathizers prepared for armed confrontation in the countryside. One *cabecilla* in Mérida district itself, Juan Jiménez, went about distributing guns to the peons of a sympathetic planter, informing them in no üncertain terms that "*now* what Delio Moreno needs is fighters, not votes."[34]

President Madero similarly hedged his bets. Even as he called for free and democratic elections and publicly lectured both Yucatecan candidates that violent, repressive acts to gain an advantage should be avoided at all costs, he rushed additional troops to his Pinista clients. This two-track strategy was not lost on the Morenistas. Carlos R. Menéndez, Moreno Cantón's chief adviser and editor of the Morenista daily, *La Revista de Mérida*, observed with sarcasm that the president was waging democracy in Yucatán with troops from central Mexico.

> At the rate our democratic government is militarizing the region, soon we will even have soldiers in our soup. Praise be to President Madero's hallowed concept of "effective suffrage."[35]

Early in September, Madero visited Yucatán to campaign for Pino Suárez as well as for his own candidacy in the upcoming presidential elections. The Morenistas seized the opportunity to stage public rallies of their own, still hoping that Madero would come to his senses and realize that it was the CEI, not Pino's PA, that had the popular mandate to rule the state. Whereas the Pinistas strained to turn out hundreds to hear the president, even when they dispensed free meals and transportation, the Morenistas assembled veritable multitudes at their rallies.[36] Still, the president had no intention of dropping his support for Pino Suárez, who for some time had been an intimate of the Madero family and would soon join Madero as vice presidential candidate on the national ticket.[37]

When Madero made a series of highly partisan speeches in an effort to lend his "coattails" to the Tabasqueño, the Morenistas finally realized that Mexico City would once again deny them. They abruptly discontinued their appeal to Madero as the republic's "Apostle of Democracy" and attacked him as a latter-day Díaz.

> It is sad how history has repeated itself. In June 1909, he came to us, humble and idealistic, hounded by the authorities, a victim of the *mano dura*. . . . Then he was "loco Pancho Madero." . . . Today he returns to Yucatán as "el señor don Francisco I. Madero," in all his splendor. He is a plenipotentiary whose signs now have the force of orders. . . . And now, as he returns, the triumphant conqueror, "the leader," he no longer addresses a humble crowd but the silk hats, the fine frock coats, the starched collars, the perfumed handkerchiefs, and kaiserlike mustachios—in short, "the eleventh-hour Maderistas," the very same crowd that prostrated itself before General Porfirio Díaz . . . when he, too, arrived like Caesar in Yucatán.[38]

As the campaign wore on, the Pinistas proved themselves every bit as adept at rigging an election as the Molinistas were before them. Morenista rallies in Hunucmá and a variety of other district seats were violently dispersed by federal troops and gangs of unemployed Yaquis. A number of local CEI leaders were roughed up and imprisoned without being charged; several sat out the campaign in jail. Felipe Carrillo Puerto, now a key Morenista organizer in Motul, became the object of an assassination plot and was jailed when he killed his assailant in self-defense. In certain localities, campesinos were threatened with the *leva* if they did not vote for Pino. Pinista officials often denied the CEI railroad access; trains that did carry Morenistas to political rallies were attacked, often with loss of life.[39]

Ultimately, on September 27, 1911, the Pinistas stole the election, announcing that Pino Suárez had defeated Delio Moreno Cantón by about nine thousand votes. This tally was regarded as inconceivable by anyone who knew the region firsthand. In Sotuta *partido*, for example, the Pinistas claimed to have received more votes than the number of inhabitants. Carlos R. Menéndez wryly observed that there was more democracy in Yucatán than in Switzerland, because "not only have almost all the eligible voters voted in some places, in others many more people voted than actually exist. This could only result from truly 'effective suffrage.' "[40]

In the months following the elections, President Madero's cause was further undermined in the state because the political mechanisms employed by Governor Pino Suárez and his successors continued to remind Yucatecos of the recent Porfirian past. For example, Pino, the first of four interim Maderista governors imposed on the state, attempted to run Yucatán and run for the vice presidency of the nation at the same time. His constant trips out of state reminded locals of Olegario Molina's frequent absences and hampered any momentum the new regime could muster.

To make matters worse, Porfirian-style nepotism reached into the upper echelons of the state government. Pino's brothers-in-law, Nicolás Cámara Vales and Alfredo Cámara Vales, became the governors of Yucatán and Quintana Roo territory, respectively, once Pino assumed the vice presidency. For good measure, Nicolás's son was named director of the United Railways of Yucatán.[41]

Even more difficult for many to swallow was the presence of "eleventh-hour Maderistas" (read, Molinistas) in important posts in the state bureaucracy.[42] Following Madero's designation of Pino Suárez, Morenista Manuel Arrigunaga had predicted that "Pino will be surprised to find himself trapped in the Molinistas' web. . . . Don Olegario still has far more influence than people realize." Indeed, by the end of 1911, the Pinistas had already promoted the candidacies of Manuel Sierra Méndez and Luis Curiel for federal deputy and senator, respectively.[43] Even more egregious was the inclusion in Governor Cámara Vales's cabinet of Tomás Castellanos Acevedo, an unsavory Molinista *jefe político* who was generally considered to reside politically in Avelino Montes's hip pocket.

Castellanos was popularly known as "El Financiero," a nickname that suggested a predilection for commercial speculation and a nose for business transactions of more dubious repute. When he was appointed to head the state's new henequen regulating commission in 1912, Yucatecos sarcastically joked that Governor Cámara Vales had put the fox in charge of the henhouse.[44] Morenistas viewed the governor as a nullity: Molina and Montes, they argued, still called the shots in the governor's office through their representative, "El Financiero." In 1912, when Montes effected a forced sale of much of the stock held by the Comisión Reguladora and the agency effectively ceased to operate, most Yucatecans suspected that Castellanos had colluded with him.[45] Significantly, when Don Olegario Molina and Enrique Muñoz Arístegui returned earlier in the year to confer with members of their *camarilla*, it was "El Financiero" who coordinated the visit. The Morenista press likened Molina's homecoming to the majestic planet Saturn being surrounded by its tiny orbiting moons.[46]

Abuses continued to erode Pinista legitimacy. The *jefatura política*, that symbol of Porfirian malice, persisted, and Pinista prefects rode roughshod over political opponents in the countryside. Of course, to secure stability and protect the monocrop, *jefes* had little recourse but to clamp down on the rural violence that wracked the state between 1911 and 1913. Nevertheless, it was the Maderista opening that initially had empowered the popular classes, and few rural dwellers could now respect the "rule of law" when it so clearly resembled the practices of the past.

Actually, in many districts (Hunucmá, Maxcanú, Progreso, Motul, Tixkokob, Izamal, Valladolid, Tizimín, Sotuta, Espita, Tekax, and Ticul), the prefects *themselves* were holdovers from the Porfirian past, typically hardline Molinista *caciques* (like Castellanos) whom Pino had merely confirmed in their posts.[47] In other strategic districts, such as Mérida, Pino had replaced popular Morenista bosses (like the charismatic Alfonso Cámara y Cámara) with his own political hacks.[48] No wonder the *jefes políticos*, members of their staffs, and imposed municipal authorities remained prize targets for rural insurgents throughout 1911 and 1912.

Finally, strong-arm tactics carried out by these same political bosses also continued, as the Pinistas censored and harassed the local press after a brief summer of freedom in 1911. The Morenistas whipped up anti-Maderista sentiment throughout the state, still using as one of their chief weapons an inflammatory press that regularly sensationalized and occasionally even invented violent episodes in the countryside to prove that the Pinistas were incapable of keeping the peace. Led by Carlos R. Menéndez's *Revista de Mérida* and a host of ephemeral partisan newspapers and broadsheets, the Morenistas patently abused the newly won freedom of the press. Yet beneath the yellow journalism often lay an accurate critique of Maderismo's glaring abuses: imposed governors and municipal officials, rigged elections, nepotism, and abuses by prefects.[49] The Pinistas replied in Porfirian fashion, smashing presses and closing down newspapers, jailing editors (including Menéndez) for libel, and countering the bad press they received with their own yellow journalism.[50]

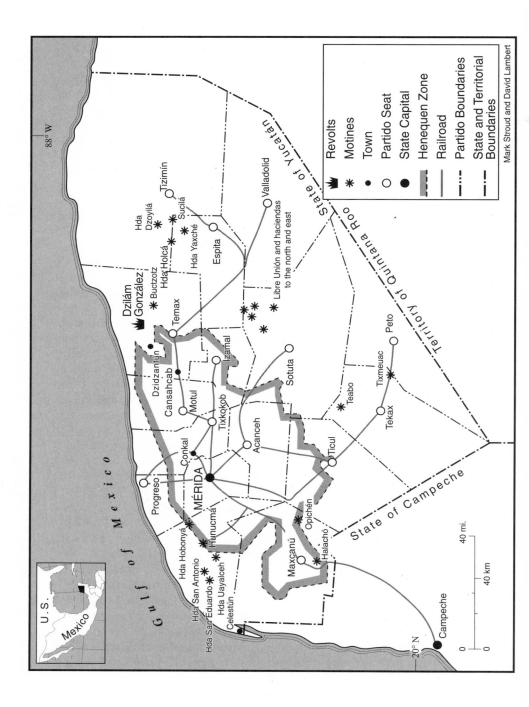

## The Crows Take Flight

What Yucatán's rival elites did not fully consider as they constructed their far-flung patronage networks, then mobilized them to contest state power, was that "their" incipient rural insurgents had agendas of their own, which were rarely congruent with the elites' rather limited political proj-ects. Almost inexorably, through several seasons of upheaval—from the aborted Candelaria conspiracy in the fall of 1909 through the failed re-bellion in Valladolid during the spring of 1910 to the more freewheeling revolts that now erupted with increasing frequency under Maderismo—locally based popular mobilization and protest had begun to evolve a life of its own, one that took little heed of elite political posturings or fraudulent election returns. Yucatán's competing elites seemed to have fulfilled the old Spanish proverb, "Raise crows and one day they'll peck out your eyes." Try as they might, they could no longer successfully harness the rage that ex-ploded in peripheral areas like Hunucmá, the Puuc, and the districts east and south of Temax. Moreover, as 1911 gave way to 1912, such popular in-surgency increasingly spilled over into the henequen zone, where it threat-ened the economic taproot of monoculture and elite rule itself (see Maps 8.1 and 8.2).

The remainder of this chapter examines the escalation in popular insur-gency in some detail. First we reconstruct the significant episodes from the ground up—that is, from the perspective of the participants themselves. Then we reflect more broadly on the problems of causation and conscious-ness that are embedded in the revolts, and we raise larger epistemological questions for students of collective action and protest.

### "BANDITRY" IN HUNUCMÁ

Both Morenistas and Pinistas made appeals to the campesinos of Hu-nucmá during the 1911 gubernatorial campaign. Their efforts were an at-tempt to add the northwestern district to their column and to protect their local planter supporters from the seemingly random pattern of criminal violence that continued to reign there. The incumbent Pinistas seemed to have the upper hand: Hunucmá *partido* had always maintained a certain independence in terms of political alignment, and the Cantonistas/More-nistas had made few inroads there since the 1890s.[51] The Pinistas, more-over, had assiduously courted Feliciano Canul Reyes, a popular *cabecilla* whom the *gente decente* both feared and loathed. Following the elections, in the face of some planter opposition, Pino Suárez appointed this so-called Chief of the Brigands and two of his lieutenants to the town council in Hunucmá's district seat. Surely, the Pinista *camarilla* supposed, "banditry" would now cease and the district might get back to business as usual.[52]

Instead, rural violence in Hunucmá reached unprecedented levels. De-spite Canul Reyes's strategic appointment, the Pinistas had miscalculated

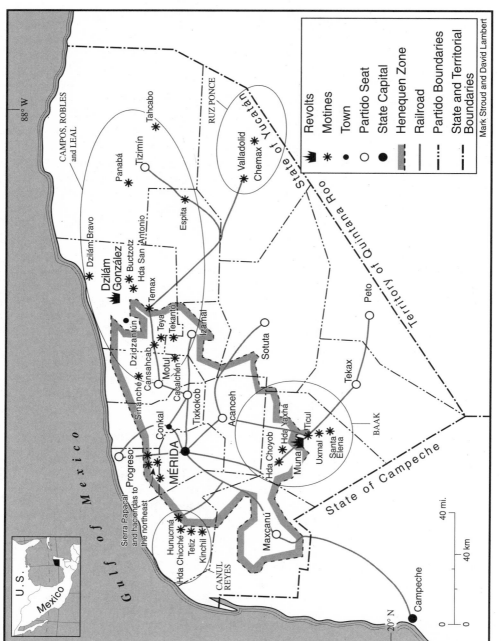

*Map 8.2.* Yucatán: 1912–March 1913.

Mark Stroud and David Lambert

**Legend:**

| Symbol | Label |
|--------|-------|
| Revolts | |
| Motines | |
| Town | |
| Partido Seat | |
| State Capital | |
| Henequen Zone | |
| Railroad | |
| Partido Boundaries | |
| State and Territorial Boundaries | |

in two crucial areas. First, they had confirmed the former Molinista *jefe político*, José María Vargas, in his post, then winked as the unpopular *cacique* applied his customary strong-arm tactics—now exclusively against the Morenistas—during the election campaign. On one occasion, Vargas harassed a CEI rally of campesinos and artisans with two hundred mounted troops, trampling several of the participants.[53] Second, and even more damaging, the Pinistas had utterly ignored the weighty social issues that had initially fueled endemic levels of Hunucmense "banditry." Pino soon removed Vargas as prefect, but in January 1912, Vargas's successor, Enrique Cámara, still painted a bleak picture for his boss in Mérida.

> The criminal happenings that darken this *partido* are numerous and proceed with near impunity. The greater portion of these are violent crimes against property and person: the destruction of estates, homicide, assault, and robbery.[54]

The specific details of this "crime wave" deserve attention. For despite the state's official view, and the impression conveyed by various versions in the elite press, the pattern of violence in Hunucmá was hardly random. What the planters and their supporters interpreted as—or at least labeled—"mindless savagery" and "criminal barbarism" can be read from another perspective as a species of guerrilla war directed by elements of the district's embattled peasantry against the great estates.[55]

Some of the testimonies of the Hunucmense rebels themselves—mediated to be sure, by the state courts—evoke the inversive, uncompromising quality of this violence. Apart from their "fighting words," that spew of expletives directed against exploitative planters, their agents, and complicit state officials in the heat of the moment, the insurgents often commented quite lucidly on what motivated their actions. Enrique Díaz, like many insurgents a *jornalero* who lived in the pueblo of Hunucmá but worked at the Hacienda San Eduardo, told his mother and sister before an attack on that estate that "he was leaving to meet up with others to carry out a revolution." His compatriot, Eleno Pech, bragged to fellow Hunucmenses of his own part in the raid, adding, "We won't quit until we screw Don Secundino Maldonado" [San Eduardo's notoriously brutal *hacendado*]." Ignacio Coyoc, a third participant, recalled that fellow *jornalero* Guillermo Canul had recruited him for the raid over a period of at least two months, repeatedly emphasizing the need "to form a movement to do away with the wealthy *caballeros* in this district."[56]

Of course, the insurgents' intentions, their rudimentary "ideology" if you will, was also inscribed in their deeds. In this guerrilla campaign, proprietors' houses and fields were burned, their machinery destroyed, their loyal retainers killed. Yet while the damage was certainly extensive, the violence was neither arbitrary nor gratuitous. The targets were always chosen purposefully by the Hunucmense insurgents, and none of the three rival elite factions remained exempt from their depredations.

From August to December 1911, insurgent campesinos carried out a series of well planned hit-and-run actions against some of the most powerful planters in the district. Consider the operations mounted against the Hobonya, San Eduardo, San Gerónimo, Concepción, Uayalceh, Mucuyche, San Pedro, and San Antonio Yaxche henequen plantations.[57] Led by Herminio Balam and Feliciano Canul Reyes (who never let his status as a town councilman deter him from participating in this *other* arena of peasant politics), village-based insurgents from the municipalities of Tetiz, Kinchil, Ucú, and Hunucmá operated in small, mobile bands that never exceeded 60 men and were welded together by ties of community and kinship. Now in masks or blackface, now disguised as national guardsmen, the insurgents rustled livestock, robbed payrolls, and looted hacienda treasuries and company stores. They also burned fields, vandalized the residences of administrators and planters, and—in the best Luddite fashion—smashed fiber decorticating machines, tore up stretches of Decauville tram tracks, and knocked over kilometers' worth of the stone markers that delimited the henequen fields of each estate.

Invariably, these incursions by villagers enlisted some support among the peons of these estates, many of whom were, of course, the insurgents' kith and kin. In several cases, such attacks helped to provoke jacqueries on neighboring haciendas. The rebels naturally were not above intimidating ("pressing") peons to join them or at least not to denounce them later to the authorities. The peons at San Antonio Yaxche and San Pedro would later report that the insurgents made it clear to them that life would "not be worth much for those of you who give us away."[58]

The rebels also purposefully targeted, then typically dispatched victims in a brutal, ritualistic manner that had the elements of a public execution. They often made an elaborate effort symbolically to negate the power of the *patrón* and to manifest the inversion in power relations that was being played out. For example, at San Pedro, Bonifacio Yam, a despised retainer of the *hacendado*, Pedro Telmo Puerto, was decapitated with a machete in the presence of the peons. An old-timer later recalled that this "act of justice" was quite a contrast from the public floggings of lazy or disorderly servants that he and his fellows had been obliged to witness during "the age of slavery."[59] At Hoboyna, Herminio Balam slit the throat of Miguel Negrón, the estate's paymaster, from ear to ear, then drank from the rivulet of spurting blood out of the palm of his hand. "How sweet and tangy [*agridulce*] the blood tasted," he would later observe to family members and confidants.[60]

Indeed, after years of exploitation and racial degradation, Hunucmá's Maya villagers and peons suddenly found themselves enthusiastically discussing their actions in the *tienditas* and at the Saturday-night *jaranas* (dances). "I lit the dynamite that blew up the boiler," offered Fulano. "I knocked down the stone markers around the new henequen field," commented Mengano. "Imagine," interjected Zutano, "all those fine clothes were paid for with the loot he [the *hacendado*] extracted from the ribs of our pueblo."[61]

Given this discourse of insurgency, as well as the agrarian roots that fed it, it is not surprising that contemporary observers often compared Hunucmá's revolutionary experience with that of Zapatismo in Morelos. Yet what Yucatecan elites chose to compare was not the social or revolutionary dimension of each conflict but the brigandage and savagery they imagined to lie at the core of each movement. Speaking for the Morenistas, Carlos R. Menéndez pointed out that at least the Morelenses fought "out in the open" and, after extorting that region's sugar planters, allowed their estates to remain in production. By contrast, Yucatán's "criminal Zapatismo has declared war to the death on the planters," and "commits its savage criminal atrocities under cover of darkness."[62]

Because it would not entertain, let alone redress, Hunucmense social grievances, and because it had failed miserably in its efforts to co-opt or crush the insurgency, the Pinista regime continued to label the rebels "bandits." It is significant that the government meted out rather lenient sentences to those few brigands it managed to catch—another sign of its weakness and its decision to treat symptoms rather than to address underlying problems.[63] Not until years later, when more progressive revolutionary governments recognized the legitimacy of certain agrarian claims in the district, did social banditry in Hunucmá finally begin to abate.

## "POPULAR MORENISMO" IN THE SOUTH AND EAST

Morenista elites fared little better than their Pinista rivals in their efforts to control the disorderly clienteles they had mobilized at the grassroots. Despite their bickering, Morenista elites shared the same world view as their Pinista counterparts. They, too, espoused a return to the political liberalism of Benito Juárez. Beneath their ideological statements and rhetorical embellishments was a desire—certainly on the part of the *heneque-neros* who dominated each faction—to return to the traditional nineteenth-century model of political power that would permit them to garner their share of the henequen spoils. Such elite liberalism, as we have seen, had all the while sanctioned the breakup of village *ejidos* in the name of progress.

Personal testimonies and programmatic statements captured by the authorities reveal that Yucatán's popular rebels were also imbued with liberalism, but of a very different stripe. Consider the extraordinary, rambling "epic poem" titled "El 15 de septiembre," written by Rigoberto Xiu, the young Morenista insurgent from Muna. Xiu's liberalism invoked liberal heroes and causes like Hidalgo and independence, Juárez and the war against the French. Yet consonant with so many of the personal testimonies of other insurgents, the liberal tradition to which Xiu appealed was not the inevitable march of progress that the elites celebrated; it was a bloody, often bleak, but utterly "moral" struggle over centuries to preserve individual freedom and dignity against external forces of oppression.[64] Unfortunately for the Morenistas, as Maderismo lingered on, this dissonance only grew louder, underscoring the adversarial relationship between the elite leadership in Mérida and its motley collection of rebels in the countryside.

As we have seen, the Morenista leadership had certainly done its spadework. Few other Mexican *camarillas* had so laboriously cultivated such an extensive network of patronage and clientele. From the glory days of Don Pancho Cantón's military and political career through the more recent failures of nephew Delio Moreno Cantón's gubernatorial bids, the faction had identified and maintained cadres of supporters in the countryside, as well as promoted an active network of intelligence and communication with them. If court testimonies, the regional press, and oral history interviews regarding the period's riots and revolts shed light on anything, it is the depth and persistence of Morenista networks in the countryside.

The linchpins of these networks remained the *cabecillas* of the free villages on the periphery of the henequen zone. These local chiefs had access not only to Mérida and the interior *cabeceras* but also to the large estates, typically through commercial and labor arrangements involving them and their kin. After 1909, as the pulse of regional politics quickened, the Morenista *camarilla* provided hingemen like José Loreto Baak, Pedro Crespo, and Juan Campos money, arms, and, most important, increased status in their local, factionalized spheres, in return for their continued loyalty.

Loyalty, however, meant involvement in a political arena that had turned increasingly violent. Some local chiefs, such as Crespo in Temax and Elías Rivero in Peto, refused to campaign as actively as they had before the fall of Díaz. Such campaigning could mean weeks, even months in the bush, and they had already spent substantial time away from their plots and families. Crespo, for example, informed the CEI in Mérida that he would certainly look after things in and around Temax but would leave the guerrilla campaign in north-central and eastern Yucatán to his former lieutenant, Manuel Fausto Robles, and to Juan Campos.[65] Thus the seasons of upheaval during Maderista rule gave some *cabecillas*, such as Robles and Espita's Juan Leal, their first opportunity to lead in their own right. Leal, like Robles and so many other rural chiefs, was an independent artisan-smallholder who had run afoul of the politics of imposition practiced by the local *jefe político*.[66]

Of critical importance, these village-based *cabecillas* attempted to build (or extend) contacts on neighboring estates that were not affiliated with Morenismo. From personal experience or through trusted contacts, they came to know who were the "good" and "bad" overseers, what constituted the *jornaleros'* principal grievances, and how and through whom to exploit them. They found out which artisans, medical personnel, merchants, and itinerant peddlers came onto the estates, and how often. They were therefore in a position to transmit intelligence up and down the patron-client chain and, to the extent that they remained inclined to do so, to implement Morenismo's plan of rural insurgency at the grassroots.

As the seasons of upheaval ran their course between 1909 and 1913, Morenismo's rural organization became increasingly elaborate and institutionalized. The countryside was divided into several "revolutionary zones," each assigned to specific "companies." These companies of irregular insurgents were, in turn, ordered by ranks (*sargentos, cabos, cornetas,* and *soldados*); and, like local leaders throughout the republic during the tumultuous first revolutionary decade, the local *cabecillas* began to arrogate to themselves inflated officer status (*coronel, jefe de operaciones,* and so on).[67] Meanwhile, a number of intermediate strata cemented the relationship between city and countryside. Agitators and propagandists like Tomás Pérez Ponce and Felipe Carrillo Puerto continued to organize targeted populations of artisans and campesinos in Hunucmá and Motul, respectively. Similarly, the *camarilla* still depended on a myriad of information brokers, couriers, and spies—types who ran the gamut from respected planters, journalists, and intellectuals to holders of rural plots, sympathetic hacienda administrators, *turcos* selling their wares on the dusty backroads, and, in two colorful cases, an eccentric peddler of patent medicines and a mysterious "tall white *huach* [non-Yucatecan] with a pockmarked face."[68]

Because they had reason to remain loyal to their traditional patrons and because they typically held Pino Suárez and "his arrogant, hypocritical clique of sissies and foreigners" in contempt, the popular Morenista chiefs remained steadfast clients of the CEI until its demise several years later.[69] For example, in the wake of Díaz's fall, Crespo and Robles had demanded a private audience with Pino in Mérida for the sole purpose of alerting him that, although they were demobilizing their forces, their followers would remain armed and could be activated "on a moment's notice." Then, in case the new Pinista regime had not gotten the message, they left Pino's office shouting "'Viva Delio Moreno Cantón!' . . . at point-blank range in the Governor's face."[70]

José Loreto Baak's devotion to the Cantón *parentesco* was even more pronounced. Local historians still recount a telling—and rather chilling—episode that took place in September 1911, when Madero accompanied Pino Suárez to the Puuc to endorse the latter's candidacy for governor. During a brief whistle-stop in Muna, Mexico's president found himself seated across the table from Baak, the local *cacique*. Efforts by Pino and Madero to engage the rustic Baak in conversation went nowhere; he merely glowered at the politicians he regarded to be Morenismo's sworn enemies. Later in the afternoon, as Madero addressed Muna's inhabitants in the plaza, Baak's displeasure became visceral. He left the gathering and cabled a terse message to Delio Moreno Cantón and Carlos R. Menéndez in Mérida: "I've got Pino and Madero here with me; what do you want me to do with them?"

Apparently, only a frantic response by these CEI leaders to "do nothing!" avoided implicating the party in a grisly episode with monumental national consequences.[71]

On several occasions after the September 1911 electoral farce and its equally fraudulent December sequel, the Morenista *cabecillas* dutifully organized uprisings in their localities as part of a regional insurrectional strategy coordinated at CEI headquarters in Mérida. These broader actions in turn were timed to coincide with national Reyista, Orozquista, and Felicista conspiracies against the Madero regime. Of course, Yucatán's rural chiefs knew little about the turns anti-Maderista politics were taking at the national or even the regional level, and cared less. They were more interested in the individual bargains they struck with specific Morenista patrons—bargains that afforded them strategic advantages in their struggles for local power and that seemed to justify the risks they took.

While individual *cabecillas* might keep faith with their elite sponsors, collectively their behavior became increasingly worrisome to elites. Not only did many *cabecillas* themselves exhibit a propensity for voluntarism and seemingly "unrestrained violence" (the words are Moreno Cantón's); they occasionally lost control of the operations they led or provoked. During the fall of 1911, throughout 1912, and into 1913, haciendas were overrun by marauding bands that took the initiative to "liberate" peons and property alike—occasionally from the very Morenista elites who had initially authorized the mobilization. Popular Morenismo was spinning out of control and the results were often as horrifying for Morenista elites as for their factional rivals.

For example, in Ticul *partido*, José Loreto Baak reassembled hundreds of his former clients and waged a guerrilla war against the Pinista authorities on his home turf. After storming the armories of national guard detachments and summarily "bringing to justice" abusive police and municipal officials, Baak became "the law" in the municipalities of Muna and Santa Elena. Furthermore, he frequently used his status as "Morenista revolutionary chief" as a cover for criminal profiteering, preying on (and in several instances brutally murdering) wealthy planters and merchants he conveniently labeled Pinistas.[72] Early in 1913, local notables in the Puuc representing all three *camarillas* signed an open letter condemning his activities and censuring the CEI for naively inflating "the heroic myth of Loreto Baak."[73]

Whatever his intentions or motives might have been, Baak came to be *perceived* as a hero by increasing numbers of campesinos from the sierra who now joined his forces. For instance, the recruits included a contingent of *jornaleros* who had risen on the Chacinicche, Yaxha, and Choyob estates on the outskirts of Muna. Old deferential habits on these estates were giving way to a new assertiveness and empowerment: the riots were triggered when the overseer of Chacinicche refused to yield to a peon on the dance floor at a Saturday-night *jarana*. Expletives turned into threats, and when the *encargado* could not defuse the situation by firing his pistol in the air, the workers made good on their threats. After administering a savage beating to the overseer, the peons fled into the bush shouting *vivas* to Loreto Baak.[74]

The planters sadly observed that social control was disintegrating up and down the Puuc by late 1911. In November, popular Morenista insurgents captured Halachó, a good-sized *cabecera*, and held it for two days. The good news for CEI headquarters was that these unlettered Maya insurgents had toppled the imposed Pinista government amid shouts for Don Delio Moreno Cantón. The bad news was that after capturing the plaza and raiding the local barracks they had knocked out telegraphic communications with Mérida and had begun naming their *own* municipal authorities. Ultimately, the state was forced to call upon federal and state troops from neighboring Campeche to crush the rebellion.[75]

On the heels of the news from Halachó came equally disturbing revelations regarding a series of jacqueries and mutinies on estates in Tekax district in the more remote, southern Puuc. Here, what had begun as an attempt to arm peons in support of a regional Morenista rebellion to protest the fraudulent elections quickly degenerated into murder, indiscriminate violence, and looting directed against the district's wealthy inhabitants. Apparently, Morenista propagandists had assured some local peons that their debts had been erased and they were free to go. With little to check it now, the force of rumor transmitted the rebellion almost instantaneously throughout the southern Puuc. Droves of workers deserted their estates, but often not before venting their rage on local symbols of privilege and authority.[76]

These scenarios of insurgency would be reenacted, in one form or another, in the eastern districts of the state. Administrators and overseers on estates in Motul, Espita, Tizimín, and Valladolid consistently warned their bosses late in 1911 that peons "were in a foul and aggressive mood," one that "Morenista agitators" were successfully exploiting.[77] Meanwhile, district prefects and the courts remarked on the disturbingly high levels of arson and bombings, rustling and theft.[78] In mid-September, apparently armed by the Morenistas, peons mutinied on Olegario Molina's hacienda, Holcá, and other Espiteño estates. Only emergency measures by the Pinista (ex-Molinista) prefect, which included calling in troop reenforcements and jailing thirteen peons, temporarily preserved Pinista rule in Espita and Tizimín.[79]

Nevertheless, following their electoral failure in September, the Morenistas stepped up their activities in the east. As we have seen, the renewed Morenista guerrilla campaign in Temax was now under the command of Juan Campos and Manuel Fausto Robles. During the spring of 1911, the campaign had remained largely focused in Temax; in the late fall, as the CEI pursued a more coordinated regional strategy, rebel movements spread rapidly into the neighboring districts. Dividing the north-central and eastern parts of the state into "revolutionary zones" of responsibility, the small, tactically mobile commandos of Campos, Robles, and the Espiteño chief, Juan Leal, roamed the countryside at will, effectively controlling the *partidos* of Temax, Tizimín, and Espita. By the middle of 1912, they threatened to extend their sphere of control into Izamal to the south and Motul to the west—two of the henequen zone's richest districts. In the final days of 1912, the Morenista *guerrilla* widened even further when Miguel Ruz Ponce, the former *cabecilla* (and fugitive) from the 1910 Valladolid revolt, suddenly opened a new front in the far eastern part of Valladolid, around Chemax.[80]

Municipalities such as Teya and Suma in southwestern Temax and Tekantó, Kantunil, Sudzal, and Tepakan in northeastern Izamal proved to be fertile recruiting areas for these popular Morenista chiefs. Here, villagers still nursed grievances about Porfirian *caciquismo* and the irregular distribution of their *ejidos* in the late 1880s, the 1890s, and the first decade of this century.[81] Consequently, when Campos's forces rampaged through Teya and Tekantó in May 1912, dynamiting municipal offices and burning several Pinista and ex-Molinista officials alive, villagers, recent guard recruits, and peons on a variety of estates rallied behind them. Many willingly signed "pledges of support"—others were "persuaded" to do so—while some left their communities and guardposts on the spot to join Campos's guerrilla force.[82]

In certain localities, just as they had done in the spring of 1911, Campos and Robles officiated at ceremonies in which peons were freed from their debts and agreed to fight for the "Morenista revolution" for two pesos a day.[83] This new economic arrangement became a powerful selling point for the CEI's rebellion. On one occasion, which the state court meticulously documented, two campesinos from Cansahcab (Temax district) engaged in an animated exchange concerning the economic opportunities of insurrection while relieving themselves against a wall.[84] Increasingly, in Temax, Espita, and Izamal, *jornaleros* began to inform overseers rather matter-of-factly that their masters could neither protect them nor provide sufficiently for them.[85] On the other hand (and particularly in localities where agrarian grievances did not burn with great immediacy), *cabecillas* also encountered savvy workers who still needed to be convinced about the economics of insurgency. "Bueno, *jefe*," a prospective recruit inquired after a Morenista chief had made his appeal to peons at the Hacienda Suytunchen, "and how much is this revolution of yours prepared to pay its fighters?"[86]

Clearly, then, the *guerrilla* mounted by Morenista *cabecillas* like Campos, Robles, Leal, and Ruz Ponce involved large numbers of campesinos and a good deal of complexity in terms of the participants' actions and motivations. Nevertheless, as far as the Pinista government was concerned, all these actions "had the character of banditry," perpetrated by "a handful of robbers and assassins."[87] Just as it had done in labeling peasant resistance in Hunucmá as banditry, the state here sought to strip the Morenista insurgents' actions of any claim to political legitimacy.

Yet no amount of labeling, surveillance, or repression could save Maderismo and its Pinista clients, so delegitimized had they themselves become in the eyes of both the *gente decente* and the popular classes by mid- to late 1912. For the elites, the last straw was the spread of bona fide revolt and jacquerie to the outskirts of the state capital itself. In early May, Morenista insurgents, drawn mostly from the pueblo of Sierra Papacal, launched a series of raids just northwest of Mérida on henequen estates owned by some of Pinismo's wealthiest planter supporters.[88]

The attacks were well prepared in advance. *Cabecillas* from Sierra Papacal conferred with CEI leaders in Mérida over a period of weeks to coordinate a strategy for the raids. They and other Morenista villagers then infiltrated the estates under cover of their jobs as part-time workers. Strengthened by commitments of cash and arms from the CEI, these insurgents attempted to recruit the peons, employing arguments that appealed to their economic interest, moral sensibilities, and family ties (in many cases, the peons had been born in or around Sierra Papacal and were blood relations). In addition, efforts were made, with some success, to cultivate and recruit authority figures on the estates, including schoolteachers, overseers and foremen, many of whom were also originally from Sierra Papacal or other nearby pueblos.

Although their preparations were thorough, Morenista elites quickly came to doubt the wisdom of their strategy. What they intended as a "controlled mobilization"—hit-and-run actions that would inflict losses on rival planters, point up the Pinistas' inability to guarantee the social peace, and ultimately topple the administration—began to show symptoms of a racially tinged class war. Before his raid on Suytunchen, Pinista Juan Berzunza's opulent *finca*, *cabecilla* Juan Jiménez exhorted his men that the time was ripe "to let the devil take these Pinista cowards." He bragged that soon he himself would "finish off these *dzules* in the mouth of my shotgun." Days later, as the revolt spread, Jiménez and his lieutenants addressed impromptu workers' committees on several neighboring estates (Yaxche, Cheuman, San Ignacio, and Nocac). This time, Jiménez not only encouraged workers on Pinista estates to burn henequen fields, rob cattle, kill overseers; he also began to make veiled threats against Morenista planters. "When Don Delio Moreno triumphs," he warned, "Manuel Peón [the proprietor of Nocac] will pay dearly."[89]

With armed bands now controlling Hunucmá and much of the southern and eastern parts of the state, and jacquerie and revolt now threatening to engulf the heart of the henequen zone itself (see Map 8.2), Yucatán's rival elite factions finally recognized the urgency of a joint strategy to *demobilize* the countryside.

"*Cria cuervos* (raise crows) and one day they'll peck out your eyes," Morenista intellectual Carlos R. Menéndez observed, applying the old Spanish proverb to the plantocracy's dilemma. Neither Pinistas nor Molinistas piped up to challenge him.[90] The message was clear. Much in the manner of the nineteenth-century Caste War, the mass participation of campesinos in these rebellions had begun to infuse the struggle with an element of local resistance to elite domination that was now cause for real alarm among the same elites that had initially invited that participation. Once again on the nation's far periphery, in the absence of a strong central state, Maya villagers and significant numbers of peons were attempting to reconfigure the boundaries of regional society and politics. They were fleeing restrictive labor arrangements, targeting the property and persons of abusive elites and their agents, and in certain noteworthy cases, building clienteles that would later be consolidated into new power domains (*cacicazgos*) when the Mexican Revolution gained a foothold in Yucatán after 1915.

What, then, could elites do late in 1912 to defuse this growing insurgency? The Liga de Acción Social redoubled its efforts to convince fellow planters of the need for improved labor conditions and rural schools. Their work paid some dividends. Faced with popular revolt, a growing number of *hacendados* felt compelled, at least in the short run, to make greater concessions; or as Alan Knight has put it for Mexico as a whole, "to wheedle and promise, as well as repress."[91] In addition, the CEI made a more serious effort to rein in its own popular *cabecillas*.[92] Yet these private-sector initiatives were at best halfway measures, and they were not matched by significant changes in Pinista government policy. As 1912 gave way to 1913, the political climate in the state eerily mimicked that of Muñoz Arístegui's last year in office: *la mano dura* endured even as liberal reform was stillborn. Indeed, the Maderista state's very "response to popular rebellion . . . implied a derogation of liberal principle, and a revival of both Porfirian methods and Porfirian interests."[93]

Ultimately, Yucatecan elites could only hope that the discredited and isolated Maderista regime would be toppled by a coup—and sooner rather than later. Indeed, probably nowhere in the republic was the architect of this eventual putsch, General Victoriano Huerta, more enthusiastically received than in Yucatán. The assassinations of Madero and Pino Suárez in February 1913 were gleefully welcomed by rival Morenista and Molinista elites, which, by and large, approved of Huertismo's Porfirista solution to the problems of "banditry" and "anarchy" (read, popular insurgency).[94] Huerta's imposition of authoritarian military rule institutionalized a political stalemate among Yucatán's three contending elite factions; nevertheless, it also allowed them an opportunity to reach an accommodation—an *acomodamiento de desleales*—that would preserve the social peace.

With the issue of state power resolved, at least temporarily, justice was meted out Porfirian style—with alternating shrewdness and verve. The Huertista government declared a general amnesty, then made it clear, in a run of edicts and local court decisions, that "banditry"—that is, new crimes against property, resistance to authority—would be punished with the greatest severity.[95] To be sure, Yucatán (like any society, even a highly controlled one) did not lack "professional" criminals: thieves and rustlers had plied their trade before the seasons of upheaval, and found even greater possibilities during them. Yet early in 1913, the use of the term *banditry* by the Huertista state and Yucatán's three elite *camarillas* was an attempt to seize the discursive high ground to meet a specific *political* challenge. Much like the more recent concept of terrorism, banditry became more a part of the "metalanguage of crime" than a specific crime in itself. It allowed the state and the planter class to mark violent or potentially violent behavior by "dangerous classes" in society.[96] Only months earlier, Morenista and Pinista elites had been in the habit of referring approvingly to at least some of these "bandits" (that is, "their" bandits) as "revolutionaries" and "insurgents." From the "bandits'" standpoint, their activities remained essentially the same. In Hunucmá, as we have seen, they operated as individuals, in small informal groups, or in larger rebel bands, depending on the options that circumstances provided, but always with a view to defending the remnants of a shrinking agrarian patrimony and settling accounts with despised power figures.

While several villagers were made examples, sent before a firing squad for rustling and robbery, the military state solicitously courted and ultimately cut deals with the most strategically placed popular *cabecillas*. In exchange at least for their quiescence, local chiefs in the Puuc and the eastern part of the state, who had demonstrated their ability to turn out hundreds of fighters, were granted a measure of political autonomy—always their principal goal. Some received commissions in the state militia, and for several the deal seems to have been sweetened with a choice piece of land. Once it had addressed the principal flashpoints of popular insurgency, the Huertista state mopped up less organized factional violence and rioting, bundling suspects off to jail, where they usually languished for a month or two before being appropriately chastened and released. By mid-1913, the Yucatecan countryside was once more essentially demobilized.

## Postmortem: Reflections on Campesino Consciousness

Understanding the consciousness of participants in rather fleeting moments of rural collective action—episodes that rarely leave a historical trace or any cultural residue—is admittedly no easy task. As rich as they are, contemporary judicial testimonies and recently gathered oral traditions permit us to speak with greater confidence about the character of Yucatán's mobilizations than about the motivations of the villagers and peons who joined or refused to join them. Indeed, many students of social movements wonder whether we can ever determine individual motivations with any degree of accuracy. The task is even more daunting when we must work retrospectively, with incomplete data. Particularly in the tumultuous context of riots and rebellions, the insurgents themselves may not even be conscious, at the moment they join a band, of what motivates them. One Yucatecan peon, Marcos Chan, tersely remarked at his trial, "They asked me if I wanted to join them, and I said yes."[97] How can we begin to know what went through his mind? How can we know if he would have acted differently a day or a week later if presented with the same choice? Durkheim wrote, "Intent is too intimate a thing to be interpreted by another. It even escapes self-observation."[98] Some structuralists find the exercise of assessing motivation so subjective (and some would add, so "trivial") that they completely discourage asking why people acted and seek only to understand how they acted and with what outcomes.[99]

These critics raise a valid point. A careful reading of the Yucatecan court records suggests that individual campesinos may have joined or refused to join insurgent bands for a plethora of conscious (often interlinked) motivations, including economic calculations, family and fictive kin ties and responsibilities, and an urge for revenge. Beyond these surface motivations, no doubt, other unconscious, psychologically based factors entered into individual behavior choices. For example, psychologists (beginning with Le Bon's aristocratic and racialist treatment at the turn of the century) have documented the collective lowering of thresholds of inhibition in mobs, and other crowd phenomena.[100] As we saw in the San Pedro Chimay riot earlier in this chapter, some episodes of Yucatecan insurgency resembled public fiestas, in which large concentrations of people, occasionally accompanied by the community band, defected en masse.[101]

And what role did gender relations play in motivation? In certain cases we found mothers, wives, and sisters egging on their male relations, in effect challenging the *machismo* of their men. In one notable example—which led to a jacquerie—Martina Ek graphically exhorted her husband and son to take action against an estate overseer: "C'mon, why don't you kill that bastard now that you have the chance; you can bet he wouldn't go soft on you!"[102] On numerous other occasions, village-based campesinos hid male relations from state security forces pursuing them for "banditry" and "sedition," and frequently "took the heat" for them. As we have seen, not infrequently women also led initiatives in the pueblos to resist their men's forced conscription into the army or national guard. These actions often provoked verbal and physical attacks on the women by state agents, which infuriated their menfolk and gave rise to celebrated local riots and revolts in which both men and women played active roles.[103]

Here Temma Kaplan's conceptualization of "female consciousness" in working-class struggles in Spain and Mexico, as well as other parts of Latin America and the developing world, is particularly helpful for understanding the motivation of these *campesinas yucatecas* (and, by extension, that of their male relations). The lives of these campesinas revolved around their perceived role as nurturers and preservers of life in the family and community. When their obligation (and perceived *right*) to feed and protect their loved ones was threatened by police, military recruiters, and other agents of the state, they not only challenged their men to perform their own customary roles, they engaged in disruptive behavior in the public arena. Thus, in mounting an effort to obtain their customary rights as family caretakers, these campesinas politicized the networks of everyday life. In the process, they often became outlaws and were generally judged by their betters to have "made spectacles of themselves."[104]

Certainly a variety of conscious and unconscious motivations and variables, as well as numerous other contingencies, come into play when we ponder why individuals participate in riots and rebellions. We might say that the political behavior of insurgent groupings is typically *overde-termined*, the product of multiple and complex social and cultural well-springs.[105] But ultimately, in grappling with these episodes of resistance and rebellion, we feel compelled to attempt a general explanation of why they took place and why villagers and peons decided to join them—to offer at least a proximate cause.

In order to do this, we are obliged to look beyond individual insurgents' own beliefs about their actions; rather we must read these beliefs against the structural considerations that affected the individual as a member of a group or groups and as a part of a larger social formation. Effectively, this means that the full range of "external" power relations must be considered, in addition to people's own "internal" perceptions of their conditions and behavior.[106]

In Chapter 6, we sketched out the dynamic relations of domination in the henequen zone during the final years of the Porfiriato. Similarly, we examined the severe threat that the expansion of the fiber estates posed to the existence of the poor but free villagers on the zone's less controllable fringes. This threat, we showed, was often compounded by the abuses of collusive political authorities at a juncture when the economy was deterio-rating but political space was widening. Often such egregious acts by *jefes políticos* or other identifiable superiors—which in the case of one notori-ous political boss routinely included the expectation of the "right of first night"—had the effect of transforming routine suffering into an unbearable sense of outrage so propitious to rebellion.[107]

E. P. Thompson provides a salutary guidepost for the challenging task of understanding the consciousness of villagers and peons during episodes of insurgency. He writes,

> The consciousness of a worker is not a curve that rises and falls with wages and prices; it is an accumulation of a lifetime of experience and socializa-tion, inherited traditions, struggles successful and defeated. . . . It is this weighty baggage that goes into the making of a worker's consciousness and provides the basis for his behavior when conditions ripen . . . and the mo-ment comes.[108]

Thompson's insight may be profitably read against the evidence of the period. Hingemen often received an ambivalent reception when they ar-rived on henequen estates seeking adherents between 1909 and 1913.[109] Bad as conditions had become, many peons still eschewed a strategy of direct confrontation. They probably believed that, as in the past, such actions were doomed to failure, and that the spoils temporarily to be won were not worth the loss of the modicum of security the estate still provided—not to mention the potential loss of life. Some required more information before standing up to the master, and assertively sought it. We have seen that in a variety of cases, individuals and groups of peons essentially *negotiated* pay levels with arriving *cabecillas*. In another instance, after a hurried discussion among themselves following the arrival of a Morenista band, several peons served notice to their master on the spot: "*Patrón*, we're leaving your service because of the violence and uncertain state of things."[110] The recollections of one of them suggest that familial responsibilities and longstanding grievances played an important part in the calculus that was done.[111]

The peons did not perceive all *henequeneros* to be losing their grip, however; nor did all *henequeneros* abandon paternal incentives. While conditions were generally deplorable, they varied from estate to estate. No doubt, many servants favored a strategy of continuing to extract what security they could and resisting the demands of monoculture in more "routine," less risky ways. Some peons, such as Alonso Patrón Espadas' *acasillados* at Sacapuc, remained genuinely loyal (and even affectionate) to a patron widely renowned for his generosity and kindness.[112]

Like the leaders of other peasant or slave revolts, Yucatán's *cabecillas* were not above "pressing" to secure recruits. Nor could they afford to be in challenging such a formidable monocultural regime. We have seen that efforts were first made to appeal—in Maya—to the ties of family and communal origin that frequently bound villagers and peons, as well as to invoke shared grievances of class and ethnicity. When they had the luxury of time, the insurgents would also throw open the doors to the hacienda store, slaughter the landowner's cattle, and fete the peons with an impromptu banquet—thereby demonstrating largesse and solidarity while pointing up the *señor's* impotence. Moreover, *cabecillas* always made a point of first attempting to woo or coerce those personnel on the estate who had a high degree of influence with the peons: the schoolteachers, overseers, foremen, and drivers. This task became easier when the *cabecillas'* intelligence suggested that such individuals, who inhabited rural society's middle ranks, might be disgruntled with their current arrangements and chafing for advancement. It was only when these various inducements and recruiting strategies failed that *cabecillas* began to intimidate the peons directly, first threatening and then making violent examples of the master's favorite servants. Typically, the insurgents threatened the assembled peons with razing their huts, burning their cornfields, and confiscating their possessions if they did not join the revolt—and with worse if they betrayed them to the authorities.[113]

Of course, a debate has always swirled around the uses of what Eugene Genovese, writing in the context of Afro-American slave revolts, calls "revolutionary terror." Genovese uses the term descriptively, even approvingly.

The sense is that leaders of slave revolts or peasant insurgencies appreciate that their mobilizations do not proceed in the abstract. Yucatán's *cabecillas* knew that whatever sympathies the peons might have harbored for their cause, they had long been conditioned to submission and would be fearful under any circumstances of a resort to violence. That being the case, such peons had to be made "to confront a new reality." Genovese writes,

> [Rebels] who have not lost their senses must conclude that they will have no prospects until the cost of collaboration rises to the level of the cost of rebellion. For only then will people be free to choose sides on grounds of duty. And it serves no purpose to pretend that "innocent"—personally inoffensive and politically neutral—people should be spared. The oppressor needs nothing so much as political neutrality to do business as usual: It is his *sine qua non*. He who wills liberation in a context that does not permit peaceful change wills revolutionary terror. No slave revolt that hesitated to invoke terror had a chance.[114]

Of course, this need to employ force to generate solidarity—a seeming contradiction in terms—has universally led insurgents' opponents to ignore pressing's *unifying function*. The "official mind" of the state has regarded pressing solely as proof of the coercive nature of rebellion—or at least portrayed it as such. Indeed, Yucatecan planters and state authorities did not stop talking about servants who had been "seized" or "forced" by "outsiders" into a growing "contagion," and many latter-day historians have drawn much the same conclusions.[115] But such one-sided depictions of pressing, Indian historian Ranajit Guha points out, fail to grasp the essential ambiguity of the phenomenon, which is symptomatic of a lack of uniformity in peasant consciousness itself: "For no class or community is ever so monolithic as completely to rule out lags or disparities in its members' response to a rebellion." In this context, Guha contends, pressing "is primarily an instrument of . . . unification and not of punishment." Insurgents use "their mass and militancy . . . to resolve a contradiction among the [subaltern] themselves, not between [them] and their enemies."[116]

The record reveals that, willingly or after some persuasion, hundreds, even thousands of peons took the risk and joined rebellious villagers in these popular insurgencies. Yet if the freewheeling Maderista riots and revolts could bring *comuneros* and *acasillados* together around shared grievances and identities, such alliances were always exceedingly fragile. Despite shared oppression and ties of kinship and communal origin, over the long haul it was extraordinarily difficult to mobilize a diverse peasantry balkanized by different social and productive relations. Contemporary testimonies are rife with references to long-running animosities and vendettas between villagers and peons. Indeed, the Maderista uprisings could just as easily drive villagers and peons farther apart as bring them together. The heat of the moment brought simmering antagonisms to a boil, and the revolts could provide a convenient cover for settling old scores. "Look, Juan, there he is, one of those chicken thieves from [Hacienda] Suytunchen," an insurgent screamed to a fellow villager from Sierra Papacal; "let's 'cure' the bastard of his bad habit once and for all."[117]

In Yucatán and elsewhere during the epic revolution—the rosy claims of some populist historians notwithstanding—villagers and peons were rarely amalgamated into durable alliances. Much less did they constitute a campesino class that struggled against landowners.[118]

Again, this is not meant to undercut the popular character of these revolts, only to delimit its reach. The *cabecillas* who directed Yucatán's Maderista insurgency provided a brand of leadership to villagers on the periphery of the henequen zone that was eminently popular: homegrown, locally focused, and organically legitimate in the sense of the Weberian model of "traditional authority."[119] Such authority both reflected and helped to shape the character of insurgency during the seasons of upheaval. As we have seen, these leaders had no encompassing national or even regional vision. They responded to, and by their actions reinforced, their followers' determination to preserve autonomy and subsistence and at the same time to undermine, actually and symbolically, the authority of the dominant class and the state. Their "ideology," we would reiterate, was written in their acts, and occasionally emerges in the rare, terse testimonies they left. Pedro Crespo, it will be recalled, told reporters: "Our goal is to overthrow the authorities and then see what happens." Crespo's ally, Juan Campos, repeatedly told his son that he aimed "to fight tyranny and slavery and remain a free man."[120]

Because of the rather parochial, defensive nature of popular authority and ideology, Yucatán's popular movement was destined to be rather fragmented and brittle. The village-based *cabecillas* might successfully mobilize and represent their local clienteles, but they often feuded with and repressed factional rivals. They could barely make common cause (and never lasting alliances) with neighboring pueblos, let alone with the peons.

We should emphasize that we are not affirming any larger theoretical judgment about peasant consciousness—that it is narrowly obsessed with local struggles over land, subsistence, or a desire simply to be left alone. Nor are we validating essentialist notions that the little world of the village or hacienda bounded the peasants' ideological horizon. Our earlier emphasis on the appropriation and reformulation of liberal ideology by Yucatecan peasants should make this clear. Moreover, scholars working on the Andes have persuasively argued that peasants often had a keen awareness of political worlds beyond the immediate locale, and possessed a flexibility of consciousness far more complex than the predictable parochial obsessions with land, autonomy, or subsistence security.[121]

Nevertheless, given the formidable constraints imposed by Yucatán's monocultural regime, particularly an "idiom of power" that effectively combined reinforcing elements of isolation, coercion, and paternalistic security, it seems legitimate to conclude that a parochial orientation and a defensive obsession with local rights did indeed prevail among the *yucateco* peasantry during the seasons of upheaval. Strong peasant communities had ceased to exist in the northwestern henequen zone long before the Caste War and the subsequent onslaught of monoculture. Even on the fringes of monoculture, peasant villages were stratified and contentious, communal bonds were fragile, and they could only be mobilized to confront a serious external threat.

Against long odds and operating within narrow parameters, then, Yucatecan campesinos generated their own species of popular movement between 1909 and 1913. Through a critical reading of largely state-mediated sources and more recent oral testimonies, we have teased out the elements of an unmistakable discourse of protest among the region's villagers and peons. To be sure, Yucatán's rural movement was a far cry from the telluric groundswells that populist writers have conjured up for regions like Morelos and Chihuahua during the same period (though such depictions may themselves be overwrought).[122] Still, it is no exaggeration to suggest that the motley bands of campesinos that rampaged during Yucatán's seasons of upheaval cast a pall over the plantocracy and ensured that henequen monoculture's ferocious regime would not go unchallenged.

Of course, the plantocracy would weather that challenge; indeed, it would manage to keep the Mexican Revolution at arm's length until 1915. How did the old order tenaciously, obstinately cling to power in the peninsula while the rest of Mexico burned? We now examine the demobilization of the countryside that began in earnest in the middle of 1913 under the Huerta regime. It was during Huertismo that Yucatán's querulous ruling class would begin to mount its last stand.

## CHAPTER 9

# A Troubled Peace, Spring 1913–
# Spring 1915

There is much to give thanks for. Jacobin furor has subsided in our
state.... [The revolutionary governor] has learned to wink at many things.
—Blano Castellanos to the archbishop, Christmas Day, 1914

I t was as if the clock had been turned back to a bygone era.
Avelino Montes's elegant black landau pulled up solemnly before the Cámara del Congreso, joining those of Yucatán's *gente
decente*, who preened and awaited the chance to pay their respects to the
new governor—once again a military man. Molinistas, Morenistas, and former Pinistas; representatives of the Liga de Acción Social and the Cámara
Agrícola—all were in attendance that first morning in February 1914.

And they were glad to be there. As he took possession of the governorship, Victoriano Huerta's proconsul, General Prisciliano Cortés, read from
an old and reassuring script: one that insisted on progress, but only after
order was no longer in doubt. Yucatán would have its rural schools (land
reform was never mentioned), but the first order of business was putting a
reliable rural militia in place. What it could—and now would—do without
was partisan political strife. "The well-being of the State," the general in-
toned, "will be guaranteed only by the disappearance of its divisive parties.
Only then will Yucatecos hear the one voice that counts, that of peace,
truth, and harmony."[1]

Much as they relished—indeed, lived for—participation in the political
arena, Yucatán's erstwhile elite factions now seemed resigned, at least temporarily, to putting their rivalries in abeyance and lending their support to
President Huerta's military solution to insurgency in Mexico. The next day,
and for days to come, in his editorials in the Morenista daily *La Revista de
Yucatán*, Carlos R. Menéndez, himself a politician to the marrow of his
bones, heartily endorsed Governor Cortés's repudiation of civilian politics.

He exhorted Yucatecans to give up their fruitless political competition and struggle in nonpartisan fashion "for truth, justice, and the fatherland"—the platitudes enshrined in Huertismo's national slogan. He expressed satisfaction that in place of his paper's former daily coverage of riots and robberies in local villages and hacienda communities, he could now offer his readers full-page pictorials celebrating the free fiestas, fireworks displays, and motion pictures that inaugurated the new government's rule.[2]

Rhetoric aside, Yucatán's elite *camarillas* and notable families had no intention of renouncing politics—least of all the Morenistas. Of all the factions, they had been quickest to court Huerta following his ouster of Madero and Pino Suárez in February 1913. As the *camarilla más popular*— that is, most highly mobilized—they now had reason to expect that with Huerta's assumption of power, their decades in the political wilderness would finally end in the statehouse. Leaving nothing to chance, they had collaborated closely with the Huertistas in effecting the transition that removed power from their bitter enemies, the Pinistas. With Madero and Pino's corpses still warm, CEI leader Delio Moreno Cantón had offered himself to Huerta as a roving ambassador for the new regime.[3]

Mexico's new military dictator immediately sought to cash in on Moreno Cantón's offer. Huerta's secretary of war put the warship *Veracruz* at the CEI leader's disposal; and on March 9, 1914, after a year and a half in exile, Don Delio returned home to a hero's welcome. In Mérida and during a series of well-publicized whistle stops throughout the state's interior, Moreno Cantón told thousands of partisans decked out in red ribbons that "Yucatán wants peace and tranquility, but a peace that can be managed only by the National Army."[4] He assured them that he would stand for governor once the state had been "pacified."[5]

Between speaking engagements, Moreno Cantón met with CEI officials and local *cabecillas*, federal military officers, and the emissaries of a defeated Pinismo to iron out details of the demobilization of the Yucatecan countryside. These arrangements would include a provision of safe conduct for Pinista *jefes políticos*. Repeatedly, in his speeches and extensive interviews with the national and regional press, Moreno Cantón emphasized how important it was for Yucatán's working people to remain at their jobs. He appealed particularly to villagers and peons, who held the state's productive future in their hands, urging them to "avoid the intrigues of outside agitators, register their complaints directly with their patrons, and return contently to their labors."[6]

Meanwhile, Morenista journalists echoed the party line every morning in the *Revista de Yucatán*. Carlos R. Menéndez and his rising star at the paper, Felipe Carrillo Puerto, publicized the benefits of the new era, in which, for the first time in recent memory, the state's government would no longer be "divorced from the people it governed."[7] In the countryside, popular Morenista *cabecillas*, acting on their own volition (but with the CEI's full support), cut individual deals with Huertismo that brought them out of the bush with full pardons. In return for local autonomy—which included license to despoil their defeated Pinista rivals—some of these chiefs pledged their direct support to the new regime; others guaranteed their acquiescence. In a few notable instances, local *cabecillas* incorporated themselves and their retainers directly into the Huertista military machine. Faced increasingly with troop shortages in its national campaign against a reconstituted revolutionary coalition, the federal government shrewdly identified these popular local chiefs as ideal agents for its military draft. But such unsavory work did not come cheap. *Cabecillas* such as Miguel Ruz Ponce and José Loreto Baak extracted high-ranking military commissions and other material inducements for their cooperation. Even then, Loreto Baak ultimately had to be coerced into accepting his post.[8]

## Pacto Social, Política Militar

Despite all the Morenistas' efforts in both city and countryside, and despite months of informed speculation in local society that Morenista rule lay just in the offing, Delio Moreno Cantón never became governor. The Huertistas wooed Morenismo, playing on its illusions and cravings like a hussy toying with a sugar daddy. The U.S. consul himself was fooled by the come-on, reporting late in 1913 that General Cortés had issued orders to the *jefes políticos* to "elect" Moreno Cantón.[9] In the end, the disappointed Morenista suitors realized how foolish they had been.[10] Cortés's own assumption of the governorship and his denunciation of partisan civilian politics merely formalized a policy of rule by trusted generals that had guided Huertismo, both in Yucatán and across the nation, from the outset.[11] A contextual reading of Carlos R. Menéndez's editorials reveals a jilted party forced to sulk privately while praising the *acomodamiento de desleales* that Huertismo saw fit to impose on Yucatán's elite factions.

For the Molinistas and former Pinistas, Huertismo's preemption of formal politics was less of a hardship. Neither *camarilla* was in a position to compete seriously in the electoral arena anyway. The Molinistas still bore the stigma of the final years of Muñoz Arístegui's regime, and they had learned to live in the political shadows. There, many had creatively reinvented themselves as Pinista "democrats"; it was now a much easier task to assume the guise of committed Huertistas.[12] The more recently defeated and discredited Pinistas similarly had no other political alternative than to work with the military dictatorship. Pinista elites, particularly the planters, were forced to balance the moral costs that attended collaboration with Pino's executioners against the military protection that Huertismo provided against rural insurgents in the countryside. Moreover, the new military rulers needed the Pinistas' bureaucratic expertise in affecting an orderly administrative transition.

It is not surprising, therefore, that large landowners like Felipe G. Solís or Tomás and Pastor Castellanos—Molinistas turned Pinistas—now rushed to take up positions in the new regime. Or even that savvy Pinista intellectuals and politicians, such as the reform-minded Calixto Maldonado and Dr. Agustín Patrón Correa, initially joined the new administration and sought to orient its policies in the social sphere. What is baffling, perhaps, is the haste with which members of Pino's own *parentesco*—including three of his brothers-in-law—hastened to collaborate with the military government that had usurped him.[13] Apart from adducing crass individual opportunism, the only other compelling explanation for such unseemly complicity lies in the great fear of Maya rebellion that the seasons of upheaval had unleashed in elite circles. So palpable and pervasive was this dread that none of the three elite factions was immune from it, and all were prepared, if necessary, to pay a price for the *pacto social* that Huertismo would enforce—even at the cost of forswearing electoral politics and betraying family loyalties.

The military regime kept its side of the bargain. In the weeks and months following its actual assumption of power in the peninsula in March 1913, Huertismo demobilized the countryside and protected elite persons and property more effectively than any regime in recent memory. With local Morenista *cabecillas* like Juan Campos, Manuel Fausto Robles, Pedro Crespo, José Loreto Baak, Elías Rivero, and Miguel Ruz Ponce helping to ensure the social peace in their bailiwicks in Temax, the Puuc, and areas on the state's southeastern frontier, uprisings (though not all forms of protest) virtually ceased. In Hunucmá, on the other hand, the new state (like its predecessors) could cut no deals, but it did bring the full weight of its police power down on "these local bandits."[14] Still, fed by the villages that survived in the interstices of the district's great henequen estates, the "infrapolitics" of Hunucmense resistance continued unabated, albeit now more often clandestinely and in smaller, more informal groups.[15]

Throughout the state as a whole, the Huertistas increased the size of the constabulary and created new rural militia units—in the latter case by accelerating conscription.[16] The government rehired José Prats y Blanch, who had earned a reputation for brutal effectiveness as head of the secret police during the Olegariato. With Prats back on the job, it seemed only fitting that the Huertistas would recondition the Hotel Bolados for an expanded number of "guests."[17]

They also militarized the court system. From mid-1913 through January 1914, the state replaced all the existing municipal justices of the peace with its own appointees, then added a new military jurisdiction to Yucatán's judicial hierarchy. In the past, criminal cases had flowed from the municipal justices of the peace or the district court judges to the appellate levels in Mérida (the *juzgado segundo del crimen* and the *tribunal superior de justicia*). Now, cases would travel through the lower-level courts and then, at the discretion of these civilian courts (working closely with the Huertista district prefect and military commandant, who were often the same individual), they might be "excused" and sent directly to the *juez instructor militar.* This special military judge was empowered to deal summarily with cases that were deemed "politically motivated," and his decision was not subject to appeal.[18]

Close examination of the state's judicial archives for the period of effective Huertista rule (early March 1913 through July 1914) bears out the "efficiency" of the militarized judicial regime.[19] Courts attended expeditiously to their business, typically bringing prisoners to trial the same month they were jailed (a marked change from the much slower-moving benches of previous administrations). In the absence of cases prosecuting riot and rebellion—which had been preempted by the regime's draconian style of rule—the courts concerned themselves mostly with punishing the perpetrators of robbery, arson, assault, and other infringements of private property and persons. One is inevitably struck by the excessive nature of the courts' sentences compared to those of their Maderista predecessors, particularly in those cases in which only small amounts of property were taken and no violence was employed against the property owners (for example, campesinos squatting for periods on marginal estate lands).

In one especially poignant case, a campesino named Francisco Várguez made his *milpa* on a few hectares of a rocky, infertile hill on the Hacienda San Antonio Huchim, in the southeastern *partido* of Tekax.[20] He did so for several years, seemingly with the consent of the *hacendado*, Saturnino Torres. But when Torres, after a personal disagreement in 1914, pressed charges for loss of rents, the district court made clear that the campesino's squatting would be "treated as robbery" and the maximum sentence imposed. Várguez spent well over a year in jail (doing *fagina* for the state), then was ordered to pay Torres financial compensation in the amount of one hundred pesos. This was an impossible fine for Várguez or any campesino to pay, and no doubt resulted in debt peonage to Torres—which may well have been the motivation behind the initiation of the original suit.

In this and numerous other cases adjudicated in 1913–14—many of them in districts that had figured more centrally in the Maderista seasons of upheaval than had Tekax—when we seek to make sense of the relationship of punishment to crime, we are left with one inescapable conclusion: this was highly punitive justice, intended to send a political message to the rabble who had run amok in the countryside. The message was that they had taken their last liberties with their betters.

## Business as Usual?

So it seemed, at a casual glance, that little had really changed as a result of the Maderista seasons of upheaval except that, in contrast to 1910, a military man now sat in the Governor's Palace. Travelers and foreign diplomats observed that in Yucatán, the old order appeared once more to be in full flower, "the Porfiriato without Don Porfirio."[21] The plantocracy began to breathe a collective sigh of relief and to turn its attention back to its

TABLE 9.1

U. S. Market Prices for Yucatecan Henequen,
1902–14

(cents per kilogram)

| Year | Average price |
|------|---------------|
| 1902 | 21.65 |
| 1903[a] | 17.86 |
| 1904 | 16.43 |
| 1905 | 15.31 |
| 1906 | 13.97 |
| 1907 | 12.32 |
| 1908 | 9.53 |
| 1909 | 10.54 |
| 1910 | 9.35 |
| 1911 | 8.16 |
| 1912[b] | 10.41 |
| 1913 | 13.97 |
| 1914 | 16.15 |

SOURCE: Askinasy, 100–101.
[a]Year of Molina-Harvester collaboration.
[b]Year of "First Reguladora" valorization scheme.

source of wealth, henequen's "green gold." As one historian has aptly put it, "while the rest of Mexico made war, Yucatán made money."[22]

Henequen was booming. After a decade of generally depressed fiber prices following the International Harvester merger and the onset of that company's collaboration with Molina-Montes in 1902, price quotations for fiber began to rise in 1912, then surged forward in 1913 and 1914 (see Table 9.1). The initial rise reflected the short-lived success of the 1912 "First Reguladora's" valorization campaign. The more sustained price trend was a product of world market forces, as North American cordage companies adjusted to a shortage of manila hemp and anticipated the effects of impending world war by frantically buying up existing hard fiber stocks.

Not surprisingly, the prime beneficiaries of the new boom were the past masters of the trade, the members of the Molina-Montes *parentesco*. Already by far the largest block of producers in the state and still, through Montes's export house, the exclusive export agents for International Harvester's U.S. cordage trust, the Molinistas possessed a liquidity that the rest of the plantocracy bitterly envied. In the next few years, this capital advantage would not only enable the clan to improve its commanding position in the fiber trade, it would also enable the *camarilla* to reassert its primacy in the elite political arena by early 1915.

Indeed, in 1913, as in every year since 1910, it really did not matter who sat in the statehouse; the Molinistas reigned supreme in the economic and social spheres. Their preponderance of capital, their partnership with the most powerful U.S. cordage manufacturers, and their control over regional and international marketing and transportation (railways, warehousing, shipping), which such capital and connections made possible, put them

TABLE 9.2
*Henequen Exports, 1913*

| Exporter | Bales | Percentage of total |
|---|---|---|
| Avelino Montes | 632,810 | 75.62 |
| Arturo Pierce | 158,518 | 18.94 |
| Compañía de Hacendados Henequeneros de Yucatán | 30,380 | 3.60 |
| Comisión Reguladora del Mercado del Henequén | 14,434 | 1.72 |
| Haro y Cía | 485 | 0.13 |
| Escalante y Cía | 121 | 0.03 |
| Miguel Gómez | 100 | 0.03 |
| Cámara de Comercio de Yucatán | 100 | 0.03 |
| Julio Blanco | 2 | — |
| Total | 836,950 | 100.00 |

SOURCE: *EA*, Dec. 1913, p. 813.

well beyond the reach of the state's ineffectual henequen regulating commission. Then again, before the arrival of Alvarado and the Mexican Revolution in 1915, the liberal state had no interest in establishing the kinds of regulations that could have brought the Molinistas back to the pack. Such regulations smacked of "bolshevism" to the planters. Thus, the Molinistas merely waited out each feeble attempt to circumvent their control of production and valorize the price beyond the levels that International Harvester negotiated with them.

One way or another, Montes's *casa exportadora* ultimately got its fiber. In most cases, liens against future production sufficed to keep indebted planters from participating in valorization arrangements. When such price-boosting campaigns were launched, they usually did not have the war chests to keep fiber off the market long enough to realize a decent price. In one celebrated instance late in 1912, when the regulatory commission was able to work out a financing arrangement on seventy thousand bales with the Banco Nacional, Montes and Molina used their connections in the capital to buy back the stocks from the bank. It did not hurt that the Comisión Reguladora's leading official at the time was none other than Tomás Castellanos Acevedo, "El Financiero," a longtime client of the *parentesco*.[23]

A 1914 report submitted to the state government by independent investigators revealed the regulatory commission's pathetic performance in one terse sentence: "Of the 208,632 bales of fiber sold by the Comisión Reguladora since its inception [in 1912] until September 10, 1914, Avelino Montes has purchased 168,399 bales, while only 40,233 have been sold to all other buyers."[24] As Tables 9.2 and 9.3 show, the Montes *casa*'s share of the trade actually increased under Huertismo. From its already preponderant portion of about 63 percent during the Maderista years, the *casa*'s share rose to 75 percent in 1914.[25] In light of this data, it is hard to discount the rumors that emanated from the Cámara Agrícola during the first half of 1914 that Gov-

TABLE 9.3
Henequen Exports, 1914

| Exporter | Bales | Percentage of total |
|---|---|---|
| Avelino Montes | 708,557 | 73.40 |
| Arturo Pierce | 179,847 | 18.50 |
| Compañía de Hacendados Henequeneros de Yucatán | 65,134 | 6.75 |
| Comisión Reguladora del Mercado del Henequén | 9,553 | 0.99 |
| Escalante y Cía | 1,320 | 0.27 |
| Miguel G. Gutiérrez | 202 | 0.04 |
| Izmael González | 100 | 0.02 |
| José Díaz y Díaz | 99 | 0.02 |
| Alfredo Sandoval | 50 | 0.01 |
| Total | 964,862 | 100.00 |

SOURCE: EA, Dec. 1914, p. 1016.

ernor Cortés himself had become an agent for Montes, and was receiving fifty thousand pesos monthly to undermine the Reguladora's power to regulate. During the general's watch, the state commission sold another forty thousand bales to Montes.[26]

No wonder Montes's wealth and power began to take on mythic proportions in regional society. Yucatecans joked about "being as rich as Montes"; rumormongers and gossip columnists speculated about the size of his fortune and the things it enabled him to do. On one occasion it was reported that a ship had docked at Progreso to bring Don Avelino five hundred thousand pesos (three hundred thousand of it in gold); possibly more money, the writer joked, than was currently on deposit in the Banco Nacional.[27]

The Molinista parentesco's economic clout translated into a predominant social role. The clan did not just set the standard of fashion in the privileged circles of Mérida and Progreso, it also shaped the contours of daily life in the countryside. While the parentesco, like other elite factions, had a few enlightened reformers, on the whole its members spearheaded the plantocracy's efforts to resurrect the social regime that had characterized the region during the halcyon days at the turn of the century. Like other historical classes that depended on slave or coerced labor, Yucatán's henequen kings were loath to change the plantation system that had so bountifully enriched and aggrandized them. "Scientific" thought and "modern" fashion had their place, but not in the social regimes of their plantations. When the Revista de Yucatán conducted a survey of planter attitudes toward labor reform late in 1913, the most common response (and the newspaper's position as well) was that "in principle" a free labor market and freedom of movement were satisfactory future options, but that the state should not rush precipitously toward them.[28]

Most observers were struck by the planters' apparent success at turning back the clock. Signs abounded. The flogging of peons remained a regular feature on estates; *fagina* continued to be exacted of campesinos by both planters and district prefects; and as late as May 1914, yet another pueblo saw its traditional village lands surveyed and parceled.[29]

No one was more impressed by the degree of planter control than Esteban Flores, the special agent of the Huertista government's Labor Department who toured the Yucatecan countryside in March 1914 to assess living and working conditions on the henequen estates.[30] Flores's visit was the result of a lobbying effort by the Cámara Agrícola to persuade the Ministry of Development to arrange for the transportation of campesinos displaced by revolutionary violence elsewhere in the country, with a view to addressing Yucatán's continuing labor shortage. In other words, the Cámara and ministry officials hoped to use Flores's report as publicity to attract peons to the henequen estates. The more progressive planters in the Cámara also saw the venture as an important step in their campaign to bring a free labor regime to the region's monoculture.

Both the "progressives" and, eventually, Flores, however, soon realized the extent of the opposition arrayed against them. The Cámara Agrícola had sent a letter to all planters of note, requesting permission for Flores to visit their particular estates. The letter emphasized the mission's long-term advantages in terms of labor acquisition and attempted to allay fears that Flores might be another muckraking John Kenneth Turner. Nevertheless, many planters took weeks to reply, some flatly turned down a visit, and Olegario Molina and Avelino Montes ignored the request completely. When Flores sought the support of interim governor Sebastián García to influence planters to open up their estates, he found him "ill and indisposed." In the end, Flores inspected sixteen estates of varying size, but few of the state's largest plantations. Many properties he inspected belonged to the so-called reformers.

Once he arrived on the estates, Flores encountered further obstacles. Only one of the sixteen proprietors gave Flores unmediated access to his work force; the rest insisted on accompanying him or delegating the overseer to do so, and all demanded the right to provide an interpreter of their choosing, typically an overseer. (Flores would later indicate his surprise to discover that, after decades—indeed, centuries—of tutelage, most of the Maya work force still could not speak, let alone read, Spanish.)

Not surprisingly, few peons were forthcoming in their response to Flores's queries regarding their working and living conditions. Some candidly refused to speak in the presence of their masters, and after awhile Flores concluded that "it was useless to conduct interviews under such circumstances." Still, despite the surveillance, two peons told Flores that they had been badly beaten by overseers. In one case, the beating had led to flight and further punishment; in another to an inability to work for a stretch of time.

Flores's report painted a highly disturbing portrait of the henequen estates' "patriarchal regime," a portrait that, had it been disseminated publicly, would no doubt have stirred memories of Tomás Pérez Ponce's indictment of the Molinas' brutality at Xcumpich almost a decade earlier. Pushing aside the euphemisms of "debts" and "accounts," Flores pointed out that enslavement, isolation, and coercion of the Maya persisted; that everywhere compensation was inadequate; and that disease had reached alarming levels. Gastroenteritis now accounted for roughly one-third of all hacienda deaths; pellagra remained an unremitting scourge.[31] In 1912 a measles epidemic had caused 1,812 deaths—roughly one-eighth of all mortality in the state—with a disproportionate number of those deaths occurring in the countryside. Furthermore, despite all the politically motivated promises by public officials and *hacendados*, "to date, little or nothing has been accomplished [on the issue] of rural schools."

Flores had no intention of being written off as a Cassandra, particularly because the purpose of his mission was to provide some selling points for labor contractors seeking to attract workers to the peninsula. He therefore applauded the fledgling efforts of reformers in the Cámara Agrícola to sell meaningful (that is, market-generated) "free labor" to the plantocracy. He also pointed out improvements in the wage rates, housing, food, and medical care that *some* planters were providing for their workers (particularly on estates that were remote from the principal urban centers and that apparently were governed by a more benign brand of paternalism).

Unfortunately, corroborating evidence bears out more the negative thrust of Flores's report than its few hopeful addenda. Indeed, documentation of some of the most egregious cases of planter cruelty and state complicity across the entire period of our study was found in the judicial archives for the Huertista period. Consider, for example, the notorious "San Nicolás incident" in late September 1913, a blot on the history of plantation monoculture every bit as dark as the Xcumpich affair, and one that, like Xcumpich, still plays on the regional imagination.[32]

San Nicolás was a henequen estate in the district of Motul, just west of Temax in the northwestern part of the henequen zone. Motuleño planters like San Nicolás's owner, Crescencio Novelo, liked to brag that their *partido* produced some of the best fiber in the state; and in truth, only a handful of the district's haciendas were larger and more profitable than San Nicolás.[33] Novelo had done what he could to keep the estate out of harm's way during the seasons of upheaval. He had provided a contingent of conscripts in 1910 to crush the Valladolid revolt, and then, like many members of Motul's principal *parentesco*, the Campos-Palma clan, he had backed the incumbent Pinistas. Unfortunately for him, however, San Nicolás lay in the path of Morenista *cabecilla* Juan Campos's rampage through Temax, Izamal, and eastern Motul in May 1912.[34] The estate suffered some physical damage and a production setback as its peons joined the Morenistas or fled into the bush. These events formed the backdrop for what transpired at San Nicolás less than a year later.

The evidence suggests that the abuses that subsequently took place on the estate were meant as a payback for those peons who had thrown in their lot with Campos or had merely shouted *vivas* to the Morenistas when they occupied the estate. The agents of the *patrón*'s vengeance were the estate's overseer, Pedro Pinto, and several of his henchmen, all of whom had probably suffered humiliation at the hands of Campos's band. According to six of San Nicolás's peons who subsequently presented themselves as eyewitnesses in court, after the day's work had ended on September 21, 1913, Pinto and his men seized two of the estate's Maya peons, Miguel Chan and his brother Mónico, and subjected them to a night of grueling torture. First Pinto and his foreman, Nicolás Pérez, flogged them with a thick henequen cord, then with a wire. After that they were led to the hacienda jail, hosed down, and made to sleep in their wet clothes, receiving periodic beatings with a wooden switch throughout the night. The following morning, the Chans were paraded before the assembled peons, brought to the overseer's office, and again pummeled thoroughly by Pinto's men. When they recovered from the beatings, both men were forced to work wearing leg irons (*grillos*) until their shins were reduced to a bloody pulp.[35] Instead of cultivating henequen in the estate's fields, they were forced to pound lime in a nearby cave from 8 to 5 daily, after which they spent their nights in the hacienda jail. It was later revealed that they had been working in irons and following the same routine of hard labor for the preceding five months as well.

As soon as they were restored to their "normal" work routine, the brothers pressed charges against Pinto and his men. The trial proved a farce, because the district judge was Elías Campos, Novelo's brother-in-law. When the Chans' mother brought the leg irons to court and sought to testify, she was thrown out of the chamber. Judge Campos, furthermore, gave little weight to the testimonies of the six Maya eyewitnesses, likening the men collectively to "a blank tablet on which nothing is written." By contrast, the bench gave great credence to the defendants' explanation of what had transpired: namely, that the brothers were bullies "insulting various people" at the hacienda store, and that when they drew their knives, Pinto, San Nicolás's *agente municipal*, "intervened to prevent a scandal." In the ensuing melée, the defendants explained, the Chans had been injured. Judge Campos ultimately dismissed the case for lack of strong evidence.

So glaring was this miscarriage of justice that it could not be swept under the carpet, even in elite circles. The brothers sought to appeal the decision to the state appeals court (*tribunal superior de justicia*). The high court agreed to hear the case, admitting that "it treat[ed] serious events, on whose clarification rest[ed] the good name of the state." The court also recognized that "a serious enmity" existed between the overseer and the peons. Yet despite the court's judicious handling of the appeal, the Chan brothers never received justice.[36] They were forced to settle for a degree of responsiveness from the court system. This suggests something of a parallel with the plantation regime of the antebellum U.S. South, where, as Eugene Genovese and others have shown, the law sought to fulfill a hegemonic function, providing at least the appearance of a disinterested standard of justice in the minds of the subordinate class.[37]

How to understand such a pattern of excessive elite behavior? As we have suggested, planter recalcitrance about altering the social order and an urge for revenge in the wake of the seasons of upheaval go a long way toward explaining this backlash. But unlike contemporary observers and more recent historians who view the social history of Huertismo in Yucatán as largely an uncontested revisiting of the Porfiriato on the region's working classes,[38] we would suggest that the vehemence of the planter and state response owed much to their bitter realization that the clock *could never* be turned back. Forces had been unleashed and struggles redefined during the period 1909–13 that would continue to find expression at society's grass-roots throughout 1913–14 and thereafter, once the Mexican Revolution established itself under General Salvador Alvarado.

By 1913, in remote, oligarchical Yucatán as in other parts of Mexico, old, deferential habits had begun to give way to a new assertiveness and empowerment—to what one historian has called "a new plebeian insolence."[39] The judicial records and a smattering of press reports reveal a variety of complaints by plantation overseers and the masters themselves that their peons no longer doffed their hats or kissed their hands.[40] The very fact that Maya peons would petition planter-run courts to institute criminal proceedings against their patrons in cases like San Nicolás, *and* that they could count on the solidarity of substantial groups of fellow workers, first in their initial ordeal on the estate and then for months, even years thereafter, during their subsequent ordeal in the state courts, speaks volumes about this boundary change in campesino consciousness.

Although the Huertista government instructed the regional press to keep news of this trend out of its papers (a directive much in keeping with the elite publishers' and editors' own interests, at least during the early, honeymoon period of Huertista rule), substantial evidence of campesinos' changing attitudes embedded itself in the rich criminal testimonies of the period. When the state's reinforced, increasingly mobile military apparatus made direct confrontation suicidal, disgruntled peons and villagers adapted their forms of protest accordingly. In addition to litigation, verbal and symbolic forms of noncompliance, labor absenteeism, well-chosen acts of arson, and other clandestine attacks and appropriations marked campesino infrapolitics.[41]

In one particularly novel episode in October 1913, which caught the attention of the authorities and the local elite but never made it into print, a group of Maya campesinos from the pueblo of Chichimilá, near Valladolid, set off a "henequen bomb" one night on the doorstep of the municipality's most powerful merchant-*hacendado*, Diego Alcocer. Manufactured from tightly wound pieces of castoff henequen fiber, bits of leather, and a measure of gunpowder, the "bomb" exploded with a deafening roar, chasing the merchant out into the street in his underwear. Charging emotional distress to himself and his family, Alcocer sought to press charges against eight villagers with whom he had ongoing labor disagreements. Ultimately, however, in the face of denials of wrongdoing by the "Chichimilá Eight," the local authorities threw out the charges, discreetly suggesting to the merchant that he had come closer to dying of embarrassment than of fright.[42]

State and plantocracy were forced to confront new challenges in urban society as well. The artisanate's nascent mutualist societies and workingmen's associations of the 1900s had given way by the early 1910s to active union organizing centered on the transportation sector of the export economy. Urban labor celebrated its first real triumph in the Progreso longshoremen's strike of 1911. Unions in the port had continued to gather strength during the years of Maderismo, and by 1913, along with the new, active Unión Obrera de los Ferrocarrileros based in Mérida, they constituted the twin foci of the labor movement.[43]

In May 1913, as the price of fiber began to take off, five unions representing Yucatán's dockworkers presented their employers, the *casas exportadoras*, with a new tariff schedule that mandated pay hikes of 25 to 50 percent. They argued that while they had benefited from increases following the 1911 strike settlement, their compensation was hopelessly inadequate in the face of surging prices for basic necessities.[44] They knew that hacienda wages were kept artificially low even as fiber quotations had begun to soar. Far from exhibiting any solidarity with the Maya *jornaleros*, however, these urbanites were merely staking their own claim to a larger share of the proceeds of Yucatán's modernization. When Progreso's exporters and commission agents, led by Avelino Montes, made what the former deemed a "conciliatory" (if modest) counter-offer, the dockworkers effectively mobilized a general strike in early June that eventually included railway and tram workers and gained the endorsement of the powerful labor federation of Veracruz.[45]

In contrast to 1911, this time the state played hardball with the strikers. After the government declared that it would no longer honor strikes, Huertista troops "ensured the social peace," protecting the Cuban engineers and other replacement workers brought in to maintain railroad and tram service. Later the government posted troops on the trains themselves and at all railway yards and offices.

Before the strike could seriously cripple the movement of fiber, the workers accepted federal arbitration, ultimately receiving only a fraction of their demands. They acquiesced in the face of a government ultimatum ordering all unions in the state to disband and threatening massive arrests if the order was not obeyed. In the months following the June strike, management in the railway and tram sectors carried out economic reprisals on strike participants.[46] The state's tactics of repression and union busting forced the nascent labor movement underground and pointed up its inadequacies.[47] Yet while this latest round of labor militancy produced a clearcut victory for management, it came at the cost of deepening antagonism in a sector of urban society whose support the plantocracy would urgently need in the near future.

## The Social Pact Begins to Unravel

By mid-1914, Yucatecans at all points on the social spectrum had come to find Huertismo odious—ironically, the regional elites most of all. More than any other factor, the exigencies of national politics had seen to that. To pay for an escalating military campaign on several fronts against the Villista, Zapatista, and Carrancista revolutionaries who challenged his dictatorship, Huerta tapped Yucatán's rich henequen revenues through increased taxes and "patriotic contributions" (read, forced loans). In addition, the expanded war required new recruits, and Yucatán was expected to shoulder some of the burden by stepping up the dreaded *leva*. Straitened household incomes and overworked bodies were nothing new for the poor. But when the full effect of the national state's demands on the plantocracy's own sources of capital and labor began to sink in, Yucatán's elite *camarillas* became incensed. The prospect of reduced profits and a shrinking labor force was not even the worst of it. A renewed wave of protest in some of the traditional rural problem areas during the summer of 1914 convinced regional elites that the new federal policies were themselves destabilizing the social pact that had made Huertismo palatable in the first place.

As we have seen throughout this book, Yucatecan elites had often been prepared to work with military intervenors from the central plateau so long as the generals acted in the planters' best economic and social interests. But when they felt their interests endangered or betrayed, Yucatecan *camarillas* were quick to mount regionalist and occasionally even separatist challenges to federal rule.[48] The tenor of regional politics from the latter half of 1913 to the first months of 1915 provides a classic illustration of this historical pattern.

By 1913, Yucatán was already a milch cow for the federal government, contributing close to ten million pesos a year in taxes to Mexico City. This was regarded as such a heavy burden, the U.S. consul reported, that it already had provoked some loose talk in the cafés about secession.[49] Further federal demands could only aggravate the situation, particularly those that persisted in targeting the already put-upon henequen industry. Thus, when General Cortés barged into the treasury office of the Comisión Reguladora on two occasions in late 1913 and early 1914 and helped himself to about two million pesos as a "patriotic contribution" for Huerta, *henequeneros* were outraged. After all, this was the same individual who was already doing everything in his power to render the Reguladora a nullity. The planters' anger failed to subside when they learned that in January 1914, Cortés had decreed a special tax of one centavo per kilogram on exported henequen to raise revenues to pay back the forced loan.[50]

Bad as all this was, it represented something of a concession to *hene-*

*quenero* opposition. Initially, Huerta had intended to exact a five-million-peso loan, which would have been defrayed by a two-centavo tax on exported fiber. He relented only in the face of a spirited lobbying effort by the Cámara Agrícola.[51] Joined by their allies in the regional press, such as Carlos R. Menéndez, the planters vehemently protested that they had already contributed a hefty amount to the "pacification" of the state and the nation, and that unlike the rebellious northern states, Yucatán was not a drain on the federal budget. More important, they reminded Huerta and Cortés that however desperately the federal war effort needed an injection of funds, it made no sense to devastate the source of all regional wealth, the henequen industry.[52] In the end, however, *henequeneros* were obliged to stand by helplessly as Huerta's special taxes ate up the new profits they might have reaped from a steady rise in world hard fiber prices.[53]

Even more problematic was the aggressively managed military draft. Its consequences were felt across the entire social spectrum. Late in 1913, Huerta sent a message to Cortés that he wanted fifteen hundred Yucatecan conscripts right away and was likely to need more in the months ahead.[54] Furthermore, he ordered that all Yaquis be repatriated for military service, a shrewd request, given their demonstrated abilities as warriors in Sonora and more recently in Yucatán during the seasons of upheaval.[55]

Daily throughout November and December 1913, carloads of white-clad campesinos poured into the Mérida railroad station from the state's interior. Then, amid poignant scenes of lamentation and farewell involving sweethearts, parents, wives, and children, the draftees departed to join embattled Huertista regiments in the center and north of the republic.[56] Yet despite the supervisory role of *cabecillas* like Baak and Ruz Ponce in the conscription process—halfhearted, to be sure, in Baak's case—violent protest and desertion were also a near-daily occurrence.[57] These Yucatecan campesinos had grown up hearing war stories of family and friends who had left to fight "overseas" or on the frontier against the *cruzob* and rarely had returned.[58] Indeed, the press had only recently reported that of the 173 conscripts from Valladolid who had left the state in 1910, only 43 had returned.[59] And in the district's pueblos and smaller settlements, where gossip and the embroidery of oral traditions served as the people's newspaper, talk of casualties from this most recent *contingente de sangre* ("blood quota") surely had inflated losses manyfold.

As the national campaign turned against the Huertistas, and as popular resistance and *cabecilla* noncompliance took their toll on recruitment in the state, Governor Cortés modified his strategy. He sent out a circular to all prefects and municipal presidents offering the rank of major as a reward to anyone who delivered 100 men to the federal army, that of lieutenant colonel for 150 recruits, and full colonel to anyone providing 200 conscripts.[60] But when few takers appeared, local Huertistas returned to more customary strong-arm tactics in both the city and the countryside. Apart from the usual complaints that peasant villagers had been seized and impressed, cases were reported of artisans, railroad workers, and white-collar clerks being dragged from their workplaces and shipped to the northern front.[61]

The planters' opposition to the draft began primarily as a pocketbook issue. They wondered publicly how the federal government, so cognizant of their perennial labor shortage, could carry off actual or potential workers, then turn around and expect to increase its tax revenues from the mono-crop.[62] Privately, it must have galled them that a loss of workers precluded increasing production sufficiently to realize the windfall that otherwise seemed assured by the current robust fiber prices. The Cámara Agrícola was particularly exercised about the decision to repatriate the Yaquis, many of whom, it contended, had become reliable workers, well acclimated to their new region.[63]

In the following months, the planters, individually and through the Cámara Agrícola, sought to offset the *leva* by arranging to import outside workers to Yucatán. Their efforts were invariably frustrated. The draft had preempted the Labor Department's earlier project to bring northern Mexican colonists to Yucatán, which had triggered agent Flores's visit. A variety of other initiatives also failed. For example, the planters turned to the employment of deported military prisoners from Morelos and Baja California, who for health reasons had been disqualified from combat. These unfortunates, a sympathetic journalist reported (in a manner that recalled Turner's *Barbarous Mexico*), were "sold like beasts of burden to the henequen *hacendados* . . . at 70 pesos a head."[64] Finally, as the labor situation grew increasingly desperate, wealthy planters began to lure, litigate, and even organize raids for peons from the estates of their rivals—giving rise to a series of ugly court cases in 1914.[65]

Few other issues had the capacity to divide local society against itself or set its members against the state as did *la leva*. Indeed, the short tenure of Yucatecan civilian governors Arcadio Escobedo and Felipe Solís, both replaced by generals brought in from outside the state, had much to do with each one's refusal to jeopardize the social peace by enforcing the draft according to the central government's draconian specifications.[66] And forced military service was one of the principal issues that eventually played into a renewal of violence in the countryside in the summer of 1914.

By the spring of 1914, the Huertistas were well aware that their legitimacy was being seriously compromised—even in Yucatán, one of Mexico's last oligarchical redoubts. Then, on April 21, the U.S. occupation of Veracruz—Woodrow Wilson's trump card in his crusade of moral diplomacy against Mexico's dictator—gave the regime one last, brief opportunity to recapture the popular imagination. Unlike other regions of Mexico, particularly the north, Yucatán had little visible U.S. presence, except for the Progreso consulate and a few modest homes and businesses there and in the capital. Nevertheless, in his rhetoric for the occasion, General Cortés masterfully played on historical regional fears of an invasion from without to construct images of a greater national identity.

Will we permit the mercenary *yanqui* to invade the Peninsula . . . without defending our national territory in hand-to-hand combat if need be? Will we permit the ignoble enemy of our race to penetrate our homes and dispose of our lives, honor, and property at will? Never, Yucatecos![67]

For the next several days, Yucatecos from all walks of life, in cities and rural *cabeceras*, imagined the national community that the governor had evoked. They participated in heated public demonstrations, smashed the windows and doors of North American businesses and residences (the occupants of which sought refuge on vessels off the port of Progreso), and dabbled with the possibility of forging broader bonds across class and ethnic lines.[68] And then the invasion scare was over, a manufactured crisis whose moment had passed. It remained to be seen what the political and cultural residue of this brief, participatory exercise in solidarity would be were Yucatán actually invaded. Indeed, the local population would not have very long to wait.

Huerta was defeated and gone by mid-July, leaving Governor Cortés to manage a deteriorating and potentially explosive social situation. Once again, a power vacuum at the center was creating political space for popular movements to maneuver at the grassroots. Not only did long-standing grievances like the appropriation of village lands or abuses by *jefes políticos* remain unresolved, they were exacerbated by the accumulation of excesses under Huertismo. This was particularly evident in districts like Hunucmá and Valladolid, which had seen the fabric of communal and family life cruelly torn by the implementation of the draft. Complicating this unsettled juncture even further were the effects of famine brought on by yet another locust plague. Corn and basic necessities were scarce; moreover, Avelino Montes and the Casa Escalante between them were importing most of the corn that sustained the region—and making a killing in the process.[69] As Carlos R. Menéndez surveyed the volatile political scene against the backdrop of a retail economy that worsened daily, he fretted in his column, "in the countryside, hunger makes a bad adviser."[70]

Before the victorious Constitutionalists could replace the Huertista regime in Yucatán in mid August, the countryside witnessed uprisings in the far eastern (Valladolid) and western (Hunucmá and Maxcanú) parts of the state. Even more disturbing to regional elites, violence flared briefly on the beaches of Progreso, during the fashionable summer season, no less.

In remote Chemax pueblo in the district of Valladolid, the issue was rather clear-cut.[71] More than a dozen Maya villagers trained their hunting pieces on Antonio Sansores, the town's telegraph operator, riddled him with buckshot, and hacked him to pieces when he tried to escape. The motive was not hard to find: Sansores, a white, middle-aged Campechano who had recently come to Chemax to take up his job, had also set himself up as a military recruiter and was reaping the attendant rewards. The Campechano had been a marked man for some time, the court record suggests; the actual *ajusticiamiento* came in late July, after the district's chief recruiter, Miguel

Ruz Ponce, had left the district and Huerta had fallen. So well timed was the "execution," in the midst of the transition to Constitutionalist rule, that the state was unable or fundamentally unwilling to prosecute the case effectively. Wisely, it conducted an investigation, detained several of the suspected perpetrators, and then, after a reasonable amount of time had passed, let them go for lack of evidence. Because the Chemaxeños' action had been circumscribed and its goals had been accomplished, it brought no further repercussions in the municipality.

Hunucmá and Maxcanú were an entirely different story. In these western districts, the villagers' unremitting struggle to protect their land and local autonomy merely entered a new phase in July and August 1914. Once again, in the absence of a repressive military state, campesinos were free to press their own agendas on longtime class adversaries. Earlier in the year, when a village-based *jornalero* from Kinchil, Felipe Cauich, was asked why he had suddenly used a lead pipe to bash in the head of the sleeping overseer on the estate where he had worked for years, he replied simply: "I hated him." The court's investigation revealed that the administrator had worked Cauich hard after hours, but also that the estate was locked in a long-term contest for a portion of Kinchil's *ejidos*.[72]

In July, the members of a neighboring Hunucmense pueblo, Tetiz, faced off against another *hacendado*, Diego María Solís, when the latter closed off a road that gave them access to their communal lands. The dispute dated back to 1904, when the planter had alienated a portion of the village's land, which included the road. Now, only state attempts to mediate the dispute prevented full-scale violence.[73] Just a month later, such violence did break out around Kinchil. Kinchileños killed the overseer of yet another nearby estate, then raided still more properties, recruiting peons as they went. That the *motín* did not escalate into a broader rebellion was largely due to inter-village rivalry: Kinchil's historic grievances lay not only with the surrounding haciendas but also with Tetiz, with which it had long disputed agrarian boundaries.[74]

In Maxcanú in late August, local villagers mounted an evening attack on the district seat, capitalizing on the ill-defined transition to Carrancismo to lash out at a number of hated institutions and symbols. Most of the witnesses were convinced that this raid was coordinated with "known elements from Hunucmá." First the insurgents sacked the police station; then they macheted in the doors of the town's political offices and leading commercial establishments, one of which also served as the district courthouse. Still not satisfied after setting fire to Maxcanú's main stores, the masked invaders looked for additional targets and happened on one of the town's most prosperous citizens, Eulogio Ponce, napping on a bench outside the police station. In the next few minutes they vented on the poor merchant decades of bitterness and rage, shooting him point-blank and cutting him to ribbons with their machetes. An eyewitness later described the final symbolic act of the *facciosos* (insurgents): "They split open his head as if it were a ripe melon and dashed his brains on the doors and walls of the *jefatura política.*" All in all, a rather graphic rendition of "Down with bad government." Shouting "Viva Carranza!" and alerting the rest of the town to the dangerous blaze they had set ("*¡fuego, muchachos!*"), they disappeared into the night.[75]

Of all the uprisings late that summer, the one that sent the most shivers through the regional elite was that led by *cabecilla* Lino Muñoz against the prefect of Progreso on August 18. The initial phase of the *tumulto* even included an extended shootout on the beach, only meters away from some of the most elegant vacation homes along the seawall. After years of wishful thinking that "the revolution" could not reach them there, the elite saw violence and chaos arrive suddenly and literally on their doorstep.[76]

Apart from its unusual setting, the uprising at the port had all the earmarks of a classic popular revolt. Few districts anywhere in Mexico could claim such a cruel and incompetent political authority as Colonel José María Ceballos, a military "lifer" from the interior of the republic. Even normally unflappable, conservative U.S. consul J. W. Germon was appalled by the prefect's antics, which had managed to alienate virtually every group in society: " 'bleeding' merchants of funds . . . forcing men into the army for not following personal orders . . . , forceable and exorbitant taxes . . . ridiculously heavy fines for petty offenses, injustice on all sides, and lastly, dedicating the aforementioned funds for his own personal uses." As if all this were not enough, added Consul Germon (trying to be discreet), Ceballos had raised additional enmity with his "questionable attitude toward young girls." In just the two months preceding the August uprising, his car was riddled with bullets and the passenger train on which he was said to be traveling was derailed.

Progreseño milkman Lino Muñoz was determined that the third time would be the charm. A democratic idealist and former Pinista militant who revered the memory of Madero and Pino, Muñoz had ample reason to despise Huertismo and Ceballos on ideological grounds alone. But his anger was also personal. Ceballos had harassed Muñoz for his political activities, jailing him for sedition, then freeing him on the proviso that he report every afternoon to the prefect's office to be publicly dressed down with vulgarities. The prefect had also made untoward advances to Muñoz's fifteen-year-old daughter. Needless to say, as he plotted his revenge, the milkman had no shortage of potential insurgents. Among his several hundred supporters were *porteños*, Meridanos, and former Pinista allies, such as the Canul Reyes brothers from Hunucmá. Like Progreso, the neighboring district had been victimized by the *leva* that Ceballos managed.

Still, the port was defended by a respectable contingent of *federales* from the Sixteenth Battalion, and even though the rebels benefited from the element of surprise in a midnight attack, the battle was no turkey shoot. In a 40-minute shootout that meandered from the central plaza to the seawall to the water's edge, fourteen people were killed, including Hunucmá's longtime *cabecilla*, Feliciano Canul Reyes. Ultimately, however, after several of the federal officers were killed, the majority of their troops defected to the rebels, who then laid their hands on Ceballos. The colonel had taken refuge on the top floor of the town hall, from which he had been directing the battle against the insurgents.

At first the rebels tied Ceballos to a tree in the public square and prepared to shoot him. But Muñoz and others were determined that the hated prefect should "die like the animal he is." After pleading in vain for mercy, Ceballos was taken to the public slaughterhouse, where his throat was slit and his corpse drained of blood. His violent political career ended on a meat hook.

In the midst of all this barbarity and death, Muñoz and his lieutenants rode about the beach, eerily assuring midnight bathers that they were in no danger—reassurances that were rendered even more absurd when the city's lights went out. (Those who could had taken refuge in small boats offshore as soon as the first shots were fired.) The macabre night ended with Progreso's new *cabecilla* paying respects to Pino Suárez's widow, Doña María Cámara Vales, while his subordinates forced Ceballos's widow to part with her jewel box and $25,000 in cash. The next morning, passersby gasped as they walked through the white port city whose main streets were now stained red with blood.

Lino Muñoz secured arms and ammunition from the federal barracks and about $2,500 from various public offices in the port, then moved his force—now swollen to almost six hundred men—into Hunucmá district. With Canul Reyes gone, Muñoz was now acknowledged as chief of the district's organized resistance. Making camp at the Hacienda Tacubaya, which he now designated as the "General Headquarters of Constitutionalism" in Yucatán—Constitutionalism being "la única revolución"—Muñoz began his siege of the *cabecera* on behalf of the national movement's "First Chief," Venustiano Carranza. In the next few days, insurgents at Kinchil declared themselves for Muñoz and Carranza, and groups elsewhere in the state began to challenge Huertista authorities in the name of Constitutionalism.[77]

Horrified that a replay of Maderismo—or worse—lay in the offing, Yucatán's elites appealed to General Cortés. He in turn beseeched the nascent Carranza government to terminate his lame-duck status and impose order in the countryside.[78] Shortly thereafter, as Carranza's governor-designate, Colonel Eleuterio Avila, prepared to sail for Yucatán, Carlos R. Menéndez wondered with some concern whether the new, "revolutionary" regime would soothe "class rancors and tensions" or further exacerbate them.[79]

## The Domestication of a Revolutionary Governor

Eleuterio Avila's posting represented something of a homecoming. Almost 40 years old, distinguished and diplomatic in bearing, Avila was a

Yucatecan by birth and a military engineer by trade. He had become a revolutionary in the normal course of seeking advancement in the world of clientelist politics. A pragmatic technocrat rather than an ideologue—a trait he shared with many Constitutionalist leaders—Avila did not come to Carrancismo; he was brought to it in its first days by Manuel Anaya, his political patron, who also happened to be the First Chief's *compadre*. Despite a lackluster military record during a series of campaigns in the north, Avila's connections and his status as a native son prompted Carranza to look his way when Yucatán fell into the Constitutionalist column. Yet for all his time away, Avila came back to Yucatán with some baggage that perhaps the First Chief had not checked over: Avila's family (from Valladolid) had important regional attachments; brother José had served for many years as an attorney for Olegario Molina's *parentesco*.[80]

Avila was determined to resist the pull of family ties and aggressively pursue his proconsular duties. Don Venus would need a reliable surrogate in the peninsula. Access to Yucatán's rich henequen revenues was crucial if the Carrancistas were to consolidate their control over all of Mexico. They now faced a strong challenge from a coalition of the Villistas and Zapatistas, whose repudiation of Carranza's leadership after Huerta's defeat had shattered the old Constitutionalist alliance and thrown the nation into a revolutionary civil war. In a bold move, Carranza had moved the headquarters of his rump movement to Veracruz, there to command the Gulf's booming oil and henequen economies, which might enable him to trump his opponents in a national war of attrition.

To Avila, however, it was clear from the outset that he would have to walk a fine line in governing Yucatán. Constitutionalism—indeed, any reformist current in the Mexican Revolution—would have to start almost from scratch in distant, conservative Yucatán.[81] Moreover, Carranza (who stood at the far right of his own movement) sent no progressive intellectual cadres to the peninsula with Avila, and made it clear that the fifteen hundred troops that accompanied him would soon be needed on the battlefronts of the nation's center and north. Plainly, Avila was being asked to do a proconsul's job with no proconsular muscle. To achieve even a modicum of success in the economic realm, he would have to reach an accommodation with the plantocracy. And the price of such an accommodation would probably be a tabling of the kind of social reforms to which many Constitutionalist leaders were passionately committed. Thus, without substantial support from Mexico City, Avila almost certainly would be forced into the compromising embrace of his own, dominant *parentesco*, the Molina-Montes family.

The first order of business after his arrival in early September was to defuse unrest in the countryside. This was a priority that regional elites heartily endorsed and for which prospects were good, at least in the short run. Even before his boat docked, Governor Avila sent an envoy to confer with Lino Muñoz in Hunucmá. The *cabecilla* quickly agreed to end his revolt, reconcentrate his forces in the municipalities of Kinchil and Samahil, and form a "revolutionary headquarters" in Kinchil that would serve the new government. The latter, for its part, agreed to give Muñoz and his forces a certain autonomy in Hunucmá, authorizing the *cabecilla* to name municipal authorities in Kinchil and neighboring Tetiz and to control "banditry" (factional rivals?) in the area. Amid a popular mood of triumph and festivity, Muñoz distributed a generous ration of maize to all of Kinchil's households—grain he had recently taken from the storehouses of the surrounding haciendas. In the following days and weeks, Avila himself made several visits to the countryside and reached similar understandings with other popular chiefs throughout the state.[82] Elite *camarillas* breathed a long sigh of relief.[83]

Following Carranza's directives, Governor Avila went beyond merely ad hoc measures to establish control over the state. All Huertista laws were nullified; the federal army was disbanded, replaced by Avila's fifteen hundred Mexican Constitutionalist troops; and martial law was temporarily declared on September 10. When a disgruntled employee set off a bomb in one of Mérida's residential neighborhoods, he was quickly apprehended and shot, and his body was publicly displayed to deter future acts. The same fate befell one of the Avila's own soldiers who was caught stealing, and, not much later, one of Olegario Molina's peons, who had killed a campesina on Hacienda Chochoh.[84]

In short order, the despised *jefaturas políticas* were abolished and replaced by Constitutionalist *comandancias militares*. The state militia was fortified. A new rural unit, the *guardias territoriales*, was created in each district, under the authority of the military commandant.[85] Unfortunately, however, with the bulk of his initial fifteen hundred troops now awaiting reassignment, the governor was obliged in the next few months to permit ex-Huertista officers and troops to find their way back into the state security forces. Moreover, José Prats y Blanch was retained in his position as chief of the secret police (now known as the judicial police).[86] The consequences of collaborating with former Huertistas would be severe.

Finally, Avila sought to disarm the general populace. He prohibited the sale of firearms and—save for some special deals with prominent *cabecillas* allowing their retainers to bear arms—he required that citizens turn in their guns within eight days of his decree or run afoul of martial law. When rural patrons pointed out that peons needed their antique shotguns to supplement their sparse diet with meat, Avila empowered the *hacendados* to return the shotguns to those workers they judged "sufficiently responsible." Villagers not tied to patrons or party to special *cabecilla* arrangements would apparently lose access to arms and the right to hunt—a significant deprivation. Thus, Avila's modification of the disarmament decree was crucial. It sent planters the message that revolution or not, they could continue to deal with "their own," rewarding the subservient and disciplining the disorderly.[87]

While individual members of the elite might indignantly criticize the harshness of the penalties meted out to transgressors of martial law, collectively the plantocracy was well pleased with the revolution's attempts to bring order out of chaos.[88] Almost everything else that Avila attempted, however, provoked controversy, either with the planters or with Avila's superiors in Mexico City. Perhaps no measure was as controversial as the September 11 decree that abolished debt peonage. Certainly the planters saw it coming: Carranza's northern brain trust had indicated its intention to reform the brutal, "medieval" labor regimes that persisted in Mexico's southeastern states. Avila himself had visited the henequen plantations and expressed some disapproval.[89] In his inaugural speech on September 9, the governor remarked portentiously, "The common people [of Yucatán] will once more become citizens and stop being pariahs."[90]

Still, the planters would not reconcile themselves to the inevitable. Even four years into Mexico's new revolutionary era, few of them had made any provisions for an end to peonage. Now, all existing debts were declared null and void, and *jornaleros* had the right to stay on their current estates or leave them, as they pleased.[91] Most planters, no doubt projecting their own deep-seated guilt regarding the treatment of their workers, feared the worst. Even the moderate "reformers" feared widespread defections and hoped to hedge their bets with some form of government involvement in the implementation of the law. The editor of the Cámara Agrícola's publication, *El Agricultor*, implored the governor "to make certain that the decree . . . is not misunderstood by the Indians," otherwise, "guided by primitive values . . . [they will] flee to the forest, denying the state a great source of wealth."[92]

Not surprisingly, the actual results were mixed. Undoubtedly, the decree set back production schedules on many plantations.[93] Individually and in groups, peons left as soon as word of *la salvadora ley* (the redemptive law) found its way onto their estates. Most of these peons left temporarily, moving back and forth between the estate and their home pueblos, savoring the first taste of freedom. A few never came back; determined to make *milpa* on their own land, they traveled for that privilege to remote reaches in the southeastern part of the state.[94] In many cases, planters reaped what they had sown. Haughty, insensitive proprietors like Hacienda Choyob's Pascual Gamboa—who had recently bought the estate as an investment, had kept his wage scale among the lowest in the state, and had already suffered one riot—saw most of his work force pick up and leave.[95] Avelino Montes was a bit more fortunate: one of his peons at Yokat wandered off, but the rest took advantage of emancipation to negotiate better wages and conditions. They bluntly told the overseer that without such improvements, they would soon be gone.[96]

In contrast, two of the state's leading reformers, Alonso Patrón Espadas and Manuel Rodríguez Acosta, suffered no defections on their model estates, Sacapuc and San Diego, respectively. Patrón Espadas, as we have seen, was a pioneer in the rural school movement, and like his father, Joaquín, he always took a sincere interest in his *jornaleros*. Rodríguez Acosta was an exponent of education, thrift, sobriety, and free labor. He was proud to say, "we've done away with San Lunes at San Diego." In 1913–14 he introduced a savings plan for his workers and a music school for their children while encouraging a number of his field hands to become mechanics and platform drivers. When the peonage decree was issued, each proprietor read it aloud in Maya as well as in Spanish and made sure the peons understood all of its provisions. At Sacapuc, workers responded by shouting *vivas* to the governor and Don Alonso, then went back to work.[97]

As it turned out, if peons did not leave the estate quickly, they lost their opportunity to leave at all. After the initial shock wore off, most planters responded aggressively to the decree, suppressing knowledge of it on their estates, relocating groups of workers to more remote locations, and mounting a ferocious lobbying effort to the governor.[98] Once again, the governor saw fit to modify one of his decrees; in the case of *la salvadora ley*, he modified it out of existence. Less than a fortnight after the law was published, Avila issued a circular to the local military commandants, rephrasing the terms of "liberation": now servants had to "specify the locale where they would reside, which is restricted to other estates or towns in Yucatán." He further emphasized: "Not for any reason will they be allowed to depart for the forest or to any other locale where this government has not established its authority."[99] This from a Mexican revolutionary proconsul! The words seem more appropriate for the Spanish viceroys who centuries ago sought to reimpose imperial authority over the *mita* workers-turned-*forasteros* in Alto Peru.

In other circulars, issued in rapid succession, Avila added the proviso that peons could not leave estates without first giving the *patrón* fifteen days' warning; then he sought to punish any agent of the state who "made dangerous propaganda" (for example, sharing information that other estates were paying higher wages). The implication was clear: the state was making it impossible for peons to leave, and anything short of advising them to stay was irresponsible behavior detrimental to production of the monocrop.[100]

Two to three weeks following the initial decree, few peons were going anywhere, even to neighboring estates. Several more weeks later, Ignacio Peón, one of the region's wealthier planters, candidly summed up the impact of "liberation" in his regular correspondence with Yucatán's archbishop, Martín Tritschler y Córdoba: "Had it been enforced, it would have brought radical transformations to our state, [but] as things stand, it is not significantly affecting the *henequeneros* under the current administration."[101]

Avila's resolve to enforce Constitutionalism's customary hard line against the church also gave way in the face of persistent elite protest and negotiation. Things started out promisingly enough for the government, with anticlerical decrees in October and November expelling foreign priests and restricting "unsanitary" religious practices.[102] But by the December holiday season the campaign—always mild in comparison to the attack on the church that would later be mounted by revolutionary leaders Salvador Alvarado and Felipe Carrillo Puerto—had run out of steam.[103] Archbishop Tritschler y Córdoba, sitting out the revolution in Havana, received a rather benign assessment of Avila's policies from his Molinista confidant in Mérida, Blano Castellanos: "[They] do not go beyond the bounds of decency; they follow a course . . . that is not firm but adaptable, malleable."[104]

More radical Constitutionalist revolutionaries and some historians have found this malleability in virtually every area of Avila's rule, taking it as evidence that he merely succumbed to the attentions, amusements, and bribes of the large planters and clergymen, "surrender[ing] himself into the arms of the reaction."[105] Did the pull of *parentesco* ultimately drag him into the Molinista orbit, as planter Joaquín Peón suggested to the archbishop?[106]

Numerous allegations and a good deal of circumstantial evidence exist to support such a notion. Among the allegations is the charge that Avila received "a very fine hacienda" and "a regular sum of money" from "the enemies of the Revolution"; that his administration, brief as it was, presided over the liquidation of the Comisión Reguladora; and that from mid-December 1914 on, Avila consistently opposed Carrancista demands for increased taxes on the regional monocrop or an increased commitment of Yucatecan state forces to fight Constitutionalism's battles in the Bajío and the north.[107]

It may well be that Avila was seduced (or "bought off") by his wealthier relations. He certainly was entertained and effectively lobbied by them.[108] But there is no smoking gun to confirm charges of an outright bribe (it would be surprising if there were), and those charges came mostly from opportunistic Carrancista officials whose careers had much to gain if Avila's were discredited.[109] As for Avila's personal integrity, moreover, impressive proof comes from the technocratic governor's meticulous accounting and probity in official dealings. During the first two months of his administration, Avila kept scrupulous records of an eight-million-peso forced loan he levied on the wealthiest planters in the state—records that would seem to exonerate him from similarly motivated charges of embezzlement and corruption.[110]

Regarding the Reguladora's demise, circumstantial evidence again weighs on both sides of the issue. To be sure, the "First Reguladora"—the one institution that had sought to stymie Montes's dominance of the market—expired on Avila's watch, but the governor did pass a decree early in his tenure that sought to end small-planter financial dependence on the Molina-Montes *parentesco*. He declared null and void all debts payable in henequen (that is, fiber liens) and called a six-month moratorium on all debts to moneylenders.[111] The point to be made here, though, is that Montes's control of the market late in 1914 was so pervasive that the Reguladora was *already* moribund (calls for its burial came from various quarters) and the moratorium on debts and liens was in no way enforcible. As an interim caretaker of a weak liberal state, Avila did not have the power seriously to affect either equation. At this time more than ever before, the Molinista *parentesco* was the only significant regional force in Yucatán's monocrop economy.

Finally, there is the matter of Avila's consistent opposition to Carranza's revolutionary government on the issues of henequen revenues and overseas military service. The source of his opposition might be narrowly interpreted as an abiding concern with protecting the interests of his *parentesco*, which had the most to lose in the face of escalating federal demands. The evidence suggests, however, that Avila's behavior was not nearly so instrumentalist. Early in his tenure, he aggressively implemented the directive from the First Chief and his finance minister, Luis Cabrera, to raise $8 million via "patriotic contribution" from the wealthiest planters in the state. The most powerful Molinistas were obliged to pay the heftiest amounts: Avelino Montes, $250,000; Olegario Molina, $200,000; Augusto L. Peón, $200,000; Manuel Cirerol and the Regil brothers (Pedro and Alvaro), $150,000 each.[112] Moreover, subsequent attempts by the wealthiest planters to gain reductions in their contributions typically met with little success.[113] In less than two weeks, Avila delivered three-quarters of the target figure; ultimately he collected $7.2 million—none of which was ever repaid.[114]

We would argue that when push came to shove on these issues, between mid-December 1914 and late January 1915, when he was replaced as governor, it was Avila's own sensibilities as a Yucateco—an elite Yucateco certainly, though not one who identified himself narrowly as a Molinista—that dictated his decision to stand with the regional elite against the economically driven policies of the Constitutionalist revolution. Avila had been briefed on the resistance Huerta had encountered when he escalated his demands for revenues and conscripts. Compared to the ultimatums that Carranza and Cabrera were presenting him, the Huertista initiatives seemed modest indeed. On top of the $8 million *empréstito*, the Carrancistas proposed a 1.5-centavo tax on each kilogram of fiber exported. The figure would later be increased to 3 centavos per kilo.[115] Avila, who had previously counseled against further exactions, arguing instead for at least some repayment on the initial loan, now pleaded with his superiors that the present policy amounted to "killing the goose that laid the golden egg." Indeed, such an unfair tax would be likely to be "swept away by public outcry" and perhaps might even spark an armed revolt.[116]

In the same letter, the governor also counseled a rethinking of Mexico City's plan to renew the draft and ship local battalions to central and northern Mexico. Most disconcerting was Carranza's insistence that the most reliable Yucatecan force, the 800-man Cepeda Peraza Battalion, which included about 350 Yaquis, be immediately mobilized. General Curiel had formed this battalion at the end of the Porfiriato; Avila himself had reorganized it as a rural police force. The governor took great pains to point out to his superiors how charged an issue overseas military service remained in

the popular regional mind: "You . . . do not appreciate the particular idio-
syncracies of the Yucatecan people. One must observe them, study them, in
order to know what strategy is most suitable to pursue." It would do no
good, Avila insisted, to tell Yucatecans that they must now "sacrifice for the
welfare of the fatherland" if no attempt were made to understand the values
and sensibilities that informed their own notions of *sacrificio* and *patria*.[117]

Avila knew that in registering these objections, he was committing political suicide. Nor could he have been under any illusions that Carranza
and Cabrera would take his advice, locked as they were in a mortal struggle
with Villismo that was nearing its climax in the Bajío early in 1915. A savvy
revolutionary politician able to surmount (or circumvent) the obstacles to
advancement up until his tenure in Yucatán, he ended that tenure galled by
the no-win situation in which he found himself. Ultimately, he reluctantly
accepted the directive of his national patron regarding the call-up of the
Cepeda Peraza Battalion, but he never recanted on the fiber tax. On January 4, the very day he was to begin the mobilization of the Cepeda Peraza,
the regiment mutinied, peppered the Governor's Palace and central plaza
with gunfire, then fled eastward in open revolt.[118] Three weeks later, the
disillusioned governor was on board a steamer en route to answer to an
angry Carranza.[119]

It was clear that a strong wind was about to blow from Mexico's central
plateau, and Avila's elite *paisanos* began to brace themselves. The Constitutionalist taxmen would be back in force at the customs houses; meanwhile, a renegade battalion of conscripts remained at large in the countryside. On the other hand, the old order was still standing; it had domesticated
its first revolutionary governor and had kept unwanted reforms to a bare
minimum. The archbishop's Molinista confidant wrote to His Eminence
on Christmas Day, 1914, in an expansive mood. There was much to give
thanks for: "Jacobin furor has subsided in our state. After the publication of
many laws at the start of his revolution, Señor Avila has learned to wink at
many things."[120]

The *henequenero* elite was disturbed by Avila's departure. Don Olegario's nephew, Julio Molina Font, wrote shortly thereafter, "He was a
man of order, and although he was imposed on us, we will certainly miss
him."[121] Unfortunately for the planters, the next wave of revolutionary
leaders would be more revolutionary, less educable, and not from Yucatán.

## CHAPTER 10

# *Last Stand of the Oligarchs, Spring 1915*

We [were] a hodgepodge of men and boys . . . Indians fresh from the henequen fields . . . mestizos immaculately decked out in their traditional
whites . . . employees, students, merchants, *hacendados*—all motivated
by a common desire to defend our city and *terruño*.
> —Julio Molina Font, on the "State Sovereignty Force,"
> March 1915

You disgraceful sons of privilege! They told us that you were going to give
us quantities of corn, clothing, even money. . . . You better show us these
things, all of them, if you want us to show you what we from the east can
do for you.
> —Leader of a detachment of "Mayan sharpshooters and
> deerhunters" to a detachment of elite Yucatecan troops,
> March 1915

If, in the words of one local commentator, Governor Eleuterio
Avila's weak salvo of reform "didn't even graze the flanks of the
old order," the program of his Carrancista successor, General
Toribio de los Santos, took dead aim at its heart.[1] A radical *norteño* with no
personal ties in the region, de los Santos immediately put the oligarchy on
notice that he would carry out "shocking new reforms." Unlike his predecessor, he "did not favor conciliation," but rather a "big broom" to sweep
away the harmful vestiges of the past.[2] During a tumultuous two-week
reign, de los Santos breathed new life into Avila's moribund peonage decree,
rescinding all the riders that had previously nullified its impact and outlaw-
ing the system of payment in scrip that underwrote the hacienda store.
Further, he required planters to finance the creation of rural schools, and to
ensure that campesinos had sufficient time to attend them, he mandated an
eight-hour workday.[3]

## Revolution and Counterrevolution

As serious a challenge as these measures posed to the planters' social regime, they were merely a warmup for what came next. De los Santos broached the unthinkable in monocultural Yucatán: he declared his intention to implement agrarian reform—to take lands away from the *henequeneros* and give them to the campesinos. Invoking the provisions of the Carrancista agrarian law of January 6, 1915—a measure that had been urged on the conservative First Chief by Constitutionalist radicals as a means of stealing the thunder of the more agrarian and populist Villistas and Zapatistas—de los Santos created the first local agrarian commissions in the state during the final days of January.[4] With agrarian reform, the revolution had finally arrived, and the planters feared that it would be only a matter of time before the henequen fields were turned over to their *jornaleros*.

But the general did not just issue decrees against the *hacendados'* interests; he humiliated the master class at every turn, virtually rubbing its face in change. Aided by a flying squad of *huach* (Mexican) propagandists and orators whose politics ran the gamut from Jacobin to Marxist, de los Santos publicly taunted the proud, chauvinistic Yucatecos, calling them "parasites" and "freeloaders" at best, "reactionaries" and "enemies of Revolutionary Mexico" at worst.[5] Thus, Constitutionalist activist Jesús Urueta pointed out that after five years of revolution throughout the republic, property in Yucatán remained "concentrated in feudal fashion," and "slavery flourished."[6] Urueta's more fiery socialist colleague, Adolfo León Osorio— the so-called *Príncipe de la Palabra* (Prince of Orators)—went even further, abandoning any pretense of civility. In one highly publicized speech, he remarked that he had yet to find in the state capital "either an honorable woman or a man of dignity." In another, he thundered,

> The Yucatecan people are . . . degenerates. If they are to be freed from their miserable state they must trade in the Bible for guns and dynamite; they must be shocked into a realization of what the Revolution is all about. . . . Until Yucatán and its people suffer, they will not have the right to claim the benefits of our glorious . . . Revolution.[7]

Previously, Mexican revolutionary appeals had been made to Yucatecans in an inclusive, patriotic spirit, inviting them to imagine themselves as part of a grander, more progressive national community. Now, under the de los Santos regime, Yucatecans were being defined out of the *patria*, and in a particularly mean-spirited fashion. In the weeks ahead, the Carrancista national state would have to deal with the backlash generated by the rhetorical excesses of its local agents. Indeed, the very notion of *patria* would be called into question in Yucatán, as the planters sought to gain the support of the popular classes for a regionalist struggle whose underlying purpose was to roll back de los Santos's social reforms.

Ordinarily, the planters' strategy would not have had a prayer of succeeding. De los Santos plausibly assumed that *class* rhetoric and social reforms would be sufficient to win the hearts and minds of Yucatán's exploited and disgruntled campesinos, workers, artisans, and intellectuals. It was reported that on various occasions, León Osorio's "rude indictments of capitalism in Yucatán" had been "wildly applauded by the people."[8] And de los Santos took steps to shore up his support among urban workers and the middle sectors. In early February, he provided additional work for Progreso's longshoremen, ordering that regular railroad service be stopped on the outskirts of the port, then levying a special tax on the city's tramcars. He also pledged to give greater autonomy to municipal governments—always a paramount issue for liberal intellectuals and middle-class town dwellers.[9]

Nevertheless, in only a fortnight and despite a program that was truly redistributive in its conception, the general managed to offend virtually every segment of regional society. Apart from the insults he hurled against the *patria chica*, which offended rich and poor alike, de los Santos's regime was rent with contradictions that nullified the appeal of its reform initiatives. Even as the general boasted that "the reactionaries would be unmasked . . . and punished," he was selling Avelino Montes the three hundred thousand bales of fiber still controlled by the moribund Comisión Reguladora, and for half the current price![10] Such behavior did little to endear him to the reform-minded *henequeneros* (and other regional critics) who had traditionally sought to limit the power of the Molina-Montes *parentesco*. Neither did the arbitrary execution of several merchant-*hacendados* in the Tekax jail by one of the general's principal officers, who was intoxicated at the time.[11] And while de los Santos's stance on peonage was undoubtedly popular among *jornaleros*, the singlemindedness with which he pursued conscription (including the call-up of all Yaquis for service in central Mexico) left many to ascribe other motives to his defense of labor.[12] Finally, early indications suggested that the implementation of the administration's policy of *municipio libre* was seriously flawed. Old political bosses were replaced by the general's handpicked military commandants; while these officers uniformly espoused the principle of a "free municipality," some had already begun to abuse their power like the *jefes políticos* of old.[13]

The planters found a kindred spirit and a timely instrument for their revenge against de los Santos in federal colonel Abel Ortiz Argumedo. A Veracruzano who had taken up residence in Mérida as a young man, Ortiz Argumedo had been an accountant before the revolution. Hitching his fortunes to Avila's rising star in the Carrancista movement after a flirtation with Huertismo, the dapper, charismatic, and uncommonly ambitious bookkeeper had been appointed military commandant of Mérida during Avila's tenure in the statehouse.[14] But he had been summarily dismissed from the influential position following de los Santos's assumption of the governorship; the general preferred his own man, the more radical Colonel

Alfredo Breceda. When Ortiz Argumedo was subsequently sent on the trail of Colonel Patricio Mendoza and the renegade Cepeda Peraza Battalion, the opportunistic Ortiz Argumedo wasted little time in proposing to Mendoza an alliance that would combine their forces against "the usurper," de los Santos.

Significantly, the pact was consummated in Temax, and former Morenista chief Juan Campos, who had become disaffected with Constitutionalism's increased *leva*, threw in his lot with the incipient rebellion. With the assistance of Campos and other local chiefs in Valladolid and the eastern part of the state, the conspirators soon boasted a force larger than that of de los Santos. Carranza had moved his best troops to central Mexico to fight Villa; meanwhile, the *guardias territoriales* were composed largely of dissident Yucatecans, including many ex-Huertistas. In a series of brief engagements on February 11, the rebels defeated the Constitutionalist federals. Lino Muñoz, the lone popular *cabecilla* who remained loyal to de los Santos, ultimately came to appreciate the hopelessness of the assignment, and dispersed his four-hundred-man Hunucmá militia without an engagement. De los Santos took custody of the funds in the state treasury and fled to Campeche. On February 12, Ortiz Argumedo rode triumphantly into Mérida and promptly installed himself as interim governor and military commander of the state.[15]

We have every reason to suspect that the state's biggest planters, led by the Molina-Montes *parentesco*, were instrumental in fomenting both the rebellion and the Temax alliance, which had initially committed itself to the reinstatement of Eleuterio Avila. That was certainly the perception at the time, and it was aired frequently in the planters' correspondence with exiled Archbishop Tritschler y Córdoba.[16] The oligarchy's probable complicity is reinforced by Ortiz Argumedo's actions: no sooner had he taken power than he summoned a delegation of superplanters and merchants to the Governor's Palace—a delegation dominated by members of the Molina-Montes clan. At this meeting, each planter agreed to contribute to the new regime the amount of taxes he had paid for all of 1914, and each merchant, one-half of his 1914 tax payments.[17] Several weeks later, Ortiz Argumedo levied an additional two-centavo tax on each kilo of fiber exported, with one-half the assessment earmarked specifically for "extraordinary" costs "in defense of the state's sovereignty."[18] The same oligarchs who had cried bloody murder at each previous Constitutionalist assessment now willingly signed off on these far greater exactions. Indeed, the elite press consistently referred to them as a "patriotic contribution," not a "loan."[19]

Nor did the oligarchy's support end there. On February 15, Ortiz Argumedo's ruling "junta of state sovereignty" formed a commission of six *hacendados* and merchants, at least four of whom were leading Molinistas: Ricardo Molina, José de Regil, Julián Aznar, and Domingo Evia. On March 11, the commission sailed for the United States via Cuba with a letter of credit in the amount of U.S. $480,000, earmarked for the purchase of arms and materiel. The credit had been arranged through Avelino Montes.[20]

In short order, the rest of the elite fell into line behind the Molina-Montes *parentesco*. The initial audience with Ortiz Argumedo had included token representation by former Morenistas and Pinistas.[21] On February 23, by unanimous vote, the Liga de Acción Social, the principal vehicle of the state's reformist planter wing, announced its "strong sympathy" for the junta's "patriotic struggle to protect the state's sovereignty." In a patent exercise in casuistic logic, the Liga pointed out that while its policy was not to affiliate with political parties, "this effort to improve our political situation is certainly the basis of our social improvement as well, which remains the Liga's primary goal."[22] The Liga, along with officials from the Cámara Agrícola, also agreed to help the new junta on the diplomatic front, forming a delegation to negotiate with Carrancista agents on board the U.S. steamer *Morro Castle* off the coast of Progreso.

This diplomatic initiative was critical to Ortiz Argumedo's government. Even as he began to prepare for the possibility of war, the opportunistic caudillo continued to pledge his complete loyalty to the First Chief and Constitutionalism. He characterized his movement as one intended to protect the "*constitutional* sovereignty of Yucatán." The new junta meant to shore up Constitutionalism's long-term prospects in the region in the face of blatant outrages perpetrated by a rogue military officer who had worked at cross purposes with the national movement's guiding principles.[23]

Clearly, Ortiz Argumedo never bargained on having to mount a defense of the region against the army of his national patron. Quite likely, he and his planter sponsors assumed that if Mexico City failed to sanction his interim government, it would send back Avila or some compromise candidate. But as the days became weeks and the First Chief steadfastly refused to acknowledge the junta's direct communiqués, Ortiz Argumedo found himself sliding down the slippery slope toward military confrontation. Hence his attempt to buy time, enlisting moderate elite mediators like the officials of the Liga de Acción Social and the Cámara Agrícola or the military commander of Quintana Roo, General Arturo Garcilazo. Garcilazo, who over the course of a mid-February fact-finding mission had developed pronounced sympathies for the planters and their cause, essentially recommended that the First Chief institute proceedings against de los Santos and legitimize Ortiz Argumedo's ruling junta.[24]

Don Venus, through his new chief proconsul for southeastern Mexico, General Salvador Alvarado, responded promptly and tersely to Garcilazo's mediation, serving notice to the Yucatecans that beneath all the rationales and euphemisms he considered their political posture to be one of rebellion, pure and simple. Mexico City would not treat with Yucatán *poder a poder*, entertaining justifications of sovereignty. In Alvarado's words, the options were plain.

If, as you claim, there is no armed revolt . . . no one need have any fear. [You need] only obey the orders that come from these headquarters. Yet [your] inexplicable conduct . . . has led us to believe in the existence of a reaction-ary revolt, and for that reason measures have been taken to suppress it with the same force that has been employed against the traitor, Francisco Villa. Our gunboats blockade the coast . . . and prevent the entry of provisions and materiel. In the meantime a large military force complete with artillery is marching to take Mérida, . . . just as was done in the case of Puebla.[25]

But things had gone too far in the region to admit surrender as a pos-sibility. The Constitutionalists were determined to settle accounts with Yucatán, and, based on his reputation as a former Magonista, Alvarado appeared to Yucatecos every bit as radical as de los Santos—if anything, more ideologically committed. Its bridges burned, the plantocracy came together for one last stand, ironically under the auspices of its erstwhile leaders, the Molinistas. Although "state sovereignty" had not initially been the principal motivation behind the Argumedista revolt, as February turned into March, regional autonomy became virtually the only issue on people's minds in the major urban centers.[26]

To be sure, it was only sound politics for ruling elites to mobilize their counterrevolutionary movement under such a banner in a state that nur-tured so many historical grievances against the nation. But such an instru-mentalist view does not explain the dynamic, expressive process of identity construction that was taking place in cities like Mérida and Progreso in early March 1915. As a military confrontation brewed, elite Yucatecans and members of the middle and working classes came to internalize the justness and inevitability of their antifederal position. The U.S. consul reported that in the major cities "there has been unusual interest . . . in this new demand for the rights of the State of Yucatán to manage its own affairs"; a U.S. special agent went even further, arguing that "the ultimate object [of the present movement] is a separate and independent state."[27] On February 16, a member of the Argumedista junta proudly boasted before a gathering of thousands, "Yucatán has been a lamb, but [now] it has been transformed into a lion!"[28]

The revels of the February carnival season only enhanced the heady, altered political climate that pervaded the state capital. Yucatecans collec-tively fended off their immense fear by engaging in a series of bravura politi-cal performances; and in the process, many came to inhabit the roles they were playing. For example, after reminiscing at length in a public speech about Yucatán's past struggles with Mexico, "with the kind of feeling that only ideas deeply rooted in the regional soul can summon," Argumedismo's most spellbinding orator, Manuel Irigoyen Lara, turned to the present.

So what are we afraid of? I don't see any great phantasm. Who recalls the childhood tale of "El Tucho" (the bogeyman)? Your mother told you: "If you don't stop crying, I'll call 'El Tucho.'" But when we got older, we realized there was no *tucho*, it was just a kid's tale, and we were no longer afraid. Well, now, Yucatecos, we are that child . . . and the *tucho* is the great, unspoken danger we feel. But if we look at that danger in the light of day, we see it for the straw man, for the child's tale it really is. My friends, it's Shrove Tuesday; God bless us! Put on your masks and costumes, mount your floats![29]

All the while, as Alvarado's seven-thousand-man Army of the Southeast drew steadily closer, the official and elite press tapped out a daily drumbeat of optimism. Headlines read, "All of Mérida under arms!" "We live through and for Yucatán!" and (anticipating Churchill) "These are our finest hours!"[30] Elegantly dressed ladies of the oligarchy, such as Alicia Molina Font and Paulina de Evia, bolstered morale by distributing gifts and provisions to the troops, which included members of their immediate families.[31] Regionalist bravado soared even higher when Yucatecan saboteurs smuggled a bomb aboard the *Progreso*, an armed Constitutionalist transport that was blockading the port of the same name. Amid taunts and shouts of glee, the ship blew up and sank in the port's shallow waters, temporarily breaking the blockade.[32]

It was in this invigorated political climate that the sons of the elite, joined by an admixture of their employees and clients in the artisan and service sectors, hastened to volunteer for the battalions of the state militia. Julio Molina Font, then not yet eighteen and a student at the prestigious Instituto Literario, later recalled that not only "were we prepared to offer our lives in the service of Yucatán's Sovereignty," but enlistment was the "macho thing to do."[33]

The bubble of self-delusion eventually had to burst. When fighting finally broke out on March 13 in Halachó district near the Campeche border, the counterrevolution was summarily crushed by Salvador Alvarado's larger, immensely more experienced invading army. Alvarado was one of Carranza's most decorated military men; many of his troops were battle tested after numerous campaigns in other theaters of the revolution. Outnumbering the Yucatecans anywhere from slightly less than two to one to as many as ten to one (contemporary estimates vary widely), the general's forces were well armed and accompanied by artillery support and even a small squadron of airplanes.[34]

By contrast, the Yucatecans were a motley crew: poorly armed and more poorly trained.[35] In their memoirs, elite survivors of the campaign recalled the heterogeneous make-up and undisciplined character of the local troops. For example, Olegario Molina's nephew, Julio Molina Font, wrote,

> We [were] a hodgepodge of men and boys whose ages ranged from 15 to 60. . . . There were Indians fresh from the henequen fields in aprons brandishing machetes; mestizos immaculately decked out in their traditional whites and heeled sandals; employees, students, merchants, *hacendados*— all motivated by a common desire to defend our city and *terruño*. . . .

Particularly among us, the students [of the Instituto Literario] and the merchants and employees of the Commerce Battalion, good humor replaced
worry; games, jokes, and goofing around marked our behavior up and down
the line. When one recently named officer . . . looking for a pretext to
discipline us, came up to "Marat" Manzanilla, a particularly rebellious
spirit, he refused to return the traditional salute to his superior. "Do you
know who I am?" the lieutenant bore down threateningly on "Marat."
"Look, guys," our friend shot right back, "an *oficialito* who doesn't even
know his own name!" The haughty officer withdrew from us with his tail
between his legs, as we split our sides laughing.[36]

A closer look at the Yucatecan "State Sovereignty Force" based on a non-
elite memoir and reports from Alvarado's camp (as well as on these elite
accounts), provides a more nuanced picture of its character. It is clear that
the two most celebrated regiments, the Commerce and Regional Battalions,
were composed overwhelmingly of wealthy students and merchants and
their most trusted employees. The urban labor movement, still smarting
from its repression over the last several years, was conspicuous in its absence. And while some members of the urban poor rounded out the ranks of
these battalions, they were often the clients and retainers of elite patrons,
such as the nameless mestizo Molina Font mentions on several occasions to
underscore the broad-based character of the Commerce Battalion.

[This] mestizo was an old acquaintance of ours, who maintained a certain
deference toward me and my brother Hugo, having worked for many years
with my uncle. He was constantly asking me what it was that he should do:
stay and fight with the Battalion or return to Mérida? I avoided responsibility for providing direct counsel, remarking only that "I am going to
stay." His immediate reaction was: "Bueno, Molinita, if you stay, then I'll
stay too."[37]

In the only working-class memoir of the campaign that we have, Wenceslao Moguel argues that paternalism does not provide the sole explanation for the poor's participation in the two urban battalions; the *leva* is also
significant. Moguel bitterly observes that recruitment in the capital "involved outright shanghaiing." Once they "enlisted," "volunteers" were reduced to "little more than abject slaves . . . who were then transported to the
slaughterhouse of the front, [where they were] obliged to protect the privileges of thieves and liars."[38]

In the rural areas, the numbers of Yucatán's *guardias territoriales* were
swelled by a variety of means. A number of *hacendados* who had some
prospect of trusting their work forces contributed contingents of *mache-
teros*. Don Sixto García, for example, who was renowned for the bond he
maintained with his peons, turned out workers from six of his estates in the
western part of the state; his son, "Sixtito," was one of the chief officers in
the state force.[39]

Other tried-and-true clientelist networks were also tapped. As they had under Maderismo, elites and the state sought to woo powerful local *cabecillas* into an alliance. In a few strategic locales, such popular chiefs became linchpins of the sovereignty movement: Juan Campos (a newly minted colonel) in northern Temax; Pedro Pablo Ruz in Valladolid and the remote southeastern recesses of the state; the Vargas brothers in the Puuc.[40] Significantly, however, in the great majority of cases, the most powerful *cabecillas* (for example, Pedro Crespo in Temax, José Loreto Baak in the Puuc) rejected such overtures, preferring to sit out the battle and later come to terms with General Alvarado's administration. They knew the revolutionaries would have much more to offer them and their campesino clienteles than the beleaguered planters.[41]

In rural locales where neither regionalist propaganda, planter paternalism, nor *cabecilla* clientelism yielded recruits, the Argumedista junta made other appeals. In the henequen zone it offered a salary of two pesos a day to volunteers, substantially more than they could make in the fields.[42] In more remote eastern areas such as Sotuta, Valladolid, and Tizimín, the state broadcast appeals reminiscent of the dangerous promises made to free Maya campesinos before the Caste War. Potential Maya recruits were variously offered foodstuffs, gifts, cash, land, and tax relief, as well as the provision of arms and ammunition. In his memoirs, Lorenzo González Reyes recalled one occasion during the campaign on which he and his elite classmates from the Instituto Literario were severely reproached by the leader of one such eastern delegation of "Mayan sharpshooters and deerhunters."

> Well, all of you who have been in school, will you do us the favor of telling us just when you plan to begin [giving us the things you promised]? You disgraceful sons of privilege! They told us that you were going to give us quantities of corn, clothing, even money, but they didn't tell us when. You better show us these things, all of them, if you want us to show you what we from the east can do for you.[43]

About this incident González Reyes observed,

> That handful of Indians from the remote eastern settlements had been promised once again what we always promise them, that things will get better. They hope for today what they have hoped for through the centuries, and will continue hoping for tomorrow. They have never been afraid to use their arms to gain a result commensurate with so much sacrifice.[44]

González Reyes had only praise for these backwoods Indian hunters. Yucatecan elites and federal soldiers alike spoke about their marksmanship in reverential terms: "Wherever they aim, they put a bullet."[45] Unfortunately for the oligarchy, there were not enough of them, and many melted away into the bush after the first lopsided engagements with the overwhelming federal force.

Desertion from the Yucatecan forces by both elites and Maya recruits was common, and for good reason. Ortiz Argumedo and his general staff

initially deceived several local regiments. Told they were going on maneuvers to Progreso, the troops instead were rushed directly to the front at
Halachó.[46] Others, fed a steady diet of misinformation about the size, capacity, and motives of the federal force in the days before the battle, fled as soon
as the hopelessness of their assignment became clear in the trenches.[47] The
official press demonized the federals as "a horde of pillaging locusts," as
*huaches* who despised the peninsula and were hell bent on razing henequen
fields and raping Yucatecan women.[48] One of the elite defenders of Halachó,
small planter Alberto J. Márquez, reflecting later on the junta's misleading
propaganda regarding Alvarado's army, concluded,

> [I joined the rebellion] because I was swept up in patriotic sentiments and
> fears that my native land was gravely threatened. This belief, I have come to
> appreciate, was engendered . . . by Ortiz Argumedo's fraudulent claims
> about state sovereignty on the heels of General de los Santos's despotic acts
> and insults. . . . I did what I did . . . to defend my *terruño* against a danger that
> I now know was essentially fabricated.[49]

But if, by hook or by crook, the plantocracy mustered anywhere from
seven hundred to four thousand troops, much more striking is the refusal of
the great majority of Yucatecan campesinos and workers to fight. This refusal, plus the mass desertion of conscripts that took place during the brief
campaign, must be seen as something of an informal referendum against the
old order, a refusal to answer its last, desperate call in extremis. In about 40
hours—the time it took to rout state forces in engagements at Hacienda
Blanca Flor, Poc Boc pueblo, and Halachó—oligarchical rule was swept
away. Yucatecan casualty lists were littered with the *juventud dorada*, the
cream of the divine caste: Molinas, Peóns, Manzanillas (including the brash
"Marat"), Ponces, Cámaras, and Cantóns, to name but a few.[50]

As the debacle played itself out, with ad hoc Constitutionalist firing
squads dispatching the officers of the insurrection, several members of the
elite managed to save themselves by doing what under any other circumstances would have been unthinkable: mimicking the hoi polloi. Lying
about their last names (Julio and Hugo Molina Font became merely Font),
stripping away or rending their respectable city attire, and feigning the deliberate, Maya-inflected speech of the countryside, several scions of the
oligarchy fooled their Mexican captors and evaded the firing squad.[51] When
Salvador Alvarado was informed of the unauthorized retribution being
meted out by certain of his lieutenants, he put a stop to the carnage and
made provisions for most of these planter sons to return to their homes in
Mérida and Progreso.[52]

By then, however, most of those residences were long vacant. Benito
Aznar reported to the archbishop that the state capital "was practically
deserted," and so were many of the elegant houses on the great estates.[53]
Most of the powerful elder Molinistas, for example, were already in Cuba
(where Don Olegario had resided for several years) or New Orleans (where

Don Avelino had just set up operations). Judging from their correspondence, they did not arrive empty-handed. Rafael Peón Losa, who had taken up residence with several other former oligarchs in the Crescent City, provided the archbishop with the following commentary of life in exile:

> Really, we live in a small, furnished palace. This life has its advantages, but also its shortcomings. I do not know how long I can hold out like this: I am so bored I can neither pray nor write.[54]

Meanwhile, the plantocracy's tarnished champion, Abel Ortiz Argumedo, was also living the good life in *Yanquilandia*, in New York City. Indeed, the governor had been among the first to depart, before Alvarado's lieutenants began mopping up at Halachó. The erstwhile caudillo had never intended to match strategies with Alvarado; instead, he had carefully mapped out his avenue of escape. A full two weeks before hostilities began, Ortiz Argumedo had borrowed more than a million pesos from the Banco Peninsular Mexicano, using government-owned henequen as collateral. Then, when the shooting began, he rounded up whatever remained in the state treasury and, on March 17, fled for Cuba.[55]

The last tracks Ortiz Argumedo left in local archives suggest that he was very soon up to his old tricks in New York. Midway through 1916, Alvarado's administration learned that he was being charged in a New York court for stealing 375,000 pesos from two U.S. citizens who had previously resided in Yucatán. The Americans had entrusted Ortiz Argumedo with their savings for safekeeping during the sovereignty revolt, and he had promised to return the funds in person at a later date in New York City. That later date, of course, never arrived.[56]

Long before that, however, Ortiz Argumedo had become a mere footnote to the region's receding oligarchical past. Its present and future now lay with the Mexican Revolution, which on March 19, 1915, in the form of Alvarado's victorious army, entered the state capital unopposed.

## Revolutionary Legacies

Without question, Alvarado's assumption of power drastically changed the rules of the political game. His proactive, redistributionist regime (1915–18) marked a radical departure from the weak liberal state of the old order. Under Alvarado, through the state's creation of unions, cooperatives, resistance leagues, and a political party, working people (particularly organized urban workers) were given an increased stake in the region's political economy. Then, after the general's departure from the state in 1918, populism gave way to a heterodox brand of Yucatecan socialism under the leadership of Felipe Carrillo Puerto (1918–24). Networks of popular mobilization, unionization, and *concientización*, orchestrated by an expanded state party, the Partido Socialista del Sureste, engaged a much greater number of campe-

sinos, even penetrating, if only temporarily, some of the state's largest henequen estates. Although Carrillo Puerto's socialist road came to an end with
his assassination in January 1924, many of the seeds of political mobilization that he sowed would sprout a decade later under the national regime of
President Lázaro Cárdenas (1934–40).[57]

None of this substantial political and social transformation would have
been possible had there been no Constitutionalist "revolution from without." Nothing less, as we have seen, could have wrenched the oligarchy's
iron grip from the levers of political and economic power in 1915. Yet in
another sense, it is wrong-headed to press the model of a "revolution from
without" too far. General Alvarado found a host of ready supporters for his
bourgeois revolutionary project among the campesinos, workers, intelligentsia, and petty bourgeoisie when he arrived in the peninsula in March
1915.

This is hardly surprising. For, as we have seen throughout this volume,
members of the popular classes had been militating for social change in one
form or another, at one political juncture or another, in one coalition or
another, since 1909, if not the turn of the century. Yucatán's political history since the inception of the Porfiriato represented a progressive widening
of political participation through an expansion of elite clientelist networks.
By about 1905, these networks, organized around rival *camarillas*, had
come to include significant numbers of artisans and urban workers; during
the period 1909–13, the political arena widened to include the participation
of newly unionized workers and peasant villagers, the latter through the
efforts of brokers or popular *cabecillas*.

At every stage of this process, the political participation of the popular
classes and their articulation of social demands had to be held carefully in
check by the ruling elites. Planter factions needed the support of expanding
clienteles, but they could not afford to lose their status as patrons. Before
Alvarado's invasion, the plantocracy barely managed this delicate political
balancing act; indeed, in 1913, they managed it only with the support of
Huerta's military dictatorship.

Thus, in 1915, the capacity for participation in a transformative revolutionary project already existed among Yucatán's popular classes; it would
only increase thereafter through encouragement by an activist state. Indeed, recent research on both the Alvarado and Carrillo Puerto administrations suggests that if anything, their state and party bureaucracies may not
have moved *quickly enough* to meet the political and social demands already pending or unleashed by their revolutionary rhetoric. (Such sluggish-
ness is a common revolutionary syndrome: witness the plight of Salvador
Allende's Popular Unity government in Chile in the early 1970s or Nicaragua's Sandinistas in the 1980s).[58]

Two powerful images that emerge from documents in the state judicial
archives suggest that the potential for such revolutionary politics *from below* already existed among villagers and peons at Alvarado's arrival. Less

than a month after Alvarado's assumption of power, village-based insurgents had resumed their militant acts of "banditry" in Hunucmá district, raiding Hacienda Chicche, the estate of one of their perennial antagonists, Diego María Solís. Revolution or not, their agrarian struggle would go on.[59]

Months later, Alvarado would also detect signs of a new militance among certain groups of *peones acasillados*. No sooner had he installed military tribunals to redress agrarian and other labor grievances than he was inundated with petitions from peons demanding that *hacendados* raise their wage schedules and improve their working conditions. In one colorful instance in September 1915, the positive decision rendered by a revolutionary tribunal was not enough to satisfy Juan Córdova, leader of a delegation of peons from Hacienda Xcumya in Progreso district. He continued to rail about the haughtiness and cruelty of his overseer and the depressed nature of wages until he was found in contempt and forcibly removed from the chamber. Before being dragged out, he threatened to launch a movement to blow up the hacienda's decorticating plant. The presiding military commandant detained Córdova for almost a week so that "such incendiary behavior not promote class antagonisms harmful to production and the spirit of work"—the guiding principles of Alvarado's new modernizing, reformist regime. Alvarado himself immediately ordered a broader investigation into peon activism throughout the henequen zone.[60]

The validation by Alvarado's regime of the political careers of such powerful local *cabecillas* as Pedro Crespo, José Loreto Baak, and Elías Rivero (and, later, Carrillo Puerto's legitimation of Juan Campos's revolutionary *cacicazgo*) provides yet another indication of campesino empowerment—and of the revolutionary state's strategy to harness it. Contemporary testimonies and the interviews we conducted with old-timers in several fringe municipalities suggest that the precipitous rise of those local chiefs was as satisfying to their campesino followers as it was disconcerting to the *hacendados* (and occasionally to the revolutionary state as well). Such *cabecillas*, who under Alvarado and Carrillo Puerto would consolidate their clienteles into intermediate power domains, midway between larger regional political machines and purely local fiefdoms, have received far too little attention in the Mexican revolutionary historiography.[61]

No doubt a series of culturally informed, longitudinal studies of such *jefes menores* or intermediate *caciques*—the "flesh of the Revolution," in the words of Carleton Beals—would go a long way toward creating the historiographical synthesis of the Mexican Revolution that appears to lie in the offing.[62] Such studies would focus on the relations these chiefs forged with the emerging revolutionary state on the one hand, and with their local clienteles on the other. Our investigation of several of Yucatán's *cabecillas* has enabled us to trace them from their beginnings as notable political actors in 1909–10, through the consolidation of their power domains in the 1910s and early 1920s, until their demise or transformation into official party functionaries in the 1930s (even the 1940s, in Pedro Crespo's case). It has also cautioned us to reject neat interpretations of the Mexican Revolution and encouraged us to fit together elements from both populist and revisionist interpretations.

Along with new populists such as Alan Knight, we would argue that local chiefs such as Crespo, Campos, Baak, and Rivero dispensed a kind of leadership to the *comuneros* of Yucatán's fringe municipalities that was homespun and truly popular, albeit rather parochial in its vision. Such *cabecillas* heeded and, through their actions, reinforced their clienteles' overwhelming desire to preserve their autonomy as *hombres libres*, as free cultivators. Where such organic leadership and organization were weak or virtually absent, among the ethnically diverse "settlements" (we hesitate even to call them true communities) of estate peons in the heart of the more systematically controlled henequen zone, the forms of protest were different. Resistance normally took on a more "routine," day-to-day quality, escalating into short-lived eruptions of violence that were often provoked by incursions of *cabecilla*-led bands between 1910 and early 1913.

Because of the rather insular, defensive nature of popular authority, Yucatán's popular movement was doomed to be a brittle and balkanized one. The pueblo-based chiefs might successfully mobilize their own local followings, but they often violently repressed factional rivals and only with great difficulty made common cause (and seldom enduring alliances) with neighboring entities, much less the peons tied to estates.

For a variety of reasons, then, it is not really surprising that the popular movement led in Yucatán by the new men of the 1910s was welded without great difficulty (and often with their assistance) into the ever-more-powerful national state of the 1920s and 1930s. In a sense, Yucatán, despite its marked regionalism, provides a vivid illustration of what is increasingly regarded as a commonplace of Mexican political culture and revolutionary history: namely, the propensity of local popular elements and movements—invariably undemocratic themselves—to react at first with suspicion, then to cooperate with caution, and finally to serve to legitimate the authoritarian regional and national caudillos and the institutionalized regime they ultimately established.

Pedro Crespo, *cacique* of the village of Temax and central Yucatán from about 1911 until he died in 1944, whose early career we have already examined, serves to illustrate this principle.[63] Representing the grievances of most Temaxeños (as well as harboring his own personal vendetta against an abusive *jefe político* who killed his father), Crespo rebelled in 1911, then reached a series of separate understandings with Maderismo, Huertismo, revolutionary Yucatán's homegrown variant of "socialismo," and ultimately with what evolved into current Priismo. But it is too easy to argue, in the manner of the revisionists, that Pedro Crespo "sold out." Up to the 1930s, political life in Temax and its environs proceeded with a high degree of local autonomy from the state, largely because of Crespo's shrewdness.

Moreover, under his *cacicazgo*, Temaxeños received most of their traditional village lands back. Then later, during the Great Depression, with
henequen irreversibly in decline, Crespo skillfully negotiated an arrangement with the most powerful planters and the state to keep fields in production and minimize layoffs.

To the day he died, Crespo lived in much the same manner as his rustic
followers. He spoke Maya among friends, wore the collarless white *filipina*
shirt, and lived in the *kaxna*, the traditional wattle-and-daub cottage with
thatched roof. What interested him most was political power, not wealth.
The Mexican Revolution had offered him a chance, and he had seized it. He
viewed himself, and is still regarded in Temax, as a *líder nato*, a born local
leader, a chief. As such, he did what was necessary to preserve, even extend
his power domain. This entailed constant political vigilance and negotiation: deals might be made with powerful planters and *had* to be made with
an ever more muscular, bureaucratic state, but they never called on Crespo
to sell out his clientele, accumulate great wealth and leave Temax for Mérida. Indeed, precisely because he was a *líder nato*, he was incapable of
transcending his locality and breaking with the political culture that had
produced him.

In the process, Pedro Crespo played an important role in promoting
those routines and rituals of rule that, when all is said and done, allow the
Mexican Revolution to stake its claim as part of a longer-running *cultural*
revolution in modern state formation.[64] Organizing local *ligas de resistencia* and, later, official party clubs and youth groups, scheduling weekly
cultural soirées, officiating at patriotic acts of commemoration (such as the
anniversary of the death of Revolutionary Martyr Felipe Carrillo Puerto),
and energetically promoting "socialist education" and baseball teams in
some of the remotest pueblos and hacienda communities of north-central
Yucatán, Crespo effectively bridged the cultural gap between Temaxeños
and the revolutionary state for several decades.[65] Today, more than 40 years
after his death, Crespo remains at the service of the state's cultural project.
Duly incorporated into the Revolutionary Pantheon beside more famous regional icons like Alvarado and Carrillo Puerto, he is commemorated when
the revolution's litany of triumphs is read in Temax every November 20.

Some of Yucatán's other *cabecillas* were more ruthless and economically acquisitive than Crespo; nevertheless, they approximate him far
more than they do Carlos Fuentes's dark fictional composite, Artemio
Cruz. All ruled over factionalized, stratified local worlds; all sought a balance between the centralizing new state and its project of capitalist transformation on the one hand, and their own local clienteles on the other,
while clinging to political power (whether it be control of local agrarian
commissions, municipal presidencies, or other vehicles). Those like Crespo
(or Peto's Elías Rivero) who managed this balancing act, who were particularly able to translate between popular and state ideologies, endured.[66]

Those not as politically or culturally adroit (such as José Loreto Baak and Juan Campos) were replaced by factional contenders who took their turn at applying the new rules of the game in a time-honored political culture.[67]

## Final Reflections

To date neither revisionist nor populist historians have provided a particularly satisfying treatment of how the postrevolutionary state was formed. It is one thing to affirm, with the revisionists, an essential continuity in the Porfirian and revolutionary elites' desire to create a national, capitalist society. It is quite another to deny agency to popular political cultures and reduce their leaders to mere instruments of an emerging Leviathan state. We would contend that in Yucatán and elsewhere, the revolutionary process forever changed the terms by which the Mexican state would be formed. Indeed, it is the state's partial incorporation of *popular demands* since 1920 that helps to distinguish Mexico from countries like Peru and El Salvador today. As Florencia Mallon has pointed out recently, one has only to juxtapose the contrasting images of Cuauhtémoc Cárdenas and Peru's Sendero Luminoso to appreciate this point. For Mexico's latter-day Cardenistas, challenging the "official party," the struggle is clearly circumscribed within the framework of the revolution, the nation, and the state; for the Senderistas, it is about the total bankruptcy of the Peruvian state and the absence of a nation.[68] We might add that, as their movement's name indicates, even the Maya guerrilla fighters of Chiapas, the Zapatista Army of National Liberation, have framed their struggle in the context of a proud agrarian tradition that the state itself did much to create.

At the same time, our Yucatecan data also compel us to subject romantic populist approaches to much closer scrutiny. The data challenge us to specify just what is so popular about "the popular," and caution us against applying facile, essentialist notions of class, communal, and ethnic solidarity to real social worlds. As we have seen, Yucatán's diverse peasantry had for many decades been divided by different social and productive relations; strong, solidary pueblos had been eroded in the henequen zone in the eighteenth century—long before the Caste War, let alone the onset of the fiber boom. Even on the periphery of monoculture, peasant communities were riven by economic stratification and contention; horizontal bonds were fragile, and often were strengthened only in the face of a major external threat.

In a recent, richly suggestive essay, "The Production of Culture in Local Rebellion," Gavin Smith argues that peasant participants in the relatively successful present-day Peruvian land invasions he has studied "are committed both to the importance of difference among them and simultaneously to the ongoing production of an image of themselves as internally homogeneous and externally distinctive." In other words, with communal heterogeneity a given, points of difference must constantly be negotiated, and *contentiousness* becomes an integral part of the process whereby community and a culture of resistance are forged. In the case of the Peruvian land invaders, such "acting in unity . . . required a *continuous process* of . . . negotiation of meanings—a process, moreover, in which the attainment of cultural unity was never complete but was always unfinished business throughout the intense periods of resistance."[69] Smith's thesis deserves to be tested in the Mexican revolutionary context, although written and oral sources rarely support such fine-grained historical ethnography. In the case of Yucatán, embattled campesinos rarely had the autonomy or mobility that Smith's *comuneros* possessed. Thus, although negotiated strategies of resistance were essential in the face of monoculture's onslaught, they were difficult to achieve, and tenuous at best.

Similarly, we have seen that ethnic identity was anything but "primordial" or solidary; Maya ethnicity had undergone important reconstructions since the days of the Yucatec Maya's "collective enterprise of survival" during the colonial period. Long before the turn of this century, regional elites and the state consciously distinguished Yucatán's Maya-speaking villagers and estate workers from the rebel Maya who had never capitulated after the Caste War. What is more important, northwestern campesinos had come to distinguish *themselves* from such *cruzob* and *pacífico* separatists, against whom many of their relatives had fought, in 1847 and subsequently, as conscripts in the state militia. Indeed, so great was the fear of *cruzob* and *pacífico* reprisals among villagers living close to the southeastern zone of refuge that it spurred mutinies against state military recruiters and figured prominently in several of the Maderista-era uprisings.

Yes, Yucatán generated a popular rural movement during the Mexican Revolution's early years, but these seasons of upheaval were a far cry from the inexorable national groundswells conjured up by such writers as Frank Tannenbaum, José Valadés, or more recently, John Mason Hart. The broadranging histories of such populists, past and present, provide heroic images and stirring accounts, to be sure; but Yucatán's revolutionary experience (as well as others only now being reappraised) alert us to other perspectives and histories that such universalizing renditions tend to elide or pass over entirely.[70]

Anthropologist and cultural critic Néstor García Canclini observes, "Often descriptions of class struggles give the impression that while they are being undertaken it is as if all interaction were suspended—just as in a lift; as though inside each class, relations were impersonal and between persons unknown to one another. There is no drama."[71] The personal testimonies that provide small windows onto Yucatán's seasons of upheaval are suffused with drama (or dramas). They reveal complex actors who in no sense can be likened to the homogeneous occupants of an elevator, carried from one level—or historical stage—to another. Their contestation of Yucatán's old order is manifestly a history of stops and starts, of ambiguity and contingency as well as structure. True to E. P. Thompson's thought that history is "the restless discipline of context," we have approached contestation in this book from a variety of angles and counterpoints: the global economy, nation, state, district, and locality. While our effort has left us holding some loose ends, we hope it has also contributed to a better understanding of the period of transition that joined the decline of the Porfirian old regime to the emergence of the new revolutionary state.

*Reference Matter*

# Notes

Complete publication information for the works cited in short form is given in the References, pp. 369–93.

## ABBREVIATIONS

| | |
|---|---|
| *AD* | *Acción Democrática* |
| AGEY | Archivo General del Estado de Yucatán |
| RJ | Ramo de Justicia |
| RPE | Ramo del Poder Ejecutivo |
| RT | Ramo de Tierras |
| AGN | Archivo General de la Nación |
| RM | Ramo de Madero |
| RTr | Ramo de Trabajo |
| AGN, SCOP | Archivo General de la Nación, Secretaría de Comunicaciones y Obras Públicas |
| *AHR* | *American Historical Review* |
| ANEY | Archivo Notarial del Estado de Yucatán |
| *APSR* | *American Political Science Review* |
| ARE | Archivo de Relaciones Exteriores |
| ASA-C | Archivo de la Secretaría del Arzobispado, Correspondencia, 1914–1919 |
| AVC | Archivo Venustiano Carranza |
| BCRM | Biblioteca Carlos R. Menéndez |
| *BE* | *Boletín Estadística* |
| *BECA* | *Boletín de la Escuela de Ciencias Antropológicas de la Universidad Autonóma de Yucatán* |
| CGPD | Colección General Porfirio Díaz |

| | |
|---|---|
| CJD | Colección Jorge Denegre V. |
| *CSSH* | *Comparative Studies in Society and History* |
| *CTJ* | *Cordage Trade Journal* |
| *CyR* | *Constitución y Reforma* |
| *DdY* | *Diario de Yucatán* |
| *DdH* | *Diario del Hogar* |
| *DO* | *Diario Oficial* |
| *DY* | *Diario Yucateco* |
| *EA* | *El Agricultor* |
| *EC* | *El Ciudadano* |
| *ECdE* | *El Crédito del Estado* |
| *EcM* | *El Economista Mexicano* |
| *ED* | *El Demócrata* |
| *EdC* | *El Eco del Comercio* |
| *EI* | *El Imparcial* |
| *EP* | *El País* |
| *EPC* | *El Padre Clarencio* |
| *EPn* | *El Peninsular* |
| *EPop* | *El Popular* |
| *ElUn* | *El Universal* |
| *ES* | *El Sufragio* |
| *ET* | *El Tiempo* |
| FCUY | Ferrocarriles Unidos de Yucatán |
| GPO | Government Printing Office |
| *HAHR* | *Hispanic American Historical Review* |
| *HM* | *Historia Mexicana* |
| *IAEA* | *Inter-American Economic Affairs* |
| IHC | International Harvester Company |
| IHCA | International Harvester Company Archives |
| INAH | Instituto Nacional de Antropología y Historia |
| INEHRM | Instituto Nacional de Estudios Históricos de la Revolución Mexicana |
| *JEH* | *Journal of Economic History* |
| *JLAS* | *Journal of Latin American Studies* |
| *JSH* | *Journal of Social History* |
| *LC* | *La Campana* |
| *LD* | *La Democracia* |
| *LO* | *La Opinión* |
| *LARR* | *Latin American Research Review* |
| *MH* | *Mexican Herald* |
| *MS/EM* | *Mexican Studies/Estudios Mexicanos* |
| NA | U.S. National Archives |
| *NYT* | *New York Times* |
| *NdY* | *Novedades de Yucatán* |
| *PP* | *Past and Present* |
| *PL* | *Periodista Libre* |
| *RdM* | *La Revista de Mérida* |
| *RdY* | *La Revista de Yucatán* |
| *RUY* | *Revista de la Universidad Autonóma de Yucatán* |
| SPC | Simón Peón Collection |
| UNAM | Universidad Nacional Autónoma de México |

VdP      *La Voz del Pueblo*
VdR      *La Voz de la Revolución*
YHE      *Yucatán: Historia y Economía*

## CHAPTER 1

1. The official story depicts "The Mexican Revolution" in schematic and uncritical fashion as the supreme moment of popular resistance in the nation's history; as a virtually spontaneous agrarian revolution that swept up the entire nation in a clean break with an essentially "feudal" past. Interestingly, this orthodoxy neatly codifies the interpretation that had first appeared in the 1920s and 1930s in works of sympathetic foreign commentators (e.g., Frank Tannenbaum, Ernest Gruening, Eyler Simpson) and revolutionary chroniclers (José Valadés, Jesús Silva Herzog)—all of whom wrote when the social revolution was at high tide.

2. Many of the restraints that the Porfirian state had imposed on popular movements were lifted during the Maderista interlude, and extremely divergent local movements began to emerge in Mexico's different regions. Surprisingly, except for important work on Morelos, Puebla, and Tlaxcala in Mexico's core, or more recently on northern San Luis Potosí and the Comarca Lagunera, little has been done to explain the mobilization of these movements or to examine their fate. Yet as the present work will demonstrate, they are highly important in understanding the character of the "epic revolution" (1910–17) and the kind of state that emerged from it. See Womack, *Zapata and the Mexican Revolution*; Buve, "Peasant Movements, Caudillos, and Land Reform"; LaFrance, *Mexican Revolution in Puebla*, and "Puebla: Breakdown of the Old Order"; Ankerson; Falcón, *Revolución y caciquismo*; and Meyers, "Second Division of the North." For a review of the surprisingly sparse literature on Maderista mobilizations, see LaFrance, "Many Causes."

3. For the Mexican Revolution's "conquest" of oligarchical Yucatán, see Joseph, *Revolution from Without*, esp. 1–10.

4. We have been considerably influenced by a burgeoning comparative literature that bridges social history, anthropology, historical sociology, and cultural studies and seeks to formulate new approaches for rethinking the multifaceted relationships between power, culture, and resistance. Some representative titles include J. Scott, *Domination and the Arts of Resistance*, and his earlier *Weapons of the Weak*; Guha and Spivak, as well as the annual publication of the journal *Subaltern Studies*, ed. Guha; Corrigan and Sayer; Stern, *Resistance, Rebellion, and Consciousness*; O'Brien and Roseberry; and McClure and Mufti.

5. Or, as Jean and John Comaroff call them, narratives of "challenge and riposte." See their *Of Revelation and Revolution*; cf. Seed's critique in "Colonial and Postcolonial Discourse." An even greater danger looms in Seed's repeated suggestions that we dismiss the study of "narratives of resistance and accommodation" as a worthy analytical pursuit and fix our attention primarily on the "discourses" of colonial and postcolonial domination. To be sure, materialist analyses of power must be augmented by poststructural linguistic and cultural studies. Indeed, the latter have proved an effective antidote to romantic "tales of adaptation and response" that rely on "notions of oppositional identity as untouched, authentic, and unproblematically created." But to dismiss the recent theoretical and empirical contributions of Scott and a generation of resistance scholars as irrelevant or obsolete is surely to overstate the case. For Seed's latest statement and a gentle but effective critique by literary scholar Rolena Adorno, see Seed, "More Colonial and Postcolonial Discourses," quotes, 149; Adorno, esp. 136–37; and the forum of commentary

and debate in *LARR* 28:3 (1993), 113–52. For a broader critique of recent polemics between "Foucauldians" and "Marxists" that "turn . . . complementary perspectives into hegemonic claims and counterclaims," see Cooper, "Postscript" to "Africa and the World Economy," esp. 194–95; Mallon, "Dialogues Among the Fragments" (the same volume's concluding essay); and Mallon, "Promise and Dilemma."

6. See, e.g., Abu-Lughod; Isaacman, "Peasants and Rural Social Protest," 236.

7. See, e.g., the treatment of hegemony in Joseph and Nugent, *Everyday Forms of State Formation*, esp. the editors' introduction and the essays by Florencia Mallon, William Roseberry, and Derek Sayer.

8. Katz, "Rural Uprisings in Mexico."

9. The essays cited in n. 7 adopt a similar position.

10. Florencia Mallon kindly brought this quotation to our attention.

11. This notion of a state of play in cultural relations owes much to Hall, esp. 235. For a fuller development of this conceptualization, see Joseph and Nugent, "Popular Culture and State Formation in Revolutionary Mexico," in *Everyday Forms of State Formation*, 3–23.

12. Cf. Clendinnen.

13. See, e.g., Benjamin and McNellie, esp. pt. 1; Voss; Balmori, Voss, and Wortman; Wasserman, *Capitalists, Caciques, and Revolution*; Benjamin, "Passages to Leviathan" and *A Rich Land, A Poor People*; Jacobs; Aguilar Camín; and Saragoza.

14. See, e.g., Katz, *Secret War*; Wasserman, *Capitalists, Caciques, and Revolution*; Wells, *Yucatán's Gilded Age*; Joseph, Wells et al., *Yucatán y la International Harvester*; Meyers, "Politics, Vested Rights, and Economic Growth"; and Hart, *Revolutionary Mexico*.

15. See, e.g., Joseph, *Rediscovering the Past*, 137; and Beezley, "Opportunities for Further Regional Study."

16. Cf. Stearns; Judt; Fox-Genovese and Genovese. Two Brazilian studies provide models for examining the links between a regional political elite and the dominant economic class. See Lewin; and Weinstein.

17. Cf., however, Graham's fine, multilevel study of politics in imperial Brazil, *Patronage and Politics*.

18. Significant exceptions are Wasserman, *Capitalists, Caciques, and Revolution*; Mallon, *Defense of Community*; the Brazilian regional studies by Weinstein and Lewin; and Topik, *Political Economy of the Brazilian State*. By contrast, Graham's work on Brazilian patronage politics would benefit immeasurably if the economic dimension were integrated.

19. We are leery of abstract characterizations that all too frequently—and rapidly—change into reifications. We use terms like *populists* and *revisionists* to indicate salient trends, not to sanction procrustean "schools" of interpretation. Womack's writings, for example, engage elements of both camps. The author of the definitive study of Emiliano Zapata and the popular movement he led (*Zapata and the Mexican Revolution*), Womack has more recently advanced a revisionist thesis in particularly provocative terms. While admitting that peasant movements and labor unions became significant forces and that Mexican society underwent "extraordinary crises and serious changes from 1910 to 1920," Womack now argues that continuity clearly took precedence over change: "The crises did not go nearly deep enough to break capitalist domination of production. The great issues were issues of state. . . . [The] subject is therefore no longer so much social revolution as political management." Though popular movements were important, "their defeat and subordination mattered more." "Mexican Revolution, 1910–1920." On "revisionism," see Bailey; Carr; Brading; and Fowler-Salamini. In his provocative two-volume study,

*The Mexican Revolution,* Alan Knight makes a forceful case for the existence and powerful influence of truly popular revolutionary movements. See also Hart, *Revolutionary Mexico;* and the final chapter of Tutino's *From Insurrection to Revolution.* Knight and Hart build on the old orthodoxy advanced 60 years ago by Tannenbaum (e.g., in *Peace by Revolution*) and others (see n. 1).

20. Knight, *Mexican Revolution,* 1: xi.

21. See Tocqueville.

22. See Knight, book review essay.

23. See, e.g., Jean Meyer, *Cristero Rebellion;* and Córdova, *La ideología de la Revolución Mexicana.* For a detailed critique of the "revisionists" (and "neo-populists"), see Joseph and Nugent, "Popular Culture and State Formation," esp. 5–12.

24. See esp. the aforementioned works of Tannenbaum and Hart. Knight's masterful synoptic history, *The Mexican Revolution,* is less vulnerable to this critique. While it forcefully argues the case for a popular agrarian revolution, it is far more sensitive to regional and local nuance, and it consistently seeks to historicize the broad issues it narrates (not for nothing does it run to well over a thousand pages!). Still, while Knight has achieved a theoretical recognition of what the popular classes realized in historical practice—namely the articulation of distinctive forms of social consciousness and experience—he has not grounded that popular presence and consciousness in a sustained analysis of popular culture. To be sure, he was constrained by his sources and the considerable demands of writing a narrative that embraced all of Mexico.

25. For an engrossing collection of essays that serves as a model for this kind of approach, see O'Brien and Roseberry.

26. See Joseph and Nugent, "Popular Culture and State Formation"; and Mallon, "Promise and Dilemma," for critiques of essentialist readings of popular culture and references to the lively ongoing debate in Asian studies about how to conceptualize subaltern politics and consciousness. For a provocative recent exchange, see Prakash, "Writing Post-Orientalist Histories"; O'Hanlon and Washbrook; and Prakash, "Can the 'Subaltern' Ride? A Reply to O'Hanlon and Washbrook."

27. In their anthology, Joseph and Nugent attempt to introduce the kind of synthesis of populist and revisionist approaches to revolutionary and postrevolutionary Mexico that is called for here.

28. For an examination of the literature on the Mexican Revolution and its aftermath in Yucatán, see Joseph, *Rediscovering the Past,* chap. 5.

29. For a representative conservative view, see Gamboa Ricalde, esp. vol. 1; cf. Betancourt Pérez's orthodox Marxist treatment, *La problemática social.* Some professional (mostly foreign) scholars have chosen—in the best revisionist fashion—to inflect the pivotal role of non-ideological, self-serving "warlords": see, e.g., Franz, chaps. 1–3.

30. Here and elsewhere in this book, to enter into wide-ranging theoretical discussions, we will define peasants (or campesinos) in the broad sense: as rural cultivators from whom an economic surplus is extracted in one form or another by nonproducing classes. It should be clear from the discussion here that it is not our intention to homogenize peasants and campesinos or essentialize them as purely economic actors. When appropriate, we will employ other terms to characterize the various structural and cultural differentiations encompassed by such a broad construction of peasantry.

31. Rutherford, 127. Of course, revisionists are particularly prone to such depictions; see the trenchant discussion in Knight, "Intellectuals in the Mexican Revolution."

32. See, e.g., Betancourt Pérez, *La problemática social.*

33. The slowness with which Mexicanists and Latin Americanists have taken up questions of *mentalidad* and culture has drawn a variety of comments: see Vanderwood; Van Young, "Mentalities"; and Joseph, "On the Trail of Latin American Bandits." For the important advances that have been made to date see ibid., n. 66, 128, 138; and Mallon, "Promise and Dilemma," 1500–1504.

34. E.g., Moore, *Social Origins of Dictatorship*; Wolf, *Peasant Wars*; Paige; Tilly; Skocpol, *States and Social Revolutions*, and "What Makes Peasants Revolutionary?" Of these, Paige, Tilly, and Skocpol were the least preoccupied with questions of peasant consciousness.

35. Abu-Lughod, 41.

36. On indigenous peoples, see, e.g., Stern, *Peru's Indian Peoples*, and *Resistance, Rebellion, and Consciousness.* On slaves and freedmen, E. Genovese, *Roll, Jordan, Roll*; Levine; Craton; and Taussig. On blacks, e.g., Jean Comaroff, *Body of Power, Spirit of Resistance*; Comaroff and Comaroff, *Of Revelation and Revolution.* On Indians and Asians, Guha, *Elementary Aspects of Peasant Insurgency*; J. Scott, *Weapons of the Weak*; Scott and Kerkvliet; Stoler.

37. Knight, "Intellectuals in the Mexican Revolution"; cf. Isaacman, "Peasants and Rural Social Protest," esp. 253–63; Watts, esp. 117.

38. See the PRI's oblique references to externally trained "professionals of violence," reported in *New York Times*, Jan. 7 and 9, 1994.

39. Van Young, "To See Someone Not Seeing," 135–36. Van Young's qualification of the "inarticulate" label strikes us as particularly important. The present study will demonstrate just how expressive peasants are, whether literate or not.

40. Ibid., 150. Actually, in "Eighteenth Brumaire," 239, Marx refers to French peasants as "isomorphous magnitudes, much as potatoes in a sack form a sack of potatoes."

41. Tutino, *From Insurrection to Revolution*, 23; and "Agrarian Social Change," 102.

42. Hamnett, 189.

43. Knight, *Mexican Revolution*, 1: 167, 79.

44. See Van Young's judicious review of the collection's strengths and weaknesses in "To See Someone Not Seeing," esp. 148–50.

45. Taylor, "Banditry and Insurrection."

46. Meyers, "Second Division of the North."

47. Van Young, "To See Someone Not Seeing," 136.

48. Cf. discussion in ibid., 151.

49. Criminal court records apparently are particularly scarce for the "epic revolution" (1910–17). In many localities the Porfirian state rather quickly fell into rebel hands, and courts, police stations, and government offices were sacked. Even when this did not happen, the criminal justice system experienced severe dislocation during the violent revolutionary decade and left a much less comprehensive body of documentation for social historians. Yucatán's rather different experience—an "extended Porfiriato" followed by a relatively nonviolent "conquest" by federal troops in 1915—has provided us with a research bounty that few Mexicanists enjoy.

50. Van Young, "To See Someone Not Seeing," esp. 153–55; quotations, 154. In his review of the works of Tutino, Hamnett, and Knight, Van Young provides some examples of unwarranted inferential leaps, all suggesting that while these scholars are particularly reticent in imputing motives and beliefs to elite actors, they rarely hesitate where campesinos are concerned.

51. Again, no doubt partly for the reasons Van Young discusses, ibid. For a critical

review of a large body of literature on modern Latin America that has utilized judicial and other criminal records, see Joseph, "On the Trail." For the effective use of criminal records in research on the colonial period see, e.g., Taylor's pathbreaking work, *Drinking, Homicide, and Rebellion*; Stern, *Peru's Indian Peoples*; and Aufderheide, "Order and Violence." The uncatalogued, disorganized state of the voluminous nineteenth- and twentieth-century documentation in AGEY, RJ has no doubt discouraged more than one researcher. Without aids and sometimes with 50 or more files, each from one to three feet thick(!), for each year, judicial research becomes an extraordinarily labor-intensive enterprise, even for tandems or teams of investigators. The judicial files for the colonial period and the first half of the nineteenth century are much less extensive, and partially organized. Most notably, Yucatecan social historian José Arturo Güémez Pineda has consulted them in his studies of rustling and routine forms of Maya resistance and accommodation. See Güémez Pineda, which is an abridged version of his *tesis de licenciatura* for the Universidad Autónoma de Yucatán.

52. The following discussion draws on Guha, *Elementary Aspects*; and several essays in Guha and Spivak, notably Guha, "Prose of Counter-Insurgency," 45–86. For a fuller discussion, see Joseph, "On the Trail," esp. 18–25.

53. See, e.g., our discussion in Chapter 8 of an extraordinary, rustic "epic poem," "El 15 de septiembre," which the authorities captured in 1909 on the person of one Rigoberto Xiu, a village-based insurgent from the Puuc region of Yucatán.

54. Cf. the insightful discussion of these thorny issues of "textuality" for an earlier period in Van Young, "Sliding Sideways," and "To See Someone Not Seeing," esp. 151; see also Taylor, *Drinking, Homicide, and Rebellion*, esp. 64–65, 90–92.

55. Guha, "Prose of Counter-Insurgency," 61. Here, too, the Comaroffs' notion of a "rhetoric of contrasts" is illuminating. See "Madman and the Migrant."

56. Guha, *Elementary Aspects*, 17. For a revealing case that illustrates how the officials of the British Raj routinely characterized insurgent Indian dacoits (bandits), see Winther.

57. Van Young, "Mentalities," 344, 350.

58. The phrase *standard manipulationist vocabulary* is borrowed from Billingsley's discussion of the Chinese state's depiction of brigands, *Bandits in Republican China*, xiv.

59. Morse, esp. 151–77; and Van Young, "Mentalities," 344–45.

60. Van Young, "Mentalities," 345.

61. Barthes, 115.

62. White, 36; see also Alonso, esp. 33–37. For an illuminating essay that deftly employs these deconstructionist insights for a much earlier period, see Seed, "Failing to Marvel."

63. In addition to Guha, *Elementary Aspects*, 78–106, see Foucault, 178–85; and Turton.

64. These documents represent cases heard by a variety of courts at two jurisdictional levels. Around the turn of the century there were three civil and three penal courts of law (*juzgados*) in Mérida, and a variety of courts of first instance (*juzgados de primera instancia*) in the countryside, all of which had justices of the peace. A superior court (*juzgado superior*), comprising six magistrates, functioned as the state's appellate tribunal in Mérida. While the documentation from these courts is massive and rich, the data are always uneven and incomplete. Civil cases have been periodically inserted into piles of documentation marked Ramo Penal, and vice versa. Research in AGEY, RPE, and CGPD has consistently turned up copies of criminal records no longer found in RJ. Not surprisingly, a few significant gaps exist;

e.g., case materials for the Valladolid rebellion of 1910. Moreover, the ravages of climate, insects, rodents, reptiles, irregular staffing, and several relocations in the past decade alone—all generally attributable to insufficient government funds for upkeep—have taken their toll on extant files.

65. Gramsci, 195–96, 246–47; cf. Genovese, *Roll, Jordan, Roll,* 25–27.

66. The standard work on the Caste War remains Reed. See also Bricker, chap. 8; and Rugeley, "Origins of the Caste War." For a discussion of the war's tremendous material and symbolic consequences for the region, as well as trends in scholarship since Reed, see Joseph, *Rediscovering the Past,* chap. 3.

67. J. Scott, *Domination and the Arts of Resistance,* chap. 7.

68. Taylor, *Drinking, Homicide, and Rebellion,* 76.

69. Cf. ibid., 64–65, 90–92.

70. Given our study's central goals and circumscribed geographical and temporal parameters, as well as the abundant corroborating materials (e.g., the regional press, oral histories, ethnographies), we did not find it necessary to engage in the quantification of criminal data that was so fashionable only a few years back. The incomplete, fragmented nature of the judicial documentation, furthermore, may not permit sophisticated quantification. Of course, such exercises can yield rich dividends, particularly in broader studies for more remote eras; witness Van Young's recent efforts to produce a statistical profile of 1,200 Mexican independence-era insurgents captured between 1810 and 1815. Van Young's computer-aided analysis is meant to discover basic social characteristics of class, ethnicity, occupation, origin, age, etc. and, if possible, to reconstruct full-bodied career portraits. For some tentative results of this exercise, see Van Young, "In the Gloomy Caverns." We have a much more intimate knowledge of our protagonists, several of whose careers will be reconstructed in the pages that follow.

71. Historians of early modern Europe have been particularly creative in using court records and other official sources to analyze peasant culture and discourse. See, e.g., Sabean, esp. 1–36; Burke; Ginzburg.

72. Taylor, *Drinking, Homicide, and Rebellion,* 77; E. P. Thompson, "Peculiarities of the English."

CHAPTER 2

1. Benjamin, "Regional Politics," 27.

2. Alan Knight characterizes Díaz's strategy as one based "on some lingering legitimacy, as well as on coercion, and the coercion was selective and limited, not indiscriminate." *Mexican Revolution,* 1: 35.

3. Literally "the unveiling," or "uncovering," it referred to the moment when Don Porfirio announced his choice for the statehouse. A good description of how Don Porfirio chose his governors is found in Valadés, *El porfirismo,* 1: 28–29.

4. On the basis of data found in CGPD, Carol Lee Carbine has demonstrated that the Porfirian practice of selecting Yucatán's governors began immediately after the triumph of the Tuxtepec rebellion. See Carbine, 14. President Manuel González continued the practice during his administration. See Cosío Villegas, *Historia moderna,* 1: 598.

5. Quoted in Valadés, *El porfirismo,* 1: 58.

6. Knight, *Mexican Revolution,* 1: 37–39.

7. Baqueiro, *Reseña geográfica,* 183. The state almost matched this mark during 1911, the first year of Maderismo, with six governors.

8. Cantón Rosado, 61–62.

9. On the telegraph, see Valdés Acosta, 3: 289–90. On railways: Wells, "All in the Family." On telephones, Ferrer de Mendiolea, 105.

10. Seventeen of Mexico's 27 governors in 1886 were military officers. Valadés, *El porfirismo*, 1: 16–17.

11. General Octavio Rosado, who was governor from 1882 to 1886, proved a notable exception to the rule. Born in Sisal, Yucatán, the son of Caste War hero Eulogio Rosado, the general was brought back by González to curb infighting between supporters of outgoing governor Manuel Romero Ancona and aspiring candidate General Francisco Cantón. Romero Ancona protested bitterly and plotted intrigues against Rosado's *destape*. See Cosío Villegas, *Historia moderna*, 1: 598–99. Despite such opposition, Rosado brought a short-lived peace to the contending *camarillas* by surrounding himself with advisers from both factions. López, *El verdadero Yucatán*, 14, 34.

12. E.g., Hernán Menéndez Rodríguez contends that Colonel Daniel Traconis, governor from 1890 to 1894, was controlled by Carlos Peón Machado's *camarilla*; "he was the Peoncistas' right hand." Peón Machado parleyed this statehouse influence to feather his own nest, succeeding Traconis as governor in 1894. Menéndez Rodríguez, "La agonía del proyecto liberal."

13. On Romero Ancona's officious actions, see Acereto, esp. 333. For a critical assessment of his administration, see Pérez Peniche, *Reseña histórica*, 10. For a discussion of the 1885 campaign, see *Solemne protesta*.

14. Cosío Villegas, *Historia moderna*, 1: 104–6.

15. *Exposición que los habitantes*.

16. An exhaustive social science literature discusses patron-client relationships, or clientelism. For a useful introduction, see S. Schmidt et al. J. Scott defines the patron-client relationship as "a special case of dyadic (two-person) ties involving a largely instrumental friendship in which an individual of higher socioeconomic status (patron) uses his own influence and resources to provide protection or benefits, or both, for a person of lower status (client) who, for his part, reciprocates by offering general support and assistance, including personal services, to the patron." J. Scott, "Patron-Client Politics." See also Powell; Wolf, "Kinship, Friendship"; Foster; and Strickon and Greenfield.

17. The expression is borrowed from Leal's insightful piece.

18. The phrase *ideology of hierarchy* appears in Richard Graham's study of patronage during the Brazilian empire. Other useful studies of clientelism include Hay; and Flory. It is interesting that standard narrative accounts of Yucatecan politics ignore the phenomenon; see, e.g., Urzáiz Rodríguez; Acereto; and Bolio Ontiveros, *Yucatán en la dictadura*.

19. A more nuanced discussion of paternalism on henequen haciendas follows in Chap. 6.

20. The degree of coercion present in the dyadic relationship depends on a number of factors. J. Scott writes: "If the client has highly valued services to reciprocate with, if he can choose among competing patrons, if force is available to him, if he can manage without the patron's help . . . then the balance will be more nearly equal. But if, as is generally the case, the client has few coercive or exchange resources to bring to bear against a monopolist-patron whose services he desperately needs, the dyad is more nearly a coercive one." "Patron-Client Politics," 104.

21. Valadés, *El porfirismo*, 1: 64. Both Menéndez Rodríguez and Bulnes state that Baranda was Cantón's stepbrother. The Barandas were the sons of Pedro Sainz de Baranda, who operated a profitable textile factory in Valladolid before the Caste War. See Cline, "Aurora yucateca"; Zayas Enríquez, *El Estado de Yucatán*, 240; and Camp.

22. On Baranda's key role in 1897, see Menéndez Rodríguez, "La agonía."

22. For an informative, albeit apologetic, biography of Pancho Cantón, see Cantón Rosado.

23. Max Weber subdivides charismatic leadership into traditional legitimacy, which exists in patrimonial societies, and rational legitimacy, found in formal bureaucratic structures. Cantón's evolution as a regional politician bridges this critical transition from traditional to modern society. Often the terms *caudillo* and *cacique* are used interchangeably, but we distinguish between a caudillo, such as Cantón, whose clientelistic network blanketed the entire state, and *caciques*, whose power domains were much more circumscribed. Paul Friedrich defines a *cacique* in "caudillesque" fashion: "a strong and autocratic leader in local and regional politics whose characteristics informal, personalistic, and often arbitrary rule is buttressed by a core of relatives, 'fighters,' and dependents and is marked by the diagnostic threat and practice of violence." See "Legitimacy of a Cacique"; and Wolf and Hansen.

24. Maximilian found Yucatecan elites to be some of his most fervent supporters. Local imperialists held Mérida for almost a month after the battle of Querétaro, which sealed Maxmilian's fate. After the siege of Mérida, Cantón and fellow monarchists were exiled to Cuba, but they returned to the peninsula months later to stage an unsuccessful uprising against the Liberal government. Urzáiz Rodríguez, chap. 2.

25. For a critical view of the general by a Molinista supporter, see López, *El verdadero Yucatán*, 48. Cantón might have been a model for García Márquez's fictional caudillo, Colonel Aureliano Buendía, who in surreal fashion led and lost 32 rebellions. Both Cantón and Buendía enjoyed charmed careers, survived repeated attempts on their lives, and shared the uncanny ability to snatch moral, if not political, victories from military defeats. The dour Buendía was cast as a reluctant warrior, while the charismatic Cantón was always spoiling for a good fight; their sense of political essentials was the same. See García Márquez.

26. On Cantón's brush with the firing squad see Cantón Rosado, 48–49; and Baranda's description, in Cantón Rosado, 163. García Márquez's fictional Buendía, also sentenced to the firing squad, avoided a similar fate. García Márquez, 129–32.

27. Baranda's brief is in Cantón Rosado, 158–65.

28. On various Cantonista uprisings, see Urzáiz Rodríguez, *Del imperio*, chapter 2. As subinspector, Cantón secured arms, ammunition, and supplies to outfit his soldiers, thereby reinforcing his military strength in eastern Yucatán. Cosío Villegas, *Historia moderna*, 1: 316. Cantón's rewards were all the more remarkable because he joined the Tuxtepec rebellion very late, only eighteen days before the government of Miguel Lerda de Tejada fell in Yucatán. Acereto, 332.

29. Colonel Teodosio Canto, quoted in Cosío Villegas, *Historia moderna*, 1: 318.

30. On the 1878 governor's race, see Lapointe, 139–41, quotation, 140. For data on the 1882 gubernatorial campaign and liberal opposition to Cantón, see López, *El verdadero Yucatán*, 34. Just as Díaz selected governors, so too he picked seats in the federal congress. State governors recommended a slate of deputies and senators, which was sent to Interior Minister Manuel Romero Rubio's private secretary, Rosendo Pineda. Romero Rubio (until his death in 1895) and Pineda would adjust the lists as they deemed appropriate and then present them to Díaz for approval. Occasionally, Díaz chose deputies to represent districts other than their own. See Valadés, *El porfirismo*, 1: 36.

31. López, *El verdadero Yucatán*, 48.

32. It is interesting that two of Cantón's chief aides, Alfonso Cámara y Cámara and José María Iturralde, left liberal *camarillas* to assist Cantón in his successful run for the statehouse.

33. Clientelistic ties and political influence also were brought to bear on key appointments in the church hierarchy. See CGPD, Cantón to Díaz, 22:8:003808, Mar. 18, 1897; Alarcón to Díaz, 22:9:004085, Mar. 3, 1897; and Acereto, 343.

34. Knight, *Mexican Revolution*, 1: 15.

35. Some notable examples of creole historiography include Ancona; Baqueiro, *Ensayo histórico*; and Molina Solís. For a recent analysis of creole historical writings, see Wells, "Los capítulos olvidados." Certain factions actually created their own armies, including many Maya recruits who later would turn on the white Yucatecans. On the demographic consequences of the war, see Joseph, *Rediscovering the Past*, 36–40.

36. González y González. For an overview of the literature on historical generations, see Spitzer, who relies on Julián Marías's definition of a historical generation: "a group born within a zone of dates and sharing a structure of *vigencias*—the binding customs, collective usages, traditions, and beliefs that define the real social existence of each individual." Spitzer, 1356.

37. In 1868, liberals closed the Seminario Conciliar de San Ildefonso, which had educated the sons of the elite for centuries. That same year, Carrillo y Ancona and Domínguez Elizalde opened the Colegio Católico. *Diccionario Porrúa*, 1: 380, 663. Not to be outdone, liberals opened the Instituto Literario in 1867; it included schools of medicine, pharmacy, law, and a normal school for primary and secondary teachers. Olegario Molina was the institute's first director. See Ruz Menéndez, *Aportaciones*; and Carranza y Trujillo.

38. Menéndez Rodríguez asserts that the church, trying to rebuild its economic clout after Maximilian's defeat, pressured local elites to tithe themselves voluntarily, and that the Molina family was instrumental in raising funds for the diocese. This relationship benefited both the Molinistas, economically, and the church, which gained political leverage during Molina's gubernatorial administration (1902–10). The church's machinations infuriated "Jacobin" liberals like the followers of Carlos Peón Machado. See Menéndez Rodríguez, "La alianza clero-Molina." Nevertheless, the church enjoyed some success after Molina was named governor. In 1904 Bishop Martin Tritschler published an edict linking tithe payments to production on henequen haciendas. *Hacendados* were required to pay one centavo per arroba (25 pounds of henequen fiber) or face possible excommunication. See Savarino, "La iglesia ausente."

39. Grafting Comtean and Spencerian scientific politics to "conservative-liberal" models found in the Spanish and French republics, Porfirian intellectuals like Justo Sierra Méndez fashioned a constitutional rationale for authoritarianism and a unifying political myth. See Hale, *Transformation of Liberalism*; and Córdova, chap. 1. Menéndez Rodríguez argues that Carlos Peón Machado and his *camarilla* were orthodox liberals who found themselves out of step with the national government. See "La agonía."

40. Alan Knight breaks down Mexican liberalism into three broadly defined categories: a popular or folk liberalism appropriated by campesinos; a developmentalist tradition that became the guiding philosophy of the Porfirian intelligentsia; and the urban middle class's limited interpretation of constitutional principles. See Knight, "El liberalismo mexicano." We will return to this typology in the next chapter. See also Hernández Chávez. By contrast, Moisés González Navarro sees two strains of liberals: "individualistic" and "social." The Reform Laws were the successful culmination of the "individual" project of liberals like José María Luis Mora and Miguel Lerdo de Tejada, while social liberals—and here he discusses an eclectic group ranging from Guillermo Prieto to Justo Sierra—continued to debate how best to arrest

Mexico's social problem. González Navarro, "Tipología del liberalismo mexicano." Henry C. Schmidt provides a useful overview of the "historiology" of Mexican liberalism in "Toward the Innerscape." See also Reyes Heroles; Hale, *Mexican Liberalism in the Age of Mora*; and Covo.

41. Typical was the reaction by opponents of Traconis, who in 1890 protested the imposition of his candidacy for governor. See Cosío Villegas, *Historia moderna*, 9: 461.

42. CGPD, Manuel Sierra Méndez to Díaz, memorandum, "Apuntes breves sobre la situación actual de Yucatán, las providencias que sería conveniente tomar al inciarse la Campaña de Indios y sobre algunos otros puntos que se relacionan con la misma campaña," 22:14:006780-95, June 9, 1897. Yucatán attempted to secede from Mexico on two occasions in the late 1830s and early 1840s. We elaborate on the strategic uses of separatism in Yucatán in Wells and Joseph.

43. Bolio Ontiveros emphasizes this point when he writes of Pancho Cantón's charismatic flair: "he had a certain following among the masses, who followed him without understanding his political ideas, and, in truth, he himself did not understand those ideas." *Yucatán en la dictadura*, 21.

44. Zayas Enríquez, *El Estado de Yucatán*, 253.

45. CGPD, Sierra Méndez memorandum, "Apuntes breves."

46. On private clubs that influenced local politics, see Sierra Villarreal, "Prensa y lucha política." Intellectuals Manuel Sales Cepeda and Rodolfo Menéndez de la Peña led short-lived literary societies and informal discussion groups. See Gamboa Ricalde, 1: 227. *Pimienta y Mostaza* appeared from 1892 to 1894 and from 1902 to 1903. See Canto López, "La imprenta y el periodismo," 50. On Masonic lodges, see Pérez Alcalá, *Ensayos biográficos*, 177.

47. Wolf, "Aspects of Group Relations," 97.

48. For a thoughtful discussion of the "theater of elections" see Graham, chap. 4.

49. See Sabato, "Citizenship, Political Participation," and "Relations Between Civil Society and the Political System."

50. Escalante Gonzalbo, 286. See also Emmerich.

51. A good description of *empleomanía* is found in Perry, 12.

52. CGPD, Sierra Méndez memorandum, "Apuntes breves."

53. Bulnes, *Whole Truth*, 28.

54. Yucatán was divided into seventeen *partidos* during the Porfiriato. The administrative head of each district was the *cabecera*.

55. E.g., *Exposición que los habitantes*; and *Solemne protesta*. Here, regional political parties were taking a cue from Díaz's presidential campaigns. In 1896, his party, the Círculo Nacional Porfirista, presented him with "a magnificent album which contained five hundred thousand signatures" calling for his reelection. García Granados, 3: 9.

56. Lázaro Pavia to Yanuario Manzanilla, quoted in Menéndez Rodríguez, "La agonía," 5.

57. Bolio Ontiveros, *Yucatán en la dictadura*, 16. Ephemeral papers were created for a specific purpose (e.g., an electoral campaign) and published only as long as the purpose lasted. On 1890 political propaganda and a complete list of publications, see Pérez Peniche, *Reseña histórica*, 29. Cf. Cosío Villegas' long count of 24 opposition newspapers, *Historia moderna*, 9: 461. The names of the newspapers changed, but the tactics remained the same throughout the Porfiriato. The 1910 Molinista machine, for instance, cranked out ten newspapers' worth of political propaganda. A complete list of the newspapers supporting the Molinistas in Mexico City and Yucatán is found in López, *El verdadero Yucatán*, 65.

58. By 1903, two-thirds of all Mexican governors were civilians and, as Knight relates, "those [military officers] who survived and prospered politically were those, like [Bernardo Reyes], who displayed administrative talents as well as military skills." Knight, *Mexican Revolution*, 1: 17.

59. Traconis's ineptitude was only part of the problem. State revenues declined largely because of weak fiber prices, which in turn depressed the regional economy. It is instructive to note that during the Porfiriato, those governors who had the good fortune to rule during periods of high fiber prices, such as Guillermo Palomino (1886–89) and Olegario Molina (1902–6), are considered to have been the state's best administrators, while those who governed during bust cycles, such as Octavio Rosado, Traconis, and his successor, Carlos Peón Machado, are not held in high regard. Traconis's fiscal difficulties were so embarrassing, however, that he was forced to take the unprecedented step of publishing a summation of his administration's actions and accomplishments one year before his term ended, to justify his actions. Pérez Peniche, *Reseña histórica*, esp. 122–28.

60. Peón Machado, who had fought with Molina against the empire and had served briefly as vice governor in Eligio Ancona's administration when the Tuxtepec rebellion broke out, inherited the mantle of liberal leadership in the state. Menéndez Rodríguez, "La agonía."

61. The ensuing analysis integrates standard primary and secondary accounts of the 1897 campaign with detailed correspondence in CGPD. Given the historiographical controversy surrounding this event, it is surprising that the rich cache of letters and memoranda in the Díaz archives has never been analyzed previously.

62. Jacqueline Rice's research on the 1892 Liberal Union convention, the nucleus of what came to be known as the *científicos*, confirms the significant role regional expatriates played in national politics. See Rice.

63. On Peón Machado's extended residence in Mexico City, see Cosío Villegas, *Historia moderna*, 9: 461–67. Cantón's connections with Baranda and his stay in the capital as a deputy and a senator have already been noted. Molina, who eagerly embraced the *científico* clique, cemented his ties when his daughter married federal deputy Carlos Casasús, son of prominent *científico* Joaquín Casasús. Molina also spent the two years before he became Yucatán's governor living in the Distrito Federal, serving as Oaxaca's senator (1900–1902). See Camp, 41, 147–48. Technically, Molina remained governor of Yucatán until 1910, but in late 1906 he joined Díaz's cabinet as minister of development. His gubernatorial term was filled by Enrique Muñoz Arístegui.

64. For a discussion of these cliques see Chapter 3; Katz, "Mexico: Restored Republic and Porfiriato," esp. 38–39; Leal; and Guerra, esp. 1: chap. 2.

65. Bulnes identifies the *científico* inner circle as "a group of intellectuals, never exceeding fifteen in number, organized with the idea of reforming the dictatorship, making it as liberal and just as possible, and unquestionably expecting to be named the successors of the dictatorial power." *Whole Truth*, 213.

66. Its leaders included General Manuel González and, later, General Bernardo Reyes. Rodolfo Reyes traces the origins of the *científico-militar* split to the 1893 gubernatorial election in Coahuila. Romero Rubio and his private secretary, Rosendo Pineda, supported the reelection of Colonel Garza Galán, while Bernardo Reyes wanted a change. From that moment on, Rodolfo Reyes contends, each side was suspicious of the other. *De mi vida*, 19. Ramón Prida dates the split earlier: in 1892, with Reyes's opposition to the *científico*-controlled National Liberal Union.

67. Naturally the newspaper was edited by a relative—nephew Delio Moreno Cantón.

68. Menéndez Rodríguez, "La agonía."

69. Cantón's braintrust included several erstwhile conservatives who would fill important posts in his administration. See Bolio Ontiveros, *Yucatán en la dictadura*, 22; Acereto, "Historia política," 341.

70. Peón Machado also reorganized statewide tax-collection procedures and carried out the federally mandated abolition of intrastate sales taxes (*alcabalas*), a move that generated a significant increase in revenues but annoyed many Yucatecans. Roberto Casellas Rivas, Peón Machado's treasurer, reported that the new property appraisal method yielded $26,850,192 (pesos) in its first year, five times the amount collected the previous year by the old method. Casellas Rivas argued that the new system was necessary because in the past, the state, perennially in debt, had been forced to borrow money from the private sector to pay employees' salaries. CGPD, Casellas Rivas to Díaz, 22:22:010669-70, Aug. 6, 1897; and Peón Machado to Díaz, 22:7:003143, Mar. 12, 1897. Throughout the book, the dollar sign refers to pesos unless otherwise noted.

71. CGPD, Díaz to Cantón, 22:4:001660, Feb. 11, 1897.

72. CGPD, Cantón to Díaz, 22:8:003918, Feb. 26, 1897. On Gran Club organizing, see Alfonso Cámara y Cámara to Díaz, 22:6:002781-82, Mar. 10, 1897.

73. CGPD, Peón Machado to Díaz, 22:5:002297, Feb. 6, 1897.

74. Díaz to Peón Machado and Vice Governor José Palomeque, 22:4:001590, Feb. 18, 1897. Cantón, instructed by Díaz, kept the secret. In the Feb. 11 letter, Díaz said he would send Cantón a secret "code for telegraph messages with clear instructions for its use." Cantón had heard the good news even before receiving Díaz's letter: Baranda had sent a telegram on Feb. 13 to a mutual friend, state deputy José Domínguez Peón, which arrived first. CGPD, Cantón to Díaz, 22:4:001589, Feb. 17, 1897.

75. Menéndez Rodríguez, "La agonía."

76. Throughout June, both *camarillas* sent Díaz hundreds of signatures; e.g., 22:16:007965-8000. Both *camarillas* heavily utilized political propaganda; 46 political publications appeared throughout the state during the 1897 campaign. González Padilla, *Yucatán: política y poder*, 16–17.

77. See, e.g., CGPD, Convención Democrática Yucateca to Díaz, 22:11:005176, Mar. 1897; and Arcadio Escobedo to Díaz, 22:12:005896, Apr. 27, 1897. The Cantonistas' blistering attack on Manzanilla's tactics is found in *LO*, May 22, 1897, no. 8.

78. CGPD, Peón Machado, quoted in Escobedo, to Díaz, 22:8:003719, Mar. 19, 1897. In his private correspondence to the president, Peón Machado was not as circumspect. He inveighed repeatedly against the opposition, labeling them "intransigent conservatives" and warning Díaz of Cantón's friendship with the federal *jefe de la zona*, Lorenzo García. Peón Machado to Díaz, 22:7:003143 and 22:8:003117, Mar. 12 and 20, 1897.

79. CGPD, letters to Díaz from Peoncista supporters, 22:6:002783 and 22:6:002794, Mar. 1897; Díaz to Domínguez Peón, 22:8:003686, n.d.; and Domínguez Peón to Díaz, 22:9:004451, Apr. 3, 1897.

80. The delegates were Convención chief Manzanilla, who was also treasurer of the Mérida City Council; José E. Castillo, a judge; Manuel Irigoyen Lara, in charge of the Mérida Ministerio Público office; Arturo Escalante Galera, director of the Escuela Correccional; and Aurelio Gamboa, a state deputy. The Cantonista press made political hay of the commission's ties to Peón Machado's administration. *LO*, Apr. 10, 1897, no. 2, and May 8, 1897, no. 6. The Mexico City daily *ElUn* reported that the Peoncistas sharply criticized Joaquín Baranda's meddling during their interview. See González Padilla, *Yucatán: política y poder*, 18.

81. CGPD, Díaz to Peón Machado, 22:10:004928, Apr. 8, 1897.

82. Peón Machado hoped that his successor would be his vice governor, Dr. José Palomeque. CGPD, Peón Machado to Díaz, 22:10:004886, Apr. 23, 1897. Díaz's paternalistic reply was brief but unhelpful: "I will always value my personal friends." Díaz to Peón Machado, 22:10:004887, n.d.

83. Molina had economic reasons for supporting Cantón, and according to Menéndez Rodríguez, both Molinistas and Cantonistas strongly supported the clergy. For further discussion of the economic factors, see Chapter 4. On the clergy, see Menéndez Rodríguez, "La alianza clero-Molina." On Molina's support for Cantón, see Valadés's citation of a letter from Molina to Rosendo Pineda, June 11, 1897, in *El porfirismo*, 1: 28–29; and Menéndez Rodríguez, who documents two letters from Molinistas to Díaz and a fabricated letter written by supporters of *científico* Manuel Sierra Méndez in Cozumel. The Cozumel letter was made to look as if it were written by the Convención Democrática Yucateca; it called for Peón Machado's reelection long after the Convención had switched horses and was backing Palomeque. The Peoncistas hurriedly disavowed the dirty trick. Menéndez Rodríguez, "La agonía," 7.

84. *LO*, June 19, 1897; *CyR*, May 9, 1897. Both also quoted in González Padilla, *Yucatán: política y poder*, 17–18.

85. On the arrest: CGPD, District Judge Castellanos to Díaz, 22:12:005663-64, May 15, 1897. The Cantonista press denied that its supporters had anything to do with the bombing. *LO*, May 4, 1897, no. 5. On García's warnings: CGPD, García to Díaz, 22:14:006750, June 9, 1897.

86. CGPD, Alvino Manzanilla to Díaz, 22:13:006279, May 9, 1897. For a discussion of rabble-rousing priests and Carlos Peón Machado's vigorous protest to Bishop Crescencio Carrillo y Ancona, see Menéndez Rodríguez, "La agonía."

87. CGPD, Baqueiro to Díaz, 22:9:004249-51, Mar. 26, 1897; Vales Castillo to Díaz, 22:18:00832, June 4, 1897; and Dondé Cámara to Díaz, 22:12:005810-12, May 7, 1897. José María Iturralde, a Cantonista and a former governor, conveyed similar sentiments to Díaz, 22:20:009999-010000, July 16, 1897.

88. CGPD, Díaz to Manzanilla, 22:15:007459, June 17, 1897. It should be emphasized that Díaz's policy of watching and waiting to see how provincial politics played out during the course of a gubernatorial campaign was his custom. See Martínez and Chassen, esp. 534–35.

89. Menéndez Rodríguez, "La agonía."

90. *DdH* and *ET* reported that the Cantonistas were beaming when they left their one-and-a-half-hour meeting with Díaz. Cosío Villegas, *Historia moderna*, 9: 461–67.

91. Mérida's *jefe político* had banned public demonstrations in early July. CGPD, Escobedo to Díaz, 22:21:010418, Aug. 13, 1897; Urzáiz Rodríguez, 133–34. Here Cantón's downtown home is the one on Calle 64 and 63, not the palace built between 1904 and 1911 on the Paseo de Montejo. The text of Cantón's acceptance speech is reproduced in Cantón Rosado, 184–86.

92. In 1872, when Cirerol attempted to extend his gubernatorial term for two more years, Cantón led a rebellion against the governor. Cantón Rosado, 52–56. It may well be that this ancient vendetta resurfaced in 1911, when Morenistas (the Cantonistas' descendants) razed Cirerol's sugar mill, Catmís, in Peto *partido*, and brutally murdered his sons. See Chap. 7; and CGPD, Cámara y Cámara to Díaz, 22:21:010489-97, Aug. 17, 1897.

93. Menéndez Rodríguez cites two letters, dated Aug. 9 and 10, 1897, the former from Eligio Erosa in Espita to Peoncista leader Aurelio Gamboa, the latter from Santiago Osorio to Manzanilla, suggesting that the incumbents were ready to fight

Cantón's imposition. Menéndez Rodríguez argues that many liberal *hacendados* and merchants, who had joined the Gran Club Liberal because they resented Peón Machado's economic policies, were appalled by Cantón's *destape* and returned home to the liberals. This is difficult to believe, because it posits that elites would be deserting the Cantonista *camarilla* at precisely the moment when they would be rewarded for their support. Menéndez Rodríguez, "La agonía."

94. Most accounts either castigate or exonerate one of the political groups in question. For the Cantonista version, see *RdM*, Aug. 15, 1897, no. 3285. Peón Machado's position is brought out in some judicial documents found in the private collection of Menéndez Rodríguez: "Instancia del Lic. Alvino Manzanilla pidiendo que el Juzgado del Distrito se avoque el concocimiento de la causa que se sigue al Juez local por los sucesos del 11 de agosto en la plaza principal de Mérida," 1897; and "Escrito a la Suprema Corte de Justicia sobre el amparo que le dictó contra mi [Manzanilla] con motivo de los sucesos del 11 de agosto de 1897," 1898. The most dispassionate analysis comes from an eyewitness, Felipe Pérez Alcalá, "Los sucesos del 11 de agosto." Pérez Alcalá was a longtime friend of Pancho Cantón but held a post in the Peón Machado administration. Even though his retelling favors the incumbents, it is the most plausible. We rely heavily on his discussion.

95. Indeed, this was not the first time that the Plaza de las Armas would live up to its name. Meridanos remembered that in 1873, Cantón's followers confronted authorities in the plaza with tragic results. Menéndez, *Noventa años*, 172–74.

96. CGPD, Pérez Alcalá to Díaz, 22:21:010173-82, Aug. 14, 1897; and Urzáiz Rodríguez, 134.

97. CGPD, Traconis to Díaz, 22:20:009917, July 22, 1897.

98. Pérez Alcalá, "Los sucesos"; CGPD, Cámara y Cámara to Díaz, 22:21: 010489-97, Aug. 17, 1897. Acereto blames Peón Machado for not taking stronger measures. Acereto, 341.

99. Pérez Alcalá, "Los sucesos."

100. CGPD, Escobedo to Díaz, 22:21:010418, Aug. 13, 1897; Cantón to Díaz, 22:22:010644-46, Aug. 14, 1897; Pérez Alcalá, "Los sucesos"; and Cosío Villegas, *Historia moderna*, 9: 467.

101. AGEY, RJ, "Toca al certificado de constancias librado con motivo del recurso de apelación interpuesto por el Lic. Serapio Rendón como defensor de Federico Aguilar contra el auto de formal prisión dictado en la causa que se le sigue por ultrajes a un funcionario público," caja 296, 1897.

102. Ibid. corroborates the positive steps taken by Cámara y Cámara and Moreno Cantón.

103. CGPD, Cantón to Díaz, 22:22:010644-46, Aug. 14, 1897; and Pérez Alcalá, "Los sucesos."

104. The Cantonista newspaper wrote twelve years later that after the shooting began in the plaza, some partisans went to Pancho Cantón's residence and implored him to arm his followers, but he refused. *LC*, Aug. 11, 1909.

105. Casualty figures vary. Pérez Alcalá states three dead and six wounded were attended to that night. Urzáiz Rodríguez, 136, says that two of the wounded died soon thereafter. Menéndez Rodríguez, "La agonía," with access to Carlos Peón's private archives, contends that casualties amounted to three dead and eleven wounded. But *LC*, Aug. 11, 1909, twelve years after the altercation, gives a detailed accounting of the incident, including names and occupations of the casualties. That estimate is used here.

106. CGPD, Escobedo to Díaz, 22:21:010418, Aug. 13, 1897; and Cantón to Díaz, 22:22:010644-46, Aug. 14, 1897.

107. CGPD, Pérez Alcalá to Díaz, 22:21:010187-91, Aug. 18, 1897.

108. CGPD, Peón Machado to Díaz, 22:23:011240, Aug. 14, 1897.

109. Altercations took place in Valladolid, where a national guard colonel shot at the house of a prominent Cantonista; in Temax, where rocks were thrown at Pancho Cantón's railway depot; and in Izamal, where the national guard ripped down Cantonista posters. On the Valladolid incident see *RdM*, Aug. 17, 1897, no. 3286. On incidents in Temax and Izamal, see CGPD, Cámara y Cámara to Díaz, 22:21:010489-97, Aug. 17, 1897.

110. The *jefe político*'s report, which places the blame squarely on the Cantonistas, is found in *DO*, Aug. 12, 1897.

111. CGPD, "Noticias de las causas instruidas con motivo de los sucesos del 11 de agosto de 1897 que están pendientes de resolución," 26:27:010711-712, Oct. 15, 1897.

112. CGPD, Cámara y Cámara to Díaz, 22:21:010489-97, Aug. 17, 1897. Urzáiz Rodríguez, 138, believes that Peón Machado advised the state deputies that the struggle was lost and that they should acquiesce to the new regime.

113. CGPD, Peón Machado to Díaz, 22:23:011227, Aug. 25, 1897.

114. CGPD, Díaz to Peón Machado, 22:23:011228, Aug. 31, 1897.

115. Ibid.

116. Menéndez Rodríguez, "La agonía." Peón Machado's problems were far from over, however. He would be a casualty of the 1907 panic (see Chap. 4).

117. *RdM*, Dec. 28, 1897; and "Escrito a la Suprema Corte." Indeed, by 1901, Manzanilla felt comfortable enough to ask Díaz to help him secure a position for his son in Olegario Molina's administration. In the spirit of "let bygones be bygones," Díaz complied and told Manzanilla he would personally write Molina. CGPD, Manzanilla to Díaz, 26:24:009487; and Díaz to Manzanilla, 26:24:000488, Sept. 26, 1897.

118. See Lapointe, esp. chap. 8; Canto López, *El territorio de Quintana Roo*; and Echánove Trujillo. *Cruzob* is the Mayanized plural of the word *cross*. The rebel Maya referred to themselves as the "people of the cross." From 1850 on, their rebellion was fueled by a revitalization movement centering on a miraculous Maya-speaking cross. See Reed, pt. 3; Bricker, 103–18; Joseph, *Rediscovering the Past*, 44–48.

119. The state government stationed troops in Valladolid and Tekax to protect the area from *cruzob* incursions and offered settlers a five-year exemption from the *leva*. Sentries (or *bomberos*, because they detonated bombs to alert settlers) were stationed on the fringes of these frontier communities. González Navarro, *Raza y tierra*, 216; Pérez Peniche, *Reseña histórica*, 44, 79.

120. See Wells, *Yucatán's Gilded Age*, 95–96.

121. On the sacking of Tixhualahtún, see Acereto, 335; and Lapointe, 146. On Rubio Alpuche's proposal, see González Navarro, *Raza y tierra*, 216.

122. Acereto, 347–48.

123. Ibid., 346.

124. Lapointe, 141.

125. Pérez Peniche, *Reseña histórica*, 51–52.

126. Lapointe, 144–47.

127. Konrad, esp. 152–54.

128. CGPD, Sierra Méndez to Díaz, 22:18:008610, June 15, 1897.

129. See Katz, "Mexico: Restored Republic," 14, 42–46; and Hu-Dehart, *Yaqui Resistance*.

130. CGPD, General Ignacio Bravo to Díaz, 30:25:009756, June 23, 1905.

131. Néstor Rubio Alpuche published a detailed commentary on Yucatán's claim to British Honduras, arguing convincingly that the British were entitled only to have usufruct over Belize. *Belice, apuntes históricos*. The national government believed

that the Yucatecan public was mistaken in claiming that Belize belonged to Mexico and that Great Britain had usurped the territory. While it was true that Belize pertained to the Captaincy General of Yucatán, and that the concessions to cut wood given to English colonists did not imply a loss of territorial sovereignty, it was also no less certain that Belize had never pertained to Mexico as an independent nation. Those who said Mexico had a right to British Honduras, Foreign Minister Ignacio Mariscal argued, would have to use the same reasoning regarding Guatemala's claim to Chiapas, a claim that Mexicans had long and bitterly contested. See García Granados, 3: 26–28.

132. See Pérez Peniche, *Reseña histórica*, 53–55. For an overview of Mexican-British diplomacy, see Cosío Villegas, *Historia moderna*, 5: 715–916. Although Díaz agreed in principle with British diplomats on the boundary treaty in 1889, he delayed signing the treaty until 1893 because of Yucatecan opposition. Lapointe, chap. 8.

133. Konrad, 153; Lapointe, 152–53. On the documents discovered at the Colonial Record Office, Konrad, personal communication, Dec. 9, 1992.

134. See Baranda, 2: chaps. 11–12.

135. Luis Cabrera, categorizing *científicos*, placed Manuel Sierra Méndez along with other prominent attorneys, just below the most powerful members of the clique. Cosío Villegas, *Historia moderna*, 9: 858.

136. E.g., CGPD, Sierra Méndez to Díaz, June 6, 9, 16, and 29, 1897. Typical was a memo including a copy of the *British Honduras Government Gazette*, where the colonial secretary, E. B. Sweet-Escott, described the circumscribed conditions under which licensed and unlicensed merchants were permitted to sell guns, powder, and shot. In another report, Sierra Méndez relayed military intelligence from a trusted informant, British merchant J. E. Plummer, who had just met with *cruzob* and *pacífico caciques* in Belize. The *pacíficos* received their name after ending their rebellion and signing a truce with the state government in 1853. On the *pacíficos*, see Bojórquez Urzáiz, "Estructura agraria" and "Regionalización de la política agraria"; and Joseph, *Rediscovering the Past*, 44–52.

137. The idea for a federal territory did not originate with Sierra Méndez; interestingly, it was advanced by General Teodosio Canto in the late 1870s. Díaz believed that the time was not right for such an initiative. Lapointe, 143–44.

138. Sierra Méndez said he had broached the subject of the land grants with Governors Traconis and Peón Machado, and both had favored the idea. But they were too weak to pass such a law through their legislatures because it threatened the interests of powerful landowners, who feared that their peons would forsake the henequen zone to homestead on the public lands. CGPD, Sierra Méndez to Díaz, "Apuntes breves." The secretary of development also toyed with the idea, but nothing came of it. González Navarro, *Raza y tierra*, 216–17.

139. Menéndez Rodríguez, "La agonía."

140. CGPD, Sierra Méndez to Díaz, "Apuntes breves."

141. On El Cuyo, see Konrad, 157–58, and Lapointe, 149. Also "Extract of Report Presented by Mr. Angel Rívas."

142. See Menéndez Rodríguez, "La agonía." Nowhere in the copious 1897 correspondence between Peón Machado and Díaz in CGPD is there the slightest indication that the governor did not back federal development policies. See esp. Peón Machado to Díaz, 22:13:006349, May 1, 1897. In 1894 Peón Machado raised an objection to the Mariscal–St. John treaty and insisted that the treaty include a clause permitting Mexican ships unrestricted access to the Bay of Chetumal. This apparently helped delay the treaty's ratification until 1897. Lapointe contends that Peón Ma-

chado and his wealthy relatives, the Escalantes, were exploring investment possibilities with British and North American entrepreneurs in the region. Lapointe, 152–53.

143. CGPD, Sierra Méndez to Díaz, "Apuntes breves," June 1897.

144. Ibid. It is interesting that even a trusted political confidant like Sierra Méndez was kept guessing about the *destape* at that late date. Four years later, Don Porfirio heeded Sierra Méndez's call for a civilian in the statehouse, choosing the technocrat Molina to succeed Pancho Cantón.

145. Lapointe, *Los mayas rebeldes*, 94–95, 153–54.

146. For a detailed discussion of the FCSO project, see Wells, *Yucatán's Gilded Age*, chap. 4. From the outset, the project was so risky that it had difficulty attracting investors from Mexico City, Yucatán, and abroad. The company went bankrupt in 1901 after laying less than fifteen kilometers of track.

147. CGPD, Cantón to Díaz, Apr. 28, 1897.

148. Quoted in Cantón Rosado, 185.

149. CGPD, Sierra Méndez to Díaz, 22:11:005259-65, n.d. [spring 1897].

150. CGPD, Sierra Méndez to Díaz, "Apuntes breves"; Sierra Méndez to Díaz, "Apuntes sobre la campaña de indios presentando en cróquis explicatorio de ellos," 22:17:008128-40, July 12, 1897; and Cantón Rosado, 71–73.

151. By 1901 the State Treasury was depleted and was forced to take out a loan of three hundred thousand pesos from the Banco Nacional. In June 1901, the federal government assumed payment of state national guard salaries. Wells, *Yucatán's Gilded Age*, 105–6.

152. Baranda, 2: 122.

153. Mestre Ghigliazza, 257.

154. Ibid. On the losses sustained by federal and state forces during the Caste War, see AGEY, RPE, "Documentos que se refiere a los reemplazos remitidos como contingente de sangre de esto Estado en los años de 1907 para atrás," Sept. 9, 1902. On the state's heavy financial expenditures, see the document *Memoria de los actos del Gobernador Constitucional*, 26. Molina asked that blacks from Belize replace Maya campesinos; Díaz agreed. Requests to reduce Yucatán's recruits for the war effort are found in CGPD, Cantón in Díaz, 26:31:012330-31, Oct. 31, 1901; and Molina to Díaz, 26:33:013178, Dec. 4, 1901.

155. Cantón's correspondence with Díaz is found in Cantón Rosado, 194–200. Mena Brito wildly claims that in the summer of 1901, Díaz offered Cantón a second term as governor and then told him about the upcoming partition. But according to this polemical account, Cantón turned down his president because of the federal government's plan to create a new territory. Mena Brito, 2: 180.

156. Wells, "All in the Family."

157. CGPD, Sierra Méndez to Díaz, 26:32:012568 and 012591, Nov. 7 and 15, 1901. The dismemberment of Yucatán was unconstitutional, according to the eminent jurist Emilio Rabasa. See Rabasa, 236.

158. CGPD, Molina to Díaz, 26:33:01373, Dec. 3, 1901. The local press waged a fierce campaign over the establishment of the new territory. The Cantonista paper, *RdM*, opposed the partition, while *EdC*, the Molinista paper, agreed with the federal government's position. See, e.g., *RdM*, Nov. 17, 1901; and *EdC*, Feb. 6, 1902.

159. Lapointe, 165.

160. On Plummer, see CGPD, Sierra Méndez to Díaz, 26:29:011216-7, Oct. 4, 1901; and Díaz's response, 011218, undated. Both Molina's and Peón Losa's concessions were contracted out to Plummer. Lapointe, 214; Wells, *Yucatán's Gilded Age*, 106–10.

161. See Konrad, 154–59; Wells, *Yucatán's Gilded Age*, 106–10.

162. On the failed concessions, see Wells, *Yucatán's Gilded Age*, 106–10; Konrad, 154–59, quote, 159.

163. Rogelio Fernández Guell, quoted in Bulnes, *The Whole Truth*, 129.

164. Knight, *Mexican Revolution*, 1: 20.

165. *LC*, Aug. 11, 1909.

## CHAPTER 3

1. For an authoritative review of the historical literature on the Porfirian regime, see Benjamin and Ocasio-Meléndez.

2. The last gasp of regional *caciquismo* occurred in 1893, when small revolts led by disgruntled military officers broke out in Coahuila and Guerrero. Díaz moved quickly to crush the rebellions and execute the ringleaders. See Iturribarría, 252.

3. López-Portillo y Rojas and Bulnes paint a picture of a scheming, conniving dictator, while García Granados's interpretation is more judicious. López-Portillo y Rojas; Bulnes, *El verdadero Díaz*; and García Granados, esp. 3: 68, 172–73. Biographies of the dictator provide ample evidence to sustain both views; e.g., Beals, *Porfirio Díaz*; Zayas Enríquez, *Porfirio Díaz*; Godoy; Fornaro; and Hannay. For an overview of the biographical literature see Cosío Villegas, "El porfiriato: su historiografía."

4. Sierra, 361–62.

5. Bulnes, *Whole Truth About Mexico*, 17.

6. Olegario Molina (Yucatán) and Enrique Creel (Chihuahua), both *científicos*, were named secretary of development and secretary of foreign relations, in 1907 and 1910, respectively.

7. Bulnes, *Whole Truth*, 116.

8. Quoted in García Granados, 3: 64.

9. Don Porfirio had perfected the art of divide and rule during the 1880s when, under the guise of "conciliation," he played off cabinet ministers who supported Manuel González against former Lerdistas and ex-Tuxtepecistas. Prida, 1: 80, 83.

10. In 1896, e.g., responding to an executive initiative, a reform was rushed through Congress mandating that in the event that the president was disabled, the secretary of foreign relations (followed by the secretary of *gobernación*) would substitute until Congress named a replacement. Cosío Villegas, *Historia moderna*, 9: 341–43.

11. Baranda and his faction subsidized *La Patria*, while the *científicos* gave four thousand pesos a month to *El Universal*. Ibid., 9: 854. Rodolfo Reyes also worked tirelessly through the press to defame the *científicos*. *De mi vida*, 23. See also Didapp, *Partidos políticos, Gobiernos militares*, and *La nación y sus gobernantes*.

12. Bulnes, *Whole Truth*, 114.

13. García Granados, 3: 54.

14. The *científicos* were not a political party per se but an aristocratic elite that served at the dictator's pleasure. For a good analysis, see Iturribarría, 248.

15. Cosío Villegas, *Historia moderna*, 9: 381.

16. In early March 1898, Limantour journeyed to Monterrey to meet with General Reyes and discuss the presidential initiative. Valadés contends that Díaz's trip to Monterrey in December, with Limantour in tow, was a good-faith effort by the dictator to fashion a compromise. *El porfirismo*, 1: 53. Not surprisingly, Rodolfo Reyes demurs, contending that Díaz played the two off against each other. *De mi vida*, 23. See also Cosío Villegas, *Historia moderna*, 9: 397–99; and Niemeyer, 91–109.

17. *Whole Truth*, 118.

18. See Valadés, *El porfirismo*, 1: 57; and Castillo, 36, 69. All Limantour could do from then on was lamely protest that he had never had any interest in partisan politics and was content to stay on as treasury minister. See Limantour, "Documentos inéditos." Bulnes cites Limantour's failing health as another reason why the compromise fell apart. *El verdadero Díaz*, 315–16. In 1903, when Limantour obviously was no longer a threat to Díaz in the upcoming election and when the minister was under serious attack by his opponents, the dictator took the extraordinary step of publishing a defense of Limantour's nationality in the *Diario Oficial*, repudiating the Baranda *dictamen*. García Granados, 3: 35–39, 80.

19. Castillo, 22–24, 33, 116.

20. On González Cosío, see Valadés, *El porfirismo*, 1: 7–12; García Granados, 3: 6; and Castillo, 33.

21. Prida compiled an interesting, if flawed, scorecard of the governors' support for the competing factions. Overrating his group's position, Prida believed that the *científicos* counted on the support of ten governors, with seventeen enemies and four "indifferent." Prida, 1: 110. See also Cosío Villegas, *Historia moderna*, 9: 849–50.

22. See, e.g., Guerra.

23. Prida, 1: 105–6.

24. The liberal argument is made by Didapp, *Partidos políticos*; the *científico* response can be found in Sierra; and Bulnes, *El verdadero Díaz*, 78–79.

25. Prida, 1: 83; Hale, *Transformation of Liberalism*, 137n; Cosío Villegas, *Historia moderna*, 9: 758–61; Bulnes, *El verdadero Díaz*, 183; and García Granados, 2: 251–52.

26. Valadés, who had access to Baranda's personal archive, cites his mercurial personality. *El porfirismo*, 1: 57. Beals branded Baranda a false symbol of liberalism. *Porfirio Díaz*, 287. Castillo, a journalist who wrote for the Barandista press, naturally portrayed his *patrón* as a *puro*. Castillo, 31–33.

27. For a partial list of journalists the regime arrested throughout the 1880s and early 1890s, see Beals, *Porfirio Díaz*, 267–71.

28. García Granados, 2: 35. See also Bulnes, *El verdadero Díaz*, 52; and Beals, *Porfirio Díaz*, 283–84. On the harassment of García Granados, see Prida, 1: 97. On Baranda's appointment of friends and clients to the judiciary, see Castillo, 126. Prida also wrote firsthand of Porfirian press persecution. Prida, 1: 85–86. Even U.S. ambassador Henry Lane Wilson, an otherwise strong advocate of the dictatorship, wrote in his *Diplomatic Episodes* of a "lame, incompetent, corrupt judiciary." Quoted in Beals, *Porfirio Díaz*, 295.

29. Castillo, 101.

30. Although the congressional debate swirled around Sierra's call for constitutional reform, a bill to ensure judicial autonomy clearly reflected the rival factions' growing rift. After all, to debate constitutional niceties during the dictatorship's heyday was not only futile, it was nearly absurd. Barandistas rightfully saw the initiative as a premeditated attack on their patron, which, if successful, would threaten their livelihood. The metropolitan newspapers, reflecting the political fault lines of the national *camarillas*, worked overtime spewing invective to persuade the deputies and, more important, the president to endorse their position. This first pitched battle between the *científicos* and Baranda ended in defeat for Sierra. After a watered-down version of the bill passed the House of Deputies, Díaz let the matter die in the Senate; he had little interest in fostering an independent judiciary. Hale sees the defeat of the measure as the death knell of doctrinaire liberalism, which "after 1893 . . . [had] an increasingly underground and ultimately revolutionary history in which classic liberal precepts became infused with new doctrines of social radicalism." *Transforma-*

*tion of Liberalism*, 121. See also Cosío Villegas, *Historia moderna*, 9: 670–76. In a quintessentially Porfirian move, Justo Sierra became chief justice of the Supreme Court soon after the measure died in Congress.

31. The reasons for Baranda's resignation are unclear. Those who have speculated include García Granados, 3: 74–75; Bulnes, *El verdadero Díaz*, 317–18, 332; Beals, *Porfirio Díaz*, 353; Castillo, 43, 69–71; and Prida, 1: 93. Baranda turned down a post as ambassador to France. He was later named to the board of directors of the Banco de Londrés y México. Castillo, 1: 154–55. He did not disappear from the political scene, however. Some historians believe he staged the controversial 1908 Creelman interview, in which Díaz intimated that he might be ready to step down and which ultimately undermined the *científicos'* succession plans. Cosío Villegas, *Historia moderna*, 9: 505. Bulnes, who plainly lost no love for the former secretary of justice, wrote, "The hatred for the Baranda family can only be calculated by using logarithmic tables." *El verdadero Díaz*, 332.

32. The aristocratic treasury minister had earned the military's lasting enmity when he slashed its budget and reduced the size of the army. Cosío Villegas, *Historia moderna*, 9: 346, 401, 616–18.

33. Valadés, *El porfirismo*, 1: 60; R. Reyes, 23; Luna, 68–69; García Granados, 3: 79; Niemeyer, 107–9; and Bryan, "Mexican Politics in Transition," 103.

34. Cosío Villegas, *Historia moderna*, 9: 433–34.

35. By 1911 the cabinet was filled with *científicos*. Ibid., 9: 346–48, 397–99, 401, 417, 616–18, 846–47; García Granados, 3: 179; Limantour, *Apuntes sobre mi vida política*, 136–37, 142–43; and Bulnes, *El verdadero Díaz*, 340. On the creation of the vice presidency, see García Granados, 3: 172; and Luna, 80, 93. See also Querido Moheno, esp. chap. 3.

36. Nor did Yucatán alone feel the effects of the political shakeup. Two key states, Oaxaca and Chihuahua, also elected *científico* governors, in 1902 and 1903, respectively. See Martínez and Chassen.

37. Molina shared the *científicos'* preference for secondary and professional education. Yucatán's professional school budget in 1900 amounted to $217,326; by 1907 it had risen to $412,958. Twenty percent of the state's budget was spent on education in 1910; indeed, Yucatán spent more money on education per inhabitant than any other state. Despite this impressive record, little of it went toward primary schools. González Navarro, in Cosío Villegas, *Historia moderna*, 4: 674–75.

38. This analysis is gleaned from largely apologistic accounts of his first term. See Urzáiz Rodríguez, 141–72; *Mensajes del (Gobernador Constitucional)*; Novelo; Casasús; and Carreno. For more on the public works projects, see Chap. 5.

39. A perfect example of the criticism is in *EPC*, Jan. 17, 1904. The nepotism controversy was not limited to Yucatán. Bulnes ably demonstrates that Díaz's ministers took good care of their relatives. *El verdadero Díaz*, chap. 7.

40. For a fuller examination of the far-flung economic empire of Molina and his *parentesco*, see Wells, "Family Elites."

41. *EPC*, Dec. 13, 1903.

42. Escoffié, who became Yucatán's journalistic gadfly, was arrested on 51 separate occasions. Interview, Menéndez Rodríguez, July 5, 1987.

43. AGEY, RJ, "Causa instruida a Carlos P. Escoffié por el delito de calumnia," caja 730, 1909.

44. The regime took a series of steps in the mid-1880s to crack down on freedom of the press. Not only was an author liable for his columns, but the editor, printer, and even those who distributed the newspaper could be jailed. Prida, 1: 99–101. For similar tactics in Oaxaca, see Martínez and Chassen, 529.

45. On the Magonistas, see Flores Magón; Anderson, "Mexican Workers"; Cockroft; and Brown. A. Knight emphasizes the Magonistas' middle-class appeal in "Intellectuals in the Mexican Revolution." Ricardo Flores Magón graphically recounts the horrors of Belém in Silva Herzog, 1: 65–66; and Fornaro, chap. 7.

46. Quotations from Pérez Ponce, 5–6. He was not stretching the truth when he proudly declared that he was steeped in the tradition of doctrinaire liberalism. One strain of Mexican liberalism harked back to Reforma intellectuals, such as Ponciano Arriaga and Ignacio Ramírez, and emphasized social justice. Pérez Ponce's difficulties with Peón Machado's administration came to a head when Mérida's district prefect allegedly tried to have him shot, right in front of the police station. Pérez Ponce killed his aggressor, was sentenced to jail for homicide for a year and a half, but was released when authorities conceded that he had acted in self-defense. On his exploits, see González Padilla, *Yucatán: política y poder*, 117–19, n. 27, which includes a biography written by three revolutionary generals, Antonio J. Villarreal, Cándido Aguilar, and Ramón Frausto. The biography was published on Apr. 23, 1917, in *ED*.

47. It is interesting that the story appeared in *Regeneración* before it was published in *Verdad y Justicia*. See *EPC*, Mar. 19, and June 11, 1905; and AGEY, RJ, "Toca a la causa seguida a Tomás Pérez Ponce por falsedad," caja 676, 1908. Audomaro Molina took exception to the charges. He invited Trinidad Sánchez Santos, editor of *EP*, to visit his haciendas and see how his peons were treated; then Molina published a pamphlet, *Constancias judiciales*, which sought to rebut—for the entire *hacendado* class—the muckraking journalism of Pérez Ponce and the Magonistas. Molina declared that his peons were well treated, well paid, and better off than the workers of many industrialized European nations. The label *negreros* (slavemasters), however, would not go away. During the last years of the Porfiriato, the Magonistas would return to haunt the Yucatecan elite. They persuaded North American socialist journalist John Kenneth Turner in 1909 to come and see firsthand the horrors of plantation life for indebted peons. Turner's sensational exposé, "Barbarous Mexico," serialized in *American Magazine*, provided the basis for a "black legend" that many still accept for Porfirian Yucatán. Significantly, campesinos still often refer to the prerevolutionary period as "the time of slavery." See González Navarro, *Raza y tierra*, esp. 206–8, and Cosío Villegas, *Historia moderna*, 4: 226–27.

48. Instead, Pérez Ponce was charged with slandering Audomaro Molina's reputation, as well as fraud—a trumped-up charge; the courts lamely argued that Canché's testimonial had not been properly witnessed. Tomás's brother Tirso was the defense attorney, later joined by other labor activists, including Urbano Espinosa. The judge who arrested both Tomás and Escoffié was Ignacio Hernández, known as "El Gran Turco" and, according to *EPC*, Audomaro Molina's good friend. After the arrest, the case was remanded to a trial judge, Miguel Losa, a prominent *hacendado* and another close Molina friend. *EPC*, Mar. 19, 1905.

49. The fraud charge was later overturned, but the state court of appeals sustained the indictment for defamation of character. AGEY, RJ, "Toca a la causa seguida a Tomás Pérez Ponce."

50. AGEY, RJ, "Urbano Espinosa, injurias a un funcionario público," caja 704, 1908. Espinosa was later absolved of the charges.

51. Molina responded by asking *científico* Joaquín Casasús to intercede on his behalf and ask Díaz to ensure that the Supreme Court denied the defendants' judgment. (Molina's daughter was married to Casasús's son.) Casasús wrote to Díaz, "I think it would set a grave precedent . . . if lawyers could enter the prison freely." CGPD, 30:24:009555, July 21, 1905. The high court, not surprisingly, rebuffed the defendants.

52. *La Humanidad*, Sept. 1, 1907.

53. Ibid., Sept. 8, 1907.

54. AGEY, RJ, "Toca a la causa seguida a José Dolores Sobrino Trejo y Agustín Pardo por conato de rebelión, apología de este delito, ataques a la Constitución del Estado y difamación contra éste," caja 685, 1908. Local officials had already targeted Sobrino Trejo as a troublemaker. See Gamboa, *Alcancé vivir*, 8.

55. Gamboa, *Alcancé vivir*, 7–11.

56. See Fornaro, chaps. 7, 8.

57. When *RdM*'s editor, Carlos R. Menéndez, finally opposed Molinista "continuismo" during the 1910 gubernatorial campaign, the newspaper's offices were ransacked and its printing presses smashed by unknown assailants. Menéndez was certain that Molinista thugs were the culprits. AGEY, RJ, "Causa seguida contra Alfonso Cámara y Cámara y socios por el delito de rebelión," 1909. Augusto L. Peón, a prominent Molinista and onetime president of the Mérida city council, held a controlling interest in *EdC*.

58. *RdM* did permit Tomás Pérez Ponce and his brother Tirso to publish letters criticizing the government's high-handed tactics and the lack of due process. Tomás's letter was written from prison. See Apr. 25. 1905. A new daily, *EPn*, was launched in March 1904 by Tabascan emigré José María Pino Suárez, who would later lead the Maderista opposition to the regime. Although *EPn* did oppose a second term for the governor, Pino Suárez preferred to raise social concerns, such as the plight of the working classes, particularly the evils of debt peonage and the use of bounty hunters to return escaped henequen workers. Yet even *EPn*'s muted criticism brought conflict with state authorities.

59. Solís Cámara, 26.

60. González Padilla, *Yucatán: política y poder*, 105; and CGPD, Molina to Díaz, 27:32:012757-60, Sept. 22, 1902; Cantón to Díaz, 27:26:010237-38, Sept. 17, 1902; Díaz to Molina, 27:27:010716, Sept. 23, 1902; Molina to Díaz, 27:34:013489, Oct. 29, 1902.

61. *RdM*, July 12, 1905. See also Apr. 4 and May 2, 1905.

62. Directors Primitivo Díaz and Federico Suárez were brought from Cuba. *EPC*, Oct. 18, 1903, no. 10.

63. Quoted in González Padilla, *Yucatán: política y poder*, 104.

64. For a comparative perspective on the *jefe político*'s role in the regulation of Porfirian town life, see French, "Progreso Forzado" and "In the Path of Progress"; and Romana Falcón, "Force and the Search for Consent."

65. See Knight, *Mexican Revolution*, 2: 25–26; and Beezley, "Madero: The 'Unknown' President," 4–5.

66. Some prefects were harder to remove than others because they had the support of local *hacendados*. E.g., Colonel Carlos Tapia was entrenched in Ticul *partido* for twelve years before Molina's arrival, despite his officious behavior. CGPD, Molina to Díaz, 26:30:011884, Oct. 28, 1901.

67. González Padilla, "La dirigencia política," 126–27.

68. Not surprisingly, documentation of collective action against management is meager. Only a few examples of (unsuccessful) organized working-class protest appear between the 1880s and the 1900s: two incidents involving railway workers and one dockworkers' strike. See Wells, "All in the Family"; and *EcM*, Jan. 17, 1903, no. 16.

69. For more detail on the urban working-class movement, see Spenser; Quintal Martín, "Breve historia"; Sierra Villarreal, unpublished ms.; Villanueva Mukul; and Gamboa, *Alcancé vivir*.

70. Knight, "Working Class and the Mexican Revolution," 58–59.

71. For a more detailed discussion of La Industrial, see Joseph and Wells, "Corporate Control of a Monocrop Economy."

72. Here we concur with Knight, who writes that these proletarians "eschewed both armed revolutionary commitment and violent street confrontations. . . . The political order was (broadly speaking) accepted. . . . Given half a chance, the organized working class opted for unionism and reformism." "Working Class," 71. Cf. Hart, *Revolutionary Mexico*, chap. 2.

73. See Parlee; and Hart, *Revolutionary Mexico*.

74. Knight has constructed a useful typology of the Porfirian urban working class, distinguishing the classic proletariat from three kinds of artisans: an embattled sector that unsuccessfully fought to hold its jobs against the new industrial regime; a dynamic artisanate that benefited materially from the Porfirian modernizing impulse; and village artisans who remained largely unaffected by the changes occurring in the provincial cities. The second type was most prominent in Yucatán. They "were familiar with the urban environment, which they and their families had long inhabited; they were neither recent rural migrants, nor classic proletarians . . . nor yet were they part of the large lumpenproletariat, the unemployed, the underemployed, vagrants, beggars, and criminals who constituted the *pelados*." "Working Class," 64.

75. Gamboa, *Alcancé vivir*, 7–11.

76. See Cosío Villegas, 4: 350–52.

77. For a discussion of working-class ideologies during the Porfiriato, see Anderson, *Outcasts in Their Own Land*, esp. the conclusions.

78. On worker-peasant alliances, see Buve, "Protesta de obreros"; and J. Meyer, "Historia de la vida social."

79. Federal officials also were preoccupied with "agitators." See Anderson, *Outcasts*, 174–75.

80. CGPD, Molina to Díaz, 30:40:015702, Oct. 30, 1905.

81. Ibid. Muñoz Arístegui picked up where Molina left off, deporting two Catalonian anarchists in the fall of 1907. Anderson, *Outcasts*, 314.

82. Gamboa, *Alcancé vivir*, 11; Villanueva Mukul, 126–27.

83. On Molinista organizing, see CGPD, Unión Popular Antirreeleccionista to Díaz, 30:27:010725-41, Aug. 7, 1905.

84. The Molinista newspaper, *EdC*, pushed for a constitutional amendment to permit its candidate to stand for reelection as early as January 1905. *RdM*, Jan. 19, 1905.

85. On Molina's nomination and the claim of eight thousand supporters, see CGPD, Molina to Díaz, and Díaz's response, 30:27:010751-52, Aug. 14 and 22, 1905; and Sierra Méndez to Díaz, 30:26:010118, Aug. 11, 1905. *EP* put the figure at four thousand.

86. *EP*, Aug. 23, 1905, cited in Cosío Villegas, *Historia moderna*, 9: 464–65.

87. Ibid., 465. For the names of the nominating committee members, all prominent Molinistas, see CGPD, Sierra Méndez to Díaz, 30:26:010118, Aug. 11, 1905.

88. *RdM*, Aug. 11, 1905.

89. To ensure tranquility and avert another *tumulto*, Muñoz Arístegui denied the opposition a permit to hold a counterdemonstration that evening. Pérez Alcalá, an informant during the 1897 campaign, continued to keep Díaz abreast of political affairs during the summer and fall of 1905. He reported that before August 10 the opposition had distributed "socialist" propaganda, and that local merchants had sold the Unión Popular pistols and ammunition. CGPD, Pérez Alcalá to Díaz, 30:27:010537, Aug. 17, 1905.

90. Urzáiz Rodríguez, 152–55.

91. The stroke left the general with a speech impediment. On Cantón's health problems, see López, 35, 54–55.

92. CGPD, Unión Popular to Díaz, Aug. 7, 1905.

93. González Padilla lists the following Unión Popular newspapers: *EPC, Verdad y Justicia, El Crítico, La Unión Popular,* and *El Pueblo Juez. Yucatán: política y poder,* 27.

94. Ibid.

95. While this exceptional report provides an unusually detailed description of Mérida's urban working classes during the 1905 campaign, we have not come across a comparably fine-grained analysis for the 1909–13 era. Unless otherwise noted, the following discussion draws on the secret police report, appended to a memorandum from Sierra Méndez to Díaz, CGPD, 30:31:012117-46, Sept. 23, 1905 (hereafter cited as secret police report).

96. E.g., CGPD, Cámara y Cámara to Díaz, 30:37:014521, n.d.

97. Quoted in secret police report.

98. *DdH,* Aug. 15, 1905, cited in Cosío Villegas, *Historia moderna,* 9: 466.

99. *RdM,* Aug. 19, 1905.

100. Secret police report.

101. Pérez Alcalá tried to convince Díaz that although the arrest appeared political, it really was not. Meneses responded that the suit was not only political but personal, noting an unusual conflict of interest: Arturo Castillo Rivas was both Molina's state treasurer and an heir to the estate of Meneses's wife, Mercedes Zavala Castillo. CGPD, Pérez Alcalá to Díaz, 30:29:011572-73, Sept. 4, 1905; Unión Popular to Díaz, 30:30:011732-36, Sept. 12, 1905; Meneses to Díaz, 30:36:014298, Sept. 22, 1905; and Meneses to Díaz, 30:40:015742, Nov. 21, 1905. All Meneses's letters were written from Juárez Penitentiary. See also *RdM,* Sept. 4, 1905.

102. On Ancona's murder, see Beals, *Porfirio Díaz,* 383.

103. Poblett Miranda, 15.

104. CGPD, Unión Popular to Díaz, Aug. 7, 1905. The Maya traditionally quarried *sahcab* as a construction material.

105. Ibid.

106. Quoted in Cosío Villegas, *Historia moderna,* 9: 465.

107. Quoted in secret police report.

108. Ibid.

109. Ibid.

110. Ibid. For a detailed discussion of the water problems created by the paving of the city streets, see Chap. 5.

111. Quoted in secret police report.

112. Ibid.

113. Ibid.

114. Rodney Anderson explains: "Article 4 of the constitution provided for freedom of the individual to contract, and Article 5 provided for freedom to withdraw from labor contracts, theoretically guaranteeing the right of workers to strike. Moreover, Article 9 provided for freedom of organization." *Outcasts,* 33. Porfirian penal code revisions had limited workers' right to strike. See Knight, "El liberalismo," 83, n. 81.

115. Guelatao, outside the city of Oaxaca, was Juárez's birthplace.

116. Epstein, "Understanding the Cap of Liberty," 117. See also Hunt.

117. Quoted in secret police report. Elsewhere in this speech, Avila referred to the city's complete name, Progreso de Castro, in honor of the city's founder.

118. Here again we concur with Knight that this appeal to traditional liberalism

by working-class intellectuals illustrates that they had much more in common with the middle class than with the rural peasantry. Knight, "Intellectuals in the Mexican Revolution."

119. Quoted in secret police report.

120. Knight, "Intellectuals in the Mexican Revolution," 21.

121. See Epstein, "Bred as a Mechanic"; and Kolakowski, 3: 240–41.

122. Gramsci, 3–4.

123. Epstein, "Bred as a Mechanic."

124. Quoted in secret police report.

125. Knight has uncovered similar animosity in other parts of Mexico. "Working Class," 58–59.

126. Anderson, *Outcasts*, 325. See also Knight, "El liberalismo," 75.

127. Secret police report.

128. CGPD, Sierra Méndez to Díaz, 30:31:012117, Sept. 23, 1905.

129. Cited in *RdM*, Sept. 6, 1905.

130. CGPD, Unión Popular to Díaz, 30:30:011732-36, Sept. 8, 1905; Sierra Méndez to Díaz, 30:37:014521, n.d.

131. CGPD, Cantón to Díaz, 30:31:012025, Sept. 19, 1905; and Díaz's reply, 012026, Sept. 28, 1905.

132. In addition to Cantón, Traconis, and Castillo, the potential candidates were Antonio Espinosa and Julio Rendón. All but Traconis were well-known Cantonistas. CGPD, Unión Popular to Díaz, 30:30:011774-78, Sept. 19, 1905; and Díaz's response, 30:30:011779, Sept. 28, 1905.

133. CGPD, Castillo to Díaz, 30:34:013228, Oct. 17, 1905; Castillo to Díaz, 30:37:014768-69, Oct. 31, 1905. Díaz's reply, 30:37:014771, Nov. 7, 1905, thanked Castillo for his decision. The figure for the size of the rally is a Molinista's conservative estimate. Pérez Alcalá to Díaz, 30:34:013380-81, Nov. 8, 1905.

134. *EPC*, Dec. 3, 1905; CGPD, Molina to Díaz, 30:40:015712, Nov. 7, 1905.

135. The discussion of the events surrounding the unrest in Kanasín draws on *RdM*'s thorough reporting of the incident on Nov. 29, 30, and Dec. 1, 1905.

136. *RdM*, Dec. 1, 1905.

137. Ibid.

138. Urzáiz Rodríguez, 154–55.

139. In addition to his political experience, Muñoz Arístegui had served as president of the Molinista Banco Yucateco, manager of La Industrial, and board member of the Hospital O'Horan. See Gamboa Ricalde, 1: 18; and Camp, 151–52.

140. Curiel was so well thought of in Yucatán that he was made an honorary citizen of the state. Gamboa Ricalde, 1: 93–94. See also Camp, 59–60. It comes as no surprise that Curiel was Cámara y Cámara's *compadre*.

141. On General Cantón's financial difficulties, see Wells, "All in the Family." On Moreno Cantón's bankruptcy, see López, 54–55; for his election in the *camarilla*, see Chaper 7.

142. On the origins of Maderismo and Pinismo in Yucatán, see Gamboa Ricalde, 1: 227; Quintal Martín, "Breve historia"; and Poblett Miranda. Ironically, Pino Suárez was the great-grandson of Pedro Sainz de Baranda, father of Joaquín Baranda and stepfather of Francisco Cantón.

CHAPTER 4

1. This section draws heavily on Joseph, *Revolution from Without*; Wells, *Yucatán's Gilded Age*; and Joseph and Wells, "Corporate Control of a Monocrop Economy."

2. Coatsworth estimates that export production rose from 9.3 percent of GDP at the beginning of the Porfiriato to 17.5 percent by 1910, more than twice as fast as the domestic sector. "State and the External Sector." For a thoughtful discussion of Latin America's economic problems and various theories raised to explain its underdevelopment, see Sheahan. On the competition between British and North American investment in Mexico during the Porfiriato, see Thorup.

3. Topik, "Image of Prosperity."

4. Quoted in A. Schmidt, 23.

5. Topik, "Economic Role of the State," 140. See also Coatsworth, "Obstacles to Economic Growth."

6. Not all Mexican tropical products enjoyed henequen's success in securing external markets during the Porfiriato. Products such as sugar, tobacco, and cotton experienced impressive gains but served the domestic market. Coffee and rubber did find markets abroad but never earned more than a marginal share of the world market. Henequen, chicle, and vanilla fared much better, dominating their international markets. Topik, "Image of Prosperity."

7. The only notable *casa* that managed to steer clear of regional politics during the 1890s and early 1900s was Henry W. Peabody and Company. Represented locally by the British consul, Arturo Pierce, the Boston-based firm seems to have made a conscious decision to refrain from meddling in *la política*—in which its foreign status would have put it at a distinct disadvantage. Unlike the other Yucatecan houses, Peabody shunned investments in regional railway companies, banks, and henequen's attendant service industries, which required more political clout. The Pierce-Peabody operation was thus the least horizontally integrated among the major henequen firms and had the least to gain from the concessions, contracts, and patronage that politicians offered. This astute noninterventionist policy may also help explain Peabody's longevity in the henequen trade. By limiting its business investments to planter advances and henequen exports, it insulated itself somewhat from the worst effects of the peninsula's periodic recessions.

8. Much of Urcelay's business went to the Deering Harvesting Machine Company during the Cantón administration.

9. Topik has written a thoughtful piece on the evolution of what Hilferding calls "finance capital" and defines as "the unification of capital. The previously separate spheres of industrial, commercial, and bank capital are now brought under the common direction of high finance, in which the masters of industry and of the banks are united in a close personal association." See Topik, "Emergence of Finance Capital," Hilferding quotation, 301; and Chernow.

10. Between January 1907 and December 1914, 55 articles concerned either directly or indirectly with IHC's role in the henequen market appeared in one local publication alone: *EA*, the Cámara Agrícola's propaganda arm. See Benjamin, "International Harvester." A stinging indictment of the trust by the muckraking Yucatecan journalist Carlos P. Escoffié Zetina is found in his *EPC*; see esp. the issue of June 27, 1909.

11. *EcM*, Sept. 1, 1906, 477. It should be noted that although it consistently criticized the "trust," the Cámara Agrícola was also an umbrella organization of *hacendados* and merchants, some of whom belonged to the Molinista faction.

12. A thorough discussion of the Compañía's attempts to finance its valorization scheme is found in *EA* throughout 1907 and 1908. See esp. Jan. 1, 1908, no. 13, and Feb. 1, 1908, no. 14.

13. Ibid., Dec. 1, 1907, no. 12.

14. *CTJ* 36, no. 11 (June 4, 1908).

15. For a detailed discussion of the role of advances in the henequen economy, see Wells, *Yucatán's Gilded Age*, 36–37.

16. Wells, "Family Elites."

17. IHCA, doc. file no. 2395, Daniels to Mr. Charles Deering, Aug. 15, 1905. *Sisal* was the preferred term for henequen fiber among contemporary North American cordage interests, although actually it is a different species from henequen. The latter was the fibrous agave exported from Yucatán.

18. Ibid.

19. Víctor Rendón's testimony, U.S. Senate, *Importation of Sisal and Manila Hemp*, 1: 26; Quintal Martín, "Breve historia."

20. *RdM*, May 29, 1908.

21. Besides Quintal Martín, "Breve historia," 56–57, see Barber, chap. 2.

22. *Importation of Sisal*, 2: 775.

23. Although many members of the elite held the Molinistas responsible for the Compañía Cooperativa's failure, only circumstantial evidence links Molina-Montes to the collapse of the combination.

24. *RdM*, Nov. 4, 1907.

25. *CTJ* 36, no. 11 (June 4, 1908), 1.

26. *DY*, June 1, 1907. For a perceptive treatment of the role speculators played in the henequen market, see *RdM*, Oct. 22, 1911.

27. *RdM*, May 15, 1908; and *MH*, May 23, 1908.

28. *RdM*, May 21, 1908; and *MH*, May 23, 1908.

29. *EI*, June 20, 1907.

30. Menéndez, *Noventa años*, 163.

31. Whether or not Molina and Montes proposed the third line as a ploy to force a merger is conjecture, but such tactics were common in Mexico and the United States during the Gilded Age. The company, organized with a working capital of six hundred thousand pesos, included among its shareholders two Molina sons-in-law, Rogelio Suárez and Avelino Montes, and Molinista ally Agustín Vales Castillo. ANEY, Ramón Escalante Pinto, oficio no. 17, Sept. 8, 1899; and Suárez Molina, *Don Rogelio Víctor Suárez*, 26–27.

32. On the mortgage, see AGN, SCOP, 23/270-1, "Informe sobre el balance general del Ferrocarril de Mérida a Campeche," 1902. On the number of shares, see ANEY, José Patrón Zavlegui, vol. 95, Apr. 21, 1900, 671–77. The Peóns were such a powerful economic force in the peninsula that they had a slew of investments with rival political factions. See Wells, "Family Elites."

33. Cantón Rosado, 70.

34. Railway mergers occurred regularly throughout Mexico during the last decade of the Porfiriato. For a discussion of this trend see Calderón, esp. 572–73.

35. Rendón's testimony, *Importation of Sisal*, 1: 26.

36. Ibid. On IHC's designs on the FCUY, see U.S. Dept. of Commerce, *International Harvester Company*, 149–50.

37. *DY*, June 12, 1908.

38. *EcM*, Aug. 17, 1907, 428.

39. AGN, SCOP, 23/460-2, *Informes del Consejo de Administración del FCUY de 1903*, pamphlet (Mérida: Tipografía y Litografía Moderna, 1904). On the shares controlled by the various factions, see Barceló Quintal, "El ferrocarril."

40. AGN, SCOP, 23.

41. *EI*, Jan. 18, 1904.

42. AGN, SCOP, 23/460-2, *Informes del Consejo de Administración del FCUY de 1907*, pamphlet (Mérida: Tipografía y Litografía Moderna, 1908). On the Escalantes'

financial problems with Thebaud, see AGEY, RJ, "Cuaderno de prueba de confesión ofrecida por el apoderado del síndico del Thebaud Brothers en el juicio ordinario que sigue contra el Banco Peninsular Mexicano y socios," 1909; and *DY*, Dec. 30, 1908.

43. Arrieta Ceniceros, esp. 146.

44. Topik argues that the Mexicans deserted silver for the gold standard for essentially political reasons. Among the most important: the financial hegemony of gold-rich British financiers; major gold strikes—in California and Australia in the mid-nineteenth century, South Africa and Alaska at the turn of the century—which created a sufficient gold reserve; increased silver production, which overwhelmed demand after the 1890s; and the increasing difficulty of stabilizing the price relationship between silver and gold. Topik, "Image of Prosperity."

45. For a trenchant analysis of the 1905 reform, see Topik, "La Revolución, el estado, y el desarrollo." See also Pletcher; María y Campos; and Hart, *Revolutionary Mexico*, 169–77.

46. In fairness, it should be noted that during Escalante Peón's tenure, management made notable improvements in the FCUY, including the complete renovation of the *vía ancha* (wide-gauge tracks). According to Escalante Peón's last *informe*, more than four million pesos were spent on these improvements. See Arrieta Ceniceros, 145–46.

47. AGN, SCOP, 23/460-2, *Informes del Consejo de Administración del FCUY 1908* (Mérida: Compañía Editorial Yucateca, 1909).

48. Another casualty of the financial panic was Rodulfo G. Cantón's Mérida-Peto railway, the only family-managed company left in the peninsula. Rodulfo had steadfastly refused to sell out to the FCUY despite an attractive offer from the Escalantes. The Mérida-Peto was brought down ultimately by a heavy debt service of more than $3.2 million and the turbulent economic climate. In late 1908, the company went into receivership and was purchased at a bargain price of $2.1 million by the FCUY, despite the trust's own considerable financial difficulties. ANEY, Tomás Aznar Rivas, vol. 1, book A, Jan. 16, 1909, 16–99.

49. Arrieta Cencieros, 150.

50. AGN, SCOP, 23/460-2, *Informes del Consejo de Administración del FCUY de 1909* (Mérida: Imprenta de la Lotería del Estado, 1910), and *Informes . . . 1910*.

51. *Importation of Sisal*, 1: 74.

52. Leo Browne's testimony, ibid., 2: 1030–31. The Escalantes were accused of precisely the same machinations when they controlled the FCUY. Arrieta Cencieros, 147.

53. ANEY, Tomás Aznar Rivas, Mar. 31, 1908, oficio no. 6, 809–57.

54. ANEY, Patricio Sabido, Oct. 5, 1908, oficio no. 17, 2013–20, and June 5, 1907, 1465–74.

55. AGEY, RJ, "Cuaderno de prueba"; and *DY*, Dec. 30, 1908. On the Thebaud brothers, see Irigoyen, "Don Us Escalante."

56. Menéndez, *Noventa años*, 186–87. As if the banks did not have enough problems, local newspapers reported the embezzlement of $740,000 from the Banco Yucateco on Jan. 5, 1908. Although three culprits were arrested and convicted, the untimely robbery undermined the credibility of the already weakened regional banking industry and paved the way for the fusion of the two banks. Menéndez, *Noventa años*, 8, 267.

57. AGEY, RJ, "Cuaderno de prueba"; and pamphlet, *Cuál es el valor*.

58. AGEY, RJ, "Cuaderno de prueba."

59. *RdM*, Sept. 12, 1907.

60. Witness the havoc wreaked on international financial markets (sardonically

referred to as the "tequila effect") following the "meltdown" of the Mexican peso in 1995. For an earlier but still insightful discussion of the reciprocal role peripheral areas can play in the world economy, see Cardoso and Faletto.

61. *EI*, June 8, 1907; and *MH*, May 9, 1907.

62. Thebaud's receivers would later claim in court that it was not only illegal but unethical to place Muñoz Arístegui in the position of *comisión* president because, in all likelihood, this liquidating commission might find itself taken to court by one of its creditors. *Cuál es el valor*, 41.

63. *EPC*, 1908–9.

64. AGEY, RJ, "Cuaderno de prueba"; *Informes y balances*, esp. 4–16; and *DY*, Dec. 30, 1908, Mar. 16, 1909, June 14, 1909, June 18, 1909, Aug. 30, 1909. It is significant that *DY*, a Molinista paper, gave so much space to the Escalante failure. *RdM*, owned and operated by Delio Moreno Cantón, leader of the opposition party in Yucatán, gave the Escalantes' misfortunes only marginal coverage.

65. Edward B. Bayley's testimony, *Importation of Sisal*, 2: 1013.

66. *DY*, June 14, 1909.

67. For an alternative case of how familial elites were able to resurrect themselves from bankruptcy, see Wells, *Yucatán's Gilded Age*, 144–50.

68. *Cuál es el valor*, 49.

69. The letters rogatory cross-examination in New York District Court, fall 1909, is found in AGEY, RJ, "Cuaderno de prueba." Letters rogatory were used more recently in the criminal investigation of the 1976 car bombing of Chilean diplomat Orlando Letelier. See Branch and Propper, 174–75 and 406–11.

70. See the letter from the Escalantes' attorney, Néstor Rubio Alpuche, to Díaz, in CGPD, 34:25:011990, July 6, 1909; and a letter from Eusebio Escalante Peón thanking Díaz for his intervention, 34:28:013994, Aug. 13, 1909.

71. *EPC*, July 6, 1909.

72. E.g., the Compañía Agrícola del Cuyo y Anexas, a multidimensional agricultural property in the eastern portion of the state valued at well over one million pesos before the panic, was auctioned for just over two hundred thousand pesos by the Compañía Comercial. Menéndez, *Noventa años*, 183.

73. *In the District Court*, vol. 3, *Testimony of Witnesses for the Petitioner*, 414.

74. Daniels's testimony, ibid.; and Alexander Legge's testimony, *Importation of Sisal*, 2: 1162.

75. Because Montes was the source, it makes sense that he would have a special interest in the rise of worker unrest in Yucatán at this time. His own hacienda, Oxcúm, located just outside Umán, six kilometers south of Mérida, had seen a workers' uprising in 1907, when 110 peons marched from the hacienda to Umán's municipal hall to protest the imprisonment of three co-workers. But to say that all of Yucatán was on the brink of revolution early in 1909 certainly would have been an exaggeration. See *RdM*, Sept. 5, 1907.

76. M. J. Smith's testimony, *Importation of Sisal*, 2: 1605.

77. *EPC*, Nov. 28, 1909.

78. See Joseph and Wells, "Corporate Control," 88–89.

79. IHCA, doc. file no. 2395, Daniels to Legge, July 16, 1909.

80. Bayley's testimony, *Importation of Sisal*, 2: 968.

81. IHCA, Daniels to Legge. IHC had funneled money to Montes and Molina before the 1909 corner and would continue to do so after the unsuccessful combination. IHCA, doc. file no. 2395, Daniels to Cyrus McCormick, Jr., Oct. 2, 1906. Indeed, Daniels later admitted under oath in the IHC antitrust trial that Montes was IHC's agent in Yucatán, when he responded positively to the following question: "Well he

[Montes] was the man who was handling matters for you down there?" *In the District Court*, 3: 419.

82. *DY*, June 21, 1909.

83. Ibid.

84. Smith's testimony, *Importation of Sisal*, 2: 1250. This amount covered Montes's profits on the original 220,000 bales. In 1909 IHC would purchase more than 450,000 bales from Montes S. en C., so Montes's profits were quite a bit more than $103,000.

85. Legge's testimony, *Importation of Sisal*, 2: 998.

86. *In the District Court*, 3: 414; IHCA, doc. file no. 2395, Daniels to Montes, June 30, 1909.

87. IHCA, doc. file no. 2395, Daniels to Montes, July 7, 1909.

88. *In the District Court*, 3: 416.

89. *Importation of Sisal*, 2: 1250.

90. Baker Library, Plymouth Cordage Records, File H, Drawer 2, article from *Boston Globe*, Dec. 10, 1914; Dewing; and *CTJ* 6: 1 (Jan. 1, 1893), 15.

91. Baker Library, Peabody Records, HL-3, Bayley to Arturo Pierce, Sept. 22, 1909.

92. Ibid.                 93. Ibid.

94. Holmes.           95. Peabody Records, Bayley to Pierce.

96. A look at IHC's twine profits during the first ten years of the century indicates that although profits dipped in 1909 and 1910 in comparison to other years, IHC still made a profit despite the failure of the combination. See *In the District Court*, 3: 416.

97. Haber, 83. See also Walker.

98. Quoted in Topik, "La Revolución, el estado," 100.

99. Haber has found that profits in manufacturing were spotty at best.

100. Ibid., 192.

101. Lamoreaux defines a horizontal combination as the simultaneous merger of many or all competitors in an industry into a single, giant enterprise. Lamoreaux, 1.

102. See Chandler, *Visible Hand* and *Scale and Scope*.

103. Idem, *Scale and Scope*, 34–35.

104. Idem, *Visible Hand*, 409.

105. Ibid., 10.

106. Lamoreaux presents a formal economic model of dominant firm pricing strategy, 100–101.

## CHAPTER 5

1. Cf. E. P. Thompson's classic treatment of the problem in "Time, Work-Discipline, and Industrial Capitalism," 56–97. What exactly constituted Porfirian ideology (or even whether it was a coherent ideology) has been subject to some dispute, as has the *científicos'* relative influence on Díaz. The finer points of the ruling Porfirian *mentalité* are discussed in Córdova, chap. 1; Hale, *Transformation of Liberalism*; Guerra; Knight, *Mexican Revolution*, 1: chap. 1; Katz, "Mexico: Restored Republic"; and French, "Peaceful and Hardworking People." Beezley likens the Porfirian agenda to a fad or craze sweeping the nation; a "persuasion" rather than a coherent ideology. *Judas at the Jockey Club*, 13–14.

2. French, "In the Path of Progress," 95.

3. Ibid., 96. The "long nineteenth century" was a notorious period of moral surveillance and repression. Cf. Hobsbawm, *Age of Capital*, 273–83; and Stone, 666.

4. Roche, 272. Cf. French, "Progreso Forzado."

5. In their stimulating recent discussions of hegemony, British sociologists Nich-

olas Abercrombie, Stephen Hill, and Bryan S. Turner argue plausibly that before "late capitalism," if so-called dominant ideologies incorporated any segment of society, it was the dominant class itself, not subaltern groups. They argue that this happened mostly because the apparatus of ideological transmission largely affected the dominant class. See *The Dominant Ideology Thesis* and their more recent edited volume, *Dominant Ideologies*, which puts their theoretical model to a comparative empirical test.

6. For an examination of the difficult relations between the federal government and the states during the early Porfiriato, see Cosío Villegas, *Historia moderna*, vols. 9 and 10; and Perry.

7. Not all regional elites went quietly; indeed, not all subscribed to the *científicos'* aggressive model of economic transformation. Some provincial elites tested their mettle against Díaz, particularly during his first few terms; but by the late Porfiriato, most had acquiesced to national dominance and turned their attention to squabbling with rival political factions. See, e.g., Langston; Wasserman, esp. chap. 2; Avila; and Falcón, "Raíces."

8. Bataillon, 52–53; and Kandell, 371. Economic historian Topik's analysis of the 1908–9 budget reveals that almost 45 percent of the entire national budget was spent in the Federal District. Topik has little doubt that the federal government siphoned funds from the states and spent them in the capital. "Much of the treasury outlays were funded by revenues captured in the provinces and deposited in the capital. . . . Mexico's financial supremacy was at the expense of the rest of the country." "Economic Domination," 192.

9. For a discussion of Mexico City's dominance, see Topik, "Economic Domination"; and Kandell, 370. In 1890, e.g., 92 percent of all credit extended in the country originated in Mexico City; by 1910, more than half the 3.5 billion pesos of foreign investment had been channeled through the Federal District's commerce, banking, public utilities, and industry.

10. Although the industrial sector grew considerably during the late Porfiriato, the Federal District was not the principal beneficiary. See Haber; and Topik, "Economic Domination." The northern frontier, driven by a mining boom, new industries, and U.S. proximity, grew dynamically. Some excellent monographs on this phenomenon include Cerutti; Saragoza; Wasserman; and Aguilar Camín.

11. Topik, "Economic Domination." Even if the center did not benefit as much as certain regions on the periphery, the railroad unquestionably encouraged immigration to the burgeoning national capital. Useful works on the railroad's role in the national economy include Coatsworth, *Growth Against Development*; Calderón; and A. Schmidt.

12. The Federal District included the capital and the surrounding suburbs. To avoid confusion, we use the terms *Federal District* and *Mexico City* interchangeably throughout this chapter. For a comprehensive treatment of Mexico City, see Gortari Rabiela and Hernández Franyuti; and González Polo.

13. Pani, vii–viii. This is not to imply that municipalities were ever very strong in Mexico (or Latin America) after independence. Two thoughtful syntheses of the city in Latin America are Cardoso; and Scobie.

14. Beezley incorporates some of the lively travelers' accounts in *Judas at the Jockey Club*.

15. In 1886 *ET* gibed, "to move about the capital, we need canoes instead of carriages." Quoted in Kandell, 371.

16. Government publicists bragged that the project was "an eternal pedestal to the glory of the . . . country that will bear witness for future generations that at the end of

the nineteenth century, Mexico had monuments it could display with pride to the civilized countries of the Old World." Ibid., 372.

17. On the drainage project, see *Memoria de las obras;* González Navarro, "México en una laguna"; Cosío Villegas, *Historia moderna,* 4: 117–30; and de Gortari Rabiela and Hernández Franyuti, 2: 359–65. Kandell relates that the drainage system did not function properly when inaugurated in March 1900; a series of adjustments was needed during the last decade of the Porfiriato. Kandell, 371–72. Pani recounts the city's health problems in detail; so does González Navarro, *Población y sociedad.*

18. During the Porfiriato the city's population doubled, to one-half million; its area quintupled, as neighboring haciendas, ranches, indigenous barrios, and municipalities turned into suburbs. See Morales; and Gortari Rabiela and Hernández Franyuti, 2: 83–154.

19. Díaz y de Ovando. For a discussion of the influence of French architectural styles in these new neighborhoods, see Fernández, 173–81, also excerpted in de Gortari Rabiela and Hernández Franyuti, 2: 137–44.

20. For an amusing account of the mistake-ridden paving episode, see Beezley, *Judas at the Jockey Club,* 9–10.

21. The most comprehensive treatment of the Federal District's social ills is found in Cosío Villegas, *Historia moderna,* vol. 4.

22. The Federal District reported four hundred murders in 1900 out of a population of one-half million. By contrast, France, a nation of 39 million, reported 840 murders. One Mexican politician sadly lamented, "our lowest classes are 40 times more criminal than those in France." Ibid., 4: 451; Kandell, 370. On the overcrowded prisons and the government's efforts to correct the problem, see Rohlfes, "Police and Penal Correction."

23. Sierra, 360.

24. Ibid., 360–64; Guerrero; and Roumagnac. Recent studies on criminality during the Porfiriato and the Revolution have enhanced our understanding of the often fractious relationship between government authorities and the urban working poor. See Buffington; and Piccato.

25. Cosío Villegas, *Historia moderna,* vol. 4. The Porfirian propagandists' rationale for the drainage and sewer system emphasized the federal government's conviction that it could play a significant role not only in improving *chilangos'* health but in regenerating their morals. See *Memoria de las obras.*

26. Pani, 67.

27. Ibid. Although Pani's work was not published until 1916, he based his conclusions on data from 1910 and 1911. The death rate per thousand inhabitants in the Federal District was 49.51 in 1900; the national average was 33.61. *Estadísticas sociales,* 160–61.

28. Cosío Villegas, *Historia moderna,* 4.

29. Beezley, Martin, and French; Beezley, "La cultura de la calle"; Kandell, 362; and Rohlfes, esp. chap. 4.

30. Lecumbérri Penitentiary, opened in 1900, was a testament to the technocrats' scientific ideas about penal reform. Yet many political prisoners were never housed in the modern penitentiary but left in hellish Belém prison. On the imprisonment of labor organizers and political dissidents see Hart, *Anarchism,* esp. chaps. 6 and 7; Anderson, *Outcasts in Their Own Land;* and Cockroft.

31. Davies; Boyer; Moreno Toscano, "Cambios en los patrones"; and Knight, *Mexican Revolution,* 1: 41.

32. Although Monterrey, which exploded from a sleepy town of 14,000 to a city of

79,000 during this period, relied on an indigenous industrial plant, it also benefited from the railroad and from substantial foreign investment in neighboring mines. See Saragoza, chaps. 1 and 2.

33. With its economic surge after independence, Yucatán stands in sharp contrast to the rest of Mexico, which had difficulty recovering from the ravages of a protracted war against Spain. On Yucatán's postindependence economy, see Suárez Molina, *La evolución económica;* and Cline, "Regionalism and Society."

34. Mérida *partido* included the city, its suburbs, and neighboring haciendas and pueblos. Remmers, citing Rubio Mañé's *Archivo histórico de la historia de Yucatán, Campeche y Tabasco* and a reliable state report, estimates that Valladolid *partido's* population (51,605) increased by more than 140 percent between 1796 and 1846. Peto *partido*, the center of the southeastern sugar industry, also had more inhabitants (51,004) than Mérida district (48,004) in 1846. Remmers, 5, 95.

35. Remmers's lengthy dissertation (see esp. pts. 2 and 3) examines the war's impact, demographic and otherwise, on the northwest and, to a lesser extent, on the frontier region.

36. See Boyer, 149. Mexico did not take a national census until 1895; therefore the figures for 1803 and 1877 in Table 5.1 represent demographic "guesstimates," based partly on unreliable local population counts. Even the national census figures must be used with care; González Navarro, e.g., believes that they underestimate the number of residents. See Cosío Villegas, *Historia moderna*, 4: 7–12. In a further demonstration of these figures' unreliability, Boyer provides an estimate for 1869 of 30,000, precisely the figure the *Historia moderna* team cites for 1877.

37. A lively historiographical debate persists on whether the Caste War precipitated the rise of monoculture in the peninsula's northwestern quadrant. See Irigoyen, *Fué el auge;* and Quintal Martín, *Yucatán. Carácter de la guerra.* Cf. Chardon, 138–42; and Remmers, 4, 386–87.

38. Baqueiro, *Reseña geográfica*, 117.

39. Remmers, 646–47.

40. Seminario de la Historia Moderna de México, 27–29.

41. Remmers, 646.

42. Seminario, 29; Boyer, "Las ciudades."

43. This section draws on Wells, "All in the Family."

44. AGN, SCOP, 23/162-1, "Datos estadísticos para la Memoria Presidencial del Ferrocarril de Mérida a Peto," 1902.

45. AGN, SCOP, 23/283-1, "Informes técnicos y estadística del movimiento de pasajeros y de carga en el Ferrocarril de Mérida a Peto," 1896.

46. Henequen fiber averaged 70 to 75 percent of all the freight hauled by the peninsular railways. AGN, SCOP, 23/163-1, "Estadística del movimiento de pasajeros y carga del Ferrocarril de Mérida a Peto," 1900–1901.

47. For a good summation of the relationship between the steamship and the growth of cities in late nineteenth-century Latin America, see Scobie.

48. Trade with central Mexico was disappointing. At first, the use of sail rather than steam vessels in the coastal trade meant freight and insurance costs 25 and 50 percent higher, respectively, than those tendered by foreign steamship carriers. Remmers, 711–12. Moreover, until the late Porfiriato, service from Veracruz and Tampico was irregular at best.

49. The new port, the brainchild of Juan Miguel Castro and Simón Peón, opened after a tense, drawn-out battle with two rival entrepreneurial teams that preferred the cities of Sisal and Celestún. See Castro; and Remmers, 651–53.

50. On the banking industry see Barceló Quintal, "El desarrollo de la banca"; and Suárez Molina, *La evolución económica*. On the opening of running accounts and *henequeneros'* overextensions, see Wells, *Yucatán's Gilded Age*, chaps. 3 and 5.

51. Although *turco* became a catchall for anyone who came from the Middle East, most of those who did were Christians. Many became merchants and petty traders, operating in both the city and the countryside. As *turcos* proved themselves able businessmen and displaced native petty traders, they often incurred harsh discrimination from local residents.

52. The largest number of Mexican nationals came from neighboring Campeche and distant Sonora. Yaqui prisoners of war were transported from Sonora to Yucatecan henequen estates after 1900. On the Yaquis, see Hu-DeHart, "Pacification of the Yaquis"; Chacón, 99–100, 146–47; and Wells, *Yucatán's Gilded Age*, 163–67. In 1910 a total of 2,757 Yaquis lived in Yucatán. Cosío Villegas, *Historia moderna*, 4: 258–59. For comparative data on internal immigration, see *Estadísticas sociales*, 77–86.

53. Of all foreigners residing in Yucatán in 1910, 61 percent lived in Mérida. Just under 40 percent were Chinese; 17.98 percent, Cuban; 12.31 percent, *turcos*. Despite the influx, together the immigrants never amounted to more than 5 percent of the population. According to the national census, the total number of foreigners living in the state increased from 1,268 in 1895 to 4,678 in 1910. Two-thirds of these foreign immigrants were men. *Estadísticas sociales*, 34–35, 194, 196, 199–200.

54. Yucatán had the third-largest number of professionals in the country. The service sector grew from just over 15,000 to almost 26,000 during the same period. Seminario, 49, 51, 57.

55. E.g., Guanche; and *Directorio Domínguez*. For an analysis of the capital's population, see Hansen; and Hansen and Bastarrachea M.

56. Because the peninsula was a backwater throughout the colonial period, with few valuable commodities for the Spanish to exploit, Mérida's colonial architecture and infrastructure paled in comparison to provincial capitals like Puebla and Guadalajara. See Farriss, 31–32.

57. Arnold and Frost, 65.

58. Quoted in Cosío Villegas, *Historia moderna*, 4: 82–83.

59. Carlos Peón Machado, Yucatán's first civilian governor during the Porfiriato (1894–97), did try to introduce a number of progressive reforms, but his administration coincided with one of the era's worst economic recessions. His most notable accomplishments were a series of educational reforms and the completion of the new Juárez Penitentiary, begun by his military predecessors Guillermo Palomino and Daniel Traconis. As a harbinger of things to come, during Peón Machado's administration, streets that had been quaintly named after animals and the like were now rechristened numerically, in good positivist fashion. Urzáiz Rodríguez, 123–31.

60. As late as 1889, butchers still hung meat out in the open air in the Plaza de las Armas. Local authorities agreed that this practice was a public health menace. After the market was completed, peddlers and itinerant merchants who had regularly sold their wares in the plaza found themselves being ushered away by the now more visible city police. AGEY, RPE, "Expediente relativo e la concesión hecho al Amado Carrillo para construir un mercado en esta ciudad," Jan. 7, 1889.

61. See Stephens; Arnold and Frost; and Turner (witness, e.g., the epigraph at the beginning of this chapter). Other useful descriptive commentaries on Mérida's growth are found in Hijuelos Febles; Ruz Menéndez, *Mérida: bosquejo biográfico*; and Dulanto.

62. Mérida also witnessed the opening of its first movie theater during the Olegariato (1908). Hansen and Bastarrachea M., 75.

63. For a reconstruction of the physical layout and general tenor of life in these neighborhoods at the end of the nineteenth century (as well as ca. 1940), see Redfield, 19–35.

64. See, e.g., *EI*, Jan. 18, 1904, May 25, 1904, Apr. 18, 1905, May 2, 1905, and Jan. 4, 1906.

65. Preparations for the unique visit were covered in both the local press and *EI*: see, e.g., Nov. 2, 1905, and Dec. 10, 1905. A thorough description of Díaz's trip to Yucatán is found in González Navarro, *Raza y tierra*, chap. 6. See also Chapter 3 of this work.

66. Sierra, quoted in *Album conmemorativo*, 11, 17, 41–42.

67. A stunning pictorial of the garish architecture is found in "Mérida de Yucatán."

68. *Directorio Domínguez.*

69. E.g., *RdM*, Nov. 14, 1893.

70. Groups of dancing "Indians" wearing masks, crowns, and deer feathers went from house to house, singing in Maya. Cosío Villegas, *Historia moderna*, 4: 708. The elite's copying of Indian culture is chronicled in Beezley's *Judas at the Jockey Club.* Beezley contends that as the upper class appropriated European and North American culture during the late Porfiriato, it gradually discarded its superficial interest in indigenous culture.

71. Arnold and Frost, 65.

72. Butler. Besides storage tanks, one of the capital's prime mosquito-breeding places was the baptismal fonts of neighborhood churches.

73. E.g., one of the FCUY's first cost-cutting moves amid the 1908 financial crisis was to let the insurance lapse on its warehouses in Mérida and Progreso. AGN, SCOP, 23/460-2, *Informes del Consejo de Administración del FCUY de 1908* (Mérida: Compañía Editorial Yucateca, 1909).

74. *MH*, Aug. 12, 1909.

75. Ibid.

76. For a representative sample of the criticism that opponents dished out to the Molina regime, see *EPC*, Jan. 17, 1904.

77. *Estadísticas sociales*, 15.

78. *EdC*, Nov. 25, 1903, Nov. 28, 1903.

79. *RdM*, July 8, 1908.

80. *EdC*, Feb. 25, 1903.

81. *EPn*, Apr. 20, 1906.

82. *RdM*, July 8, 1908. In 1907, *EI*, a Mexico City daily with a correspondent in Mérida, reported that the end of the public works binge had created a glut in the housing market because many Spanish and Mexican nationals had left the state and returned home after the *obras públicas* were completed. One thousand properties were reported vacant that year. *EI*, May 17, 1907.

83. CGPD, 34:37:018248-51, Antonio Rodríguez Caballero to Porfirio Díaz, Nov. 2, 1909.

84. For a small sample of the morals cases prosecuted, see, in AGEY, RJ: on pornography, "Causa a Rufino Fernández y socio por ultrajes a la moral pública," 1908, caja 668; on gambling, "Toca a la causa seguida a Arcadio Segura, Luciano Sosa, Pablo Ruíz, Ninfo Domínguez, y José Guadalupe Rojas por el delito de juego prohibido," 1908, caja 691; on vagrancy, "Causa seguida a Moisés Pereira por el delito de vagancia," 1908, caja 691; on prostitution, *EPC*, Oct. 4, 1903.

85. *EPC*, 1903–9. Conflating the images of Don Olegario and *el papa* was no accident: Escoffié was anticlerical and a partisan of the Flores Magón brothers' Partido Liberal Mexicano. Recent work on the Catholic church in Porfirian Yucatán, moreover, indicates that the Molina administration and the church hierarchy worked together in a number of areas to pursue their respective agendas. See Savarino, "La iglesia ausente."

86. *EPC*, Sept. 27, 1903. Cf. French, "In the Path of Progress," 95–98, and "Progreso Forzado," for a discussion of an even less successful campaign to regulate Porfirian Chihuahua. *Aguardiente* was the preferred drink of the working poor; during Molina's administration the number of *aguardiente* factories in Yucatán dropped precipitously from 56 to 13, and the number of registered distilleries fell from 68 to 15. Statewide production fell from 1.2 million liters annually in 1898–99 to 237,064 in 1910–11. The reasons for this sharp decrease are difficult to discern. Certainly Molina's temperance policy played a role, but the state also placed a tax on liquor establishments that no doubt hurt the industry. Two other factors may have been significant: the increasingly oligopolistic nature of all entrepreneurial activity in late Porfirian Yucatán and the importation of cheaper brands of *aguardiente*. *Estadísticas sociales*, 120–23.

87. What is most interesting about the report is that in 1907, appreciably more Mexican nationals (174) and foreigners (134) were involved in criminal activities than Yucatecans (93). *DO*, Jan. 10, 1908. Certainly, the regime feared that immigrants perpetrated many of the "political crimes" in Mérida and Progreso during the late Porfiriato (see Chap. 3).

88. During Molina's administration, sales from the prison shop totaled $77,872.38. Of this amount, $51,944.92 paid prison operating expenses, and the rest went to inmates. Casasús, 75–77; and *MH*, Mar. 6, 1910.

89. Governors had to sign off on the release of each prisoner, which only added further administrative delays to the process. *EPC* regularly described the oppressive prison treatment. See, e.g., Dec. 13, 1903; May 15, June 19, and July 3, 1904. Escoffié's numerous fabled brushes with the law were uncovered in AGEY, RJ, 1909, boxes 730 and 736; and in Menéndez Rodríguez interview, July 5, 1987.

90. The following description of Juárez Penitentiary is drawn from Rendón's memo, CGPD, 34:36:017853-859, n.d., Fall 1909. Rendón was counsel for a group of men accused of embezzling one-half million pesos from the Banco Yucateco, and his outspoken and public defense of his clients evoked the enmity of Elías Amábilis, a Molinista state legislator. See Menéndez Paz.

91. Molina added the death penalty in his penal reform. Yucatán was one of several states to follow the federal blueprint. Cosío Villegas, *Historia moderna*, 4: 448–52.

92. *EPC*, Dec. 13, 1903; May 15, June 19, and July 3, 1904.

93. On the limited access to lawyers, see CGPD, 30:24:009555, Joaquín D. Casasús to Díaz, July 21, 1905. Rendón's and Escoffié's complaints were corroborated by three inmates who wrote to Díaz of horrendous conditions. CGPD, 27:31:012044, Benito Báez, Andrés Ramírez, Nicamedes Moo to Díaz, Oct. 20, 1902.

94. See Foucault.

95. Knight, *Mexican Revolution*; Womack, *Zapata and the Mexican Revolution*.

CHAPTER 6

1. *EC*, June 10, 1911.

2. We use several terms to characterize rural workers in Yucatán during the Porfiriato. *Campesino*, used in a broad sense, indicates any rural dweller or cultivator. *Jornalero* is a generic term for agricultural worker, and we use it freely to embrace henequen workers, tenants, and part-timers (specifically called *luneros*, or Monday men, in Yucatán). *Peones acasillados* are permanent resident peons tied to the henequen estate through the mechanism of debt. *Comuneros*, on the other hand, are "free" peasants who may or may not own land, but live in village communities and

are not tied by debt to neighboring haciendas. The analytical difficulty of capturing the diverse range of relationships and experiences in a single construct—e.g., "peasantry" or "campesinado"—has motivated a number of Latin Americanists, Africanists, and Asianists to try to "unpack" such terms. In so doing, they have emphasized the development of historically specific categories of rural cultivators, a strategy we have adopted in the present work. For recent discussions that usefully grapple with the problem of defining peasantry, see Isaacman, 205–7, 219–21; and Gould, 6–8.

3. The henequen zone lies within a radius of 70 to 80 kilometers of Mérida (see Map 6.1).

4. Wolf, *Peasant Wars*, introduction. Tutino writes more explicitly, "In places where the most radical economic changes of the Porfiriato occurred, where established peasant communities were suddenly incorporated into the export economy as export producers, there was little revolutionary insurrection after 1910." *From Insurrection to Revolution*, 296.

5. A recent portrayal of the Yucatecan *peón acasillado* as quiescent is found in Knight, *Mexican Revolution*, 1: 89. For a general discussion of the literature on henequen workers during the Porfiriato, see Wells, *Yucatán's Gilded Age*, chap. 6.

6. This point is developed more fully in Wells, "From Hacienda to Plantation," 112–42, 269–75. On the transformation of the Caribbean sugar industry, see Moreno Fraginals, "Plantations in the Caribbean"; and Schnakenbourg.

7. In a seminal article written more than three decades ago, Wolf and Mintz attempted rigorously to define haciendas and plantations. A hacienda is "an agricultural estate operated by a dominant landowner . . . and a dependent labor force, organized to supply a small-scale market by means of scarce capital in which the factors of production are employed not only for capital accumulation but also to support the status aspirations of the owner." By contrast, a plantation is "an agricultural estate operated by dominant owners (usually organized into a corporation) and a dependent labor force, organized to supply a large-scale market by means of abundant capital, in which the factors of production are employed primarily to further capital accumulation without reference to the status needs of owners." Although this ideal typology simplifies complex institutions, it points up key differences in property ownership, capitalization, markets, and landowners' desire for conspicuous consumption.

8. Wolf and Mintz, 390.

9. Ibid., 401.

10. Georg Hegel's penetrating insight in *The Phenomenology of Mind* is particularly appropriate here: personal power taken to an extreme ultimately contradicts itself, "for total domination can become a form of extreme dependence on the object of one's power, and total powerlessness can become the secret path to control of the subject that attempts to exercise such power." Quoted by Patterson, 2.

11. Mason, 11.

12. Ibid.

13. The following discussion draws heavily on Patterson, chap. 1.

14. Marx, *Capital*, 1: 77, also cited in Patterson, 19.

15. Designed by *henequeneros* to limit workers' mobility and autonomy, the three mechanisms were often so mutually reenforcing that it is sometimes difficult to delineate where one began and another left off. The hacienda store, e.g., served many functions. It gave *henequeneros* a surefire mechanism for raising workers' debts (coercion). By providing basic foodstuffs and household items, it diminished the resident peons' need to leave the property to purchase goods, thereby minimizing

potentially disruptive contact with neighboring villagers and agitators (isolation). Through the sale of corn, beans, and other staples, it ensured subsistence for resident peons (security). In sum, it was a perfect vehicle for appropriating labor in a scarce market, because it facilitated dependency and immobility while conveying a measure of convenience and security to landless peons. For heuristic purposes, however, we will break down these three interrelated mechanisms to clarify how the idiom of power was conveyed to the *jornaleros* and villagers who lived in the henequen zone. Their strategic convergence, however, must always be kept in mind.

16. Peniche Rivero, "Mujeres, dotes y matrimonios," 6; idem, "Gender, Bride-wealth, and Marriage," 74–89. See also Gill, "Campesino Patriarchy," esp. chaps. 4 and 5.

17. In some cases, the traditional wattle-and-daub huts gave way to whitewashed masonry. Gill, "Campesino Patriarchy," 110. See also García Cantón, 26.

18. Wells, *Yucatán's Gilded Age*, 161–62.

19. E.g., Gill, "Campesino Patriarchy," 111.

20. Moisés González Navarro provides several examples of blatant land-grabbing by government officials and *hacendados* who used laws on vacant public land to usurp lands from neighboring smallholders and *ejidos*. Even Secretary of *Fomento* Olegario Molina was accused of fraudulently acquiring 2,179 hectares of land in Tizimín *partido*. See Cosío Villegas, *Historia moderna*, 4: 193.

21. Betancourt Pérez, *Revoluciones y crisis*, 52.

22. Suárez Molina, *La evolución económica*, 1: 160.

23. See Farriss.

24. For a comprehensive examination of Yucatán's ecology, see Wilson.

25. For a discussion of the henequen zone's poor soil and low corn yields, see Shuman, chap. 5.

26. The demand for firewood from locomotives alone was prodigious. The FCUY estimated that in 1912, all four rail lines utilized 61,600 *tareas* of firewood a year at a cost to the company of $133,082.63. A *tarea* was commonly defined as 2 *varas* by 2 *varas* by ¾ *vara* (1 *vara* equals 33 inches). A *tarea* weighed roughly 46 kilograms. AGN, SCOP, 23/453-1, "Informe de los trabajos ejecutados en los años 1901, 1912 y 1922."

27. Runaway contract workers were even easier to find. González Navarro cites the case of a Huastecan *jornalero* enticed by unscrupulous agents with offers of high wages to leave his native San Luis Potosí and come to Yucatán with his family. When he discovered that his daily wage was 48 centavos instead of the promised 2 pesos, he tried twice to return home; local authorities captured him and returned him to his estate. On his third try, he successfully escaped but had to leave his family behind in Yucatán. Cosío Villegas, *Historia moderna*, 4: 225.

28. Farriss makes a strong case for the migratory propensity of the colonial Yucatec Maya; see esp. chap. 12.

29. Wells, *Yucatán's Gilded Age*, 105, n. 30.

30. See, e.g., Bojórquez Urzáiz, "El Yucatán de 1847," "Crisis maicera," and "Regionalización de la política."

31. See, e.g, CGPD, Memo, Sierra Méndez to Díaz, "Apuntes breves," 22:14: 006780-95, June 9, 1897. Cf. AGEY, RJ, "Toca a la causa seguida a Juan Jiménez y socios por el delito de provocación al delito de rebelión," 1913. It is common knowledge that in Yucatán the term *mestizo* has come to differ from the standard Mexican usage. It connotes a person or attribute—that is, a style of dress or abode—that is at root Maya but has been influenced over time by Hispanic culture. Yucatán's unique ethnic categories are discussed in R. Thompson; Bricker, 92, 253; and Hansen, 122–41.

32. E.g., interviews, Ku Peraza and Trejo Hernández; Campos Esquivel; Zozaya Ruz; and Tut de Euán; Chris Gill, personal communication, June 23, 1996.

33. E.g., AGEY, RJ, "Toca a la causa seguida a Hermenegildo Nah y socio por los delitos de robo y destrucción en propiedad ajena por incendio," 1912; "Toca a la causa seguida a Visitación González y Magdalena Alcocer de González, por injurias a funcionario público y resistencia a la autoridad," 1914.

34. This aphorism appeared in contemporary travelers' accounts, e.g., Arnold and Frost, 324, and is cited in numerous secondary treatments of Yucatán's "Age of Slavery."

35. Wells, *Yucatán's Gilded Age*, 159.

36. CGPD.

37. Occasionally, Díaz would ask his handpicked governors to look into specific complaints from individuals, but it is difficult to discern whether the problems themselves were ever addressed. CGPD.

38. Wells, *Yucatán's Gilded Age*, 176–77.

39. Baerlein, 19–20, 182; Knight, "Mexican Peonage," 61.

40. Quoted in Wells, *Yucatán's Gilded Age*, 178.

41. Sometimes whipping was not applied "in moderation." Pedro Chin, a *jornalero* on Hacienda San Antonio, died from a whipping by the *mayordomo*. Cosío Villegas, *Historia moderna*, 4: 26. Also see the file of correspondence between *hacendado* José María Peón and his *encargado*, Quintín Baqueiro. Peón berates Baqueiro for his excessive beating of peons, which has prompted several to flee and required Peón to hire a costly bounty hunter to round them up. In a draft letter to his overseer, Peón snaps: "If you wanted to teach him a lesson by punishing him physically, I could understand it, but did you have to nearly kill him, Don Quintín?" SPC, Box 8, Oct.–Dec., 1887.

42. Quoted in Knight, "Mexican Peonage," 61.

43. AGEY, RJ, "Flagelación a Julio Pérez," 1912.

44. In some cases, escaped campesinos remanded to the hacienda had the cost of their return—typically, the fee paid to the bounty hunter—added to their debt. See Gill, "Campesino Patriarchy," 114.

45. Wells, *Yucatán's Gilded Age*, 157.

46. Knight, "Mexican Peonage," 51. For samples of such contracts for personal services dating from the 1870s, see SPC, Box 3.

47. AGEY, RJ, "Incidente promovido por el apoderado de D. Dolores Guerra de Mendoza pidiendo la suspensión del remate de la hacienda Xcuyum," 1895; quotation from *ECdE*, July 15, 1895; and Wells, *Yucatán's Gilded Age*, 157.

48. A recent study of peonage in Puebla and Tlaxcala during the Porfiriato noted that some *acasillados* actually sought to increase their indebtedness, believing that the size of the debt was a measure of social status on the hacienda. Nickel, *Peonaje*, 54–55. While data on this for Yucatán are lacking, many *acasillados* clearly built up extremely large debts during the Porfiriato. Whether they considered the debt irrelevant and consequently borrowed as much as estate management allowed, or whether they did regard debt to be a symbol of status remains unclear.

49. AGEY, RJ, "Acusación presentada por el C. Juan Bautista Chan contra el Juéz Segundo de Paz de Tahmek," 1912. One point not addressed in Chan's grievance was how a *jornalero* could pay such an enormous sum, given that the daily rural wage at that time was approximately one peso. Without other financial assistance, it would have been difficult to raise that much money to liquidate a debt.

50. The use of scrip varied from hacienda to hacienda and only in rare cases was negotiable at shops in nearby towns. On payment by token or scrip, see Leslie and Pradeau.

51. Although many *jornaleros* were paid by the piece rather than with a set daily wage so as to boost production levels, it would be wrong to infer that these "rural proletarians" were wage earners in the modern sense. *Henequeneros* never made any pretense that these wages were meant to foster either a money economy or a free labor market in the henequen zone. For an interesting discussion of debts and wages on henequen and maize haciendas in Yucatán during the boom, see Gill, "Regional Variation," chap. 3. See also Wells, "From Hacienda to Plantation"; and Joseph, *Rediscovering the Past*, 59–81. As if to add insult to injury, some hacienda records tell us that proprietors enhanced their *jornaleros'* indebtedness by charging for breakfast. AGEY, RJ, "Tercer cuenta de administración de la finca San Pedro sujeta al juicio hipotecario promovido por la representación de Don Perfecto Eduardo Bolio Rendón y continuando por Don Wenceslao Lizarraga Patrón contra Doña Mercedes Irigoyen de Herrera," 1911, and "Segunda cuenta de administración que rinde el depositario de la finca sujeta al juicio que siguen los Sres. Avelino Montes S. en C. contra Marcos Díaz Cervera," 1911.

52. AGEY, RJ, "Cuenta de administración de la Compañía Agrícola del Cuyo y anexas, S.A.," 1910.

53. Quoted in García Quintanilla and Millet Cámara.

54. The concept is discussed at length in Tutino, *From Insurrection to Revolution*.

55. Knight, "Mexican Peonage," 64.

56. Not all *hacendados* prohibited corn cultivation. See Gill, "Campesino Patriarchy," 131–32.

57. See García Quintanilla and Millet Cámara. But cf. the account of foreign traveler Baerlein, who reported in 1913 that Maya peons were permitted to carry guns for hunting after work. Baerlein, 156.

58. Pellagra, a scourge in Europe throughout the eighteenth century (in Spain it was called Asturian leprosy), first appeared in the New World in Yucatán in the 1880s. García Quintanilla and Millet Cámara argue persuasively that this date was no coincidence; this was precisely when *henequeneros* began to undercut the fundamental security of subsistence by severing the Maya's tie to the *milpa*. Not until 1914 did a U.S. Public Health Service scientist prove conclusively that pellagra was not caused by toxic corn. See García Quintanilla and Millet Cámara; García Quintanilla; and Arjona.

59. Cited in García Quintanilla and Millet Cámara. Imports of corn increased, despite a federal tax on foreign corn, because trade patterns favored foreign suppliers over national merchants. See Kaerger, 22; Wells, *Yucatán's Gilded Age*, 170–74.

60. Gill, "Campesino Patriarchy," esp. 130–31. In "Honor and Social Control," Gill argues that on the southwestern fringe of the henequen zone, planters still provided *milpa* for their *acasillados*.

61. Knight, "Mexican Peonage," 64.

62. The following discussion is informed by the pioneering research of Gill, "Campesino Patriarchy" and "Honor and Social Control"; and Peniche Rivero, "Clase, género y cultura" and "Mujeres, matrimonios y esclavitud."

63. Gill, "Honor and Social Control," 2.

64. Quoted in Peniche Rivero, "Clase, género y cultura."

65. Ibid.

66. On Yaqui laborers, see Wells, *Yucatán's Gilded Age*, 164. More research is needed into gender relations on the henequen estates during the boom. We need to understand more thoroughly how patriarchy, as practiced by both master and servant, influenced the mechanisms of isolation, coercion, and security, and how the institution evolved as labor and economic conditions deteriorated during the last

decade of the Porfiriato. Equally important, we need to know how campesinas characteristically may have resisted and accommodated themselves to this double oppression. A more general discussion of peon resistance follows in the next section.

67. Although the predominantly Maya *acasillado* settlements lacked even the attenuated organizational and cultural resources of the zone's embattled village communities, they were not entirely bereft of cultural resources and affinities, most notably the family and religion.

68. This is also a classic illustration of the isolation mechanism at work. Alejandra García Quintanilla, personal communication, Nov. 20, 1987.

69. AGEY, RJ, "Diligencias en la averiguación del delito atentado contra la libertad de la menor Eleuteria Ek, denunciado por Micaela López," 1908, caja 658.

70. Farriss, 268–69.

71. See, e.g., García Cantón.

72. R. Scott; Moreno Fraginals, *El ingenio.* For reviews of the historiographical debate over Cuban working conditions, see F. Knight, "Caribbean Sugar Industry"; and Wells, "Terrible Green Monster."

73. R. Scott, 19.

74. Cosío Villegas, *Historia moderna,* 4: 529–30.

75. The social history of the Maya family has yet to be written. Our general observations for the late nineteenth- and early twentieth-century henequen zone are derived from a variety of sources, including AGEY, RJ and the regional press, and are informed by the ethnohistorical (e.g., Farriss) and ethnographic literature.

76. Finley, chap. 2, prefers to characterize slaves as "outsiders" rather than as "deracinated." Space limitations and incomplete data prevent us here from reconstructing patterns of resistance for the henequen zone's imported workers (Yaquis, Asians, central Mexican deportees, and *enganchados*). Non-Maya labor and resistance (and the difficulties attending its study) are discussed in Joseph, *Rediscovering the Past,* chap. 4, esp. 70–81.

77. James Harrington, *A System of Politics,* quoted in E. Genovese, *From Rebellion to Revolution,* vi.

78. J. Scott, *Weapons of the Weak,* "Resistance Without Protest," and more recently *Domination and the Arts of Resistance.* In the third book, Scott develops a more elegant and general model of "infrapolitics." Scott cannot (and does not) take full credit for focusing attention on "quiet" forms of struggle that do not result in insurgency. He acknowledges that his work builds on previous studies by scholars working in other areas on similar agrarian themes; e.g., E. Genovese, *Roll, Jordan, Roll;* and Adas. For a provocative, state-of-the-art survey of peasant resistance in its various forms, see Stern, "New Approaches."

79. J. Scott, "Resistance Without Protest," 450.

80. Hobsbawm, "Peasants and Politics," 12; also cited in J. Scott, "Resistance Without Protest," 424.

81. J. Scott, "Resistance Without Protest," 422; cf. *Weapons of the Weak,* chap. 7. Scott points out, e.g., that the accumulation of thousands of individual acts of tax evasion, theft, or desertion can seriously disrupt elite establishments and even destabilize regimes.

82. While hacienda records and mortgage suits (*juicios hipotecarios*) inform about such categories as wages, debts, production, machinery, property values, and goods on hand in the *tienda de raya,* they say little about the day-to-day interaction of management and labor. AGEY, RJ contains isolated references to shirking, footdragging, etc. (see n. 84 below), but note the absence of such detail in *hacendado* memoirs; e.g., García Cantón; and G. Molina Font.

83. An example of this vague impressionism is found in the 1971 documentary film *Mexico: The Frozen Revolution*, in which an old-timer is interviewed about the nature of labor relations during the henequen boom. Citations of the sparse oral historical literature are found in Joseph, *Rediscovering the Past*, chap. 4 and epilogue.

84. E.g., for shirking: AGEY, RJ, "Denuncia que hace Lorenzo Díaz de varios hechos delictuosos cometidos por Federico Trejo," 1910, and "Toca a las diligencias practicadas en averiguación de las lesiones que presenta Francisco Lugo contra Temístocles Correa Gutiérrez," 1914. For footdragging, noncompliance, and insubordination: ibid., "Toca a la causa seguida a Antonio Puc y socios por los delitos de motín y destrucción de propiedad," 1911. See also the letter to *hacendado* José María Peón from one of his *encargados* which laments that "owing to the torpor of Cab [a peon], we couldn't clear the land before the burning season." Letter from ? [Muna] to Peón, March 20, 1876, SPC, Box 4, Folder 26.

85. E.g., for rustling and theft: AGEY, RJ, "Causa seguida a Severiano Baas y socios, por el delito de abigeato," 1911, and "Toca a la causa seguida a Hermenegildo Nah y socio por los delitos de robo y destrucción de propiedad ajena por incendio," 1912. For arson and sabotage: ibid., "Toca a la causa a Santiago May por el delito de destrucción en propiedad ajena por incendio," 1908, caja 674; ibid., "Denuncia que hace Manuel Ríos de destrucción de propiedad ajena," 1914.

86. E.g., AGEY, RJ, "Cuenta de administración de la finca San José Kuché y su anexa San Francisco correspondiente a un més corrido de 25 de julio a hoy, agosto 25 de 1897," 1897. The comparative slavery literature contains an abundant discussion of feigned illness as resistance. The contemporary travelers' accounts by Baerlein and Turner, among others, contain a variety of planter complaints regarding the laziness and drunkenness of their peons.

87. *DO*, Jan. 9, 1908.

88. For examples of deaths attributed to "alcoholic congestion," see AGEY, RJ, "Toca a las diligencias practicadas en averiguación del motivo de la muerte de Manuel J. Chávez," 1913, and "Toca a las diligencias practicadas en averiguación del motivo de la muerte de Victoriano Chan," 1913.

89. Thus far, we have not attempted to quantify the criminal data in AGEY, RJ. The data's disorganized and incomplete nature would render such an exercise extremely difficult and highly problematic.

90. J. Scott, *Weapons of the Weak*, 302.

91. Gill, "Campesino Patriarchy," 146. Gill argues that by punishing his wife, this peon "reasserted his patriarchal domination."

92. A perfect case in point is found in AGEY, RJ, "Toca a la causa seguida a Manuel Baas por el delito de destrucción en propiedad ajena por incendio," 1912. Baas claimed that he was in a "total alcoholic stupor" when he burned down a hut. He was given a very lenient sentence.

93. See, e.g., the characterization of Maya campesinos in AGEY, RJ, "Toca a la causa seguida a Hermenegildo Nah y socio," 1912, and "Toca a la causa seguida a Visitación González y Magdalena Alcocer de González por injurias al funcionario público y resistencia a la autoridad," 1914.

94. For a fascinating discussion of the colonial judicial system's attitude toward alcohol abuse that has yielded important insights for the present work, see Taylor, *Drinking, Homicide, and Rebellion*.

95. AGEY, RJ, "Toca a la causa seguida a Santiago May," 1908, caja 674. One *mecate* equals approximately one acre.

96. The following is a sample of other unusually severe sentences for property crimes: AGEY, RJ, "Toca a la causa seguida a Felipe Medina por el delito de destruc-

ción ajena por incendio," 1908 (seven years, nine months for burning a house); "Toca a la causa seguida a Pedro May y socios por el delito de robo," 1912 (two years, six months for stealing a modest quantity of corn); "Toca a la causa seguida a Francisco Várguez por destrucción de propiedad ajena," 1914 (one year for illegally making *milpa* on eight hectares of a *hacendado*'s forest). Cf. the lenient sentence for murder in ibid., "Toca a la causa seguida a Manuel Fernández y Antonio Tos por el delito de homocidio," 1908, caja 680 (five years, six months for killing another *jornalero*). The eighteenth-century English courts similarly upheld the sanctity of private property. See Hay.

97. Menéndez, *Noventa años*, 137.

98. For a frustrated investigation, see AGEY, RJ, "Toca a la causa seguida a Pedro Chí por el delito de destrucción de propiedad ajena por incendio," 1912.

99. J. Scott, "Resistance Without Protest," 452.

100. For a discussion and critique of Scott's argument, see Joseph, "On the Trail of Latin American Bandits."

101. Gaumer.

102. A number of contemporary observers, including General Salvador Alvarado and Yucatecan poet Antonio Mediz Bolio, commented on the incidence of suicide among peons during the boom. See Carey, 78, n. 29. The problem apparently was not limited to Yucatán. Other contemporary observers blamed it on gambling, cynicism, superstition, bad business, unrequited love, and impugned honor. Cosío Villegas, *Historia moderna*, 4: 428–29. It is interesting that studies of the colonial Yucatec Maya by Nancy Farriss and Grant Jones have not uncovered a high incidence of suicide. Farriss and Jones, personal communications, winter and spring 1988. This may reflect differences in social conditions or recordkeeping. The Porfirian state was probably more disposed, and certainly far better equipped, to investigate violent deaths in the countryside, filing a detailed judicial report of each episode.

103. AGEY, RJ, "Diligencias en averiguación de la muerte de José María Eb, vecino que fué de la hacienda San José," 1912. Pellagra sometimes drove its victims to socially aggressive acts, including murder. Typically the victims were close relations or fellow peons. In 1912, Hermenegildo Puc beat Desideria Canul senseless in her hammock with his sandals. Puc believed that Canul was a witch who had cast a spell on him, "darkening his sight and refusing to make him well." The court ruled that pellagra had so diminished the defendant's senses that he was not responsible for his actions. Indeed, Puc was taken to the Ayala Asylum in Mérida for treatment. Ibid., "Toca a la causa seguida a Hermenegildo Puc por el delito de homicidio," 1912.

104. We are indebted to García Quintanilla, who first alerted us to this ritualistic Maya method of suicide. See, e.g., AGEY, RJ, "Diligencias con motivo del suicidio de Candelario Cauich, sirviente de la finca Chunkanán," 1913; "Diligencias con motivo de la muerte de Vicente Cen," 1908, caja 714; "Diligencias en el suicidio del que se cree llamarse Valerio Godoy, verificada en la Hacienda Vista Alegre," 1897, caja 296; "Toca a las diligencias practicadas en averiguación de la muerte de Enrique Canché Piña," 1912. These are poignantly descriptive episodes, but multiple references from RJ could be provided for any year in this study.

105. Quoted in J. E. S. Thompson, 301. Sylvanus Morley, relying on Bishop Diego de Landa, does not specify a special heaven for suicide victims but insists that suicides by hanging, warriors killed in battle, sacrificial victims, women who died in childbirth, and priests all automatically went directly to the Maya paradise. Morley, 194.

106. Morley, 203; J. E. S. Thompson, 301.

107. Quoted in Morley, 194. Redfield, in a ca. 1930s ethnographic study of a com-

munity outside the henequen zone, suggests (with no elaboration) a different cultural understanding of suicide: "The cenotes are also the openings to the underworld; the suicide, the worst of all sinners, hurls himself into the cenote to pass directly into hell." Redfield, 119.

108. Of course, the southeastern rebel Maya's creation of a Speaking Cross cult following the Caste War provides the most celebrated example of the reformulation of established forms and symbols within an ongoing, dynamic process of resistance.

109. Savarino, "La iglesia ausente."

110. In *Boletín Eclesiástico del Obispado de Yucatán*, Mar. 8, 1909, 35–38, cited by Savarino, "La iglesia ausente," 15.

111. Savarino, "La iglesia ausente."

112. See Knight, *Mexican Revolution*, 1: 64–65, and Katz, "Mexico: Restored Republic," 62–68.

113. Gill, "Regional Variation," chaps. 3 and 4, provides an acute microhistorical analysis of the involution of labor conditions, the tightening of credit, and the threat to the peons' security of subsistence during the final years of the Porfiriato. Particularly promising is Gill's preliminary discussion of planter appropriation of household labor, 39–40, 60–61.

114. For an insightful and devastating critique of such models, see Aya, "Theories of Revolution," and "Popular Intervention."

115. *RdM*, Sept. 20, 1909. The hacienda belonged to Luisa Hübbe de Molina, sister-in-law of Olegario Molina, Yucatán's richest planter and leader of the dominant oligarchical faction.

116. Ibid., Sept. 5, 1907; *EI*, Sept. 6, 1907.

117. See *DO*, *RdM*, and *DY*, Mar. 8–12, 1911. The revolt is analyzed in Chapter 7.

118. Gill, "Campesino Patriarchy," 89. Not surprisingly, campesino rebels routinely cut telegraph wires and often torched the poles as well. See, e.g., *DO*, Apr. 23, 1888.

119. It is nonetheless dangerous to overemphasize either the novelty or the threat in these episodes. Not until ca. 1910 were they reported consistently, and then, frequently exaggerated, at least by the regional press tied to the elite factions contesting the Molinista oligarchy. Long a repressed and cowed institution, the opposition press dramatically increased its coverage of henequen zone unrest after the national Madero rebellion opened political space. See Sierra Villarreal. Some indication of increasing rustling and banditry on the fringes of the henequen zone appears in AGEY, RJ, "Testimonio de la causa seguida a Herminio Balam y socios por los delitos de homocidio y robo por asalto," 1911, and "Diligencias practicadas con motivo del asalto y robo hecho a Absalón Vázquez, administrador de la finca Uayalceh," 1911.

120. Wolf's venerable ideal construct, the "closed corporate peasant community," has little applicability for Yucatecan peasants either in the henequen zone or on its fringes. Wolf himself has reflected on the utility of the concept in light of recent research. See "Vicissitudes."

121. See, e.g., the controversy surrounding the latest of many attempts to survey Muna's *ejido. RdM*, Mar. 8, July 29, Oct. 3, 8, Nov. 28, 30, Dec. 6, 1910. For a general discussion of the complexities of the ejidal issue, see *DO*, Aug. 9, 1911; Gamboa Ricalde, 1: 133–37; Chacón, "Yucatán and the Mexican Revolution," 118–19; and Franz, 34.

122. CGPD contains a particularly poignant case of how authority could be abused to dispossess a smallholder of his parcel. Gregorio Escamilla, a modest mason from Halachó, petitioned President Díaz when the district prefect denied him his parcel. The prefect, it turned out, was having an affair with Escamilla's wife at the

same time that he was distributing Halachó's *ejidos*. After Escamilla's wife left him, the *jefe político* conveniently justified the denial of land by arguing that Escamilla was no longer the head of a household and thereby not entitled to an allocation. Instead, the *jefe* awarded the parcel to Escamilla's estranged wife—now his own mistress. CGPD, 34:25:012455, June 22–23, 1909.

123. See *DO*, June 26, 1915; AGEY, RPE, "Informe del inspector administrativo del departamento de Temax, Capitán E. González, al Gobernador Salvador Alvarado," July 4, 1917; Ibid., "Informe del inspector administrativo del departamento de Temax, José A. Erosa, al Gobernador Alvarado," Sept. 15, 1917; and Chacón, "Yucatán and the Mexican Revolution," 51–54. The agrarian surveys Alvarado commissioned from 1915 to 1917—the results of which are reported in *DO* or contained in *informes* to the governor—have been invaluable to this study, not only in documenting patterns of ejidal dispossession and land accumulation but also in establishing the power and status of elites and village insurgents alike. We are grateful to Ramón Chacón for initially calling our attention to these materials.

124. For a discussion of the impact of the *pacífico* truce on agrarian relations in the southern Puuc, see Bojórquez Urzáiz, "Regionalización de la política agraria," and "Estructura agraria y maíz"; and Joseph, *Rediscovering the Past*, 46–52.

125. Our discussion of agrarian resistance in Santa Elena before 1910 draws on Stephens, 1: 204–24; *EdC*, Feb. 10 and Apr. 4, 1885; AGEY, RPE, Sección de Fomento, Manuel Sierra Méndez to Francisco Cantón, Mar. 22 and May 10, 1900, Secretary of *Fomento* Leal to Cantón, Oct. 10, 1900; Sección de Ticul, Colonel Carlos Tapia to Cantón, Aug. 31, 1901; Sección de Hunucmá, Angel R. Rosado to Cantón, Oct. 29, 1900, and Audomaro Reyes to Cantón, Mar. 14, 1901; Gill, "Campesino Patriarchy," 93–94; and Wells, *Yucatán's Gilded Age*, 103–4.

126. For similar acts of resistance to railroad surveying in Maxcanú and Peto, see *EdC*, Sept. 15 and 26, 1891; Wells, *Yucatán's Gilded Age*, 102–3; and Coatsworth, "Railroads, Landholding," 69.

127. See the agrarian surveys for Maxcanú and Hunucmá districts, respectively, in *DO*, July 30 and Apr. 16, 1917.

128. The ensuing discussion draws on AGEY, RJ, "Primer cuaderno de prueba instrumental que ofrece el representante del Ministerio Público en la causa seguida a José Encarnación Huichim y socios por el delito de homicidio perpetrado a la persona Feliciano Chi," 1908, caja 679; AGEY, RT, "Plano de los terrenos de las fincas Santa María Acú, Sihó, San Diego, Kankabchen y lotes de Cepeda y Halachó, 1916; Escobedo; Koh interview; López, 106; and Gill, "Campesino Patriarchy," 91–92.

129. It is ironic that Rendón, who for twenty years worked as a public defender for the indigent, should so eloquently defend a powerful *hacendado* in this case. For biographical details, see Menéndez Paz.

130. *EdC*, Mar. 20, 1880, Apr. 26, May 7, 1892, Sept. 17, 1895; *DO*, Apr. 24, May 27, 1892, July 3, 1895; *RdM*, Apr. 24, 28, May 1, 29, 1892, Aug. 10, 1897; and Gill, "Campesino Patriarchy," 85–86.

131. AGEY, RPE, "Informe del inspector administrativo del departamento de Temax, Capitán E. González, al Gobernador Alvarado," July 4, 1917; Campos Esquivel interviews.

132. These conclusions are supported by the agrarian surveys for Temax *partido* in *BE* 9: 7 (Mar. 1, 1902), 49–52; *DO*, Sept. 21, 1917; interviews, Campos Esquivel, Dec. 26, 1986, and Jan. 2, 1987; and Zozaya Raz. For the expansion of the Manzanilla estate, San Francisco, at the expense of adjacent smallholders, see Cisneros Canto, 49–50.

133. AGEY, RJ, "Causa seguida contra Pedro Crespo y socios por el delito de homi-

cidio, rebelión y robo," 1911; Zozaya Raz interview (Crespo); AGEY, RJ, "Toca a la causa seguida a Felipe Carrillo Puerto por los delitos de ultrajes a funcionario público y golpes simples," 1907, caja 614; *EC*, Aug. 19, 1911 (Carrillo Puerto); AGEY, RJ, "Causa seguida a Manuel Fausto Robles por el delito de lesiones," 1907, caja 629; *DY*, Mar. 6, 1911 (Robles); AGEY, RJ, "Causa seguida a Benjamín Cuevas Lope y socios por el delito de ultrajes a funcionario público," 1909 (Baak); Ibid., "Causa seguida contra José Policarpo Mendoza y socios por el delito de rebelión," 1912; *DO*, Aug. 14, 1911 (Leal). Details for several of these cases are provided in Chaps. 7 and 8.

134. In addition to interviews with Campos Esquivel and Zozaya Raz, see interviews with Doña Salustina Tut, viuda de Braulio Euán; Ku Peraza; and Trejo Hernández. See also *DY*, Mar. 6, 1911.

135. Zozaya Raz interview.

136. Although not a mestizo or a smallholder on the fringes of monoculture, Felipe Carrillo Puerto, the future revolutionary and socialist leader, similarly ran afoul of Molinista authorities and launched his career as a political broker in Motul *partido* during the 1907–11 period. An autodidact intellectual who worked in the countryside as a mule driver, carter, railroad conductor, and butcher, Carrillo Puerto became fluent in Maya as a young man. His agitation for an end to debt peonage and greater dignity for Maya workers led to continuing persecution by Motul's wealthy planters and their political allies. See AGEY, RJ, "Toca a la causa a Felipe Carrillo Puerto por los delitos de ultrajes a funcionario público y golpes simples," 1907, caja 614; and *EC*, Aug. 19, 1911. See also Joseph, *Revolution from Without*, 188–91.

PART II

1. To our knowledge, the term *hingeman* first appeared in P. Brown.

2. Tutino, *From Insurrection to Revolution*, 22.

CHAPTER 7

1. Unlike the national politics of late-Porfirian *camarillas* and *bloques del poder* (which have been little studied, and hence occupy the first part of this work), Madero's national movement and rebellion have received extensive examination, and require only circumscribed treatment here. The two best book-length studies of Maderismo, both of which duly emphasize regional factors, are Knight, *Mexican Revolution*, esp. vol. 1; and Guerra, *Le Mexique*. For a briefer, synoptic account, see LaFrance, "Many Causes." Two political biographies of Madero, written 40 years ago but still useful, are Cumberland, *Mexican Revolution*; and Ross, *Francisco I. Madero*.

2. Moreno Cantón, owner of *RdM*, was also a regional poet of some repute and, of course, Pancho Cantón's nephew. For biographical details, see *DdY*, Mar. 10, 1963, and *Homenaje del Diario de Yucatán*, 17–18. Pino Suárez, founder of *EPn* (see Chap. 3), would become best known as vice president in the ill-fated Madero administration (1911–13). For details of his life and regional political career, see Quintal Martín, *Lic. José María Pino Suárez*, esp. 65–66.

3. Womack, "Mexican Revolution," 82.

4. Civeira Taboada, "Francisco I. Madero," 57.

5. López, *El verdadero Yucatán*, 74.

6. A good summation of the two party platforms is found in Chacón, "Yucatán and the Mexican Revolution," 83–85; see also González Rodríguez, "Cuatro proyectos," esp. 80–83. In a provocative recent contribution, "Reinterpretación histórica," Yucatecan historian Menéndez Rodríguez emphasizes the Pinistas' progressive social

position, basing his argument on the finding that Pino's *camarilla* included many former supporters of Carlos Peón Machado, who he maintains was a sincere, even radical, reformer. By contrast, he argues, the Morenistas were merely latter-day Cantonistas, recycled Conservatives, and imperialists. Menéndez relies on Peón's previously untapped personal papers, which have come into his possession; he intends to develop his arguments in a forthcoming book on Yucatecan liberalism, which will focus on Peón's strategic role. For a preliminary statement, see "La agonía," 3–8.

7. One acerbic Molinista commentator, Alfonso López, railed against the Morenistas for their "unpleasant manipulation of the fairer sex." Patronizingly, he censored the women's transgression of customary boundaries: "These [political] gatherings . . . create anything but a favorable impression. The *señoritas* arrive in luxury automobiles, elegantly attired for a gala event, only to militate at the podium! And from lips that were meant to whisper sweet words of conciliation pour harsh, injurious diatribes that are as false as they are unbecoming." To validate his critique, López invoked similarly disapproving remarks by one of Mérida's leading female schoolteachers (also a Molinista), who objected to the tactic of using women as "the cannon fodder of the political campaign." López, *El verdadero Yucatán*, 67–68.

8. Nevertheless, Chacón, "Yucatán and the Mexican Revolution," 83–84; and Menéndez Rodríguez, "Reinterpretación histórica," rightly emphasize that the Pinistas enlisted many of the most talented members of the state's intellectual and political elite, namely, Calixto Maldonado, Alonzo Alonso, and Crescencio Jiménez Borreguí. Several of these Pinista intellectuals would endure in state political life well into the revolutionary era, serving in the Alvarado and Carrillo Puerto regimes.

9. Pinista broadsheet, part of *PL*, n.d., 1911, Biblioteca Carlos R. Menéndez.

10. López, *El verdadero Yucatán*, 69; Franz, 19.

11. Civeira Taboada, "Francisco I. Madero," 50; Franz, 19–20.

12. AGEY, RJ, Pino Suárez to Rigoberto Xiu, Sept. 9, 1909, in "Causa seguida a Rigoberto Xiu y socios por el delito de rebelión," 1909.

13. CGPD, Muñoz Arístegui to Díaz, Aug. 22, 1909, 34:29:014427.

14. CGPD, Muñoz Arístegui to Díaz, Sept. 28, 1909, 34:31:015141-43.

15. See CGPD, Muñoz Arístegui to Díaz, Sept. 13 and 21, 1909, 34:32:015777-79/34:32:015736-38; and López, *El verdadero Yucatán*, 64.

16. AGEY, RJ, "Acusación presentada por Crescencio Aguilar y socios contra el jefe político de Valladolid por abuso de autoridad," box 725, 1909.

17. CGPD, Muñoz Arístegui to Díaz, Sept. 28, 1909, 34:31:015141-43; Chacón, "Yucatán and the Mexican Revolution," 86, n. 126.

18. CGPD, Muñoz Arístegui to Díaz, Oct. 19, 1909, 34:33:016363-68.

19. According to one witness at an important organizing session of the party leaders, Pancho Cantón, although present, categorically refused to participate in any uprising against Porfirio Díaz. AGEY, RJ, "Causa seguida contra Alfonso Cámara y Cámara y socios por el delito de rebelión," 1909.

20. López, *El verdadero Yucatán*, 64.

21. On Oct. 29, the house of Alfonso Cámara y Cámara's mother, whose name was Candelaria, as well as the nearby Church of the Candelaria, a few blocks south of the center of the city, were both searched in a futile effort to find the ringleader, Alfonso himself. He was finally arrested two weeks later, but by then the plot had acquired its name.

22. Quoted in AGEY, RJ, "Causa seguida contra Alfonso Cámara y Cámara y socios"; see also López, *El verdadero Yucatán*, 82. For additional details on how the Candelaria revolt was supposed to unfold, see CGPD, Muñoz Arístegui to Díaz, Oct. 12 and 19, 1909, 34:33:016356/016363-68.

23. AGEY, RJ, "Causa seguida a Rigoberto Xiu." The captured documents are corroborated by published accounts of the CEI's strength and the size of its rallies. E.g., Baerlein, 110, puts Morenista membership at around five thousand shortly after the party's creation. Nevertheless, the Molinistas still retained some support in the countryside. See Aboites, 58–59; and Batt, esp. 208, who show that in Espita *partido*, local *hacendados* actually switched their allegiance from the Cantonistas to Molina and successfully managed dissent—at least initially.

24. We are indebted to Hernán Menéndez Rodríguez for introducing us to the colloquial political use of these terms.

25. AGEY, RJ, "Causa seguida a Rigoberto Xiu."

26. Ibid.

27. To make matters worse, Col. Juan Bautista Ramírez, the state militia officer who was to lead the revolt on Mérida's San Sebastián barracks with a force of 140, lost his nerve and fled the state with the funds intended for the military effort. See Chacón, "Yucatán and the Mexican Revolution," 87–88.

28. CGPD, Muñoz Arístegui to Díaz, Oct. 5, 1909, 34:35:016745-50.

29. AGEY, RJ, "Expediente formado con motivo de la queja presentada por Crescencio Jiménez contra Enrique Muñoz Arístegui relativo a una indemnización que hace acceder a ciento veinte y cinco mil pesos," 1916.

30. *ES*, Oct. 15, 1909. Carlos R. Menéndez, editor of *RdM*, managed to escape arrest by fleeing the state. Carlos Escoffié, who moved to Campeche to continue his work on *EPC*, was not so lucky. See Chap. 3.

31. CGPD, CEI partisans to Díaz, Oct. 12, 1909, 34:33:016456-64; Muñoz Arístegui to Díaz, Nov. 2, 1909, 34:36:017634-36; Sra. Cámara y Cámara to Díaz, Nov. 20, 1909, 34:36:017979-84.

32. Civeira Taboada, "Francisco I. Madero," 58–59, quotation, 81.

33. Menéndez, *La primera chispa*. Cf. Betancourt Pérez, *La problemática social*, which, while it takes issue with Menéndez's thesis, implicitly endorses the traditional historiographical preoccupation with the episode.

34. See, e.g., the Molinista organ, *LD*, June 27, 1910; and *DO*, Jan. 3, 1911.

35. In one important methodological respect, the Valladolid rebellion is unique in our study. Unlike the other major revolts of the 1909–13 period, this one has no criminal court records preserved in AGEY, RJ; at least none that have found their way into the bundles designated pre-1915. We have depended largely on the Porfirio Díaz Papers in CGPD, the regional press, memoirs, and secondary accounts for the reconstruction that follows. See esp. Menéndez, *La primera chispa*; Baqueiro Anduze; Jiménez Borreguí; Betancourt Pérez, *La problemática social*; Gamboa Ricalde, 1: 49–71; Urzáiz Rodríguez, 357–58; Bolio Ontiveros, *Yucatán en la dictadura*, 49–57; Berzunza Pinto, "Las vísperas"; Civeira Taboada, "Francisco I. Madero," 87–103; Chacón, "Yucatán and the Mexican Revolution," 90–97; and Franz, 30–36. We also benefited from interviews with Mario Menéndez Romero (now deceased), the son of Carlos R. Menéndez; and the longtime regional historian and activist, octogenarian Antonio Betancourt Pérez.

36. *DY*, Jan. 6, 1910.

37. Chacón, "Yucatán and the Mexican Revolution," 90, leaning on Baqueiro Anduze, 314–17, maintains that Jiménez Borreguí penned the revolt's Plan of Dzelkoop. In his memoirs, Jiménez downplays his enthusiasm for the revolt, essentially claiming that he was blackmailed into participating by the Morenista conspirators, who threatened to leak his associations with them to the Molinista authorities. See Jiménez Borreguí, 9–10; Betancourt Pérez, *La problemática social*, 16, 19–20; Betancourt Pérez interview.

38. Quoted in Civeira Taboada, "Francisco I. Madero," 91; see also Bolio Ontiveros, *Yucatán en la dictadura*, 49–56.

39. For Ramírez Bonilla and Ruz Ponce's role in the Candelaria, see AGEY, RJ, "Causa seguida contra Alfonso Cámara y Cámara y socios." Although we have found no evidence confirming Alcocer's participation in the 1909 conspiracy, he, too, had spent some time in jail several months before the Valladolid revolt for "suspected subversive activities." Franz, 31.

40. Fabela, 11: 114–18.

41. Cantón's own role in the conspiracy remains uncertain. Hoping to distance himself from the revolt, Don Pancho journeyed to Mexico City on June 12 to put himself willingly under house arrest, offer obeisance to Díaz, and thereby vindicate himself of accusations in the Molinista press that he was the brains behind the rebellion. See *DY*, June 13, 1910; CGPD, Francisco Cantón to Díaz, Aug. 29, 1910, May 1, 1911, 35:23:011420-21/36:17:008037. See also n. 19. Still, the Valladolid rebels went into battle shouting *vivas* to General Cantón and Delio Moreno Cantón, and *mueras* to Olegario Molina. See *DO*, June 21, 1910.

42. E.g., see *LD*, June 15, 1910; cf. Betancourt Pérez, *La problemática social*; Betancourt Pérez interview.

43. For a trenchant analysis of a similar case, the ties of cultural dependency that bound estate workers to patrons in peripheral zones of prerevolutionary Nicaragua, see Gould.

44. Arnold and Frost, 122; *EdC*, Oct. 7, 1902; Dumond, esp. 109, 123; Gill, "Campesino Patriarchy," 79–81. For a particularly graphic illustration of the deep-seated animosity Maya *comuneros* harbored toward whites around Valladolid, see AGEY, RJ, "Toca a la apelación interpuesta contra el auto que negó la libertad provisional bajo protesta de José Isabel Mena y Pedro Solís López, procesados por el delito de resistencia a los agentes de la autoridad," box 666, 1908. In this case, when *dzules* entered the pueblo of Dzitnup during a saint's day fiesta, they were informed, "This is *our* bullfight, and not for the white race."

45. Fabela, 11: 114–18.

46. It is interesting that at one point, Ruz Ponce and Ramírez Bonilla actually inquired into the possibility of speaking with the rebel Indians east of Valladolid about joining their revolt. A sympathetic local Maya smallholder, Felipe Chí, informed them that these Maya "would only run away at first sight." CGPD, Muñoz Arístegui to Díaz, Feb. 27, 1911, 36:8:003879-87. For some recent (but very preliminary) findings that suggest a more engaged political posture on the part of the Indian rebels beyond Valladolid and Tizimín, see Medina Un.

47. For an eyewitness account of the prefect's grisly end, see CGPD, report by captured insurgent Teodoro Núñez, included in Muñoz Arístegui to Díaz, Feb. 27, 1911, 36:8:003879-87.

48. Several authorities claim the battle was shorter; e.g., Berzunza Pinto, "Las vísperas," 78–80; Chacón, "Yucatán and the Mexican Revolution," 94.

49. Alcocer, mounted on a fresh horse, rescued a disoriented, semi-inebriated Ruz Ponce amid a hail of bullets. Together they fled east into Quintana Roo, finding sanctuary among a group of rebel Maya who had never surrendered to the Mexican state. Shortly thereafter, Ruz Ponce "romanced the daughter of the Maya chief and married her following indigenous customs." See Baqueiro Anduze, 294–95. Once the Díaz regime fell, however, and without warning, Ruz Ponce deserted his new family and the man who had saved his life, and returned to Mérida. Enraged by Ruz Ponce's flight, the Maya *cacique* ordered the execution of Claudio Alcocer. Ruz Ponce, as we will see in subsequent chapters, would opportunistically reintegrate himself into

local politics, first with the Maderistas, later with the Huertistas. On the unusual escape and subsequent fates of these *cabecillas*, see also Betancourt Pérez, *La problemática social*, 23–26; Jiménez Borreguí, 13–14.

50. E.g., see Gamboa Ricalde, 1: 57.

51. Menéndez, *La primera chispa*, 129.

52. Moreno Cantón cited in AGEY, RJ, "Causa seguida a Rigoberto Xiu."

53. Therefore the popular insurgencies led by the *cabecillas* Pedro Crespo, Juan Campos, and José Loreto Baak were also notoriously poorly armed.

54. Menéndez, *La primera chispa*, 120; Betancourt Pérez, *La problemática social*, 21; Betancourt Pérez interview. Cf. the moralistic language of Ramírez Bonilla's final reflections with that of the Plan of Dzelkoop.

55. Interviews with ex-*jornaleros* on the Yaxcopoil estate, 1984–85; Montalbano.

56. Bolio Ontiveros, *Yucatán el la dictadura*, 57–62.

57. *RdM*, Aug. 3, 5, 1910.

58. See, e.g., Aya, "Theories of Revolution Reconsidered."

59. The following reconstruction of Pedro Crespo's early political career and *guerrilla* in north-central Yucatán in 1911 draws extensively on Joseph and Wells, "Rough-and-Tumble Career of Pedro Crespo," esp. 27–34. That essay rests principally on AGEY, RJ, "Causa seguida contra Pedro Crespo y socios por los delitos de homicidio, rebelión, y robo," 1911; the partisan regional press (e.g., *DY, RdM*); and interviews with two old-timers who have firm recollections of the period: Campos Esquivel, son of one of Crespo's closest political allies; and Zozaya Raz, Crespo's successor as revolutionary *cacique* in the Temax district.

60. Zozaya Raz interview. In Yucatán the term *mestizo* differs from the standard usage. See Chap. 6, n. 31. Cf. Paul Friedrich's characterization of Primo Tapia—a more renowned agrarian "hingeman" in Naranja, Michoacán, during the 1920s—as "very Indian, but very savvy." *Agrarian Revolt*, 72.

61. Drawing on conventional secondary accounts, Chacón, "Yucatán and the Mexican Revolution," 98, highlights Crespo's initial dissidence with Molinismo. But existing accounts fail to note that in early 1909, Crespo (perhaps with some reluctance) was already working for Muñoz Arístegui's election. See *LD*, Jan. 15, 1909; Zozaya Raz interview.

62. *DY*, Mar. 6, 8, June 2, 1911.

63. Interviews, Zozaya Raz; Campos Esquivel, Jan. 2, 1987.

64. See AGEY, RJ, "Causa seguida contra Pedro Crespo." Although the court testimonies convey some confusion as to whether Herrera murdered Crespo's father or brother, the oral traditions we gathered in Temax leave little doubt that Don Cosme Damián Crespo was the victim.

65. AGEY, RJ, "Causa seguida contra Pedro Crespo."

66. At the end of the Porfiriato, Alfonso López made the interesting observation, "The burial of Juan Carnaval is a new wrinkle that has been added to Carnival festivities." *El verdadero Yucatán*, 137. For a persuasive symbolic analysis that explores how to "read" patterns of ethnic conflict from such historical accounts of Yucatecan carnival, as well as from observing present-day rituals, see Bricker, 150–54. For a more general discussion of the dynamics of popular "voice under domination" that considers rituals of reversal such as carnival, see J. Scott, *Domination and the Arts of Resistance*, chap. 6, esp. 172–82.

67. Crespo's band remained poorly armed even after sacking the barracks. Only half his men had old hunting pieces; the rest carried *coas* (henequen harvesting implements) and machetes. *DY*, Mar. 6, 1911; Zozaya Raz interview.

68. *RdM*, May 16, 1911. By the fall of 1911, Morenista insurgent networks clearly were more fully articulated. (See Chap. 8.)

69. Castillo, formerly the *encargado* of Hacienda San Luis, not only had become disaffected with the *patrón*, Ricardo Méndez; he also had family ties with villagers who had joined the Crespo revolt. *DY*, Mar. 8, 1911; Zozaya Raz interview. Here and in many of the other episodes we examine in this and the following chapter, kin (real or fictive) and communal affiliations played a significant role in shaping individual choices of whether or not to participate in a given event or movement.

70. *RdM*, May 16, 1911; cf. *DY*, Mar. 6, 1911.

71. Campos Esquivel interviews. Cf. the oral traditions regarding the Campos insurgency gathered in Villanueva Mukul, 124–36. Reading the local lore Villanueva collected about Campos evokes more often a Robin Hood, one of Hobsbawm's idealized "noble robbers," than a flesh-and-blood insurgent. For an analysis and critique of such constructions, see Joseph, "On the Trail of Latin American Bandits."

72. *DY*, Mar. 6, 1911.

73. Campos Esquivel interview, Dec. 26, 1986.

74. For his later career, see Joseph and Wells, "Rough-and-Tumble Career," 34–40.

75. This northwest-southeast arc of pueblos rather closely approximated the geography of the Caste War in the late 1840s and 1850s. The phrase *un hombre libre* remains embedded in the memory and discourse of the descendants of the rebels from these transitional zones. Interviews, Campos Esquivel, Zozaya Raz.

76. AGEY, RJ, "Causa seguida a Rigoberto Xiu." The following reconstruction of the Peto-Catmís insurgency rests on AGEY, RJ, "Causa seguida a Elías Rivero y socios por los delitos de rebelión, homicidio, destrucción de propiedad ajena, y ataques a la libertad individual y robo," 1911; AGEY, RJ, "Acusación formulada por don Arturo Cirerol contra don Máximo Sabido, Jefe Político de Peto, por los delitos de abuso de autoridad y allanamiento de morada," 1913; a variety of regional press accounts; and interviews with two octogenarian Petuleños who recalled the events in question, Ku Peraza and Trejo Hernández.

77. See the *jefe político*'s devastating critique of Peto's inexperienced and inadequate (ten- to twelve-man) garrison, which also applies generally to the lamentable state of Yucatán's militia throughout much of the period 1910–13. AGEY, RJ, "Acusación . . . Arturo Cirerol."

78. AGEY, RJ, "Causa seguida a Elías Rivero"; *DY*, Mar. 3, 4, 1911.

79. Ku Peraza and Trejo Hernández interviews.

80. *El Popular*, Apr. 17, 1923.

81. Ku Peraza and Trejo Hernández consistently used this term in their discussions of hacienda life in Peto District before the revolutionary period; cf. Iglesias.

82. The Cirerols also owned a string of henequen properties elsewhere in the state.

83. AGEY, RJ, "Acusación . . . Arturo Cirerol."

84. See, e.g., *DY*, Mar. 4, 1911.

85. AGEY, RJ, "Acusación . . . Arturo Cirerol." Emphasis ours.

86. Ku Peraza interview. To punctuate the point, Ku first referred to the sexual act in Maya.

87. AGEY, RJ, "Acusación . . . Arturo Cirerol."

88. NA, RG 59, Consul G. B. McGoogan to Secretary of State, Mar. 11, 1911, 812.00/985.

89. Ku Peraza interview. Cf. the government's more conservative estimate of its losses (40) in Civeira Taboada, "Francisco I. Madero," 112.

90. AGEY, RJ, "Causa seguida a Elías Rivero."

91. Unfortunately, conditions at Catmís would remain scandalous until the work force was mobilized and reforms were introduced by socialist governor Felipe Carrillo Puerto in the early 1920s. See Joseph, *Revolution from Without*, 213–14.

92. Ku Peraza and Trejo Hernández interviews. Rivero's bust, like that of Crespo, today graces the Pantheon of Revolutionary Heroes, established by the Partido Revolucionario Institucional in Mérida's main cemetery.

93. *DY*, morning and afternoon editions, Mar. 4, 1911.

94. See, e.g., the skittish reaction in the press to unrest in the Opichén-Maxcanú area roughly a fortnight after the events in Peto. *DO*, Mar. 18, 1911. Months later, planters openly worried about an alliance between their restive *jornaleros* and the eastern *rebeldes*, which, if consummated, might "destroy property and civilization in the peninsula." *EA*, July 1911, 305. Needless to say, paranoia had been even more intense during the Valladolid revolt, given the rebel Maya pillaging of that city during the Caste War. See, e.g., *DY*, June 9, 1910; Menéndez, *La primera chispa*, 13–16; Berzunza Pinto, "Las vísperas," 77–79.

95. See, e.g., *DO*, July 13, 1911.

96. Civeira Taboada, "Francisco I. Madero," 108. See also Bolio Ontiveros, *Yucatán en la dictadura*, 57–62; and Domínguez.

97. For a discussion of resistance to conscription and desertion as less confrontational but highly effective historical forms of peasant resistance, see J. Scott, *Weapons of the Weak*, esp. 30–32, 291–94.

98. Our reconstruction of this episode leans heavily on Domínguez, which in turn is based on extensive oral history interviews in Yaxcabá and Sotuta. All interviews cited in this section were conducted by Domínguez.

99. Interview, Clotilde Cob, Nov. 8, 1977.

100. Interview, Vilo Llanes, Dec. 15, 1977.

101. Cob interview, Nov. 8, 1977.

102. Cob interview, Oct. 2, 1977.

103. *Jefe político* of Sotuta, quoted in Domínguez, 190.

104. Unidentified informant [Clotilde Cob?], quoted in Domínguez, 190.

105. Ibid.

106. Ibid.

107. *RdM*, Mar. 8, 1911; *DO*, July 13, 1911; Gamboa Ricalde, 1: 88.

108. *DO*, July 13, 1911.

109. CGPD, Muñoz Arístegui to Díaz, Mar. 8, 1911, 36:11:005280-282.

110. Gamboa Ricalde, 1: 88.

111. On Curiel and his brief interregnum, see Gamboa Ricalde, 1: 88–111; see also Franz, 40–43; and Chacón, "Yucatán and the Mexican Revolution," 101–4. On Díaz's earlier use of such tactics, see Chap. 2.

112. *RdM*, Apr. 28, 1911, esp. editorial, 1.

113. Significantly, Muñoz Arístegui's ham-fisted repressive tactics in the wake of the Valladolid rebellion caused such a popular furor that even the Molinistas were appalled. Indeed, they periodically entreated Díaz to send Don Olegario back to pick up the pieces. On one occasion, Molina actually journeyed to Yucatán briefly (on the pretext of Muñoz's ill health) to defuse a gathering political crisis. *DY*, Jan. 15, 1910; Gamboa Ricalde, 1: 43; Chacón, "Yucatán and the Mexican Revolution," 88–89.

114. CGPD, Curiel to Díaz, May 16, 1911, 36:18:008671.

115. *DO*, Mar. 28, Apr. 24, July 13, 1911; NA, RG 59, McGoogan to Secretary of State, Mar. 19, 1911, 812.00/990; Gamboa Ricalde, 1: 96–97. As we will see, however, forced conscription would again rear its ugly head.

116. The committee's report is in *RdM*, May 30, 1911. (See also Chapter 8.)

117. *DO*, Mar. 27, Apr. 17, May 24, 31, 1911; *RdM*, Apr. 25, 28, May 12, 20, 31, 1911; AGEY, RJ, "Acusación . . . Arturo Cirerol."

118. *DO*, Apr. 19, 1911. Díaz, in dire straits in his national battle against the Maderistas, had agreed to Curiel's recommendation of amnesty on the condition that Yucatán's rebels lay down their arms and declare that they were revolting against local conditions and not against the federal government. CGPD, Curiel to Díaz, Mar. 21, 1911, 36:12:005637-38; Díaz to Curiel, Mar. 28, 1911, 36:12:005640.

119. Chacón, "Yucatán and the Mexican Revolution," 102–4.

120. See, e.g., *RdM*, June 25, 1911.

121. See, e.g., ibid., May 16, 1911.

122. Our reconstruction of the Muna rebellion and the early political career of José Loreto Baak draws on AGEY, RJ, "Causa seguida a Benjamín Cuevas López y socios por el delito de ultrajes a funcionario público," 1909; AGEY, RJ, "Diligencia practicada con motivo de la destrucción del plano original de los ejidos en este pueblo, denunciado por el Ingeniero de estos ejidos," 1911; *DO*, June 2, 1911; *RdM*, May 23, 27, 30, June 2, 1911; *DY*, May 28, 1911; *Renacimiento*, July 22, Aug. 5, 1911; Gamboa Ricalde, 108–11; and Gill, "Campesino Patriarchy," 94–96.

123. For an even longer historical perspective on the origins of the revolt, see Chapter 6.

124. Unlike the Peto insurgents, but very much like their Valladolid counterparts and those in most of the other episodes under scrutiny, the large force of Muna rebels was poorly armed. The minority that carried old shotguns had only eight to ten rounds to draw on; the rest wielded machetes. Gamboa Ricalde, 1: 110.

125. SPC, Arrigunaga to "Mintola," June 1, 1911, Manuel Arrigunaga Private Correspondence, Box 1.

126. Ibid.

## CHAPTER 8

1. The following discussion of the San Pedro Chimay riot rests on AGEY, RJ, "Toca a la causa seguida a Antonio Puc y socios por los delitos de motín y destrucción de propiedad," 1911.

2. Ibid. *Salpicón* is a popular Yucatecan stew.

3. Ibid.

4. In *Drinking, Homicide, and Rebellion*, Taylor suggests that during the colonial period, Indian defendants routinely played off of such demeaning white perceptions of them and constructed their courtroom defenses accordingly.

5. *DO*, July 12, 1911; Chacón, "Yucatán and the Mexican Revolution," 117–18; Gamboa Ricalde, 1: 122–23; see also Manuel Arrigunaga's earlier correspondence to "Minta." SPC, Letter, June 9, 1911, Private Correspondence, Box 1.

6. *DO*, June 15, 1911; *EA*, July 1911, 299–307; Chacón, "Yucatán and the Mexican Revolution," 120–24.

7. *DO*, Aug. 16, 1911; *EA*, July 1911, 305. Enrique Cámara, Víctor Rendón, and Manuel Arrigunaga comprised the planter delegation to the new Madero government. For a detailed account of the delegation's lobbying efforts, see SPC, Arrigunaga to "Minta," June 9 and 16, 1911.

8. Ibid., July 8, Aug. 16, 1911.

9. Ibid., Aug. 16, 1911.

10. *EA*, July 1911, 299; Chacón, "Yucatán and the Mexican Revolution," 120–21.

11. AGEY, RPE, José María Pino Suárez, "Un manifiesto al pueblo yucateco," June 14, 1911; Chacón, "Yucatán and the Mexican Revolution," 116.

12. *EA*, July 1911, 302–3.

13. Cámara Zavala, 125–26.

14. The most complete treatment of the twelve conferences and the plantocracy's larger debate over rural education and social reform may be found in Betancourt Pérez, *La verdad sobre el origen*; Chacón, "Yucatán and the Mexican Revolution," chap. 2, esp. 121–31 (much of which is reprinted in "Rural Educational Reform," pt. 2); and Bolio Ontiveros, "Historia de la educación." The following discussion draws on these works and two publications by the Liga itself: Liga de Acción Social, and Correa Delgado.

15. Quoted in Liga de Acción Social, 84–85.

16. Quoted in ibid., 67–69.   17. Ibid.

18. Ibid., 94–95.   19. Ibid., 188.

20. Correa Delgado, 51–52; Betancourt Pérez, *La verdad*, 24.

21. *DO*, Aug. 30, 1911.

22. Bolio Ontiveros, "Historia de la educación," 193; Gamboa Ricalde, 1: 143. For a celebratory account of Manzanilla's establishment of a school at San Francisco (and of his paternalism in general), see Cisneros Canto, esp. 116, 50–53.

23. Chacón, "Yucatán and the Mexican Revolution," 131 (our emphasis). Cf. Gamboa Ricalde, 1: 142–43.

24. *DO*, Aug. 9, 1911.

25. Chacón, "Yucatán and the Mexican Revolution," 118–20; Gamboa Ricalde, 1: 137.

26. For one notorious episode of flogging that actually found its way into the judicial process, see AGEY, RJ, "Flagelación a Julio Pérez," 1912. For a revealing case of excessive *fagina* abuse and the authorities' successful efforts to cover their tracks, see AGEY, RJ (no cover page), accusation of abuse of public power brought against the *jefe político* of Temax, Pastor Castellanos Acevedo, by Luciana Chi, 1912.

27. E.g., in 1912, when Avelino Montes foreclosed on the San José henequen estate in Acanceh district, it was pointed out that many peons' debts had just risen into the two-hundred- to four-hundred-peso range. *DO*, Dec. 28, 1912.

28. For the continuing use of bounty hunters, see, e.g., AGEY, RJ, "Séptima cuenta de administración de la finca rústica San Isidro y anexa que presenta el señor Roberto Hernández en el juicio hipotecario promovido por Pedro Solís Cámara contra Claudio Canul," 1911.

29. This phrase appeared often in the propaganda of the rival Morenistas: see, e.g., the broadsheet distributed with an ephemeral Morenista newspaper that encouraged "the real people of Yucatán" to repudiate the Campechanos, Tabasqueños, Laguneros, and Yaquis who poured into the state to work for Pino Suárez, himself a Tabascan. *AD*, Sept. 10, 1911.

30. We are indebted to Hernán Menéndez Rodríguez for introducing us to this aphorism. Personal communication, July 15, 1987.

31. For a more detailed treatment of the failure of such valorization schemes, including "the first [1912] Comisión Reguladora," see Joseph, *Revolution from Without*, 137–38; see also Chap. 4.

32. This was not the first or the last time that elite factional struggles had these consequences on local political fabrics; indeed, they show striking parallels with both the Caste War of 1847 and the struggles between socialists and liberals that took place during the subsequent Salvador Alvarado and Felipe Carrillo Puerto regimes (1915–24). Regarding the Caste War, see Reed; and Bricker, chap. 8; for revolutionary politics after 1915, see Joseph, *Revolution from Without*, pt. 2 and 3.

33. Moreno Cantón, CEI "Program of Government," cited in Civeira Taboada, "Francisco I. Madero," 131.

34. AGEY, RJ, "Toca a la causa de Juan Jiménez y socios por el delito de provocación al delito de rebelión," 1913. Emphasis ours.

35. *RdM*, July 2, 1911.

36. Chacón, "Yucatán and the Mexican Revolution," 110–11; cf. Mena Brito's (hyperbolic) assertion that 90 percent of Mérida was present at one CEI rally(!). Mena Brito, 2: 273.

37. Menéndez Rodríguez recalls that Morenistas like his grandfather, Carlos R. Menéndez, frequently made bitter comments about Pino's close ties to President Madero's brother Gustavo. Interview, July 24, 1987.

38. Carlos R. Menéndez, quoted in Civeira Taboada, "Francisco I. Madero," 151, 154–56.

39. AGN, RM, "El centro electoral independiente al pueblo yucateco," Sept. 14, 1911, paquete 19; AGEY, RJ, "Toca a la causa seguida a Felipe Carrillo Puerto," 1912; *DO*, July 13, Sept. 14, 1911; *RdM*, Aug. 12, 17, Sept. 13, 1911; *NdY*, July 21, 1968; Carrillo Puerto, 7–12; Chacón, "Yucatán and the Mexican Revolution," 111–12; and Franz, 45–46.

40. C. R. Menéndez, Editorial, *RdM*, Sept. 26, 1911, p. 2; AVC, Heriberto Barrón to Carranza, Aug. 3, 1916; Civeira Taboada, "Francisco I. Madero," 162–63; Franz, 47.

41. *EC*, Jan. 24, 1911.

42. Ibid., Jan. 11, 1912.

43. SPC, Arrigunaga to "Minta," June 16, 1911; *DO*, Dec. 20, 1911.

44. The ephemeral Morenista press (e.g., *VdP, EC*) was virtually obsessed with "El Financiero" during the second half of 1911 and into 1912. See, e.g., *VdP*, Dec. 21, 1911, and throughout January 1912. For other unflattering characterizations of Castellanos Acevedo at the time, see *DdH*, Jan. 24, 1912; and Fabela, 1: 160.

45. *VdP*, Dec. 21, 1911; *RdY*, Oct. 5, 1912; Joseph, *Revolution from Without*, 137–38. Rumors also circulated wildly among Yucatán's lesser planters that Madero himself was collaborating with Montes to seal the fate of the beleaguered Comisión Reguladora. AGN, RM, Faustino Escalante to Madero, Feb. 7, 1912, paquete 2–16.

46. *EC*, Jan. 11, 1912.

47. See, e.g., *DO*, Jan. 3, 1912; *RdM*, Aug. 30, 1911. (The more ephemeral Morenista press, e.g., *VdP, EC*, contained the same scathing references to *continuismo* after *RdM* was closed down in Dec. 1911.) See also *DdH*, Jan. 24, 1912; and Civeira Taboada, "Francisco I. Madero," 141–46.

48. *DO*, June 9, 1911.

49. The Pinistas stole the Dec. 1911 elections as blatantly as they had the earlier round in Sept. For the "cooked" electoral tallies by *partido*, see *DO*, Dec. 16–Jan. 17, 1911. Note particularly the incredible, often lopsided, Pinista victories in districts such as Motul, Temax, and Ticul, where popular Morenista *cabecillas* (e.g., Felipe Carrillo Puerto, Pedro Crespo, Juan Campos, and José Loreto Baak) clearly held sway.

50. AGEY, RJ, "Causa seguida a Carlos R. Menéndez y socios por el delito de rebelión," 1912; AGEY, RJ, "Toca a la apelación interpuesta por Carlos R. Menéndez contra el auto de su formal prisión en la causa que se le sigue a Jorge Rath y socios por el delito de rebelión," 1912; *RdY*, July 4, 14, 1912; Chacón, "Yucatán and the Mexican Revolution," 114–15. For a bitter commentary on Pinismo's strong-arm tactics, see the earliest issues of the short-lived, polemical *EC*, founded by Morenistas in Dec. 1911 when the regime closed *RdM* and jailed Menéndez.

51. We are grateful to local historian Menéndez Rodríguez for the insight regard-

ing Hunucmá's nineteenth-century history, a point that was confirmed in later discussions with local residents.

52. *DO*, July 12, 13, Dec. 22, 1911.

53. Ibid., July 12, 1911; Civeira Taboada, "Francisco I. Madero," 14–15.

54. Cámara to Pino Suárez, cited by José Delgado Lujan, Secretaria del Tribunal Superior de Justicia, in AGEY, RJ, "Causa seguida a Guillermo Canul y socios por los delitos de daño y destrucción de propiedad ajena," 1912.

55. See, e.g., the retrospective editorial in *RdY*, May 6, 1913.

56. AGEY, RJ, "Causa seguida a Guillermo Canul."

57. The ensuing discussion draws on the following criminal court records in AGEY, RJ: "Causa seguida a Herminio Balam y socios por los delitos de homicidio y robo por asalto," 1911; "Toca a la causa seguida a Herminio Balam y socios por los delitos acumulados de encubridor de homicidio, destrucción de propiedad ajena y robo," 1913; "Diligencias practicadas con motivo del asalto y robo hecho a Absalón Vázquez, administrador de la finca Uayalceh," 1911; "Causa seguida a Guillermo Canul."

58. AGEY, RJ, "Toca . . . de Herminio Balam."

59. Ibid.; Interview, Ek.

60. AGEY, RJ, "Causa seguida a Herminio Balam."

61. See, e.g., AGEY, RJ, "Causa seguida a Guillermo Canul."

62. *RdY*, May 6, 1913.

63. See, e.g., the mild sentence handed down in AGEY, RJ, "Causa seguida a Herminio Balam." Murderers typically received about two years. It is instructive to contrast such leniency during the seasons of upheaval with the harsh sentences routinely meted out for robbery and other property crimes during the late Porfiriato.

64. Handwritten ms., "Poecía para el 15 Septembre," AGEY, RJ, "Causa seguida a Rigoberto Xiu y socios," 1909. Of course, such popular constructions of liberalism (cf. the artisans' voices in Chap. 3) were not unique to Yucatán. The Morelos Zapatistas' Plan de Ayala, e.g., professed deep admiration for Juárez and concluded with the liberal slogan "Reform, Liberty, Justice, and the Law." For rich discussions of nineteenth- and twentieth-century popular liberalism, see Knight, "Intellectuals in the Mexican Revolution"; Mallon, *Peasant and Nation*; and Guardino.

65. Interviews, Campos Esquivel and Zozaya Raz. Robles, originally from Peto, was a mason and middling plotholder. He bitterly resented the Molinista authorities in Temax, who in 1907 had sent him to prison for 36 days for his involvement in a fight over a rather routine commercial matter. AGEY, RJ, "Toca a la causa seguida a Manuel Fausto Robles por el delito de lesiones," box 629, 1907; *DY*, Mar. 6, 1911. In March 1911 he helped Crespo depose and execute Temax's brutal *jefe político*, Antonio Herrera (see Chap. 7), and became Crespo's second in command.

66. Leal owned two decent-sized plots on the eve of the Mexican Revolution. See *DO*, Dec. 18, 1916. He was ousted from the Dzitas town council by the Pinistas. See *DO*, Aug. 14, 1911. Details regarding the revolt he led may be culled from several court cases treating the Morenista guerrilla campaign, most notably AGEY, RJ, "Causa seguida contra José Policarpo Mendoza y socios por el delito de rebelión," 1912.

67. On the incipient organization and rank structure of the Morenista uprisings, see, e.g., AGEY, RJ, "Causa seguida contra José Policarpo Mendoza"; and "Informe que rinde al Supremo Gobierno del Estado el Jefe Político del Partido de Temax, del resultado de sus operaciones en persecución de los rebeldes comandados por el cabecilla Manuel F. Robles," *DO*, Jan. 12, 1912. The latter appends several intercepted Morenista documents that reveal a heightened organizational capacity.

68. See the following, in AGEY, RJ: for a hacienda administrator, "Causa seguida a Bernabé Escalante por suponérsele presunto cómplice del delito de homicidio, para la continuación respecto a José Osorio, Juan Campos y socios," 1912. On the *turcos* and the *huach*, "Toca a la causa seguida a Juan Jiménez." On the patent medicine peddler, "Toca a la causa seguida a Julio Rodríguez y socios por el delito de rebelión," 1912.

69. Campos Esquivel interview, Dec. 26, 1986. The quotation is Campos Esquivel's firm recollection of his father's sentiments regarding Pino and his *camarilla*.

70. *EPn*, July 1, 1911.

71. Interviews, Menéndez Romero, July 17, 1987; Menéndez Rodríguez, July 15, 24, 1987—the son and grandson, respectively, of Carlos R. Menéndez. The Menéndezes possess the actual cable that Baak sent to Moreno Cantón and Carlos R. Menéndez at the *RdM* offices.

72. AGEY, RJ, "Denuncia de Isabel Carrillo Vda. de Villalobos, contra Loreto Baak y socios," 1913; *RdY*, Oct. 25, 26, 27, 30, 1912.

73. Broadside, "Al público," May 24, 1913, found in binder, "Varios Periódicos," BCRM. The broadsheet was a response to a Morenista editorial by "Augusto Miquis" (one of the pen names of Carlos R. Menéndez) in *RdY*, May 8, 1913. Cf. the Pinistas' earlier, sarcastic indictment of that "model citizen . . . José Loreto Baak," in the ephemeral paper *Renacimiento*, July 15, 1911.

74. *RdY*, Oct. 8, 1912; Menéndez Romero interview, July 17, 1987.

75. AGEY, RJ, "Toca a la causa a José Dolores Cauich y socios por los delitos de rebelión, robo, y destrucción de propiedad ajena," 1912; *RdM*, Dec. 4, 5, 1911; cf. the misleading account of the revolt that appears in ARE, unsigned letter, Dec. 16, 1911, L-E-737, R-67-6, 1–3, repeated in Franz, 48.

76. AGEY, RJ, "Causa seguida contra Carmen Och y socios por el delito de homicidio y rebelión," 1911; "Toca a la causa seguida a Hermenegildo Nah y socio por los delitos de robo y destrucción de propiedad ajena por incendio," 1912; *RdY*, Oct. 19, 25, 1912. Recent works by resistance scholars such as Guha (of the "subaltern studies" school) and J. Scott contribute insights on the uses of rumor and gossip in galvanizing both ephemeral and more durable episodes of peasant protest. In *Elementary Aspects* Guha argues, "rumor is both a *universal* and *necessary* carrier of insurgency in any preindustrial, preliterate society." Chap. 6, esp. 251. Clearly, few riots occur without rumors to incite, accompany, and intensify the violence; and no society, however controlling or repressive, can effectively screen out rumor and gossip—witness the case of Yucatán's de facto slave society. Moreover, solidarities and community itself can be "generated by the uncontrollable force of [rumor's] transmission." Ibid., 257. Thus the belittling manner in which official discourse treats rumor as "lies" or "bazaar gup" is "a clear acknowledgment of the correspondence between the public discourse of rumour and the popular act of insurrection." Ibid., 258, 259. See also Scott's provocative reflections on the anonymity and transitivity of gossip and rumor in building the "subcultures of resistance" that later fuel episodes of popular protest and revolt. *Domination and the Arts of Resistance*, 140–48.

77. AGEY, RJ, Diligencias practicadas a solicitud del señor Osvaldo González para la averiguación del autor o autores del delito de rebelión y conspiración para un levantamiento armado de los jornaleros de la finca Yaxche," 1911.

78. See AGEY, RJ, "Causa seguida a Manuel Canché y socios por los delitos de asonada, homicidio, destrucción de propiedad ajena," 1911; see also AGEY, RJ, 1912, for an extensive, if incomplete, set of documents inventorying the month-by-month caseload of each of the state's district and appellate courts during 1911 and 1912.

79. AGEY, RJ, "Diligencias practicadas . . . Osvaldo González."

80. See, e.g., *RdY*, Nov. 19, Dec. 16, 19, 20, 1912, Feb. 22, 26, 1913.

81. See the discussion of this subregion's agrarian structure in Chacón, "Yucatán and the Mexican Revolution," 51–52, which rests on the inventory of rural properties undertaken by the Alvarado regime in 1915. *DO*, June 26, 1915.

82. Our discussion of the extended Campos-Robles guerrilla campaign draws on the frightened accounts in *DO*: e.g., Dec. 28, 1912, Jan. 3, 1913; and the elite press: e.g., *RdY*, Oct. 20, Nov. 19, Dec. 19, 20, 1912, as well as several extremely rich court cases cited below.

83. AGEY, RJ, "Causa seguida a Bernardino Canul, Ramón May y Gabino Huchim, por los delitos de destrucción de propiedad ajena y lesiones," 1913; "Toca a la causa seguida a Fernando Mateo Estrada y socios por el delito de rebelión," 1913; *DO*, Dec. 28, 1912.

84. AGEY, RJ, "Causa seguida a Bernardino Canul, Ramón May y Gabino Huchim."

85. AGEY, RJ, "Causa seguida contra José Policarpo Mendoza"; "Toca a la causa seguida a Juan Jiménez."

86. AGEY, RJ, "Toca a la causa seguida a Juan Jiménez"; Campos Esquivel interview, Dec. 26, 1986.

87. *DO*, July 29, 1912, Jan. 3, 1913.

88. The following discussion draws on AGEY, RJ, "Toca a la causa seguida a Juan Jiménez," an extraordinarily rich criminal case comprising a file of well over one hundred pages. Although Sierra Papacal and the henequen estates that surrounded it were located in Mérida *partido*, they lay in close proximity to Ucú municipality in the rebellious *partido* of Hunucmá.

89. Jiménez, Sierra Papacal's *agente municipal* and leader of the local national guard detachment, apparently had come to feel betrayed by his erstwhile patron, Manuel Peón. Irritated and frightened by the *cabecilla*'s excessive violence against Pinista planters, as well as by Jiménez's escalating class rhetoric and actual work stoppages on his own estate, Nocac, the Morenista Peón had blown the whistle on Jiménez, requesting troops from the state authorities.

90. Interviews, Menéndez Romero, July 15, 1987, and Betancourt Pérez. Cf. a similar Morenista observation in *RdY* June 3, 1912.

91. Knight, *Mexican Revolution*, 1: 221. See also, e.g., Cámara Zavala, which promotes the Liga reform initiatives in the wake of the Maderista uprisings.

92. For example, several attempts were made in 1912 to bring *cabecillas*, such as Campos and Robles or their lieutenants (e.g., Juan Osorio), "in from the bush." Such attempts, typically made through the intercession of trusted couriers and friends, were unsuccessful before the consolidation of the Huerta regime. See AGEY, RJ, "Causa seguida a Bernabé Escalante"; "Toca a la causa seguida a Julio Rodríguez."

93. Knight, *Mexican Revolution*, 1: 333. See also Chacón, "Yucatán and the Mexican Revolution," 115.

94. For expressions of great relief among the Morenistas, sample the coverage of Maderismo's demise and the consolidation of Huertismo in *RdY*, late Feb. and Mar. 1913; see esp. Delio Moreno Cantón's endorsement of the new regime, Mar. 10. For the Molinistas' embrace of Huertismo, see Gamboa Ricalde, 1: 220–22; and Chacón, "Yucatán and the Mexican Revolution," 142–43. Cf. the similarly enthusiastic embrace of Huertismo by Oaxacan elites in Sánchez Silva.

95. For the amnesty declaration, see *DO*, Mar. 6, 1913. We base this conclusion on a careful examination of criminal court cases and executive decrees (*DO*) for 1913. We present the details of Huertismo's demobilization and repression of the popular movement in the next chapter.

96. Indeed, even banditry's etymological origins (the Latin *bannire*, to banish) suggest this process of exclusion, in which a boundary was created between the bandit and society (cast in even bolder relief with the analogous term *outlaw*). For a fuller discussion of the state's use of labeling to criminalize popular protest and resistance, which draws on a venerable Anglo-Saxon literature on the sociology of deviance, as well as the recent linguistic turn in critical inquiry associated primarily with French scholarship, see Joseph, "On the Trail of Latin American Bandits," esp. 18–25.

97. AGEY, RJ, "Toca a la causa seguida a Juan Jiménez."

98. Durkheim, 201.

99. See, e.g., Foweraker; and Skocpol, *States and Social Revolutions*, esp. 16–18.

100. Le Bon. For a broader discussion of psychological approaches to crowd activity, see Rudé, esp. 3–16; and Van Young, "Mentalities and Collectivities," 337–53.

101. E.g., *RdM*, May 16, 1911; see also n. 1. Of course, European social historians, such as E. P. Thompson and George Rudé, have also focused on the "moral content"—the appeal to customary rights or "natural justice"—that informed (eighteenth- and nineteenth-century English and French) crowd phenomena and enhanced their "capacity for swift, direct action." See E. P. Thompson, "Patrician Society," 401, and "Moral Economy"; cf. Rudé, esp. chaps. 14 and 15. It is significant that several of Yucatán's uprisings took place on days celebrating patron saints. Not only did *aguardiente* lower inhibitions, but such collective celebrations served to bind members of the community together, providing "time out" to reflect on shared grievances and demands. Cf. Taylor's discussion of late colonial uprisings in *Drinking, Homicide*, 118–19. For recent discussions of the sociocultural significance of folk Catholic celebrations in revolutionary-era Yucatán, see Savarino, "La iglesia ausente"; Fallaw, "Maya into Mexicans," and "El atlas parroquial de 1935."

102. AGEY, RJ, "Toca a la causa seguida a Luis Uc y socios por los delitos de amenaza de injurias," 1913. In her insightful essay, Martin examines a similar discourse. In the colonial mining society of Chihuahua, women would taunt their husbands as "effeminate cooks" and "cowardly hens" for their willingness to give in too easily to their employers' terms. Their manhood challenged, these workers often trudged back to the workplace and held out for a better offer.

103. See, e.g., AGEY, RJ, "Toca a la apelación interpuesta por María Isabel Reyes y Agustina Poot contra el auto de fecha 20 de mayo de 1914 en que se les declara formalmente presas, en la causa que se les sigue por el delito de ultrajes a funcionarios públicos," 1914. Here, wife and mother-in-law shielded insurgent *cabecilla*, were verbally abused and fondled by police, and fought back, provoking an uprising. Cf. Stern's insightful discussion of a "gendered etiquette of revolt" in eighteenth-century Mexican villages. Stern, *Secret History of Gender*, 189–213.

104. Kaplan, "Female Consciousness," 566. See idem, "Women and Communal Strikes," esp. 444–46 on the Mexican Gulf region; and "Making Spectacles of Themselves." Cf. Logan, which discusses female consciousness in present-day urban contexts, particularly Mérida, where many housewives are recent arrivals from the countryside.

105. Joseph, "On the Trail," and "Resocializing," esp. 166. Cf. Van Young, "Mentalities and Collectivities." J. Scott trenchantly observes, "Once all the structural factors that might shed some light on [outbreaks of protest and insurgency] have been considered, there will be a large and irreducible element of voluntarism left." *Domination and the Arts of Resistance*, 217. He cautions us, therefore, to leave some analytical space for historical breaks, for moments when things change dramatically, almost in Jekyl-Hyde fashion; for possibilities that are immanent in practices that on the surface would seem to indicate otherwise.

106. Taylor, *Drinking, Homicide*, 128–42; and Stern, "New Approaches," 3–25, provide insightful discussions of the relationship between peasant consciousness and structural relations of power in the genesis of rural insurgencies.

107. Cf. the thesis developed by Moore, *Injustice*, esp. 468–71. See also Tutino, *From Insurrection to Revolution*, chap. 1.

108. Thompson quoted in Winn, v.

109. Episodes that reveal much of this ambiguity and complexity are AGEY, RJ, "Toca a la causa seguida a Pedro Chi por el delito de destrucción de propiedad ajena por el incendio," 1912; and "Toca a la causa seguida a Juan Jiménez."

110. AGEY, RJ, "Causa seguida a José Policarpo Mendoza"; interview, Parra.

111. Parra interview.

112. Interviews with Menéndez Rodríguez, Apr. 13, 1987; García Quintanilla, June 9, 1985; Cruz.

113. Two court cases that document pressing in particularly rich detail are AGEY, RJ, "Causa seguida contra José Policarpo Mendoza," and "Toca a la causa seguida a Juan Jiménez."

114. Genovese, *From Rebellion to Revolution*, 11. For equally pertinent accounts of the dynamics of pressing in actions by eighteenth- and nineteenth-century Indian *ryots*, nineteenth-century English peasants, and former slaves in the postbellum "rice kingdom" of South Carolina and Georgia, see Guha, *Elementary Aspects*: Hobsbawm and Rudé; and Foner, chap. 3, respectively.

115. AGEY, RJ, 1910–13; Gamboa Ricalde, vol. 1; Betancourt Pérez, *La problemática social*; Franz, chaps. 1–3. See also the periodic reports of U.S. consuls, which echo the perspective of state officials and the planter elite, in NA, RG 84, 1910–13.

116. Guha, *Elementary Aspects*, 188–98, quotations, 197–98.

117. AGEY, RJ, "Toca a la causa seguida a Juan Jiménez."

118. In *Revolutionary Mexico*, Hart advances, in most extreme fashion, the populist notion of a peasantry unified in struggle.

119. Here, it should be noted, we are in agreement with Knight's characterization of the leadership of the Mexican Revolution's popular movement as a whole. Knight, *Mexican Revolution*.

120. See Chap. 7, n. 72, 73.

121. See, e.g., the essays in Stern, *Resistance, Rebellion, and Consciousness*, esp. chaps. 1, 2, and 9.

122. See esp. Tannenbaum, or any of the several classic populist treatments by Silva Herzog and Valadés; more recently, Hart, *Revolutionary Mexico*. Knight's magnum opus, *Mexican Revolution*, is less deserving of such criticism. Unlike other populists, Knight is consistently alive to regional variation. He refuses to deduce mechanically the behavior and consciousness of historical actors from structural relations of production or, worse, to assume that they are the product of some preexisting consciousness.

## CHAPTER 9

1. Quoted in *RdY*, Feb. 2, 1914; see also interview, Betancourt Pérez.

2. E.g., see *RdY*, Feb. 2, 22, 26, 1914. For additional coverage of the new regime's free bread and circuses, see *DO*, Jan. 28, 1914.

3. *RdY*, Feb. 28, Mar. 6, 9, 1913.     4. Ibid., Mar. 10, 1913.

5. Ibid., Mar. 25, 1913.     6. Ibid.

7. See, e.g., Ibid., editorial by "Augusto Miquis" [Carlos R. Menéndez], Feb. 2,

1914; cf. the earlier interviews with and editorials by Menéndez (a.k.a. "Miquis" and "Parmenion") throughout 1913 (e.g., Mar. 29, Oct. 13), all of which similarly indict Maderismo-Pinismo for being authoritarian and estranged from the people.

8. See, e.g., AGEY, RJ, "Toca a la causa seguida a Julio Rodríguez y socios por el delito de rebelión," 1913 (negotiations to bring in Juan Campos and members of his band). On Baak, see AGEY, RJ, "Denuncia de Isabel Carrillo Vda. de Villalobos, contra Loreto Baak y socios," 1913; *RdY*, Mar. 27, Apr. 8, May 21, June 1, 1913; on Ruz Ponce, see *RdY*, Feb. 26, May 21, June 1, Nov. 22, 26, 1913, July 25, 1914.

9. NA, RG 59, U.S. Consul William Gracey, Progreso, to Chargé d'Affaires Nelson O'Shaughnessy, Nov. 5, 1913, 812.00/9781.

10. By the end of March, Moreno Cantón was back in Mexico City, and shortly thereafter he abandoned his political career. He died less than three years later in the Federal District. *Homenaje*, 18; *DdY*, Mar. 10, 1963.

11. For a discussion of Huerta's policy of militarizing state politics, see M. Meyer, 95–108.

12. Witness the case of the wealthy Molinista planter Arcadio Escobedo, who was named interim governor soon after Pinista Nicolás Cámara Vales was forced to resign on Feb. 26, 1913. Escobedo stayed in office until July 9, 1913; after little more than a week of rule by former Pinista—and Molinista—Felipe G. Solís, Huerta appointed General Eugenio Rascón interim governor. (Finally, in September, the dictator turned the interim position over to fellow general Prisciliano Cortés, who in short order was declared "elected" to the office. All told, from late 1910 to late 1913, the state had fourteen governors. For a complete list, see *RdY*, Dec. 13, 1913.)

13. On the defection of Pinistas (and Molinistas) to Huertismo, see Chacón, "Yucatán and the Mexican Revolution," 142–45. For the incorporation of the Castellanos Acevedo brothers, Felipe G. Solís, Patrón Correa, and Maldonado into the Huertista government, see *DO*, Apr. 10, July 1, 24, 1913. For the report from Carrancista secret agent David Berlanga, June 1913, that Nicolás Cámara Vales, Pino's brother-in-law, had allied himself with Huertismo, see Fabela, 14: 275–80. Calixto Maldonado and Arcadio Zentella were the other two brothers-in-law who opted to join the Huertista government in Yucatán.

14. In a report released early in 1914, the Huertista government announced that it had "opportunely repressed disorder and crimes against people and property" in Hunucmá. *DO*, Jan. 7, 8, 1914.

15. E.g., see AGEY, RJ, "Causa seguida a Juan Martín y socios por los supuestos delitos de homicidio, robo, destrucción a la propiedad, e incendio," 1914; "Denuncia del señor Manuel Ríos (destrucción de propiedad ajena)," 1914; "Toca a la causa seguida a Felipe Cauich por el delito de homicidio," 1914; "Toca a la apelación interpuesta por María Isabel Reyes y Agustina Poot . . . en la causa que se les sigue por el delito de ultrajes a funcionarios públicos," 1914.

16. *DO*, Jan. 8, 1914.

17. On Prats's rehiring, see *RdY*, Apr. 9, 1913. On the "renaissance" of the Juárez Penitentiary under Huertismo, see *RdY*, Mar. 19, 1914.

18. *RdY*, Feb. 18, 1914; *DO*, Jan. 1, 8, 1914.

19. The following conclusions are based on an analysis of hundreds of criminal files in AGEY, RJ, 1913–14, particularly a series of monthly inventories prepared for the state judiciary by the clerks of each court. Rich, though incomplete, these documents summarize the caseloads of first-instance and appellate courts throughout the state, and typically note alleged crimes, verdicts, and numbers of prisoners involved.

20. AGEY, RJ, "Toca a la causa seguida a Francisco Várguez por destrucción de

propiedad ajena," 1914. The defendant's attorney characterized the land on which Várguez squatted as "poor land [that] contains no precious woods"—a point the prosecution did not dispute.

21. E.g., see the report, dated May 27, 1914, by the national Department of Labor's special agent, Esteban Flores, on social conditions in Yucatán in March 1914. AGN, RTr, Departamento de Trabajo, caja 9, exp. 20; later published, with commentary, in Flores D.

22. Franz, 58.

23. *RdY*, Sept. 26, 1912; *EA* (Oct. 1912), 571–72.

24. The 1914 report by Graciano Ricalde and Tomás Ojeda to Governor Eleuterio Avila was published five years later as *Informe acerca de las operaciones*; quotation, 15.

25. Contemporaries alleged that Arturo Pierce remained a party to the notorious pact between Harvester and Molina-Montes to control production and keep prices as low as possible. See, e.g., Gamboa Ricalde, 1: 142–43; C. Reyes, esp. 181–83; Chacón, "Yucatán and the Mexican Revolution," 131. It is clear that Pierce had collaborated with the Molinistas and IHC on various occasions, but in the absence of documentation that would constitute a "smoking gun," such allegations cannot be proved for the 1913–14 period. If they were true, and the market share controlled by Pierce's *casa* were added to that of Montes's *casa*, the Molinista *parentesco* would have controlled upwards of 94 percent of the trade in 1914!

26. The allegations regarding Cortés's collaboration with Montes and the hefty bribe are stated matter-of-factly in Gamboa Ricalde, 1: 200–201; and repeated in Chacón, "Yucatán and the Mexican Revolution," 150–51, and in the Betancourt Pérez interview. (Gamboa Ricalde wrote about events and arrangements he had experienced or noticed as a politically engaged member of Meridano society.) For evidence of the sales to Montes and repeated laments that the Reguladora had practically ceased its activities under Cortés's administration, see *EA* (Oct. 1913), 774, and (July 1914), 917–18.

27. *RdY*, Nov. 22, 1913.

28. E.g., ibid., Dec. 11, 1913. The paper's editor and publisher, Carlos R. Menéndez, tried to put the best face on an unsavory situation. Admitting that "Yucatán is the only place in the world where such a system of debts exists," he also pointed out that labor conditions had recently improved on some estates and that some planters were moving toward free labor in a piecemeal, de facto manner.

29. On flogging, see, e.g., AGEY, RJ, "Toca a la causa seguida a Pedro Pinto y socios por los delitos de lesiones y atentados contra la libertad individual," 1914, and "Toca a las dilgencias practicadas en averiguación de las lesiones que presenta Francisco Lugo contra Temístocles Correa Gutiérrez," 1914. On *fagina*, see "Toca a la causa seguida a Leopoldo Marín, vecino de Oxkutzcab, por ultrajes a funcionario público." For the continuing measurement and parceling of village lands, see *DO*, May 22, 1914. The pueblo in question was Yaxkukul in the *partido* of Tixkokob. For the Spanish crown's original conferral of the *ejido* to the pueblo, see Barrera Vásquez.

30. The following discussion draws on the actual report, found in AGN, RTr, caja 9, exp. 20, May 27, 1914.

31. Judicial investigations into a series of gruesome suicides by Maya peons in the advanced stages of pellagra certainly bear out Flores's observation. See, e.g., AGEY, RJ, "Toca a las diligencias practicadas en averiguación de la muerte de Francisco Tuc," 1914 (peon throws himself down well); "Diligencias con motivo de la muerte de Martín Can," 1914 (peon found hanging on door of beekeeping shed); "Diligencias

con motivo de la muerte de María Francisca Cetzal," 1914 (peon's wife hangs herself in full view of patron's residence).

32. The following discussion draws on AGEY, RJ, "Toca a la causa seguida a Pedro Pinto"; *RdY*, Sept. 21, Oct. 1, 3, 5, 1913. Other cases of lesser renown and degree could be cited. See, e.g., AGEY, RJ, "Toca a las diligencias . . . Francisco Lugo."

33. For San Nicolás's privileged position in the agricultural economy of Motul municipality and district, see the agrarian survey of properties in *DO*, Aug. 20, 1917.

34. It should be remembered that Juan Campos was a humble campesino from Temax district and no relation to the elite Campos-Palma *parentesco* of Motul, of which Crescencio Novelo was a member.

35. A photo of the leg irons appeared in *RdY*, Oct. 3, 1913.

36. Unfortunately, the file in the AGEY, RJ, and the press accounts are incomplete. Thus, while we know a great deal about the lower court's deliberations, we know much less about the appellate case—only that the defendants were never convicted.

37. See E. Genovese, *Roll, Jordan, Roll*, 25–49.

38. See, e.g., Gamboa Ricalde, 1: chap. 16; Franz, chap. 3; Chacón, "Yucatán and the Mexican Revolution," chap. 2.

39. Knight, *Mexican Revolution*, 1: 169.

40. See, e.g., AGEY, RJ, "Incendio en la finca Texán," 1913, on peons' absolute failure to observe customary deference; and *RdY*, Mar. 31, 1914, wherein angry peons confront their *encargado* "without doffing their hats . . . and with a disrespectful attitude."

41. As we saw in Chapter 6, arson always represented the most fearsome of the "weapons of the weak"—potentially terrible in its destruction, difficult to protect against or to prosecute successfully. During 1913–14 the districts of Hunucmá and Maxcanú alone saw three major episodes of arson, the most dramatic in late April at Hacienda San Antonio Chel, the large estate of Molinista superplanter Augusto L. Peón. In a matter of moments, the blaze consumed almost four thousand *mecates* of fiber in four fields, a loss of eighty thousand pesos. See AGEY, RJ, "Denuncia del señor Ríos"; and *RdY*, Apr. 30, 1914. For the other episodes in Hunucmá and Maxcanú, see AGEY, RJ, "Incendio en la finca Texán," and "Toca a las diligencias practicadas en averiguación del delito de destrucción de la propiedad por incendio denunciado por Próspero Patrón," 1914. According to the agrarian survey conducted by General Alvarado's revolutionary government in 1916, Augusto Peón's San Bartolomé Texán and San Antonio Chel were easily the two most valuable henequen estates in Hunucmá municipality. See *RdY*, Apr. 16, 1917.

42. AGEY, RJ, "Toca a las diligencias practicadas con motivo de una bomba que estalló en la casa de Diego Alcocer," 1914.

43. NA, RG 59, Gracey, Progreso, to H. L. Wilson, June 4, 1915, 812.5045/62; Spenser, 220–27; Franz, 87–88. The railroad workers' union was founded in late April 1911. See Durán Rosado, 3.

44. Travelers and military officials from Mexico City and other parts of the republic consistently commented on the high cost of living in the peninsula. See, e.g., the remarks of Constitutionalist governor General Toribio de los Santos, in a letter to Venustiano Carranza, Jan. 14, 1915, CJD, roll 3.

45. NA, RG 59, Gracey to Wilson, June 4, 1913, 812.5045/62; Gracey to Secretary of State, June 14, 1913, 812.5045/63; Franz, 87; Chacón, "Yucatán and the Mexican Revolution," 151–52. The port workers sought an increase of about 25 percent; Montes argued for something in the range of 8 to 10 percent—a position from which he had not significantly budged in about six months. See *RdY*, Dec. 17, 1913.

46. NA, RG 59, Gracey to Secretary of State, Nov. 8, 1913, 812.00/9781; *RdY*, Feb. 3, 1913; Betancourt Pérez interview; Chacón, "Yucatán and the Mexican Revolution," 152–53.

47. For detailed coverage of the strike and an evaluation of its impact, see Durán Rosado.

48. Witness the separatist activity in the peninsula in response to centralist policies in the 1830s and 1840s. See Reed, chaps. 1, 2.

49. *EA* (Oct. 1913), 784; NA, RG 59, Gracey to Secretary of State, Apr. 22, 1913, 812.00/7363.

50. NA, RG 59, O'Shaughnessy to Secretary of State, Jan. 25, 1914, 812.00/10684; *DO*, Jan. 16, 1914; Gamboa Ricalde, 1: 223–25; Chacón, "Yucatán and the Mexican Revolution," 149–50.

51. *EA* (Oct. 1913), 784; NA, RG 59, Gracey to Secretary of State, Oct. 31, 1913, 812.00/9698.

52. *EA* (Oct. 1913); *RdY*, Nov. 1, 9, 1913, esp. Carlos R. Menéndez's editorials.

53. For one *hacendado*'s discussion of the relationship between taxes and profits, see G. Molina Font, esp. 80.

54. NA, RG 59, Gracey to Secretary of State, Nov. 22, 1913, 812.00/10019.

55. *RdY*, Apr. 16, 1914.

56. See the day-to-day human interest coverage of the draft in *RdY*, Nov. 21–26, 1913. See also NA, RG 59, Gracey to Secretary of State, Nov. 22 and Dec. 2, 1913, 812.00/10019/10165.

57. See, e.g., *RdY*, Nov. 22, 26, 1913. It is instructive that, judging from press accounts and judicial evidence, both recruiting for the draft and resistance to it were most pronounced in three of the rural districts where the Maderista insurgency had been most active: Hunucmá, Temax, and Valladolid. This has several possible explanations, none of them mutually exclusive. First, as we have seen, the Huertistas sought to co-opt local chiefs who might recruit their own retainers for military service (e.g., Ruz Ponce). Second, it was in those areas where campesinos were well mobilized and determined to defend their autonomy that recruitment stirred the greatest passions and made the fewest inroads. Third, the Huertistas may have been determined (and advised by local planters) to use the *leva* as an instrument of pacification and repression in "bandit-infested" zones. While no hard evidence has surfaced to corroborate such a conscious policy, the interviews with Campos Esquivel, Dec. 26, 1986, and Betancourt Pérez strongly support this argument.

58. Campos Esquivel interview, Dec. 26, 1986.

59. *RdY*, Nov. 22, 1913.

60. *DO*, June 4, 1914.

61. *RdY*, May 16, 1914.

62. See, e.g., the editorials about this question in *RdY*, Nov. 1913, *passim*.

63. See, e.g., *RdY*, Apr. 16, 1914; cf. the similar assessment of the Yaquis by Governor Eleuterio Avila in AGEY, RPE, Avila to Carranza, Jan. 3, 1915.

64. Ceballos Rodríguez, 86. Tragedy had already befallen the main body of about 280 deported Zapatista troops who constituted the Second Company of the Sixteenth Federal Battalion, which was stationed in Mérida. In the wee hours of the morning of Aug. 19, 1913, the Zapatistas had mutinied at the Mejorada Barracks, then held off local troops for several hours before being subdued. After the bloody battle, a military court had harshly punished the company's members: the leaders were executed, and the others sent to penal camps in Quintana Roo. See *DO*, Aug. 20, 1913, Jan. 8, 1914; NA, RG 59, Consul J. W. Germon, Progreso, to Secretary of State, Aug. 20, 1913, 812.00/8511.

65. E.g., AGEY, RJ, "Toca a las dilgencias practicadas en averiguación del delito de ataques a la libertad individual denunciado por Pedro Concha y atribuido a José Marcelino y Benjamín Zapata," 1914; "Querella del Alonso Patrón Espada contra el ex-Jefe Político de Mérida, Tomás Castellanos Acevedo, por los delitos de defamación y atentados contra la libertad individual," 1914; "Acusación de Alonso Patrón Espada contra Tomás Castellanos A.," 1914; *RdY*, Apr. 10, 1913. Planters had long coveted control over workers on neighboring estates but rarely had attempted to co-opt them. In these cases, Felipe G. Cantón and Tomás Castellanos Acevedo used their clout in the Pinista and Huertista regimes to seize and litigate control over groups of workers from the estates of the Zapata and Patrón Espadas families, respectively, but the courts ultimately nullified their efforts.

66. See the argument to this effect in *RdY*, July 9, 1913.

67. *DO*, Apr. 21, 1914, special supplement.

68. Ibid., Apr. 28, 1914; NA, RG 59, Germon to Department of State, Apr. 23, 1914, 812.00/11783.

69. Discussion of these conjunctural factors dominates regular reports on Yucatán's political economy in *RdY* and *DO*, ca. May through October 1914. On the maize shortage and Montes and Escalante's involvement in the trade, see, e.g., *DO*, May 13, Sept. 10, 1914; *RdY*, July 8, 9, Sept. 5, 1914.

70. *RdY*, Sept. 4, 1914.

71. Our account of the Chemax episode draws on AGEY, RJ, "Toca a la apelación interpuesta por Mateo Knil contra el acto de Formal Prisión, en la causa que por el delito de homicidio se sigue contra éste y socios," 1914; and *RdY*, July 30, 1914.

72. AGEY, RJ, "Toca a la causa seguida a Felipe Cauich."

73. For the standoff regarding "Solís's road" and its historical determinants, see *RdY*, July 12, 16, 29, Aug. 5, 8, 1914.

74. Ibid., Aug. 26, 28, 1914.

75. AGEY, RJ, "Toca a la causa seguida a Juan Martín"; "Toca al recuso de apelación interpuesta contra el auto de formal prisión dictado contra Juan Martín y socios en la causa que se les sigue por los delitos de homicidio, robo, y destrucción de propiedad ajena," 1914. Four of the campesinos (all but Martín bearing Maya surnames) were apprehended. Unfortunately, neither of these incomplete files provides any information regarding the disposition of the case.

76. The following narrative account is based on *RdY*, Aug. 9, 15, 19, 20, 1914; NA, RG 59, Germon to Secretary of State, Aug. 20, 1914, 812.00/13125; C. Escoffié.

77. *RdY*, Aug. 21, 23, 25, 26, 1914; C. Escoffié.

78. For white society's fears that "the *clase indígena* was again giving itself up to insurrection and drunkenness," see *RdY*, Aug. 26, 1914. For Cortés's SOS call to the Constitutionalists, see AVC, Governor Cortés to General Eduardo Hay, Secretary of War and Navy, Aug. 27, 1914.

79. Editorial by "Parmenion," *RdY*, Sept. 4, 1914.

80. Ibid., Aug. 27, Sept. 16, 1914; Gamboa Ricalde, 1: 225–26; Mena Brito, 3: 52–55; J. Molina Font, 3; Chacón, "Yucatán and the Mexican Revolution," 160–61. The most prestigious client of José Avila's law practice was Joaquín Casasús, the noted Porfirian *científico*, whose family was closely allied with the Molinas through marriage.

81. On this point and many others regarding the Avila regime, this chapter draws on the informative account provided in Chacón, "Yucatán and the Mexican Revolution," chap. 3.

82. *RdY*, Sept. 6, 9, 10, Dec. 21, 1914.

83. See, e.g., column by "Augusto Miquis," *RdY*, Sept. 13, 1914.

84. *DO*, Sept. 10, 28, 1914; *RdY*, Sept. 16, 1914; NA, RG 59, Germon to Secretary of State, Sept. 11, 1914, 812.00/135252.

85. *DO*, Sept. 21, Nov. 21, 1914. U.S. military and diplomatic sources reported that Avila had bolstered the state's military capacity by recruiting nine hundred Yaquis into the "Pino Suárez" Battalion, thereby suggesting that Huertista military recruiters had transported few if any Yaquis from the state. NA, RG 59, Commanding Officer, Detached Atlantic Squadron, to Secretary of the Navy, Nov. 7, 1914, 812.00/13286.

86. AGEY, RPE, Toribio de los Santos to Carranza, Jan. 14, 1915; *RdY*, Nov. 29, 1914.

87. *DO*, Sept. 26, Oct. 2, 1914; *RdY*, Sept. 27, 1914; AGEY, RPE, Daniel Sánchez, Juez de Paz, Suma, to Governor Carlos Castro Morales, Nov. 17, 1919. We thank Ramón Chacón for bringing this reference to our attention.

88. For such penalties see, e.g., NA, RG 59, Germon to Secretary of State, Sept. 11, 1914, 812.00/13252; J. Molina Font, 3.

89. Chacón, "Yucatán and the Mexican Revolution," 168–69.

90. *RdY*, Sept. 10, 1914.

91. *DO*, Sept. 12, 1914.

92. Joaquín García Ginerés, "El nuevo régimen," *EA* (Sept. 1914), 748. Cf. the almost identical language in Menéndez's editorial in *RdY*, Sept. 13, 1914.

93. *DO*, Oct. 17, 1914.

94. In the absence of statistical data, we have only informed speculation regarding the extent of permanent flight. See Chacón, "Yucatán and the Mexican Revolution," 170. For one Yucatecan intellectual's memories of the event, see Rosado Vega, 105.

95. *RdY*, Mar. 31, Sept. 17, 1914.

96. Ibid., Sept. 17, 1914.

97. Ibid., Mar. 3, 1914; Sept. 15, 17, 1914.

98. Gamboa Ricalde, 2: 225.

99. *DO*, Sept. 22, 1914.

100. Ibid., Sept. 24, 1914; AGEY, RPE, Avila to Comandante Militar of Mérida, Sept. 28, 1914; *RdY*, Sept. 21, 1914.

101. ASA-C, Peón to Tritschler y Córdoba, Nov. 14, 1914. For a biting critique of Avila by a Cuban labor organizer that reaches much the same conclusion, see Loveira, 25–27.

102. *DO*, Nov. 14, 1914; *RdY*, Nov. 17, 1914; AGEY, RPE, Avila to Carranza, Oct. 7, 1914. The Constitutionalists prohibited as "unsanitary" the use of holy water, the kissing of sacred images, and the presence of cadavers or their remains in religious buildings.

103. For an incisive treatment of the church under both Avila and Alvarado, see Chacón, "Yucatán and the Mexican Revolution," chaps. 3, 4, and "Salvador Alvarado and the Roman Catholic Church."

104. ASA-C, Castellanos to Tritschler y Córdoba, Dec. 25, 1914. For his part, Avila wrote to Carranza, "While I have acted entirely in accord with our principles, I have done so without wounding the religious sensitivities of my fellow Yucatecans. . . . I have reached an agreement with the present head of the Church in the state [and] he has taken the steps necessary to avoid abuses in outward worship." AVC, Avila to Carranza, Oct. 7, 1914.

105. Loveira, 23.

106. Peón went so far as to suggest that the governor was the creature of José T. Molina, Don Olegario's nephew. ASA-C, Peón to Tritschler y Córdoba, Sept. 12

and Nov. 14, 1914. This instrumentalist position has also been adopted by Chacón, "Yucatán and the Mexican Revolution," chap. 3; Berzunza Pinto, "El constitucionalismo"; and Mena Brito, vol. 3, esp. 73, 81.

107. See, e.g., CJD, Toribio de los Santos to Carranza, Jan. 14, 1915, roll 3 (bribes from reactionaries); *DO*, Sept. 14, 1914 (liquidation of the Reguladora); and Chacón, "Yucatán and the Mexican Revolution," chap. 3 (opposition to Constitutionalist demands).

108. Ibid., 184; Mena Brito, 3: 73, 81.

109. Most notably the radical Constitutionalist, General Toribio V. de los Santos, who replaced Avila as governor and liked to draw invidious comparisons with his Yucatecan predecessor. See, e.g., AGEY, RPE, de los Santos to Carranza, Jan. 14, 1915. For a discussion of de los Santos's brief, chaotic tenure, see the next chapter.

110. For Avila's extensive accounting on the loan, see AVC, Avila to Carranza, Nov. 6, 1914; Gamboa Ricalde, 2: 271. For the charges of corruption, see Mena Brito, 3: 53–56.

111. Pasos Peniche, 67–68; Chacón, "Yucatán and the Mexican Revolution," 176–77.

112. *DO*, Sept. 28, 1914; AGEY, RPE, "Relación de los contribuyentes para el empréstito de ocho millones de pesos," Dec. 24, 1914. See also *RdY*, Oct. 1, 1914 (list of individuals and amounts owed), and Oct. 31, 1914 (new decree extending participation in the "contribution" to those with a capital between twenty thousand and one hundred thousand pesos).

113. See, e.g., the cries and lamentations that populate the personal correspondence of various prominent planters to the archbishop of Yucatán in October 1914: ASA-C, Ignacio Peón to Tritschler y Córdoba, Oct. 10; Alfredo Peón to Tritschler y Córdoba, Oct. 31. On one occasion, however, wealthy Molinista Rafael Peón Losa was granted an exemption because of alleged economic hardship. ASA-C, Peón Losa to Tritschler y Córdoba, Nov. 5, 1914.

114. AVC, Avila to Carranza, Oct. 7, 1914; Gamboa Ricalde, 2: 261–73.

115. AGEY, RPE, telegram, Cabrera to Avila, Dec. 15, 1914; letter, Cabrera to Avila, Jan. 23, 1915.

116. AGEY, RPE, Avila to Cabrera, Dec. 15, 1914, also cited in Gamboa Ricalde, 2: 291.

117. AGEY, RPE, Avila to Cabrera, Dec. 15, 1914. Avila was a favorite of the U.S. consulate because he "did not encourage the radical changes" that animated some Constitutionalist Jacobins. At the same time, Consul W. P. Young praised Avila for his acute understanding of local hopes and fears. NA, RG 59, Young to Secretary of State, Oct. 29, 1915, 812.00/17559.

118. *DO*, Jan. 7, 1915; NA, RG 59, Young to Secretary of State, Jan. 12, 1915, 812.00/14262; Bolio Ontiveros, *Yucatán en la dictadura*, 83–85.

119. The First Chief would later tell Salvador Alvarado that Avila's sustained opposition to his policies was "the best proof of the antipatriotic behavior of Governor Avila and the wealthy classes in Yucatán." AVC, Carranza to Alvarado, Feb. 16, 1915.

120. ASA-C, Blano Castellanos to Tritschler y Córdoba, Dec. 25, 1914. Contrast this optimism with the worried, apocalyptic tone that had characterized planter correspondence to the archbishop in the early days of Avila's administration. Rafael Peón Losa had observed in November 1914, "I fear we may have to suffer as never before. God free us from more calamities." ASA-C, Peón Losa to Tritschler y Córdoba, Nov. 5, 1914.

121. J. Molina Font, 12.

CHAPTER 10

1. Quoted in Berzunza Pinto, "El constitucionalismo," 274.
2. E.g., see *DO*, Jan. 28, 1915; *RdY*, Feb. 10, 1915.
3. *DO*, Feb. 4, 8, 1915. For a comprehensive discussion of de los Santos' controversial initiatives, see Chacón, "Yucatán and the Mexican Revolution," 188–98; and Gamboa Ricalde, 2: 315–19.
4. *DO*, Feb. 4, 1915; Berzunza Pinto, "El constitucionalismo," 282–83.
5. E.g., see de los Santos' "Manifesto to the People of Yucatán," in *DO*, Jan. 28, 1915; cf. AVC, Carranza to de los Santos, Jan. 30, 1915; NA, RG 59, Young to Secretary of State, Feb. 11, 1915, 812.00/14454; J. Molina Font, 1; Chacón, "Yucatán and the Mexican Revolution," 188–92. *Huach* is a colloquial, derogatory Yucatecan term for people from the interior of the republic, chiefly military personnel and manual laborers.
6. Quoted in Berzunza Pinto, "El constitucionalismo," 279–80.
7. Quoted in M. Escoffié Z., *De la tierra prometida*, 70–80.
8. AVC, L. Andrade to Gustavo Espinosa M., Jan. 15, 1915; see also AVC, Calixto Maldonado to Carranza, Jan. 9, 1915.
9. NA, RG 59, Young to Secretary of State, Feb. 11, 1915, 812.00/14459; Franz, 91–92.
10. *DO*, Jan. 28, 1915; Gamboa Ricalde, 2: 316–17.
11. Gamboa Ricalde, 2: 332–33.
12. Ibid., 331.
13. NA, RG 59, Young to Secretary of State, Feb. 11, 1915, 812.00/14154; Franz, 91–92.
14. For Ortiz Argumedo's background and early career, see Gamboa Ricalde, 2: 324–25; J. Molina Font, 17–18; *RdY*, Feb. 13, 1915.
15. This distillation of the events leading to Ortiz Argumedo's coup draws on NA, RG 59, Young to Secretary of State, Feb. 23, 1915, 812.00/14154/14561; Campos Esquivel interviews, Dec. 26, 31, 1986; Gamboa Ricalde, 2: 318–19, 331; Villaseñor, esp. 34; Mena Brito, 3: 109–17; and J. Molina Font, 15–16.
16. See, e.g., ASA-C, Benito Aznar to Tritschler y Córdoba, Feb. 12, 1915; Chacón, "Yucatán and the Mexican Revolution," esp. 196.
17. *DO*, Feb. 26, 1915; AGEY, RPE, Ignacio Magaloni, State Treasurer, to Federico Escalante et. al., Feb. 24, 1915; J. Molina Font, 21; M. Escoffié Z., *De la tierra*, 93–94; Chacón, "Yucatán and the Mexican Revolution," 209.
18. *DO*, Feb. 27, 1915.
19. See, e.g., *RdY*, Feb. 27, 1915; *DO*, Feb. 26, 1915.
20. AGEY, RPE, "Nota del vice consul de España, Rogelio Suárez, relativa a los agravios y perjuicios ocasionados al súbdito español, Avelino Montes," May 1916; Chacón, "Yucatán and the Mexican Revolution," 209–10. One can only speculate whether IHC provided some or all of this capital. We know that IHC had about U.S. $6 million in cash in Montes's safe during the Argumedista revolt, and that of the 200,000 bales stored at Progreso, the company owned 112,000. Montes was one of the principal backers of the Junta of State Sovereignty and undoubtedly made a strong case for IHC support. The capital in question was a relatively modest investment for a big company like IHC, moreover, and a very wise one if it could at least buy the time to move IHC stocks out of Progreso at a chaotic political moment. In mid-March, with the Yucatecan junta about to fall, IHC arranged to evacuate its capital and records via Eduardo Robledo, manager of the Casa Montes (Montes him-

self had already fled), on the U.S. gunboat *Des Moines*. NA, RG 59, H. L. Daniels to U.S.S. *Washington*, Mar. 19, 1915, 812.61326/32; Clements, esp. 484; Chacón, "Yucatán and the Mexican Revolution," 222–27.

21. Clearly, though, J. Molina Font's characterization of the delegation and the resulting junta as a "regional stew [*puchero regional*] . . . with all political hues represented, from pale yellow to flaming red [a clear reference to Morenismo]," is an exaggeration, and a self-serving one at that. J. Molina Font, 21.

22. AGEY, RPE, Gonzalo Cámara Zavala to Ortiz Argumedo, Feb. 23, 1915; *DO*, Feb. 26, 1915.

23. Telegram, Ortiz Argumedo to Carranza, Feb. 12, 1915, published in *DO*, Feb. 13, 1915. Emphasis ours. See also Berzunza Pinto, "El constitucionalismo," 283–84.

24. Garcilazo, who was warmly received by Meridano society, on Feb. 18 indiscreetly declared at a banquet in his honor, "If, perchance, I might one day be called on to act in a military capacity against the just complaints of the Yucatecan people, I would sooner resign my commission as a soldier." That same day, he had advanced the case for state sovereignty in a cable to Carranza and Alvarado. His advocacy cost him his command and his life: arrested in late February by Alvarado, he was courtmartialed for treason and shot. Most of his force of 450 later defected to Ortiz Argumedo. See AGEY, RPE, Garcilazo to Alvarado, Feb. 18, 1915; *DO*, Feb. 18, 19, 20, Mar. 9, 1915; *RdY*, Feb. 19, 27, 1915.

25. AGEY, RPE, Alvarado to Garcilazo and Ortiz Argumedo, Feb. 18, 1915.

26. See, e.g., Pacheco Cruz, 52.

27. NA, RG 59, W. P. Young to Secretary of State, Feb. 23, 1915, 812.00/14561, John R. Silliman to Secretary of State, Mar. 3, 1915, 812.00/14484.

28. *RdY*, Feb. 17, 1915.

29. Ibid.

30. See, e.g., *RdY*, Feb. 17, Mar. 15, 1915.

31. Ibid., Feb. 22, 1915.

32. NA, RG 59, Young to Secretary of State, Mar. 3, 1915, 812.00/14561; *RdY*, Mar. 1, 1915; Gamboa Ricalde, 2: 338–39.

33. J. Molina Font, 22–23; see also the memoirs of then fellow student González Reyes.

34. Valadés, *Historia general*, 4: 273–77; Berzunza Pinto, "El constitucionalismo," 288–89. On Alvarado's early career, see Joseph, *Revolution from Without*, 99, 330, n. 24. Valadés, Berzunza Pinto, 289, and Chacón, "Yucatán and the Mexican Revolution," 216, put the size of the Yucatecan forces at four thousand. Franz, 97, relying on Gamboa Ricalde, 2: 350, estimates only seven hundred. From the descriptions of the campaign in several memoirs, the latter figure seems too low. Most commentators place the Constitutionalist force between seven thousand and eight thousand.

35. Young elite recruit J. Molina Font candidly observed, "Our marksmanship was never on a par with our military zeal; I never saw a single enemy soldier bite the dust." In his journal of the campaign, he mentions only one training exercise for his regiment: a battle simulation held March 11 at Sodzil, a large henequen estate owned by "Tío Olegario." J. Molina Font, 28, 52 (quotation); see also Gamboa Ricalde, 2: 350. Virtually every contemporary source makes some mention of the Yucatecans' old and inadequate firearms.

36. J. Molina Font, 36, 18, 45.          37. Ibid., 41–42.

38. Moguel, 56–57.                        39. González Reyes, 30–31.

40. See, e.g, *DO*, Feb. 27, Mar. 3, 9, 11, 1915; Campos Esquivel interviews, Dec. 26, 31, 1986; interview, Juan Campos, ca. 1962, cited in Berzunza Pinto, "El constitucionalismo," 295.

41. Interview, Zozaya Raz.

42. González Reyes, 20–21.

43. Ibid., 33.

44. Ibid.

45. Ibid., 48. In *his* memoirs, the chauvinistic Yucateco M. Escoffié Z. avers hyperbolically, "our magnificent Maya marksmen . . . fired volleys so frighteningly accurate that they felled more than two men with the same bullet." *¡Ya!* 135.

46. Moguel, 78; Berzunza Pinto, "El constitucionalismo," 289; Franz, 97.

47. Interview, Ku Peraza. Ku claimed that as a seventeen-year-old Maya conscript in the *guardias territoriales*, he "fled the retribution of the overwhelming federal forces." For the Argumedista campaign of propaganda and misinformation, see *RdY*, Feb. 28–Mar. 16, 1915; Villaseñor, 51; Pacheco Cruz, 53; and Chacón, "Yucatán and the Mexican Revolution," 215–16.

48. Cf. the negative portrayals of the federal army reported in González Reyes, 50; and *RdY*, Mar. 10, 1915.

49. AGEY, RPE, Márquez to Alvarado, Aug. 5, 1915.

50. J. Molina Font, 89. According to local historian Bolio Ontiveros, the Yucatecans suffered 450 dead and many more wounded, the Carrancistas a mere 34 dead and 129 wounded. See *Yucatán en la dictadura*, 100–101.

51. J. Molina Font, 70–71, 78.

52. Ibid., 66; Moguel, 95–96. More than 40 Yucatecans were shot before Alvarado could intervene.

53. ASA-C, Aznar to Tritschler y Córdoba, Mar. 25, 1915. Also see *NYT*, Mar. 21, 1915; NA, RG 59, Young to Secretary of State, Mar. 30, 1915, 812.000/14961; NA, RG 84, Young to Secretary of State, Mar. 30, 1915, 812.61326/56. The U.S. consul exaggerated the exodus to the point of absurdity, reporting that half of Mérida fled before the *federales'* arrival.

54. ASA-C, Peón Losa to Tritschler y Córdoba, Apr. 20, 1915.

55. *VdR*, Aug. 31, 1915; AGEY, RPE, Ortiz Argumedo to State Treasurer, Mar. 3, 1915, Ortiz Argumedo to Banco Peninsular Mexicano, Mar. 3, 1915.

56. AGEY, RPE, "Anexos referentes a los asuntos que se ventilan en la ciudad de Nueva York con motivo del asunto Abel Ortiz Argumedo," May 12, 1916. We are grateful to Ramón Chacón for initially providing us with this reference; copies of the most relevant documents in the expediente were also found in AGEY, RJ, 1915.

57. For an analysis of Yucatán's participation in the Mexican Revolution after 1915, see Joseph, *Revolution from Without*; Paoli; Paoli and Montalvo; Sierra Villarreal and Paoli Bolio.

58. See, e.g., Eiss; Savarino; Fallaw, "Peasants, Parties and Hacendados." Among the issues campesinos contested with the state during the 1915–24 period were the pace of land reform and the legitimacy of land invasions; the right to cut firewood on the planters' property; *comuneros'* attempts to control or open roads closed by *hacendados*; *acasillados'* efforts to leave the henequen estate; access to life's basic commodities, which could escalate into sackings of hacienda stores (often by women); campesinas' attempts to challenge domestic labor arrangements set by patrons; the recovery of children and minors kept as unpaid household servants by *hacendados*; and campesinos' struggles to defend their folk Catholic festivals against the attack of Alvaradista anticlericalism.

59. AGEY, RJ, "Diligencias asalto y robo en la finca Nohuayun," 1915. Things seemed to get worse before they got better, under the impact of Alvarado's reforms. Before the end of the year, the volume of *hacendado* complaints was so large that the government warned, "in Hunucmá the times of Nero reign." AGEY, RPE, Oficina de Información y Propaganda, n.d., 1915. See also Eiss.

60. AGEY, RJ, "Diligencias contra Juan Córdova," 1915; interview, Betancourt Pérez.

61. But see Joseph, "Caciquismo and the Revolution"; Joseph and Wells, "Rough-and-Tumble Career of Pedro Crespo"; Buve, "Jefes menores," and Falcón, *Revolución y caciquismo.*

62. Beals, *Mexican Maze*, chap. 13.

63. The following discussion draws on AGEY, RJ, "Causa seguida contra Pedro Crespo y socios"; *EPop*, Mar. 16, 23, 1922; *Tierra* 24 (Oct. 1923), 13; 5th ser., 3 (June 1930), 20; *DdY*, Nov. 27, 1928; interviews, Zozaya Raz, and Campos Esquivel, Dec. 26, 1986, Jan. 2, 1987; Joseph and Wells, "Rough-and-Tumble Career"; and Joseph, *Revolution from Without*, 209–12.

64. Corrigan and Sayer.

65. For an examination of how the official party used baseball in Yucatán during the 1920s and 1930s to mobilize popular support and *forjar patria* in both socio-cultural and infrastructural terms, see Joseph, "Forging the Regional Pastime." The state's campaign was so successful that baseball has become the regional pastime, an anomaly in a nation where *fútbol* is typically the people's game.

66. Elías Rivero controlled Peto for Alvarado and Carrillo Puerto and remained a force there until his death in 1947. Over the course of his political career, he was widely reputed to have "come into money." Interviews, Ku Peraza and Trejo Hernández. When Rivero died, he was buried in Mérida's main cemetery near Carrillo Puerto, and his name, like Crespo's, was enshrined in the Rotonda de los Socialistas Distinguidos.

67. Campos's political career was marked by ups and downs. Imprisoned for two years by Alvarado for his participation in the Argumedista episode, he was ultimately released by Carrillo Puerto, and soon became one of the stalwarts of Don Felipe's Partido Socialista del Sureste (PSS). In the early 1920s, Campos and Crespo together ruled over north-central Yucatán, and Campos held a variety of public offices: municipal president of Dzilám González, president of Dzilám's *liga de resistencia*, deputy in the state legislature, and, briefly, federal deputy. With Crespo, he helped introduce baseball to Temax and neighboring districts. Nevertheless, following Carrillo Puerto's assassination, Campos was unable to accommodate the more conservative local and national states and was soon forced to settle back into the life of a small merchant and rancher in his native Dzilám González. Campos interview; Campos Esquivel interviews, Dec. 26, 1986, Jan. 2, 1987; *EPop*, Mar. 16, 1922; Joseph and Wells, "Rough-and-Tumble Career," 35–37; Joseph, *Revolution from Without*, 209–12. Baak's *cacicazgo* in the Puuc also peaked under Carrillo Puerto's regime; in the early 1920s, his influence extended as far east as Sotuta. His decision in December 1923 to desert the PSS during the de la Huerta rebellion cost him a secure political career once the party returned to power in 1924. Enmeshed thereafter in a series of bloody encounters with factional rivals, Baak was ultimately gunned down by his enemies in 1926. *RdY*, Dec. 17, 1923; Joseph, *Revolution from Without*, 210–12, 271, 365, n. 33; Redfield and Villa Rojas, 26.

68. See Mallon, "Reflections on the Ruins," and *Peasant and Nation.*

69. Smith, 181, 204.

70. See, e.g., the "postrevisionist" studies by Jan Rus (highland Chiapas), Daniel Nugent and Ana María Alonso (western Chihuahua), and Marjorie Becker (northwestern Michoacán) in Joseph and Nugent. Again, Knight's *Mexican Revolution* is less vulnerable to such criticism. See our Chapter 8, n. 122.

71. García Canclini, 476. Jeff Rubin kindly brought this quotation to our attention.

# References

A list of abbreviations used in this bibliography precedes the Notes, pp. 295–97.

## ARCHIVES AND MANUSCRIPT COLLECTIONS

Archivo General de la Nación, Mexico City
  Ramo de Gobernación, Secretaría de Comunicaciones y Obras Públicas
  Ramo de Madero
  Ramo de Trabajo
Archivo General del Estado de Yucatán, Mérida
  Ramo de Justicia
  Ramo del Poder Ejecutivo
  Ramo de Tierras
Archivo Notarial del Estado de Yucatán, Mérida
Archivo de la Secretaría del Arzobispado, Mérida
  Correspondencia, 1914–1919
Archivo de la Secretaría de Relaciones Exteriores, Mexico City
Baker Library, Harvard University Graduate School of Business Administration, Cambridge
  Henry W. Peabody and Company Records, 1867–1957
  Plymouth Cordage Company Records
Biblioteca Carlos R. Menéndez, Mérida
Centro de Estudios de Historia de México, Condumex, Mexico City
  Manuscript Collections
  Archivo Venustiano Carranza
Colección General Porfirio Díaz, Universidad Iberomamericana, Mexico City
Colección Jorge Denegre V., Instituto Nacional de Antropología e Historia, Mexico City
International Harvester Company Archives, Chicago

Hernán Menéndez Rodríguez Papers, Mérida
Simón Peón Collection, Special Collections Division, University of Texas at Arlington Library, Arlington
U.S. National Archives, Washington, D.C.
  Record Group 59, Records of the Department of State Relating to the Internal Affairs of Mexico, 1910–1929
  Record Group 84, U.S. Department of State Consular Post Records: Progreso

PERIODICALS

*Acción Democrática*, Mérida
*El Agricultor*, Mérida
*Boletín de Estadística*, Mérida
*La Campana*, Mérida
*El Ciudadano*, Mérida
*El Crédito del Estado*, Mérida
*Constitución y Reforma*, Mérida
*Cordage Trade Journal*, New York
*El Demócrata*, Mérida
*El Diario del Hogar*, Mexico City
*El Diario de Yucatán*, Mérida
*Diario Oficial*, Mérida
*Diario Yucateco*, Mérida
*El Eco del Comercio*, Mérida
*El Economista Mexicano*, Mexico City
*La Humanidad*, Mérida
*El Imparcial*, Mexico City
*Mexican Herald*, Mexico City
*New York Times*, New York
*Novedades de Yucatán*, Mérida
*La Opinión*, Mérida
*El País*, Mexico City
*El Padre Clarencio*, Mérida
*El Peninsular*, Mérida
*Periodista Libre*, Mérida
*El Popular*, Mérida
*Renacimiento*, Mérida
*La Revista de Mérida*, Mérida
*La Revista de Yucatán*, Mérida
*El Sufragio*, Mérida
*El Tiempo*, Mexico City
*Tierra*, Mérida
*El Universal*, Mexico City
*Verdad y Justicia*, Mérida
*La Voz del Pueblo*, Mérida
*La Voz de la Revolución*, Mérida
*Yucatán Nuevo*, Mérida

PRINTED DOCUMENTS AND SECONDARY SOURCES

Abercrombie, Nicholas, Stephen Hill, and Bryan S. Turner, eds. *Dominant Ideologies*. London: Unwin Hyman, 1990.

——. *The Dominant Ideology Thesis.* London: Allen and Unwin, 1980.

Aboites, Luis. *La Revolución Mexicana en Espita, Yucatán (1910–1940).* Mérida: Maldonado Editores, 1985.

Abu-Lughod, Lila. "The Romance of Resistance: Tracing Transformations of Power Through Bedouin Women." *American Ethnologist* 17, no. 1 (1990): 41–55.

Acereto, Albino. "Historia política desde el descubrimiento europeo hasta 1920." In C. Echánove Trujillo, *Enciclopedia Yucatanense,* 3: 5–388.

Adas, Michael. "From Avoidance to Confrontation: Peasant Protest in Precolonial and Colonial Southeast Asia." *CSSH* 23, no. 2 (Apr. 1981): 217–47.

Adorno, Rolena. "Reconsidering Colonial Discourse for Sixteenth- and Seventeenth-Century Spanish America." *LARR* 28, no. 3 (1993), 135–45.

Aguilar Camín, Héctor. *La frontera nómada: Sonora y la Revolución Mexicana.* Mexico City: Siglo XXI, 1977.

*Album conmemorativo de las fiestas presidenciales.* Mérida: Imprenta Gamboa Guzmán, 1906.

Alonso, Ana María. "The Effects of Truth: Re-Presentations of the Past and the Imagining of Community." *Journal of Historical Sociology* 1, no. 1 (Mar. 1988): 33–57.

Ancona, Eligio. *Historia de Yucatán desde la época más remota hasta nuestros días.* 2nd ed. 5 vols. Mérida/Barcelona: Imprenta de M. Heredia Arguelles/Jaime Jepús Roviralta, 1889–1905.

Anderson, Rodney D. "Mexican Workers and the Politics of Revolution, 1906–1911." *HAHR* 54, no. 1 (Feb. 1974): 94–113.

——. *Outcasts in Their Own Land: Mexican Industrial Workers, 1906–1911.* DeKalb: Northern Illinois University Press, 1976.

Ankerson, Dudley. *Agrarian Warlord: Saturnino Cedillo and the Mexican Revolution in San Luis Potosí.* DeKalb: Northern Illinois University Press, 1984.

Arjona, Fernando. *Breves apuntes sobre la pelagra.* Mérida: n.p., 1898.

Arnold, Channing, and Frederick J. Tabor Frost. *The American Egypt: A Record of Travel in Yucatán.* London: Hutchinson, 1909.

Arrieta Ceniceros, Lorenzo. "Importancia económica y social de los ferrocarriles en Yucatán. Empresas y grupos económicos: 1876–1915." *Estudios Políticos* 5, nos. 18–19 (1979): 113–56.

Askinasy, Siegfried. *El problema agrario de Yucatán* (Mexico: Ediciones Botas, 1936).

Aufderheide, Patricia A. "Order and Violence: Social Deviance and Social Control in Brazil, 1780–1840." Ph.D. diss., University of Minnesota, 1976.

Avila, Ricardo. "¡Así se gobierna, señores!: el gobierno de José Vicente Villada." In Rodríguez O., *Revolutionary Process in Mexico,* 15–32.

Aya, Rod. "Popular Intervention in Revolutionary Situations." In Charles Bright and Susan Harding, eds., *Statemaking and Social Movements: Essays in History and Theory,* 318–43. Ann Arbor: University of Michigan Press, 1984.

——. "Theories of Revolution Reconsidered: Contrasting Models of Collective Violence." *Theory and Society* 8 (1979): 39–99.

Baerlein, Henry. *Mexico: Land of Unrest.* London: Herbert and Daniel, 1913.

Bailey, David C. "Revisionism and the Recent Historiography of the Mexican Revolution." *HAHR* 58, no. 1 (Feb. 1978): 62–79.

Balmori, Diana, Stuart Voss, and Miles Wortman, eds. *Notable Family Networks in Latin America.* Chicago: University of Chicago Press, 1984.

Baqueiro, Serapio. *Ensayo histórico sobre las revoluciones de Yucatán desde el año 1840 hasta 1864.* 3 vols. Mérida: vols. 1, 2, Imprenta de M. Heredia Arguelles, 1878–79; vol. 3, Tipografía de Gil Canto, 1884.

——. *Reseña geográfica, histórica y estadística del Estado de Yucatán.* Mexico City: Francisco Díaz de León, 1881.

Baqueiro Anduze, Oswaldo. *La ciudad heroica: historia de Valladolid*. Mérida: Imprenta Oriente, 1943.

Baranda, Joaquín. *Recordaciones históricas*. 2 vols. Mexico City: Tipográfica Económica, 1913.

Barber, Gerald. "Horizon of Thorns: Yucatán at the Turn of the Century." Master's thesis, Universidad de las Américas, Cholula, Puebla, 1974.

Barceló Quintal, Raquel. "El desarrollo de la banca y el henequén." *YHE* 29 (July–Aug. 1982): 3–24.

———. "El ferrocarril y la oligarquía henequenera." *YHE* 26 (July–Aug. 1981): 23–54.

Barrera Vásquez, Alfredo. *Documento n.1 del deslinde de tierras en Yaxkukul, Yuc*. Mérida: INAH, 1984.

Barthes, Roland. "Introduction to the Structural Analysis of Narratives." In Barthes, *Image/Music/Text*, trans. Stephen Heath. New York: Hill and Wang, 1977.

Bataillon, Claude. *La ciudad y el campo en el México central*. Mexico City: Siglo XXI, 1972.

Batt, Rosemary L. "The Rise and Fall of the Planter Class in Espita, 1900–1924." In Brannon and Joseph, *Land, Labor, and Capital*, 197–219.

Beals, Carleton. *Mexican Maze*. Philadelphia: Book League of America, 1931.

———. *Porfirio Díaz: Dictator of Mexico*. Westport: Greenwood Press, 1971.

Beezley, William H. "*La cultura de la calle*: Holidays, Holy Days, Mexican Virtue on Parade." Paper presented at the 8th Conference of Mexican and North American Historians, San Diego, Oct. 18–20, 1990.

———. *Judas at the Jockey Club and Other Episodes of Porfirian Mexico*. Lincoln: University of Nebraska Press, 1987.

———. "Madero: The 'Unknown' President and His Political Failure to Organize Rural Mexico." In George Wolfskill and Douglas W. Richmond, eds., *Essays on the Mexican Revolution: Revisionist Views of the Leaders*, 1–24. Austin: University of Texas Press, 1979.

———. "Opportunities for Further Regional Study." In Benjamin and McNellie, *Other Mexicos*, 275–300.

Beezley, William H., Cheryl English Martin, and William E. French. "Constructing Consent, Inciting Conflict." Introduction to *Rituals of Rule, Rituals of Resistance*, ed. William H. Beezley, Cheryl English Martin, and William E. French, xiii–xxxii. Wilmington: Scholarly Resources, 1994.

Benjamin, Thomas. "International Harvester and the Henequen Marketing System in Yucatán, 1898–1915." *IAEA* 31 (Winter 1977): 3–19.

———. "Passages to Leviathan: Chiapas and the Mexican State, 1891–1947." Ph.D. diss., Michigan State University, 1981.

———. "Regional Politics." In Benjamin and McNellie, *Other Mexicos*, 27–31.

———. *A Rich Land, A Poor People: Politics and Society in Modern Chiapas*. Albuquerque: University of New Mexico Press, 1989.

Benjamin, Thomas, and William McNellie, eds. *Other Mexicos: Essays on Regional History, 1876–1911*. Albuquerque: University of New Mexico Press, 1984.

Benjamin, Thomas, and Marcial Ocasio-Meléndez. "Organizing the Memory of Modern Mexico: Porfirian Historiography in Perspective, 1880s–1980s." *HAHR* 64, no. 2 (May 1984): 323–64.

Benjamin, Thomas, and Mark Wasserman, eds. *Provinces of the Revolution: Essays on Regional Mexican History, 1910–1929*. Albuquerque: University of New Mexico Press, 1990.

Berzunza Pinto, Ramón. "El constitucionalismo en Yucatán." *HM* 12, no. 2 (Oct.–Dec. 1962): 274–95.

——. "Las vísperas yucatecas de la Revolución." *HM* 6, no. 1 (July–Sept. 1956): 75–88.

Betancourt Pérez, Antonio. *La problemática social: ¿primera chispa de la Revolución Mexicana?* Mérida: Academia Yucatanense de Ciencias y Artes/Gobierno del Estado, 1983.

——. *Revoluciones y crisis en la economía de Yucatán.* 2nd ed. Mérida: Maldonado Editores, 1986 [1953].

——. *La verdad sobre el origen de las escuelas rurales en Yucatán.* Mérida: Editorial Zamná, 1971.

Betancourt Pérez, Antonio, and Rodolfo Ruz Menéndez, eds. *Yucatán: textos de su historia.* 2 vols. Mexico City: SEP/Instituto Mora/Gobierno del Estado de Yucatán, 1988.

Bethell, Leslie, ed. *The Cambridge History of Latin America.* 8 vols. Cambridge, U.K.: Cambridge University Press, 1986.

Billingsley, Philip. *Bandits in Republican China.* Stanford: Stanford University Press, 1988.

Bojórquez Urzáiz, Carlos. "Crisis maicera de la comunidad campesina yucateca en la segunda mitad del siglo XIX." *BECA* 6 (Mar.–Apr. 1979): 46–52.

——. "Estructura agraria y maíz a partir de la 'guerra de castas.'" *RUY* 20 (Nov.–Dec. 1978): 15–35.

——. "Regionalización de la política agraria de Yucatán en la segunda mitad del siglo XIX." *RUY* 21 (May–Aug. 1979): 32–45.

——. "El Yucatán de 1847 hasta 1851: breves apuntes sobre el trabajo y la subsistencia." *BECA* 5 (Nov.–Dec. 1977): 18–25.

Bolio Ontiveros, Edmundo. "Historia de la educación pública y privada hasta 1910." In C. Echánove Trujillo, *Enciclopedia Yucatanense,* 4: 153–92.

——. *Yucatán en la dictadura y la Revolución.* Mexico City: Talleres Gráficos de la Nación, 1967.

Boyer, Richard L. "Las ciudades mexicanas: perspectivas de estudio en el siglo XIX." *HM* 22, no. 2 (1972): 142–59.

Brading, D. A., ed. *Caudillo and Peasant in the Mexican Revolution.* Cambridge, U.K.: Cambridge University Press, 1980.

Branch, Taylor, and Eugene M. Propper. *Labyrinth.* New York: Viking, 1982.

Brannon, Jeffery T., and Gilbert M. Joseph, eds. *Land, Labor, and Capital in Modern Yucatán: Essays in Regional History and Political Economy.* Tuscaloosa: University of Alabama Press, 1991.

Bricker, Victoria. *The Indian Christ, the Indian King: The Historical Substrate of Maya Myth and Ritual.* Austin: University of Texas Press, 1981.

Brown, Lyle C. *The Mexican Liberals and Their Struggle Against the Díaz Dictatorship, 1900–1906.* Mexico City: Mexico City College Press, 1956.

Brown, Peter. *Society and the Holy in Late Antiquity.* Berkeley: University of California Press, 1982.

Bryan, Anthony T. "Mexican Politics in Transition, 1900–1913." Ph.D. diss., University of Nebraska, 1969.

Buffington, Robert. "Revolutionary Reform: The Mexican Revolution and the Discourse on Prison Reform." *MS/EM* 9, no. 1 (1993): 71–94.

Bulnes, Francisco. *El verdadero Díaz y la Revolución.* Mexico City: Editorial Nacional, 1967.

——. *The Whole Truth About Mexico: The Mexican Revolution and President Wilson's Part Therein, As Seen by a Científico.* Detroit: Blaine-Etheridge, 1972 [1916].

Burke, Peter. *Popular Culture in Early Modern Europe.* New York: Harper and Row, 1978.

Butler, Joseph H. "Hydrogeologic Constraints on Yucatán's Development." *Science* 86, no. 4164 (Nov. 1974): 591–95.

Buve, Raymond Th. "Jefes menores de la Revolución Mexicana y los primeros avances en la consolidación del estado nacional: el caso de Tlaxcala (1910–1920)." Unpublished ms., 1985.

——. "Peasant Movements, Caudillos, and Land Reform During the Revolution (1910–1917) in Tlaxcala, Mexico." *Boletín de Estudios Latinoamericanos y del Caribe* 18 (June 1975): 112–52.

——. "Protesta de obreros y campesinos durante el Porfiriato: unas consideraciones sobre su desarrollo e interrelaciones en el este de México central." *Boletín de Estudios Latinoamericanos* 13 (1972): 1–25.

Calderón, Francisco R. "Los ferrocarriles," *HM* 7: 483–634.

Cámara Zavala, Gonzalo. "La Liga de Acción Social." In "Distinguidos autores yucatecos." *Yucatán: artículos amenos acerca de su historia, leyendas, usos, costumbres, evolución social, etc.*, 125–29. Mérida: Alvaro Salazar, 1913.

Camp, Roderic A. *Mexican Political Biographies, 1884–1935*. Austin: University of Texas Press, 1991.

Canto López, Antonio. "La imprenta y el periodismo." In C. Echánove Trujillo, *Enciclopedia Yucatanense*, 5: 5–107.

——. *El territorio de Quintana Roo y Yucatán*. Mérida: Gobierno del Estado, 1954.

Cantón Rosado, Francisco. *Datos y documentos relativos a la vida militar y política del Sr. General Brigadier Don Francisco Cantón*, ed. Carlos R. Menéndez. Mérida: Talleres de la Compañía Tipográfica Yucateca, 1931.

Carbine, Carol Lee. "The Indian Policy of Porfirio Díaz in the State of Yucatán, 1876–1910." Ph.D. diss., Loyola University of Chicago, 1977.

Cardoso, Fernando H. "The City and Politics." In Jorge Hardoy, ed., *Urbanization in Latin America: Approaches and Issues*, 157–90. New York: Anchor/Doubleday, 1975.

Cardoso, Fernando H., and Enzo Faletto. *Dependency and Development in Latin America*. Berkeley: University of California Press, 1979.

Carey, James C. *The Mexican Revolution in Yucatán, 1915–1924*. Boulder: Westview Press, 1985.

Carr, Barry. "Recent Regional Studies of the Mexican Revolution." *LARR* 15, no. 1 (1980): 3–14.

Carranza y Trujillo, Ramón. *El Instituto Literario de Yucatán*. Mexico City: n.p., 1938.

Carreno, Alberto María. *Licenciado Don Olegario Molina*. Mexico City, n.p., 1925.

Carrillo Puerto, Acrelio. *Lo que no se olvida: Felipe Carrillo Puerto*. Mérida: n.p., 1964.

Casasús, Francisco A. "Ensayo biográfico del licenciado Olegario Molina Solís." *RUY* 14, no. 81 (1972): 68–95.

Castillo, José R. *Historia de la revolución social en México*. Mexico City: n.p., 1915.

Castro, Juan Miguel. *El triunfo de la verdad en favor de El Progreso*. Mérida: n.p., 1866.

Ceballos Rodríguez, Alfredo. "Yucatán en tiempo de V. Huerta." *El Paso del Norte*, Oct. 27, 1915, cited in Franz, "Bullets and Bolshevists," 86.

Cerutti, Mario. *Burguesía y capitalismo en Monterrey, 1850–1910*. Mexico City: Claves Latinoamericanas, 1983.

Chacón, Ramón D. "Rural Educational Reform in Yucatán: From the Porfiriato to the Era of Salvador Alvarado, 1910–1918." *The Americas* 42, no. 2 (Oct. 1988): 207–28.

——. "Salvador Alvarado and the Roman Catholic Church: Church-State Relations in Revolutionary Yucatán, 1914–1918." *Journal of Church and State* 27, no. 2 (1985), 245–66.

——. "Yucatán and the Mexican Revolution: The Pre-Constitutional Years, 1910–1918." Ph.D. diss., Stanford University, 1982.

Chandler, Alfred D., Jr. *Scale and Scope: The Dynamics of Industrial Capitalism.* Cambridge, MA: Harvard University Press, 1990.

——. *The Visible Hand: The Managerial Revolution in American Business.* Cambridge, MA: Harvard University Press, 1977.

Chardon, Roland E. P. *Geographic Aspects of Plantation Agriculture in Yucatán.* Washington, D.C.: National Academy of Sciences/National Research Council, 1961.

Chernow, Ron. *The House of Morgan.* New York: Atlantic Monthly Press, 1990.

Civeira Taboada, Miguel. "Francisco I. Madero contra Carlos R. Menéndez." Unpublished ms., 1974.

Clements, Kendrick A. "A Kindness to Carranza: William Jennings Bryan, International Harvester, and the Intervention in Yucatán." *Nebraska History* 57 (Winter 1976): 476–90.

Clendinnen, Inga. "Understanding the Heathen at Home." *Historical Studies* (Melbourne, Australia) 18, no. 72 (Apr. 1979): 435–41.

Cline, Howard F. "The 'Aurora Yucateca' and the Spirit of Enterprise in Yucatán: 1821–1847." *HAHR* 27, no. 1 (1947): 30–60.

——. "Regionalism and Society in Yucatán, 1825–1847: A Study in 'Progressivism' and the Origins of the Caste War." In *Related Studies in Early Nineteenth-Century Yucatecan Social History.* 3 parts. Microfilm Collection of Manuscripts on Middle American Cultural Anthropology, no. 32. Chicago: University of Chicago Library, 1950.

Coatsworth, John. *Growth Against Development: The Economic Impact of Railroads in Porfirian Mexico.* DeKalb: Northern Illinois University, 1981.

——. "Obstacles to Economic Growth in Nineteenth-Century Mexico." *AHR* 83, no. 1 (Feb. 1978): 80–100.

——. "Railroads, Landholding, and Agrarian Protest in the Early *Porfiriato.*" *HAHR* 54, no. 1 (Feb. 1974): 48–71.

——. "The State and the External Sector in Mexico, 1800–1900." Paper presented at the Latin American Studies Association meeting, Mexico City, Sept. 1983.

Cockcroft, James D. *Intellectual Precursors of the Mexican Revolution, 1900–1913.* Austin: University of Texas Press, 1968.

Comaroff, Jean. *Body of Power, Spirit of Resistance.* Chicago: University of Chicago Press, 1985.

Comaroff, John, and Jean Comaroff. "The Madman and the Migrant: Work and Labor in the Historical Consciousness of a South African People." *American Ethnologist* 14, no. 2 (1987): 191–209.

——. *Of Revelation and Revolution: Christianity and Colonialism in South Africa.* Chicago: University of Chicago Press, 1992.

*Constancias judiciales que demuestran no existir esclavitud en Yucatán y que son falsas las imputaciones hechas en el libelo difamatorio titulado "Carta Abierta."* Pamphlet. Mérida: Imprenta de la Lotería del Estado, 1905.

Cooper, Frederick. "Africa and the World Economy." In Cooper et al., *Confronting Historical Paradigms,* 187–201.

Cooper, Frederick, Allen F. Isaacman, Florencia E. Mallon, William Roseberry, and Steve J. Stern. *Confronting Historical Paradigms: Peasants, Labor, and the Cap-*

*italist World System in Africa and Latin America*. Madison: University of Wisconsin Press, 1993.

Córdova, Arnaldo. *La ideología de la Revolución Mexicana: la formación del nuevo régimen*. Mexico City: Ediciones Era, 1973.

Correa Delgado, Manuel. *Breve relación histórica de la Liga de Acción Social: sus principales trabajos durante los cincuenta años de su existencia*. Mérida: Díaz Massa, 1959.

Corrigan, Philip, and Derek Sayer. *The Great Arch: English State Formation as Cultural Revolution*. Oxford: Basil Blackwell, 1985.

Cosío Villegas, Daniel. "El porfiriato: su historiografía o arte histórico." *Extremos de América* (1949): 113–82.

———, ed. *Historia moderna de México*. 9 vols. Mexico City: Editorial Hermes, 1955–1972.

Vol. 1. *El porfiriato, la vida política interior*, primera parte.

Vol. 4. *El porfiriato: la vida social*, by Moisés González Navarro.

Vol. 5. *El porfiriato: la vida política exterior*, primera parte.

Vol. 6. *El porfiriato: la vida política exterior*, segunda parte.

Vol. 9. *El porfiriato: la vida política interior*, segunda parte.

Covo, Jacqueline. *Las ideas de la Reforma en México (1855–1861)*. Trans. María Francisca Mourier-Martínez. Mexico City: UNAM, 1983.

Craton, Michael. *Testing the Chains: Resistance to Slavery in the British West Indies*. Ithaca: Cornell University Press, 1982.

*¿Cuál es el valor y cuál es el alcance de la convención que se dice ajustada entre la Sociedad "E. Escalante e Hijo" y sus acreedores?* Pamphlet. Mérida: n.p., 1911.

Cumberland, Charles C. *The Mexican Revolution: Genesis Under Madero*. Austin: University of Texas Press, 1952.

Davies, Keith A. "Tendencias demográficas urbanas durante el siglo XIX en México." *HM* 21 (1972): 481–537.

Dewing, Arthur S. *A History of National Cordage Company*. Cambridge, MA: Harvard University Press, 1913.

Díaz y de Ovando, Clementina. "La ciudad de México en 1904." *HM* 24 (1974): 122–44.

*Diccionario Porrúa de historia, biografía y geografía de México*. 3rd ed. 2 vols. Mexico City: Editorial Porrúa, 1970.

Didapp, Juan Pedro. *Gobiernos militares de México: los ataques al ejército y las maquinaciones políticas del partido científico para regir los destinos nacionales*. Mexico City: Tipografía de J. I. Guerrero y Compañía, 1904.

———. *La nación y sus gobernantes ante la historia y la conciencia colectiva*. Mexico City: Tipografía de los sucesores de F. Díaz de León, 1905.

———. *Partidos políticos de México: la política del dinero y la política del patriotismo disputando la sucesión de la presidencia del país*. Mexico City: J. Gil, 1903.

*Directorio Domínguez para 1908 de las ciudades de Mérida, Campeche, San Juan Bautista y Veracruz*. Mexico City: Talleres de Imprenta y Fotograbado de "Arte y Letras," 1907.

Domínguez, José Luis. "Situación política en el partido de Sotuta (1911–1916)." In Blanca González et al., eds., *Yucatán: peonaje y liberación*, 178–205.

Dulanto, Enrique. "Apuntes históricos y anecdóticos sobre Mérida." In "Mérida de Yucatán," 7–61.

Dumond, David E. "Independent Maya of the Late Nineteenth Century: Chiefdoms and Power Politics." In Grant Jones, ed., *Anthropology and History in Yucatán*, 103–38. Austin: University of Texas Press, 1977.

Durán Rosado, Esteban. *La primera huelga ferrocarrilera de Yucatán*. Mérida: Imprenta Oriente, 1944.

Durkheim, Emile. *Suicide: A Study in Sociology*. New York: Free Press, 1966 [1951].

Echánove Trujillo, Carlos A., ed. *Enciclopedia Yucatanense*. 8 vols. Mexico City: Gobierno de Yucatán, 1944–47.

Echánove Trujillo, Ramón. *Una tierra en disputa: Belice ante la historia*. Mérida: Universidad de Yucatán, 1951.

Eiss, Paul. "At the Limits of Control: Provisional Land Reform During Alvarado's Revolution, Yucatán, 1915." Unpublished ms., 1994.

Emmerich, Gustavo Ernesto. "Las elecciones en México, 1808–1911: ¿sufragio efectivo? ¿no reelección?" In Pablo González Casanova, ed., *Las elecciones en México: evolución y perspectivas*, 41–67. Mexico City: Siglo XXI, 1985.

Epstein, James. " 'Bred as a Mechanic': Plebeian Intellectuals and Popular Politics in Early Nineteenth-Century England." Unpublished ms., 1989.

——. "Understanding the Cap of Liberty: Symbolic Practice and Social Conflict in Early Nineteenth-Century England." *PP* 122 (Feb. 1989): 75–118.

Escalante Gonzalbo, Fernando. *Ciudadanos imaginarios: memorial de los afanes y desventuras de la virtud y apología del vicio triunfante en la República Mexicana—tratado de moral pública*. Mexico City: El Colegio de México, 1992.

Escobedo, Arcadio. *En defensa de Faustino Méndez (El crimen de Cepeda)*. Mérida: n.p., 1908.

Escoffié, Carlos P. "Primeros episodios de la Revolución Constitucionalista en Yucatán," *DdY*, Jan. 1, 1939.

Escoffié Z., Manuel M. *De la tierra prometida*. Havana: Casa Editora Metodista, 1918.

——. *¡Ya! Libro de buenos yucatecos*. Mérida: n.p., 1955.

*Estadísticas sociales del Porfiriato, 1877–1910*. Mexico City: Secretaría de Economía, Dirección General de Estadística, 1956.

*Exposición que los habitantes de la capital y de todos los municipios del Estado hacen a la H. Legislatura del mismo pidiendo la reforma del artículo 45 de la Constitución Local, en el sentido de la reelección del Gobernador del Estado*. Progreso: Establecimiento Tipográfico de El Faro, 1889.

"Extract of Report Presented by Mr. Angel Rívas, Receiver Appointed at the Meeting of the Creditors of the Negociación Agrícola El Cuyo y Anexas," 1911, unpublished ms., courtesy Rodolfo Ruz Menéndez.

Fabela, Isidro, and Josefina Fabela, eds. *Documentos históricos de la Revolución Mexicana*. 27 vols. Mexico City: Editorial Jus, 1960–73.

Falcón, Romana. "Force and the Search for Consent: The Role of the *Jefaturas Políticas* of Coahuila in National State Formation." In Joseph and Nugent, eds., *Everyday Forms of State Formation*, 107–34.

——. "Raíces de la Revolución: Evaristo Madero, el primer eslabón de la cadena." In Rodríguez O., *Revolutionary Process in Mexico*, 33–56.

——. *Revolución y caciquismo: San Luis Potosí, 1910–1938*. Mexico City: El Colegio de México, 1985.

Fallaw, Ben. "El atlas parroquial de 1935." *Unicornio: Suplemento Cultural de ¡Por Esto!* 116 (June 13, 1993): 3–9.

——. "Maya into Mexicans(?): Anticlericalism, Prohibition, and the Politics of Social Reform in Revolutionary Yucatán, ca. 1925–1940." Paper presented at the 9th Conference of Mexican, Canadian, and U.S. Historians, Mexico City, Oct. 27–29, 1994.

——. "Peasants, *Caciques*, and *Camarillas*: Rural Politics and State Formation in Yucatán, 1924–1940." Ph.D. diss., University of Chicago, 1995.

Farriss, Nancy M. *Maya Society Under Colonial Rule: The Collective Enterprise of Survival*. Princeton: Princeton University Press, 1984.

Fernández, Justino. *El arte del siglo XIX en México*. Mexico City: Imprenta Universitaria, 1967.

Ferrer de Mendiolea, Gabriel. *Nuestra ciudad: Mérida de Yucatán (1542–1938)*. Mérida: Talleres Gráficos "Basso," 1938.

Finley, Moses. *Ancient Slavery and Modern Ideology*. New York: Viking, 1980.

Flores D., Jorge. "La vida rural en Yucatán en 1914." *HM* 10 (Jan.–Mar., 1961): 470–83.

Flores Magón, Enrique. *Peleamos contra la injusticia: Enrique Flores Magón, precursor de la Revolución Mexicana, cuenta su historia a Samuel Kaplan*, ed. Samuel Kaplan. 2 vols. Mexico City: Libro Mex, 1960.

Flory, Thomas. *Judge and Jury in Imperial Brazil, 1808–1871: Social Control and Political Stability in the New State*. Austin: University of Texas Press, 1981.

Foner, Eric. *Nothing But Freedom: Emancipation and Its Legacy*. Baton Rouge: Louisiana State University Press, 1983.

Fornaro, Carlo de. *Díaz: Czar of Mexico*. New York: International Publishing, 1909.

Foster, George M. "The Dyadic Contract: A Model for the Social Structure of a Mexican Peasant Village." *American Anthropologist* 63, no. 6 (1961): 1173–92.

Foucault, Michel. *Discipline and Punish*. Trans. Alan Sheridan. New York: Pantheon, 1977 [1974].

Foweraker, Joe. *Making Democracy in Spain: Grass-Roots Struggle in the South, 1955–1975*. New York: Cambridge University Press, 1989.

Fowler-Salamini, Heather. "The Boom in Regional Studies of the Mexican Revolution: Where Is It Leading?" *LARR* 28, no. 2 (1993): 175–90.

Fox-Genovese, Elizabeth, and Eugene Genovese. "The Political Crisis of Social History." *JSH* 10 (Winter 1976): 204–20.

Franz, David A. "Bullets and Bolshevists: A History of the Mexican Revolution in Yucatán, 1910–1924." Ph.D. diss., University of New Mexico, 1973.

French, William E. "In the Path of Progress: Railroads and Moral Reform in Porfirian Mexico." In Clarence B. Davis and Kenneth E. Wilburn, Jr., with Ronald Robinson, eds., *Railway Imperialism*, 85–102. New York: Greenwood Press, 1991.

——. " 'Peaceful and Working People': The Inculcation of the Capitalist Work Ethic in a Mexican Mining District (Hidalgo District, Chihuahua), 1880–1920." Ph.D. diss., University of Texas at Austin, 1990.

——. " 'Progreso Forzado': Workers and the Inculcation of the Capitalist Work Ethic in a Mexican Mining District." Paper presented at the 8th Conference of Mexican and North American Historians, San Diego, Oct. 18–20, 1990.

Friedrich, Paul. *Agrarian Revolt in a Mexican Village*. 2nd ed. Chicago: University of Chicago Press, 1977.

——. "The Legitimacy of a Cacique." In Marc J. Swartz, ed., *Local-Level Politics: Social and Cultural Perspectives*, 243–69. Chicago: Aldine, 1966.

Fuentes, Carlos. *The Death of Artemio Cruz*. New York: Farrar, Straus and Giroux, 1964.

Gamboa, Ceferino. *Alcancé vivir la Revolución social. Breves apuntes de las realidades de mi vida*. Mérida. Secretaría de Educación, 1961.

Gamboa Ricalde, Alvaro. *Yucatán desde 1910*. 3 vols. Veracruz and Mexico City: Imprenta Standard, 1943–55.

García Canclini, Néstor. "Culture and Power: The State of Research." *Media, Culture, and Society* 10 (1988): 467–97.

García Cantón, Alberto. *Memorias de un ex-hacendado henequenero*. Mérida: n.p., 1965.

García Granados, Ricardo. *Historia de México desde la restauración de la república en 1861 hasta la caída de Porfirio Díaz.* 4 vols. Mexico City: Editorial Andrés Botas e Hijo, 1912–28.

García Márquez, Gabriel. *One Hundred Years of Solitude.* New York: Harper and Row, 1970.

García Quintanilla, Alejandra. "Hambre y progreso en Yucatán: la epidemia de pelagra en 1889 y 89." Unpublished ms., 1995.

García Quintanilla, Alejandra, and Luis Millet Cámara. "Milpa y henequén, salud y enfermedad en la hacienda henequenera a fines del siglo XIX." Unpublished ms., 1991.

Gaumer, George F. "Pellagra in Yucatán." *American Medical Journal* 38 (1910): 89–101.

Genovese, Eugene D. *From Rebellion to Revolution: Afro-American Slave Revolts in the Making of the New World.* Baton Rouge: Louisiana State University Press, 1979.

——. *Roll, Jordan, Roll: The World the Slaves Made.* New York: Pantheon, 1974.

Gill, Christopher J. "Campesino Patriarchy in the Times of Slavery: The Henequen Plantation Society of Yucatán, 1860–1915." Master's thesis, University of Texas, Austin, 1991.

——. "Honor and Social Control in Plantation Societies: The Lowlands of Antebellum South Carolina and Georgia and the Henequen Plantation Society of Yucatán, Mexico." Paper presented at the 2nd Congreso Internacional sobre Cultura Yucateca," Mérida, Oct. 7–9, 1993.

——. "Regional Variation and Patterns of Resistance: The Henequen Boom in Yucatán, 1880–1915." Senior honors thesis, University of Michigan, 1987.

Ginzburg, Carlo. *The Cheese and the Worms: The Cosmos of a Sixteenth-Century Miller.* Trans. by John and Anne Tedeschi. Baltimore: Johns Hopkins University Press, 1980.

Godoy, José F. *Porfirio Díaz, President of Mexico: The Master Builder of a Great Commonwealth.* New York: Putnam, 1910.

González y González, Luis. *Pueblo en vilo: microhistoria de San José de Gracia.* Mexico City: El Colegio de México, 1972.

González Navarro, Moisés. "México en una laguna." *HM* 4, no. 4 (1955): 506–22.

——. *Población y sociedad en México (1900–1970).* 2 vols. Mexico City: UNAM, 1974.

——. *Raza y tierra: la guerra de castas y el henequén.* 2nd ed. Mexico City: El Colegio de México, 1979.

——. "Tipología del liberalismo mexicano." *HM* 32, no. 2 (1982): 198–225.

González Padilla, Beatriz. "La dirigencia política en Yucatán, 1909–1925," in Millet Cámara et al., *Hacienda y cambio social,* 103–166.

——. *Yucatán: política y poder (1897–1929).* Mérida: Maldonado, 1985.

González Polo, Ignacio. *Reflexiones y apuntes sobre la ciudad de México.* Mexico City: Departamento del Distrito Federal, 1984.

González Reyes, Lorenzo. *Los defensores de Halachó, marzo de 1915.* Mérida: n.p., 1960.

González Rodríguez, Blanca. "Cuatro proyectos de cambio en Yucatán," in Millet Cámara et al., *Hacienda y cambio social,* 77–102.

González Rodríguez, Blanca, et al., eds. *Yucatán: peonaje y liberación.* Mérida: FONAPAS-Yucatán et al., 1981.

Gortari Rabiela, Hira de, and Regina Hernández Franyuti, eds. *La ciudad de México y el Distrito Federal: una historia compartida.* 4 vols. Mexico City: Instituto Mora, 1988.

Gould, Jeffrey. *To Lead as Equals: Rural Protest and Political Consciousness in Chinandega, Nicaragua, 1912–1979.* Chapel Hill: University of North Carolina Press, 1990.

Graham, Richard. *Patronage and Politics in Nineteenth-Century Brazil.* Stanford: Stanford University Press, 1990.

Gramsci, Antonio. *Selections from the Prison Notebooks of Antonio Gramsci,* ed. and trans. by Quintin Hoare and Geoffrey Nowell Smith. London: Lawrence and Wishart, 1971.

Guanche, Víctor, ed. *Directorio de la ciudad de Mérida.* Mérida: Tipografía y Litografía Moderna, 1903.

Guardino, Peter. "Peasants, Politics, and State Formation in Nineteenth-Century Mexico: Guerrero, 1800–1855." Ph.D. diss., University of Chicago, 1991.

Güémez Pineda, José Arturo. "Everyday Forms of Maya Resistance: Cattle Rustling in Northwestern Yucatán, 1821–1847." In Brannon and Joseph, eds., *Land, Labor, and Capital,* 18–50.

Guerra, François-Xavier. *Le Mexique: de l'ancien régime à la Révolution.* 2 vols. Paris: L'Harmattan, 1985.

Guerrero, Julio. *El génesis del crímen en México: estudio de psiquiatría social.* Mexico City: Librería de la Viuda de Ch. Bouret, 1901.

Guha, Ranajit. *Elementary Aspects of Peasant Insurgency in Colonial India.* Delhi: Oxford University Press, 1983.

——. "The Prose of Counter-Insurgency," in Guha and Spivak, *Selected Subaltern Studies,* 45–86.

Guha, Ranajit, and Gayatri Chakravorty Spivak, eds. *Selected Subaltern Studies.* New York: Oxford University Press, 1988.

Haber, Steven H. *Industry and Underdevelopment: The Industrialization of Mexico, 1890–1940.* Stanford: Stanford University Press, 1989.

Hale, Charles A. *Mexican Liberalism in the Age of Mora, 1821–1853.* New Haven: Yale University Press, 1968.

——. *The Transformation of Liberalism in Late Nineteenth-Century Mexico.* Princeton: Princeton University Press, 1989.

Hall, Stuart. "Notes on Deconstructing 'the Popular.'" In Raphael Samuel, ed., *People's History and Socialist Theory,* 227–40. London: Routledge and Kegan Paul, 1981.

Hamnett, Brian R. *Roots of Insurgency: Mexican Regions, 1750–1824.* Cambridge, U.K.: Cambridge University Press, 1986.

Hannay, David. *Díaz.* New York: Kennikat Press, 1977 [1917].

Hansen, Asael T. "Change in the Class System of Mérida, Yucatán, 1875–1935." In Moseley and Terry, *Yucatán: A World Apart,* 122–41.

Hansen, Asael T., and Juan R. Bastarrachea M. *Mérida: su transformación de capital colonial a naciente metrópoli en 1935.* Mexico City: INAH, 1984.

Hart, John Mason. *Anarchism and the Mexican Working Class, 1860–1931.* Austin: University of Texas Press, 1987.

——. *Revolutionary Mexico: The Coming and Process of the Mexican Revolution.* Berkeley: University of California Press, 1987.

Hay, Douglas. "Property, Authority, and the Criminal Law." In Douglas Hay, Peter Linebaugh, and E. P. Thompson, eds., *Albion's Fatal Tree: Crime and Society in Eighteenth-Century England,* 17–63. New York: Pantheon, 1975.

Hernández Chávez, Alicia. *La tradición republicana del buen gobierno.* Mexico City: El Colegio de México, 1993.

Hijuelos Febles, Fausto. *Mérida: antigua y moderna.* Mexico City: Ediciones del Centro Yucateco, 1946.

Hilferding, Rudolph. *Finance Capital: A Study of the Latest Phase of Capitalist Development.* Trans. by Morris Watnich and Sam Gordon. London: Routledge and Kegan Paul, 1981.

Hobsbawm, Eric J. *The Age of Capital.* New York: Scribners, 1975.

———. *Bandits.* Revised ed. New York: Pantheon, 1981.

———. "Peasants and Politics." *Journal of Peasant Studies* 1, no. 1 (Oct. 1973): 3–22.

Hobsbawm, Eric J., and George Rudé. *Captain Swing.* London: Lawrence and Wishart, 1969.

Holmes, G. F., comp. *What Every Farmer Should Know About Binder Twine in 1910.* 2nd ed. North Plymouth, MA: Plymouth Cordage Company, 1910.

*Homenaje del Diario de Yucatán al Lic. D. Delio Moreno Cantón en el centenario del nacimiento del prócer yucateco.* Mérida: Biblioteca Carlos R. Menéndez, 1963.

Hu-DeHart, Evelyn. "Pacification of the Yaquis in the Late Porfiriato: Development and Implications." *HAHR* 54, no. 1 (Feb. 1974): 72–93.

———. *Yaqui Resistance and Survival: The Struggle for Land and Autonomy, 1821–1910.* Madison: University of Wisconsin Press, 1984.

Hunt, Lynn. *Politics, Culture, and Class in the French Revolution.* Berkeley: University of California Press, 1984.

Iglesias, Esther L. "Historias de vida de campesinos henequeneros." *Yucatán: Historia y Economía* 2 (May–June 1978): 3–15.

*Informes y balances presentados por la Comisión Liquidora a los acreedores de los Señores E. Escalante Peón en las asambleas de 27 y 28 de septiembre y 12 y 13 de marzo de 1909.* Mérida, 1909.

*In the District Court of the United States for the District of Minnesota, United States of America vs. International Harvester Co.,* et al. 14 vols. Washington, D.C., 1919.

Irigoyen, Renán. *¿Fué el auge del henequén producto de la guerra de castas?* Mérida: Henequeneros de Yucatán, 1947.

———. "Don Us Escalante, precursor de la industria henequenera." *Revista de Estudios Yucatecos* 1 (Feb. 1949): 17–52.

Isaacman, Allen F. "Peasants and Rural Social Protest in Africa." In Cooper et al., *Confronting Historical Paradigms,* 205–317.

Iturribarría, Jorge F. "Limantour y la caída de Porfirio Díaz." *HM* 10, no. 2 (1960): 243–81.

Jacobs, Ian. *Ranchero Revolt: The Mexican Revolution in Guerrero.* Austin: University of Texas Press, 1984.

Jiménez Borreguí, Crescencio. *Nostalgias durante su destierro en los años 1909–1911.* Mérida: Imprenta Oriente, 1938.

Joseph, Gilbert M. "Caciquismo and the Revolution: Carrillo Puerto in Yucatán." In D. A. Brading, ed., *Caudillo and Peasant in the Mexican Revolution,* 193–221.

———. "Forging the Regional Pastime: Baseball and Class in Yucatán." In Joseph L. Arbena, ed., *Sport and Society in Latin America: Diffusion, Dependency, and the Rise of Mass Culture,* 29–61. Westport: Greenwood Press, 1988.

———. "On the Trail of Latin American Bandits: A Reexamination of Peasant Resistance." *LARR* 25, no. 3 (1990): 7–53.

———. *Rediscovering the Past at Mexico's Periphery: Essays on the Modern History of Yucatán.* Tuscaloosa: University of Alabama Press, 1986.

———. " 'Resocializing' Latin American Banditry: A Reply." *LARR* 26, no. 1 (1991), 161–74.

———. *Revolution from Without: Yucatán, Mexico, and the United States, 1880–1924.* Rev. ed. Durham: Duke University Press, 1988 [1982].

Joseph, Gilbert M., and Daniel Nugent, eds. *Everyday Forms of State Formation:*

*Revolution and the Negotiation of Rule in Modern Mexico.* Durham: Duke University Press, 1994.

Joseph, Gilbert M., and Allen Wells. "Corporate Control of a Monocrop Economy: International Harvester and Yucatán's Henequen Industry During the Porfiriato." *LARR* 17, no. 1 (1982), 69–99.

——. "The Rough-and-Tumble Career of Pedro Crespo." In William H. Beezley and Judith Ewell, eds., *The Human Tradition in Latin America: The Twentieth Century*, 27–40. Wilmington: Scholarly Resources, 1987.

Joseph, Gilbert M., Allen Wells, et al. *Yucatán y la International Harvester.* Mérida: Maldonado, 1986.

Judt, Tony. "'A Clown in Regal Purple': Social History and the Historians." *History Workshop* 7 (1979): 66–94.

Kaerger, Karl. *Agricultura y colonización en México en 1900.* Trans. by Pedro Lewin and Gudrun Dohrmann. Mexico City: Universidad Autónoma Chapingo, 1986 [1901].

Kandell, Jonathan. *La Capital: The Biography of Mexico City.* New York: Random House, 1988.

Kaplan, Temma. "Making Spectacles of Themselves: Women's Rituals and Patterns of Resistance in Africa, Argentina, and the Contemporary United States." Paper presented at the National Humanities Center, Research Triangle Park, NC, Nov. 1992.

——. "Female Consciousness and Collective Action: The Case of Barcelona, 1910–1918." *Signs* 7, no. 3 (Spring 1982): 545–66.

——. "Women and Communal Strikes in the Crisis of 1917–1922." In Renate Bridenthal, Claudia Koonz, and Susan Stuard, eds., *Becoming Visible: Women in European History*, 2nd ed., 428–49. Boston: Houghton Mifflin, 1987.

Katz, Friedrich. "Mexico: Restored Republic and Porfiriato, 1876–1910." In Bethell, *Cambridge History of Latin America*, 5: 3–78.

——. "Rural Uprisings in Mexico." Unpublished ms., n.d. [1981].

——. *The Secret War in Mexico: Europe, the United States and the Mexican Revolution.* Chicago: University of Chicago Press, 1981.

——, ed. *Riot, Rebellion, and Revolution: Rural Social Conflict in Mexico.* Princeton: Princeton University Press, 1988.

Knight, Alan. "Intellectuals in the Mexican Revolution." Paper presented at the 6th Conference of Mexican and U.S. Historians, Chicago, Sept. 1981.

——. "El liberalismo mexicano desde la Reforma hasta la Revolución (una interpretación)." *HM* 35, no. 1 (1985): 59–91.

——. "Mexican Peonage: What Was It and Why Was It?" *JLAS* 18, no. 1 (May 1986): 41–74.

——. *The Mexican Revolution.* 2 vols. Cambridge, U.K.: Cambridge University Press, 1986.

——. "The Working Class and the Mexican Revolution." *JLAS* 16, no. 1 (1984): 51–79.

——. Book review essay. *JLAS* 16, no. 2 (1984): 523–27.

Knight, Franklin W. "The Caribbean Sugar Industry and Slavery." *LARR* 18, no. 2 (1983): 219–29.

Kolakowski, Leszek. *Main Currents of Marxism.* 3 vols. New York: Oxford University Press, 1978.

Konrad, Herman. "Capitalism on the Tropical Forest Frontier: Quintana Roo, 1880s to 1930." In Brannon and Joseph, *Land, Labor, and Capital*, 143–71.

LaFrance, David. "Many Causes, Movements, Failures, 1910–1913: The Regional Nature of Maderismo." In Benjamin and Wasserman, *Provinces of the Revolution*, 17–40.

——. *The Mexican Revolution in Puebla, 1908–1913: The Maderista Movement and the Failure of Liberal Reform*. Wilmington: Scholarly Resources, 1989.

——. "Puebla: Breakdown of the Old Order." In Benjamin and McNellie, *Other Mexicos*, 77–106.

Lamoreaux, Naomi. *The Great Merger Movement in American Business, 1895–1904*. New York: Cambridge University Press, 1985.

Langston, William S. "Centralization Against State Autonomy." In Benjamin and McNellie, *Other Mexicos*, 55–76.

Lapointe, Marie. *Los Mayas rebeldes de Yucatán*. Zamora: El Colegio de Michoacán, 1983.

Leal, Juan Felipe. "El estado y el bloque en el poder en México, 1867–1914." *HM* 23, no. 2 (1974): 700–21.

Le Bon, Gustave. *The Crowd: A Study of the Popular Mind*. 6th ed. London: E. Benn, 1952 [1909].

Leslie, Edwin C., and A. F. Pradeau. *Henequen Plantation Tokens of the Yucatán Peninsula*. Washington, D.C.: Organization of International Numismatics, 1972.

Levine, Lawrence. *Black Culture and Black Consciousness: Afro-American Thought from Slavery to Freedom*. New York: Oxford University Press, 1977.

Lewin, Linda. *Politics and Parentela in Paraíba: A Case Study of Family-based Oligarchy in Brazil's Old Republic*. Princeton: Princeton University Press, 1987.

Liga de Acción Social. *Trabajos de la "Liga de Acción Social" para el establecimiento de las escuelas rurales de Yucatán*. Mérida: Imprenta Empresa Editora, 1913.

Limantour, José Ives. *Apuntes sobre mi vida política*. Mexico City: Porrúa, 1965.

——. "Documentos inéditos de José Ives Limantour: apuntes relativos a una conversación habida con el Sr. Presidente en presencia de los Sres. Ramón Corral y Olegario Molina." *Trimestre Político* 1, no. 1 (1975): 125–38.

Logan, Kathleen. "Women's Participation in Urban Protest." In Joe Foweraker and Ann L. Craig, eds., *Popular Movements and Political Change in Mexico*, 150–59. Boulder: Westview Press, 1990.

López, Alfonso E. *El verdadero Yucatán: boceto social-político-financiero*. 2nd ed. Mérida: Tipografía de la Crónica Nacional, 1910.

López-Portillo y Rojas, José. *Elevación y caída de Porfirio Díaz*. 2nd ed. Mexico City: Editorial Porrúa, 1975.

Loveira, Carlos. *El obrerismo yucateco y la revolución mexicana*. Washington, D.C.: Law Reporter Printing Company, 1917.

Luna, Jesús. *La carrera pública de Don Ramón Corral*. Mexico City: Sepsetentas, 1975.

Mallon, Florencia E. *The Defense of Community in Peru's Central Highlands: Peasant Struggle and Capitalist Transition, 1860–1940*. Princeton: Princeton University Press, 1983.

——. "Dialogues Among the Fragments: Retrospect and Prospect." In Cooper et al., *Confronting Historical Paradigms*, 371–401.

——. *Peasant and Nation: The Making of Postcolonial Mexico and Peru*. Berkeley: University of California Press, 1994.

——. "The Promise and Dilemma of Subaltern Studies: Perspectives from Latin American History," *AHR* 99, no. 5 (Dec. 1994): 1491–1515.

——. "Reflections on the Ruins: Everyday Forms of State Formation in Nineteenth-Century Mexico," in Joseph and Nugent, *Everyday Forms of State Formation*, 69–106.

María y Campos, Alfonso de. "Los científicos y la reforma monetaria de 1905." *Estudios Políticos* 5, nos. 18–19 (1979): 157–88.

Martin, Cheryl English. "Popular Speech and Social Order in Northern Mexico, 1650–1830." *CSSH* 32, no. 2 (Apr. 1990): 305–20.

Martínez, Héctor G., and Francie R. Chassen. "Elecciones y crisis política en Oaxaca: 1902." *HM* 39, no. 2 (1989): 523–54.

Marx, Karl. *Capital*. 3 vols. New York: International Publishers, 1967 [1867].

———. "The Eighteenth Brumaire of Louis Bonaparte." In David Fernbach, ed., *Surveys from Exile*. New York: Vintage Books, 1974 [1852], 143–249.

Mason, Philip. *Patterns of Dominance*. London: Oxford University Press, 1971.

McClure, John, and Aamir Mufti, eds. (for *Social Text Collective*). *Postcolonialism and the Third World*. Durham: Duke University Press, 1992.

Medina Un, Martha. "Dominación y movilización campesina en Yucatán a principios del siglo XX." In Luis A. Várguez Pasos, ed., *Memorias: segundo encuentro sobre investigaciones en ciencias sociales*, 30–40. Mérida: Universidad Autónoma de Yucatán, 1990.

*Memoria de los actos del Gobernador Constitucional del Estado de Yucatán, General Francisco Cantón. En el cuatrenio de 1 de febrero, 1898 a 31 de enero de 1902*. Mérida: Gobierno del Estado, 1902.

*Memoria de las obras del sistema de drenaje profunda del Distrito Federal*. 3 vols. Mexico City: Departmamento del Distrito Federal/UNAM, 1975.

Mena Brito, Bernardino. *Reestructuración histórica de Yucatán*. 3 vols. Mexico City: Editores Mexicanos Unidos, 1967.

Menéndez, Carlos R. *Noventa años de historia de Yucatán (1821–1910)*. Mérida: La Revista de Yucatán, 1937.

———. *La primera chispa de la Revolución Mexicana: el movimiento de Valladolid en 1910*. Mérida: La Revista de Yucatán, 1919.

Menéndez Paz, Arturo. *Serapio Rendón (1867–1913) en la Revolución Mexicana*. Mérida: Gobierno del Estado, 1986.

Menéndez Rodríguez, Hernán. "La agonía del proyecto liberal: Carlos Peón frente a la dictadura." *Unicornio: Suplemento Cultural de ¡Por Esto!* (Sept. 22, 1991), 3–8.

———. "La alianza clero-Molina: el resurgimiento económico de la Iglesia Católica en Yucatán." *Unicornio: Suplemento Cultural de ¡Por Esto!* (Oct. 10, 1993), 3–11.

———. "Reinterpretación histórica: Salvador Alvarado y Carlos Peón." *Unicornio: Suplemento Cultural de ¡Por Esto!* (June 14, 1992), 3–11.

*Mensajes del (Gobernador Constitucional) C. Lic. Olegario Molina al Congreso de Yucatán, 1902–1906*. Mérida: Gobierno del Estado, 1906.

"Mérida de Yucatán." In *Artes de México* 20, nos. 169–70 (1960).

Mestre Ghigliazza, Manuel. *Efemérides biográficas*. Mexico City: Imprenta Aldina, Robredo y Rosell, 1945.

Meyer, Jean A. *The Cristero Rebellion: The Mexican People Between Church and State, 1926–1929*. Trans. Richard Southern. Cambridge, U.K.: Cambridge University Press, 1976.

———. "Historia de la vida social." In *Investigaciones contemporáneas sobre la historia de México: memorias de la tercera reunión de historiadores mexicanos y norteamericanos*, 373–406. Mexico City/Austin: UNAM/El Colegio de México/University of Texas, 1971.

Meyer, Michael C. *Huerta: A Political Portrait*. Lincoln: University of Nebraska Press, 1972.

Meyers, William K. "Politics, Vested Rights, and Economic Growth in Porfirian Mexico: The Company Tlahualilo in the Comarca Lagunera, 1885–1911." *HAHR* 57, no. 3 (Aug. 1977): 425–42.

———. "Second Division of the North: Formation and Fragmentation of the Laguna's Popular Movement, 1910–11." In Katz, *Riot, Rebellion, and Revolution*, 448–86.

Millet Cámara, Luis, José Luis Sierra Villarreal, Blanca González Rodríguez, and Beatriz González Padilla, eds., *Hacienda y cambio social en Yucatán*. Mérida: Maldonado, 1984.

Moguel, Wenceslao. *El milagro del santo de Halachó*. Mérida: Editorial Mayab, 1938.

Moheno, Querido. *¿Hacia dónde vamos? Bosquejo de un cuadro de instituciones políticas adecuadas al pueblo mexicano*. Mexico City: Talleres de I. Lira, 1908.

Molina Font, Gustavo. *La tragedia de Yucatán*. Mexico City: Editorial Jus, 1941.

Molina Font, Julio. *Halachó, 1915*. Mérida: Editora Internacional de México, n.d.

Molina Solís, Juan Francisco. *Historia de Yucatán desde la independencia de España hasta la época actual*. 2 vols. Mérida: Talleres Gráficos de La Revista de Yucatán, 1921–27.

Montalbano, William D. "Africa Locust Plague May Become Worst Recorded in Modern Times." *Los Angeles Times*, Apr. 24, 1988, p. 20.

Moore, Barrington, *Injustice: The Social Bases of Obedience and Revolt*. White Plains, NY: M. E. Sharpe, 1987.

——. *Social Origins of Dictatorship and Democracy: Lord and Peasant in the Making of the Modern World*. Boston: Beacon Press, 1966.

Morales, María Dolores. "La expansión de la ciudad de México en el siglo XIX: el caso de los fraccionamientos," in Moreno Toscano, *Ciudad de México*, 189–200.

Moreno Fraginals, Manuel. *El ingenio: complejo económico social cubano del azúcar*. 3 vols. Havana: Editorial de Ciencias Sociales, 1978.

——. "Plantations in the Caribbean: Cuba, Puerto Rico, and the Dominican Republic in the Late Nineteenth Century." In Manuel Moreno Fraginals, Frank Moya Pons, and Stanley L. Engerman, eds., *Between Slavery and Free Labor: The Spanish-speaking Caribbean in the Nineteenth Century*, 3–21. Baltimore: Johns Hopkins University Press, 1985.

Moreno Toscano, Alejandra. "Cambios en los patrones de urbanización en México, 1810–1910." *HM* 22 (1972): 179–87.

——, ed. *Ciudad de México: Ensayo de construcción de una historia* (Mexico City: INAH, 1978).

Morley, Sylvanus. *The Ancient Maya*. 3rd ed. Rev. by George W. Brainerd. Stanford: Stanford University Press, 1956.

Morse, Richard M. "The Heritage of Latin America." In Louis Hartz, ed., *The Founding of New Societies*, 123–77. New York: Harcourt, Brace, 1964.

Moseley, Edward H., and Edward D. Terry, eds. *Yucatán: A World Apart*. Tuscaloosa: University of Alabama Press, 1980.

Nickel, Herbert J. *Paternalismo y economía moral en las haciendas mexicanas del porfiriato*. Puebla: Comisión Puebla, Gobierno del Estado, 1989.

——. *Peonaje e inmovilidad de los trabajadores agrícolas en México: la situación de los peones acasillados en las haciendas de Puebla y Tlaxcala*. Trans. Catalina Valdivieso de Acuña. Bayreuth: Universität Lehrstäuhle Geowissenschaften, 1980.

Niemeyer, Eberhardt V., Jr. *El general Bernardo Reyes*. Trans. Juan Antonio Ayala. Monterrey: Gobierno del Estado de Nuevo León, 1966.

[Novelo, José Inés?]. *Yucatán 1902–1906*. Mérida: n.p., 1907.

O'Brien, Jay, and William Roseberry, eds. *Golden Ages, Dark Ages: Imagining the Past in Anthropology and History*. Berkeley: University of California Press, 1991.

O'Hanlon, Rosalind, and David Washbrook. "After Orientalism: Culture, Criticism, and Politics in the Third World." *CSSH* 34, no. 1 (Jan. 1992): 141–67.

Pacheco Cruz, Santiago. *Recuerdos de la propaganda constitucionalista en Yucatán*. Mérida: Editorial Zamná, 1953.

Paige, Jeffrey. *Agrarian Revolution: Social Movements and Export Agriculture in the Underdeveloped World.* New York: Free Press, 1975.

Pani, Alberto. *Hygiene in Mexico: A Study of Sanitary and Educational Problems.* New York: Putnam, 1917.

Paoli, Francisco J. *Yucatán y los orígenes del nuevo estado mexicano: gobierno de Salvador Alvarado, 1915–1918.* Mexico City: Ediciones Era, 1984.

Paoli, Francisco J., and Enrique Montalvo. *El socialismo olvidado de Yucatán.* Mexico City: Siglo XXI, 1977.

Parlee, Lorena M. "The Impact of United States Railroad Unions on Organized Labor and Government Policy in Mexico (1880–1911)." *HAHR* 64, no. 3 (Aug. 1984): 443–76.

Pasos Peniche, Manuel. *La intervención estatal en la industria henequenera.* Mexico City: Imprenta Moctezuma, 1951.

Patterson, Orlando. *Slavery and Social Death: A Comparative Study.* Cambridge, MA: Harvard University Press, 1982.

Peniche Rivero, Piedad. "Clase, género y cultura en la hacienda henequenera de Yucatán. El control de la fuerza de trabajo durante el Porfiriato (1870–1901)." Paper presented at the 2nd Congreso Internacional sobre Cultura Yucateca," Mérida, Oct. 7–9, 1993.

——. "Gender, Bridewealth, and Marriage: Social Reproduction on Henequen Haciendas in Yucatán (1870–1901)." In Heather Fowler-Salamini and Mary Kay Vaughan, eds., *Women of the Mexican Countryside, 1850–1990: Creating Spaces, Shaping Transitions,* 74–89. Tucson: University of Arizona Press, 1994.

——. "Mujeres, dotes y matrimonios: lógica simbólica y función de las deudas de los trabajadores de la hacienda henequenera de Yucatán durante el Porfiriato." Paper presented at the 8th Conference of Mexican and North American Historians, San Diego, Oct. 18–20, 1990.

——. "Mujeres, matrimonios y esclavitud en la hacienda henequenera durante el porfiriato." *Historias* 17 (1987): 125–37.

Pérez Alcalá, Felipe. *Ensayos biográficos. Cuadros históricos. Hojas dispersas.* Mérida: La Revista de Yucatán, 1914.

——. "Los sucesos del 11 de agosto en Mérida." In Carlos R. Menéndez, ed., *Noventa años de historia de Yucatán,* 539–44.

Pérez Peniche, Rodolfo S. *Reseña histórica de la administración del C. Coronel Daniel Traconis, 1890–1892.* Mérida: Gamboa Guzmán, 1893.

Pérez Ponce, Tomás. *Las coronas del General Salvador Alvarado.* Mexico City: n.p., 1918.

Perry, Laurens Ballard. *Juárez and Díaz: Machine Politics in Mexico.* DeKalb: Northern Illinois University Press, 1978.

Piccato, Pablo. " 'El Paso de Venus por el Disco del Sol': Criminality and Alcoholism in the Late Porfiriato." *MS/EM* 11, no. 2 (Summer 1995): 203–241.

Pletcher, David. "The Fall of Silver in Mexico, 1870–1910, and Its Effect on American Investment." *JEH* 18 (Mar. 1958): 33–55.

Poblett Miranda, Martha. *José María Pino Suárez: semblanza.* Mexico City: Instituto Nacional de Estudios Históricos de la Revolución Mexicana, 1986.

Powell, John W. "Peasant Society and Clientelistic Politics." *APSR* 64, no. 2 (1970): 411–25.

Prakash, Gyan. "Can the 'Subaltern' Ride? A Reply to O'Hanlon and Washbrook." *CSSH* 34, no. 1 (Jan. 1992): 168–84.

——. "Writing Post-Orientalist Histories of the Third World: Perspectives from Indian Historiography." *CSSH* 32, no. 2 (Apr. 1990): 383–408.

Prida, Ramón. ¡De la dictadura a la anarquía! Apuntes para la historia política de México durante los últimos cuarenta y tres años. 2 vols. El Paso: Imprenta de El Paso de Norte, 1914.

Quintal Martín, Fidelio. "Breve historia de Yucatán durante la última década del porfiriato (1901–1910)." BECA 11, no. 65 (1984): 43–62.

———. Licenciado José María Pino Suárez, liberal revolucionario (1869–1913). Mérida: Gobierno del Estado, 1985.

———. Yucatán. Carácter de la guerra campesina en 1847: una síntesis interpretiva. Mérida: Universidad de Yucatán, 1976.

Rabasa, Emilio. La constitución y la dictadura: estudio sobre la organización política de México. 4th ed. Mexico City: Editorial Porrúa, 1968.

Redfield, Robert. The Folk Culture of Yucatán. Chicago: University of Chicago Press, 1941.

Redfield, Robert, and Alfonso Villa Rojas. Chan Kom: A Mayan Village. Chicago: University of Chicago Press, 1950.

Reed, Nelson. The Caste War of Yucatán. Stanford: Stanford University Press, 1964.

Remmers, Lawrence J. "Henequen, the Caste War, and the Economy of Yucatán, 1846–1883: The Roots of Dependence in a Mexican Region." Ph.D. diss., University of California, Los Angeles, 1981.

Reyes, Candelario. "Historia del henequén de Yucatán en su aspecto político-económico durante las cuatro décadas del siglo XX." México Agrario 2, no. 4 (1940): 179–89.

Reyes, Rodolfo. De mi vida: memorias políticas. Madrid: Biblioteca Nueva, 1929.

Reyes Heroles, Jesús. El liberalismo mexicano. 3 vols. Mexico City: Universidad Nacional Autónoma de México, 1957–61.

Ricalde, Graciano, and Tomás Ojeda. Informe acerca de las operaciones consignadas en los libros de contabilidad de la Comisión Reguladora del Mercado del Henequén en el período de tiempo corrido desde el 1 de mayo de 1912 hasta el 10 de septiembre de 1914, presentado al gobernador del estado por Graciano Ricalde como componente de la comisión especial instituida para investigar, examinar y depurar los manejos de la citada Comisión Reguladora. Mérida: Imprenta Constitucional, 1919.

Rice, Jacqueline Ann. "The Porfirian Political Elite: Life Patterns of the Delegates to the 1892 Unión Liberal Convention." Ph.D. diss., University of California, Los Angeles, 1979.

Roche, Daniel. The People of Paris: An Essay in Popular Culture in the Eighteenth Century. Trans. Marie Evans. Leamington Spa, Hamburg: Berg Publishers, 1987.

Rodríguez O., Jaime E., ed. Patterns of Contention in Mexican History. Wilmington: Scholarly Resources, 1992.

———, ed. The Revolutionary Process in Mexico: Essays on Political and Social Change, 1880–1940. Los Angeles: UCLA Latin American Center, 1990.

Rohlfes, Laurence J. "Police and Penal Correction in Mexico City, 1876–1911: A Study of Order and Progress in Porfirian Mexico." Ph.D. diss., Tulane University, 1983.

Rosado Vega, Luis. El desastre. Havana: Imprenta "El Siglo XX," 1919.

Ross, Stanley R. Francisco I. Madero: Apostle of Mexican Democracy. New York: Columbia University Press, 1955.

Roumagnac, Carlos. Los criminales en México: ensayo de psicología criminal. Mexico City: Tipografía "El Fénix," 1904.

Rubio Alpuche, Néstor. Belice, apuntes históricos y colección de tratados internacionales relativos a esta colonia británica. Mérida: n.p., 1894.

Rudé, George. *The Crowd in History: A Study of Popular Disturbances in France and England, 1730–1848.* New York: Wiley, 1964.

Rugeley, Terry. "Origins of the Caste War: A Social History of Rural Yucatán, 1800–1847." Ph.D. diss., University of Houston, 1992.

Rutherford, John. *Mexican Society During the Revolution: A Literary Approach.* Oxford: Oxford University Press, 1971.

Ruz Menéndez, Rodolfo. *Aportaciones para el estudio de la historia del Instituto Literario de Yucatán.* Mérida: Instituto Literario de Yucatán, 1967.

———. *Mérida: bosquejo biográfico.* Mérida: Maldonado, 1983.

Sabato, Hilda. "Citizenship, Political Participation, and the Formation of the Public Sphere in Buenos Aires, 1850s–1880s." *PP* 136 (Aug. 1989): 139–63.

———. "Relations Between Civil Society and the Political System in Latin America: A Historical Perspective." Paper presented at the National Humanities Center, Research Triangle Park, NC, Apr. 1993.

Sabean, David W. *Power in the Blood: Popular Culture and Village Discourse in Early Modern Germany.* New York: Cambridge University Press, 1984.

Sánchez, Ricardo, Eric Van Young, and Gisela Von Wobeser, eds. *La ciudad y el campo en la historia mexicana.* 2 vols. Mexico City: UNAM, 1992.

Sánchez Silva, Carlos. *Crisis política y contrarrevolución en Oaxaca (1912–1915).* Mexico City: INEHRM, 1991.

Saragoza, Alex M. *The Monterrey Elite and the Mexican State, 1880–1940.* Austin: University of Texas Press, 1988.

Savarino, Franco. "La iglesia ausente. Catolicismo y disidencia en Yucatán, 1900–1920." Paper presented to the 9th Conference of Mexican, Canadian, and U.S. Historians, Mexico City, Oct. 27–29, 1994.

———. "Pueblo, élites y dinámica política local en el proceso revolucionario: el caso de Abalá, Yucatán, 1915–1924." *Historias* 30 (Apr.–Sept. 1993): 61–77.

Schmidt, Arthur. *The Social and Economic Effects of the Railroad in Puebla and Veracruz, Mexico, 1867–1911.* New York: Garland, 1987.

Schmidt, Henry C. "Toward the Innerscape of Mexican Historiology: Liberalism and the History of Ideas." *MS/EM* 8, no. 1 (1992), 117–38.

Schmidt, Steffen W., Laura Guasti, Carl. H. Landé, and James C. Scott, eds. *Friends, Followers, and Factions: A Reader in Political Clientelism.* Berkeley: University of California Press, 1977.

Schnakenbourg, Christian. "From the Sugar Estate to Central Factory: The Industrial Revolution in the Caribbean (1840–1905)." In Bill Albert and Adrian Graves, eds., *Crisis and Change in the International Sugar Economy, 1860–1914,* 83–93. Norwich, England: ISC Press, 1984.

Scobie, James. "The Growth of Latin American Cities, 1870–1930." In Bethell, *Cambridge History of Latin America,* 4: 233–66.

Scott, James C. *Domination and the Arts of Resistance: Hidden Transcripts.* New Haven: Yale University Press, 1990.

———. "Patron-Client Politics and Political Change in Southeast Asia." *APSR* 67, no. 1 (Mar. 1973): 103–27.

———. "Resistance Without Protest and Without Organization: Peasant Opposition to the Islamic *Zakat* and the Christian Tithe." *CSSH* 29, no. 3 (July 1987): 417–52.

———. *Weapons of the Weak: Everyday Forms of Peasant Resistance.* New Haven: Yale University Press, 1985.

Scott, James C., and Benedict J. Tria Kerkvliet, eds. "Everyday Forms of Peasant Resistance." *Journal of Peasant Studies* 13, no. 2 (1986) (special issue).

Scott, Rebecca. *Slave Emancipation in Cuba: The Transition to Free Labor, 1860–1899.* Princeton: Princeton University Press, 1985.

Seed, Patricia. "Colonial and Postcolonial Discourse." *LARR* 26, no. 3 (1991): 181–200.

———. "'Failing to Marvel': Atahualpa's Encounter with the Word." *LARR* 26, no. 1 (1991): 7–32.

———. "More Colonial and Postcolonial Discourses." *LARR* 28, no. 3 (1993): 146–52.

Seminario de la Historia Moderna de México. *Estadísticas económicas del porfiriato: fuerza de trabajo y actividad económica por sectores.* Mexico City: El Colegio de México, 1965.

Sheahan, John. *Patterns of Development in Latin America: Poverty, Repression, and Economic Strategy.* Princeton: Princeton University Press, 1987.

Shuman, Malcolm K. "The Town Where Luck Fell: The Economics of Life in a Henequen Zone Pueblo." Ph.D. diss., Tulane University, 1974.

Sierra, Justo. *The Political Evolution of the Mexican People*, ed. Edmundo O'Gorman. Trans. Charles Ramsdell. Austin: University of Texas Press, 1969.

Sierra Villarreal, José Luis. "Prensa y lucha política en Yucatán, 1895–1925." Mimeograph. Centro Regional del Sureste, INAH, Mérida, 1984.

Sierra Villarreal, José Luis, and José Antonio Paoli Bolio. *Cárdenas y el reparto de los henequenales.* Mérida: Consejo Editorial de Yucatán, 1986.

Silva Herzog, Jesús. *Breve historia de la Revolución Mexicana.* 2 vols. Mexico City: Fondo de Cultura Económica, 1960.

Skocpol, Theda. *States and Social Revolutions.* Cambridge, U.K.: Cambridge University Press, 1979.

———. "What Makes Peasants Revolutionary?" *Comparative Politics* 14, no. 3 (1982): 351–75.

Smith, Gavin. "The Production of Culture in Local Rebellion." In O'Brien and Roseberry, *Golden Ages, Dark Ages*, 180–207.

*Solemne protesta del pueblo yucateco contra la candidatura del Lic. Manuel Romero Ancona.* Mérida: Imprenta del Eco del Comercio, 1885.

Solís Cámara, Fernando. *Bosquejo biográfico de Olegario Molina Solís.* Mexico City: American Book Publishing Company, 1907.

Spenser, Daniela. "Workers Against Socialism? Reassessing the Role of Urban Labor in Yucatecan Revolutionary Politics." In Brannon and Joseph, *Land, Labor, and Capital*, 220–42.

Spitzer, Alan B. "The Historical Problem of Generations." *AHR* 78, no. 3 (Dec. 1973): 1353–85.

Stearns, Peter. "Social and Political History." *JSH* 16, no. 3 (1983): 366–83.

Stephens, John Lloyd. *Incidents of Travel in Yucatán.* 2 vols. New York: Harper and Brothers, 1843.

Stern, Steve J. "New Approaches to the Study of Peasant Rebellion and Consciousness: Implications of the Andean Experience." In Stern, *Resistance, Rebellion, and Consciousness*, 3–25.

———. *Peru's Indian Peoples and the Challenge of the Spanish Conquest: Huamanga to 1640.* Madison: University of Wisconsin Press, 1982.

———. *The Secret History of Gender: Women, Men, and Power in Late Colonial Mexico.* Chapel Hill: University of North Carolina Press, 1995.

———, ed. *Resistance, Rebellion, and Consciousness in the Andean Peasant World, 18th to 20th Centuries.* Madison: University of Wisconsin Press, 1987.

Stoler, Ann. *Capitalism and Confrontation in Sumatra's Plantation Belt, 1870–1979.* New Haven: Yale University Press, 1985.

Stone, Lawrence. *The Family, Sex, and Marriage in England, 1500–1800.* London: Penguin, 1977.

Strickon, Arnold, and Sidney M. Greenfield, eds. *Structure and Process in Latin*

*America: Patronage, Clientage, and Power Systems.* Albuquerque: University of New Mexico Press, 1972.

Suárez Molina, Víctor M. *Don Rogelio Víctor Suárez: caballero español. Breve relato de su vida y gesta.* Mérida: Talleres de Impresión Díaz Massa, 1949.

——. *La evolución económica de Yucatán: a través del siglo XIX.* 2 vols. Mexico City: Ediciones de la Universidad de Yucatán, 1977.

Suárez Navarro, Juan, General. "Informe sobre las causas y el carácter de los frecuentes cambios políticos ocurridos en Yucatán . . ." In Betancourt Pérez and Ruz Menéndez, *Yucatán: textos de su historia,* I: 54–56.

Tannenbaum, Frank. *Peace by Revolution: Mexico After 1910.* New York: Columbia University Press, 1933.

Taussig, Michael. *The Devil and Commodity Fetishism in South America.* Chapel Hill: University of North Carolina Press, 1980.

Taylor, William B. "Banditry and Insurrection: Rural Unrest in Central Jalisco, 1790–1816." In Katz, *Riot, Rebellion, and Revolution,* 205–46.

——. *Drinking, Homicide, and Rebellion in Colonial Mexican Villages.* Stanford: Stanford University Press, 1979.

Thompson, E. P. "The Moral Economy of the English Crowd in the Eighteenth Century." *PP* 50 (Feb. 1971): 76–136.

——. "Patrician Society, Plebeian Culture." *JSH* 7, no. 4 (1974), 382–405.

——. "The Peculiarities of the English." *Socialist Register* (1965). Reprinted in Thompson, *The Poverty of Theory and Other Essays,* 35–91. New York: Monthly Review Press, 1978.

——. "Time, Work-Discipline, and Industrial Capitalism." *PP* 38 (Dec. 1967): 56–97.

Thompson, J. Eric S. *Maya History and Religion.* Norman: University of Oklahoma Press, 1970.

Thompson, Richard. *The Winds of Tomorrow: Social Change in a Maya Town.* Chicago: University of Chicago Press, 1974.

Thorup, Cathryn. "La competencia económica británica y norteamericana en México (1887–1910): el caso de Weetman Pearson." *HM* 31, no. 4 (Apr.–June 1982): 599–641.

Tilly, Charles. "Revolution and Collective Violence." In Fred I. Greenstein and Nelson Polsby, eds., *Handbook of Political Science.* 8 vols. Reading, MA: Addison-Wesley, 1975. 3: 483–85.

Tocqueville, Alexis de. *The Old Regime and the French Revolution.* Trans. Stuart Gilbert. New York: Anchor/Doubleday, 1955 [1856].

Topik, Steven C. "Economic Domination by the Capital: Mexico City and Rio de Janeiro, 1888–1910." In Sánchez, Van Young, and Von Wobeser, *La ciudad y el campo,* I: 185–97.

——. "The Economic Role of the State in Liberal Regimes: Brazil and Mexico Compared, 1888–1910." In Joseph L. Love and Nils Jacobsen, eds., *Guiding the Invisible Hand: Economic Liberalism and the State in Latin American History,* 117–44. New York: Praeger, 1988.

——. "The Emergence of Finance Capital in Mexico." In Virginia Guedea and Jaime E. Rodríguez O., eds., *Five Centuries of Mexican History/Cinco siglos de historia de México.* 2 vols. Mexico City/Irvine, CA: Instituto Mora/University of California, Irvine, 1992. 2: 227–42.

——. "Exports Under the Porfiriato." Unpublished ms., n.d.

——. "The Image of Prosperity: The Porfirian Export Boom in Comparative Perspective." Paper presented at the 9th Conference of Mexican, Canadian, and U.S. Historians, Mexico City, Oct. 27–29, 1994.

——. *The Political Economy of the Brazilian State, 1889–1920*. Austin: University of Texas Press, 1985.

——. "La Revolución, el estado y el desarrollo económico en México." *HM* 40, no. 1 (1990): 79–144.

Turner, John Kenneth. *Barbarous Mexico*. Austin: University of Texas Press, 1969.

Turton, Andrew. "Patrolling the Middle-Ground: Methodological Perspectives on Everyday Peasant Resistance." *Journal of Peasant Studies* 13, no. 2 (Jan. 1986): 36–48.

Tutino, John. "Agrarian Social Change and Peasant Rebellion in Nineteenth-Century Mexico: The Example of Chalco." In Katz, *Riot, Rebellion, and Revolution*, 95–140.

——. *From Insurrection to Revolution in Mexico: Social Bases of Agrarian Violence, 1750–1940*. Princeton: Princeton University Press, 1986.

Urzáiz Rodríguez, Eduardo. *Del imperio a la revolución, 1865–1910*. Mérida: Gobierno del Estado, 1971.

U.S. Department of Commerce, Bureau of Corporations. *International Harvester Company*. Washington, D.C.: GPO, 1913.

U.S. National Archives, *Records of the Department of State Relating to the Internal Affairs of Mexico, 1910–1929* (RG 59), Microfilm Publication 274 (Washington, D.C.: GPO, 1959).

U.S. Senate. Committee on Agriculture and Forestry. *Importation of Sisal and Manila Hemp: Hearings Before the Sub-Committee of the Committee on Agriculture and Forestry*. 2 vols. Washington, D.C.: GPO, 1916.

Valadés, José C. *Historia general de la Revolución Mexicana*. 10 vols. Mexico City: Manuel Quesada Brandi, 1963–1967.

——. *El porfirismo: historia de un régimen*. 2 vols. Mexico City: Editorial Patria, 1948.

Valdés Acosta, José María. *A través de las centurias*. 3 vols. Mérida: Talleres "Pluma y Lapiz," 1926.

Van Young, Eric. "In the Gloomy Caverns of Paganism: Popular Culture, the Bourbon State, and Rebellion in Mexico, 1810–1821." In Christon I. Archer, ed., *The Mexican Wars of Independence, Empire, and Early Republic*. Lincoln: University of Nebraska Press, forthcoming.

——. "Mentalities and Collectivities: A Comment." In Rodríguez O., *Patterns of Contention in Mexican History*, 337–53.

——. "To See Someone Not Seeing: Historical Studies of Peasants and Politics in Mexico." *MS/EM* 6, no. 1 (Winter 1990): 133–59.

Van Young, Eric. "Sliding Sideways: Text and Context in the Mexican Wars of Independence." Paper presented at the annual meeting of the American Historical Association, Chicago, Dec. 1991.

Vanderwood, Paul. "Building Blocks But Yet No Building: Regional History and the Mexican Revolution." *MS/EM* 3, no. 2 (Summer 1987): 421–32.

Villanueva Mukul, Eric. *Así tomamos las tierras: henequén y haciendas en Yucatán durante el porfiriato*. Mérida: Maldonado, 1984.

——. "La formación de las regiones de Yucatán." In Othón Baños Ramírez, ed., *Sociedad, estructura agraria y estado en Yucatán*. Mérida: Universidad Autónoma de Yucatán, 1990, 167–203.

Villaseñor, Roberto. *El separatismo en Yucatán: novela histório-política*. Mexico City: Andrés Botas, 1916.

Voss, Stuart F. *On the Periphery of Nineteenth-Century Mexico: Sonora and Sinaloa, 1810–1877*. Tucson: University of Arizona Press, 1982.

Walker, David W. *Kinship, Business, and Politics: The Martínez del Río Family in Mexico, 1824–1867.* Austin: University of Texas Press, 1986.

Wasserman, Mark. *Capitalists, Caciques, and Revolution: The Native Elite and Foreign Enterprise in Chihuahua, Mexico, 1854–1911.* Chapel Hill: University of North Carolina Press, 1984.

Watts, Michael. "Struggles Over Land, Struggles Over Meaning." In Reginald G. Golledge, Helen Couclelis, and Peter Gould, eds., *A Ground for Common Search,* 31–51. Goleta, CA: Santa Barbara Geographical Press, 1988.

Weinstein, Barbara. *The Amazon Rubber Boom, 1850–1920.* Stanford: Stanford University Press, 1983.

Wells, Allen. "All in the Family: Railroads and Henequen Monoculture in Porfirian Yucatán." *HAHR* 72, no. 2 (May 1992): 159–209.

———. "Los capítulos olvidados del pasado yucateco: la política del Siglo Diecinueve en perspectiva historiográfica." In Pablo Serrano Alvarez, ed., *Del pasado, presente y futuro de la historiografía regional de México.* Mexico City: UNAM, forthcoming.

———. "Family Elites in a Boom-and-Bust Economy: The Molinas and Peóns of Porfirian Yucatán." *HAHR* 62, no. 2 (May 1982): 224–53.

———. "From Hacienda to Plantation: The Transformation of Santo Domingo Xcuyum," in Brannon and Joseph, eds., *Land, Labor, and Capital,* 112–142.

———. "The Terrible Green Monster: Recent Literature on Sugar, Coffee, and Coerced Labor in the Caribbean." *LARR* 23, no. 2 (1988): 189–205.

———. *Yucatán's Gilded Age: Haciendas, Henequen, and International Harvester, 1860–1915.* Albuquerque: University of New Mexico Press, 1985.

Wells, Allen, and Gilbert M. Joseph. "Modernizing Visions, *Chilango* Blueprints, and Provincial Growing Pains: Mérida at the Turn of the Century." *MS/EM* 8, no. 2 (Summer 1992): 167–215.

White, Hayden. *The Content of Form.* Baltimore: Johns Hopkins University Press, 1987.

Wilson, Eugene M. "Physical Geography of the Yucatán Peninsula," In Moseley and Terry, *Yucatán: A World Apart,* 5–40.

Winn, Peter. *Weavers of Revolution: The Yarur Workers and Chile's Road to Socialism.* New York: Oxford University Press, 1986.

Winther, Paul C. "Contemporary Dacöity and Traditional Politics in South Asia." *University of Oklahoma Papers in Anthropology* 18, no. 2 (Fall 1977): 153–66.

Wolf, Eric R. "Aspects of Group Relations in a Complex Society: Mexico." In Dwight Heath and Richard Adams, eds., *Contemporary Cultures and Societies of Latin America,* 85–101. New York: Random House, 1965.

———. "Kinship, Friendship, and Patron-Client Relations in Complex Societies." In Michael Banton, ed., *The Social Anthropology of Complex Societies,* 1–22. New York: Praeger, 1966.

———. *Peasant Wars of the Twentieth Century.* New York: Harper and Row, 1969.

———. "The Vicissitudes of the Closed Corporate Peasant Community," *American Ethnologist* 13, no. 2 (May 1986): 325–29.

Wolf, Eric R., and E. C. Hansen. "Caudillo Politics: A Structural Analysis." *CSSH* 9, no. 2 (1967): 168–79.

Wolf, Eric R., and Sidney W. Mintz. "Haciendas and Plantations in Middle America and the Antilles." *Social and Economic Studies* 6 (1957): 380–412.

Womack, John, Jr. "The Mexican Revolution, 1910–1920." In Bethell, *Cambridge History of Latin America,* 5: 79–153.

———. *Zapata and the Mexican Revolution.* New York: Knopf, 1968.

Zayas Enríquez, Rafael de. *El Estado de Yucatán. su pasado, su presente, su porvenir.* New York: J. J. Little and Ives, 1908.

——. *Porfirio Díaz.* New York: Appleton, 1908.

INTERVIEWS

Antonio Betancourt Pérez, Mérida, August 10, 1984.

Jesús Campos Esquivel, Dzilám González, December 26, 31, 1986; January 2, 1987.

Lina Cruz, Sacapuc, June 10, 1985.

Marcos Ek, Hunucmá, June 7, 1982.

Alejandra García Quintanilla, Mérida, June 9, 1985; November 20, 1987.

Chablé Koh, Cepeda, January 1989, courtesy of Christopher J. Gill.

Marcos Ku Peraza, Peto, June 14, 1982, courtesy of Marie Lapointe and Lucy Defresne.

Mario Menéndez Romero, Mérida, July 14, 17, 1987.

Hernán Menéndez Rodríguez, Mérida, April 13, 1987; July 5, 15, 24, 1987.

Encarnación Parra, Libre Unión, Oct. 24, 1984.

Alicia Trejo Hernández, Peto, June 14, 1982, courtesy of Marie Lapointe and Lucy Defresne.

Salustina Tut de Euán, Opichén, August 12, 1991.

Melchor Zozaya Raz, Temax, December 31, 1986.

# Index

In this index an "f" after a number indicates a separate reference on the next page, and an "ff" indicates separate references on the next two pages. A continuous discussion over two or more pages is indicated by a span of page numbers, e.g., "57–59." *Passim* is used for a cluster of references in close but not consecutive sequence.

Library of Congress Cataloging-in-Publication Data
Wells, Allen.
Summer of discontent, seasons of upheaval : elite politics and
rural insurgency in Yucatán, 1876–1915 / Allen Wells and Gilbert M.
Joseph
    p.   cm.
Includes bibliographical references and index.
ISBN 0-8047-2655-8 (cloth)
ISBN 0-8047-2656-6 (pbk.)
    1. Yucatán (Mexico : State)—Politics and government.   2. Mexico—
Politics and government—1867–1910.   3. Mexico—Politics and
government—1910–1946. 4. Oligarchy—Mexico—Yucatán (State)—
Political activity—History.   5. Insurgency—Mexico—Yucatán
(State)—History.   I. Joseph, G. M. (Gilbert Michael).
II. Title.
F1376.W45   1996
972'.65—dc20
96-10471   CIP
          r96

⊗ This book is printed on acid-free, recycled paper.

Original printing 1996

Last figure below indicates year of this printing:

05  04  03  02  01  00  99  98  97  96